How to
Find a Scholarship Online

How to
Find a Scholarship Online

Shannon R. Turlington

McGRAW-HILL

New York   San Francisco   Washington, D.C.   Auckland   Bogotá
Caracas   Lisbon   London   Madrid   Mexico City   Milan
Montreal   New Delhi   San Juan   Singapore
Sydney   Tokyo   Toronto

McGraw-Hill

*A Division of The **McGraw·Hill** Companies*

1 2 3 4 5 6 7 8 9 0   AGM/AGM   0 9 8 7 6 5 4 3 2 1 0

0-07-136511-7

This book was set in Minion by Pro-Image.

Printed and bound by Quebecor World/Martinsburg.

McGraw-Hill books are available at special quantity discounts to use as
premiums and sales promotions, or for use in corporate training
programs. For more information, please write to the Director of Special
Sales, Professional Publishing, McGraw-Hill, Two Penn Plaza, New York,
NY 10121-2298. Or contact your local bookstore.

This book is printed on recycled, acid-free paper containing a
minimum of 50% recycled de-inked fiber.

Contents

CONTENTS

CONTENTS

CONTENTS

CONTENTS

ACKNOWLEDGMENTS

I would like to thank my agent, Martha Kaufman-Amitay, my editor at McGraw-Hill, Nancy Mikhail, and the entire McGraw-Hill team who worked so hard to bring this book to its final form. I would also like to thank Luke, Del, and Frisbee for putting up with me while I spent so many nights and weekends working on the manuscript. Finally, thanks to all of the scholarship sponsors, without whom this book would not be possible—they should be commended for helping a lot of deserving students realize their dreams.

INTRODUCTION

College. The word probably fills you with both excitement and uneasiness. Excitement because going to college means you'll be out on your own for the first time in your life, meeting new people, learning new things, having new experiences. Uneasiness because you're probably wondering how in the world you're going to pay for it all.

Paying for college has become increasingly more difficult, as we've all heard on the news. In recent years, college tuition has increased at an average rate of 8 percent each year, far outpacing the rise of inflation. At the same time, financial aid awards from traditional sources like the federal government and the schools have dwindled. Winning scholarships from private sources has become an important way for college and graduate students to make up the difference.

In order to find money for college, you need to take the initiative to search out the scholarships for which you are well qualified. But locating scholarships is often a time-consuming process. You have to page through gigantic books to hunt down the scholarships you might qualify for, only to find when you apply that important information, like the application deadline or the eligibility requirements, has changed since the book was published. But with the growing popularity of the Internet, that situation has changed. Now scholarship programs are being publicized on the Web, making it easier for you to find up-to-date information and enabling you to submit applications quickly.

How the Internet Can Help

The Internet is the most powerful tool you can have in your arsenal when you start searching for scholarships. It can drastically reduce the time you spend hunting down the scholarships that you are eligible to apply for, it can reduce your costs when requesting scholarship information, and it can even enable you to apply effortlessly by submitting electronic applications. If you use the Internet wisely, you should be able to track down and apply for more scholarships than you possibly could otherwise. This book will show you how to do just that.

First, the Internet can make it faster and easier to hunt for scholarships for which you would make a good candidate. On the Web, you'll find complete information about all kinds of scholarship programs, including programs sponsored by private foundations, professional associations, state and federal governments, corporations, and other groups. You can also search for scholarship money offered by the colleges themselves, including money from academic departments, athletic scholarships, awards for minorities and female students, and academic scholarships for incoming freshmen. Finally, if you don't find the scholarship information online, you can still track down a contact that you can write for information about awards. For instance, you can search for sources of scholarships like your city and county government, your parents' employers and associations, religious and ethnic organizations, and many others. This book will tell you how to perform every step of your scholarship search, so that you'll overlook no potential source of money for college.

After you locate the scholarships that you want to apply for, the Internet makes learning about them much easier. One secret to winning scholarships is only applying for those awards for which you are truly qualified. On the scholarship's Web site, you can learn exactly what the eligibility requirements are, and you don't have to worry about that information being out of date. Another secret to winning scholarships is presenting yourself in the application as the absolute best candidate. You do this by showing how well you fit the sponsor's mission and objectives in offering the award. On the scholarship's Web site, you can read about the sponsor's history, what it hopes to accomplish in awarding the scholarship, and the winning qualities that the sponsor is looking for in applicants. You can then use this information to craft the best application possible, greatly increasing your chances of winning. This book will show you how to put together a winning application package and how to present yourself in the best possible way in every part of that package.

Finally, the Internet makes applying for scholarships easier and cheaper, which means that you can apply for more awards. Previously, if you wanted to apply for a scholarship, you had to request an application form by mail and send a self-addressed, stamped envelope with your request. You then had to wait for the application to arrive, which meant that you risked either missing the deadline or not composing the best application package in order to get it in on time. But with the Internet, the cost and wait have been eliminated in most cases. Most scholarship Web sites provide application forms on the site that you can download and print right away. In some cases, you can actually fill out and submit the application online. This book will tell you exactly how to deal with all of the kinds of applications you'll find on scholarship Web sites and how to submit electronic applications.

The Internet makes all other steps of the college application process easier, as well. For instance, you can use the Internet to apply for financial aid from federal and state govern-

ments and from your school, which will go a long way toward helping you pay for college. (Don't worry—this book will tell you how to do that.) And you can use the Internet to research potential colleges, contact admissions and financial aid officers, decide where to apply, and even send in your college applications. Did you know that many colleges waive the application fee if you apply online? While applying to college can still be a nerve-wracking process, using the Internet as much as you can makes that process quicker, easier, and cheaper.

Remember that Web site addresses and Web pages change frequently and without warning. If you cannot locate a particular scholarship at the address given, try going to the top of the site by entering only the first part of the Web address and then searching the site or drilling down through the menus to locate the scholarship information.

What You'll Find Inside

This comprehensive directory of online scholarship programs further simplifies the process of hunting down scholarships on the Internet. The first half of the directory gives advice on all aspects of applying for scholarships, from how to use them to help pay for college, to how to craft applications that stand out from the crowd, to how to avoid scholarship scams.

Here's what you'll find in Part I:

- Chapter 1, "The Scoop on Scholarships," gives an overview of all kinds of financial aid, explains how to apply for federal, state, and college aid online, and tells the truth about how scholarships fit into the financial aid picture, blowing away many commonly held misconceptions. This chapter also tells you how to use scholarships effectively to pay your tuition bills and how to ensure that you get as much help with paying for college as you can.

- Chapter 2, "Using the Internet to Find Scholarships," explains how to hunt down all kinds of scholarships online, using both searchable scholarship databases and other methods in order to ensure that you find as many awards as possible. This chapter also provides sound suggestions for searching for scholarships out in the "real world," honestly evaluating your qualifications, and selecting the scholarships to apply for, the ones that you have the best chance of winning.

- Chapter 3, "Turning in a Winning Scholarship Application," goes over the process of crafting a perfect application package, from start to finish. You'll find out what scholarship judges are looking for in applicants, how to complete online application forms, how to write an outstanding essay, how to get the most effective letters of recommendation, and even how to get through an interview. Finally, you'll discover the most common mistakes other students make when completing scholarship applications and how to avoid them.

- Chapter 4, "Avoiding Scholarship Scams," guides you through the major pitfall of searching for scholarships online. Scholarship scams are becoming increasingly more prevalent, especially on the Web, but in this chapter you'll learn how to recognize the signs of a scam, how to evaluate suspicious scholarship programs, and how to report a scam if you do find one.

The second half of the book lists over 3,500 online scholarships, categorized so you can quickly pinpoint the awards that you qualify for. Each listing details at a glance all the important facts you need, including the sponsoring organization, deadline, award amount, and eligibility requirements. The listing also tells

you exactly how to locate the most up-to-date information about the scholarship at the program's Web site, how to apply online, and any pitfalls to watch out for. In each section you'll find cross references to scholarships listed in other parts of the book that also fit that category, so you won't miss any awards that you might qualify for. With this timely information at your fingertips, you can quickly locate and apply for more scholarships than ever before, resulting in more dollars for college.

Here's what you'll find in the listings:

- Chapter 5, "General Scholarships," lists scholarships that almost everyone can apply for, including academic scholarships, essay contests, science and technology competitions, and general contests.

- Chapter 6, "Academic and Career Interest Scholarships," lists scholarships that specify a particular major or career. Most of these scholarships are aimed at graduating high school seniors and college undergraduates.

- Chapter 7, "Graduate School Scholarships," lists scholarships and fellowships intended for students in graduate, medical, and professional programs, again categorized by field of study.

- Chapter 8, "Extracurricular Activity Scholarships," lists scholarships for students with particular hobbies, interests, and activities outside of school. In this chapter you'll find artistic and athletic scholarships, awards sponsored by clubs, sororities, and fraternities, and scholarships for students who work.

- Chapter 9, "Scholarships for Members of Minority and Ethnic Groups," lists scholarships intended for African American, Asian American, Hispanic, and Native American students, as well as awards aimed at particular ethnic groups, such as Greek and Portuguese students.

- Chapter 10, "Scholarships for Students with Disabilities and Medical Conditions," lists scholarships intended for students with physical disabilities or medical conditions, including students who are physically challenged, hearing impaired, or visually impaired.

- Chapter 11, "Religious Affiliation Scholarships," lists scholarships that specify that applicants adhere to a particular religion or Christian denomination.
- Chapter 12, "Gender-Based Scholarships," lists scholarships that specify that applicants either be female or male. The majority of these awards are targeted at female students.
- Chapter 13, "Military Service Scholarships," lists scholarships for students who join the Armed Forces, Reserve Officers Training Corps (ROTC), or National Guard and who agree to serve their country after receiving a college degree.
- Chapter 14, "Family Affiliation Scholarships," lists scholarships that you may qualify for by virtue of who you're related to. These include awards offered by employers, professional associations, unions, civic groups, and military groups, as well as government-sponsored scholarships for children of veterans and public safety officers.
- Chapter 15, "Residence-Specific Scholarships," lists scholarships that specify that applicants live in a particular state, city, or county. These awards are categorized by state and include a section specifically for Canadian students.
- Chapter 16, "College-Specific Scholarships," lists the Web sites of colleges and universities that provide detailed information about scholarships available to students of that school, including online applications in many cases.

Who This Book Is for

This book is aimed at all students who can use scholarships to help pay for higher education, including high school students getting ready to apply to college, current college undergraduates, adult students returning to school, and students in graduate, medical, and professional programs. This is the only scholarship directory to exclusively focus on Internet-based scholarship programs. Offering in-depth scholarship advice and comprehensive listings of online scholarships, *How to Find Scholarships Online* should be the only scholarship directory any student needs.

PART I

FINDING AND WINNING SCHOLARSHIPS

Winning scholarship money is a long process that requires a lot of work and dedication. Locating scholarships that you are qualified for is only the first step. Next you have to win those scholarships by impressing the judges with an outstanding application package, complete with essays, letters of recommendation, and other supporting documents. This book not only helps you find scholarships, but it guides you through the process of applying for them and winning them. These first four chapters share the secrets of finding and winning scholarships.

First, learn how scholarships fit into the financial aid package as a whole. Then, discover how to search for scholarships both on the Internet and out in the "real world." Find out how to put together an application package that makes an impression. And understand how to avoid the scholarship scams that have become so prevalent. If you follow the tips given in the following chapters, you'll be way ahead of the pack when it comes to winning money for college.

THE SCOOP ON SCHOLARSHIPS

Before you start your scholarship hunt, you should understand how financial aid works and how scholarships integrate into the total financial aid package that you will receive from your college. Scholarships will probably make up the smallest part of any financial aid package that your school gives you. In your search for scholarships, don't overlook other forms of financial aid.

This chapter provides an overview of the entire process of applying for and receiving financial aid. This process is pretty much the same no matter which college, university, community college, or other postsecondary school you choose to attend. You will discover where scholarships fit in with other forms of financial aid and how they help pay for college. You will also learn the truth behind scholarship myths that you may have heard.

For most students, financial aid is the key to acquiring a higher education. But many students and their parents do not take the time to understand what may seem, at first glance, an extremely complex procedure. After reading the overview of financial aid presented in this chapter, take the time to investigate further. Plenty of books describe the financial aid system in greater detail. The financial aid officer at the college you plan to attend is another valuable resource who can answer your questions and help you figure out financial aid. Finally, turn to the Internet for more information. The U.S. Department of Education gives a thorough overview of financial aid at http://www.ed.gov/studentaid. Another excellent repository of financial aid information is FinAid at http://www.finaid.org.

Financial Aid—The Big Picture

"Financial aid" refers to the entire gamut of programs that help students pay for higher education, ranging from the largest federal programs to the smallest locally sponsored scholarships. Understanding exactly what kinds of financial aid you can get and where that money is coming from will put you in a much stronger position when it comes time to evaluate financial aid awards from different colleges and negotiate for more aid.

Types of Financial Aid

Financial aid can be broken down into four broad categories: grants, loans, work-study programs, and scholarships.

Grants are awards that you do not have to repay. They are typically based on financial need. That is, you must prove that you need the grant money to pay for college in order to receive a grant. Grants typically come from public sources of financial aid, such as the federal government and your state's government.

Loans are aid that must be repaid, and they usually make up the largest part of the financial aid package. The federal government sponsors the largest student loan program, called the Stafford Loan program. These loans are a very good deal; they carry lower interest rates and more flexible repayment terms than private loans, and you don't even have to start repaying them until six months after you get your degree. You may be eligible for federal student loans whether or not you have financial need, and your parents can even borrow under this program. If you are not eligible, you can take out a private loan, which usually must be cosigned by your parents. While it is a bit more expensive to borrow from private banks and other organizations than through the Stafford Loan program, these loans still carry lower interest rates than consumer loans, such as the kind of loan you would get to buy a car.

Work-study programs enable you to earn your keep. In return for financial aid dollars, you must work a part-time job on-campus. You may get a job in the library or the cafeteria, or you may actually do work that is relevant to your field, such as working in a lab or assisting a professor. While the federal government sponsors the largest work-study program, your college decides what job to give you. Work-study awards typically make up the smallest part of the financial aid package.

Scholarships are gift aid, just like grants. But unlike grants, scholarships are usually awarded based not on financial need, but on merit. You may receive scholarships because you get good grades, are an excellent athlete, perform service in your community, or have an artistic talent. You may also receive scholarships based on who you are. Scholarship money goes to minorities, women, members of religious groups, veterans and dependants of veterans, and the disabled. Scholarships typically come from private sources, such as corporations, foundations, nonprofit groups, churches, and the schools themselves. Usually you must apply for them separately from other forms of financial aid.

Who Gives Financial Aid?

So who gives away all this money to help you go to college? Financial aid dollars come from four major sources: federal government, state government, colleges and universities, and private organizations.

Aid From Federal Government

The federal government is the largest source of financial aid, providing nearly 70 percent of the aid dollars awarded each year. There are three major federal financial aid programs: the Pell Grant program, campus-based programs, and the Stafford Loan program.

Pell Grants go only to the neediest students, those students who come from low-income families and disadvantaged backgrounds. Individual grants range from $400 to $3,000, with the average award falling around $1,700. The Pell Grant program is an entitlement program. Those students who qualify automatically receive a Pell Grant, as long as they apply for financial aid before the final deadline. Most of you will not qualify for a Pell Grant, though.

The colleges and universities administer the *campus-based* programs. These awards come in the form of a grant called the Federal Supplemental Educational Opportunity Grant, a work-study program called Federal Work-Study, and a very low-interest loan called the Federal Perkins Loan. The federal government gives each school a certain amount of money that it can award under the campus-based programs, and the school doles out the money to students there according to its own policies and formulas. Once that money is gone, it is really gone—no more campus-based aid can be given out until the next year's allotment comes through. For that reason alone, you should apply for financial aid as early as possible, before all the money is gone. Like the Pell Grant, awards from campus-based programs typically go to the neediest students.

The federal financial aid program that most students benefit from is the *Stafford Loan* program, which provides low-interest student loans. Students with financial need remaining after subtracting aid from other sources can borrow a subsidized Stafford Loan to cover all or part of the remaining need. With a subsidized loan, the government pays the interest while the student attends college and for six months after graduation. So students who borrow under this program have time to start working before they must start making loan payments, and the overall amount that must be repaid is less.

Even if you do not have financial need, you can still borrow under the Stafford Loan program to help pay for college. In that case, you must borrow an unsubsidized loan. You may opt to postpone repayment until after you graduate, but interest will accrue during the entire time that you are in college.

Even your parents can borrow under the Stafford Loan program. Stafford Loans that go to parents are called PLUS Loans. PLUS Loans are also low interest, although they cost a bit more than the Stafford Loans that go directly to students. Unlike student loans, though, they do not have any borrowing limits, and they can be used to make up both the family contribution and any financial need remaining after the college determines your financial aid award.

How do you apply for all of these financial aid programs? You only have to file one form, called the Free Application for Federal Student Aid (FAFSA). As the name implies, applying for federal financial aid is free. You will learn how to file the FAFSA later in this chapter.

Aid From State Government

State governments are the second-largest source of financial aid dollars. All 50 states have some kind of financial aid program in place, and collectively they award 6 percent of all available financial aid. The amount of financial aid money you will receive depends greatly on where you live. Some states—California, Illinois, New Jersey, New York, and Pennsylvania, in particular—are just more generous than others.

Kinds of state financial aid programs vary greatly from state to state, ranging from grants to low-interest loans to entitlement programs for the dependents of public officers killed or disabled in the line of duty. Ninety percent of state-sponsored financial aid is awarded based on financial need. Of the non-need-based, state-sponsored aid programs, the biggest chunk of cash goes into academic scholarships. You don't have to be ranked number one in your class to win scholarships from your state. Some states encourage students to enter needed professions, such as teaching or the health professions, by offering scholarships in exchange for service. Some states have large scholarship programs serving minority populations like African-Americans, Native Americans, and Hispanics. Others give out full-tuition scholarships to low-income students to encourage those students to stay in school.

If you are just starting college, the state where you went to high school is the state that gives you financial aid. You will continue to be eligible for financial aid money from that state as long as your parents can claim you as a dependant on their income tax forms, even if you go to college in another state. Just keep in mind that you are much more likely to qualify for financial aid money from your state if you attend an in-state school. Of course, the biggest state-sponsored financial aid programs are the public colleges and universities in your home state, which offer reduced tuition to in-state students. If you happen to live in a state that boasts an excellent public university system, you probably will not find a better bargain when it comes to higher education.

Each state has an agency that oversees most of the financial aid distributed by the state and administers the state's financial aid programs. Your state's financial aid agency is the best source of up-to-date, comprehensive information about the aid programs offered by your state. You can access a directory of state financial aid agencies with their addresses, phone numbers, and links to their Web sites on the FinAid site at http://www.finaid.org/otheraid/state.phtml.

Aid From Colleges and Universities

Next to the federal and state governments, colleges and universities are the largest contributors to the financial aid pot. Colleges have 5 billion dollars in their own funds to help students pay those exorbitant tuition bills. Just like the government, colleges award aid in the forms of grants, loans, and work-study programs, all based on financial need. But colleges are also a very large source of merit-based scholarships. Usually you apply for these scholarships simply by applying for admission to the college and submitting an application for financial aid. The financial aid office will tell you about any school-funded scholarships that you qualify for, so your research efforts in this area don't have to be as extensive as when searching for scholarships offered by private groups.

Be prepared to do a little detective work when searching for scholarships from your college, though. You may be eligible for scholarships offered by individual academic departments within the school, for instance. You may also qualify for athletic scholarships, artistic scholarships, or club-sponsored scholarships. You will learn how to hunt down all kinds of college-sponsored scholarships in Chapter 2, "Using the Internet to Find Scholarships."

Colleges and universities differ greatly in how they award financial aid. Some schools have a lot more money to give, simply because they have larger endowments. Some schools, particularly the more prestigious Ivy League colleges and universities, do not give out merit-based scholarships at all; all of the aid these schools award is based entirely on financial need. Others give out a lot of merit scholarships, particularly if they are trying to recruit gifted students or create a more diverse student body. If winning scholarships from your college is crucial to helping you afford to go to school, do a little research before you decide where to apply. Find out who the college gives financial aid to and how much aid the typical student receives; also ask if that aid is need-based or merit-based. An admissions officer or financial aid officer at the college should be willing to answer all of your questions about financial aid and scholarships awarded by the school.

Private Sources of Financial Aid

Private sources of financial aid include corporations, nonprofit groups, charitable foundations, churches, professional associations, unions, clubs, sororities and fraternities, and community organizations. Altogether, these groups give away the smallest amount of financial aid—less than 5 percent—but most of those dollars are awarded in the form of merit-based scholarships (although private groups also award a small number of grants and loans). Most of the scholarships listed in this book are sponsored by private organizations.

Applying for Financial Aid

Everyone who plans to go to college or graduate school should apply for financial aid, even those who don't think they will qualify. The formula for determining who gets financial aid and who doesn't is so complicated that no one can guess whether they will receive aid or how much aid they will get. Even if financial aid pays for only a small part of the tuition bill, that is still money that your family doesn't have to pay out of their pockets. Besides, applying for financial aid is often the only way to apply for merit-based scholarships sponsored by your college or university.

The first thing you should do is meet with a financial aid officer at each college where you are applying for admission. Schedule this meeting during the campus visit, and be sure to bring your parents along. If you cannot visit campus, then contact a financial aid officer by phone or e-mail.

The financial aid officer can tell you exactly what you need to do to apply for financial aid at that college. Find out the deadlines for applying for aid, and get copies of all required forms. The financial aid officer can also answer all of your questions about financial aid. Don't hesitate to ask about any part of the process, no matter how basic your questions may seem. Applying for financial aid is a complex, often daunting process, and very few people understand it right from the start. The financial aid officer's job is to help you, so take advantage of this valuable resource.

Even if you haven't decided where you're going to go to college yet, you should apply for financial aid at each school where you are applying for admission. Financial aid is often awarded on a first-come, first-served basis, so if you wait until the acceptance letters arrive in May, you will most likely miss out. The financial aid package that each school offers you can often help you make up your mind about where to go.

The first step in applying for financial aid is always the same, no matter which community college, four-year college, or university you end up attending. First, you must file the FAFSA, which enables you to receive financial aid from federal government programs. You only have to file one copy of the FAFSA, even if you are applying for admission to several colleges; simply indicate on the FAFSA which schools should receive the results. (You will have to reapply for financial aid every year that you remain in college or graduate school.)

Plan to file the FAFSA on or as soon after January 1 of your senior year in high school as possible. The earlier you apply, the faster you'll receive your results and the more aid you are likely to get. Since most schools award financial aid dollars first to those students who apply first, it really does benefit you to get your application in early.

According to the U.S. Department of Education, which processes the FAFSA, filing the FAFSA on the Internet is the fastest way to apply for financial aid. It also results in the fewest errors, since the computer checks for mistakes before sending in your application, which saves you even more time. Go to http://www.fafsa.ed.gov and follow the instructions to complete the electronic version of the FAFSA.

Make sure to find out what the requirements for applying for financial aid from your state and from your college are, so you won't miss out on any aid dollars. In most cases, the FAFSA also functions as an application for aid from your state and college, as well as from the federal government. So you will very likely only have to complete and submit one financial aid application form, the FAFSA. Some states require students to submit a separate form to apply for state-sponsored aid programs, though. Your guidance counselor or financial aid officer can tell you what financial aid forms your state requires and when the deadline for applying for state-sponsored aid is.

Some colleges, particularly the more prestigious private schools, require a separate financial aid application called the College Scholarship Service (CSS) Financial Aid PROFILE, which uses a different formula than the FAFSA to determine financial aid eligibility. You can register for the CSS/Financial Aid PROFILE in your high school guidance office, in college financial aid offices, and on the Internet at http://www.collegeboard.org/finaid/fastud/html/proform.html. You will receive a paper application in the mail approximately one week after registering, or you can complete the online version of the form at http://profileonline.cbreston.org. The financial aid officer at each college where you are applying for admission can tell you if the CSS/PROFILE or any other institutional financial aid applications are required to receive financial aid from that school.

About four weeks after you file the FAFSA—sooner if you applied online—you will receive a Student Aid Report (SAR). This form tells you what your Estimated Family Contribution (EFC) is, based on your family's financial circumstances as reported on the FAFSA. The EFC is the amount of money that your family as a whole is expected to contribute to the cost of your college education.

Look the SAR over carefully and correct any mistakes you find right away, following the instructions given on the form. After all errors have been corrected, the colleges can decide how much to award you in financial aid and what kinds of aid to give you.

To make this determination, the financial aid officer first figures out what your financial need is. Financial need equals the total cost of attending that college—including tuition, fees, room and board, books, and miscellaneous expenses like lab fees, special equipment, and disability services, if required—minus the EFC. So if the total cost of attending your first-choice college is $20,000 per year, and your EFC is $5,000, then your financial need would be $15,000.

Don't expect to receive the total amount of your financial need in financial aid awards, though. Colleges are not obligated to fulfill all of your financial need, and different schools have very different policies to determine how much aid to give to each student. Some colleges first fulfill the financial need of the neediest students. Others fulfill need on a first-come, first-served basis, so those students who apply for financial aid late may not receive any awards at all, regardless of how much financial need they have. And some schools fulfill a percentage of every student's need, but never all of the need for any student. Some colleges even make admission decisions based on how much financial need the applicant has, rejecting those students who are least able to pay. It's a good idea to ask an admissions officer or financial aid officer what the financial aid policies of the college are before you apply.

Soon after you receive your acceptance letter, you will also receive a financial aid package from the college. This package tells you how much total financial aid you received and what kinds of aid you got. Look over each financial aid package carefully before deciding which one to accept. A smaller financial aid package that contains more grants and scholarships may be more desirable than one that relies heavily on loans, leaving you with a lot of debt after you graduate.

If you are unhappy with the financial aid package that you got from your favorite college, you can always try to negotiate a better package with the financial aid officer. You will be in a better negotiating position if you can document special financial circumstances that the financial aid applications didn't take into account. If your family cares for an elderly relative, if you are disabled with special expenses, or if you are a single parent, you may very well qualify for more aid. Likewise, if you are a particularly desirable applicant—an outstanding student, accomplished artist, or talented athlete, perhaps—you may be able to negotiate for more aid as an incentive to attend that college. In those cases, you should also discuss the financial aid package with an admissions officer, who may be able to locate more merit-based scholarships for you.

How Scholarships Fit in

Scholarships are a very attractive form of financial aid. First, you don't have to pay them back. Also, you usually don't have to demonstrate financial need to win a scholarship, which makes them a viable alternative for middle-class students who don't qualify for much financial aid. Since scholarships often reward you based on what you have accomplished or based on who you are, you may be eligible for a large number of scholarships even if you aren't a stellar student.

Scholarships typically come from private groups rather than public sources of financial aid such as federal and state governments. For that reason, you must apply for scholarships separately than for other forms of financial aid. You can usually apply for federal, state, and college aid programs by filling out just one form, the FAFSA. You often must complete and mail in a separate application for each scholarship you want to win.

The only exceptions to this rule are scholarships sponsored by the colleges. Often these scholarships are awarded based on your admissions application or financial aid application, or both. In some cases, though, you do have to file separate scholarship applications to be considered for some scholarships awarded by the college, particularly the most prestigious academic scholarships. The athletic department, arts department, and individual academic departments may also require separate application forms for their scholarships. An admissions officer or financial aid officer can tell you exactly what forms you need to file to be considered for college-sponsored merit scholarships.

Unfortunately, scholarships make up a relatively small part of the financial aid picture—much smaller than many people believe. According to the U.S. Department of Education, only 4 percent of all undergraduate, graduate, and professional school students receive a privately sponsored scholarship, and the average award is only $1600. With the time that you must spend searching for scholarships that you are eligible to receive and filling out dozens of applications, the rewards may not seem worth it.

Nonetheless, hundreds of millions of dollars are awarded in the form of private scholarships each year—not an amount to take lightly. Even winning just a few hundred or a few thousand dollars in scholarships can make the difference in being able to afford your top-choice college. With the high costs of college

these days, every little bit helps. Just remember to go after the big awards available from federal, state, and college financial aid programs first and early, and then concentrate your efforts on picking up private scholarships.

Turning to Scholarships to Help Pay for College

Many students believe that if they win several scholarships from private sources, those awards, combined with the financial aid they receive from the federal government, state government, and their school, will result in a free ride to college. Unfortunately, scholarships are usually not the answer to your problems paying for college. You must report every scholarship dollar that you receive to the financial aid office at your school. Those scholarship awards are factored into your overall aid award, thus reducing the total amount of financial aid the college was originally going to give you. Your EFC remains exactly the same.

So scholarships are not free money awarded over and above the financial aid that you have already received. They won't make a dent in what you are expected to pay for college. That is one good reason why you should concentrate on getting aid through the federal, state, and college channels first. You are much more likely to receive more money from these sources than from private scholarship programs.

Searching and applying for scholarships requires an enormous amount of work. You will have to spend hours in front of the computer looking for scholarships that you qualify for. You will then have to spend even more time learning about each scholarship program, completing lengthy application forms, writing essays, gathering letters of recommendation, and making sure that your application package is absolutely perfect. Successful scholarship winners report that they spent 10 to 14 hours on every application they submitted. And since scholarship awards tend to be low, you must submit dozens of applications to win a significant amount of money.

Why then should you pursue scholarships at all? Depending on your specific financial situation, scholarships may help you pay for college in a better way.

First, if the bulk of your financial aid comes in the form of loans, winning scholarships can reduce your debt burden. When the financial aid officer adds your scholarship winnings to your financial aid package, the first thing that should be subtracted is aid from loans. If grant aid is taken away instead, you need to schedule an appointment to discuss the situation with your financial aid officer, or shop around for a better financial aid package.

Second, your school may give you very little aid or no financial aid at all, regardless of how much financial need you have. Likewise, you may not have a lot of financial need, or any need at all. In those cases, winning scholarships will help reduce your out-of-pocket expenses when paying for college.

Depending on which college you decide to attend, winning a scholarship can make a very big difference if you don't qualify for a lot of financial aid. Suppose that after you apply for financial aid, your EFC is $10,000. If you decide to attend an Ivy League school that costs $30,0000 a year, you will qualify for $20,000 in financial aid. If you receive a $5,000 scholarship, though, that money is combined with the rest of your financial aid package. You will still have to pay $10,000 out of your own pocket. But if you go to State U, which costs $9,000 a year, you will not qualify for any financial aid at all, since your EFC is higher than the total cost of attending the college. If you receive a $5,000 scholarship in that case, you will reduce your out-of-pocket contribution to $4,000, making it significantly cheaper to attend that

college. Since many scholarship awards are based on factors other than financial need, students who qualify for very little financial aid are eligible for a large number of scholarships.

Finally, winning scholarships is impressive. It gives you plenty of what you might call "prestige points." These honors look good on your resume, which could help you later when you apply to graduate school or job hunt. They may even help you win more scholarships in later years.

Common Misconceptions about Scholarships

Many myths and misunderstandings about scholarships get passed around the halls of high schools and among the parents of students getting ready to go to college. Before you start hunting for scholarships, you should understand the truth behind these misconceptions so you will not be taken in by them.

Unawarded Scholarships

The biggest myth about scholarships is that billions of dollars' worth of scholarship money goes unclaimed each year, just waiting for a savvy student like you to come along and scoop it up. Scholarship search services are mostly to blame for this myth, which they use in an effort to get you to hand over your money to them (you'll learn more about these search services in Chapter 4, "Avoiding Scholarship Scams").

The truth, according to most college financial aid offices, is that almost all available scholarship money is given out each year. The scholarships that are not awarded usually have highly restrictive eligibility requirements or strict deadlines. When you hear that 75 percent of all private financial aid went unclaimed last year, you should understand that that figure does not refer to scholarships at all. What it actually refers to is tuition assistance offered by companies to their employees (which means that if you are currently employed and considering going back to school, you should ask your human resources office about available educational benefits).

Free Rides

Many people mistakenly believe that scholarships are typically large awards that can provide a free ride to college. As you have already learned, scholarships rarely help pay for your EFC, because the scholarship awards are added into the total amount of financial aid that you have already received and an equal amount of aid from other sources is subtracted. Also, scholarship awards are typically small, often under $1,000, and you may not even be able to renew the scholarship for all four years of college. Winning a few scholarships can help you make a dent in what you must pay for higher education, but you should be prepared to dip into your savings or take out a student loan all the same.

Certainly, a few scholarship programs pay full tuition. Competition for the biggest prizes is fierce, however, and they typically go to students with the best possible qualifications. Even if you have perfect grades and test scores, you can't count on winning a full-tuition scholarship. Someone out there may have a better community service record than you, or more leadership experience.

Because scholarship awards are typically low, and because private scholarship programs are the smallest sources of financial aid dollars, you are much more likely to receive a lot more money from other sources of financial aid, especially the federal government. If you want or need a free ride, you will probably have to depend on a patchwork quilt of aid made up of grants, loans, work-study, and scholarships. Therefore, you should explore all sources of financial aid open to you, particularly federal and state programs, student loans, and aid from your school.

Do not neglect scholarships altogether, though. No financial aid award is too small. As you have already learned, winning a scholarship can help you by reducing the amount of student loans you have to take out or by making up for financial aid that you did not receive. Even a $100 scholarship can pay for a semester's worth of books. Just recognize that the bulk of your financial aid will probably not come from scholarships, and prioritize your time wisely in order to take advantage of all financial aid programs open to you.

Scholarships Only Go to the Best

Many students believe that because their grade point averages are just average or because they don't have a great athletic talent, they don't have a hope of winning any scholarships. While it is true that the largest scholarship awards go to the academic and athletic all-stars, those make up only a very small percentage of all the scholarship programs that are open to you.

Many scholarship programs do not even consider academic or athletic ability, or consider these as secondary requirements. Most programs are tailored to a small percentage of the population—students who plan to study microbiology, for instance, or students who have an amateur radio license. Your unique qualities are probably what will win you scholarships, whether you have an unusual hobby, plan to study a particular subject, or even live in a particular place. So while you may not qualify for the national scholarships or the huge athletic awards, you may easily find that you are best in your field when it comes to the smaller scholarships with more restricted eligibility requirements. Keep hunting for those scholarships—don't give up before you start.

The most important qualities in winning scholarships are not grades and athletic ability, but determination and persistence. The students who are most likely to win scholarships are the ones who put in the hard work hunting down the scholarships they are well qualified for, crafting professional application packages, and getting them to the right place at the right time. Think of applying for scholarships as a job—put in the time and the effort, and you will probably get paid.

USING THE INTERNET TO FIND SCHOLARSHIPS

The first step in winning scholarships is to hunt down those scholarships for which you are most qualified. While thousands of scholarship programs are out there, no one will just hand the money to you. You have to search it out. There is no central place where scholarships are advertised, and no book or database can claim to list all available awards. Therefore, you must use every resource at your disposal to search for scholarships to put together the most complete list possible of scholarships that you have a good chance of winning.

Many scholarship application deadlines come early in the school year, often before second semester starts. Many scholarships are awarded on a first-come, first-served basis, and some scholarship programs may stop accepting applications early if they receive too many. It pays to start your search early. Start hunting for college scholarships during your sophomore or junior year of high school.

There are scholarships for students at all levels of study, from graduating high school seniors through the doctoral level, so don't give up your scholarship hunt once you reach college. Actually, more scholarship programs are aimed at college upperclassmen than at entering freshmen. Your school probably awards several scholarships to continuing students, and you may also find scholarships sponsored by your major department, academic organizations, and fraternities and sororities. Colleges also give special scholarships to transfer students and to nontraditional students—adult students who are returning to higher education after spending time in the workforce or as homemakers. Consider the scholarship search to be an ongoing process that you will continue all through college and graduate school.

In this chapter you'll learn how to conduct a scholarship search efficiently and come up with good results. You'll find out what kinds of scholarships are available and where to start looking for them, both on the Internet and out in the "real world." You'll also discover out how to evaluate your unique qualifications and match those characteristics to scholarship programs so that you end up applying only for those scholarships that you truly have the best chance of winning.

Kinds of Scholarships

There are as many different kinds of scholarships as organizations that sponsor scholarship programs. Each scholarship sponsor has a different goal it wants to accomplish by awarding scholarship money. So even if you do not have the best grades or the most prowess on the athletic field, you shouldn't give up the scholarship search. Chances are that you are uniquely qualified for scholarships that you never even considered.

This section describes the major types of scholarships that you can search for. You'll find listings of each type of scholarship in Part II of this book.

Academic Scholarships

Academic scholarships are rewards for students who have already demonstrated their academic talents. These scholarships go to the students with the best grades, the highest test scores, and the most challenging courseloads. Some are awarded only to valedictorians and salutatorians. While some private organizations sponsor academic scholarships, most are awarded by the colleges themselves and by state governments. If you have outstanding academic qualifications, you should seek out these scholarships.

Contests

Many contests aimed at young people award scholarships as prizes. While some contest results are as random as the Publisher's Clearinghouse Sweepstakes, most actually reward the entrants' academic and artistic talents. Some contests award top prizes to the best essays or speeches written on a particular subject. Others reward students for science, technological, or Internet projects. Another category of contests gives prizes to students who enter the best artwork, photograph, cartoon, creative writing sample, or musical performance. If you have talent in any of these areas, you should seek out contests that award scholarships. Just be aware that entering a lot of contests can be a time-consuming process since you will often have to write an essay or put together a project in addition to completing the application form.

In addition to the individual contests listed in Part II of this book, you can get a list of contests approved by the National Association of Secondary School Principals from their Web site. Since these contests are preapproved, you know they are not scams and are worth spending your time on. You can download the list of contests at http://www.nassp.org/publications/contest_activities/index.html.

Career and Academic Interest Scholarships

A large number of scholarships go to college and graduate school students who want to study a specific field or pursue a particular career. These scholarships are usually sponsored by academic organizations, professional associations, industry groups, companies, and academic departments within a college. State and federal governments also sponsor career-oriented scholarships to entice students into entering needed professions, such as the sciences, health professions, and teaching. To be eligible, you often have to declare a major or otherwise demonstrate to the scholarship judges that you are serious about pursuing the field of study that the scholarship supports. If you already know what you want to study, you should definitely look for these scholarships. To find them, ask your professors about scholarship opportunities, and join the campus chapter of your field's professional association. Also watch for scholarship opportunities posted on your major department's Web page.

Athletic Scholarships

Athletic scholarships don't just go to the all-stars on the football, basketball, and baseball fields. Scholarships are awarded for practically every sport, including archery, badminton, bowling, crew, fencing, gymnastics, lacrosse, sailing, skiing, and synchronized swimming. You simply have to seek out these less well-known awards.

Athletic departments of colleges and universities sponsor most athletic scholarships. The biggest schools will woo the best jocks in the most popular sports, of course. If you can't compete in that arena, look at smaller colleges and universities with ambitious sports programs. Though your skills may not have gotten you far at Big State U, the smaller college may be happy to have you and willing to supply scholarship money to entice you to attend.

If you decide to pursue athletic scholarships, start searching for them early—as early as your sophomore year in high school. Your coach can probably recommend colleges that have strong programs in your sport. Numerous college guides break down athletic scholarships by sport to make your search easier. Contact the coaches for your sport at each college you are interested in attending, and inquire about scholarship opportunities. Put together an athletic résumé that lists your accomplishments in the sport, your stats, your coach's name, the camps or summer programs you have attended, the honors you have won, and anything else that you think will improve your chances for winning a scholarship. You might also include a letter of recommendation from your coach, newspaper clippings about your athletic accomplishments, and even a videotape showing you in action.

Federal law requires that colleges and universities offer an equal amount of scholarships to female athletes as to male athletes. Therefore, most colleges have large scholarship programs open to female athletes but the competition for those dollars is not as great. If you are a woman and play a sport, do not overlook this lucrative source of funding.

Community Service Scholarships

Performing community service, while personally rewarding, can also help you win scholarships. While you are in high school, look for ways that you can volunteer in your community. You can serve in local hospitals, animal shelters, retirement homes, and libraries. Or you can help out with hotlines, mentoring programs, literacy programs, and community clean-ups. You are certain to find opportunities for community service that match your particular interests. And all your hard volunteer work is likely to pay off in scholarship money. Many scholarship programs seek out students with strong backgrounds in community service, and some are intended solely to reward students for outstanding service efforts. (Your community service record will look good to college admissions committees, as well.)

Club and Hobby Scholarships

Joining clubs and participating in extracurricular activities looks good on your college applications because it shows that you are well rounded and have interests outside of school. But clubs and extracurricular activities are also a major source of scholarships. If you belong to any kind of afterschool club or have a particular hobby, look for scholarships that support your interest. You may be surprised at what you find out there. There are scholarships for students with passions for ham radio, bowling, horseback riding, marching band, and gardening, to name a few. Other big sponsors of scholarships include academic honors societies, sororities and fraternities, scouting groups, service organizations, 4-H, Future Farmers of America, and Future Business Leaders of America.

Minority and Ethnic Scholarships

A large number of scholarships are awarded exclusively to members of minority groups, both as a way to open opportunities to traditionally disadvantaged groups and to entice minorities into schools and professions where they have been underrepresented. These scholarships are sponsored by state governments, colleges and universities, and private groups like professional associations, corporations, and charitable foundations. If you are a member of a minority group—African-American, Hispanic, Pacific Islander, Native American, or Alaskan Native—you will be eligible for a wide range of lucrative scholarship programs. Take advantage of them.

In addition to minority scholarships, some scholarships are aimed at specific ethnic groups, such as students with a Hellenic, Portuguese, Italian, Polish, Asian, or Norwegian background. Ethnic associations most often sponsor these scholarships. If you know your ethnic background and can document it, you should seek out these awards.

A growing group of minority scholarships are scholarships for gay, lesbian, bisexual, and transsexual students. These scholarship programs often require that you identify yourself as a gay, lesbian, bisexual, or transsexual person. They are also awarded to students who are active volunteers in the gay and lesbian community.

Scholarships for Students with Disabilities

If you have a disability or a long-term medical condition, you may very likely be eligible for scholarship money. The best source of information about such scholarships is the office of disability support services at your college or university. National advocacy groups for the disabled and state governments are also major sources of disability scholarships.

Religious Affiliation Scholarships

Many organized religious groups are big sources of scholarship money, particularly for students who intend to enter the ministry or attend colleges affiliated with the church. Some religious groups also provide educational loans to their members. To learn about such scholarships, start by asking your local religious leader. You will have a better shot at winning religious scholarships if you have been active in your religious community and have performed community service.

Gender-Based Scholarships

Just as many scholarship programs are awarded exclusively to minorities, many target female students in an effort to entice women into professions where they are traditionally underrepresented or to provide them the same opportunities as men. If you are a female student, you should seek out scholarships targeted at women in your field of study sponsored by corporations, professional associations, academic groups, and your school. Athletic schol-

arships are another big source of funding for female students, as you have already learned. A unique category of scholarships for women is beauty pageants. If you feel comfortable with entering pageants, you may find them a lucrative source of college funding.

There are not as many scholarships for men as there are for women, but there are a few. Groups like the Boy Scouts and fraternities often sponsor these awards.

Military Scholarships

The military is a huge source of funding for college. If you enlist in a branch of the Armed Forces, you will become eligible for the Montgomery GI Bill, an education benefits program that can pay your entire tuition bill. Or you can elect to join the Reserve Officers Training Corps (ROTC) while in college, which provides two-, three-, and four-year scholarships to eligible members; in return, you are expected to serve as an officer in the Armed Forces after you graduate. For more information on the Montgomery GI Bill and the ROTC, contact your local recruiter or your on-campus ROTC office.

Veterans are eligible for educational benefits from the Veterans Administration, as well as scholarships from civic groups, state governments, and military-related foundations. If you are a veteran and you would like to pursue a higher education, you should look into all sources of educational benefits open to you. For more information about educational benefits for veterans, visit the U.S. Department of Veterans Affairs' Web site at http://www.gibill.va.gov.

Family Affiliation Scholarships

You may be eligible for scholarships because of who your parents are. Your parents' employers may provide scholarships to the dependents of employees; the human resources office at your parents' companies can tell you more about such programs. If your parents belong to professional associations, unions, civic organizations, fraternities or sororities, or clubs, you may be eligible for scholarship money from them, as well. You may also get a legacy scholarship if you attend the same college as one of your parents. Sit down with your parents and make a list of potential sources of scholarship money.

A large number of scholarships are available for the dependents of veterans, military officers, and public safety officers like police officers, firefighters, and correctional officers, particularly if they were disabled or killed in the line of duty. If either of your parents fits into one of those groups, search out scholarship programs offered by civic organizations, veterans' groups, and state governments. Finally, if one of your parents is disabled, you may also be eligible for scholarship money from your state.

Regional Scholarships

As you have already learned, states offer a lot of scholarship money to their residents. But regional scholarships programs do not stop at the state level. You may also be able to locate scholarships for students living in your county, city, or school district sponsored by local governments, Chambers of Commerce, and community foundations. Local scholarships are often easier to win because the competition for them is not so great, so you should definitely apply for as many as you can find. The best sources of information about local scholarships are your newspaper and library, which often publish scholarship announcements.

College-Sponsored Scholarships

As you already know, the college or university that you attend is a huge source of scholarship money. An admissions officer or financial aid officer can tell you about college-wide merit- and need-based scholarships that you might qualify for. Also seek out scholarships from your academic department, the clubs you join, the athletic teams you play for, and your sorority or fraternity.

Tips for the Search—Both Online and Off

Be thorough in your search for scholarship. Many scholarships, particularly college and local scholarships, are underpublicized, but these are also the awards that you are most likely to win. Therefore, you cannot just search one computer database or leaf through one scholarship guide and call your search finished. Take advantage of as many sources as you can to build as complete a list of scholarships as possible. If you take the time to perform a thorough search, you are much more likely to end up with some scholarship money.

Scholarship Search Services

The Internet provides an invaluable resource for finding scholarships: electronic scholarship search services. A number of Web sites now provide access to huge databases of scholarships that you can quickly search just by filling out an electronic form. The best news is that these scholarship search services are all free!

Searching these databases is the best investment of your time. In just a few hours you can compile a long list of scholarships that you are well qualified for. Combine that with searching books like this one, and you will probably find more scholarships than you will have time to apply for.

You can connect to all of the following free scholarship search services on the Internet:

- CASHE: http://www.cashe.com/runsearch.html
- College Board: http://www.collegeboard.org/fundfinder/html/ssrchtop.html
- CollegeNET Mach 25 Scholarship Search: http://www.collegenet.com/mach25
- CollegeQuest: http://www.collegequest.com
- Embark.Com: http://www.embark.com/UserProfile/login.asp
- FastAid: http://www.fastaid.com
- FastWeb: http://www.fastweb.com
- FreSch!: http://www.freschinfo.com
- GoScholarshipSearch: http://www.gocollege.com/goscholarshipsearch/index.html
- ScholarAid: http://www.scholaraid.com
- Scholarships 101: http://208.225.207.218/scholarships101
- StudentAwards.Com: http://www.studentawards.com (for Canadian students only)
- *U.S.News* Scholarship Search: http://www.usnews.com/usnews/edu/dollars/scholar/search.htm

Most scholarships search services require you to fill out a personal profile listing your individual characteristics and accomplishments. The program then combs the database of scholarships to find those that you may be eligible for, according to the information that you gave in the profile. Therefore, you should be as accurate as possible when completing the profile in order for the program to come up with the best list of scholarships for you. Read the instructions carefully before you get started.

Typically, your scholarship search results will provide a lot of useful information about the scholarship, including eligibility requirements, the amount awarded, the deadline for application, and an address where you can write to get an application form. To request a scholarship application via the mail, write a brief, polite note indicating your name, your year in school, the name of the school you attend, and the scholarship that you want to apply for. Always include a self-addressed, stamped envelope for the reply.

Since no scholarship database is complete, you should take the time to search as many of them as possible. Of course, you will come up with some duplicates, but performing multiple searches is the only way to be sure that you have found all the scholarships for which you are qualified. Besides, the searches are free and don't take very long to complete, so what have you got to lose (except for scholarship awards)?

More Places to Search for Scholarships on the Internet

This book lists over 3,500 scholarships that you can find information about on the Internet. You can even apply for most of them online or download application forms directly from the scholarship program's Web site. But like any guide, this book cannot list every scholarship program. You should also do some detective work on your own to find scholarships for which you are uniquely qualified. Fortunately, with the entire Internet at your disposal, that search should not take you very long.

Your first stop should be the Web sites of all the colleges where you are applying for admission (or the college you already attend). You'll find a list of all college Web sites at http://www.mit.edu:8001/people/cdemello/univ.html, or you can search for your school on Yahoo! (http://www.yahoo.com). Often the Web address is easy to guess if you remember that college Web sites always end in .edu. For instance, Duke's Web site is http://www.duke.edu, and the University of North Carolina's Web site is http://www.unc.edu.

College Web sites are often gold mines of scholarship information, if you know where to look for it. First, check the admissions page, which often lists merit scholarships. Then, go to the financial aid page, which may also list merit scholarships. Check out the page for your academic department to discover if any scholarships for your field of study are mentioned. The Web site may also contain information about artistic, athletic, study abroad, and ROTC scholarships sponsored by the school. Graduate students should check the graduate school section of the site, which often lists university-sponsored fellowships and fellowships from external sources. Besides scholarship and fellowship listings, you will probably find online applications, the names of people you can contact for more information, and tips for preparing scholarship applications.

Next, look for local scholarships. Check the Web site for your state's financial aid agency (a list of these agencies, with links to their Web sites can be found at http://www.finaid.org/otheraid/state.phtml). These sites list state-sponsored financial aid programs and tells you how to apply for state aid. Next, search for home pages of your county government, city government, local civic organizations, community foundations, and high school. Any of these might list scholarship opportunities.

But don't stop there. Try to think of other Web sites where you might find scholarship listings. These can include the Web sites of your parents' employers and professional associations, the home pages of any clubs you belong to, and your church's Web site.

Finally, turn to the major search engines, like HotBot (http://www.hotbot.com), Excite (http://www.excite.com), and AltaVista (http://www.altavista.com). If you just search for the word "scholarship," though, you will find hundreds of thousands of matches, more than you can possibly look at. Most of the matches will not match your qualifications anyway. But if you are looking for scholarships with very specific qualifications, search engines are the most effective tools to employ. For instance, if you play chess and want to track down chess scholarships, search one of the major search engines for the phrase "chess scholarship." While you may not come up with the names of any specific scholarships, you should at least find some

colleges that award chess scholarships where you can apply for admission.

Searching Offline

While the Internet is an invaluable research tool and can make your scholarship search significantly easier, you will not find every scholarship publicized online. Therefore, you should expend some effort out in the real world, as well.

The first place to start is in your own community, where you will likely find the most scholarships that you are qualified for, scholarships that are least likely to be publicized on the Internet. The following are some places in your hometown where you can look for scholarship announcements:

- Your high school guidance office or college academic department
- Your church, synagogue, or temple
- Local government offices
- The Chamber of Commerce
- Your employer
- Your parents' employers
- Clubs, athletic teams, academic societies, and other organizations you belong to
- Clubs, unions, professional associations, and civic groups that your parents belong to
- Civic and public service organizations
- Your local library, where scholarship announcements are often posted
- Your local newspaper, which scholarship announcements are often published

Next, look for scholarships at each college where you are applying for admission. When you plan a campus visit, schedule appointments with an admissions officer and with a financial aid officer. These people are your best sources of information about college-sponsored scholarships. While you are on campus, contact the head of the academic department where you plan to study to inquire about subject-specific scholarships. If you are an athlete, visit the coach of your sport to ask about scholarship opportunities. If you are an artist, dancer, actor, or musician, visit the appropriate art department to inquire about scholarships for majors and nonmajors; be prepared to audition or submit samples of your work if requested. Also get in touch with the faculty advisors of any extracurricular activities you plan to participate in, such as the newspaper or debate club, to find out if any scholarships are available for students with that interest. If you plan to go to graduate school, visit the graduate office both at the college you currently attend and the universities where you intend to apply for admission to learn about funding opportunities for post-graduate studies.

If you haven't yet decided where to apply for college, invest in a good college guide. These guides provide important details about each college that can give clues to where you are most likely to find scholarships that match your talents and interests. You can learn what the strongest academic departments are, for instance; money from industry groups and corporations often gravitates toward schools with strong academic departments in that field. You can also learn what athletic teams and extracurricular activities the school sponsors, which helps you determine which activities they might provide scholarships to promote. If you look out for potential scholarship opportunities when you start your college search, you may discover colleges where you never would have thought of applying but that are willing to give you the money, academics, and extracurriculars that you are looking for.

If you still have time to devote to your scholarship search, go to the library and consult Gale's Encyclopedia of Associations. This reference is one of the most valuable resources for a scholarship search (but it is very expensive, which is why you should look for it at the library). It lists names and contact information for professional associations, industry groups, ethnic societies, religious groups, and advocacy groups for minorities, women, and the disabled. Make a list of all the groups that have a connection with your field of study or background qualities. Then send a brief letter to each group to inquire about scholarship opportunities (include a self-addressed, stamped envelope for the reply). You may be surprised at what unpublicized scholarship programs you may turn up.

Finally, take the PSAT/NMSQT during your junior year in high school. Not only will this help you prepare for the SAT I, but if you score high enough, you may also qualify for National Merit Scholarships. These prestigious scholarships are given out by the National Merit Scholarship Corporation and by college and corporate sponsors. Some colleges work extra hard to recruit National Merit finalists because of the prestige that winning the award brings to the institution. So although the actual scholarship received by National Merit finalists is not that large, it can earn you offers of more attractive financial aid packages as schools try to recruit you.

Evaluating Your Qualifications

The key to winning scholarship money is to find awards that you are well qualified for and expend your efforts in applying for them. No matter how good a student you are, if you don't match the eligibility requirements for a particular scholarship, you don't have a hope of winning it.

It will help your scholarship search efforts if you make a list of all of your achievements, interests, and other qualifications before you start. Creating this personal profile can help you think of scholarship programs that you might have otherwise overlooked. The profile will also come in handy when you start filling out scholarship applications and writing essays. You can even give a copy of it to people you ask to write letters of recommendation for you, to make their jobs easier.

To help you think about the kinds of qualifications that will win you scholarships, go to one of the online scholarship search services listed in the previous section of this chapter. Each scholarship search service requires you to fill out a form listing your personal characteristics, which are then matched with scholarship programs. After filling out the form, print out a copy of it or make a note of your answers. After you perform a number of online scholarship searches, you should have enough information to put together a personal profile.

Any of the following factors could qualify you for a scholarship, so include them all when drawing up your personal profile:

- Gender
- Race or ethnic background
- Citizenship
- The state, county, and city where you live
- The name of your college, or the name of your high school and the colleges where you applied for admission
- Any disabilities that you have or your parents have
- Your year in school
- Your grade point average
- Your class rank
- Your PSAT/NMSQT score
- Your SAT I or ACT scores
- The field you plan to major in
- Your strongest academic subjects
- Academic awards you have won
- Special academic programs you have completed
- Sports you actively participate in
- Student government positions you have held

- All clubs and other organizations you belong to
- Hobbies you actively pursue
- Artistic talents or pursuits (visual arts, photography, dance, drama, music, or creative writing)
- Your employers, present and past
- Internships you have completed
- Community service and volunteer activities you participate in
- Religious organizations you are affiliated with
- Military service you have completed
- Where your parents are employed and their occupations
- All professional associations, unions, clubs, sororities, fraternities, civic groups, and other organizations your parents belong to
- The colleges your parents attended
- Whether your parents are veterans or currently active in any branch of the Armed Forces or the National Guard

Selecting the Scholarships You Should Apply for

Applying for scholarships is a time-consuming process. You should only spend your time applying for scholarships that you have the best chance of winning.

The first thing to remember is to limit your applications to the scholarships where you match all of the eligibility requirements. Many students believe that if they take a scattershot approach and apply for each and every scholarship they find, they are bound to win something. Not so. If you do not meet the scholarship's often rigid eligibility requirements, you application goes straight into the trash—literally.

Before deciding whether to apply for a scholarship, check your qualifications against the eligibility requirements listed on the scholarship's brochure or Web page. Look for a minimum grade point average and make sure you measure up. Also check if a year of study or number of college credits is specified; these usually must be listed on your transcript in order for you to qualify for the scholarship.

Next, check residency requirements. Many scholarship programs specify a state residency. If you are a dependant student—if your parents can still claim you as a dependant on their tax returns—then your state of residence is the state where your parents live, not the state where you attend college. You may be asked to provide proof of residency, such as a driver's license or an income tax return.

Find out if you need to belong to the sponsoring group to be eligible for the scholarship. If the sponsor is a professional or academic association, one of the requirements is likely to be membership in the group. Usually you can join by checking a box on the scholarship application, but you may have to submit the first year's membership dues along with the application.

Some scholarship programs do consider financial need when deciding who to give money to. If you have already applied for federal financial aid, you should have a good idea of how much financial need you have. But if you haven't filed the FAFSA or received the results, consider your family income when estimating your financial need. Most scholarship sponsors will not consider you needy if your parents make a decent income, particularly when you are competing against families who make $20,000 a year or less. So don't apply for scholarships that factor in financial need unless you are sure that you have need and you can demonstrate this to the scholarship committee. If you need help making this decision, the financial aid officer at your college can often provide a good reality check.

These are just a few of the eligibility requirements that you are likely to run into when

you start searching for scholarships. Other scholarship programs may specify that you have a particular ethnic background or minority status, that you belong to a particular religion, or that your parents belong to the sponsoring group or be employed in a particular profession. If you don't understand all of the eligibility requirements, contact the scholarship's sponsor by phone or e-mail to clarify them.

Just because you meet all of a scholarship's eligibility requirements does not mean that you are a good candidate to win that scholarship. Some scholarship programs are very competitive. These programs usually also require the most effort in terms of writing essays, gathering letters of recommendation, and submitting additional materials with your application for the scholarship. Before you decide to apply, evaluate yourself honestly to determine if you are a competitive candidate for that award. Check the profiles of past winners to see if your qualifications are similar to theirs; often you can find these profiles on the scholarship program's Web site. If the average grade point average of past winners is 4.0 and yours is 3.5, for instance, you are not very likely to win that scholarship. Or if past winners all had community service experience and you don't, you won't make a very good candidate. Other qualities that you should consider include leadership experience, creativity, ability to rise above disadvantages, and even personal character. Compare yourself to past winners in these areas to determine if the scholarship judges would think that you are a good candidate for the award.

Reading over the application form can also give you a clue as to whether you will make a good candidate for that scholarship. You should have a strong response to every question on the application. If you find questions that don't really apply to you, then that scholarship probably is not meant for you.

In your scholarship search, try to find scholarship programs where the competition is not so great. You have a much better chance of winning these awards. Instead of expending your efforts on the large national scholarship competitions, look for local scholarships. Find scholarships aimed at students of your ethnic group or gender. Remember that the more specific eligibility requirements a scholarship has, the less competition there is likely to be for that award. For instance, a scholarship for African-American microbiology students from Santa Barbara, California, will probably have very few applicants; if you fit all of those requirements, then you should definitely apply.

If you do decide to apply for a national prestigious scholarship, enlist the help of someone at your high school or college, such as your guidance counselor, financial aid officer, or academic advisor. For prestigious awards like the Rhodes Scholarship and the Truman Fellow-ship, your college will most likely have a contact in the honors office, scholarships office, or financial aid office whose job it is to help students prepare applications. Get in touch with that person as soon as you decide to apply, so that you can get all the help you will need to win such a prestigious prize.

Your scholarship search efforts should have turned up a long list of scholarships for which you are qualified to apply. To maximize your chances of winning some scholarship money, apply for as many of the scholarships you found as you can. You should apply for at least 10 scholarships every year you are in college. Just remember to spend the bulk of your time and efforts on the applications for the scholarships that you honestly feel you have the best chance of winning, which are not necessarily the scholarships with the biggest payoffs.

TURNING IN A WINNING SCHOLARSHIP APPLICATION

You may think that hunting down scholarships was a difficult job, but your hard work has not even begun yet. In fact, finding scholarships that match your qualifications is probably the easiest part. Preparing the scholarship applications will take considerably more of your time and efforts.

But taking care to put together prefect application packages is time well spent. If your application does not appear neat and professional to the scholarship judges, you won't have a chance of winning the scholarship, no matter how well qualified you are for the award. Plan to spend several hours crafting each application and putting together the supplemental materials required. The judges will expect perfection of the student to whom they award the scholarship, so perfection is what you should strive for.

Your application package must also convince the scholarship committee that they should give the award to you. You must use every part of the application package to demonstrate to the judges that you are most qualified to receive the scholarship and that you will best use the scholarship money to achieve the sponsor's goals. You also have to spend some time figuring out exactly what those goals are in order to accomplish this. This chapter will help you figure that out.

You will also learn about the different kinds of scholarship applications that you are likely to find on the Internet and how to complete each one in a way that will impress the scholarship committee. Most scholarship programs require applicants to submit additional materials, such as essays, letters of recommendation, and transcripts; this chapter will give you valuable tips on preparing each part of the application package. Finally, you'll learn about

some common mistakes that you must avoid to put yourself in the running for any scholarship award.

If you follow all of the tips that you learn in this chapter, you are guaranteed to place yourself among the top candidates for any scholarship you apply for.

What Scholarship Committees Are Looking For

Every scholarship sponsor has a reason for offering that particular scholarship. If you can figure out what the sponsor's goals for the scholarship are, you can better demonstrate in your application that you will best fulfill those goals.

The best way to do this is to learn as much as you can about the scholarship program before you start filling out the application. The scholarship sponsor's Web site will be a big help to you. Explore the Web site to find out more about the organization sponsoring the scholarship. What kind of group is it—a professional association, a charitable foundation, a civic group? Try to discover what goals the sponsor has by supporting higher education. Perhaps the sponsor wants to bring more students into a particular field or recruit students whose work will help a particular population of people. Find out what other activities the organization sponsors and what kinds of people belong to the group. Read about past winners of the scholarship to determine what qualities the sponsor is looking for in the students to whom they award scholarships.

Make notes on the qualities that you think the scholarship committee is looking for in scholarship applicants, based on what you find on the Web site. When you start filling out the application, keep those notes close to hand so that you can highlight those qualities in yourself with the information that you choose to provide in the application and essay.

Most scholarship sponsors have similar goals in awarding scholarship money. They want to give financial aid to students who are most likely to use the money to further their educational goals and who will make a valuable contribution after achieving those goals, whether that be by pursuing a worthwhile career, becoming active in the community, or mentoring to others. To achieve these objectives, scholarship judges look for applicants who have solid academics, creativity, leadership ability, and a sense of responsibility. They search out applicants who have already served in the community and who have overcome special circumstances to achieve their personal goals. These are the qualities that you should highlight in your scholarship applications.

If you cannot find enough information about the scholarship program on the Web site, you should at least find the name and address of the contact for the scholarship program. Request a printed scholarship application form in the mail. This form typically comes with a brochure or letter explaining the purpose of the scholarship. Don't forget to include a self-addressed, stamped envelope with your request.

Organizing Scholarship Applications

Since you are probably applying for 10 or more scholarships, it is a good idea to get organized right from the start. Later, when you are trying to beat deadlines and put together complete application packages, you'll be glad you did.

Once you decide which scholarships you want to apply for and have gathered all the information and application forms for them, start a file for each scholarship. On the front of the file, write the scholarship's name, the application deadline, the name of the sponsoring organization, and the sponsor's contact information, including the postal address, phone number, e-mail address, and Web site address. Put copies of everything pertaining to the scholarship in the file, including all of the information about the scholarship you receive, a copy of the completed application form and any other materials you submit, and any correspondence you receive or send regarding the scholarship. If any item of the application package becomes lost or damaged, you can simply replace it with the copy in your files. Also, if you decide to reapply for the scholarship in subsequent years, you can save time by consulting the copies you made of the scholarship information and application materials. You may even be able to reuse some of the scholarship materials, such as an essay you wrote or a letter of recommendation, in your other scholarship applications.

Also create a scholarship tracking sheet using a calendar or spreadsheet program where you can keep track of your progress on all the scholarships you are applying for. Create a column for each scholarship, noting the name of the award, the name of the sponsoring organization, the sponsor's contact information, and the date you downloaded or requested the application. Also list every item that you must submit in the application package and the application deadline. Tick off each item as you complete it, and note the date when you sent in the application package. Try to submit the application as early before the final deadline as possible, because some scholarship programs close competitions early if they receive too many applications. Also make a note on your tracking sheet of the date when you are supposed to learn whether you won the scholarship.

Completing the Online Application

Most scholarship programs that advertise on the Internet provide an application right on the Web site that you can either print out or submit electronically. This means that you do not have to request and wait for an application form to arrive by mail, which can make the difference in meeting deadlines. You are most likely to find three kinds of scholarship applications on the Internet: interactive electronic applications; printable applications in Portable Document Format (PDF); and printable, plain text applications. You will need to deal with each kind of application in a separate way.

Electronic Applications

Electronic applications can be filled out online and submitted over the Internet. These applications are interactive; in other words, you can type directly into them and click a Submit button at the end of the application form to send your responses to the sponsor. Electronic applications are the most desirable of online scholarship applications because they let you submit an application quickly and easily. In fact, some scholarship programs will not accept applications any other way.

If you find an electronic application for a scholarship for which you intend to apply, it will be tempting to go ahead and fill the application out in one sitting, and then click the Submit button. Despite the ease of submitting electronic applications, you must take as much care with them as you would with printed ap-

plication forms if you want to be seriously considered for the scholarship.

The first thing you should do is print a hard copy of the electronic application form. Your Web browser's print function is found under the File menu; most Web browsers also have a Print button on the toolbar. Choosing Print prints out the entire page that is currently displayed in the Web browser. Some applications are more than one page long, so make certain that you print out the form in its entirety. After printing out the application, make a bookmark or favorite for the scholarship's Web site so you can easily return to it when you are ready to submit the final copy of the application.

Treat your printout as a working copy of the application. You can take your time answering the questions and correct errors or make revisions as you go. If you need to gather information like grades or test scores from your school or other sources, you can take the printout with you to make notes. When you're finished filling out the application, have someone you trust read over your working copy to look for mistakes and responses that need revision.

When you are ready to fill out the application itself, return to the Web site. Consulting your working copy, carefully type your answers into every blank provided in the electronic application form. After you finish, take the time to read over your answers before clicking that Submit button. Make certain that you have made no mistakes in grammar, punctuation, and spelling and that you have completely answered every question. Then print out a copy of the application with your answers filled in that you can keep for your files. Only when you have done all of those things should you send off the electronic application.

PDF Applications

Portable Document Format (PDF) is a file format that enables documents to look exactly the same in electronic form as when they are printed. A scholarship sponsor can link a PDF version of the scholarship application to its Web site, knowing that the online version looks just the same as the printed version. That is the main reason why so many scholarship sponsors use PDF to provide electronic versions of scholarship applications for downloading over the Internet.

To read PDF files, you will need a software program called Adobe Acrobat Reader, which works with your Web browser to display PDF files inside the browser window. Adobe Acrobat Reader is free, so you should go ahead and download a copy. You will use it often, not only to print scholarship applications, but also to look at college admissions applications, brochures, and other information published on the Web. To get a copy of Adobe Acrobat Reader, go to http://www.adobe.com/products/acrobat/readstep.html and follow the instructions given for downloading and installing the program for your computer's operating system. The next time you click on a link to a PDF file (a file ending with the extension .pdf), Adobe Acrobat Reader will automatically open and display the file.

You cannot submit applications in PDF format electronically. You must print them out, complete them by hand, and mail them to the scholarship committee. Make sure to click the Print button on the Adobe Acrobat Reader toolbar rather than your Web browser's Print button, so that you will produce a properly formatted printout. Make a couple of copies of the printed application. One will be your working copy, where you can compose first drafts of your responses, correct mistakes, and make revisions. The other is your final copy; put it away in a drawer so it will stay neat and clean until you are ready to fill out the final copy of the application.

The final copy should be as neat and professional as possible. If you have access to a typewriter, it is always best to type your an-

swers. If not, print them legibly in black ink. Again, take the time to read over your application carefully. Make certain that you have not committed any errors and that you have thoroughly answered every question. If you mess up, you can always return to the scholarship's Web site and print out a fresh copy of the application.

Some application forms are published in Microsoft Word or in WordPerfect format rather than (or in addition to) PDF format. To view these application forms, you will need to have a word processing program that can open and display files in that file format installed on your computer. Save the file to your hard drive by clicking the link to it, and then open the file in Microsoft Word or a compatible program. Scholarship application files in a word processor file format have an added benefit: you can complete them in your word processor and print out a cleanly typed copy rather than complete them by hand or with a manual typewriter. If you do not have the correct program to view the file, don't worry. Often an alternative application in PDF format is provided, or the Web page tells you how to request that a printed application be sent to you.

Text Applications

Unlike PDF files, text-based applications do not require any special software to view. They simply appear in your Web browser window. They may even look like interactive forms, except you will be unable to type in the blanks or the Submit button will be missing. These are the most basic kind of scholarship application forms that you will find on the Internet.

You will also need to print out text-based applications, complete them by hand, and mail them to the scholarship committee. To print a text-based application, use your Web browser's print function. You may have to adjust the print settings to print the application so that it fits on the page. To do so, choose Page Setup from the File menu. If you are unable to print out a neat copy of the application, request a printed application form by e-mail, fax, or mail instead.

After you have printed out a few copies of the application, complete them just as you would a PDF application. Type the application if possible, and take the time to make certain that you have made no errors and that you have answered every question.

If There Is No Application

Not all scholarship Web sites provide application forms for printing or submitting over the Internet. Instead, they tell you how to request an application. Look for the fastest method, so you can be sure of meeting deadlines. For instance, if you can request an application by e-mail or fax, choose that method instead of the postal service. Some scholarship programs are very strict about requiring potential applicants to request applications through the mail, though. In those cases you will have to follow their rules.

Draft a brief form letter that you will send to every scholarship program when you need to request an application form by mail. Address the letter to the scholarship program, providing a contact name if one is given on the Web site. In the letter, state your name, the name of your school, and the field you are studying, if that seems relevant. Also, specify exactly which scholarship you are requesting an application for, since many organizations sponsor more than one. Type your letter, and make certain that it is neat and free of errors. Always enclose a self-addressed, stamped envelope with your inquiry, or you may not receive a response.

Before you submit an application that you find on a scholarship sponsor's Web site, make certain that it is the correct form. Look over the Web site to make sure that the information is not out of date. If the Web site specifies an application deadline for the previous year or otherwise has not been updated in a while, be careful—the application form or the eligibility requirements for the scholarship may have changed. In those cases, it is safest to request a printed application form directly from the scholarship sponsor.

Submitting Additional Materials

In addition to your application, you will probably have to submit some supplementary materials. These additional materials may include an essay or personal statement, a resume or curriculum vitae (CV), academic papers, proposals, samples of artwork, creative writing samples, audio tapes or videotapes of performances, letters of recommendation, official school transcripts, test score reports, and even photographs.

The most important thing to remember about submitting additional materials is to follow directions. The scholarship committee asks for these supporting documents for a reason, and if you fail to give them exactly what they ask for, they probably will not consider you for the award. Include in your application package everything requested in the application instructions, exactly as specified. Certainly do not give less than is requested, but do not send more either.

These supplementary materials give the scholarship judges a chance to get to know you as a person. An essay, letter of recommendation, or writing sample tells the judges much more about you than the brief answers to questions on an application form ever can. If you are asked to supply additional materials, take advantage of the opportunity. Use it to show the judges who you are and why you deserve to win that scholarship. In the majority of cases, it is the extra materials that help the judges decide who to award the scholarship to, not the application itself. For that reason alone, you should spend a lot of time putting together the supplemental materials and making sure that they portray you in the best light possible.

Essays and Personal Statements

The most common extra item asked for in scholarship applications is an essay or personal statement. There are as many different kinds of scholarship essay questions as there are scholarships. Some scholarship programs may request an essay of only a few paragraphs, while others may ask for an essay several pages long. Some applications provide a very specific, focused essay question, while others leave the choice of topic entirely up to you. And some scholarship judges decide who to award the scholarship to based entirely on the essay. So be prepared to spend a lot more time writing as you get ready to apply for scholarships.

Fortunately, scholarship essays as a rule are short, usually a page or less. Scholarship essays often cover the same topics as college application essays, so you may be able to reuse or revise the essays you already wrote for your college applications to include with scholarship applications. You may also be able to reuse one essay for several different scholarship applications, both this year and in future years. If you keep copies of all essays that you write for class, for college applications, and for scholarship applications, you will probably end up saving yourself a lot of time by recycling essays appropriately.

That does not meant that you should write one very general essay to use for every scholarship application. Such an essay will not win you any scholarships. Even if you reuse an essay that you have already written, you must revise it and tailor it to each individual schol-

arship. If you must write a brand-new essay to adequately address an essay question on a scholarship application, then bite the bullet and do the work. That is the only way to win scholarships.

Choosing an Essay Topic

Often the most difficult part of writing a scholarship application essay is deciding what to write about. Essay questions on scholarship applications are usually very general and open ended. In many cases you will simply be asked to provide a personal statement or to tell the scholarship committee about yourself.

When deciding on essay topics, keep in mind the reasons why you are writing the essay in the first place. You are trying to accomplish two important objectives with the essay. The first is to tell the scholarship committee more about yourself. The essay is your chance to show the judges what you are like as a person—your goals, values, personality, and experiences. The second objective is to convince the scholarship committee to award you the scholarship by proving to them that you will use the award to accomplish educational and life goals that are squarely in line with the goals of the scholarship sponsor. Make sure that any essay topic you choose fulfills both of these objectives.

Again, it pays to know something about the organization sponsoring the scholarship and its goals for awarding the scholarship. That knowledge makes it easier to choose an essay topic that is squarely in line with the mission and interests of the scholarship sponsor. If the scholarship is sponsored by a patriotic organization like the Daughters of the American Revolution or the American Legion, then your essay should touch on issues like American history, government, and the valuable contributions you can make to your country. But if the scholarship is sponsored by a minority advocacy group, the judges will probably be much more interested in hearing about the contributions you can make to the minority community and how you can promote issues that are important to that minority. Likewise, you should tailor the tone of your essay depending on who the scholarship sponsor is. The essay that you write for a church-sponsored scholarship will have a very different tone than one you write for a scholarship sponsored by an arts organization.

But you do not want to write a sanitized, bland essay that no one on the scholarship committee will remember five minutes after reading it. Your essay should express your personality and individuality. It should make you into a real person to whom the scholarship judges can imagine awarding the scholarship. The best way to do this is to describe specific events in your life that illustrate the qualities you are trying to show the scholarship judges. If leadership ability is important to the committee, then an essay describing a specific incident in your life that illustrates your leadership abilities is a good choice. If the scholarship committee values community service, then telling an anecdote about your actual experiences as a volunteer and what you learned from those experiences will make a good essay.

Start brainstorming essay topics, making a list of possible subjects that you can write about. Consult the notes that you made about the scholarship program and sponsors to start the ideas flowing. Ask yourself the following questions as you brainstorm essay topics:

- Why would the scholarship be helpful to you? How does winning this scholarship fit into your plans for the future?
- What have you always dreamed of doing? How will this scholarship help make your dreams come true?
- What are your career goals? Why did you choose a particular field of study? What

would you contribute to this field? What have you worked hard to accomplish, academically and in your personal life? Did you have to overcome any obstacles to reach your goals? What made you successful?
- What was the most difficult time of your life? What did you learn from that experience?
- What clubs or groups do you belong to, and why?
- What activities do you pursue outside of school? Why are you enthusiastic about a particular activity?
- What leadership opportunities have you had? What have you gained from those experiences?
- How have you contributed to your community? What have you gained from that experience?
- What is your employment background? What experience did you gain from your employment?
- What attributes or skills distinguish you from everyone else?
- What books, movies, or people have influenced your life in a meaningful way?

After you brainstorm a list of topics, put your list aside for a while. Give your brain time to reflect on the ideas that you came up with. You may feel especially passionate about one particular idea on your list. That is the topic you should write about—it will automatically result in a more interesting, dynamic essay. Once you settle on a topic, do not throw away your brainstorm list. Put it in your scholarship file instead. You may be able to reuse it when you have to write the next essay.

Do not pick a topic that repeats information listed elsewhere on your application, like your grade point average or test scores. Instead, use the essay as an opportunity to tell the scholarship judges things about you that they would otherwise not know. The list of your extracurricular activities on the application form tells the judges what you do after school. Use the essay as a chance to tell them why you do those things.

Finally, stay away from controversial essay topics, unless the essay question explicitly asks about them. Scholarship committees as a rule are conservative folks, and you don't want to risk turning them off by choosing an essay topic that offends them. That old adage about not discussing politics, religion, or sex in public particularly applies to scholarship essays. The only exceptions are scholarships sponsored by political or religious organizations (it is never a good idea to write about sex).

Writing a Personal Statement

One type of essay that scholarship applications frequently request is a personal statement. For instance, the essay question may ask you to simply tell the scholarship judges about yourself. It is up to you to come up with something specific to write about. Fortunately, once you write it, you can reuse it again and again.

If you are asked to write a personal statement, avoid listing your qualities or repeating information that you listed elsewhere in the scholarship application. If your personal statement sounds like a singles ad, you need to start over. Instead of listing every possible attribute and interest you have, select one or two important details that you especially want the scholarship committee to know about you. Choose qualities that you already know are important to the judges, based on your research on the scholarship program and its sponsor. Before you sit down to write, take the time to plan what image of yourself you want to sell to the judges in order to win the scholarship.

One way to write an interesting personal statement is to imagine that you are not writing about yourself, but rather about a person you particularly admire. If you set out to write about your favorite teacher, you would not simply say, "He teaches English." Instead, you would probably describe how that teacher used

his teaching skills to affect your life or make you look at the world in a different way. Try to get into this mindset when describing yourself in the personal statement. Instead of simply listing your interests, skills, or talents, for instance, choose one and tell the judges why that interest is important to you, what impact it has had on your life, and where it may lead in the future.

Making Your Essay Stand out

The scholarship committee will read hundreds of essays, most of them on similar topics with similar themes. If you want to win the scholarship, you have to make your essay stand out from the pack.

The best way to make your essay stand out is to come up with something personal and specific to write about. Choosing a broad essay topic such as what you learned from being on a sports team will result in a bland, boring essay. Instead, try to think of specific experiences you had that illustrate the qualities or achievements you want the scholarship committee to know about. The more vivid details and specific examples you can provide, the more interesting your essay will be. For instance, you might tell the story of the day you were passed over for first string on the athletic team you joined, how that made you feel, and what you did about it.

You can make your essay stronger by writing honestly about something that really happened in your life. If you try to exaggerate events or make them up, the judges will be able to tell. Do not worry that the event you choose to write about is uninteresting or that nothing exciting has ever happened to you. If you tell the story in an honest voice, it will ring true and stick in the minds of readers. It will also do the best job of showing the scholarship judges who you are and what your personality is like.

To make your essay more interesting, tell a story as if you were talking to a friend (only with better grammar). Do not write the standard five-paragraph essay that you learned in school. Use vivid, detailed language to show the readers what you are trying to describe. Include elements like dialogue and active verbs to make your essay more interesting. If you are having trouble, read some other successful essays. You will find books of good college and scholarship application essays in your bookstore and library.

Getting Help

What you say in your essay is very important, but that message won't be received if you do not take the time and care to make sure that your essay is grammatically perfect, free of spelling errors, easy to read, and easy to understand. Committing any of these common errors could earn your scholarship application a place in the reject pile.

Revise your essay as many times as possible—at least twice. With each rewrite, your essay is bound to improve. After writing a draft, put it aside for at least a day so you can come back to it with a fresh eye. When you rewrite, look for elements that you can improve to make your essay more readable and interesting.

Write a powerful introduction that does not restate the essay question but instead launches into your story in an intriguing way that hooks the reader. If your introduction is too boring, try cutting it; often the second paragraph makes a better introduction. Following the introduction, each paragraph should develop one idea and lead naturally to the next paragraph. Use detailed, specific language that shows instead of tells. Avoid passive verb construction, clichés, and very general language. The conclusion should wrap the entire essay up and state the main point of your essay.

No professional writer works without an editor, and neither should you. Have one or two people you trust read your essay and provide suggestions on revisions you can make. Your English teacher, a guidance counselor, and your parents are all good choices.

Also take advantage of help from your school. Some high schools and colleges offer scholarship or college application workshops where you can get help not only with your essays, but with preparing the entire application package. Many colleges and universities also have writing labs or free tutoring services that can give you help with crafting your essays.

You can even take advantage of free Internet resources to improve your essay, such as the following useful sites:

- Guide to Writing a Basic Essay: http://members.tripod.com/~lklivingston/essay
- *The Blue Book of Grammar and Punctuation:* http://www.grammarbook.com
- Common Errors in English: http://www.wsu.edu/~brians/errors/errors.html
- Strunk and White, *Elements of Style:* http://www.bartleby.com/141/index.html
- Paradigm Online Writing Assistant: http://www.powa.org
- A Guide for Writing Research Papers: http://webster.commnet.edu/mla.htm
- Harris, *A Handbook of Rhetorical Devices:* http://www.vanguard.edu/faculty/rharris/rhetoric.htm
- Merriam-Webster Dictionary: http://www.m-w.com/dictionary
- quoteland.com: http://www.quoteland.com
- refdesk.com http://www.refdesk.com
- *Roget's Thesaurus:* http://humanities.uchicago.edu/forms_unrest/ROGET.html

When you are certain that your essay is as perfect as you can make it, prepare the final copy. Type your essay or print it out from the computer to make it as easy to read as possible. If you must handwrite it, print in black ink, writing as legibly as possible. Read your essay over one more time, keeping an eye out for little mistakes in grammar, spelling, and punctuation. Do not rely on your spell checker when making this final check.

Résumés

You probably do not have an actual résumé yet, but you may be asked to submit one with your scholarship application. Prepare your résumé according to the standard style. Your word processor may have a template that you can use, or you can consult books on résumé writing in your local library for help on preparing résumés. Remember that since you are still a student, you should list your academic history before your employment history. Also include on your résumé a list of clubs and organizations you belong to, afterschool activities you have participated in, leadership positions you have held, unpaid internships, and volunteer work experience.

Art and Writing Samples

Scholarship programs that reward students for their artistic talents will most likely want to see samples of your artwork. If you are requested to submit art, performance, or writing samples, the most important thing to remember is to follow the directions given in the application form. The scholarship committee came up with these instructions to make their lives easier, so cooperate by following them exactly.

For example, if you are applying for a visual arts scholarship, the committee probably will not want to see your original artwork. Instead, they will request slides or photographs as samples of your work. Give them what they want in exactly the format specified. If slides are requested, do not send photographs instead. The same applies to videotapes of dance and drama performances or audiotapes of musical performances. If the scholarship application requests a 5-minute cassette tape and you send a 10-minute tape or a CD, your application will probably be disqualified.

Do not stress overmuch about preparing these materials. Scholarship judges do not expect studio-quality recordings or professional studio photographs. If you follow the instructions and provide samples of your best work, you should be fine. If you have any questions about how to prepare art, performance, or writing samples, contact the scholarship sponsor directly.

Letters of Recommendation

After essays, letters of recommendation are the most requested extra items on scholarship applications. Letters of recommendation tell the scholarship judges how other people see you. Carefully choose the people you ask to write letters of recommendation for you, and select people who know you well and can portray you in a positive light. The best people to choose are people with whom you have worked closely and who can provide specific examples of why you are a good candidate for the scholarship. Teachers or professors of classes where you participated often, attended office hours or after-class review sessions regularly, and received many favorable comments on your papers are always good choices. Depending on the nature of the scholarship for which you are applying, you might also select an academic advisor, a guidance counselor, a coach, the faculty advisor of a club you belonged to, a religious leader, a prominent member of the community, or your supervisor at work or in your volunteer job. A variety of recommendations that demonstrate your wide range of interests and activities will impress the scholarship judges, but you should also make every effort to choose recommenders who are appropriate for the scholarship. For example, sponsors of academic scholarships will prefer to receive letters from your teachers, while a letter of recommendation from your coach would be more appropriate for an athletic scholarship application. Never select a relative to write your letters of recommendation.

Ask for recommendations early, at least four to six weeks before the application deadline. Schedule an appointment with the person whom you want to write the letter of recommendation; don't just corner him or her in the hall. At the appointment, tell the person about the scholarship for which you are applying and why you think you are a good candidate to win the award. Then ask if the person would feel comfortable recommending you for that scholarship and if she or he has time to write the letter. Don't take it personally if you receive a "no" in response to this question. You want a supportive, positive recommendation, not a lukewarm one, so it's better to find out at the start if the person is willing and able to give you that.

If the person agrees to write a letter of recommendation for you, do everything you can to make his or her job as easy as possible. A letter of recommendation that contains specific examples about your qualifications and achievements can be key in winning the scholarship. To help out your letter writer, provide a list of your accomplishments, qualities, and interests, such as a copy of the personal profile that you prepared when you started your scholarship search. You might also want to give the letter writer a copy of the scholarship information and a copy of your completed application form so he or she has a better idea of what the scholarship is. Finally, spend some time talking over your qualifications for the scholarship with the letter writer to ensure that the details are fresh in his or her mind.

Also provide the letter writer with everything he or she needs to write the letter of recommendation. Make sure that he or she knows the deadline for mailing in the scholarship application. Provide any forms that the letter writer needs to complete, with all the information that you can provide, such as your name and address, already filled in. If the person works for your high school or college, ask him or her to prepare the letter on official school letterhead. If the letter of recommendation must be mailed in separately from the scholarship application, provide a preaddressed, stamped envelope that the letter writer can use. Politely remind the person when the deadline is approaching. After you receive the letter, send the person a thank-you note, and follow up to let him or her know if you won the scholarship.

You don't have to request a separate letter of recommendation each time you need one. If you plan to apply for a lot of scholarships, it will save you a lot of time if you keep a few different letters of recommendation on file, so you can simply make a copy of an appropriate letter to send with your application as you need it. If you are going after a prestigious national scholarship or a major fellowship, though, you will get better results if you solicit letters of recommendation intended just for those applications.

In some cases it is a good idea to plan ahead and request letters of recommendation before you actually need them. For instance, if you have a class with a great professor or you take part in a short-term internship, go ahead and ask for the letter of recommendation as soon as that experience is finished, while you are still fresh in your professor's or supervisor's mind. Some colleges will even keep a dossier of letters of recommendation for you and will send out the letters on official letterhead at your request.

Transcripts and Test Scores

You will probably have to submit an official transcript from your high school or college with most of your scholarship applications. Go ahead and find out what the procedures of requesting transcripts are and how long such requests take to process. Then you can make certain to request any transcripts you need in plenty of time to meet application deadlines.

When sending in transcripts, be sure to follow the instructions given in the scholarship application to the letter. Some scholarship committees prefer to receive transcripts separately, while others like to have the transcript included with the rest of the application package. In the latter case, it is important that you not open or tamper with the sealed envelope the transcript comes in, or the scholarship committee may not accept the transcript.

Also be prepared to send official reports of your standardized test scores if the scholarship application requests them. The test registration booklet and your score report tell you how to request additional score reports. You can also order additional score reports on the Internet. If you took the ACT Assessment, go to http://www.act.org/aap/scores/new_asr.html. If you took the SAT I, go to http://www.collegeboard.org/sat/html/students/scrpt02c.html. When you request the additional reports, you will have to pay a fee, so have your credit card ready. You will also have to provide the code for the scholarship program to send the score report to; if you don't find this code on the application form, contact the scholarship sponsor directly to ask what it is.

Photographs

Some scholarship applications may request that you enclose a photograph to be used for publicity purposes when the winners are chosen. Do not enclose candid snapshots or baby pictures! Instead, have a set of photographs in different sizes professionally made. Those that you do not use for scholarship applications you can give to family members.

Interviews

It is very unlikely that you will have to go to an interview, unless you are applying for a very prestigious scholarship or a graduate school fellowship. (Some performing arts scholarships may require an audition as well.) If an interview is required, don't let it intimidate you. As with every other part of the application package, you should use the interview to show the scholarship judges why you are the best person to win the award.

Treat the interview as if you were going to a job interview. Dress in a conservative, professional manner, and leave the nose ring at home. Bring copies of your résumé, the scholarship application, your essay, and your transcripts with you. You may not need them, but on the other hand, you may be very glad to have them. Plan to arrive a few minutes early. During the interview, take care with how you present yourself. Don't slouch in your chair, fidget, or chew gum. Answer questions as clearly as possible, and take the time to think over your answers. Finally, be honest; don't tell the interviewer what you think he or she wants to hear.

Think about how you might answer stock interview questions before you go to the interview. Don't memorize stock answers, though; you don't want to sound as if you are reading from a script. You also don't want to be caught without an answer to basic questions. Be prepared to discuss your educational history, employment experiences, family background, academic achievements, extracurricular activities, future plans, financial needs, and personal values.

After the interview, send the interviewer a handwritten thank-you note. That will leave a lasting good impression.

Putting the Package Together

Following directions is also essential when it comes to putting your application package together and preparing it for mailing. Do not staple or paperclip materials together, unless the application directs you to do so. Unless told otherwise, arrange the scholarship materials in the order that they are asked for in the application instructions, with the application form itself on top. Print your name and address in the top corner of every page, and affix labels to other items like tapes or photographs, in case the application materials become separated. Use a large manila envelope to keep everything neat and unwrinkled, and take it to the post office yourself to ensure that you attach the correct postage. Consider sending the application certified mail and requesting a return receipt, to make certain that the application reached its destination.

It is usually a good idea to attach a cover letter to your application package. Keep the letter brief and to the point. Type it, and keep it free of errors. In it, explain which scholarship you are applying for, the name of the college that you attend or have been accepted to (if applicable), your year in school, and a list of the materials enclosed in the application package, in the same order. It is also nice to thank the scholarship committee for their consideration.

Common Mistakes Students Make

Scholarship judges are not required to read your scholarship application. The tiniest things can get your application tossed in the wastebasket, so be scrupulous about avoiding mistakes.

Ninety percent of scholarship applications receive a rejection in the first 30 seconds after they are opened. At this point, they are usually not even read by a scholarship judge. Instead, an administrative assistant opens the envelopes and compares applications to a checklist to determine which applications get tossed and which ones go to the scholarship committee. If you want your application to make it past this initial screening process, you have to receive a "yes" for every item on that checklist by avoid-

ing the common mistakes that most of your peers will make.

Missing the application deadline is the first item on that checklist that will get your application rejected. In fact, some scholarship programs stop accepting applications before the published deadline, without warning. Send in your application as early as possible to have the best chance of winning.

The second item on the checklist is meeting all the eligibility requirements. The person who initially screens scholarship applications will check that each applicant meets every requirement, no matter how strict. If the scholarship is intended for African-American students from Orange County, California, who are sophomores in college and are majoring in journalism, then you had better meet each and every one of those criteria. If you do not, your application will never make it to the judges. That is why it is so crucial to spend time applying only for scholarships for which you are truly qualified; going after other scholarships will just be a waste of your time.

Next, the screener will check that you followed all of the application instructions exactly and that your application is complete. If the application requested an essay, two letters of recommendation, and a photograph, all of those items had better be in your packet, or your application will wind up in the rejected pile. Likewise, if that essay must be three pages long and yours is only two pages, your application will probably get tossed. Finally, you must answer every question on the application form. If you have to write "not applicable" in an application blank, then you probably are not a good candidate for that scholarship.

Neatness counts very heavily during this initial screening phase. Your application should be neatly typed or written and presented as professionally as possible. If it is wrinkled, stained, or filled out in crayon, it will very likely get weeded out. Before you even touch the final copy of the application, use a working copy to draft your response to application questions and make revisions. Then take your time preparing the final application. Avoid crossing items out or using whiteout to correct errors. If you make a mistake and must start all over again, then do so—that is the only way to ensure that your application makes it past the initial screening.

Spelling is another crucial element during this first once-over. At this point, the scholarship judges have probably received more applications than they can ever possibly read and are looking for ways to make that pile smaller. Even one spelling or punctuation mistake can earn your application a rejection. Before you put your scholarship application in the mail, proofread it twice. Try to find someone else to proofread behind you as well.

Do not add extra materials to your application package. Including an extra-long essay or a videotape of you in the school play may seem like a good way to impress the scholarship judges, but unless the application instructions specifically request such materials, chances are good that they will not be appreciated. Likewise, enclosing your application materials in a plastic binder may seem like a good way to make your application appear more professional, but it may just irritate whoever is opening the application envelopes. It is better to follow the application instructions as stringently as possible and refrain from adding any extra touches.

In the end you have no control over whom the scholarship committee chooses to award the scholarship. You can make the best case for yourself as possible by submitting a professional-looking application package with an original essay and impressive letters of recommendation. But you never can tell what, in the end, will influence the scholarship judges to choose one applicant out of the hundreds or thousands of applications they receive. If you do not win a particular scholarship, don't take it personally. Just focus on winning the next one.

Once you win a scholarship, your job may not be over. The scholarship sponsor may specify conditions that you have to meet to keep the scholarship, such as maintaining a minimum grade point average or serving in an internship. Some scholarships last only one year, while others are awarded the entire time that you are in college. Some programs specify that you can apply only once, while others let you reapply for the scholarship each year. Before accepting a scholarship, make certain that you understand what all of the conditions are and what you must do to keep or regain the scholarship. And be prepared to fill out more application forms, write more essays, and gather more letters of recommendation next year.

AVOIDING SCHOLARSHIP SCAMS

Because there are so many scholarship programs, and so many students competing for those dollars, scholarship scams have become a booming business. These fraudulent programs do their best to imitate legitimate scholarship programs sponsored by government agencies, charitable foundations, and corporations. They often employ official but meaningless names that incorporate words like "national," "federal," "foundation," "nonprofit," and "administration" to fool you. But these programs do not give you free money; rather, they try to take money from you.

Scholarship scams are especially prevalent on the Internet, primarily because the Internet has become such a useful tool for hunting down scholarships. Also, it is very easy for a scam artist to set up a Web page for what looks like a legitimate scholarship program or scholarship search service. Once the scam artist collects enough money, he or she can dismantle the Web site and disappear, eluding prosecution.

Whenever money is involved, it pays to be careful. Scam artists prey on students and their parents who are desperate to find money for college. To avoid getting taken, watch out for offers that seem too good to be true. Approach every scholarship program with caution, particularly programs you have never heard of before or programs that aren't sponsored by well-known organizations.

This chapter will help you avoid the increasing number of fraudulent scholarship offers and services that you are likely to encounter in your online scholarship search. You'll find out about the most common types of scholarship-related scams, including the growing field of fraudulent scholarship search services. You'll learn the warning signs of a scholarship scam and how to evaluate a schol-

arship program that you think may be too good to be true. Finally, you'll discover how to report scholarship scams to the proper authorities and keep other students from becoming victims.

Don't let your quest for scholarship money overwhelm your good sense. If you encounter a scholarship program or financial aid service that sets off your warning bells, listen to your instincts and look for financial aid from another source. You can always find another way to help pay for college. But if a scam artist manages to take your money, your chances of ever recovering it are minuscule.

Common Online Scholarship Scams

Most scholarship scams make their money by taking it directly from unsuspecting students desperate to find some extra dollars for college, usually by hitting students up for all kinds of fees during the scholarship application process. The scholarship sponsors may charge what they call an application fee, entrance fee, reading fee, judging fee, or administrative fee. Students may even have to pay a processing or handling fee just to receive a copy of the application form or to get more information about the scholarship.

Other scholarship scams pile on the hidden fees after you have submitted an application. For instance, you may receive a notice that you have won the scholarship, but to collect, you must pay a "disbursement" or "redemption" fee. Warning bells should immediately go off in your head if this situation occurs. No legitimate scholarship program makes you pay money in order to get the money that you have supposedly won.

One common scam of this type is to charge "taxes" on the scholarship award. This may seem like a legitimate charge; after all, no one wants to tangle with the IRS. The truth is that most scholarships are tax-free money. You have to pay taxes on a scholarship award only if you use the money for college costs other than tuition, required fees, or required supplies like books and lab equipment. If you use the scholarship money to help pay for room and board, the costs of traveling to and from campus, or a new computer for school, you will probably have to treat the scholarship as taxable income. But even in those cases, you report the income on your tax return and pay any required taxes directly to the IRS. You should never have to pay federal, state, or sales taxes to the organization giving you the scholarship.

These fees often amount to only a few dollars, low enough to seem like it won't hurt to pay when the reward could be a thousand-dollar scholarship. But since the scholarship program probably receives thousands of applications, those low fees quickly add up to a large chunk of money. For instance, say a program awarding a $1,000 scholarship charges an application fee of $10. If the program receives 1,000 applications, it has made enough money to pay the scholarship and pocket a nice profit. Most of these fraudulent scholarship programs do not award any scholarships at all, letting all of the applicants assume that they just didn't win the scholarship. Or the sponsor may award the scholarship to himself or herself. Even those fee-based scholarship programs that do actually give out a scholarship may still violate various contest and sweepstakes laws, depending on the structure of the scholarship program and the state where it is offered.

Your odds of winning a scholarship do not improve when you pay a fee to apply. Your chances of winning may actually decrease because the scholarship is more likely to be a scam. While a few legitimate scholarship programs do charge an entrance or administrative fee, the majority do not charge anything at all. Because the scholarship money comes from charitable foundations, which also pay the costs of administering the scholarship program, there is no need to charge fees to applicants. To be safe, limit your application efforts to scholarship programs that don't charge any fees to apply. If you get hit up for hidden fees after you submit an application, turn elsewhere in your hunt for money for college—chances are you have stumbled onto a scam. By the way, the majority of the scholarships listed in this guide charge no fees to applicants, and the exceptions are clearly noted in the scholarship descriptions.

Spotting the Warning Signs

It can be difficult to discern at first glance whether a particular scholarship program is fraudulent, particularly if it is one of the ones that charge hidden fees rather than ask for money up front. Most scholarship scams share several common characteristics. Look for these warning signs in each scholarship that you consider applying for, and use them to weed out potential scams.

The scholarship program contacts you first, instead of the other way around. Legitimate scholarship programs receive more applications than they can handle already. They don't need to spend time on recruiting more applicants. To win scholarships, you have to take the initiative by seeking out scholarships for which you are qualified and applying for them. Any scholarship program that comes looking for you is much more likely to try to take your money than to give you theirs.

The program claims that everyone is eligible for the scholarship. No legitimate scholarship is equally open to all applicants, without restrictions. Even if no eligibility requirements are specified, the scholarship judges still set standards for choosing the winner, such as a minimum grade point average, which are bound to eliminate some applicants. Even contests where the winner is chosen randomly usually specify age or grade level restrictions.

The sponsor insists that you must act quickly to be considered for an award. This is a typical aspect of a "hard sell," where you are pressured to buy into something without having time to think it over or let your common sense kick into gear. Legitimate scholarship programs set an application deadline that remains the same from year to year. It is your responsibility to meet this deadline; the sponsor won't remind you to get your applications in on time. If you are feeling pressured, take a step back and reevaluate the scholarship with a fresh eye to see if you can detect a scam.

The program cannot prove that it has actually awarded scholarships in the past. Most scholarship programs are proud of their accomplishments and publish a list of past recipients of the award on their Web site or in their scholarship materials. If you suspect a scholarship program of being fraudulent, request a list of past winners. If the sponsor can't furnish one or the list seems incomplete or suspicious to you, that's a good sign that you're dealing with a scam.

The program claims to have approval from the government, a particular university, the Chamber of Commerce, or the Better Business Bureau. Legitimate scholarship programs don't need to make such claims. Government departments, universities, and Chambers of Commerce don't endorse individual scholarship programs, unless they are cosponsoring the program. You can easily check on this by contacting the organization that supposedly endorsed the scholarship and asking a few simple questions about the scholarship. If that group didn't actually endorse the scholarship, they

will be glad that you informed them that their name was being used illegitimately, and they will probably take action.

Information about the scholarship is full of hype and lacks facts that you can easily verify. Do the scholarship materials read like an ad for a used car lot? Are basic facts about the scholarship missing, such as the award amount or eligibility requirements? Can you find a phone number? Is the mailing address for a post office box, mail drop, or residential address? Are the brochure and application forms full of spelling and grammatical errors, or do they just look unprofessional to you? All of these are good signs that you are not dealing with a legitimate scholarship program.

The program asks you to disclose a bank account or credit card number in order to hold the scholarship. This is one way that fraudulent scholarship programs try to take your money. Never give out information like this, not even if the sponsor insists it is required to process the scholarship that you've already won. No legitimate scholarship program needs such information or would never ask for it.

You receive notification of an award by phone rather than by mail. Every legitimate scholarship program notifies recipients of the award by letter. If a scholarship sponsor calls you to tell you that you've won the award, they will very likely then ask you to send money or provide your credit card number in order to send you the scholarship. They will also employ hard sell tactics, like pressuring you to act right away or you'll miss out. The best way to protect yourself is to hang up.

The scholarship sounds too good to be true. Your common sense is the best judge of potential scholarship scams. If all your instincts are telling you that something is not right, then something fishy probably is going on. There are thousands of legitimate scholarship programs out there, so you have no good reason to waste your time and money on one that you suspect may be a scam.

Evaluating Scholarship Programs

If you come across a scholarship that you think is a scam or otherwise illegitimate, your best option is just not to apply. Spend your efforts on searching out legitimate scholarship programs for which you are eligible.

Occasionally you may find a suspicious scholarship that you do want to apply for if it turns out to be the real thing. In those cases, take some time to research the organization sponsoring the scholarship before you apply to help determine whether the scholarship program is legitimate.

The first thing to look for is the organization's contact information, which should be published prominently on the scholarship's Web site. You should find a street address, not a post office box or a paid mail drop (such as an address at a place like Mail Boxes, Etc.). You should also find a phone number. If you cannot find the contact information on the scholarship's Web site, there are plenty of Internet sites where you can look it up, including Infospace (http://www.infospace.com), GTE SuperPages (http://yp.gte.net), and Yahoo! (http://yp.yahoo.com).

You can easily check out the sponsor's phone number and address to determine if they belong to a legitimate business or nonprofit organization. The simplest thing to do is to call up the scholarship sponsor and ask some questions of whoever answers the phone. You may be able to form a good impression of the legitimacy of the sponsoring organization from the manner and professionalism of the person on the other end of the line. That person should be able to provide concrete answers to all of your questions about the scholarship, rather than giving you the runaround or providing answers that sound like they are being read from a script. If the person who answers the phone becomes abusive or tries to give you a hard sell, that is also a bad sign. And beware if the phone number seems to be issued to a residence rather than to a business.

Next, you can investigate the sponsoring organization's address to determine whether it belongs to a legitimate business. If the address given in the contact information is a post office box, call the post office for that zip code and ask the clerk for the street address of the business using the P.O. box. The post office is required to provide this information if the owner of the P.O. box is a business. So if the post office cannot release the street address information, you know that it belongs not to a business but to a residence, which means that the scholarship is much more likely to be a scam. Also, if the business is located in a different state than the P.O. box, especially if that state is Nevada, that is another good sign that you are dealing with a scam of some kind.

Many scholarships are sponsored by nonprofit organizations. All nonprofits are required to register with the IRS as 501(3)c nonprofit organizations and file financial records that become public record. It is easy enough to check on a nonprofit's legitimacy by looking it up in a registry of nonprofit organizations, such as the one found at http://www.guidestar.org/index.html. You can also call the IRS directly to check on an organization's nonprofit status; you will sit on hold forever, but you will eventually get an answer. Another place that all nonprofit organizations must register is with their state's Attorney General or Secretary of State, so you can also call that office and ask if the organization is registered as nonprofit. Get a list of these offices and their phone numbers for the entire United States at http://www.finaid.org/scholarships/attyoffices.phtml.

If the scholarship is sponsored by a company that uses Incorporated, Inc., Corporation, or LLC in its name or otherwise identifies itself as a corporation, its articles of incorporation

41

must be on file with the state Attorney General or Secretary of State. You can call the state's corporation bureau at one of these offices and ask them to identify the status of the corporation and provide its business address and date of incorporation. This should give you a good idea whether the sponsoring corporation is a legitimate practicing business.

Finally, find out whether any complaints have been lodged against the organization sponsoring the scholarship. The Better Business Bureau is the first place to check; go to http://www.bbb.org to find a directory of Better Business Bureaus across the country. Another good place to call is the Attorney General's office in the state where the sponsor is located, to inquire if there are any open investigations into the organization, a history of complaints, or a history of action against the organization.

Scholarship Search Services

Just as profitable a business as fraudulent scholarship programs are scholarship search services that charge a fee to search for scholarships for you. Not all of these businesses are scams, but they are all a waste of money. The best of them charge a small fee—less than $50—to search the same databases for scholarships that you can now search on the Internet for free. (Turn back to Chapter 2, "Using the Internet to Find Scholarships," to review how to do this.) The worst of them charge you exorbitant amounts of money—$500 or more—and then either do nothing or print out a pitifully small list of scholarships that you don't even qualify for. No matter which kind you use, you are still throwing away your money. In fact, fewer than 1 percent of users of fee-based scholarship search services actually win a scholarship through them.

Scholarship search services will try their hardest to sell their services to you, though, and you are very likely to run into several of these businesses as you conduct your online scholarship search. Many scholarship search services claim that you cannot get the information they provide anywhere else, that they list obscure scholarships, or that billions of dollars in scholarship money are unclaimed every year. Do not believe these claims. All scholarship programs are publicized at least a little bit, so you can find out about them from other sources than the fee-based scholarship service. The "obscure" scholarships the fee-based search service lists are likely to be awards with such strict eligibility requirements that you could not possibly qualify for them. And you already know that those unclaimed financial aid dollars are in employer-sponsored tuition assistance, rather than scholarships. The scholarship that does not have a winner every year is rare indeed.

In almost every case, a fee-based scholarship search service, even a legitimate one, will not find any scholarships for you that you would not have come across on your own with some smart searching. With all of the resources at your disposal—the free scholarship databases on the Internet and the large number of scholarship guides published every year, including this one—you are bound to come up with a long list of scholarships for which you are qualified. In fact, because no one knows you like you do, you are much more likely to conduct an effective search that results in scholarships you can actually win than any fee-based search service could ever be.

Many students believe that the scholarship search services do all the work for them, which can make paying the fee worthwhile. But these services only search for scholarships for you and send you the information they find. They do not fill out applications, write essays, get letters of recommendation, or mail everything in for you. You still have to invest a great deal of your time in winning the scholarship awards. With the Internet at your disposal, searching for scholarships may be the easiest part of the process.

The guarantees that most fee-based scholarship search services offer can be tempting. You might think that you don't have anything to lose. When a scholarship search service makes promises that it cannot keep, it crosses the line and becomes a scam.

No scholarship search service can guarantee that you will win a scholarship, because they don't award the scholarships. Read the fine print. Most scholarship search services place so many ridiculous restrictions on their "guarantees" that they make it impossible to recoup your money. For instance, they may insist that in order to be eligible for a guarantee, you must apply for every scholarship they send you. Then they send you scholarships that it is impossible to apply for, such as scholarships whose deadlines have already passed. Or the service may insist on receiving rejection notices from every scholarship you applied for, when most scholarship programs do not even send out rejection notices.

If you still want to use a fee-based scholarship search service, be smart about it. Check out the company before giving it any money by using the techniques described in the "Evaluating Scholarship Programs" section earlier in this chapter. Ask your guidance counselor or financial aid officer to recommend reliable companies that students have used in the past without significant problems. Finally, don't pay more than $50 for these services; they aren't worth any more than that.

Reporting Scams

If you do get scammed by a scholarship search service or a fraudulent scholarship program, be aware that you probably will not get your money back. You should still report the scam, though, if only to prevent other students from falling for it.

First, gather all the information you have regarding the fraudulent company, including all correspondence you sent and received. Make notes about all phone and in-person communications you had with the company. If you gave your credit card number to the company, contact your credit card company and register a complaint about the charge. Any agency you report the scam to will want to see documentation of your dealings with the company.

There are several places where you can file your complaint, and you should hit as many of them as you can. First, file a complaint with the Better Business Bureau by using the electronic complaint form at http://www.bbb.org. Also register a complaint with the Federal Trade Commission by going to http://www.ftc.gov/ftc/complaint.htm, and with the National Fraud Information Center by going to http://www.fraud.org. If the U.S. postal service was involved at any point—if you sent money through the mail, for instance—you can report the scam at http://www.usps.gov/websites/depart/inspect. In your complaints, include details of what occurred, the steps you took to obtain satisfaction, and the company's response.

Next, file a complaint with the Attorney General of the state where the company is located as well as in your own state; you will find a list of Attorney General offices at http://www.finaid.org/scholarships/attyoffices.phtml. Do not expect any immediate action resulting from this complaint. The Attorney General's office does not usually act until it has received an overwhelming number of complaints. At least your complaint will be on file so that others can find it when they investigate the company.

Finally, spread the word. Tell your guidance counselor and financial aid officer about the experience, and report it in Usenet newsgroups like soc.college and soc.college-financial-aid. If the fraudulent company advertised on the Internet, you can also report it to ScamBusters (http://www.scambusters.org) and the Web Police (http://www.web-police.org), which can help get the word out. The free scholarship search services listed in Chapter 2 might also be willing to warn students about scams. FinAid is another well-trafficked Web site that will post your warning; send it to scams@finaid.org. Do not be vindictive, though. An unemotional warning that states the facts will effectively get the message out and is much more likely to be publicized than an angry rant.

PART II

ONLINE SCHOLARSHIPS

This part of the book lists over 3,500 scholarships that you can find information about, and in most cases apply for, on the Internet. The scholarships are categorized by type so that you can easily locate the awards for which you are eligible, and cross references help you find scholarships that fit into more than one category. Each scholarship listing provides the name of the award, the name of the sponsoring organization, the Web site address where you can learn more about the scholarship, the amount awarded, the number of awards given out, the application deadline, the education level that you must have attained to be eligible to apply for the scholarship, and other eligibility requirements. You will also find instructions for learning more about the scholarship and applying for it on the Web site.

While all of the information listed in this book was accurate at the time of publication, some details—particularly aplication deadlines—are likely to change from year to year. Always check each scholarship's Web site for the most up-to-date deadlines and other information before submitting an application. If the Web site appears to be out of date, contact the scholarship sponsor directly and request a printed application and informational material.

The listings in this book should help you start compiling a list of scholarships. Combine them with the results of your online scholarship search using the free search services you learned about in Part I, and you will be well on your way to winning some extra money for college.

GENERAL SCHOLARSHIPS

This chapter lists scholarship programs that the largest number of students are eligible to enter. These awards include academic scholarships, essay contests, science and technology competitions, and general contests with randomly chosen winners.

Just because these scholarships are open to most students does not mean that they are easy to win. Some of the most prestigious national scholarship programs, with the largest awards and the stiffest competition, are listed in this chapter. You will still have to meet minimum academic qualifications to compete for most of these scholarships, or you will need to have a well-developed talent for essay writing, science, or computing to put yourself in the running. But don't get scared off by scholarships that require essays or research projects. Applying for those scholarships may require more hard work, but the payoff if you win is usually well worth it, and the competition may not be so fierce because the tough entrance requirements may frighten many other students away.

Academic Scholarships

All-American Scholar Scholarship

Sponsor: United States Achievement Academy (USAA)
Web Site: http://www.usaa-academy.com/aas/aas.html
Amount of Scholarship: $100 to $1,500
Number of Awards: not given
Deadline: May 28
Education Level: high school students and college undergraduates

Eligibility: Applicant must have a minimum 3.8 GPA.

To be eligible even to apply for this scholarship, you must be nominated by a teacher or professor as an All-American Scholar. The scholarship is awarded entirely based on academic scores and achievements. If you feel that you can compete, you should persuade a teacher who knows you well to nominate you. The teacher can nominate you online by clicking the Nominations button on the scholarship's Web page and filling out the electronic nomination form (the nomination form is different for high school and college students). After you have been nominated, you will receive a biographical data form in the mail; fill this out and return it as instructed to obtain a copy of the scholarship application. Even if you don't win the scholarship, being recognized as an All-American Scholar will make a nice addition to your academic résumé. To learn more about this program and its sponsor, click the Go to USAA Site button.

Coca-Cola Scholars Scholarship

Sponsor: The Coca-Cola Company
Web Site: http://www.thecoca-colacompany.com/scholars/index.html
Amount of Scholarship: $4,000 to $20,000
Number of Awards: 250
Deadline: October 31
Education Level: high school seniors
Eligibility: Applicant must attend a high school in a participating bottler's territory.

Coca-Cola Scholars is one of the most prestigious and competitive scholarships. Every year this program awards $20,000 to 50 National Scholars and $4,000 to 200 Regional Scholars selected from applicants all over the country.

Since this scholarship is so competitive and the awards are so large, you should spend plenty of time exploring the Web site to learn about the program and the selection process. When you arrive at the site, you will see a series of links down the left-hand side. First, make sure you qualify by clicking Bottler Search and entering your city, state, and zip code to find out if your high school is located in a participating bottler's territory. If you are eligible to apply, click How It Works to learn about the selection process and the general qualities that Coca-Cola is looking for in scholarship applicants. Also click Our Scholars, where you can read detailed descriptions of past winners; this will give you an even better idea of the qualities the program is seeking in its candidates. Finally, go to the FAQs, which answer the most common questions about the scholarship program, including questions about specific eligibility requirements and application procedures. Feel free to explore the remaining links to learn who the previous year's winners were, which colleges past winners have attended, and more about the mission of Coca-Cola's educational foundation. If you choose to apply, click the Apply Online link (this link will not appear if the program is not currently accepting applications). Read the application guidelines and click the I Accept button if you agree with them. The online application form then appears in your Web browser window. To turn in your completed application, click the Submit Application button at the bottom of the page.

COHEAO Scholarship

Sponsor: Coalition of Higher Education Assistance Organizations (COHEAO)
Web Site: http://www.coheao.com/scholarframe.html
Amount of Scholarship: $500 to $1,000
Number of Awards: 6
Deadline: March 1

Education Level: college freshmen, sophomores, and juniors
Eligibility: Applicant must attend a COHEAO member college, have a minimum 3.75 GPA, and be a U.S. citizen.

Three $500 scholarships and three $1,000 scholarships are given out under this program. To find out if your college, university, community college, or technical school is a member of COHEAO, making you eligible for the scholarship, click the COHEAO Member School link. The only way to apply for this scholarship is through the Web site. Before you can access the online application, though, the Web site will check your eligibility requirements. You must provide a satisfactory response to each question asked in the Application Wizard to get a copy of the scholarship application. After answering a question, click the Next button to advance to the next question in the Application Wizard; if you don't meet one of the eligibility requirements, a Web page will appear that tells you that you were disqualified and you will be unable to access the application. Once you get to the application itself, you can choose to print out a copy and fill it out by hand or submit the electronic version of the application.

Datatel Scholars Scholarship

Sponsor: Datatel Scholars Foundation
Web Site: http://www.datatel.com/scholars_foundation/index.html
Amount of Scholarship: $700 to $2,000
Number of Awards: not given
Deadline: February 15 (deadlines may vary at different institutions)
Education Level: college undergraduates and graduate students
Eligibility: Applicant must attend a college or university that is a Datatel client site or work at a Datatel non-education site, and take at least six credit hours per semester.

Datatel Scholars is an academic scholarship intended for students at schools that use Datatel products and services and for employees of companies that use Datatel products or services, regardless of which college they attend. To verify that your school or company is a Datatel client, ask your financial aid officer, or contact the Foundation directly using the address, phone number, or e-mail address given on the Contact the Foundation page. If you attend a Datatel client school, you must apply through your school's scholarship or financial aid office; you cannot apply directly through the Web site. Likewise, if you work for a Datatel client, you must apply for the scholarship through your human resources department or CEO's office. The scholarship program's Web site will give you all the information and forms you need to apply, though. First, open the Winners Profile to learn what qualities the ideal applicant possesses; grades are very important for this scholarship, and most winners have at least a 3.7 GPA. The How to Apply link describes the process of getting nominated by your school or employer. The application instructions on this page explains the application process and judging criteria in detail; it is up to you to make certain that your school or employer follows these instructions so that your application will be accepted. You will also find a PDF copy of the application linked to this page, which you can print out to use as a working copy. Your school or employer will have official printed copies of the application to use for your final submission.

"Most Valuable Student" Scholarship

Sponsor: The Elks National Foundation
Web Site: http://www.elks.org/enf/mvs.cfm
Amount of Scholarship: $1,000 to $7,500
Number of Awards: 500
Deadline: January 14
Education Level: high school seniors
Eligibility: Applicant must live within the jurisdiction of the BPO Elks of the USA,

enroll as a full-time student at a four-year U.S. college, and be a U.S. citizen.

This scholarship program rewards the 500 top students in the United States. The 494 fourth-place winners receive $1,000 scholarships, the 2 third-place winners receive $3,000 scholarships, the 2 second-place winners receive $4,000 scholarships, and the 2 first-place winners receive $7,500. To win, applicants must advance through local, district, and state competitions to reach the national level. Many winners at the regional levels also receive scholarships. To apply, you must file an application with your local Elks Lodge; you can search for an Elks Lodge in your community at http://www.elks.org/search.cfm. The Web site does not provide a lot of information about this scholarship program, but exploring the rest of the Web site, particularly the Our Scholarships section, will help you learn more about what the Elks National Foundation is looking for in a "most valuable student."

P.L.A.T.O. Scholarship

Sponsor: P.L.A.T.O.
Web Site: http://www.plato.org/scholarship/home.htm
Amount of Scholarship: $1,000 to $10,000
Number of Awards: 67
Deadline: April 30
Education Level: high school seniors, college undergraduates, and graduate students
Eligibility: Applicant must have a minimum 2.75 GPA; enroll in an accredited two-year college, four-year college, or graduate school; and be a U.S. citizen or permanent resident.

This scholarship is awarded solely based on academic achievement; you don't even need to write an essay! Scholarship awards are distributed by geographical region. Ten $1,000 scholarships and one $5,000 scholarship are given in each region, and the national winner receives $10,000. To learn what states make up each region, look at the Awards page. The only way to apply for this scholarship is to submit the online scholarship application, located on the Scholarship Application page. Check the Questions & Answers page for valuable tips on filling out the electronic application. The application is short and won't take you very long to complete, so there is no reason not to apply. (You will receive information about the P.L.A.T.O. student loan, though.)

Sam Walton Community Scholarship

Sponsor: Wal-Mart
Web Site: http://compedge.wal-mart.com/sw_scholar.html
Amount of Scholarship: $1,000
Number of Awards: more than 2,300
Deadline: February 1
Education Level: high school students
Eligibility: Applicant must attend a participating high school.

Participating Wal-Mart stores award these scholarships directly to high schools, and the high schools then choose the scholarship winners. To find out if your high school participates, ask your guidance counselor or contact the Community Involvement Coordinator at your local Wal-Mart. This brief Web page does not provide a lot of information about the scholarship, but it does tell you a little about the application procedures and how you can learn more about the scholarship.

Search for Excellence National Scholarship

Sponsor: Delta Epsilon Iota
Web Site: http://www.deltaepsiloniota.org/excellence/index.htm
Amount of Scholarship: $1,000
Number of Awards: not given
Deadline: March 1

Education Level: college undergraduates
Eligibility: Applicant must have a minimum 3.3 GPA, have completed 30 semester hours of college coursework, and attend a participating college.

This scholarship rewards college undergraduates who exemplify the principles that Delta Epsilon Iota promotes: dedication, enthusiasm, and initiative. The Additional Information link tells you exactly what qualities the judges are looking for in scholarship winners, as well as what materials need to go in your application package. To find out if your college participates in the scholarship program, follow the Participating Colleges and Universities link. Download a PDF copy of the application form by following the Download Application link and choosing Scholarship Application. To learn more about Delta Epsilon Iota, visit the honor society's home page and read the student information.

Tribute Award Scholarship

Sponsor: Discover Card and American Association of School Administrators
Web Site: http://www.aasa.org/discover.htm
Amount of Scholarship: $1,250 to $25,000
Number of Awards: 477
Deadline: January 11
Education Level: high school juniors
Eligibility: Applicant must have a minimum 2.75 GPA, enroll in any kind of postsecondary school, and be a U.S. citizen or permanent resident.

These scholarships go to students who excel in four of five very broad areas: special talents, leadership, obstacles overcome, unique endeavors, and community service. If you can fit yourself into all of these categories, then you will make a good applicant for the award. Read the biographies of past winners published on the Web site to get a better idea of whether you can compete. Nine scholarships are awarded to finalists living in each state, the District of Columbia, and overseas: three awards of $2,500, three awards of $1,750, and three awards of $1,250. At the national level, nine awards of $25,000 are given out. You can get an application from your guidance office, or call the phone number on the Web page to request a copy.

Contests

AAA Scholarship Sweepstakes

Sponsor: AAA Financial Services
Web Site: http://www.financial.aaa.com/aaainlandauto/money/edloans/win.html
Amount of Scholarship: $1,000
Number of Awards: 10
Deadline: April 1
Education Level: high school seniors and college undergraduates
Eligibility: Open to all.

Winning this scholarship is genuinely based on luck. Scholarship winners are selected randomly out of the pool of all entrants. To enter, all you have to do is call the toll-free phone number given on the Web site and ask to be entered; you can also get the official sweepstakes rules by calling this number. In return, you will receive a copy of AAA's free Education Financing Kit. You probably won't find another scholarship that is this easy to apply for.

National High School Oratorical Contest

Sponsor: American Legion
Web Site: http://www.legion.org/orator.htm
Amount of Scholarship: $50 to $18,000
Number of Awards: 53 national scholarships
Deadline: not given
Education Level: grades 9 through 12

Eligibility: Applicant must be under the age of 20 and be a U.S. citizen or permanent resident.

This scholarship contest is a bit unusual. In order to participate, you have to write and give a speech, so students with public speaking experience or who have taken a speechwriting class in school will be better equipped to compete. The Web site outlines the contest rules and provides lots of tips for what qualities the judges are looking for in potential winners. Be sure to read the rules carefully to understand what topic your speech must cover, how long the speech should last, and even what to wear to the contests. The contest takes place in several rounds, starting at the local level. Winners at the state level receive scholarships from their state's American Legion headquarters and advance to the national level. To learn what scholarships are awarded in your state, click the State & Local Contests link. The National Contest Web page describes the prizes awarded to winners at the national level, which can be as high as $18,000. If you decide to enter this contest, you must contact your local American Legion Post or your state headquarters for an entry form; follow the link at the bottom of the page to find a directory of state headquarters offices. Your high school principal or guidance counselor may also be able to provide more information about this well-known contest.

Sallie Mae CASHE Scholarship

Sponsor: Sallie Mae Trust for Education
Web Site: http://www.cashe.com/scholarship.html
Amount of Scholarship: $1,000
Number of Awards: 50
Deadline: March 30
Education Level: any
Eligibility: Applicant must enroll in any kind of postsecondary school.

All you have to do to enter this scholarship contest is search the free Sallie Mae CASHE

Scholarship Service for scholarships, which you were probably planning to do anyway. You are automatically entered when you fill out the Online Student Profile Form, which is linked to the scholarship information page. One winner from each state is randomly chosen to win scholarships. That's all there is to it.

Take Me Away to College Scholarship

Sponsor: Calgon
Web Site: http://www.takemeaway.com/scholarship/index_2000.html
Amount of Scholarship: $500 to $2,500
Number of Awards: 2
Deadline: August 15
Education Level: high school seniors and college undergraduates
Eligibility: Applicant must enroll in a two-year or four-year U.S. college and be a U.S. or Canadian citizen or permanent resident.

This contest works a bit differently than the others. To enter, click the Enter button at the bottom of the page, then answer the three questions in the electronic entry form, keeping to the specified character limits. To check that you haven't exceeded the limits, click the Character Count button after writing your answer for each question. Twenty-five finalists are chosen from the initial applications. These finalists must then write an essay on a specific topic. The two most original essays (in the opinions of the judges) receive a grand prize of $2,500 and a runner-up prize of $500. To learn all the details about the submission and judging procedures, follow the link to the official contest rules.

Essay Contests

Anthem Essay Contest

Sponsor: Ayn Rand Institute
Web Site: http://www.aynrand.org/contests/

ant.html
Amount of Scholarship: $100 to $1,000
Number of Awards: 31
Deadline: April 1
Education Level: high school freshmen and sophomores
Eligibility: Open to all.

The Ayn Rand Institute sponsors several essay contests each year, for which entrants must write essays on one of Ayn Rand's books. This contest requests essays on the novel *Anthem*. Twenty third prizes of $100, 10 second prizes of $200, and 1 first prize of $1,000 are awarded. Specific essay questions change from year to year, so you must consult the Web page for the current year's topics. The Web page also tells you exactly how to format your submission and the address where you should mail your essay. You don't need to fill out an official application form, but you do need to format your submission correctly, or your essay won't be judged. Unfortunately, you can't read essays of past winners on the Web site, but by exploring the rest of the Ayn Rand Institute's Web site, you should gain some insight into the philosophy behind her fiction.

Elie Wiesel Prize in Ethics Essay Contest

Sponsor: Elie Wiesel Foundation for Humanity
Web Site: http://www.eliewieselfoundation.org/EthicsPrize/EPIntro.htm
Amount of Scholarship: $500 to $5,000
Number of Awards: 5
Deadline: January 21
Education Level: college juniors and seniors
Eligibility: Applicant must be a full-time student at a four-year college.

Each year the Elie Wiesel Foundation sponsors cash prizes for the best essays on ethics by college undergraduates. Suggested essay topics change from year to year and are published on the Web site. To enter, a professor who has reviewed your essay must sponsor you. It is up to you to make certain that the Faculty Sponsor Form is correctly filled out and submitted along with your essay. You can print a PDF version of the form from the Faculty Sponsor Page, along with the faculty sponsor guidelines. Get more information about the submissions procedures by following the Student Guidelines link. At the bottom of this page, you'll find two printable copies of the entry form, one in PDF format and one plain text. Five prizes are awarded in this program: two honorable mentions of $500 each, a third-prize award of $1,500, a second-prize award of $2,500, and a first-prize award of $5,000.

E-Mail Xpress Scholarship

Sponsor: E-mail Xpress
Web Site: http://www.141.com/scholarships/
Amount of Scholarship: $500 plus $100 of e-mail service
Number of Awards: 1
Deadline: January 31
Education Level: high school seniors
Eligibility: Applicant must be admitted to a postsecondary school of any kind.

For this scholarship, you must write a short essay about e-mail. As an Internet user, you should be well qualified to address this topic. To enter, fill out the electronic form at the bottom of the Web page and submit it; you can only apply over the Internet. The Web site does not provide many details about the scholarship other than the essay topic, but as the winner is chosen solely based on the quality of his or her essay, this would be a good competition for any talented writer to enter.

Fountainhead Essay Contest

Sponsor: Ayn Rand Institute
Web Site: http://www.aynrand.org/contests/tf.html
Amount of Scholarship: $1,000 to $10,000

Number of Awards: 16
Deadline: April 15
Education Level: high school juniors and seniors
Eligibility: Open to all.

This is another essay contest that rewards students for reading and writing about Ayn Rand's works. This contest is for older students and requires an essay on the novel *The Fountainhead*. To find out what the current essay topics are, you must go to the Web site. The Web site also describes exactly how long the essays must be and how they must be formatted in order to avoid disqualification. You will also find the address where you can send your essay; there is no official application form. Sixteen prizes are given to the writers of the best essays: 10 third prizes of $1,000; 5 second prizes of $2,000; and 1 first prize of $10,000. If you are unfamiliar with Ayn Rand or the philosophy of her novels, you should explore the rest of the Ayn Rand Institute's Web site—you will probably gain some insights that will help you write a better essay.

George S. and Stella M. Knight Essay Contest

Sponsor: National Society of the Sons of the American Revolution
Web Site: http://www.sar.org/youth/knightrl.htm
Amount of Scholarship: $500 to $4,500
Number of Awards: 3
Deadline: not given
Education Level: high school juniors and seniors
Eligibility: Applicant must be a U.S. citizen or permanent resident.

For this competition, entrants must write an essay about the American Revolution, the Declaration of Independence, or the framing of the U.S. Constitution. There are three scholarship prizes: a third-prize award of $500; a second-prize award of $1,000; and a first-prize award of $4,500. The Web site provides some information about acceptable essay topics, the format of the essay, and judging criteria. You must apply through a local chapter of the Sons of the American Revolution and advance through the local, state, and national levels. To find your local chapter, follow the Listing of State Society Contacts link at the bottom of the page, find the mailing address of the Society headquarters in your state, and follow the instructions for sending a letter request to that Society. You can also go to the NSSAR home page to learn more about this organization and to get ideas for your essay.

The Humanist Essay Contest Scholarship

Sponsor: The American Humanist Association
Web Site: http://www.infidels.org/org/aha/essaycon
Amount of Scholarship: $100 to $1,000
Number of Awards: 6
Deadline: December 1
Education Level: all
Eligibility: Applicant must be younger than the age of 25.

This scholarship rewards the best humanistic essays. Humanism is defined on the Web site, and your essay should fit this definition to compete for the scholarship prizes. Other than applying humanistic philosophy to your essay, the topic is left entirely up to you, although several suggestions are given on the site. You might also benefit from reading about humanism in books, on the Web, and in back issues of the magazine *The Humanist,* where the winning essays are published (you can find out how to order a free sample issue from a link on the scholarship's Web page). The Web site also tells you everything you need to know

about formatting the essay and mailing in your submission. Three awards in given in each age category, one for students between the ages of 13 and 17, and one for students between the ages of 18 and 24. Third prize is $100, second prize is $400, and first prize is $1,000. No application form is required.

National High School Essay Contest

Sponsor: United Nations Association of the United States of America (UNA-USA), United Nations Development Programme, and the Dailey Family Foundation
Web Site: http://www.unausa.org/programs/nhsessay.htm
Amount of Scholarship: $500 to $1,000
Number of Awards: 3
Deadline: April 14
Education Level: grades nine through twelve
Eligibility: Open to all.

For this competition, students must write essays about the United Nations and the United States' participation in the UN. First prize is $1,000, second prize is $750, and third prize is $500. The specific essay topic changes each year and is announced on the contest's Web site. You will also find the winning essays from past years on the site, which should provide good models for your essay. If you decide to enter the contest, go to the Student Application Kit page. There you can read the contest rules, guidelines for formatting essays, and judging criteria, and explore Internet resources that may help you write your essay. You will also find a printable copy of the Essay Cover Form and a directory of local chapters and divisions of UNA-USA. Note that you must submit your essay to your local chapter or division, rather than to a central address.

Swackhamer Peace Essay Contest

Sponsor: The Nuclear Age Peace Foundation
Web Site: http://www.napf.org/awards/swackrules.html
Amount of Scholarship: $500 to $1,500
Number of Awards: 3
Deadline: June 1
Education Level: high school students
Eligibility: Open to all.

Each year this contest solicits essays from high school students on solving the problems of war and peace. The essay topic changes annually. To find out the current essay topic and the guidelines for submitting your essay, scroll down the page until you see the contest rules; you don't need to submit an application form with your essay. First prize is $1,500, second prize is $1,000, and third prize is $500. Before you write your essay, you may find it helpful to learn more about the scholarship sponsor. The links to articles, information, and an electronic newsletter published by the sponsor at the bottom of the Web page will give you insight into the tone your essay should take. You can also read past winning essays by following the links at the very top of the scholarship information page.

Voice of Democracy (VOD) National Competition

Sponsor: Veterans of Foreign Wars of the United States
Web Site: http://www.vfw.org/vod/index.shtml
Amount of Scholarship: $1,000 to $25,000
Number of Awards: 60
Deadline: November 1
Education Level: grades 9 through 12
Eligibility: Applicant must attend a U.S. high school.

This is an audio essay competition; not only must you write an essay, but you must also deliver it as a speech (and record it on a cassette tape). The essay topic changes each year and is posted at the top of the Web site. The VOD Student Information page provides valuable information about the objectives of the contest, which will help you craft your essay. The VOD National Scholarships link lists the scholarships available under this program and their award amounts. You can also read the past year's winning essay, linked to the main scholarship information page, to get a better idea of what the judges are looking for. To learn how to apply, how to record your essay, and what the judging criteria are, go to the VOD Ready Reference page. Note that you cannot apply directly; a teacher or guidance counselor must nominate you to the local VFW Post or the State Headquarters. A directory of State Headquarters is linked to the Ready Reference page.

Young Visionaries Essay Competition

Sponsor: Denny's
Web Site: http://www.dennys.com
Amount of Scholarship: $1,000 to $25,000
Number of Awards: 11
Deadline: March 20
Education Level: high school juniors and seniors
Eligibility: Open to all.

Denny's sponsors an essay contest every year, and the grand prize, awarded to one winner, is a $25,000 scholarship. Ten $1,000 regional scholarships are also awarded. The current year's essay topic, along with the contest rules and entry form, are posted on the Web site. Be sure to read over the rules, which describe the essay topic, length, and format. After reading the rules, you can print out a copy of the entry form directly from your browser. Although the scholarship is not restricted to African-Americans, it is sponsored by African-American organizations and the essay topic is one that concerns African-Americans; therefore, African-American students may have a better chance of winning and are particularly encouraged to apply.

Science and Technology Competitions

The Collegiate Inventors Competition

Sponsor: National Inventors Hall of Fame
Web Site: http://www.invent.org/collegiate/index.html
Amount of Scholarship: $20,000
Number of Awards: 6
Deadline: June 1
Education Level: college undergraduates and graduate students
Eligibility: Applicant must be a full-time student.

This competition rewards students with talents in science, engineering, mathematics, technology, and invention. Six prizes of $20,000 each are awarded. To enter, you (or your team of up to four students) must come up with a useful, original invention and prepare a paper describing it. You will also need to recruit a faculty advisor to help you with the project and enter the competition with you. Go to the Overview page to get a general idea of what the competition is all about and what kind of inventions the judges are looking for. The FAQ page should answer your specific questions about the competition. Go to How to Enter to find out how to prepare your entry, get a checklist

of required materials, and read some valuable tips for what goes into a winning entry. You can then download a PDF copy of the official entry form by clicking the link in the top corner of the home page or the How to Enter page.

DuPont Challenge Essay Awards

Sponsor: DuPont and General Learning Communications
Web Site: http://www.glcomm.com/dupont/index.html
Amount of Scholarship: $50 to $1,500
Number of Awards: 102
Deadline: January 28
Education Level: grades 7 through 12
Eligibility: Applicant must attend a U.S. or Canadian secondary school.

This well-known science and technology essay competition awards scholarships to the best essays on a scientific or technological development, event, or theory—a very broad topic. To help you narrow your topic, check the Student Info page, which provides many tips about what makes a winning essay. There are two divisions; the Junior Division is for applicants in grades 7 through 9, and the Senior Division is for applicants in grades 10 through 12. In each division, a first-place prize of $1,500, a second-place prize of $750, a third-place prize of $500, and 48 honorable mentions of $50 each are awarded. The first-place essays are also published on the Sr. Division Winners and Jr. Division Winners pages; there is no better way to judge the qualities of a good essay than to read past winners. If you want to enter, be sure to read the Rules page, which describes exactly how the essays must be formatted. You can also print out a copy of the entry form from the Web site. Note that the entry form must be signed by your science teacher and packaged with other entries from your class, if there are any.

Duracell/NSTA Invention Challenge

Sponsor: Duracell, Inc. and the National Science Teachers Association (NSTA)
Web Site: http://www.nsta.org/programs/duracell
Amount of Scholarship: $500 to $20,000
Deadline: January 12
Number of Awards: 200
Education Level: grades 6 through 12
Eligibility: Applicant must be younger than the age of 21, and be a U.S. citizen.

To enter this contest, you (or you and a partner) must design and build a device that runs on Duracell batteries. Your entry consists of a written description of the device and its uses, a schematic of the device, and photographs of the device. If you become a finalist, you then send in the actual device for judging. To start, fill out the official entry form and submit it with your preliminary materials; note that a sponsoring teacher must sign your entry. You can print out a PDF copy of the entry form from the Web site, or order a printed entry form by calling the phone number or sending a message to the e-mail address listed on the How to Enter page. To boost your chances of coming up with a winning idea, you can submit a paper describing your idea to First Step by November 15 (in return, you will receive free batteries to use in your invention). More information about this optional step in the competition can be found on the First Step page. If you have a technical question, get free help by sending an e-mail message to an electronics professional; click Ask the Experts to learn more.

ExploraVision Awards

Sponsor: Toshiba Corporation, Toshiba American Group Companies, Toshiba America Foundation, and the National Science Teachers Association
Web Site: http://www.toshiba.com/tai/exploravision/main.html
Amount of Scholarship: $5,000 to $10,000
Number of Awards: 32
Deadline: February 2
Education Level: grades kindergarten through 12
Eligibility: Applicant must be a U.S. or Canadian citizen or permanent resident.

This competition is for teams of two, three, or four students, along with an adult team advisor, who explore a particular technology in great detail and project what that technology will be like in the future. The team must present their findings in a written paper and five graphical Web pages. The How to Enter page describes exactly what each entry must include and how to prepare and submit entries. Go to Request an Entry Kit to download and print a PDF copy of the entry form or order a printed version. Also look at the Past Winners page to read brief summaries of winning projects from previous years and get an idea of whether your project can compete. There are four entry categories: primary level for grades kindergarten through 3; upper elementary level for grades 4 through 6; middle level for grades 7 through 9; and high school level for grades 10 through 12. The 4 first-place teams in each entry category win $10,000 and the 4 second-place teams receive $5,000. Awards must be divided equally among all members of the team.

Intel International Science and Engineering Fair

Sponsor: Intel and Science Service
Web Site: http://www.sciserv.org/isef
Amount of Scholarship: $500 to $40,000
Number of Awards: 63 plus several special scholarships

Deadline: varies
Education Level: grades 9 through 12
Eligibility: Applicant must be under the age of 21.

The International Science and Engineering Fair is the ultimate science fair, with students from all over the world competing for scholarships and other prizes, and a top of scholarship prize of $40,000 awarded to the two best projects. The entire range of available scholarships is listed on the Scholarships & Awards page. For more information about this program, read the Background page. Then, go to Fair Affiliation to find a list of affiliated science fairs in your state, as well as rules and guidelines that projects entered in affiliated fairs must follow and the guidelines for judging projects. When preparing your project, you will find lots of helpful information on the Resources page. You will also find printable forms that you might need to submit with your project on the Forms & Publications page. Because this competition is so large and the rules are so complex, you should definitely enlist the help of your science teacher if you are considering entering a project. Your science teacher can help you come up with a viable project, follow the rules, properly enter your project into the competition, and act as your sponsor.

Intel Science Talent Search

Sponsor: Intel
Web Site: http://www.sciserv.org/sts
Amount of Scholarship: $5,000 to $100,000
Number of Awards: 39
Deadline: December 1
Education Level: high school seniors
Eligibility: Applicant must attend a U.S. high school or be a U.S. citizen.

The Science Talent Search is one of the oldest and most prestigious competitions recognizing the best scientific research projects. Not only will becoming a semifinalist or finalist net you scholarship money, but it is a prestigious honor that can gain you admission to the best colleges and graduate schools. The top prize is $100,000, the second-prize winner receives $75,000, the third-prize winner receives $50,000, and three $25,000 and three $20,000 awards are also given; the 30 semifinalists receive $5,000 each. Because the prestige factor is so high (and so are the scholarship awards), you should definitely enlist the help of your science teacher, who can act as your official advisor, and only enter your best work in this competition. Be sure to read the official entry rules carefully and print out a copy of the entry form exactly as directed on the Entry Rules & Forms page. The Science Talent Search is not a competition to be entered lightly. Be prepared to spend a lot of time and hard work developing a research project that can effectively compete, and get started working on your project well before the deadline so that you can turn in the best work possible. To get a good idea of what kinds of students enter the Science Talent Search and what kinds of projects win top honors, visit the Finalists page and read each winner's biography.

Junior Science and Humanities Symposium

Sponsor: U.S. Departments of the Army, Navy, and Air Force
Web Site: http://www.jshs.org/index.htm
Amount of Scholarship: $2,000 to $16,000
Number of Awards: 48
Deadline: varies
Education Level: grades 9 through 12
Eligibility: Applicant must be a U.S. citizen or permanent resident.

If you have conducted an original research investigation in the sciences, engineering, or math, you can participate in the Junior Science and Humanities Symposium (JSHS) and perhaps win scholarship prizes. Eight third-place scholarships of $2,000, eight second-place scholarships of $6,000, and eight first-place scholarships of $16,000 are awarded at the national level, plus regional winners receive $4,000 scholarships. To participate, you must present your research into one of the 48 participating regional symposia, so make certain that there is one in your geographical area before you consider applying. You can also only get application materials by contacting the director of your local regional symposium directly. Find a list of these regional symposia, along with contact information, on the JSHS Regions page. Also read the More About JSHS page to discover what the aims of the program are, how the competition works, and who is eligible to participate. If you decide to enter, be sure to download the official guidelines and score sheet, available in PDF format on the Guidelines page.

ThinkQuest Internet Challenge

Sponsor: ThinkQuest
Web Site: http://www.thinkquest.org/tqic

Amount of Scholarship: $5,000 to $15,000
Number of Awards: 15 to 45
Deadline: May 1
Education Level: high school students
Eligibility: Applicant must be between the ages of 12 and 19.

This prestigious program rewards students who have strong Internet and Web site publishing skills. Students work in teams of two or three, along with one or more adult coaches, to develop Web sites in different academic categories that can be used as learning tools by other students. First, read How to Participate to find out how to enter the competition. The Step by Step Instructions page tells you exactly how to enter your team for consideration and how to submit your application. To understand how the competition works, read the ThinkQuest Rules, which outlines the application process and the judging criteria. The FAQ also answers common questions about the competition. Be sure to look at the Judging Feedback, which details the judging criteria and provides some insight into what the judges are looking for in winning entries.

ACADEMIC AND CAREER INTEREST SCHOLARSHIPS

The scholarships in this chapter support students pursuing specific fields of study or planning to enter a particular career. Scholarships that fit primarily in another category but also specify a field of study are cross-referenced at the end of the appropriate section.

Some of these scholarships are intended for students who have only expressed an interest in a field of study or career, but many are restricted to students who have already declared their majors. Read the eligibility requirements carefully before applying to make certain that you fulfill all the conditions set by the scholarship program.

The scholarships in this chapter mainly go to graduating high school students and undergraduate college students, although some programs are also extended to graduate students. If you are a graduate student searching for scholarship money to support your studies in a particular field, turn to Chapter 7, "Graduate School Scholarships." All students should also check under the name of their college or university in Chapter 16, "College-Specific Scholarships," to find scholarships offered by their academic departments at their schools.

Accounting

Account for Your Future Scholarship

Sponsor: AccountingNet, John Wiley & Sons, and KPMG
Web Site: http://accountingstudents.proZnet.com/x6579.xml
Amount of Scholarship: $1,000
Number of Awards: 6

Deadline: December 1 and June 1
Education Level: college undergraduates and graduate students
Eligibility: Applicant must either major in accounting at an accredited college or enroll in a graduate program in accounting or taxation at an accredited university and hold a bachelor's degree in accounting; be a full-time student; and have completed at least 24 semester hours or 45 quarter hours of college coursework.

This scholarship is awarded to three outstanding accounting students two times a year, which means you have twice the opportunity to win. First, check the scholarship rules to make certain that you are eligible. You must demonstrate an interest in the relationship between technology and accounting and understand the importance of technology to the future of accounting to be in the running. The Rules page also tells you what criteria are used in selecting the winners. To apply, follow the Application link. You will have to register as a user of the Web site first, complete an optional survey, and decide whether to sign up for e-mail newsletters. Simply fill out each screen and click the Submit button at the bottom of each page to advance, and eventually you will come to the application form; bookmark this page so that you can quickly return to it later. Before going through all this, you might want to explore the rest of the AccountingStudents Web site to learn more about the site you are registering to use (follow the Home link at the bottom of the page). Scholarship winners are also announced online. Go to the News section of the site to find profiles of previous winners.

AAHCPA Undergraduate Scholarship

Sponsor: American Association of Hispanic Certified Public Accountants (AAHCPA)

Web Site: http://www.aahcpa.org/
undergra.htm
Amount of Scholarship: not given
Number of Awards: not given
Deadline: September 15
Education Level: college undergraduates
Eligibility: Applicant must enroll in or have completed an intermediate-level accounting course, have a minimum 3.0 GPA, and be Hispanic.

As explained on the scholarship's Web page, this scholarship is awarded based on academic achievement, financial need, and community involvement. In addition to the official application form, the scholarship program requires that several supporting documents be included in the application package, which are also listed on the Web page; be sure your application package is complete. To get a copy of the application, scroll to the bottom of the page and click Undergraduate Scholarship Application Form. You can fill out the form online and then print it out for mailing.

AICPA Scholarship for Minority Accounting Students

Sponsor: American Institute of Certified Public Accountants (AICPA) Foundation
Web Site: http://www.aicpa.org/members/
div/career/mini/smas.htm
Amount of Scholarship: up to $5,000
Number of Awards: around 300
Deadline: July 1
Education Level: college undergraduates and master's students
Eligibility: Applicant must be an undergraduate student with a declared major in accounting, enroll in a master's program in accounting with any undergraduate degree, or enroll in a master's program in accounting, business administration, finance, or taxation with an undergraduate degree in accounting; be a full-time student; have a minimum 3.0 GPA;

have completed 30 semester hours or 45 quarter hours of college coursework, including at least six semester hours in accounting; and be a member of a minority group.

For this scholarship, eligible minorities include African-Americans, Native Americans, Alaskan Natives, Pacific Islanders, and Hispanics. Financial need is also a factor when choosing the scholarship winners. The FAQ will give you valuable information about who is eligible to apply. You have three choices for obtaining the application form and submitting it: download a PDF version of the form from the Web site; use the fax back service as described in the FAQ; or submit the electronic application online, as well as send additional documents through the mail. Whichever method you choose, be sure to follow the instructions exactly as given.

Excellence in Accounting Scholarship

Sponsor: New York State Society of Certified Public Accountants Foundation for Accounting Education
Web Site: http://www.nysscpa.org/Archive/
other/Acctscholarship01.htm
Amount of Scholarship: $750 to $1,500
Number of Awards: not given
Deadline: April 1
Education Level: college sophomores and juniors
Eligibility: Applicant must enroll in a four- or five-year program in accounting at a New York college, have completed at least 60 semester hours of college coursework including introductory accounting courses, be a New York resident, and be a U.S. citizen or permanent resident.

The scholarship's Web page outlines the eligibility requirements and the requirements for maintaining the scholarship, so read them over carefully before applying. To be eligible, you have to enroll in a state-approved accounting program; a list of New York colleges with such programs can be found at http://www.nysscpa.org/society/Future_CPAs/futurecpas.htm. Follow the link at the bottom of the scholarship's information page to open a printable copy of the application form. Note that you must submit this application through the chairperson of your school's accounting department; you can't directly apply for the scholarship. Two kinds of awards are given out under this program: $750 for part-time students and $1,500 for full-time students.

Frank L. Greathouse Government Accounting Scholarship

Sponsor: Government Finance Officers Association (GFOA)
Web Site: http://www.gfoa.org
Amount of Scholarship: $2,000
Number of Awards: not given
Deadline: February 4
Education Level: college juniors
Eligibility: Applicant must enroll as a full-time student in an accounting program, intend to enter a career or pursue graduate study in state or local government finance, and be a U.S. or Canadian citizen or permanent resident.

To find information about this scholarship, click the Scholarships link under Services and scroll down until you see the scholarship's listing under Available Scholarships. Return to the top of the frame and follow the GFOA Forms link to get a copy of the application. Scroll down until you see the Scholarships section, and click the Frank L. Greathouse Government Accounting Scholarship link to view the application form in PDF format. The application provides a lot more information about eligibility requirements and judging criteria.

Institute of Management Accountants National Scholarships

Sponsor: Institute of Management Accountants (IMA)
Web Site: http://web.imanet.org/academia/admin/scholarship.htm
Amount of Scholarship: $2,000 to $5,000
Number of Awards: 20
Deadline: February 15
Education Level: college sophomores, juniors, and seniors and graduate students
Eligibility: Applicant must be a student member of IMA.

These scholarships are intended for students who want to pursue careers in management accounting or financial management. Twelve of the scholarships are awarded to students at four-year colleges: six $2,000 awards for rising juniors and six $3,000 awards for rising seniors. Two Two-Year Transfer Scholarships of $2,000 each go to students who have just graduated from a two-year college and plan to continue their education in a four- or five-year accounting program. Five Advanced Degree Scholarships of $3,000 each go to graduate students pursuing an advanced degree in management accounting or financial management; college seniors applying to graduate school and current graduate students are both eligible to apply. Finally, one person out of the entire pool of applicants receives the $5,000 Stuart Cameron and Margaret McLeod Memorial Scholarship. In addition, 30 finalists in each category, including scholarship winners, receive scholarships to take the Certified Management Accountant or Certified in Financial Management exam within a year of graduation. See the Web site for specific eligibility requirements in each of these award categories, as well as for selection criteria. You can also print a text or PDF version of the application from the Web site.

KSCPA College Scholarship

Sponsor: Kentucky Society of Certified Public Accountants (KSCPA) Educational Foundation
Web Site: http://www.kycpa.org/Students/college%20scholarships.htm
Amount of Scholarship: $1,000
Number of Awards: 2
Deadline: January 30
Education Level: college sophomores and juniors
Eligibility: Applicant must have completed Principles of Accounting, be enrolled in or have completed Intermediate Accounting, have a minimum overall GPA of 2.75 and an accounting GPA of 3.0, and attend a Kentucky college.

Two scholarships are given out each year under this program. The Web page doesn't provide a lot of information about the awards, but it does tell you what the eligibility requirements are and what supporting documents you must submit with your application. Contact the mailing address, toll-free phone number, or e-mail address at the bottom of the page to request an application form.

KSCPA High School Scholarship

Sponsor: Kentucky Society of Certified Public Accountants (KSCPA)
Web Site: http://www.kycpa.org/Students/highschoolscholarships.htm
Amount of Scholarship: $500
Number of Awards: 10
Deadline: March 1
Education Level: high school seniors
Eligibility: Applicant must plan to enroll in an accounting program at a Kentucky college and attend a Kentucky high school.

This scholarship is awarded based on overall academic achievement and interest in becoming a Certified Public Accountant. You don't need to submit an official application form to apply. Instead, send a letter containing the information outlined at the bottom of the Web page, along with the requested additional materials, to the address given.

MACPA Scholarship

Sponsor: Maryland Association of Certified Public Accountants (MACPA) Educational Foundation, Inc.
Web Site: http://www.macpa.org/Services/scholar.htm
Amount of Scholarship: $1,000 and up
Number of Awards: not given
Deadline: April 15
Education Level: college undergraduates
Eligibility: Applicant must have completed at least 60 total credit hours of college coursework with at least six credit hours in accounting courses (including Accounting Principles I and II), be enrolled in or completed Intermediate Accounting, be a full-time student at a Maryland college, have a minimum 3.0 GPA, demonstrate financial need, and be a Maryland resident.

In order to apply for this scholarship, you must demonstrate a commitment to pursuing a career as a Certified Public Account. You must also maintain a satisfactory level of academic progress, as described on the Web page, to keep the scholarship once you win it. To apply, submit all of the materials listed under Application Procedure, including a printout of the application form.

NJSCPA Accounting Manuscript Contest

Sponsor: New Jersey Society of CPAs (NJSCPA) and *New Jersey Business* magazine
Web Site: http://www.njscpa.org/students/manuscript.asp

Amount of Scholarship: $1,000 to $3,000
Number of Awards: 4
Deadline: February 4
Education Level: college sophomores, juniors, and seniors
Eligibility: Applicant must major in accounting at a two-year or four-year New Jersey college.

This essay contest is intended for accounting majors. First-place winners not only receive a scholarship of $3,000, but have their essays published in *New Jersey Business* magazine. Up to three additional students receive honorable mention awards of $1,000 each. The essay topic changes each year and is posted on the scholarship's Web page. You can also read the previous year's winning essay on this page. Check the Manuscript Guidelines to find out how to format your essay and how the essays are judged. You must submit your essay with the Accounting Manuscript Entry Form, which you can print out from the site.

NJSCPA College Scholarship

Sponsor: New Jersey Society of CPAs (NJSCPA)
Web Site: http://www.njscpa.org/students/college.asp
Amount of Scholarship: not given
Number of Awards: not given
Deadline: not given
Education Level: college juniors
Eligibility: Applicant must major in accounting at a four-year New Jersey college and be a New Jersey resident.

According to the brief description of the scholarship on the Web page, the chairperson of the accounting department at your college must nominate you for this award. Winners are selected based on an interview and academic achievement. If you have any questions about the eligibility requirements, contact the e-mail address or phone number given on the scholarship's Web page.

NJSCPA High School Scholarship

Sponsor: New Jersey Society of CPAs (NJSCPA)
Web Site: http://www.njscpa.org/students/highschool.asp
Amount of Scholarship: $500 to $5,000
Number of Awards: not given
Deadline: October 29
Education Level: high school seniors and part-time college undergraduates
Eligibility: Applicant must enroll in an undergraduate accounting program at a two-year or four-year college, and either be a New Jersey resident or attend a New Jersey high school.

NJSCPA also awards scholarships to graduating high school students who intend to study accounting in college. Winners are chosen based on their scores on a one-hour aptitude test, which is given each November. Awards range from a one-time grant of $500 to five-year scholarships of $3,000 to $5,000. Read the Scholarship Rules to find out exactly how the application process works, what the eligibility requirements are, the rules governing the exam, and the requirements for renewing the scholarship. Obtain a copy of the exam registration form by clicking the Application Form link and printing the contents of the window that appears (make certain that the application form is correct for the current school year).

NSA Scholarships

Sponsor: National Society of Accountants (NSA) Scholarship Foundation
Web Site: http://www.nsacct.org/scholar.htm
Amount of Scholarship: $500 to $2,000
Number of Awards: 33

Deadline: March 10
Education Level: college undergraduates
Eligibility: Applicant must major in accounting at a two-year or four-year U.S. college, have a grade average of B or better, and be a U.S. or Canadian citizen.

The Web page provides a brief overview of this scholarship program, which gives out several different awards to accounting students. Follow the How to Apply link to learn what the eligibility requirements for all of the scholarships are, what documents your application package must contain, and how winners are selected. The Special Awards section of this page describes the three special scholarships awarded under this program, in addition to the 30 general scholarships. The Stanley H. Stearman Award of $2,000 goes only to a relative of an NSA member who is also pursuing a career in accounting. The Louis and Fannie Sager Memorial Scholarship, which ranges from $500 to $1,000, is restricted to Virginia high school students who study accounting at a Virginia college. The most outstanding student in the general scholarship competition receives the Charles Earp Memorial Scholarship and an additional $200. Get a better idea of the judging criteria by looking over the qualifications of the previous year's scholarship winners; follow the Recipients link from the main page. To apply, print copies of the application and the appraisal forms, both of which are linked to the main page.

Robert Kaufman Memorial Scholarship

Sponsor: Independent Accountants International (IAI)
Web Site: http://www.iai.org/education/
Amount of Scholarship: $250 to $5,000
Number of Awards: up to 20
Deadline: March 1

Education Level: college sophomores, juniors, and seniors and graduate students
Eligibility: Applicant must enroll as a full-time student in a degree program in accounting and have a minimum 3.5 GPA in accounting.

This scholarship is awarded to students attending colleges and universities in countries around the world. Each year, several different countries are selected to be eligible for the award; these are listed at the top of the scholarship program's Web page. Make sure that the country where you attend college is one of the selected countries before you apply. The amount of the scholarship depends on the winner's financial need, although the minimum scholarship of $250 is awarded without regard for financial need. The highest consideration is given to undergraduate applicants. Obtain a copy of the scholarship application by following the link at the top or bottom of the page. Your application must be signed by an endorsing IAI member firm. To locate a firm near you, go to http://www.accountants.org, click World Search, and drill down by region, country, state, and city. Mail the application directly to the firm you choose and ask the firm to forward the application to IAI headquarters. Otherwise your application will be disregarded.

Also see the following scholarships:

- Hispanic College Fund Scholarship: Chapter 9, "Hispanic" section
- Indian Health Service Scholarships: Chapter 9, "Native American" section
- Minorities in Government Finance Scholarship: Chapter 9, "All Minorities" section
- NAFOA Student Scholarship: Chapter 9, "Native American" section
- New York State Regents Professional Opportunity Scholarship: Chapter 15, "New York" section
- State Farm Companies Foundation Exceptional Student Fellowship: Chapter 6, "Business" section

Actuarial Science

Actuarial Scholarship for Minority Students

Sponsor: Society of Actuaries and Casualty Actuarial Society
Web Site: http://www.soa.org/academic/index.html
Amount of Scholarship: varies
Number of Awards: not given
Deadline: May 1
Education Level: college undergraduates
Eligibility: Applicant must enroll in an actuarial science program or otherwise prepare for a career in actuarial science, be a member of a minority group, and be a U.S. citizen or permanent resident.

Eligible minorities for this scholarship include African-Americans, Hispanics, and Native Americans. Read over this Web page to find out what the purpose of the scholarship program, eligibility requirements, and application procedures are. At the bottom of the page is a link to the scholarship application form in PDF format.

D.W. Simpson & Company Actuarial Science Scholarships

Sponsor: D.W. Simpson & Company
Web Site: http://www.dwsimpson.com/scholar.html
Amount of Scholarship: $1,000
Number of Awards: 2 general scholarships per semester
Deadline: July 15 and November 15
Education Level: college juniors
Eligibility: Applicant must major in actuarial science, have passed at least one actuarial exam, have a minimum 3.4 GPA in actuarial science and a minimum 3.0 GPA overall, and be a U.S. citizen or permanent resident.

Read the brief description of the general scholarship program at the top of the Web page to see if you qualify. Note that additional scholarships are awarded through the mathematics departments of the eight colleges listed. If you attend any of those colleges, contact a faculty member in the mathematics department to learn more. The application form for all the scholarships (general and school-affiliated) is linked to the bottom of the page. You can fill out and submit the application online.

Also see the following scholarships:

- State Farm Companies Foundation Exceptional Student Scholarship: Chapter 6, "Business" section
- Wendell Milliman Scholarship: Chapter 14, "Employers and Professions" section

Advertising, Marketing, and Public Relations

National Ad 2 Scholarship Challenge

Sponsor: American Advertising Federation (AAF) and National Ad 2
Web Site: http://www.ad2.org/scholarship/index.html
Amount of Scholarship: $500
Number of Awards: 1
Deadline: March 29
Education Level: college sophomores and juniors
Eligibility: Applicant must major in advertising or a closely related field at a four-year U.S. or Canadian college, be a member of an AAF College Chapter, and have a grade average of C or better.

For this scholarship, you have to create an application package that demonstrates your advertising skills by really selling yourself to the scholarship judges. Follow the rules as outlined to create a print, radio, or television ad for you. Print out a copy of the entry form, which is linked to the Web page, to include with your entry. You might also want to explore the rest of the Web site to find out what National Ad 2 is all about.

Also see the following scholarships:

- AWC-DC Scholarship: Chapter 12, "Female" section
- Hispanic College Fund Scholarship: Chapter 9, "Hispanic" section
- Jessica Savitch Scholarship: Chapter 6, "Communications" section
- Roberta Thumin Scholarship: Chapter 6, "Communications" section
- State Farm Companies Foundation Exceptional Student Scholarship: Chapter 6, "Business" section

Aerospace Sciences and Engineering

AIAA Foundation Undergraduate Scholarship

Sponsor: American Institute of Aeronautics and Astronautics (AIAA) Foundation
Web Site: http://www.aiaa.org/information/student/scholarship/undergrad.html
Amount of Scholarship: $2,000 per year (renewable)
Number of Awards: at least 3
Deadline: January 31
Education Level: college freshmen, sophomores, and juniors
Eligibility: Applicant must intend to pursue a career in an aeronautics- or astronautics-related field, have completed one quarter or semester of full-time study at an accredited

college, have a minimum 3.0 GPA, and be a U.S. citizen or permanent resident.

This scholarship program awards one $2,000 scholarship to at least one rising sophomore, one rising junior, and one rising senior each year. The Web page describes the objectives of the program, the scholarship's eligibility requirements, and the selection criteria. Read this valuable information carefully to determine if you would make a good candidate. To qualify, you must plan to work in a field related to the technical activities of AIAA, so you had better understand what those activities are; go to the AIAA home page to learn more. Even though you don't have to be a member of AIAA to apply for the scholarship, you do have to become a member before you can accept it; learn more about becoming a student member by following the Membership link on the left-hand side of the page. If you would like to apply, print out a text version of the application form (make certain that this application is dated for the current school year, or order the latest application directly from the sponsor).

Donald K. "Deke" Slayton Memorial Scholarship

Sponsor: American Astronautical Society
Web Site: http://www.astronautical.org/slayton.html
Amount of Scholarship: $5,000
Number of Awards: 1
Deadline: February 1
Education Level: college juniors and seniors and graduate students
Eligibility: Applicant must major in engineering, intend to pursue a career in astronautics, have a minimum 3.5 GPA, be a full-time student at an accredited college or university, and be a U.S. citizen or permanent resident.

This scholarship is intended for students who want to pursue a career in astronautics, and applicants must demonstrate this intent through their scholastic plans. You will find more detailed information about the judging criteria on the Web page, as well as instructions for submitting the application and additional materials. Follow the link at the bottom of the page to open and print a PDF copy of the application.

LaSPACE Undergraduate Student Scholarship

Sponsor: Louisiana Space Consortium (LaSPACE)
Web Site: http://phacts.phys.lsu.edu/ugssp.html
Amount of Scholarship: $2,500 per year (renewable for four years)
Number of Awards: not given
Deadline: not given
Education Level: college undergraduates
Eligibility: Applicant must study aerospace or space sciences, be a full-time student at a participating Louisiana Space Consortium college, and be a U.S. citizen.

This Web site describes the LaSPACE undergraduate scholarship and the rationale behind offering the scholarship, which you should read in order to prepare an application that effectively demonstrates why you are the best candidate. To be eligible, you must attend a member college of the Louisiana Space Consortium (look up your college in Chapter 16 to find out if it offers the scholarship). You can renew the scholarship each year if you meet the conditions outlined on the Web page. To find out how to contact LaSPACE and obtain an application, and to learn more about the Louisiana Space Consortium in general, go to http://phacts.phys.lsu.edu.

Montana Space Grant Consortium Scholarships and Fellowships

Sponsor: Montana Space Grant Consortium
Web Site: http://www.montana.edu/wwwmsgc/Text/ScholarProgram.html
Amount of Scholarship: $1,000 to full tuition and a stipend of $15,000 (renewable)
Number of Awards: not given
Deadline: March 24
Education Level: college undergraduates and graduate students
Eligibility: Applicant must study an aerospace-related field, be a full-time student at a Montana Space Grant Consortium college or university, and be a U.S. citizen.

Under this program, scholarships for $1,000 are awarded to undergraduates, and graduate students receive full-tuition fellowships plus an annual stipend of $15,000. These awards are given to students who are studying a field related to aerospace sciences and engineering, which can include biology, chemistry, geology, physics, engineering, or computer science, depending on your academic interests and career goals. Be prepared to justify why your field of study is related to the goals of the Montana Space Grant Consortium in your application. Participating Montana campuses are listed on the Web page. If you decide to apply, print out the text application for either the undergraduate scholarship or graduate fellowship, and follow the instructions given at the bottom of the form. (Make certain that the form is correct for the current school year, or obtain a current application from the contact person listed on the page.)

NASA Nebraska Space Grant and EPSCoR Scholarships and Fellowships

Sponsor: NASA Nebraska Space Grant and EPSCoR Programs

Web Site: http://cid.unomaha.edu/ ~nasa/funding/scholar.htm
Amount of Scholarship: $500 to $2,500 per semester (renewable)
Number of Awards: not given
Deadline: varies by school
Education Level: college undergraduates and graduate students
Eligibility: Applicant must study an aerospace- or aviation-related field at a Nebraska Space Grant college or university, and be a U.S. citizen.

Two undergraduate scholarships and two graduate fellowships are offered through this program. The Undergraduate Research Scholarship awards $750 per semester to an undergraduate student to fund a preapproved research project in aerospace or aviation studies, and the Graduate Research Fellowship awards $2,500 for the same purpose to a graduate student. The Undergraduate Course Work Scholarship and the Graduate Course Work Fellowship don't require students to conduct research; rather, they give $500 per semester solely based on past academic performance. A Flight Scholarship is also available to help fund students' flight training. Women, minorities, and students with disabilities are actively recruited for this program. Most of the information about the awards, including the program's goals, selection criteria, and conditions, are listed on the application forms; click the appropriate link to open the form for the award that interests you. To be eligible to apply, you must attend one of the Nebraska State Grant member colleges, universities, or community colleges. The application forms also list eligible schools, as well as the name and phone number of each school's scholarship contact.

OSGC Scholarships

Sponsor: Ohio Space Grant Consortium (OSGC)

Web Site: http://www.oai.org/OSGC/page/ Scholarship.html
Amount of Scholarship: $2,000 to $3,000
Number of Awards: not given
Deadline: January 31
Education Level: college sophomores and juniors
Eligibility: Applicant must enroll in an aerospace-related program at an OSGC-affiliated college, and be a U.S. citizen.

This program awards two different scholarships: the Junior Scholarship gives $2,000 to rising juniors, and the Senior Scholarship awards $3,000 to rising seniors. If you win the scholarship, you will be expected to complete a research project during the award year. Look on the scholarship's Web page for links to PDF copies of the informational brochure, application form, and recommendation form. Read the brochure first to make certain that you are a good candidate for the scholarship. Minorities, female students, and students with disabilities are particularly encouraged to apply. You must attend an Ohio college affiliated with the OSGC to be eligible for the scholarships. Click the Consortium link to find a list of member colleges.

VSGC Scholarships and Fellowships

Sponsor: Virginia Space Grant Consortium (VSGC)
Web Site: http://www.vsgc.odu.edu/html/ fellowships.htm
Amount of Scholarship: $1,000 to $8,500
Number of Awards: not given
Deadline: varies
Education Level: high school seniors, college undergraduates, and graduate students
Eligibility: Applicant must study an aerospace-related field, be a full-time student at a Virginia Space Grant college or university or at a Vir-

ginia community college, have a minimum 3.0 GPA, and be a U.S. citizen.

Four scholarships are available under this program to students attending the participating colleges and universities listed at the top of the Web page. Click an award's name to learn more about it; this opens a PDF file describing the award in greater detail and providing a printable copy of the application form. Each award carries specific eligibility requirements that you should be aware of, so read the application materials carefully to make sure you qualify. Minorities, females, and students with disabilities are especially encouraged to apply for all awards in this program. The Aerospace Graduate Research Fellowship gives $5,000 of add-on financial support to graduate students in any field relevant to the aerospace sciences. The Aerospace Undergraduate Research Scholarship awards up to $8,500 to a rising college junior or senior to complete a research project. The Teacher Education Scholarship gives $1,000 to future K-12 teachers, with priority going to education majors specializing in technology education, mathematics, earth science, environmental science, or space science; high school seniors and community college sophomores are eligible to apply for this scholarship. The Community College Scholarship awards $1,500 to community college freshmen studying a technological field that supports aerospace. The award brochures also provide more information about the general goals and mission of the Virginia Space Grant Consortium.

Also see the following scholarships:

- AFCEA General Emmett Paige Scholarship: Chapter 13, "All Branches" section
- AFCEA General John A. Wickham Scholarship: Chapter 6, "Sciences" section
- AFCEA ROTC Scholarship: Chapter 13, "All Branches" section
- New Economy Technology Scholarships: Chapter 15, "Pennsylvania" section

Agriculture

California Farm Bureau Scholarship

Sponsor: California Farm Bureau Scholarship Foundation
Web Site: http://www.cfbf.com/scholar.htm
Amount of Scholarship: not given
Number of Awards: not given
Deadline: March 1
Education Level: college undergraduates
Eligibility: Applicant must plan to pursue a career in the agricultural industry, and attend a four-year accredited college in California.

The scholarship's Web page tells you who is eligible for the scholarship and what items must be included in the application package. If you decide to apply, click the link at the bottom of the page to open a text copy of the application, which you can print from your Web browser.

Careers in Agriculture Scholarship

Sponsor: Cenex/Land O'Lakes Agronomy Company
Web Site: http://www.cnxlol.com/sch.htm
Amount of Scholarship: $1,000
Number of Awards: 35
Deadline: March 1
Education Level: high school seniors
Eligibility: Applicant must enroll in a livestock- or agronomy-related program at a two-year or four-year college and be a resident of the primary Cenex/Land O'Lakes Agronomy Company trade area.

Thirty-five scholarships are awarded under this program. One qualification is that scholarships only go to students who live in the sponsor's primary trade area; to find out if you meet this requirement, follow the link to the map and locate your home state. If you decide to apply, either print the PDF application form linked to the page or send a message to the e-mail address given at the bottom of the page to request that an application be sent to you.

Clark/Taylor Higher Education Scholarship

Sponsor: Clark/Taylor Bankers Association
Web Site: http://www.csbloyal.com/scholarship.htm
Amount of Scholarship: $500
Number of Awards: 2
Deadline: March 10
Education Level: high school seniors
Eligibility: Applicant must study agriculture or business at a two-year or four-year college, have a minimum 2.0 GPA, and demonstrate financial need.

The Web page doesn't give you a lot of information about the scholarship or even provide detailed eligibility requirements. It does link to both a text and a PDF version of the application form, which you can print out, complete, and mail to the address given. Also follow the Mission link at the top of the page to learn more about the sponsor and its objectives.

NDPRB Undergraduate Scholarships

Sponsor: National Dairy Promotion and Research Board (NDPRB)
Web Site: http://www.dairyinfo.com/onlin/scholarship.html
Amount of Scholarship: $1,500 to $2,500
Number of Awards: up to 20
Deadline: March 31
Education Level: college sophomores and juniors
Eligibility: Applicant must enroll in a dairy food science, technology, or marketing program.

Nineteen scholarships of $1,500 each are awarded under this program, and the best applicant receives an additional $2,500 scholarship. The Web page describes the scholarship, what the sponsor is looking for in a successful applicant, how to submit your application, and the additional materials you must include with the completed application form. You can also download a PDF version of the application form for printing. The application form itself lists more detailed selection criteria and application instructions.

U.S. Department of Agriculture/ Woodrow Wilson Fellowship

Sponsor: U.S. Department of Agriculture
Web Site: http://www.woodrow.org/public-policy/usda/
Amount of Scholarship: full tuition
Number of Awards: 8 to 10
Deadline: not given
Education Level: college sophomores
Eligibility: Applicant must be selected as a U.S. Department of Agriculture/1890 National Scholar and attend a Historically Black 1890 Land Grant School.

This program helps college sophomores at Historically Black Colleges and Universities pursue a bachelor's and master's degree in a field of importance to the U.S. Department of Agriculture, such as agriculture, food sciences, or natural resources. If you win a scholarship, the program pays full tuition and fees during your junior and senior years in college and while you earn a master's degree; the fellowship may even continue through the doctoral level, if appropriate. Winners also receive funding to train at two summer institutes, including a salary and costs of travel. Fellows must agree to work for the U.S. Department of Agriculture one year for every year that they receive support (these conditions are spelled out in the Description of the Award and in the Eligibility Requirements).

To be eligible, you must already attend 1 of the 17 Historically Black 1890 Land Grant Schools listed under the Eligibility Requirements. You also must be nominated out of the National Scholars Program to be considered for this prestigious award; you cannot apply for it directly. The scholarship or financial aid office at your college can provide more information about the nomination process.

Walter J. Clore Scholarship

Sponsor: Washington Association of Wine Grape Growers
Web Site: http://www.wawgg.org/cloreinfo.html
Amount of Scholarship: $2,000
Number of Awards: 1
Deadline: December 31
Education Level: high school seniors and college undergraduates
Eligibility: Applicant must enroll in an area of study pertaining to the wine industry.

This scholarship is intended for students who want to pursue a career in the wine industry and who are taking a relevant curriculum in agriculture or viticulture. Preference is given to residents of Washington state, but residents of any state are free to apply. The scholarship guidelines listed on the Web site outline the eligibility requirements and selection criteria. To apply, follow the link to the text version of the application, which you can print out from your Web browser.

Also see the following scholarships:

- Competitive Edge Scholarship: Chapter 6, "Engineering" section
- Frank and Elizabeth Spencer Scholarship: Chapter 15, "North Carolina" section
- Garden Club of Georgia Scholarships: Chapter 15, "Georgia" section
- Key Club International Scholarships: Chapter 8, "Clubs" section
- Lawrence Conservation District Scholarship: Chapter 15, "Pennsylvania" section
- Michigan Farm Bureau Scholarships: Chapter 14, "Employer and Profession" section
- Missouri Department of Agriculture Scholarship: Chapter 15, "Missouri" section
- National Council of State Garden Clubs Scholarship: Chapter 6, "Horticulture" section
- National FFA Scholarships: Chapter 8, "Clubs" section
- New Economy Technology Scholarships: Chapter 15, "Pennsylvania" section
- North Carolina Tomato Growers Scholarship: Chapter 15, "North Carolina" section

Architecture

AIA/AAF Minority/ Disadvantaged Scholarship

Sponsor: American Institute of Architects (AIA) and American Architectural Foundation (AAF)
Web Site: http://www.e-architect.com/institute/scholar.htm
Amount of Scholarship: $500 to $3,000
Number of Awards: 20
Deadline: December 6
Education Level: high school seniors and college freshmen
Eligibility: Applicant must enroll in an accredited degree program in architecture, either be a member of a minority group or come from a financially disadvantaged background, and be a U.S. citizen or permanent resident.

This scholarship aids students who would not otherwise have the opportunity to enter a professional degree program in architecture. Scroll down the page until you see the AIA/AAF Minority/Disadvantaged Scholarship heading to learn more about the award. Financial need is the most important consideration when selecting scholarship winners, and it determines the amount of the award that winners receive. To receive an application, you must be nominated by your high school guidance counselor, the dean of the architecture department at your college, an architect, or someone else who can testify to your interest in pursuing architecture as a career. Print out a copy of the nomination form by following the link to Minority/Disadvantaged Scholarship at the top of the page; this form also tells you a little more about the scholarship and outlines the eligibility requirements in greater detail.

AIA/AAF Scholarship for First Professional Degree Candidates

Sponsor: American Institute of Architects (AIA) and American Architectural Foundation (AAF)
Web Site: http://www.e-architect.com/institute/scholar.htm
Amount of Scholarship: $500 to $2,500
Number of Awards: not given
Deadline: February
Education Level: college juniors
Eligibility: Applicant must enroll in an accredited professional degree program in architecture.

You will only find a little bit of information about this scholarship on the Web page, but it should be enough to determine if it is worth pursuing. Scroll down the page until you find the paragraph describing the scholarship. As you can see from the description, the dean of your architecture department or a designated scholarship committee must nominate you for the award. The Web page also lists the documents that must be included in the application package. Get more information from your college's architecture department if you are interested in applying for the award.

Also see the following scholarships:

- FFGC Scholarships: Chapter 15, "Florida" section
- Garden Club of Georgia Scholarships: Chapter 15, "Georgia" section
- Hispanic College Fund Scholarship: Chapter 9, "Hispanic" section
- New York State Regents Professional Opportunity Scholarship: Chapter 15, "New York" section

Athletic Training

See the following scholarship:

- New York State Regents Professional Opportunity Scholarship: Chapter 15, "New York" section

Atmospheric Sciences

AMS Scholarships

Sponsor: American Meteorological Society (AMS)
Web Site: http://www.ametsoc.org/AMS/amsedu/scholfel.html
Amount of Scholarship: $300 to $15,000
Number of Awards: not given
Deadline: varies
Education Level: high school seniors, college undergraduates, and graduate students
Eligibility: Applicant must plan to pursue a career in the atmospheric sciences or a related field.

This scholarship program encompasses three undergraduate scholarships, two graduate fellowships, and one essay contest. Each award is described on this Web page, followed by general instructions for applying for all of the awards and links to the application forms in PDF format. AMS/Industry Minority two-year scholarships of $6,000 go to graduating high school students who are traditionally underrepresented in the sciences, particularly Hispanic, Native American, and African-American students. AMS/Industry Undergraduate two-year scholarships of $4,000 go to rising college juniors majoring in a course of study related in some way to the atmospheric sciences. Eight different Undergraduate Scholarships are awarded to rising college seniors who are full-time students and have a grade point average of at least 3.0. These awards range from $700 to $5,000. Click each scholarship's name to open a brief description of the history of the scholarship and a biography of the person whom the award honors. You only have to submit one application form to apply for all of these scholarships. The AMS Graduate Fellowship in the History of Science awards a one-year $15,000 stipend to a student researching and writing a dissertation on the history of the atmospheric or related sciences. This is the only award listed on the Web page that does not require an official application form; instead, follow the instructions under Eligibility Criteria to put together an application package. AMS/Industry/Government Graduate Fellowships award nine-month stipends of $15,000 to master's and doctoral students in any field related to the atmospheric sciences. Finally, the Father James B. Macelwane Awards in Meteorology go to the best student papers in the atmospheric sciences. You don't need to complete an official application form for this contest; simply follow the steps under Application Procedures to submit an entry.

Aviation

AOPA Air Safety Foundation Scholarships

Sponsor: Aircraft Owners and Pilots Association (AOPA) Air Safety Foundation and University Aviation Association

Web Site: http://www.aopa.org/asf/scholarship
Amount of Scholarship: $1,000
Number of Awards: 2
Deadline: March 31
Education Level: college juniors and seniors
Eligibility: Applicant must major in a non-engineering program in aviation at a four-year college, have a minimum 3.25 GPA, and be a U.S. citizen.

Two scholarships are awarded under this program: the McAllister Memorial Scholarship and the Donald Burnside Memorial Scholarship. The top of the scholarship page gives general information about both of the scholarships, including application procedures. Follow the Information links beside each scholarship's name to find details about that award's eligibility requirements and application procedures. The only real difference between the two scholarships is the essay question that you have to answer in your application. If you decide to apply, return to the top of the page and click the Application link beside the scholarship for which you want to be considered (you can apply for both scholarships, if you like). This opens a text version of the application form that you can then print out. To learn more about the goals and activities of the AOPA Air Safety Foundation, follow the Air Safety Foundation link on the left-hand side of the page.

NBAA Aviation Scholarship

Sponsor: National Business Aviation Association (NBAA) and University Aviation Association (UAA)
Web Site: http://www.nbaa.org/scholarships
Amount of Scholarship: $1,000
Number of Awards: 5
Deadline: November 1
Education Level: college freshmen, sophomores, and juniors
Eligibility: Applicant must enroll in an aviation-related degree program at an NBAA or

UAA member institution, have a minimum 3.0 GPA, and be a U.S. citizen.

Here you will find a brief description of this scholarship, including a list of documents that must be included in the application package and a phone number to contact for more information. You can also download a PDF copy of the scholarship application. NBAA or UAA member colleges are listed at the end of the scholarship's description; you must attend one to be eligible to apply.

USAIG PDP Scholarship

Sponsor: U.S. Aircraft Insurance Group (USAIG)
Web Site: http://www.nbaa.org/scholarships
Amount of Scholarship: $1,000
Number of Awards: 3
Deadline: August 31
Education Level: college freshmen, sophomores, and juniors
Eligibility: Applicant must enroll in an aviation-related program at an NBAA member institution that incorporates the NBAA Professional Development Program, have a minimum 3.0 GPA, and be a U.S. citizen.

The Web page gives a description of the scholarship, including eligibility requirements, application instructions, and a phone number of contact for more information. You can also download a PDF copy of the application form. Eligible colleges are listed on the last page of the application form; you must attend one to qualify for the scholarship.

WAI Scholarships

Sponsor: Women in Aviation, International (WAI)
Web Site: http://www.wiai.org/scholarships/index.html
Amount of Scholarship: $500 to $1,000
Number of Awards: 5

Deadline: December 10
Education Level: college sophomores and juniors
Eligibility: Applicant must enroll in a degree program in an aviation-related field and be female.

Among the many awards given out under this program are four scholarships for female undergraduate students pursuing degrees in aviation. To learn about these scholarships, click the Available Scholarships link. Under General Scholarships, you will find two awards for college students studying aviation: the Airbus Leadership Grant, which requires a minimum GPA of 2.0 and awards one scholarship of $1,000; and the Women in Aviation International Achievement Awards, which awards $500 to two full-time students. Under the Maintenance Scholarships category, you will find two scholarships for college undergraduates studying aircraft maintenance: the Aircraft Electronics Association Aviation Maintenance Scholarship, which requires a minimum GPA of 2.75 and awards one scholarship of $1,000; and the Paul Irvin Memorial Maintenance Scholarship, which requires a minimum GPA of 3.0 and awards one scholarship of $1,000. None of the other awards is intended for college students, but you may still find a few that you would like to apply for, particularly if you need to take flight training courses (check the Flight Scholarships category). You can't apply for more than two awards, though. Once you decide which scholarships to go for, return to the main page and click the Application Guidelines link to find out how to apply. Then download the application form in PDF format by following the link from the main page. Be sure to write the name of the scholarship for which you are applying at the top of the application form and complete the section for college students.

Also see the following scholarship:

- NASA Nebraska Space Grant and EPSCoR Programs Scholarships and Fellowships: Chapter 6, "Aerospace Sciences and Engineering" section

Avionics and Aircraft Repair

AEA Educational Foundation Scholarships

Sponsor: Aircraft Electronics Association (AEA) Educational Foundation
Web Site: http://www.aea.net/EducationalFoundation/default.asp
Amount of Scholarship: $1,000 to $16,000
Number of Awards: 22
Deadline: February 15
Education Level: high school seniors and college undergraduates
Eligibility: Applicant must enroll in an accredited avionics or aircraft repair program and have a minimum 3.0 GPA.

This scholarship program gives out 19 different scholarships to students of avionics and aircraft repair. The average award is $1,000. Most of the scholarships have no eligibility requirements other than enrollment in an avionics or aircraft repair program, but you should still read through the descriptions and note the specific awards for which you are qualified. For instance, some scholarships go only to students who attend college in a particular state or in Canada. Five awards are limited attending a particular school: one $1,000 award for students at Fox Valley Technical College in Wisconsin; one $1,500 award for students at Embry-Riddle Aeronautical University (either the Florida or Arizona campus); one $3,000 award for students at the College of Aeronautics in New York; three $6,000 awards for students at Colorado Aero Tech; and one $16,000 scholarship for students at the NEC Spartan

School of Aeronautics in Oklahoma. Click the Write to Us link to find contact information for obtaining application materials. Explore the links at the top of the page to find more information about the scholarship sponsor, particularly the Who Is AEA? and Educational Foundation links.

William M. Fanning Maintenance Scholarship

Sponsor: National Business Aviation Association
Web Site: http://www.nbaa.org/scholarships
Amount of Scholarship: $2,500
Number of Awards: 2
Deadline: September 1
Education Level: college undergraduates
Eligibility: Applicant must enroll in an accredited airframe and power plant program at an approved FAR Part 147 school, and be a U.S. citizen.

This Web page provides a brief description of the scholarship, including the eligibility requirements, a list of documents that must be included in the application package, and a phone number to contact for more information. You can also download a PDF copy of the application form.

Also see the following scholarship:

- WAI Scholarships: Chapter 6, "Aviation" section

Biology

NIH Undergraduate Scholarship

Sponsor: National Institutes of Health (NIH)
Web Site: http://ugsp.info.nih.gov
Amount of Scholarship: $20,000 per year (renewable for up to four years)

Number of Awards: 15
Deadline: March 31
Education Level: college undergraduates
Eligibility: Applicant must plan to pursue a career in biomedical research, be a full-time student at an accredited college, have a minimum 3.5 GPA or be ranked in the top 5 percent of his or her class, come from a disadvantaged background, and be a U.S. citizen or permanent resident.

Along with a substantial monetary award, winners of this scholarship receive a paid summer internship at NIH. After graduation, scholarship winners must work at NIH one year for each year they received scholarship money. Learn more about the field of biomedical research and the NIH by clicking the Biomedical Research at NIH button. The Executive Summary & FAQs page provides a good overview of the scholarship program, including details on application procedures, selection criteria, and what it means to come from a disadvantaged background. Also be sure to go to the Information About the UGSP page, which describes in greater detail how to apply, how to renew your scholarship, the benefits of the award, and the service obligation it entails. If you decide to apply, follow the Scholarship Application & Renewal link, where you can fill out parts of your application online and download the other required forms.

UNCF/Merck Undergraduate Science Research Scholarship Awards

Sponsor: United Negro College Fund (UNCF) and Merck Company Foundation
Web Site: http://www.uncf.org/merck/programs/undergrd.htm
Amount of Scholarship: $25,000
Number of Awards: 15
Deadline: January 31
Education Level: college juniors

Eligibility: Applicant must demonstrate an interest in biomedical research, major in the life or physical sciences, be a full-time student at a four-year U.S. college, have a minimum 3.3 GPA, be African-American, and be a U.S. citizen or permanent resident.

This award is intended to increase the number of African-Americans entering the field of biomedical research. The scholarship consists of a substantial monetary award for college education and two paid summer internships. The main scholarship page provides a brief overview of the program and lists the eligibility requirements. To learn more, go to the Application Details page. You might also find it helpful to read the UNCF/Merck History or to compare yourself to Current Fellows (follow the links on the left side of the page). If you decide to apply, the Application Procedures page tells you how to obtain an application form and put together an application package. You can also request more information about the program and application forms by filling out an electronic form linked to this page.

Also see the following scholarships:

• National Council of State Garden Clubs Scholarship: Chapter 6, "Horticulture" section
• New Economy Technology Scholarships: Chapter 15, "Pennsylvania" section
• ZymoGenetics Scholarship for the Advancement of Science: Chapter 15, "Washington" section

Botany

See the following scholarships:

• FFGC Scholarships: Chapter 15, "Florida" section
• Garden Club of Georgia Scholarships: Chapter 15, "Georgia" section

- National Council of State Garden Clubs Scholarship: Chapter 6, "Horticulture" section

Business

Atlas Shrugged Essay Contest

Sponsor: Ayn Rand Institute
Web Site: http://www.aynrand.org/contests/atlas.html
Amount of Scholarship: $1,000 to $5,000
Number of Awards: 3
Deadline: February 15
Education Level: college undergraduates and graduate students
Eligibility: Applicant must be enrolled in a business degree program.

For this contest, you must write an essay on the Ayn Rand novel *Atlas Shrugged*. The writer of the best essay receives $5,000, second place receives $3,000, and first place gets $1,000. You will find the current year's essay questions posted on the contest's Web page, as well as the contest rules, which tell you how to format and submit your essay. You do not have to fill out an official application form to enter. If you are unfamiliar with the works and philosophy of Ayn Rand, be sure to explore the rest of the Ayn Rand Institute's Web site by following the link at the very bottom of the page; you will find the site helpful in preparing a competitive entry.

State Farm Companies Foundation Exceptional Student Fellowship

Sponsor: State Farm Companies Foundation
Web Site: http://www.statefarm.com/foundati/exceptio.htm
Amount of Scholarship: $3,000
Number of Awards: 50
Deadline: not given
Education Level: college juniors
Eligibility: Applicant must major in a business-related field, be a full-time student at a U.S. college, have a minimum 3.6 GPA, and be a U.S. citizen.

Fifty awards are given under this program each year to business students specializing in areas such as accounting, actuarial science, business administration, computer science, economics, finance, insurance, investing, management, marketing, mathematics, and statistics. The scholarship is awarded based on leadership, academic achievement, character, and potential for a business career, as described in the Selection section of the Web page. To find the program's contact information and request an application, select Foundation from the drop-down menu to the right and scroll down to the bottom of the page.

Zonta International Foundation Jane M. Klausman Women in Business Scholarship

Sponsor: Zonta International Foundation
Web Site: http://www.zonta.org/programs/descriptions.htm
Amount of Scholarship: $4,000
Number of Awards: 5
Deadline: not given
Education Level: college sophomores and juniors
Eligibility: Applicant must enroll in a business-related degree program, and be female.

To find information about this scholarship, scroll down the page until you see the Scholarship heading. There you will find the goal of the program, the eligibility requirements, and basic application instructions. No application form is available online. If you would like to apply, click the Additional Application Information link to send an e-mail message requesting that an application be mailed to you.

Also see the following scholarships:

- Avis Scholarship: Chapter 7, "Business" section
- Bank of America ADA Abilities Scholarship: Chapter 10, "Any Disability" section
- Burlington Northern Santa Fe Foundation Scholarship: Chapter 9, "Native American" Section
- Clark/Taylor Higher Education Scholarship: Chapter 6, "Agriculture" section
- Hispanic College Fund Scholarship: Chapter 9, "Hispanic" section
- Indian Health Service Scholarships: Chapter 9, "Native American" section
- Minorities in Government Finance Scholarship: Chapter 9, "All Minorities" section
- NAFOA Student Scholarship: Chapter 9, "Native American" section
- Wendell Milliman Scholarship: Chapter 14, "Employer and Profession" section
- Yes You Can (Y.Y.C.) Scholarship: Chapter 15, "Washington" section

Chemistry

ACS Scholarships

Sponsor: American Chemical Society (ACS)
Web Site: http://www.acs.org/minorityaffairs/scholars.html
Amount of Scholarship: up to $2,500
Number of Awards: not given
Deadline: February 15
Education Level: high school seniors and college freshmen, sophomores, and juniors
Eligibility: Applicant must major in chemistry or a related field at a two-year or four-year college, plan to pursue a career in the chemical sciences, have a grade average of B or better, be a member of a minority group, demonstrate financial need, and be a U.S. citizen or permanent resident.

The ACS Scholars program encompasses six different scholarships for minority students who want to study the chemical sciences and chemical technology. (Students pursuing careers in medicine or pharmacy are not eligible for these scholarships.) Eligible minorities include African-Americans, Hispanics, and Native Americans. The scholarship's Web page gives an overview of the program, lists the selection criteria for all scholarships, and lists the eligibility requirements for the different awards. Some of the scholarships are reserved for students of specific disciplines within the broad field of chemistry or students at different educational levels, and almost every scholarship is limited to a specific geographical region. Study the details of each scholarship and identify at least one for which you are qualified before applying. You don't have to apply for each scholarship separately; indicate on the application form which scholarships you want to be considered for. Under How to Apply, you will find links to PDF files that tell you exactly how to apply and enable you to download an application form for all scholarships.

Also see the following scholarships:

- Dr. Vicki L. Schechtman Scholarship: Chapter 12, "Female" section
- Nancy Lorraine Jensen Memorial Scholarship: Chapter 14, "Clubs and Community Organizations" section
- National Pathfinder Scholarship: Chapter 12, "Female" section
- New Economy Technology Scholarships: Chapter 15, "Pennsylvania" section
- NSBE Scholarships: Chapter 9, "African-American" section

- ZymoGenetics Scholarship for the Advancement of Science: Chapter 15, "Washington" section

City Planning and Land Management

See the following scholarships:

- FFGC Scholarships: Chapter 15, "Florida" section
- Garden Club of Georgia Scholarships: Chapter 15, "Georgia" section
- National Council of State Garden Clubs Scholarship: Chapter 6, "Horticulture" section
- Xerox Technical Minority Scholarship: Chapter 9, "All Minorities" section

Clinical Laboratory Science

Alpha Mu Tau Fraternity Scholarships

Sponsor: Alpha Mu Tau
Web Site: http://www.ascls.org/leadership/awards/amt.htm
Amount of Scholarship: $1,000 to $1,500
Number of Awards: not given
Deadline: varies
Education Level: college juniors and seniors and graduate students
Eligibility: Applicant must enroll in an accredited clinical laboratory science program and be a U.S. citizen or permanent resident.

Every year, Alpha Mu Tau grants four different scholarships to students in clinical laboratory science, including clinical laboratory science/medical technology, clinical laboratory technician/medical laboratory technician, cytotechnology, or histotechnology. Two scholarships are reserved for undergraduate students, one scholarship goes to graduate students, and either an undergraduate or a graduate student can win the remaining scholarship. The average award is $1,000. The scholarship program's Web page briefly describes the available awards. If you feel you qualify, send a request for an application to the address listed at the bottom of the page.

Forum for Concerns of Minorities Scholarship

Sponsor: American Society for Clinical Laboratory Science
Web Site: http://www.ascls.org/leadership/awards/fcm.htm
Amount of Scholarship: not given
Number of Awards: 2
Deadline: April 1
Education Level: college undergraduates
Eligibility: Applicant must enroll in an accredited program in Clinical Laboratory Science/Medical Technology or Clinical Laboratory Technician/Medical Laboratory Technician, demonstrate financial need, and be a member of a minority group.

The Web site does not tell you much about the scholarship, other than the eligibility requirements. If you meet those requirements, write to the postal address or e-mail address at the bottom of the page to request an application.

VSCLS Scholarship

Sponsor: Virginia Society for Clinical Laboratory Sciences (VSCLS)
Web Site: http://vscls.vavalleyweb.com/scholarship.html
Amount of Scholarship: $500
Number of Awards: not given
Deadline: December 20
Education Level: college juniors

Eligibility: Applicant must enroll in an accredited clinical laboratory science program at a Virginia college.

This scholarship is awarded to students in clinical laboratory science/medical technology, clinical laboratory technology/medical laboratory technology, cytology, and histology programs. If you would like to apply, download the scholarship brochure, guidelines, and application in Word format from the Web site.

Also see the following scholarship:

- Indian Health Service Scholarship: Chapter 9, "Native American" section

Communications

Jessica Savitch Scholarship

Sponsor: New York Women in Communications, Inc.
Web Site: http://www.nywici.org/students_scholarships_savitch.htm
Amount of Scholarship: $2,000
Number of Awards: not given
Deadline: March 27
Education Level: college sophomores, juniors, and seniors and graduate students
Eligibility: Applicant must major in a communications-related field; have a minimum 3.5 GPA in the major and a 3.0 GPA overall; and attend a college or university in Connecticut, New Jersey, or New York.

Students in communications-related fields such as broadcasting, journalism, marketing, new media, and public relations should consider applying for this scholarship. The Instructions page outlines all the steps that the successful applicant must follow, which will tell you a lot about what the scholarship committee is looking for in a scholarship winner and help you prepare your application package. At the bottom of the page is a text version of the application that you can print out and mail to the address given. Also look at the main scholarships page (click the Scholarships link), which provides some valuable tips about preparing a successful application package for this program.

Leonard M. Perryman Communications Scholarship

Sponsor: United Methodist Communications
Web Site: http://www.umcom.org/scholarships
Amount of Scholarship: $2,500
Number of Awards: 2
Deadline: March 15
Education Level: college sophomores and juniors
Eligibility: Applicant must major in communications or journalism, plan to pursue a career in religious communications, be a full-time student at a U.S. college, and be a member of a minority group.

To learn more about this scholarship, click the Leonard M. Perryman Communications Scholarship link. This opens the application form in PDF format. The first page of the form describes the purpose of the scholarship and the eligibility requirements. More detailed selection criteria are listed after the Instructions for Applying. You don't have to be United Methodist to apply, but one of the two awards given out each year is reserved for a member of the United Methodist church.

Roberta Thumin Scholarship

Sponsor: New York Women in Communications, Inc.
Web Site: http://www.nywici.org/students_scholarships_thumin.htm
Amount of Scholarship: $1,500
Number of Awards: not given

Deadline: March 27
Education Level: college sophomores and juniors
Eligibility: Applicant must major in a communications-related field, have a minimum 3.0 GPA in the major, and attend college in Connecticut, New Jersey, or New York.

This scholarship goes to students majoring in communications-related fields like broadcasting, English, journalism, marketing, new media, speech, and theatre. The Instructions page outlines all the steps that the successful applicant must follow, which will tell you a lot about what the scholarship committee is looking for in a scholarship winner and help you prepare your application package. At the bottom of the page is a text version of the application that you can print out and mail to the address given. You should also look at the main scholarship page (click the Scholarships link at the top of the page), which provides some more valuable tips about preparing a successful application package for this program.

Also see the following scholarships:

- ARRL Foundation Scholarships: Chapter 8, "Amateur Radio" section
- AWC-DC Scholarship: Chapter 12, "Female" section
- Hispanic College Fund Scholarship: Chapter 9, "Hispanic" section
- National Ad 2 Scholarship Challenge: Chapter 6, "Advertising" section
- Yes You Can (Y.Y.C.) Scholarship: Chapter 15, "Washington" section

Computer Science and Engineering

Lance Stafford Larson Student Scholarship

Sponsor: Institute of Electrical and Electronics Engineers (IEEE) Computer Society

Web Site: http://computer.org/students/schlrshp.htm#larson
Amount of Scholarship: $500
Number of Awards: 1
Deadline: October 31
Education Level: college undergraduates
Eligibility: Applicant must be a member of IEEE Computer Society and have a minimum 3.0 GPA.

This scholarship rewards the best student paper in computer science. The Web page describes the history and goals of the award and the judging criteria. Click the Application Questions link to open a template for the application form (there is no official form). You must submit your answers to these questions as a cover sheet for your entry, along with five copies of the paper itself, to the address given at the bottom of the application questions page. To find out how to join the IEEE Computer Society, scroll up to the top of the scholarship description page and click the Join button.

Microsoft National Technical Scholarships

Sponsor: Microsoft
Web Site: http://www.microsoft.com/college/scholarships.htm
Number of Awards: 10
Amount of Scholarship: $1,000
Deadline: February 25
Education Level: college sophomores and juniors
Eligibility: Applicant must major in computer science, computer engineering, or a related discipline; be a full-time student; have a minimum 3.0 GPA; and either be female or a member of a minority group.

In an effort to recruit diverse workers into the computer science field, Microsoft offers five scholarships to African-Americans, Hispanics, and Native Americans and five scholarships to women. Winners are selected based on their interest and potential in the computing and software industry, so your application must demonstrate your passion for technology in order to be competitive. Selected winners are offered paid summer internships with Microsoft. The Criteria for Scholarship Eligibility section of the Web page describes what the selection committee is looking for in scholarship recipients. To find instructions for applying, scroll down to the What Is Required to Apply? section, which describes each item that must be included in your application package.

Microsoft Women's Technical Scholarship

Sponsor: Microsoft
Web Site: http://www.microsoft.com/college/womenscholar.htm
Amount of Scholarship: full tuition (renewable)
Number of Awards: 1
Deadline: January 28
Education Level: college sophomores and juniors
Eligibility: Applicant must major in computer science, computer engineering, or a related discipline; be a full-time student; have a minimum 3.0 GPA; and be female.

This scholarship program, which is administered separately from the National Technical Scholarship program described in the previous listing, is designed to attract female students into the computing field. The scholarship covers one year's tuition and fees for the college the winner attends, and winners also receive a paid summer internship at Microsoft. The Web page describes the benefits of the scholarship, the exact eligibility requirements, and the instructions for applying; an official application form is not required.

Richard E. Merwin Student Scholarship

Sponsor: Institute of Electrical and Electronics Engineers (IEEE) Computer Society
Web Site: http://computer.org/students/schlrshp.htm#merwin
Amount of Scholarship: $3,000
Number of Awards: 4
Deadline: May 31
Education Level: college juniors and seniors and graduate students
Eligibility: Applicant must major in computer science or a well-defined computer-related field of engineering, be a member of an IEEE Computer Society student branch chapter, be a full-time student, and have a minimum 2.5 GPA.

This scholarship was designed to reward leaders in IEEE Computer Society branch chapters, so you should already be an active member before you consider applying. The brief description of the scholarship on the Web page tells you who is eligible, the selection criteria, and the documents that you must submit with your application. Click the Application Questions link to open a template for the application form (there is no official form). To learn more about the IEEE Computer Society, scroll to the top of the page, and explore the links on the left side of the page. Be sure to look at the About the Computer Society, Get Involved, Member Benefits & Services, and Volunteer Resources pages, which will help you discover exactly what the scholarship judges are looking for in an "active" member of the Computer Society.

SSQ Scholastic Grant-in-Aid

Sponsor: Society for Software Quality (SSQ)
Web Site: http://www.ssq.org/grant/gia.html
Amount of Scholarship: $500
Number of Awards: 4
Deadline: May 1
Education Level: high school seniors and college freshmen, sophomores, and juniors

Eligibility: Applicant must major or minor in a computer science field or in a field that requires the use of software at a U.S. college.

One prize is awarded to the best essay on a subject related to quality software principles at each grade level. The essay topic changes each year. To find the current essay topic and learn how to submit your essay, follow the link to the Essay Contest Details. This page also links to several Web sites that will help you research the essay topic. On the main page, you can read past winning essays, which will give you a good idea of what the scholarship judges are looking for. Finally, if you plan to enter the essay contest in the future, you can enter your name and e-mail address in a form to request notifications of when the Web site is updated with new essay topics and contest rules.

Upsilon Pi Epsilon Student Award for Excellence

Sponsor: Institute of Electrical and Electronics Engineers (IEEE) Computer Society
Web Site: http://computer.org/students/schlrshp.htm#upsilon
Amount of Scholarship: $500
Number of Awards: 4
Deadline: October 31
Education Level: college undergraduates and graduate students
Eligibility: Applicant must be a member of IEEE Computer Society, be a full-time student, and have a minimum 3.0 GPA.

This scholarship honors academic achievement and participation in computing-related extra-curricular activities. The Web page describes the history and goals of the scholarship and the judging criteria. Click the Application Form link to open a template for the application form. Your application package consists of a cover sheet with the answers to the questions on this page and all of the additional documents listed beneath the application questions;

you don't have to submit an official application form. To find out how to join the IEEE Computer Society, scroll to the top of the page and click the Join button.

Also see the following scholarships:

- AFCEA General Emmett Paige Scholarship: Chapter 13, "All Branches" section
- AFCEA General John A. Wickham Scholarship: Chapter 6, "Sciences" section
- AFCEA ROTC Scholarship: Chapter 13, "All Branches" section
- Competitive Edge Scholarship: Chapter 6, "Engineering" section
- Dr. Vicki L. Schechtman Scholarship: Chapter 12, "Female" section
- Hispanic College Fund Scholarship: Chapter 9, "Hispanic" section
- Indian Health Service Scholarships: Chapter 9, "Native American" section
- Maryland Science and Technology Scholarship: Chapter 15, "Maryland" section
- New Economy Technology Scholarships: Chapter 15, "Pennsylvania" section
- NSBE Scholarships: Chapter 9, "African-American" section
- OCECS Scholarship: Chapter 15, "Oregon" section
- San Diego County Scholarship: Chapter 15, "California" section
- Society of Women Engineers Scholarships: Chapter 12, "Female" section
- State Farm Companies Foundation Exceptional Student Fellowship: Chapter 6, "Business" section
- Wendell Milliman Scholarship: Chapter 14, "Employer and Profession" section
- Xerox Technical Minority Scholarship: Chapter 9, "All Minorities" section
- Yes You Can (Y.Y.C.) Scholarship: Chapter 15, "Washington" section

Construction

AGC Scholarships

Sponsor: Associated General Contractors (AGC) Education and Research Foundation
Web Site: http://www.agc.org/ Education_&_Training/scholarships.asp
Amount of Scholarship: $2,000 to $7,500
Number of Awards: not given
Deadline: November 1
Education Level: college undergraduates and graduate students
Eligibility: Applicant must enroll as a full-time student in a construction or civil engineering degree program at a four-year college or graduate school and plan to pursue a career in construction.

Go to the Downloadable Application Forms page to learn more about the 50 different scholarships available under this program. There are two broad programs: the undergraduate scholarship competition for college undergraduates, which gives out several $2,000 awards per year; and the graduate award competition for master's and doctoral candidates, which gives out several $7,500 scholarships. There is also an essay contest for senior-level students that awards $2,300 for the best three essays. Click the link beside each scholarship listing that you want to apply for to download a PDF application form for that award. You only need to submit one application form to be considered for all of the scholarships in each category. To learn more about the sponsor, click the Education & Research Foundation link at the bottom of the page.

NAWIC Founders' Scholarship

Sponsor: National Association of Women in Construction (NAWIC)
Web Site: http://www.nawic.org/nef
Amount of Scholarship: $500 to $2,000
Number of Awards: not given
Deadline: February 1
Education Level: college undergraduates
Eligibility: Applicant must have completed at least one term of study in a construction-related associate's or bachelor's degree program, plan to pursue a career in a construction-related field, be a full-time student, and have a minimum 3.0 GPA.

To find the scholarship information, click the NAWIC Founders' Scholarship link in the left frame. This page briefly describes the eligibility requirements, but it doesn't provide very much information about the scholarship itself. You can apply for the scholarship online by going to http://www.fastweb.com and searching for the scholarship there, or you can send an e-mail message to the address given on the scholarship information page to request that a printed application be mailed to you. Note that you don't have to be a female student to apply.

Cosmetology

Joe Francis Haircare Scholarship

Sponsor: Joe Francis Haircare Scholarship Foundation
Web Site: http://www.joefrancis.com/jfh/ scholar.html
Amount of Scholarship: $500 to $1,000
Number of Awards: 12
Deadline: June 1 and September 1
Education Level: beauty school students
Eligibility: Applicant must enroll in beauty school and be sponsored by an approved organization.

Twelve scholarships are given out each year to students who are committed to a long-term career in cosmetology. To be eligible, you must secure sponsorship from an accredited barber or cosmetology school, a licensed salon owner or manager, a full-service distributor, or a member of one of the professional associations listed on the Requirements page. Click the Apply Online link to find the application requirements and access the electronic application form, which you can submit over the Internet. You can also apply by mail, if you prefer.

Oregon Barbers and Hairdressers Grant

Sponsor: Oregon Student Assistance Commission
Web Site: http://www.osac.state.or.us/barbers_hairdressers.html
Amount of Scholarship: $600
Number of Awards: around 90
Deadline: January 1
Education Level: beauty school students
Eligibility: Applicant must enroll as a full-time student in a licensed barbering, hair design, cosmetology, or manicure program in Oregon that lasts at least nine months; demonstrate financial need; and be an Oregon resident.

This Web page tells you how to apply for the grant and details the eligibility requirements. You will need to submit the FAFSA and list the beauty school you plan to attend on the FAFSA to apply for the grant, which is primarily based on financial need. You can obtain a copy of the FAFSA from the financial aid office at your school, or return to Chapter 1 of this book to find out how to file the FAFSA online.

Criminal Justice

ASC Gene Carte Student Paper Competition

Sponsor: American Society of Criminology (ASC)
Web Site: http://www.asc41.com/cartesp.html

Amount of Scholarship: $200 to $500
Number of Awards: 3
Deadline: college undergraduates and graduate students
Education Level: April 15
Eligibility: Open to all.

This award recognizes outstanding scholarly papers in the field of criminology. Prizes of $200, $300, and $500 are given for the top three papers. Read the Specifications for Papers section of the Web page to find out how to format your paper and submit it. The Procedures for Judging Entries section describes what makes a first-place paper. Past winning papers are listed at the bottom of the page, which should give you an idea of the kinds of essay topics the judges are looking for.

ASCLD Scholarship

Sponsor: American Society of Crime Laboratory Directors (ASCLD)
Web Site: http://www.ascld.org/scholarship.html
Amount of Scholarship: $1,000
Number of Awards: 4
Deadline: late February
Education Level: college sophomores and juniors
Eligibility: Applicant must plan to pursue a career in forensic science.

This Web page describes the scholarship program, including the application process. If you feel that you qualify based on this brief overview, contact the postal address, phone number, or e-mail address at the bottom of the Web page for an application. This contact can also provide more information about the scholarship.

John Charles Wilson Scholarship

Sponsor: International Association of Arson Investigators Educational Foundation, Inc.

Web Site: http://www.fire-investigators.org/jcw.htm
Amount of Scholarship: varies
Number of Awards: 3
Deadline: February 15
Education Level: college undergraduates
Eligibility: Applicant must enroll in police or fire sciences courses and be a member of the International Association of Arson Investigators, the immediate family member of a member, or sponsored by a member.

This program awards three scholarships each year to students of the police and fire sciences, including fire investigation and related subjects. The Web page briefly describes the eligibility requirements. You can link to a printable text application from the page if you would like to apply.

Also see the following scholarship:

• North Carolina Sheriff's Association Undergraduate Criminal Justice Scholarship: Chapter 15, "North Carolina" section

Culinary Arts

American Academy of Chefs *Chaine des Rotisseurs* Scholarship

Sponsor: American Academy of Chefs and Chaine des Rotisseurs
Web Site: http://acfchefs.org/academy/aacschol.html
Amount of Scholarship: $1,000
Number of Awards: 10
Deadline: December 1
Education Level: culinary school students
Eligibility: Applicant must enroll in a full-time two-year culinary program.

Anyone enrolled in culinary school is encouraged to apply for this scholarship. You can download a copy of the application in Microsoft Word format from the Web page. If you don't own Microsoft Word, the page also links to a free program that enables you to open and print Word documents.

Ray and Gertrude Marshall Scholarship

Sponsor: American Culinary Federation, Inc. (ACF)
Web Site: http://www.acfchefs.org/educate/eduschap.html
Amount of Scholarship: not given
Number of Awards: not given
Deadline: none
Education Level: college undergraduates
Eligibility: Applicant must have completed at least one full term of an accredited culinary program, be a member of ACF, and demonstrate financial need.

You can submit an application for this scholarship at any time. Applications are reviewed and scholarships are awarded three times a year: February, June, and October. The criteria for selecting scholarship winners are listed on the Web page. Note that financial aid is an important consideration, and you will have to submit a Financial Aid Release Form, which you can print from the Web site. You can also print a copy of the application form from the site. Be sure to include all of the additional documents listed under How to Apply in your application package.

Also see the following scholarship:

• Roundtable for Women in Foodservice Scholarship: Chapter 6, "Hotel and Restaurant Management" section

Dentistry and Dental Hygiene

AADS/Oral-B Dental Hygiene Education Academic Career Scholarship

Sponsor: American Association of Dental Schools (AADS) and Oral-B
Web Site: http://www.aads.jhu.edu/DEPR/OralBScholarship.htm
Amount of Scholarship: $2,500
Number of Awards: 2
Deadline: February 21
Education Level: college undergraduates
Eligibility: Applicant must have earned an associate's degree or certificate in dental hygiene, enroll in a degree completion program, and be an individual member of AADS.

This scholarship is intended for students who want to earn bachelor's degrees in dental hygiene and pursue an academic career. You must be an individual member of AADS in order to apply. You can apply for membership right away by clicking the link on the scholarship's Web page. In the Application Process section of the Web page, you will find a link to the printable application form and a list of items that you must submit with the application. Be sure to check AADS/Oral-B Dental Hygiene Education Academic Career Scholarship on the application form to be considered for the award.

ADHA Institute for Oral Health Scholarships

Sponsor: American Dental Hygienists' Association (ADHA) Institute for Oral Health
Web Site: http://www.adha.org/students/scholarships.htm
Amount of Scholarship: varies

Number of Awards: 31 plus an unspecified number of general scholarships
Deadline: June 1
Education Level: college undergraduates and graduate students
Eligibility: Applicant must have completed at least one year of a dental hygiene program.

This page describes the 17 different scholarships available for dental hygiene students from the ADHA Institute for Oral Health. Read the descriptions of the available scholarships on the main page carefully. Each scholarship has specific eligibility requirements, such as educational level, eligible colleges and universities, minority status, grade point average, and residency. All applicants who meet the general eligibility requirements will be considered for an unnamed general scholarship even if they don't meet the requirements for one of the special scholarships listed, so all qualified students should submit an application. To obtain a scholarship application, click the link at the top of the page. This takes you to an electronic form that checks whether you are eligible; fill out and submit the form to request that an application packet be sent to you.

Also see the following scholarships:

• Health Professional Scholarship: Chapter 6, "Health Care" section
• Indian Health Service Scholarships: Chapter 9, "Native American" section
• New York State Regents Professional Opportunity Scholarship: Chapter 15, "New York" section

Design

AFCEA Copernicus Foundation Scholarship

Sponsor: Armed Forces Communications and Electronics Association (AFCEA)

Web Site: http://www.afcea.org/awards/scholarships.htm#copernicus
Amount of Scholarship: $2,000
Number of Awards: not given
Deadline: not given
Education Level: college sophomores and juniors
Eligibility: Applicant must enroll in a computer graphic design curriculum at an accredited four-year U.S. college and be a U.S. citizen.

This is actually a contest, with winners chosen based on the merits of their digital artwork. The Web page tells you how to format the artwork sample and submit it properly. It also lists the other documents that must go in the application package and tells you how to request an application form. Applications for the next award year are generally available on the Web site after June 1.

ASID Scholarships

Sponsor: American Society of Interior Designers (ASID) Educational Foundation
Web Site: http://www.asid.org/edfoundation/foundation_main.htm
Amount of Scholarship: $250 to $3,000
Number of Awards: 7
Deadline: March 10
Education Level: college undergraduates and graduate students
Eligibility: Applicant must enroll in an interior design program.

This page describes the six different scholarships offered by ASID. Each scholarship is linked directly to a PDF application form that you can open inside your Web browser and then print out. The brief description underneath the scholarship's name tells you the award amount, eligibility requirements, selection criteria, and preferences, if any. Be sure to apply for only those scholarships for which you are best qualified. Many awards require academic papers, and one requires a portfolio showcasing your work (it also is the only scholarship in this program to require an entry fee, so you may choose not to apply for that one).

IDSA Scholarships

Sponsor: Industrial Designers Society of America (IDSA)
Web Site: http://www.idsa.org/whatsnew/guidelines.htm
Amount of Scholarship: varies
Number of Awards: 5
Deadline: June 2
Education Level: college juniors and seniors and graduate students
Eligibility: Applicant must enroll as a full-time student in an IDSA-approved program in industrial design, be a member of an IDSA Student Chapter, and be a U.S. citizen or permanent resident.

One undergraduate scholarship and two graduate fellowships are given under this program. The descriptions for each award tell you who is eligible, how to submit application materials, and how applications are judged. You only have to complete one application form to be considered for all of the awards given at your educational level. Click the application link in the scholarship's description to open a printable version of the application form. To find out how to become a student member of IDSA, return to the top page of the IDSA site, and click the Join Us Membership button, where you will find an online membership application.

Mike Alesko Design Scholarship

Sponsor: International News, Inc.
Web Site: http://www.collegeplan.org/cpnsearch.htm
Amount of Scholarship: $1,000
Number of Awards: not given
Deadline: March 30

Education Level: high school seniors and college undergraduates
Eligibility: Applicant must major in fashion or graphic design, have a minimum 2.5 GPA, and demonstrate financial need.

This page describes the scholarship and the person whom it honors. Reading over this background information can help you prepare a more impressive application. If you decide to apply, you will find the scholarship application at the bottom of the page. Although the application looks like an electronic form, it is designed to be printed; you may be able to fill in the fields inside your Web browser and print the application form with your answers intact, if your browser supports this feature. Be sure to include with your application all of the additional materials listed at the bottom of the page.

Print and Graphics Scholarship

Sponsor: Graphic Arts Technical Foundation and Print and Graphics Scholarship Foundation
Web Site: http://www.gatf.org
Amount of Scholarship: not given
Number of Awards: 300
Deadline: March 1 (high school) and April 1 (undergraduate)
Education Level: high school seniors and college undergraduates
Eligibility: Applicant must plan to pursue a career in graphic communications and be a full-time student at a two-year or four-year college.

To find information about this scholarship, click the Print and Graphics Scholarship Foundation link in the left frame. This page describes the purpose of the scholarship program, eligibility requirements, selection criteria, and renewal conditions. To apply, follow the link to the PDF application form, which you can print out, complete, and mail to the address listed.

Also see the following scholarships:

- AWC-DC Scholarship: Chapter 12, "Female" section
- New York State Regents Professional Opportunity Scholarship: Chapter 15, "New York" section

Economics and Finance

AARP Andrus Foundation Undergraduate Scholarship for Study of Aging and Finance

Sponsor: Association for Gerontology in Higher Education, The Gerontological Society of America, and American Association of Retired Persons (AARP) Andrus Foundation
Web Site: http://www.aghe.org/UGbroint.htm
Amount of Scholarship: $5,000
Number of Awards: 8
Deadline: June 2
Education Level: college undergraduates
Eligibility: Applicant must study a gerontology-and-finance-related program at an accredited U.S. college, plan to work in the field of aging, be a full-time student, and have a minimum 3.0 GPA.

This scholarship program is designed to help students who are studying the specific field of finances for the aging, with the goal of working in a related career. Scholarship winners are expected to research some aspect of aging and finance. Read the scholarship overview and eligibility requirements carefully to make certain that you qualify. Follow the application procedures exactly; the checklist at the bottom of the page will help you make sure that your application package is complete. At the very bottom of the page are links to printable versions of the application form and the faculty nomination form, which must be submitted with your application.

Karla Scherer Foundation Scholarship

Sponsor: Karla Scherer Foundation
Web Site: http://comnet.org/kscheref
Amount of Scholarship: varies
Number of Awards: 25
Deadline: March 1
Education Level: high school seniors, college undergraduates, and graduate students
Eligibility: Applicant must major in finance or economics at a U.S. college or university, plan to pursue a corporate business career in the private sector, and be female.

The eligibility requirements for this scholarship are very specific, and anyone who falls outside the lines won't be considered. The scholarship is intended to help women who will someday become CEOs and CFOs of major manufacturing companies. Therefore, the scholarship is only awarded to women majoring in finance and economics, and women who plan to enter a career in the public or service sectors do not qualify. Read the scholarship information carefully to make certain that you are a good candidate. You must request a scholarship application through the mail. Be sure to follow all of the instructions given on the Web page exactly, or your request will not be honored.

Also see the following scholarships:

- Bank of America ADA Abilities Scholarship: Chapter 10, "Any Disability" section
- Betty Rendel Scholarship: Chapter 12, "Female" section
- Hispanic College Fund Scholarship: Chapter 9, "Hispanic" section
- Institute of Management Accountants National Scholarships: Chapter 6, "Accounting" section
- Minorities in Government Finance Scholarship: Chapter 9, "All Minorities" section
- NAFOA Student Scholarship: Chapter 9, "Native American" section
- State Farm Companies Foundation Exceptional Student Scholarship: Chapter 6, "Business" section
- Wendell Milliman Scholarship: Chapter 14, "Employers and Professions" section

Education

Barbara Lotze Scholarship for Future Teachers

Sponsor: American Association of Physics Teachers and Barbara Lotze Endowment for the Advancement of Physics Education in the United States
Web Site: http://www.aapt.org/aaptgeneral/lotze.html
Amount of Scholarship: $2,000
Number of Awards: 1
Deadline: December 1
Education Level: high school seniors and college undergraduates
Eligibility: Applicant must enroll in a course of study leading to a career in teaching physics, and be a U.S. citizen.

This scholarship encourages qualified students to become high school physics teachers. Applicants from Allegheny College are given first preference, but anyone may apply. You can print out a PDF copy of the application directly from the Web site, or if you have additional questions, contact the phone number or e-mail address listed.

Charles McDaniel Teacher Scholarship

Sponsor: Georgia Student Finance Commission
Web Site: http://www.hope.gsfc.org
Amount of Scholarship: $1,000
Number of Awards: 3

Deadline: not given
Education Level: college sophomores and juniors
Eligibility: Applicant must enroll as a full-time student in the department of education at a Georgia public college, plan to pursue a career in teaching, have a minimum 3.25 GPA, be a Georgia resident, and have graduated from a Georgia public high school.

To find information about this scholarship, click the State Grants link at the top of the page, and then click the Program Information link. Scroll down until you see the name of the scholarship, and click it. On this page, you will find the objectives of the scholarship, eligibility requirements, and application instructions. To be eligible, the department of education at your college must nominate you. If you are nominated, your department of education will give you the application form. Contact your academic advisor or the dean of your department to find out how to be considered for nomination at your college.

Child Care Provider Scholarship

Sponsor: Maryland Higher Education Commission and Maryland State Scholarship Commission
Web Site: http://www.mhec.state.md.us/SSA/introduction.htm
Amount of Scholarship: $500 to $2,000 (renewable for four years)
Number of Awards: not given
Deadline: June 15
Education Level: college undergraduates
Eligibility: Applicant must enroll in a child development or early childhood education academic program at a two-year or four-year college, be a full-time student or work at least 15 hours a week in a child care center, and be a Maryland resident.

To find information about this scholarship, first click the Program Description link on the left side of the page. Then scroll down through the list of scholarships until you find the Child Care Provider Scholarship link, and click it. This will take you to some general information about the award. This is a service scholarship; you must work as a child care provider in Maryland one year for every year you received scholarship money. Available grants include $500 for part-time community college students, $1,000 for full-time community college students and part-time college students, and $2,000 for full-time college students. After you read about the program, follow the link to Eligibility Criteria if you are unsure whether you qualify. You must request an application from the Maryland State Scholarship Administration; to find contact information, click Online Applications in the left frame (no application forms have actually been published online, as of this writing).

David A. DeBolt Teacher Shortage Scholarship

Sponsor: Illinois Student Assistance Commission
Web Site: http://www.isac1.org/ilaid/schols.html#DADTSSP
Amount of Scholarship: up to $5,000
Number of Awards: not given
Deadline: May 1
Education Level: college sophomores and juniors
Eligibility: Applicant must enroll in a teacher education program at an eligible Illinois college, seek certification in a teacher shortage discipline, be an Illinois resident, and be a U.S. citizen or permanent resident.

This scholarship program encourages education majors to pursue careers as public school teachers in disciplines that have been designated teacher shortage areas in the state of Illinois. Minority students are particularly encouraged to apply. The Web site outlines the eligibility requirements and the selection process. To be eligible, you must file the FAFSA and must commit to teaching in Illinois after earning your degree. The section under How to Apply tells you how to get a scholarship application; probably the fastest way is to obtain one from the education department or scholarship office at your college.

Distinguished Scholar Teacher Education Scholarship

Sponsor: Maryland State Scholarship Administration
Web Site: http://www.mhec.state.md.us/SSA/introduction.htm
Amount of Scholarship: $3,000 (renewable for four years)
Number of Awards: not given
Deadline: not given
Education Level: high school juniors
Eligibility: Applicant must enroll as a full-time student in a teacher education program at a Maryland college, have received a Distinguished Scholar award, and be a Maryland resident.

To find information about this scholarship, click the Program Description link in the left frame, and then click the Distinguished Scholar Teacher Education Program link in the list of scholarships given. To qualify, you must already have won a Distinguished Scholar award. Learn more about the Distinguished Scholar Program by clicking its link in the list of scholarships at the top of the page. You must also agree to teach in Maryland one year for each year that you receive the scholarship. If you do receive the Distinguished Scholar award, you will automatically receive an application for the teacher scholarship.

Freshman/Sophomore Minority Grant

Sponsor: Arkansas Department of Higher Education

Web Site: http://www.adhe.arknet.edu/finance/minoritygrant.html
Amount of Scholarship: $1,000
Number of Awards: not given
Deadline: not given
Education Level: college freshmen and sophomores
Eligibility: Applicant must enroll in a teacher education program at a two-year or four-year Arkansas college, plan to pursue a career in teaching, and be a member of a minority group.

This program is trying to recruit more African-Americans, Asian Americans, and Hispanics into teaching in the state of Arkansas. In addition to scholarship money, winners get the opportunity to participate in internships and other activities in the teacher education field. You must contact the appropriate official at your college to obtain more information and find out how to apply. The scholarship's Web page tells you who to contact.

FTE Undergraduate Scholarship

Sponsor: Foundation for Technology Education and International Technology Education Association (ITEA)
Web Site: http://www.iteawww.org/I3d.html
Amount of Scholarship: $1,000
Number of Awards: 1
Deadline: December 1
Education Level: college freshmen, sophomores, and juniors
Eligibility: Applicant must major in a technology education teacher preparation program, be a member of ITEA, be a full-time student, and have a minimum 2.5 GPA.

The Web page describes the eligibility requirements for the scholarship and tells you exactly what materials you need to submit to apply. An official application form is not required. The scholarship is only available to members of ITEA, but you can enclose your membership application with your scholarship application. To learn more about becoming a member, click the Membership link at the bottom of the page, then click How to Join/Renew to find a membership application in PDF format that you can print out.

ITEA/EEA-Ship Undergraduate Scholarship in Technology Education

Sponsor: International Technology Education Association (ITEA)
Web Site: http://www.iteawww.org/I3a.html
Amount of Scholarship: $1,000
Number of Awards: not given
Deadline: December 1
Education Level: college freshmen, sophomores, and juniors
Eligibility: Applicant must major in a technology education teacher preparation program, be a member of ITEA, be a full-time student, and have a minimum 2.5 GPA.

The Web page describes the eligibility requirements for the scholarship, and it tells you exactly what materials you need to submit to apply. An official application form is not required. The scholarship is only available to members of ITEA, but you can enclose your membership application with your scholarship application. To learn more about becoming a member, click the Membership link at the bottom of the page, then click How to Join/Renew to find a membership application in PDF format that you can print out.

KHEAA Teacher Scholarship

Sponsor: Kentucky Higher Education Assistance Authority (KHEAA)
Web Site: http://www.kheaa.com/prog_tchschl.html
Amount of Scholarship: $1,250 to $5,000
Number of Awards: not given

Deadline: May 8
Education Level: high school seniors, college undergraduates, and graduate students
Eligibility: Applicant must enroll as a full-time student in a teacher certification program at a participating Kentucky college, demonstrate financial need, be a Kentucky resident, and be a U.S. citizen.

If you accept this service scholarship, you must agree to teach after graduating; otherwise the scholarship becomes an interest-accruing loan. Awards are $1,250 per year for college freshmen and sophomores and $5,000 per year for upperclassmen and graduate students. Recipients are also eligible to receive smaller scholarships to pay for summer study. Because this scholarship is based on financial need, you must submit the FAFSA, along with the Teacher Scholarship Application; both forms are linked directly to the Web page. The application form also describes the eligibility criteria, service commitment, and selection process in greater detail.

Litherland/FTE Scholarship

Sponsor: Foundation for Technology Education (FTE) and International Technology Education Association (ITEA)
Web Site: http://www.iteawww.org/I3b.html
Amount of Scholarship: $1,000
Number of Awards: 1
Deadline: December 1
Education Level: college freshmen, sophomores, and juniors
Eligibility: Applicant must major in a technology education teacher preparation program, be a member of ITEA, be a full-time student, and have a minimum 2.5 GPA.

The Web page describes the eligibility requirements for the scholarship and tells you exactly what materials you need to submit to apply. You don't need to submit an official application form for this award. The scholarship is only available to members of ITEA, but you can enclose your membership application with your scholarship application. To learn more about becoming a member, click the Membership link at the bottom of the page, then click How to Join/Renew to find a membership application in PDF format that you can print out.

Martin Luther King, Jr. Memorial Scholarship

Sponsor: California Teachers Association (CTA)
Web Site: http://www.cta.org/inside_cta/training/hr_scholar_mlk.html
Amount of Scholarship: $2,000 to $5,000
Number of Awards: not given
Deadline: March 15
Education Level: high school seniors, college undergraduates, and graduate students
Eligibility: Applicant must enroll in a teacher education program, be an active member of CTA or Student California Teachers Association (SCTA) or be the dependent of a CTA member, and be a member of a minority group.

The Web page briefly describes this scholarship and lists the names of past recipients. Applications are not available on the site, but they can be requested from the contact address, phone number, or e-mail address given. To learn more about joining CTA, click the Membership link at the very bottom of the page. Or follow the Student CTA link to learn more about how to become a member of the student branch of the professional association.

Maryland HOPE Teacher Scholarship

Sponsor: Maryland State Scholarship Administration
Web Site: http://www.mhec.state.md.us/SSA/introduction.htm

Amount of Scholarship: $1,000 to $3,000
Number of Awards: not given
Deadline: March 1
Education Level: high school seniors, college undergraduates, and graduate students
Eligibility: Applicant must enroll as a full-time student in a teacher education program at a two-year or four-year college or a graduate school in Maryland, have a minimum 3.0 GPA, and be a Maryland resident.

To find information about this scholarship, click the Program Description link in the left frame, then click Maryland HOPE Teacher Scholarship in the list of scholarships given. This broad scholarship program is aimed at recruiting more teachers to work in the state. Students at two-year colleges receive $1,000 per year, and students at four-year colleges and universities receive $3,000 per year. If you accept the scholarship, you must agree to teach in Maryland one year for each year you received scholarship money, or pay back the scholarship with interest. Obtain a copy of the scholarship application from the guidance office at your high school or from your college's financial aid office. Or click the Online Applications link to find contact information for the State Scholarship Administration, from which you can directly order applications.

Minority Teacher Incentive Grant

Sponsor: Connecticut Department of Higher Education
Web Site: http://www.ctdhe.org/dheweb/mtigp.htm
Amount of Scholarship: $5,000 per year (awarded for two years)
Number of Awards: not given
Deadline: January 19
Education Level: college sophomores and juniors

Eligibility: Applicant must be enrolled as a full-time student in a teacher education program at a participating Connecticut college and be a member of a minority group.

This program recruits African-American, Hispanic, Asian-American, and Native American students into teaching in public schools in Connecticut. To participate, you must already be enrolled in a teacher education program at one of the participating colleges listed on the Web site, and the dean of the education department at your school must nominate you. Application forms are available starting August 1 of each school year. If you have already earned a college degree but are not certified as a teacher, you may still be able to take advantage of the grant program; read about the Alternate Route to Certification on the Web site to learn more.

Minority Teacher/Special Education Scholarship

Sponsor: State Student Assistance Commission of Indiana
Web Site: http://www.ai.org/ssaci/
m-teach.html
Amount of Scholarship: $1,000 to $5,000 per year (renewable)
Number of Awards: not given
Deadline: not given
Education Level: college undergraduates
Eligibility: Applicant must enroll as a full-time student in a teacher education program or a special education, occupational therapy, or physical therapy program; plan to teach in an Indiana public school after graduation; have a minimum 2.0 GPA; be an Indiana resident; and be a member of a minority group.

Although this scholarship program is open to special education, occupational therapy, and physical therapy majors, all recipients must commit to working in an Indiana public school after graduating from college. These conditions

are outlined on the scholarship's Web page. Financial need determines the amount of the scholarship, but it is not required to receive an award. Only African-American and Hispanic students are eligible to apply for the teaching scholarship. While minority status is not required if you are studying special education, physical therapy, or occupational therapy, minority applicants in these fields are still given preference. You must submit the application directly to your college; you can print it out from the Web page.

Minority Teachers of Illinois Scholarship

Sponsor: Illinois Student Assistance Commission
Web Site: http://www.isac1.org/ilaid/
schols.html#MTISP
Amount of Scholarship: $5,000 per year
Number of Awards: not given
Deadline: May 1
Education Level: college sophomores and juniors
Eligibility: Applicant must enroll as a full-time student in a teacher education program at an Illinois college, have a minimum 2.5 GPA, be a member of a minority group, be an Illinois resident, and be a U.S. citizen or permanent resident.

This program recruits African-American, Asian-American, Hispanic, and Native American students to become teachers at Illinois public schools with large numbers of minority students. The Web page describes the scholarship program and the service commitment that you must make if you receive the award. Look under How to Apply to find out how to start the application process; probably the fastest way is to obtain an application form from your college's education department or financial aid office.

Minority Teachers Scholarship

Sponsor: Arkansas Department of Higher Education
Web Site: http://www.adhe.arknet.edu/finance/mteachers.html
Amount of Scholarship: $5,000 per year (up to two years)
Number of Awards: not given
Deadline: June 1
Education Level: college juniors
Eligibility: Applicant must enroll as a full-time student in a teacher education program at a four-year college in Arkansas, have completed 60 to 90 semester credit hours of college coursework, have a minimum 2.5 GPA, be a member of a minority group, be an Arkansas resident, and be a U.S. citizen or permanent resident.

This scholarship program encourages African-American, Asian-American, and Hispanic students to become public school teachers in Arkansas. If you accept the scholarship, you must agree to teach in Arkansas for five years after graduating, although that commitment time can be reduced if you meet the conditions outlined on the Web page. You must meet many requirements before you can even be eligible for the scholarship, so be sure to read the list carefully before applying. If you decide to apply, call the toll-free number at the bottom of the Web page to request an application form.

Minority Teaching Fellows

Sponsor: Tennessee Student Assistance Corporation
Web Site: http://www.state.tn.us/tsac/grants.htm#Minority
Amount of Scholarship: $5,000 per year
Number of Awards: not given
Deadline: April 15
Education Level: high school seniors and college undergraduates
Eligibility: Applicant must enroll in a teacher education program, have a minimum 2.5 GPA, be a member of a minority group, be a Tennessee resident, and be a U.S. citizen.

This scholarship program is similar to other service scholarships for teachers. Recipients must agree to teach one year in a Tennessee public school for every year they received scholarship money. The brief description on the Web page outlines the basics of the program and the eligibility requirements. Note that high school students applying for the scholarship must meet minimum test score and class rank requirements, as well as the eligibility requirements listed above. If you want to apply, scroll to the top of the page and click the Scholarship Applications link. You will see a list of application forms in PDF format; choose the Minority Teaching Fellows application (MTEP.pdf). You can then print out a copy of the application and find out what other documents you need to submit in the application package.

North Carolina Teaching Fellows

Sponsor: North Carolina Teaching Fellows Program
Web Site: http://www.teachingfellows.org
Amount of Scholarship: $6,500 per year (awarded for four years)
Number of Awards: 400
Deadline: October 29
Education Level: high school seniors
Eligibility: Applicant must enroll in a teacher education program at a participating North Carolina college, be a North Carolina resident, and be a U.S. citizen.

This is another teaching for service program, this time for North Carolina residents. Follow the Program link to get an overview of the program and learn its history and goals. You will also find a profile of the kind of student the program is looking for, which will help you decide if you are a competitive candidate. Click the Applicants link to learn how the application process works, find a calendar or important dates, and receive answers to common questions about the program. Explore the rest of the site to learn about the activities that Teaching Fellows participate in and other benefits of joining the program. Finally, follow the Campus link to find out which colleges participate in the program and to learn more about each college's specific Teaching Fellows program and offerings. If you decide to apply, talk to your guidance counselor, or contact the address, phone number, or e-mail address given on the Program page.

NSF/STEMTEC Teaching Scholars

Sponsor: National Science Foundation (NSF) and Science, Technology, Engineering, and Mathematics Teacher Education Collaborative (STEMTEC)
Web Site: http://k12s.phast.umass.edu/ stemtec/stss/scholars/scholars.html
Amount of Scholarship: $1,000 to $5,000
Number of Awards: not given
Deadline: April 1
Education Level: college undergraduates and graduate students
Eligibility: Applicant must enroll in a teacher education program at a STEMTEC college, plan to pursue a career in math or science education, and be a U.S. citizen or permanent resident.

This program is for students who are interested in teaching science and math and who attend one of the Massachusetts colleges in the STEMTEC collaborative, which are listed on the Web page. Besides scholarship money, the program provides mentoring, advising, and other perks to help students achieve their career goals.

Most awards go to undergraduate students, and minorities are particularly encouraged to apply. Read the Scholarship Program Press Release, published on the Web site, to learn more about the program. Then go to the Application and Nomination Materials page and click the Information for New Applicants link to get details about the award, eligibility requirements, the kinds of applicants the program is looking for, and application instructions. The Application and Nomination Materials page provides all of the forms you need in both Microsoft Word and Rich Text Format (RTF), a text format that can be read by most word processors.

PROMISE Teacher Scholarship

Sponsor: Georgia Student Finance Commission
Web Site: http://www.gsfc.org/hope/ttoc.htm
Amount of Scholarship: $3,000 per year (awarded over two years)
Number of Awards: not given
Deadline: none
Education Level: college juniors
Eligibility: Applicant must enroll in a teacher education program at an eligible Georgia college, have completed between 60 and 90 credit hours of college coursework, have a minimum 3.6 GPA, and be a U.S. citizen or permanent resident.

First, read the Eligibility Requirements for Students Seeking a Bachelor's Degree in Teacher Education to make sure that you qualify for the program and that you are willing to comply with all the conditions of the scholarship. Scroll to the bottom of the Web page and click Promissory Notes to find a printable copy of the service agreement (or promissory note) that you will have to sign if you accept the scholarship; this tells you exactly what your service commitment will be. Next, follow the link to Application Process and Eligible Institutions to find out how to apply. This page also lists all of the Georgia colleges where the scholarship can be used. You can obtain an application form from your school's education department or financial aid office.

Sharon Christa McAuliffe Memorial Teacher Education Award

Sponsor: Maryland State Scholarship Administration
Web Site: http://www.mhec.state.md.us/SSA/introduction.htm
Amount of Scholarship: up to $10,000 (renewable for one year)
Number of Awards: not given
Deadline: December 31
Education Level: college undergraduates
Eligibility: Applicant must enroll in a teacher education program in a critical shortage subdiscipline at a Maryland college, have completed at least 60 credit hours of college coursework, have a minimum 3.0 GPA, and be a Maryland resident.

To find information about this scholarship, click the Program Descriptions link in the left frame, then click Sharon Christa McAuliffe Memorial Teacher Education Award in the list of scholarships. This broad scholarship program recruits students to work in the state in subject areas that don't have enough teachers. These critical shortage areas are listed in the scholarship description under How Do I Qualify? If you accept the scholarship, you must agree to teach in Maryland one year for each year you received scholarship money, or pay back the scholarship with interest. You can obtain a copy of the scholarship application from the financial aid office or education department at your college. Or click the Online Applications link to find contact information for the State Scholarship Administration, from which you can directly order scholarship applications.

Teach for Texas Conditional Grant

Sponsor: Texas Higher Education Coordinating Board
Web Site: http://www.thecb.state.tx.us/divisions/student/TeachTx
Amount of Scholarship: $5,000 per year
Number of Awards: not given
Deadline: not given
Education Level: college sophomores and juniors
Eligibility: Applicant must enroll in a teacher education program at an approved Texas college, have a minimum 2.5 GPA, receive a TEXAS Grant, have an EFC of less than $5,000, and be a Texas resident.

This scholarship program encourages Texas students to become teachers in critical shortage disciplines and areas of the state. The award is actually a student loan, but you don't have to repay it if you meet the conditions described on the Web page. The eligibility requirements are strict. One is that you must receive a TEXAS Grant; follow the link to open the grant's information page to learn more about qualifying and applying for this financial aid program. Another is that you must attend an approved college in Texas; the list is linked to the main page, or you can look up your school in Chapter 16 to see if it offers the scholarship. Finally, you must study a critical shortage subject or agree to teach in a critical shortage area (both are listed on the grant's Web page). The FAQs page can answer most of your questions about the program, including where to get application materials. If you have other questions, contact the postal address, phone number, or e-mail addresses listed at the very bottom of the page.

Tennessee Teaching Scholars

Sponsor: Tennessee Student Assistance Corporation

Web Site: http://www.state.tn.us/tsac/
grants.htm#Tennessee Teaching
Amount of Scholarship: not given
Number of Awards: not given
Deadline: April 15
Education Level: college sophomores, juniors, and seniors and graduate students
Eligibility: Applicant must enroll in a teacher education program in Tennessee, have a minimum 2.75 GPA, and be a Tennessee resident.

Under the terms of this service scholarship, recipients must agree to teach one year in a Tennessee public school for every year they received scholarship money. The description on the Web page outlines the basics of the program and the eligibility requirements. If you want to apply, scroll to the top of the page and click Scholarship Applications (one of the buttons on the left side of the page). You will see a list of application forms in PDF format; choose the Tennessee Teaching Scholars application (TTSP.pdf). You can then print out a copy of the application and find out what other documents you need to submit.

Underwood-Smith Teacher Scholarship

Sponsor: State College and University Systems of West Virginia
Web Site: http://www.scusco.wvnet.edu/
www/stserv/FCTSTUWS.HTM
Amount of Scholarship: $5,000
Number of Awards: not given
Deadline: April 15
Education Level: college sophomores, juniors, and seniors and graduate students
Eligibility: Applicant must enroll as a full-time student in a teacher education program at a West Virginia college, either have a minimum 3.25 GPA (undergraduate) or have graduated in the top 10 percent of the class (graduate), and be a West Virginia resident.

The Web page describes the eligibility requirements and conditions of this service scholarship program. It also briefly lists the criteria for choosing scholarship winners. You must apply through your school's department of education, as instructed on the Web page. Get further information about the scholarship by contacting the address given at the very bottom of the page.

WAMLE Student Scholarship

Sponsor: Wisconsin Association for Middle Level Education (WAMLE)
Web Site: http://www.wamle.org/form1.html
Amount of Scholarship: $600
Number of Awards: not given
Deadline: January 15
Education Level: college sophomores and juniors
Eligibility: Applicant must enroll in a middle-level education program at a Wisconsin college and be a student member of WAMLE.

This page briefly describes the scholarship and the eligibility requirements. You can also print out a copy of the application. If you need more information about becoming a member of WAMLE, follow the Home link at the bottom of the page to WAMLE's home page, which will answer all of your questions. You will find a printable membership application on the Information page.

Also see the following scholarships:

- Burlington Northern Santa Fe Foundation Scholarship: Chapter 9, "Native American" section
- Christa McAuliffe Scholarship: Chapter 15, "Tennessee" section
- CTA Scholarships: Chapter 14, "Unions and Professional Associations" section
- Jim Bourque Scholarship: Chapter 9, "Native American" section
- Lawrence Conservation District Scholarship: Chapter 15, "Pennsylvania" section

- Robert G. Porter Scholarship: Chapter 14, "Unions and Professional Associations" section
- VSGC Scholarships and Fellowships: Chapter 6, "Aerospace Sciences and Engineering" section
- Yes You Can (Y.Y.C.) Scholarship: Chapter 15, "Washington" section
- Zeta Phi Beta Scholarships and Fellowships: Chapter 12, "Female" section

Engineering

ASDSO Undergraduate Scholarship

Sponsor: Association of State Dam Safety Officials (ASDSO)
Web Site: http://www.damsafety.org/undergrad.html
Amount of Scholarship: up to $5,000
Number of Awards: not given
Deadline: February 15
Education Level: college sophomores and juniors
Eligibility: Applicant must enroll in an accredited civil engineering program or a related field, plan to pursue a dam-related career, have a minimum 3.0 GPA, and be a U.S. citizen.

Here you will learn what the eligibility requirements and selection criteria for the ASDSO scholarship are. This page also describes the goals of ASDSO, which will help you prepare an application package that demonstrates how you will support those goals if you win an award. A PDF version of the application form is linked at the bottom of the page.

ASME Auxiliary Scholarships

Sponsor: American Society of Mechanical Engineers (ASME) Auxiliary, Inc.

Web Site: http://www.asme.org/auxiliary/scholarshiploans
Amount of Scholarship: $2,000
Number of Awards: not given
Deadline: March 15
Education Level: college juniors and seniors and graduate students
Eligibility: Applicant must enroll in an accredited mechanical engineering program at a U.S. college or university and be a member of ASME.

This page describes five scholarships awarded by ASME: two for undergraduate students; one for master's students; one for doctoral students; and one for international graduate students. You can download a PDF or Microsoft Word version of the application form for each scholarship. Scroll to the bottom of the page to find links to Letter of Recommendation Forms, which you must submit with the application form. You can also learn about student loans for members of ASME on this page. To find out how to become a member of ASME, go to http://www.asme.org/memb.

ASME Scholarships

Sponsor: American Society of Mechanical Engineers (ASME)
Web Site: http://www.asme.org/educate/aid/scholar.htm
Amount of Scholarship: $1,500 to $8,000
Number of Awards: 44
Deadline: March 15
Education Level: college undergraduates
Eligibility: Applicant must enroll in an accredited mechanical engineering program and be a student member of ASME.

Eight different scholarship are available under this program: four $1,500 awards; one $2,000 award; two $3,000 awards; and one $8,000 award. Check the Scholarship Details and Requirements link to find out the specifics about each scholarship, including eligibility requirements, selection criteria, and award amounts. While most scholarships fall under the basic eligibility requirements listed above, some do specify residency and citizenship restrictions. To apply for any of the scholarships, return to the main page and follow the link to the application form. Check the boxes beside all the scholarships for which you want to be considered. If you aren't a member of ASME, you can go ahead and apply for membership by following the Student Member Application link on this page.

ASNE Scholarships

Sponsor: American Society of Naval Engineers (ASNE)
Web Site: http://www.navalengineers.org/ scholarships/sc_info.htm
Amount of Scholarship: $2,500 to $3,500
Number of Awards: not given
Deadline: February 15
Education Level: college juniors and seniors and master's students
Eligibility: Applicant must enroll in a naval engineering-related program, be a member of ASNE or the Society of Naval Architects and Marine Engineers (graduate students only), and be a U.S. citizen.

This page describes the goals of the general scholarship program and the basic eligibility requirements for all scholarships, including a definition of what a naval engineering-related curriculum of study is. Note that award amounts and eligibility requirements differ slightly for undergraduate and graduate students. You can also find out how scholarship recipients are chosen, which will help you present yourself as a better candidate. Follow the Scholarship News link at the top of the page to read recent announcements about the scholarship program. You can also access a PDF version of the application from a link at the top of the page. To find out how to become a mem-

ber of ASNE, go to ASNE's home page and follow the Membership link.

B. Charles Tiney Memorial ASCE Student Chapter Scholarship

Sponsor: American Society of Civil Engineers (ASCE)
Web Site: http://www.asce.org/peta/ed/ app_tin.html
Amount of Scholarship: $2,000 (renewable for two years)
Number of Awards: not given
Deadline: February 11
Education Level: college undergraduates
Eligibility: Applicant must be a National Student Member of ASCE.

This page briefly describes the eligibility requirements, selection criteria, and application procedures for the scholarship. You will find a text copy of the application form at the very bottom of the page, or you can download and print a PDF version by following a link. To learn how to become a member of ASCE, click the Membership button on the left side of the page and explore the items in the menu under See Information About Student Membership. You can even submit your membership application online. Note that you can major in any discipline of engineering or engineering technology to be eligible to join ASCE and apply for scholarships; you don't have to be a civil engineering major.

Charles E. Price Scholarship Award

Sponsor: National Technical Association
Web Site: http://www.ntaonline.org/ ceprice.htm
Amount of Scholarship: $6,000
Number of Awards: 1 (renewable for up to four years)

Deadline: September 15
Education Level: high school seniors and college freshmen
Eligibility: Applicant must major in electrical or mechanical engineering, be a member of a minority group, and be a U.S. citizen.

This page describes the scholarship in brief, including the objectives of the award program, the selection criteria, and the rules for applying. Minorities who are eligible to apply include African-Americans, Asian-Americans, Hispanics, Native Americans, and Pacific Islanders. Click the Download Application link at the very bottom of the page to find a Microsoft Word version of the application form.

Competitive Edge Scholarship

Sponsor: Wal-Mart Foundation
Web Site: http://www.walmartfoundation.org /compedge.html
Amount of Scholarship: $20,000 (awarded over four years)
Number of Awards: around 250
Deadline: not given
Education Level: high school seniors
Eligibility: Applicant must enroll as a full-time student in an eligible engineering or related field of study at a participating college; have an ACT score of 27 or higher or an SAT I score of 1100 or higher; have a minimum 3.5 GPA; be ranked in the top 10 percent of the high school graduating class; and be a U.S. citizen.

The main Web page describes the background and goals of this prestigious scholarship program. Follow the How to Apply link on the left side of the page to get more details about eligibility requirements and the application process. This page also lists eligible college majors (not all engineering disciplines are eligible), tells you how to keep the scholarship once you have won it, and provides a link to the application form in PDF format. Note that you must submit your application directly to your college, rather than to the scholarship sponsor. To find out which colleges participate in the scholarship program, click the The Schools link. Follow the The Students link to find detailed biographies of past winners, which will help you determine what qualities the sponsor is looking for in scholarship applicants.

Florida Engineering Society Scholarships

Sponsor: Florida Engineering Society
Web Site: http://www.fleng.org/awards.htm
Amount of Scholarship: $1,000 to $3,000
Number of Awards: 12
Deadline: February 15
Education Level: high school seniors and community college transfer students
Eligibility: Applicant must enroll in an accredited engineering program, have a minimum 3.5 GPA (high school students) or 3.0 GPA (community college students), be a Florida resident, and be a U.S. citizen.

Scroll down to the bottom of the page to find the brief descriptions of the $1,000 scholarship for graduating high school students and the scholarships of varying amounts for community college transfer students. Open either the application form for high school seniors or the one for community college transfers (available in both PDF and Microsoft Word formats) to learn more. Note that the junior transfer scholarships can only be used at the colleges listed on the application form, and only students enrolled in Florida community colleges can apply. Also, most of these scholarships specify the engineering disciplines that they must be used for; they are not general engineering scholarships like the high school scholarships.

IIE Scholarships

Sponsor: Institute of Industrial Engineers (IIE)
Web Site: http://www.iienet.org

Amount of Scholarship: $300 to $4,000
Number of Awards: 16
Deadline: November 15
Education Level: college undergraduates and graduate students
Eligibility: Applicant must enroll as a full-time student in an accredited industrial engineering program, be an active member of IIE, and have a minimum 3.4 GPA.

To locate the scholarship information, click the Outreach link at the top of the page, then click the IIE Honors & Awards link. The General Information page describes the goals of IIE's awards program, which may be helpful in preparing your application. Look for descriptions of the eight different scholarships offered under the program, including eligibility requirements and award amounts, on the Listing of All IIE Scholarships & Fellowships page. Four general undergraduate scholarships with awards ranging from $600 to $2,000 and one general graduate scholarship of $2,200 are available. There is also one scholarship of $300 for graduate students studying transportation, one $4,000 scholarship for female students, and one $4,000 scholarship for minority students. General eligibility requirements and selection criteria for all of the scholarships are listed at the very bottom of the page. Notice that for all scholarships but one, the head of your industrial engineering department must nominate you; the nomination form is linked to the top of the page. If you would like to apply for the IIE Council of Fellows award, you must directly request an application using the IIE Council of Fellows Request for Application Form, also linked to the top of the page. Follow the Membership link to learn more about joining IIE and to find an online student membership application.

Mercedes-Benz U.S. International/SAE Scholarship

Sponsor: Mercedes-Benz United States International and Society of Automotive Engineers (SAE) Foundation

Web Site: http://www.sae.org/students/mercedes.htm
Amount of Scholarship: $2,500
Number of Awards: 1
Deadline: April 1
Education Level: college juniors
Eligibility: Applicant must major in manufacturing engineering or a mobility-related engineering discipline at an Alabama college, be an Alabama resident, and be a U.S. citizen.

The page briefly describes this scholarship and the selection criteria. Click the Application link to open an application form that you can fill in online. You must print out the application form complete with your responses and mail it in with all the supporting documentation requested, however; you can't submit it online. To learn more about the scholarship sponsor and its goals, click the SAE Foundation link in the upper right corner of the Web page.

NACME Scholarships

Sponsor: NACME, Inc.
Web Site: http://www.nacme.org/sch.html
Amount of Scholarship: up to $20,000
Number of Awards: not given
Deadline: February
Education Level: high school seniors and college undergraduates
Eligibility: Applicant must major in engineering, be a member of a minority group, and be a U.S. citizen.

NACME offers one of the largest scholarship programs for minorities studying engineering. You can't apply directly for these scholarships. Instead, you must be nominated by or obtain applications from your college. Follow the Participating Institutions link on the left side of the page to find out which colleges award NACME scholarships. You can read about some of NACME's most prestigious programs on the Web site, though. Scroll to the bottom of the page and then explore the links under

Programs to get an idea of what kinds of scholarships are available and what kinds of applicants NACME is looking for.

Office of Nuclear Energy Undergraduate Scholarship

Sponsor: Oak Ridge Institute for Science and Education and U.S. Department of Energy
Web Site: http://www.orau.gov/orise/edu/uggrad/nuceng1.htm
Amount of Scholarship: $2,000
Number of Awards: not given
Deadline: January
Education Level: college sophomores and juniors
Eligibility: Applicant must major in nuclear engineering and plan to attend graduate school in nuclear engineering.

You will find only the bare details about this scholarship on the Web page. To receive more information, contact one of the e-mail addresses or phone numbers listed at the bottom of the page. Click the How to Apply button to find an applicaton form and instructions for submitting it. Make certain that the PDF application form is correct for the current school year before submitting it, though.

SAE Carolina Section Scholarships

Sponsor: Carolina Section of Society of Automotive Engineers (SAE)
Web Site: http://www.sae.org/students/carolina.htm
Amount of Scholarship: $1,000
Number of Awards: 2
Deadline: February 29
Education Level: high school seniors
Eligibility: Applicant must enroll in an accredited engineering program and be a U.S. citizen.

Two scholarships are available under this program. The Web page outlines the eligibility requirements, the selection criteria, and the application instructions for both scholarships and provides a downloadable Microsoft Word version of the application form.

SAE Long-Term Member-Sponsored Scholarship

Sponsor: Society of Automotive Engineers (SAE) Foundation
Web Site: http://www.sae.org/students/schlrshp.htm
Amount of Scholarship: $1,000
Number of Awards: not given
Deadline: April 1
Education Level: college juniors
Eligibility: Applicant must enroll in an engineering program and be a student member of SAE.

This Web page outlines the goals of this scholarship program and describes the application process, which requires nomination by both an SAE Faculty Advisor and the SAE Section Chair. The page also describes the selection criteria. You will find an application form that the two nominators must fill out. Although this form looks like an electronic application and you can type in the fields, it still must be printed out and mailed in; it cannot be submitted online. For more information about membership in SAE, click the Membership link in the left-hand frame of any page on the site.

Samuel Fletcher Tapman ASCE Student Chapter/Club Scholarship

Sponsor: American Society of Civil Engineers (ASCE)
Web Site: http://www.asce.org/peta/ed/app_tap.html
Amount of Scholarship: $2,000
Number of Awards: 12
Deadline: February 11

Education Level: college freshmen, sophomores, and juniors
Eligibility: Applicant must be a National Student Member of ASCE.

You will find a brief description of the selection criteria for this scholarship program under the Eligibility Requirements section of the Web page. Beneath that is a list of all the items that you must include in the application package and instructions for submitting the package. A text version of the application form is provided at the very bottom of the page, or you can link to a PDF version of the form. You may apply for student membership when you submit your application. To learn more, click the Membership button on the left side of the page and explore the items in the menu under See Information About Student Membership.

SME Scholarships

Sponsor: Society of Manufacturing Engineers (SME)
Web Site: http://www.sme.org
Amount of Scholarship: $600 to $20,000
Number of Awards: 70
Deadline: February 1
Education Level: high school seniors, college undergraduates, and graduate students
Eligibility: Applicant must enroll as a full-time student in an accredited manufacturing engineering program or a closely related engineering field at a U.S. or Canadian college or university.

To find the scholarship information, choose Education Foundation from the Quick Links menu and click the Scholarships & Fellowships link. There is a lot of information on this page; for easier reading, you can download a Word version of the scholarship information. Scholarships for different educational levels are grouped separately. There are 5 scholarships for graduating high school students, 17 scholarships for current undergraduate students, and

1 fellowship for graduate students. The average award is $1,000, and the largest award of $20,000 is available only to students who are children or grandchildren of SME members. Scroll down the page until you find the category of scholarships that fits you, then read the description of each scholarship listed to ensure you meet its specific eligibility requirements, such as residency, eligible colleges, minimum GPA, and minimum test scores. Click each scholarship's link to read detailed eligibility requirements, selection criteria, and application instructions for that award. Make a note of each scholarship for which you would like to apply. At the bottom of the main scholarship page you will find the application guidelines and submission instructions for all scholarships, as well as a link to a Word copy of the Application Cover Sheet that must be included in your application package. You must list the names of all of the scholarships that you want to apply for on this sheet.

SPE Foundation Scholarships

Sponsor: Society of Plastics Engineers (SPE) Foundation
Web Site: http://www.4spe.org/SCHL.HTML
Amount of Scholarship: $1,000 to $5,000
Number of Awards: 21
Deadline: December 15
Education Level: college sophomores, juniors, and seniors and graduate students
Eligibility: Applicant must major in a science, engineering, or related discipline in preparation for a career in the plastics industry; be a full-time student; and have a minimum 3.0 GPA.

This page describes the eight scholarships available from this program. The opening paragraph lists the basic eligibility requirements, including appropriate fields of study, and the selection criteria for all scholarships. Only the three scholarships described under Special Scholarships have specific eligibility requirements. Follow the How to Apply for Foundation Scholarships link to find more details about eligibility requirements and selection criteria, as well as instructions for submitting an application. The Application Form is linked to the bottom of this page.

SPE GCS Scholarship

Sponsor: Gulf Coast Section (GCS) and Houston Society of Petroleum Engineers (SPE) Auxiliary
Web Site: http://www.spegcs.org//speinfo/scholar.htm
Amount of Scholarship: not given
Number of Awards: not given
Deadline: February 15
Education Level: high school seniors
Eligibility: Applicant must enroll in an engineering or science program, plan to work in the petroleum industry, have a minimum SAT I score of 1100, reside in the Houston area, and be a U.S. citizen.

The Web page describes the eligibility requirements for this award and the criteria used to evaluate applicants. The page also describes the conditions for renewing the scholarship.You can download application forms in either Microsoft Word or RTF format from the site, or you can request an application by sending an e-mail message to the address given.

Also see the following scholarships:

- AFCEA General Emmett Paige Scholarship: Chapter 13, "All Branches" section
- AFCEA General John A. Wickham Scholarship: Chapter 6, "Sciences" section
- AFCEA ROTC Scholarship: Chapter 13, "All Branches" section
- AGC Scholarships: Chapter 6, "Construction" section
- AISE Steel Foundation Scholarships: Chapter 14 "Unions and Professional Associations" section
- AISES A. T. Anderson Memorial Scholarship: Chpater 9, "Native American" section
- APEGBC Entrance Scholarships: Chapter 15, "Canada" section
- ARRL Foundation Scholarships: Chapter 8, "Amateur Radio" section
- Astronaut Scholarship: Chapter 6, "Sciences" section
- Barry M. Goldwater Scholarship: Chapter 6, "Sciences" section
- Burlington Northern Santa Fe Foundation Scholarship: Chapter 9, "Native American" section
- Development Fund for Black Students in Science and Technology Scholarship: Chapter 12, "African-American" section
- Dr. Vicki L. Schechtman Scholarship: Chapter 12, "Female" section
- Hispanic College Fund Scholarship: Chapter 9, "Hispanic" section
- Maryland Science and Technology Scholarship: Chapter 15, "Maryland" section
- Nancy Lorraine Jensen Memorial Scholarship: Chapter 14, "Clubs and Community Organizations" section
- New Economy Technology Scholarship: Chapter 15, "Pennsylvania" section
- New York State Regents Professional Opportunity Scholarship: Chapter 15, "New York" section
- NSBE Scholarships: Chapter 9, "African-American" section
- NTA Science Scholarship Award: Chapter 9, "All Minorities" section
- OCECS Scholarship: Chapter 15, "Oregon" section
- San Diego County Scholarship: Chapter 15, "California" section
- Society of Women Engineers Scholarships: Chapter 12, "Female" section
- Xerox Technical Minority Scholarship: Chapter 9, "All Minorities" section

English

See the following scholarship:

- Roberta Thumin Scholarship: Chapter 6, "Communications" section

Environmental Studies

Arkansas Environmental Federation Scholarship

Sponsor: Arkansas Environmental Federation
Web Site: http://www.environmentark.org/edu/pubed.html
Amount of Scholarship: $1,500
Number of Awards: 2
Deadline: March 31
Education Level: college undergraduates and graduate students
Eligibility: Applicant must enroll as a full-time student in an environmental-related program, have completed at least 40 credit hours of college coursework, have a minimum 2.8 GPA, and be an Arkansas resident.

Two awards are given out each year to students majoring in subjects related to environmental studies, which could include environmental engineering, wildlife management, environmental health science, forestry, fisheries and wildlife, geology, or agriculture—anything with an environmental or health and safety emphasis. This page tells you more about the scholarship and organization sponsoring it. It also details the scholarship criteria. To apply, print out the text application (linked to the scholarship's Web page) and attach all of the requested additional documents.

EPA Tribal Lands Environmental Science Scholarship

Sponsor: American Indian Science and Engineering Society and U.S. Environmental Protection Agency (EPA)
Web Site: http://www.aises.org/scholarships/#EPA
Amount of Scholarship: $4,000
Number of Awards: not given
Deadline: June 15
Education Level: college juniors and seniors and graduate students
Eligibility: Applicant must major in an environmental-related field, have a minimum 2.5 GPA, be a full-time student, and be Native American.

As indicated in the scholarship description, this program awards both scholarship money and internship opportunities in EPA facilities and on Indian reservations. First, follow the link to the Scholarship Criteria to find out if you are eligible to apply. This page describes exactly what environmental disciplines can be studied under the scholarship and how to document Native American status. It also lists the items that must be included in the application package. You can download the application form in PDF format from the main page.

James L. Goodwin Memorial Scholarship

Sponsor: Connecticut Forest and Park Association
Web Site: http://www.ctwoodlands.org/scholarsh.html
Amount of Scholarship: $1,000 to $3,000
Number of Awards: not given
Deadline: April 1
Education Level: college undergraduates and graduate students

Eligibility: Applicant must enroll in a program in silviculture or forest resource management and be a Connecticut resident.

This Web page briefly describes the history of this scholarship program and the criteria used in selecting scholarship winners. If you meet the eligibility requirements, you can obtain an application form by writing to the mailing address under Where to Apply or by sending an e-mail message to the address under Where to Obtain an Application.

Larry Wimer Memorial Scholarship

Sponsor: Idaho Power Company
Web Site: http://www.idahopower.com/commnity/schol_wimer.html
Amount of Scholarship: $500 per year
Number of Awards: not given
Deadline: March 1
Education Level: high school seniors
Eligibility: Applicant must enroll as a full-time student in a forestry, wildlife, or range science program at a college or vocational-technical school in Idaho or Oregon.

This page describes the eligibility requirements, application requirements, and selection criteria for this scholarship. You can also download a copy of the application form in Microsoft Word format, if you choose to apply.

Masonic Range Science Scholarship

Sponsor: Society for Range Management (SRM)
Web Site: http://www.srm.org/scholarship.html
Amount of Scholarship: not given
Number of Awards: not given
Deadline: January 15

Education Level: high school seniors and college freshmen
Eligibility: Applicant must major in range science.

The page briefly describes the eligibility requirements for the scholarship and lists the documents required for the application package. Click Go to Application Form at the bottom of the page to open a text version of the application that you can print from within your Web browser.

Morris K. Udall Foundation Undergraduate Scholarship

Sponsor: Morris K. Udall Foundation
Web Site: http://www.udall.gov/p_scholarship.htm
Amount of Scholarship: up to $5,000
Number of Awards: 75
Deadline: February 15
Education Level: college sophomores and juniors
Eligibility: Applicant must either study an environmental field or be a Native American or Alaskan Native studying a field related to health care or tribal public policy at a two-year or four-year college, have a grade average of at least a B, and be a U.S. citizen or permanent resident.

This is a very prestigious scholarship program, and it is highly competitive. The Student Bulletin, published on the Web site in PDF format, tells you everything you need to know about the program, including a profile of a typical Udall Scholar. You can't apply directly for this scholarship; the official Udall faculty representative at your college must nominate you. Click the Faculty Representatives link to locate the name and phone number for the faculty representative at your college, whom you can contact to get more information about the nomination process at your school. Faculty representatives can also download nomination guidelines and forms from the site.

Paul W. Rodgers Scholarship

Sponsor: International Association for Great Lakes Research
Web Site: http://www.iaglr.org/as/rodgersannounce.html
Amount of Scholarship: $2,000
Number of Awards: 1
Deadline: February 29
Education Level: college juniors and seniors and graduate students
Eligibility: Applicant must intend to research an area of study related to the Great Lakes and attend an accredited four-year college or graduate school.

The Web page describes in detail what the scholarship sponsor is looking for in applicants, particularly in regard to the requirement of an interest in Great Lakes research. Follow the link at the bottom of the page to find full details on application procedures. You don't need to submit an official application form, but you do need to follow the instructions given on the Web site exactly to ensure that your application is considered.

SWANA BC Pacific Chapter Scholarship

Sponsor: British Columbia Chapter of the Solid Waste Association of North America (SWANA)
Web Site: http://www.ecowaste.com/swanabc/scholar.htm
Amount of Scholarship: $500 (Canadian)
Number of Awards: not given
Deadline: October 15
Education Level: college sophomores and juniors
Eligibility: Applicant must enroll in an environmental management or related program at a college in British Columbia, Canada.

This page describes the eligibility requirements for this scholarship and the criteria for selecting winners. You will also find a link to a PDF version of the application form and a list of supporting documents that you must submit with your application.

Truman D. Picard Scholarship

Sponsor: Intertribal Timber Council
Web Site: http://www.itcnet.org/picard.html
Amount of Scholarship: $1,200 to $1,800
Number of Awards: 14
Deadline: March 3
Education Level: high school seniors and college undergraduates
Eligibility: Applicant must study a field related to natural resources and be either Native American or Alaskan Native.

This Web page briefly outlines the eligibility requirements and application procedures for this scholarship. Graduating high school students receive $1,200 awards, and current undergraduates receive $1,800 awards. Simply follow the instructions on the Web page to submit your application; you don't need to fill out an official application form. If you have any questions about eligibility or how to prepare your application package, contact the address given at the bottom of the page.

Also see the following scholarships:

- AISES A. T. Anderson Memorial Scholarship: Chapter 9, "Native American" section
- FFGC Scholarships: Chapter 15, "Florida" section
- Garden Club of Georgia Scholarships: Chapter 15, "Georgia" section
- Georgia Water and Pollution Control Association Scholarships: Chapter 14, "Unions and Professional Associations" section
- Jim Bourque Scholarship: Chapter 9, "Native American" section
- Lawrence Conservation District Scholarship: Chapter 15, "Pennsylvania" section

- National Council of State Garden Clubs Scholarship: Chapter 6, "Horticulture" section
- NEHA/AAS Scholarship: Chapter 6, "Health Care" section
- New Economy Technology Scholarships: Chapter 15, "Pennsylvania" section
- Rockefeller State Wildlife Scholarship: Chapter 15, "Louisiana" section

Family and Consumer Sciences

See the following scholarships:

- Frank and Elizabeth Spencer Scholarship: Chapter 15, "North Carolina" section
- Missouri Department of Agriculture Scholarship: Chapter 15, "Missouri" section

Film and Television

Charles and Lucille King Family Foundation Scholarship

Sponsor: Charles and Lucille King Family Foundation
Web Site: http://www.kingfoundation.org
Amount of Scholarship: $2,500 (renewable for two years)
Number of Awards: not given
Deadline: April 15
Education Level: college sophomores and juniors
Eligibility: Applicant must major in television and film production at a four-year U.S. college.

The Frequently Asked Questions section of this Web page contains the most detailed information about scholarships available through this program, including the selection criteria. To get

an application, contact the mailing address or e-mail address listed under the last question.

David J. Clark Memorial Scholarship Grant

Sponsor: Ohio Valley Chapter of National Academy of Television Arts and Sciences
Web Site: http://www.emmyonline.org/ohiovalley/html/scholar.html
Amount of Scholarship: $3,000
Number of Awards: 1
Deadline: April 1
Education Level: college undergraduates and graduate students
Eligibility: Applicant must be a full-time broadcasting major at an accredited four-year college or university in the designated market area of stations serving the Ohio Valley Chapter.

The scholarship's Web page describes the eligibility requirements and selection criteria for the award. Also pay attention to the list of supporting documents that you must submit in addition to the application form. You can fill out the application itself and submit it directly from the Web page. To find out if your college is located in the Ohio Valley Chapter's market area, follow the link at the bottom of the page to the Ohio Valley Chapter's home page, where you will find a list of city markets under Service Area; the markets are located in Indiana, Kentucky, Ohio, and West Virginia.

Kodak Scholarship

Sponsor: Kodak and University Film and Video Foundation
Web Site: http://www.kodak.com/US/en/motion/programs/student/scholarship.shtml
Amount of Scholarship: up to $5,000
Number of Awards: not given
Deadline: not given
Education Level: college sophomores, juniors, and seniors and master's students

Eligibility: Applicant must study cinematography at a U.S. college or university offering four-year degree programs in motion picture filmmaking.

This page describes the goals of this scholarship program, who is eligible to apply, and how winners are selected. Students cannot apply for scholarships directly. Instead, the dean or chairperson of the film department at your school must request applications, and the school must nominate all candidates. An address is provided where faculty can request applications.

Also see the following scholarships:

- Jessica Savitch Scholarship: Chapter 6, "Communications" section
- Roberta Thumin Scholarship: Chapter 6, "Communications" section

Food Science and Nutrition

ADA Scholarships

Sponsor: American Dietetics Association (ADA)
Web Site: http://www.eatright.org/scholelig.html
Amount of Scholarship: $500 to $5,000
Number of Awards: 150
Deadline: February 15
Education Level: college undergraduates and graduate students
Eligibility: Applicant must enroll in a dietetics program and be a U.S. citizen or permanent resident.

The number of awards available under this program and their dollar amounts vary from year to year. Scholarship information for the next award year is available on the Web page after September. The Web page also describes the general requirements for scholarships given at different educational levels. Some of the scholarships have specific eligibility requirements, such as membership of ADA, membership of a specific dietary practice group, residency in a particular state, or minority status. Some graduate scholarships require that applicants study a specific subdiscipline of dietetics. You can apply for all of the ADA scholarships using the same application form, however. Download the application in Microsoft Word format directly from the Web page. If you are unable to view this form, you can request that a printed copy of the application form be mailed to you by sending an e-mail message to the address provided.

IFT Scholarships

Sponsor: Institute of Food Technologists (IFT)
Web Site: http://www.ift.org/careers/index.shtml
Amount of Scholarship: $1,000 to $5,000
Number of Awards: 145
Deadline: varies
Education Level: high school seniors, college undergraduates, and graduate students
Eligibility: Applicant must enroll in an IFT-approved food science or food technology undergraduate program or enroll in a master's or doctoral program in food science or food technology at any university.

To find the scholarship information, click the Awards, Scholarships & Fellowships link at the top of the page. The page that opens describes IFT's scholarships and fellowships program, which awards 112 undergraduate scholarships of amounts ranging between $1,000 and $2,250 and 33 graduate fellowships of amounts ranging between $1,000 and $5,000. Follow the links at the bottom of the page to learn more about the purpose of the awards. The Program Description and Instructions link provides the most detailed information about available scholarships and fellowships, including a list of available awards for each educational level, specific eligibility requirements for each award, selection criteria, and application procedures; definitely read this page over before deciding whether to apply. To find out if your college offers an IFT-approved program in food science or technology, follow the link to the list of such programs. Click the Download Scholarship Application Forms link to find text versions of the application forms that you can fill out in your word processor; this link also tells you how to order application materials. Be sure to download the correct application form for your educational level. You will automatically be considered for all general scholarships, although you will need to indicate on the application whether you are applying for awards with special qualifications as well.

Also see the following scholarships:

- Competitive Edge Scholarship: Chapter 6, "Engineering" section
- Indian Health Service Scholarship: Chapter 9, "Native American" section
- New Economy Technology Scholarships: Chapter 15, "Pennsylvania" section
- Roundtable for Women in Foodservice Scholarship: Chapter 6, "Hotel and Restaurant Management" section
- School Food Service Foundation Scholarships: Chapter 14, "Employer and Profession" section

Funeral Service and Mortuary Science

ABFSE Scholarship

Sponsor: American Board of Funeral Service Education (ABFSE)

Web Site: http://www.abfse.org/html/scholarships.html
Amount of Scholarship: $250 to $500
Number of Awards: not given
Deadline: March and September
Education Level: college undergraduates
Eligibility: Applicant must have completed at least one semester of an ABFSE-accredited funeral service and mortuary science program and be a U.S. citizen.

This page provides an overview of this scholarship program for funeral service and mortuary science students. The Procedures and Requirements page tells you how to prepare an application package and provides a link to the scholarship application, which you can print out from inside your Web browser.

State Funeral Directors Associations Scholarships

Sponsor: National Funeral Directors Association (NFDA)
Web Site: http://www.nfda.org/careers/scholar/state/index.html
Amount of Scholarship: varies
Number of Scholarships: not given
Deadline: varies
Education Level: college undergraduates
Eligibility: Applicant must enroll in a funeral service and mortuary science program.

Thirty-eight of the state chapters of NFDA offer scholarships to funeral service and mortuary science students who are residents of their states. To find information about a scholarship, click your state's name. Each scholarship description lists the eligibility requirements and award amounts for that particular award and provides an address and phone number that you can contact for more information and an application form.

Geography

ACSM Scholarships

Sponsor: American Congress on Surveying and Mapping (ACSM)
Web Site: http://www.survmap.org/scholar.html
Amount of Scholarship: $500 to $2,000
Number of Awards: not given
Deadline: December 17
Education Level: college undergraduates and graduate students
Eligibility: Applicant must enroll in a cartography, geodetic surveying, geodesy, geographic information system, surveying, or surveying technology program at a two-year or four-year college or graduate school.

This page describes the purpose and selection criteria for scholarships sponsored by ACSM. Five categories of eligible applicants are described under Application Instructions; make sure you fit at least one of those categories, and follow the instructions for your category. A list of scholarships and fellowships follows the Application Instructions, indicating which awards are available in each category, the amounts of the awards, and their specific selection criteria. A PDF application form for all scholarships is linked to the bottom of the Web page; be sure to check the boxes beside the names of all scholarships for which you want to be considered.

Robert E. Altenhofen Memorial Scholarship

Sponsor: American Society for Photogrammetry and Remote Sensing (ASPRS) and International Geographic Information Foundation
Web Site: http://www.asprs.org/membership.html
Amount of Scholarship: $2,000
Number of Awards: 1

Deadline: December 1
Education Level: college undergraduates and graduate students
Eligibility: Applicant must study photogrammetry and be a member of ASPRS.

To find the scholarship information, click the Awards and Scholarships link, then click the name of the scholarship in the list of awards. This section of the Web page describes the goals of this scholarship for students of photogrammetry and tells you who is eligible to apply, how to submit an application, how the application is evaluated, and the obligations of the recipient. To find the application form, return to the top of the page and click the Application Instructions link, which tells you how to complete the application. Then follow the Application Forms link to open the application in PDF format. To find out how to become a member of ASPRS, click the Individual Membership link on the left side of the page.

Geosciences

SEG Foundation Scholarships

Sponsor: Society of Exploration Geophysicists (SEG) Foundation
Web Site: http://seg.org/business/foundation/scholarships/index_body.html
Amount of Scholarship: $500 to $10,000
Number of Awards: around 100
Deadline: March 1
Education Level: high school seniors, college undergraduates, and graduate students
Eligibility: Applicant must study geophysics at a U.S. college.

This scholarship program gives out around 100 awards each year to students of geophysics at all educational levels, with an average award of $1,200. This page provides an overview of the program, its history, and the eligibility requirements. Download a PDF version of the application form by following the link in the Applications and Supporting Documents section of the Web page.

Also see the following scholarships:

- AGI Minority Geoscience Scholarship: Chapter 7, "Geosciences" section
- APEGBC Entrance Scholarships: Chapter 15, "Canada" section
- Dr. Vicki L. Schechtman Scholarship: Chapter 12, "Female" section
- New Economy Technology Scholarship: Chapter 15, "Pennsylvania" section

Government and Public Service

Donald A. Strauss Scholarship

Sponsor: Donald A. Strauss Foundation
Web Site: http://www.straussfoundation.org/scholarship_info.html
Amount of Scholarship: $10,000
Number of Awards: 15
Deadline: varies
Education Level: college juniors
Eligibility: Applicant must plan to pursue a career in public service, and be a full-time student at a participating California college.

Your college must nominate you for this scholarship, so you will have to submit your application package directly to your school. Follow the How to Apply link on the left side of the page to find important application information, including a list of scholarship contacts at each participating California college. The eligibility requirements are listed in the Guidelines section of the scholarship's Web page; preference is given to applicants from the colleges named there. Read the A Career in Public Service section to find out what fields of study

and career tracks are acceptable to the sponsor. If you win, you will have to carry out a public service project, as described under Responsibilities of Scholarship Recipient. Before applying, you should explore the rest of the Web site to learn more about this award, particularly the About Us, Project Presentations, and Sample Proposals pages.

Harry S Truman Scholarship

Sponsor: Harry S Truman Scholarship Foundation
Web Site: http://www.truman.gov
Amount of Scholarship: $30,000
Number of Awards: 75 to 80
Deadline: February 1
Education Level: college juniors
Eligibility: Applicant must commit to a career in government or public service, plan to go to graduate or professional school, be a full-time student at a participating college, be in the upper 25 percent of his or her class, have an extensive community service record, and be a U.S. citizen or national.

The Truman Scholarship is among the most prestigious awards available for college students. The bulk of the award must be used to fund graduate study. First, go to the About the Foundation page to learn what the mission of the scholarship program is. Then follow the For Potential Scholars link to learn all about the program, including its purpose, how the scholarship is awarded, eligibility requirements, nomination procedures, conditions for accepting the award, and activities that Truman Scholars participate in. This page also defines what a career in public service is. You cannot apply directly for this program. Instead, your college must nominate you. Each participating college has a Truman Faculty Representative who oversees the nomination process at the school, helps nominees prepare application materials, and submits nomination materials. Follow the For Faculty Representatives link to locate the Truman Faculty Representative at your college. You can also link to the application materials in PDF format at the bottom of this page.

Public Service Scholarship

Sponsor: Public Employees Roundtable
Web Site: http://www.theroundtable.org/scholarship.htm
Amount of Scholarship: $1,000
Number of Awards: not given
Deadline: May 19
Education Level: college sophomores, juniors, and seniors and graduate students
Eligibility: Applicant must plan to pursue a career in government, be a full-time student, and have a minimum 3.5 GPA.

This page describes the background of the scholarship program, its purpose, eligibility requirements, and selection criteria. Look at the previous year's winners to discover what kinds of students are chosen to receive this award. To find out how to submit an application and get more details about eligibility requirements, follow the link to the application form. You can also download a printable version of the application from this page.

Washington Crossing Foundation Scholarship

Sponsor: Washington Crossing Foundation
Web Site: http://www.gwcf.org/Awards.htm
Amount of Scholarship: $1,500 to $10,000 (awarded over four years)
Number of Awards: 6
Deadline: January 1
Education Level: high school seniors
Eligibility: Applicant must plan to pursue a career in government service and be a U.S. citizen.

Under this scholarship program, the first-place winner receives $10,000, the second-place win-

ner receives $7,500, and the third-place winner receives $5,000. Two additional scholarships of $2,500 and $1,500 respectively are also available. Finally, one scholarship of $5,000 is reserved for Pennsylvania residents (follow the link beside this scholarship to learn more about this particular award). To be considered, you must submit an essay on the topic described on the scholarship's information page. Follow the Official Rules link to find eligibility requirements, judging criteria, and application submission instructions. Click the Application link to find complete instructions for preparing the application package.

Also see the following scholarships:

- Betty Rendel Scholarship: Chapter 12, "Female" section
- Minorities in Government Finance Scholarship: Chapter 9, "All Minorities" section
- Robert G. Porter Scholarship: Chapter 14, "Unions and Professional Associations" section

Health Care

ACMPE Scholarships

Sponsor: American College of Medical Practice Executives (ACMPE)
Web Site: http://www.mgma.com/acmpe/scholars.html
Amount of Scholarship: $500 to $2,000
Number of Awards: not given
Deadline: varies
Education Level: college undergraduates and graduate students
Eligibility: Applicant must enroll in a degree program relevant to medical practice management or be a member of the Society for Physicians in Administration (SPA) or Anesthesia Administration Assembly (AAA).

Nineteen different scholarships are awarded under this program. Most of these scholarships are intended for medical practice management students. Follow the link on the right side of the page to open a list of all available scholarships, along with each award's specific eligibility requirements. Note that five scholarships are limited to students at specific universities. Others have residency requirements. Make a note of each scholarship for which you would like to apply. Then link to the application form, which you can print out from inside your Web browser. Be sure to check the boxes on the application form beside all of the scholarships for which you are applying. You must submit a separate cover sheet for each scholarship as well.

Hays Medical Center Scholarships

Sponsor: Hays Medical Center
Web Site: http://www.haysmed.com/scholar.html
Amount of Scholarship: $500 to $3,500
Number of Awards: 6
Deadline: varies
Education Level: college undergraduates and graduate students
Eligibility: Applicant must study an applicable health care field.

This page provides a brief description of each of the six different scholarships available, as well as specific eligibility requirements for each award, including the specific health care fields each award supports. Most scholarships are for nursing students. Many scholarships require employment at Hays Medical Center after graduation, and some scholarships are only available for current employees. Follow the link in the first paragraph to open a page where you can submit an application online. You must check the boxes beside all scholarships for

which you are applying and complete the appropriate autobiographical sketch forms.

Health Professional Scholarship

Sponsor: Washington State Higher Education Coordinating Board
Web Site: http://www.hecb.wa.gov/paying/health.htm#Health Scholarship
Amount of Scholarship: full tuition
Number of Awards: not given
Deadline: April 21
Education Level: college undergraduates
Eligibility: Applicant must enroll in an approved health care professions program.

This is a service scholarship that recruits students to work as health care professionals in shortage areas in Washington state in exchange for scholarship money. Shortage areas are listed underneath the scholarship's description on the Web page. Unlike other state-specific service scholarships, though, you don't need to be a Washington resident or attend college in Washington to be eligible. To get an application, scroll to the top of the Web page and click the Health Professional Scholarship Application link. The application also provides a lot more information about the program, eligibility requirements, selection criteria, and how the service obligation works. Note that eligible health care programs change each year; this year's eligible programs are listed on the first page of the scholarship application.

NEHA/AAS Scholarship

Sponsor: National Environmental Health Association (NEHA) and American Academy of Sanitarians (AAS)
Web Site: http://www.neha.org/scholarship.html
Amount of Scholarship: $1,000
Number of Awards: not given
Deadline: February 1

Education Level: college juniors and seniors and graduate students

Eligibility: Applicant must enroll in an environmental health sciences program or public health degree program (graduate students only) at an eligible college or university.

Read through the scholarship information to learn more about the purpose of the scholarship, the eligibility requirements, approved environmental health programs, and application procedures. Colleges and universities that offer eligible environmental health programs are listed at the bottom of the page. You will find a link to the Scholarship Application at the very bottom of the page, which you can fill out in your Web browser and then print out for mailing.

RMHC and College Fund/UNCF Scholarship

Sponsor: Ronald McDonald House Charities (RMHC) and College Fund and United Negro College Fund (UNCF)
Web Site: http://www.rmhc.com
Amount of Scholarship: $1,000 to full tuition
Number of Awards: 60
Deadline: April 1
Education Level: college sophomores
Eligibility: Applicant must major in a health care-related field at an UNCF college and have a minimum 3.0 GPA.

This page outlines the details of the scholarship program. Ten full-tuition scholarships are available, as well as 50 $1,000 scholarships. Although you don't have to be African-American to apply, the program is obviously targeted at African-American students. Application instructions are given at the very bottom of the page. Return to the top of the page to link to a PDF version of the application form. To find out what the UNCF colleges are, go to http://www.uncf.org and click the Member Institutions button.

Secretary's Award for Innovations in Health

Sponsor: U.S. Department of Health and Human Services, Health Resources and Services Administration and Federation of Associations of Schools of Health Professions
Web Site: http://www.aacn.nche.edu/Education/secawardapplication.htm
Amount of Scholarship: $1,500 to $7,500
Number of Awards: 6
Deadline: February 1
Education Level: college undergraduates and graduate students
Eligibility: Applicant must enroll in an accredited health professions program that is affiliated with the Federation of Associations of Schools of Health Professions, and be a U.S. citizen or permanent resident.

This contest awards cash prizes for the best student projects in health promotion and disease prevention. In the interdisciplinary category, first prize is $7,500, second prize is $5,000, and third prize is $3,000. In the single-discipline category, first prize is $3,500, second prize is $2,500, and third prize is $1,500. Read the Web page to learn what the purpose of the awards program is, what kinds of projects the sponsors are looking for, and what acceptable project topics are. The page also describes the eligibility requirements, contest rules, judging criteria, selection process, and available prizes. And you will find an entry cover sheet that you can print out. Note that the health care program you are enrolled in must be affiliated with a member organization of the Federation of Associations of Schools of Health Professions. These member organizations are listed at the bottom of the Web page.

Also see the following scholarships:

• Burlington Northern Santa Fe Foundation Scholarship: Chapter 9, "Native American" section

- Congressional Black Caucus Spouses Scholarships: Chapter 15, "Alabama" section
- FFGC Scholarships: Chapter 15, "Florida" section
- Health Professions Scholarship: Chapter 15, "Pennsylvania" section
- Indian Health Service Scholarship: Chapter 9, "Native American" section
- Morris K. Udall Foundation Undergraduate Scholarships: Chapter 6, "Environmental Studies" section
- Pre-Health and Armed Forces Health Professions Scholarships: Chapter 13, "Air Force and Air Force ROTC" section
- Robert G. Porter Scholarship: Chapter 14, "Unions and Professional Associations" section
- Wendell Milliman Scholarship: Chapter 14, "Employers and Professions" section
- Zeta Phi Beta Scholarships and Fellowships: Chapter 12, "Female" section

Heating, Refrigeration, and Air Conditioning

ASHRAE Scholarships

Sponsor: American Society of Heating, Refrigeration, and Air-Conditioning Engineers (ASHRAE)
Web Site: http://www.ashrae.org
Amount of Scholarship: $3,000 to $20,000
Number of Awards: 11
Deadline: varies
Education Level: college undergraduates and graduate students
Eligibility: Applicant must enroll as a full-time student in an accredited engineering or engineering technology program with a preparatory curriculum for a career in the heating, ventilating, air conditioning, and refrigeration field.

To find the scholarship information, click the Scholarships link (found under ASHRAE Activities), and then click the ASHRAE Scholarship Program Information link. This page describes all of the available scholarships, including their award amounts and specific eligibility requirements. Five $3,000 and two $10,000 scholarships are available for engineering students pursuing a bachelor's degree. Two $3,000 scholarships are available for engineering technology students, one for an associate's degree student and one for a bachelor's degree student. The graduate fellowship of $20,000 is awarded only to students at Purdue University in Indiana; the specific eligibility requirements and application procedures for this fellowship are also listed. At the bottom of the page are links to two different application forms for undergraduate scholarships. Be sure to print out the correct application for the group of scholarships for which you are applying (engineering or engineering technology).

SCHPA Scholarship

Sponsor: South Carolina Heat Pump Association (SCHPA)
Web Site: http://www.scheatpump.com/sch-wrd.html
Amount of Scholarship: $500
Number of Awards: not given
Deadline: not given
Education Level: college undergraduates
Eligibility: Applicant must plan to work in the heating and air conditioning industry after graduation and be a South Carolina resident.

This page describes the scholarship program, eligibility requirements, and requirements for renewing the scholarship. Note that employees and families of contractor members and students in engineering degree programs are given preference. Link to a printable version of the scholarship application at the bottom of the page.

Historic Preservation

Georgia Trust for Historic Preservation Scholarship

Sponsor: Georgia Trust for Historic Preservation
Web Site: http://www.georgiatrust.org/scholarship.asp
Amount of Scholarship: $1,000
Number of Awards: 2
Deadline: February 1
Education Level: college freshmen, sophomores, and juniors
Eligibility: Applicant must major in historic preservation or a related field, be a full-time student at a Georgia college, be a Georgia resident, and be a U.S. citizen.

The Web page provides a lot of information about the mission of this scholarship program and the qualities that the sponsors are looking for in awardees. Be sure to check the eligibility requirements (found under the heading Who) and the selection criteria described throughout the page. Print out a copy of the application in either text or PDF format by following the links at the bottom of the page.

Also see the following scholarship:

• Garden Club of Georgia Scholarships: Chapter 15, "Georgia" section

Horticulture

Bedding Plants Foundation Scholarships

Sponsor: Bedding Plants Foundation, Inc.
Web Site: http://bpfi.org/application.htm
Amount of Scholarship: $500 to $2,000
Number of Awards: not given
Deadline: May 1
Education Level: high school seniors, college undergraduates, and graduate students
Eligibility: Applicant must study a horticulture-related field and be a U.S. or Canadian citizen or permanent resident or attend a U.S. or Canadian college.

The Bedding Plants Foundation offers 20 different scholarships to horticulture students. You can apply for up to three of them with the scholarship application on this Web site; follow the Scholarship Application link. The application form itself gives you all the information you need to know about the scholarship program. First, check the eligibility requirements to ensure that you meet the minimum requirements for all scholarships. Most scholarships require a 3.0 grade point average, although if you have outstanding qualifications in other areas, you may be able to overcome this restriction. The application also lists all of the available scholarships, along with their specific eligibility requirements and educational levels. Find the three that you are best qualified for and make a note of them on a separate piece of paper. When you complete the application, write the name of the specific scholarship for which you are applying in the first blank on the application form; you must submit a separate copy of the application form for each of the three scholarships.

Katharine M. Grosscup Scholarship

Sponsor: Garden Club of America
Web Site: http://216.117.137.211/grosscup.htm
Amount of Scholarship: $3,000
Number of Awards: not given
Deadline: February 1
Education Level: college sophomores, juniors, and seniors and master's students
Eligibility: Applicant must study horticulture.

As indicated on this short Web page, this scholarship goes to students studying horticulture. Preference is given to students from Indiana, Kentucky, Michigan, Ohio, Pennsylvania, and West Virginia. Finalists must attend an interview in Cleveland, Ohio, so be sure this requirement won't pose a problem before you apply. A text version of the application is linked to the Web page, which you can print from inside your Web browser.

National Council of State Garden Clubs Scholarship

Sponsor: National Council of State Garden Clubs
Web Site: http://www.gardenclub.org/scholar.htm
Amount of Scholarship: $3,500
Number of Awards: 32
Deadline: March 1
Education Level: college sophomores, juniors, and seniors and graduate students
Eligibility: Applicant must major in a gardening-related subject, and have a minimum 3.0 GPA.

Applicants for scholarships in this program must study a gardening-related field, such as horticulture, floriculture, landscape design, botany, biology, plant pathology, forestry, agronomy, environmental studies, city planning, land management, or a similar subject. The scholarship program's Web page describes the application procedures and requirements, as well as the qualities for which scholarship winners are selected. Applicants must mail the application forms to the scholarship chairperson of the State Garden Club for their state. All of the state garden club scholarship chairpersons, including contact addresses and phone numbers, are listed at the bottom of the page. If the application passes the state level of judging, it is forwarded to the national scholarship committee, which decides who receives the fi-

nal awards. State garden clubs may also award scholarships to qualified applicants from their states, in addition to the national scholarships described on this Web page. You can print out a copy of the application from this page as well.

Oregon Nurserymen's Foundation Scholarships

Sponsor: Oregon Nurserymen's Foundation (ONF)
Web Site: http://www.nurseryguide.com/onfform.shtml
Amount of Scholarship: $500 to $1,000
Number of Awards: 16
Deadline: April 3
Education Level: high school seniors and college undergraduates
Eligibility: Applicant must study horticulture or a related field and be a resident of Oregon or southwest Washington.

Each year ONF awards 16 different scholarships to students attending college in Oregon and southwest Washington. Most scholarships go to students of horticulture, but award amounts, specific majors, residency requirements, and other eligibility requirements vary by scholarship. Check the list of scholarships to find those awards for which you are best qualified. You can also print out a copy of the application in PDF format from the Web page.

Sidney B. Meadows Scholarship

Sponsor: Southern Nursery Association (SNA)
Web Site: http://www.sna.org/education/sbmsef-info.html
Amount of Scholarship: $2,500
Number of Awards: 12
Deadline: May 31
Education Level: college sophomores, juniors, and seniors and graduate students
Eligibility: Applicant must enroll as a full-time student in an accredited ornamental horticul-

ture academic program at a four-year college or university, have a minimum 2.25 undergraduate GPA or 3.0 graduate GPA, be a resident of one of the states included in the SNA, and be a U.S. citizen.

The Web page provides a lot of information about the origins of the scholarship program and its goals, which will help you in preparing the application materials. Click the Eligibility link at the top of the page to jump to the detailed eligibility requirements. Note that applicants must be residents of one of the 16 states listed, although they don't have to attend school in one of those states. If you would like to apply, download a PDF version of the application form linked to the Web page, send an e-mail request to receive the application in the mail, or use the fax-on-demand service as described to get a faxed copy of the page.

Also see the following scholarships:

- FFGC Scholarships: Chapter 15, "Florida" section
- Garden Club of Georgia Scholarships: Chapter 15, "Georgia" section
- North Carolina Tomato Growers Scholarship: Chapter 15, "North Carolina" section

Hotel and Restaurant Management

AHF Scholarships

Sponsor: American Hotel Foundation (AHF)
Web Site: http://www.ei-ahma.org/ahf/scholarships3.htm
Amount of Scholarship: $500 to $5,000
Number of Awards: not given
Deadline: varies
Education Level: college undergraduates
Eligibility: Applicant must major in hospitality management.

This page describes five different scholarships given out by AHF. Read the brief descriptions to determine which scholarships you would like to compete for. The Arthur J. Packard Memorial Scholarship and the Ecolab Scholarship are open competitions for all hospitality management students. The Hyatt Hotels Fund for Minority Lodging Management Students Scholarship is restricted to minority applicants. The Rama Scholarship for the American Dream is limited to the 14 hospitality management schools listed on the page. The American Express Scholarship goes to employees of American Hotel and Motel Association members and their dependents. At the bottom of the page you will find contact information where you can request applications for any of the scholarships.

NSMH Scholarships

Sponsor: National Society of Minorities in Hospitality (NSMH)
Web Site: http://www.nsmh.org/scholarships.html
Amount of Scholarship: not given
Number of Awards: 10
Deadline: December 11
Education Level: college undergraduates
Eligibility: Applicant must enroll in a hospitality management degree program and be a member of a minority group.

This page briefly describes the program, which awards 10 scholarships to minority hospitality students, including details of application requirements and selection criteria. Contact your local chapter of NSMH or the address listed at the bottom of the page to receive more information and an application form.

Oklahoma Restaurant Association Scholarship

Sponsor: Oklahoma Restaurant Association
Web Site: http://www.okcareertech.org/mkted/ora.htm

Amount of Scholarship: not given
Number of Awards: not given
Deadline: February 1
Education Level: college undergraduates
Eligibility: Applicant must study restaurant management at Oklahoma State University, Stillwater, or Oklahoma State University, Okmulgee.

This page describes the purpose of the scholarship and the qualities the sponsor is looking for in a successful applicant. It also provides application instructions and tells you where you can get an application form (one is not available on the Web site).

Roundtable for Women in Foodservice Scholarship

Sponsor: Roundtable for Women in Foodservice (RWF)
Web Site: http://www.rwf.org/scholarship_application.shtml
Amount of Scholarship: not given
Number of Awards: not given
Deadline: not given
Education Level: college undergraduates
Eligibility: Applicant must enroll in a culinary arts, food service, food science and nutrition, hospitality, or hotel and restaurant management program in an RWF-approved college; have completed at least one semester of college coursework; and have a minimum 3.0 GPA.

This scholarship goes to students who want to pursue a career in food service or a related field. The eligibility requirements describe what you have to submit in your application package and the other conditions of the award. Note that you must attend an RWF-approved school to be eligible; the school eligibility requirements are listed directly underneath the applicant eligibility requirements. Contact information is given at the top of the page if you have any remaining questions about whether you are eligible. To apply, you must submit both the Application Cover Page and the Application Form. Both can be submitted online, but you will have to mail some documents, and you should include a printout of each form with them.

TH&MA Educational Foundation Scholarships

Sponsor: Texas Hotel & Motel Association (TH&MA)
Web Site: http://www.texaslodging.com/membersonly/ef/scholarship.phtml
Amount of Scholarship: $1,000
Number of Awards: 6
Deadline: not given
Education Level: high school seniors, college undergraduates, and graduate students
Eligibility: Applicant must enroll in a hospitality degree program at a two-year or four-year college or university in Texas and have a minimum 3.0 GPA.

Six scholarships are available for all educational levels under this program. The one with the most strict eligibility requirements is the Texas High Schools for Hospitality Scholarships, which goes to high school seniors who have completed a Texas High Schools for Hospitality program. To get an application form for your educational level, call the phone number or send a message to the e-mail address listed just beneath the scholarship descriptions. The rest of the page describes travel and tourism scholarships sponsored by other organizations, some of which you may also be interested in applying for.

Also see the following scholarships:

- BILO John Rohaley Scholarship: Chapter 8, "Work" section
- Undergraduate Merit Scholarship for College Students: Chapter 8, "Work" section
- Undergraduate Merit Scholarship for High School Seniors: Chapter 8, "Work" section

International Studies

Institute for International Public Policy Student Award

Sponsor: Institute for International Public Policy, United Negro College Fund, Woodrow Wilson National Fellowship Foundation, Hispanic Association of Colleges and Universities, American Indian Higher Education Consortium, and Association of Professional Schools of International Affairs
Web Site: http://www.woodrow.org/public-policy
Amount of Scholarship: not given
Number of Awards: not given
Deadline: not given
Education Level: college sophomores
Eligibility: Applicant must plan to pursue a career in international service, be a full-time student at a four-year college, have a minimum 3.2 GPA, and be a U.S. citizen or permanent resident.

This program enables students to pursue a degree in international affairs all the way through to the master's level in preparation for a career in international service. The goals of this prestigious scholarship program are listed at the top of the main Web page. Follow the links underneath to learn more about the program. Click the Description of Student Award link to learn more about the components of the program, including summer institutes, junior year abroad, undergraduate internships, and master's degree fellowship assistance. The Eligibility Requirements page lists the basic requirements for qualifying for the program. Minorities are particularly encouraged to apply and are given priority consideration, as described on the Selection Procedure page. The How to Apply link tells you how to obtain an application form and what items must be included in the application package.

Ronald H. Brown Service Fellowship

Sponsor: U.S. Department of Commerce and Woodrow Wilson National Fellowship Foundation
Web Site: http://www.woodrow.org/public-policy/ronbrown
Amount of Scholarship: full tuition (awarded for the last two years of college and the first year of graduate school)
Number of Awards: not given
Deadline: not given
Education Level: college sophomores
Eligibility: Applicant must commit to a career in the Commercial Foreign Service, have a minimum 3.0 GPA, and be a U.S. citizen.

This program is intended to bring academically talented students into careers in the Commercial Foreign Service, a trade promotion organization that operates around the world to support U.S. private sector interests abroad. Before you decide whether to apply, read the Description of the Commercial Foreign Service to determine if such a career is right for you. In addition to financial support, fellows attend summer institutes in public policy and international affairs, work at the Department of Commerce before graduate school, and enter a mentoring relationship with a professional in the field. In return, fellows must agree to serve a minimum of four and a half years in the Commercial Foreign Service. The How to Apply page lists the required components of the application package. If you want to apply, you must request an application by writing to the postal address or e-mail address given.

U.S. Department of State Foreign Affairs Fellowship

Sponsor: U.S. Department of State and Woodrow Wilson National Fellowship Foundation

Web Site: http://www.woodrow.org/public-policy/faf
Amount of Scholarship: full tuition (awarded for three years)
Number of Awards: not given
Deadline: February 18
Education Level: college sophomores
Eligibility: Applicant must plan to pursue a graduate degree in international studies, have a minimum 3.2 GPA, and be a U.S. citizen.

The top of the page describes the goals of this prestigious fellowship, which funds the junior and senior years of college and the first year of graduate study. This program prepares students for a career in the U.S. Foreign Service, which is described on the Description of the Foreign Service page; this page also provides more details about the goals of the fellowship program and the qualities of successful applicants. Follow the Description of the Award link to learn more about the benefits of the fellowship and the service commitment that recipients must make. The Eligibility Requirements page lists the most basic qualifications that applications have to have. Note that minorities and women are particularly encouraged to apply. Students with financial need are given priority consideration, as described on the Selection Criteria section of the site. Finally, go to the How to Apply page to request an application package using an electronic form.

Journalism

Joel Garcia Memorial Scholarship

Sponsor: California Chicano New Media Association
Web Site: http://www.ccnma.org/scholarship-info.htm
Amount of Scholarship: $500 to $2,000

Number of Awards: not given
Deadline: April 7
Education Level: high school seniors and college undergraduates
Eligibility: Applicant must plan to pursue a career in journalism, be a full-time student, be a California resident or attend college in California, and be Hispanic.

The brief description at the top of the Web page tells you about the history of this scholarship program and the criteria used to select scholarship winners. Eligibility criteria are also listed. Follow the link at the bottom of the page to find a text version of the application form that you can print. Be sure to submit all of the additional materials requested exactly as instructed.

NGLTF Messenger-Anderson Journalism Scholarship

Sponsor: National Gay and Lesbian Task Force (NGLTF)
Web Site: http://www.ngltf.org/about/messenger.htm
Amount of Scholarship: $10,000 (awarded over three years)
Number of Awards: 4
Deadline: February 15
Education Level: high school seniors and college undergraduates
Eligibility: Applicant must enroll in a Bachelor of Arts program in journalism at an accredited four-year college; be a self-identified lesbian, gay, bisexual, or transsexual; be a student member of NGLTF; and have a minimum 2.5 GPA.

This page describes the goals of this scholarship program, which will help you prepare a competitive application. It also briefly describes the internship that comes with the scholarship. Click the Guidelines link to get more details about the goals of the scholarship program, how the scholarship money is awarded, eligibility requirements, and materials that must be included in the application package. Link to a PDF version of the scholarship application at the bottom of the page. You can join NGLTF by clicking the link under Eligibility, or you can submit your membership application and dues with your scholarship application.

NPC Scholarship

Sponsor: National Press Club (NPC)
Web Site: http://npc.press.org/what/scholar.htm
Amount of Scholarship: $20,000 (awarded over four years)
Number of Awards: 1
Deadline: March 1
Education Level: high school seniors
Eligibility: Applicant must plan to pursue a career in journalism, have a minimum 2.75 GPA, and be a member of a minority group.

The top of the page briefly outlines this scholarship for minorities who want to study journalism. Scroll down to How to Qualify to find eligibility requirements and a list of items that must be submitted with your application. Click the link at the bottom of the page to open the application form, which you can fill out inside your Web browser and then print out for mailing.

RTNDF Scholarships

Sponsor: Radio and Television News Directors Foundation (RTNDF)
Web Site: http://www.rtndf.org/asfi/scholarships/application.html
Amount of Scholarship: $1,000 to $10,000
Number of Awards: not given
Deadline: May 1
Education Level: college sophomores and juniors

Eligibility: Applicant must plan to pursue a career in broadcast journalism and be a full-time student.

This page describes all of the scholarships and professional awards available from RTNDF, as well as internship opportunities for students. Follow the links at the top of the page to find more detailed information about the different awards. The RTNDF Scholarships link lists the 16 scholarships available to undergraduates, including a brief description of each award and its specific eligibility requirements. Note that many awards are restricted to minority students, and one scholarship—the George Foreman Scholarship—is limited to University of Texas at Austin students. You can only apply for one scholarship, so choose the one that you are best qualified for. Beneath the list, you can link to a PDF version of the application form. Click the FAQ link at the top of the page to find answers to additional questions about the scholarship program.

Vaughan/NAHWW Scholarship

Sponsor: Vaughan and Bushnell Manufacturing and National Association of Home Workshop Writers (NAHWW)
Web Site: http://www.hammernet.com/scholar.htm
Amount of Scholarship: $1,500
Number of Awards: 1
Deadline: June 1
Education Level: college undergraduates and graduate students
Eligibility: Applicant must intend to pursue a career in "do-it-yourself" journalism or a related technical writing field.

This page gives the bare details for this scholarship, including eligibility requirements and instructions for requesting an application form by mail. Note that all applicants must be sponsored by a member of NAHWW; a member list is sent to you along with the application.

Also see the following scholarships:

- AWC-DC Scholarship: Chapter 12, "Female" section
- Jessica Savitch Scholarship: Chapter 6, "Communications" section
- Leonard M. Perryman Communications Scholarship: Chapter 6, "Communications" section
- National Ad 2 Scholarship Challenge: Chapter 6, "Advertising, Marketing, and Public Relations" section
- NCAA Scholarships: Chapter 8, "Athletics" section
- Roberta Thumin Scholarship: Chapter 6, "Communications" section

Labor Studies

See the following scholarship:

- Robert G. Porter Scholarship: Chapter 14, "Unions and Professional Associations" section

Landscape Architecture and Design

See the following scholarships:

- FFGC Scholarships: Chapter 15, "Florida" section
- Garden Club of Georgia Scholarships: Chapter 15, "Georgia" section
- National Council of State Garden Clubs Scholarship: Chapter 6, "Horticulture" section

- New York State Regents Professional Opportunity Scholarship: Chapter 15, "New York" section

Logistics

Logistics Scholarship

Sponsor: International Society of Logistics (SOLE) and Logistics Education Foundation
Web Site: http://www.sole.org/lef.asp
Amount of Scholarship: $1,000
Number of Awards: not given
Deadline: April 15
Education Level: college undergraduates and graduate students
Eligibility: Applicant must enroll as a full-time student in a logistics-related program.

The scholarship program is described in the right-hand column of the Web page. There you will find an overview of the qualifications the scholarship sponsors are looking for in successful applicants and learn how to prepare an application package. You can also download a Microsoft Word version of the application form.

Marine Science

SEASPACE Scholarship

Sponsor: SEASPACE, Inc.
Web Site: http://www.seaspace.org/schship.htm
Amount of Scholarship: not given
Number of Awards: not given
Deadline: February 1
Education Level: college sophomores, juniors, and seniors and graduate students

Eligibility: Applicant must major in a marine science-related field, be a full-time student at a U.S. college or university, have a minimum 3.3 GPA, and demonstrate financial need.

This page describes the SEASPACE scholarship, which goes to students of marine biology, fisheries and wildlife, environmental toxicology, biological oceanography, ocean engineering, genetics, aquaculture, marine mammal zoology, and other marine science-related fields. Note that the bulk of the awards under this program are intended for graduate students. Read the introductory scholarship information to learn what qualifications you must have to be eligible to apply and what fields are eligible for study under the award. Download the application form and instructions in PDF format by following the appropriate link. You can also link to a list of past winners to see if you fit the profile of a qualified applicant. Go to the SEASPACE home page to learn more about the scholarship's sponsor.

Also see the following scholarships:

- AMS Scholarships: Chapter 6, "Atmospheric Sciences" section
- FFGC Scholarships: Chapter 15, "Florida" section
- Rockefeller State Wildlife Scholarship: Chapter 15, "Louisiana" section

Massage Therapy

See the following scholarship:

- New York State Regents Professional Opportunity Scholarship: Chapter 15, "New York" section

Materials Science and Metallurgy

ASM International Foundation Undergraduate Scholarships

Sponsor: ASM International Foundation
Web Site: http://www.asm-intl.org/ Foundation/eligib.htm
Amount of Scholarship: $500 to $10,000
Number of Awards: 34
Deadline: May 1
Education Level: college sophomores and juniors
Eligibility: Applicant must major in materials science engineering or metallurgy and be a student member of ASM International.

This page provides information about the six different scholarships awarded by ASM International. Most of them have no specific eligibility requirements other than those described above. You will also find instructions for applying for the different awards and a link to the PDF scholarship application. Learn about ASM International's National Merit Scholarship by following the link on the left side of the page; only high school students who score well enough on the PSAT to become National Merit Semifinalists are considered for this award. To learn how to become a student member of ASM International, follow the link to ASM Home on the left side of the page, and then click How to Join ASM. There you will find a page called ASM and Students, which tells you everything you need to know.

FEF Scholarships

Sponsor: Foundry Educational Foundation (FEF)
Web Site: http://www.fefoffice.org/ overview.html
Amount of Scholarship: $500 to $1,500

Number of Awards: not given
Deadline: varies
Education Level: college undergraduates and graduate students
Eligibility: Applicant must take at least one class related to cast metal technology and be a full-time student at a participating college.

The overview of this scholarship program tells you a little about the goals and how to qualify. Click the Student Standards link to learn more about the general eligibility requirements and selection criteria. To read about the named scholarships that are available, each with their own eligibility requirements and application deadlines, click the Special Scholarships link; most of these awards have residency requirements that will narrow the field of competition. The Deadlines page summarizes the application deadlines for all scholarships. You can find out at which schools the scholarships can be used by clicking the List of Schools link; underneath each school is the name of the FEF Key Professor there, who selects scholarship recipients and can tell you about other awards that may be available through this program. To register with FEF, follow the To Register link; you must register in order to be eligible to apply for scholarships. Fill out and submit the Interest Response Form to indicate the scholarship for which you would like to be considered; you can only apply for one special scholarship.

TMS Outstanding Student Papers Contest

Sponsor: The Minerals, Metals, & Materials Society (TMS)
Web Site: http://www.tms.org/Students/AwardsPrograms/PaperContests.html
Amount of Scholarship: $500 to $1,000
Number of Awards: 4
Deadline: May 1
Education Level: college undergraduates and graduate students

Eligibility: Applicant must be a student member of TMS.

This contest awards cash for the best undergraduate and graduate papers in the field of metallurgy and materials science. First prize in each division is $1,000 and second prize is $500. Be sure to read the contest details for your educational level to find out what topics you can submit papers on and other requirements. The Guidelines and Procedures section of the page describes how to format and submit your paper. You can also go ahead and apply for student membership by following the Student Member Application link at the very bottom of the page.

TMS Student Scholarships

Sponsor: The Minerals, Metals, & Materials Society (TMS)
Web Site: http://www.tms.org/Students/AwardsPrograms/Scholarships.html
Amount of Scholarship: $2,000 to $5,000
Number of Awards: 10
Deadline: May 1
Education Level: college undergraduates and graduate students
Eligibility: Applicant must enroll as a full-time student in a metallurgical or materials science engineering program and be a student member of TMS.

You can apply for up to three of the six different scholarships described on this Web page. The general selection criteria, eligibility requirements, and application procedures for all scholarships are listed at the top of the page. Download PDF versions of the Scholarship Application and Scholarship Recommendation forms by clicking the appropriate links at the bottom of the page. You can also submit a membership application online by following the Student Membership Application link at the bottom of the page.

Also see the following scholarships:

- New Economy Technology Scholarship: Chapter 15, "Pennsylvania" section
- NSBE Scholarships: Chapter 9, "African-American" section
- Xerox Technical Minority Scholarship: Chapter 9, "All Minorities" section

Mathematics

See the following scholarships:

- AFCEA General Emmett Paige Scholarship: Chapter 13, "All Branches" section
- AFCEA General John A. Wickham Scholarship: Chapter 6, "Sciences" section
- AFCEA ROTC Scholarship: Chapter 13, "All Branches" section
- AISES A. T. Anderson Memorial Scholarship: Chapter 9, "Native American" section
- Barry M. Goldwater Scholarship: Chapter 6, "Sciences" section
- Dr. Vicki L. Schechtman Scholarship: Chapter 12, "Female" section
- Maryland Science and Technology Scholarship: Chapter 15, "Maryland" section
- New Economy Technology Scholarship: Chapter 15, "Pennsylvania" section
- NSBE Scholarships: Chapter 9, "African-American" section
- NTA Science Scholarship Award: Chapter 9, "All Minorities" section
- San Diego County Scholarship: Chapter 15, "California" section
- State Farm Companies Foundation Exceptional Student Fellowship: Chapter 6, "Business" section
- Virginia BPW Foundation Scholarships: Chapter 15, "Virginia"
- Wendell Milliman Scholarship: Chapter 14, "Employer and Profession" section

Music

AMCA Music Scholarships

Sponsor: Associated Male Choruses of America, Inc. (AMCA)
Web Site: http://www.tc.umn.edu/nlhome/m042/thoma075/scholar.html
Amount of Scholarship: $500
Number of Awards: 6
Deadline: March 1
Education Level: college undergraduates
Eligibility: Applicant must major in music, be sponsored by a chorus that is a member of AMCA, and be a full-time student at a four-year college.

All of the scholarship information is published on the same Web page—just keep scrolling down to find it. Under Process, you will find a list of detailed steps that you should follow to apply for a scholarship. Under Application Form/Blank, you can request an application form be sent to you through the mail or open a printable version of the application. The Sponsorship section describes how to locate an AMCA-member chorus to sponsor your application and provides several links to information that will help you with this process. The For Choruses section of the page describes how sponsoring choruses can assist in the application process. The Frequently Asked Questions section lists the eligibility requirements and answers other questions about the scholarship program. Note that this section recommends that you highlight your vocal and choral interests, as these applicants are given preference.

Montana Bandmasters Association Scholarship

Sponsor: Montana Bandmasters Association
Web Site: http://www.3rivers.net/medriver/mba/index.htm

Amount of Scholarship: $100 to $250
Number of Awards: 2
Deadline: May 1
Education Level: high school seniors and college juniors
Eligibility: Applicant must major in music education specializing in a wind or percussion instrument at a Montana college, be nominated by a band director who is a member of the Montana Bandmasters Association, and have a grade average of at least a B.

This page briefly describes the scholarship program, but it does not tell you much. To learn more, click the link to the application form for your educational level. The application pages describe the eligibility requirements in more detail and tell you what additional materials you must submit, as well as providing links to printable scholarship applications.

Also see the following scholarships:

- "Duke" Demay Jazz Scholarship: Chapter 8, "Performing Arts" section
- Madison Jazz Society Scholarship: Chapter 8, "Performing Arts" section

Native American Studies

See the following scholarship:

- Morris K. Udall Foundation Undergraduate Scholarship: Chapter 6, "Environmental Studies" section

Norwegian Studies

King Olav V Norwegian American Heritage Scholarship

Sponsor: Sons of Norway Foundation
Web Site: http://www.sofn.com

Amount of Scholarship: $250 to $3,000
Number of Awards: not given
Deadline: March 1
Education Level: college undergraduates
Eligibility: Applicant must demonstrate an interest in Norwegian studies, be over 18 years old, and be a U.S. citizen (or be a Norwegian interested in studying American heritage).

To find information about this scholarship, click the Foundation link, then click the Scholarships and Grants link. There you will find a link to the application form in PDF format, which describes the scholarship in more detail, including the selection criteria.

Nursing

AORN Foundation Scholarship

Sponsor: Association of Perioperative Registered Nurses (AORN) Foundation
Web Site: http://www.aorn.org/foundation/scholapp.htm
Amount of Scholarship: $500 to $2,000
Number of Awards: not given
Deadline: April 1
Education Level: college undergraduates and graduate students
Eligibility: Applicant must enroll in a nursing degree program, be a Registered Nurse, and be a member of AORN.

At the top of the page you will find a link to the scholarship application in PDF format. Beneath that is detailed information about how to apply, including eligibility requirements, a list of documents that you must submit, and other conditions. Be sure to follow these instructions exactly, or your application will not be considered. To learn how to become a member of AORN, click About Us in the banner at the top of the page, and explore the links under AORN Membership.

KBOR Nursing Scholarship

Sponsor: Kansas Board of Regents (KBOR)
Web Site: http://www.kansasregents.org/academic_affairs/financial/nursing.html
Amount of Scholarship: $2,500 to $3,500 per year (renewable)
Number of Awards: not given
Deadline: May 15
Education Level: college undergraduates
Eligibility: Applicant must enroll in a nursing program at a Kansas college.

Read the first paragraph describing this service scholarship carefully. If you win a scholarship, you must commit to working as a nurse at a specific location in Kansas, and you must locate a sponsor to provide partial scholarship funding and employment after graduation. If you are willing to abide by those conditions, scroll through the rest of the page to learn more about the program, including eligibility requirements, scholarship obligations, and application instructions. To apply, obtain all the forms listed in the Recipients section of the page from your guidance counselor or your college's financial aid office.

Maryland State Nursing Scholarship and Living Expenses Grant

Sponsor: Maryland Higher Education Commission and Maryland State Scholarship Administration
Web Site: http://www.mhec.state.md.us/SSA/introduction.htm
Amount of Scholarship: $2,400 (renewable for up to three years)
Number of Awards: not given
Deadline: June 30
Education Level: high school seniors and college undergraduates
Eligibility: Applicant must enroll in a nursing program at a Maryland college, have a minimum 3.0 GPA, and be a Maryland resident.

To find information about this scholarship, click the Program Description link in the left frame, then click State Nursing Scholarship and Living Expenses Grant. This service scholarship requires one year of employment as a nurse in Maryland for every year that you receive assistance. If you have financial need, you can apply for a Living Expenses Grant for an additional $2,400 beyond the amount of the scholarship awarded. Follow the steps under How Do I Apply? to apply for this grant. Click the Online Applications link in the left frame to find contact information for the State Scholarship Administration, from which you can order application forms; no actual applications are available on the Web site as of this writing, though.

North Carolina Nurse Scholars

Sponsor: North Carolina Nurse Scholars Commission
Web Site: http://www.ncseaa.edu/nsp.html
Amount of Scholarship: $3,000 to $5,000 per year (awarded for two to four years)
Number of Awards: not given
Deadline: February 15
Education Level: high school seniors and college undergraduates
Eligibility: Applicant must enroll as a full-time student in a two-year or four-year nursing program at a North Carolina college, have a minimum 3.0 GPA, be a North Carolina resident, and be a U.S. citizen.

This is a service scholarship with some complicated conditions. First, read the list under Who Is Eligible? at the top of the left column to make certain that you qualify. The rest of the page describes the service conditions that you must commit to if you accept a scholarship, how the awards are given out, and how they can be renewed. Look under How Do I Apply? for application instructions. Follow the Apply Here link to find Word versions of the application forms and instructions that you can download.

Scott & White Nursing Scholarships

Sponsor: Scott & White Memorial Hospital
Web Site: http://www.sw.org/nursing/scholar.htm
Amount of Scholarship: $1,000 to full tuition
Number of Awards: not given
Deadline: April 15
Education Level: high school seniors, college undergraduates, and graduate students
Eligibility: Applicant must enroll in a nursing program at a participating college in central Texas.

This page describes the 15 scholarships available for all levels of nursing study under this one program. Find the kind of nursing degree that you want to pursue, and read about the scholarships available at that educational level. Most scholarships require employment at Scott & White Memorial Hospital after graduation, or they are only available to current employees and their dependents, and they are all limited to the central Texas colleges listed on the main page. Make sure that you meet all of the eligibility requirements and conditions for the scholarships for which you want to apply.

State Student Assistance Commission of Indiana Nursing Scholarship

Sponsor: State Student Assistance Commission of Indiana
Web Site: http://www.ai.org/ssaci/nur.html
Amount of Scholarship: not given
Number of Awards: not given
Deadline: not given
Education Level: college undergraduates
Eligibility: Applicant must enroll in a nursing program at an Indiana college, have a minimum 2.0 GPA, demonstrate financial need, and be an Indiana resident.

This is a service scholarship that requires students to work as a nurse in Indiana for at least two years after graduation. The conditions of accepting the scholarship are described with the other eligibility requirements on the scholarship's Web page. Contact the mailing address at the bottom of the page or your school's financial aid office to obtain an application.

Also see the following scholarships:

- Army ROTC Nurse Scholarships: Chapter 13, "Army and Army ROTC" section
- Four-Year Navy Nurse Scholarship: Chapter 13, "Navy ROTC" section
- Hays Medical Center Scholarships: Chapter 6, "Health Care" section
- Health Professional Scholarship: Chapter 6, "Health Care" section
- Indian Health Service Scholarship: Chapter 9, "Native American" section
- National Health Service Corps Scholarship: Chapter 7, "Medicine" section
- New York State Primary Care Service Corps Scholarship: Chapter 15, "New York" section
- New York State Regents Professional Opportunity Scholarship: Chapter 15, "New York" section
- Nurses, Physical Therapists, and Respiratory Therapists Scholarship: Chapter 14, "Military Personnel and Veterans" section
- Professional School Scholarship: Chapter 15, "Maryland" section

Occupational Health and Safety

KSHN Educational Scholarships

Sponsor: Kentucky Safety and Health Network (KSHN) Foundation, Inc.
Web Site: http://www.kshn.org/education/education.html
Amount of Scholarship: not given
Number of Awards: not given
Deadline: March 1
Education Level: college undergraduates and graduate students
Eligibility: Applicant must major in occupational health and safety or industrial hygiene and either attend a Kentucky college or be a Kentucky resident attending college out-of-state.

This page provides an overview of the scholarship program and outlines the eligibility requirements. Application forms are not available online but can be obtained by contacting either the phone number or e-mail address listed at the bottom of the page.

Occupational and Physical Therapy

AMBUCS Scholarships

Sponsor: AMBUCS, Inc.
Web Site: http://www.ambucs.com/scholarships.htm
Amount of Scholarship: $500 to $6,000
Number of Awards: not given
Deadline: May 15
Education Level: college sophomores, juniors, and seniors and graduate students

Eligibility: Applicant must enroll in an accredited occupational therapy, physical therapy, speech language pathology, or hearing audiology program; demonstrate financial need; and be a U.S. citizen.

This scholarship program awards a variety of scholarships to therapy students. Most awards are between $500 and $1,500, but one two-year award of $6,000 is also available. The Web page describes the types of awards, their eligibility requirements, and how to apply for all of them. You can only apply for these scholarships online; paper applications are not accepted. Follow the link at the bottom of the page to access the electronic application.

AOTF Scholarships

Sponsor: American Occupational Therapy Foundation (AOTF)
Web Site: http://www.aotf.org/html/scholarships.html
Amount of Scholarship: $150 to $2,000
Number of Awards: 71
Deadline: January 15
Education Level: college undergraduates and graduate students
Eligibility: Applicant must enroll as a full-time student in an accredited occupational therapy program, be a member of the American Occupation Therapy Association (AOTA), and demonstrate financial need.

Forty-three scholarships are available under this program. First, follow the General Information and Eligibility Requirements link to make certain that you meet the basic eligibility requirements for scholarships awarded at your educational level. The Available Awards page describes all of the scholarships, along with each award's specific eligibility requirements, if there are any. This includes a full list of state-specific scholarships sponsored through AOTF. There is also a list of scholarships for occupational therapy students sponsored by other organizations. To get more information about the AOTF scholarship program, click the Contact Us button in the top right corner of the page and contact the appropriate phone number, mailing address, or e-mail address given. No application forms are available online.

Maryland Physical and Occupational Therapists and Assistants Grant

Sponsor: Maryland Higher Education Commission and Maryland State Scholarship Administration
Web Site: http://www.mhec.state.md.us/SSA/introduction.htm
Amount of Scholarship: $2,000 (renewable for up to three years)
Number of Awards: not given
Deadline: July 1
Education Level: high school seniors and college undergraduates
Eligibility: Applicant must enroll as a full-time student in a physical therapist, physical therapist assistant, occupational therapist, or occupational therapist assistant program at a Maryland college; and be a Maryland resident.

To find information about this scholarship, click the Program Description link in the left frame, then click the link to the scholarship's name. This is a service scholarship that requires one year of employment in Maryland for every year that you receive assistance. You must submit the application form listed under How Do I Apply? to apply for this grant. Click the Online Applications link in the left frame to find contact information for the State Scholarship Administration, from which you can order application materials; no actual application forms are on the Web as of this writing, though.

NTRS Edith Ball Scholarship

Sponsor: National Therapeutic Recreation Society (NTRS)
Web Site: http://www.nrpa.org/branches/ntrs/edith.htm
Amount of Scholarship: $500
Number of Awards: 1
Deadline: August 15
Education Level: college sophomores and juniors
Eligibility: Applicant must major in an accredited therapeutic recreation program, be a student member of NTRS, have a minimum 3.5 GPA in major coursework, have a minimum 3.3 GPA overall, and be a full-time student.

This page provides an overview of the scholarship, details the eligibility criteria, and lists the documents that should be included in the application package. To find out more about NTRS and locate an online membership application, follow the link to the NTRS Home Page at the very bottom of the page.

Also see the following scholarships:

- Minority Teacher/Special Education Scholarship: Chapter 6, "Education" section
- Indian Health Service Scholarship: Chapter 9, "Native American" section
- New York State Regents Professional Opportunity Scholarship: Chapter 15, "New York" section
- Nurses, Physical Therapists, and Respiratory Therapists Scholarship: Chapter 14, "Military Personnel and Veterans" section

Ophthalmic Dispensing

See the following scholarship:

- New York State Regents Professional Opportunity Scholarship: Chapter 15, "New York" section

Optics

Michael Kidger Memorial Scholarship

Sponsor: Kidger Optics
Web Site: http://www.kidger.com/mjkms.html
Amount of Scholarship: $4,000
Number of Awards: 1
Deadline: May 1
Education Level: college undergraduates
Eligibility: Applicant must enroll in an optical design program.

Read the selection criteria for this scholarship to determine if you are eligible to apply and to find out what application materials you must submit. Be sure to follow the guidelines for the letter of recommendation also given on this page. Click the Application Form link to open a copy of the application that you can print from your Web browser.

Raymond Davis Scholarship

Sponsor: Society for Imaging Science
Web Site: http://207.199.130.150/resources/education/scholarship/rdavisscholarship.cfm
Amount of Scholarship: not given
Number of Awards: not given
Deadline: December 15
Education Level: college sophomores, juniors, and seniors and graduate students
Eligibility: Applicant must study imaging or photographic science or engineering and be a full-time student at an accredited college or university.

This page very briefly describes the eligibility requirements for this scholarship. You can also download the application form in PDF format from the page.

SPIE Scholarships

Sponsor: International Society for Optical Engineering (SPIE)
Web Site: http://www.spie.org/web/courses/schol.html
Amount of Scholarship: not given
Number of Awards: not given
Deadline: March 31
Education Level: high school seniors, undergraduate students, and graduate students
Eligibility: Applicant must pursue a course of study in optics, optical engineering, or optical science.

This page describes the goals of the SPIE scholarship program and describes all of the available awards. Look under Student Scholarships for general eligibility requirements, selection criteria, and application guidelines. You can also link to the application form in PDF format. If you keep scrolling down the page, you will find a list of special scholarships that you may qualify for. You must mark the appropriate box on the application form if you choose to apply for any of these. You will automatically be considered for all other available scholarships when you submit your application.

Pharmacy and Pharmacology

See the following scholarships:

- Indian Health Service Scholarship: Chapter 9, "Native American" section
- National Pathfinder Scholarship: Chapter 12, "Female" section
- New Economy Technology Scholarship: Chapter 15, "Pennsylvania" section
- New York State Regents Professional Opportunity Scholarship: Chapter 15, "New York" section

- Professional School Scholarship: Chapter 15, "Maryland" section

- New York State Primary Care Service Corps Scholarship: Chapter 15, "New York" section

Physician Assistant

Physician Assistant Foundation Annual Scholarships

Sponsor: American Academy of Physician Assistants (AAPA) and Physician Assistant Foundation
Web Site: http://www.aapa.org/pafprog.html#ASP
Amount of Scholarship: $2,000 to $18,000
Number of Awards: not given
Deadline: February 1
Education Level: college undergraduates and graduate students
Eligibility: Applicant must enroll in an accredited physician assistant program in the professional phase of training and be a student member of AAPA.

The scholarship section of this Web page briefly describes the eligibility requirements, selection criteria, and available awards. Eight different scholarships are available, but only the award amounts differ; the eligibility requirements are the same for all of them. Download and print the application form in PDF format by following the Applications link. To learn more about joining AAPA, follow the Student Members link. You can also apply for student membership by completing the appropriate section of the application and enclosing your dues with the form.

Also see the following scholarships:

- Indian Health Service Scholarship: Chapter 9, "Native American" section
- National Health Service Corps Scholarship: Chapter 7, "Medicine" section

Physics

SPS Scholarships

Sponsor: Society of Physics Students (SPS)
Web Site: http://www.aip.org/education/sps/scholars.htm
Amount of Scholarship: $1,000 to $4,000
Number of Awards: 3
Deadline: February 15
Education Level: college juniors
Eligibility: Applicant must be a member of SPS and be a full-time student.

This page describes the purpose of the scholarship program, the kinds of awards available, and the selection criteria. Three awards are given out under this program: one for $1,000, one for $2,000, and one for $4,000. The Web page also tells you how to get application forms and how to put together an application package. Use the checklist at the bottom of the page to make certain that your application package is complete. To find an SPS membership application that you can submit right away, go to the SPS Home Page and follow the Membership link.

Also see the following scholarships:

- AFCEA General Emmett Paige Scholarship: Chapter 13, "All Branches" section
- AFCEA General John A. Wickham Scholarship: Chapter 6, "Sciences" section
- AFCEA ROTC Scholarship: Chapter 13, "All Branches" section
- Dr. Vicki L. Schechtman Scholarship: Chapter 12, "Female" section

- Nancy Lorraine Jensen Memorial Scholarship: Chapter 14, "Clubs and Community Organizations" section
- New Economy Technology Scholarship: Chapter 15, "Pennsylvania" section
- NSBE Scholarships: Chapter 9, "African-American" section
- SEG Foundation Scholarships: Chapter 6, "Geosciences" section
- Xerox Technical Minority Scholarship: Chapter 9, "All Minorities" section

Political Science

See the following scholarships:

- Betty Rendel Scholarship: Chapter 12, "Female" section
- Jerry Clark Memorial Scholarship: Chapter 14, "Unions and Professional Associations" section
- Minorities in Government Finance Scholarship: Chapter 9, "All Minorities" section

Project Management

AACE International Scholarship

Sponsor: Association for the Advancement of Cost Engineering (AACE)
Web Site: http://www.aacei.org/newdesign/education/scholarship.html
Amount of Scholarship: $750 to $3,000
Number of Awards: not given
Deadline: November 8
Education Level: college sophomores, juniors, and seniors and graduate students
Eligibility: Applicant must enroll as a full-time student in a degree program related to total

cost management at an accredited U.S. or Canadian college or university.

The introduction to the scholarship describes what total cost management is and what the applicable fields of study are. The rest of the page lists the award amounts, eligibility requirements, and selection criteria. Download an application in PDF format by following the link at the bottom of the page.

Robert J. Yourzak Scholarship Award

Sponsor: Project Management Institute (PMI) Educational Foundation
Web Site: http://www.pmi.org/pmief/rjys.htm
Amount of Scholarship: $2,000
Number of Awards: not given
Deadline: February 15
Education Level: college undergraduates and graduate students
Eligibility: Applicant must enroll a degree program in project management or a related field.

To get more information about this scholarship other than the brief overview on the main page, follow the General Information link. This page describes the selection criteria and required parts of the application package and provides a link to the application form. You should also follow the link to the PMI Educational Foundation Home Page to learn more about the mission and goals of the scholarship's sponsor.

Wilson-Zells Academic Grant

Sponsor: Project Management Institute (PMI) Educational Foundation
Web Site: http://www.pmi.org/pmief/w-zs.htm
Amount of Scholarship: $2,000
Number of Awards: not given
Deadline: February 15

Education Level: college undergraduates and graduate students
Eligibility: Applicant must enroll in a degree program in project management or a related field.

To get more information about this scholarship other than the brief overview on the main page, follow the General Information link. This page describes the selection criteria and required parts of the application package and provides a link to the application form. Also follow the link to the PMI Educational Foundation Home Page to learn more about the mission and goals of the scholarship's sponsor.

Psychology

See the following scholarships:

- Dr. Vicki L. Schechtman Scholarship: Chapter 12, "Female" section
- Hispanic College Fund Scholarship: Chapter 9, "Hispanic" section
- National Pathfinder Scholarship: Chapter 12, "Female" section
- Zeta Phi Beta Scholarships and Fellowships: Chapter 12, "Female" section

Real Estate

CAR Scholarships

Sponsor: California Association of Realtors (CAR)
Web Site: http://www.car.org/aboutus/scholarships/index.html
Amount of Scholarship: $1,000 to $2,000
Number of Awards: not given
Deadline: May 1
Education Level: college undergraduates

Eligibility: Applicant must study a real estate-related program at a two-year or four-year California college, have completed at least 12 units of college courses, be currently enrolled in a minimum of 6 units of college coursework, have a minimum 2.6 GPA, and be a California resident.

This short page describes the scholarship program and includes a list of acceptable real estate-related fields that applicants can study. $1,000 scholarships go to students at two-year colleges, and $2,000 scholarships go to students at four-year colleges. If you would like to apply, click the Application link to access a printable copy of the application form.

George M. Brooker Collegiate Scholarship for Minorities

Sponsor: Real Estate Management Foundation
Web Site: http://www.irem.org/foundation/brooker.htm
Amount of Scholarship: $1,000 to $2,500
Number of Awards: 3
Deadline: March 15
Education Level: college undergraduates and graduate students
Eligibility: Applicant must major in real estate or a related field, have completed two courses in real estate, have a minimum 3.0 GPA, be a member of a minority group, and be a U.S. citizen.

One graduate scholarship of $2,500 and two undergraduate scholarships of $1,000 each are available under this program. First, read the purpose of this scholarship program, so you can understand its goals and prepare a better application. Then check the requirements to make sure that you qualify. This section of the scholarship's Web page also tells you what items need to go in the application package. The Stipulations section details the conditions of the award. A printable copy of the application form is provided at the bottom of the page.

Oregon Realtors Scholarship

Sponsor: Oregon Realtors Scholarship Trust
Web Site: http://or.realtorplace.com/scholarship.htm
Amount of Scholarship: not given
Number of Awards: not given
Deadline: not given
Education Level: college undergraduates
Eligibility: Applicant must enroll in a real estate-related curriculum at an Oregon college.

This page very briefly describes the scholarship program and includes a list of real estate careers that applicants can pursue. An application form is not published online. Instead, contact the mailing address or toll-free phone number at the bottom of the page to order application materials.

Religious Studies

FTE Undergraduate Fellowship

Sponsor: Fund for Theological Education, Inc. (FTE)
Web Site: http://www.thefund.org/programs/fellowships/undergrad/index.html
Amount of Scholarship: $1,500
Number of Awards: not given
Deadline: not given
Education Level: college undergraduates
Eligibility: Applicant must be considering but undecided about ministry as a career, attend a North American college, and be a U.S. or Canadian citizen.

First, read the objectives and eligibility requirements of this fellowship program to determine if you would make a good applicant. The Benefits section of the Web page describes the

monetary and other benefits of becoming an FTE Fellow. If you would like to apply, contact the e-mail address given at the bottom of the page for further information about the program.

Also see the following scholarship:

• Homeland Ministries Scholarship: Chapter 11, "Christian Church (Disciples of Christ)" section

Respiratory Therapy

Jimmy A. Young Memorial Education Recognition Award

Sponsor: American Respiratory Care Foundation
Web Site: http://www.aarc.org/arcf/young.html
Amount of Scholarship: $1,000
Number of Awards: 1
Deadline: June 30
Education Level: college undergraduates
Eligibility: Applicant must enroll in an accredited respiratory care training program, have a minimum 3.0 GPA, and be a member of a minority group.

This page describes the scholarship program and lists the required documents that must be included in the application package. Note that preference is given to students nominated by a faculty member at their school, although you can apply without such a nomination. Follow the Return link at the bottom of the page to find a link to the printable application form. Be sure to check the name of the scholarship for which you are applying on the form.

Morton B. Duggan, Jr. Memorial Education Recognition Award

Sponsor: American Respiratory Care Foundation
Web Site: http://www.aarc.org/arcf/duggan.html
Amount of Scholarship: $1,000
Number of Awards: 1
Deadline: June 30
Education Level: college undergraduates
Eligibility: Applicant must enroll in an accredited respiratory care training program and have a minimum 3.0 GPA.

This page describes the scholarship program and lists the required documents that must be included in the application package. Note that preference is given to students from Georgia and South Carolina. Follow the Return link at the bottom of the page to open a page with a link to the printable application form. Be sure to check the name of the scholarship for which you are applying on the form.

NBRC/AMP Robert M. Lawrence, MD Memorial Education Recognition Award

Sponsor: American Respiratory Care Foundation, National Board for Respiratory Care (NBRC), and Applied Measurement Professionals, Inc. (AMP)
Web Site: http://www.aarc.org/arcf/lawrence.html
Amount of Scholarship: $2,500
Number of Awards: 1
Deadline: June 30
Education Level: college sophomores and juniors
Eligibility: Applicant must enroll in an accredited respiratory care bachelor's degree program and have a minimum 3.0 GPA.

This page describes the scholarship program and lists the required documents that must be included in the application package. Follow the Return link at the bottom of the page to find a link to the printable application form. Be sure to check the name of the scholarship for which you are applying on the form.

NBRC/AMP William W. Burgin, Jr., MD Education Recognition Award

Sponsor: American Respiratory Care Foundation, National Board for Respiratory Care (NBRC), and Applied Measurement Professionals, Inc. (AMP)
Web Site: http://www.aarc.org/arcf/burgin.html
Amount of Scholarship: $2,500
Number of Awards: 1
Deadline: June 30
Education Level: college freshmen
Eligibility: Applicant must enroll in an accredited respiratory care associate's degree program and have a minimum 3.0 GPA.

This page describes the scholarship program and lists the required documents that must be included in the application package. Follow the Return link at the bottom of the page to find a link to the printable application form. Be sure to check the name of the scholarship for which you are applying on the form.

Also see the following scholarships:

- Indian Health Service Scholarship: Chapter 9, "Native American" section
- Nurses, Physical Therapists, and Respiratory Therapists Scholarship: Chapter 14, "Military Personnel and Veterans" section

Retailing

RMA Scholarship

Sponsor: Retail Merchants Association (RMA) of Greater Richmond
Web Site: http://www.retailmerchants.com/services/other/scholarship.htm
Amount of Scholarship: $1,000
Number of Awards: not given
Deadline: not given
Education Level: high school seniors and college undergraduates
Eligibility: Applicant must plan to pursue a career in retailing, enroll in a two-year or four-year degree program, and be a resident of the metropolitan Richmond, Virginia, area.

This page briefly describes the scholarship, including who may apply and the criteria for selecting recipients. Contact the mailing address or phone number listed at the bottom of the Web page to order application materials.

Sciences

AFCEA General John A. Wickham Scholarship

Sponsor: Armed Forces Communications and Electronics Association (AFCEA) Educational Foundation
Web Site: http://www.afcea.org/awards/scholarships.htm#wickham
Amount of Scholarship: $2,000
Number of Awards: not given
Deadline: May 1
Education Level: college sophomores and juniors
Eligibility: Applicant must enroll in a degree program in aerospace engineering, computer science, computer engineering, electrical engineering, electronics, mathematics, or physics; be a full-time student at a four-year U.S. college; have a minimum 3.4 GPA; and be a U.S. citizen.

You won't find a lot of information about this scholarship on the Web page—just enough to determine if you qualify. If you do, you can either download the PDF application form or find out how to request an application directly from the sponsor. Be sure to check the box for the General John A. Wickham Scholarship at the top of the application form when you complete it; you are only allowed to apply for one AFCEA-sponsored scholarship.

Astronaut Scholarship

Sponsor: Astronaut Scholarship Foundation
Web Site: http://www.astronautscholarship.org
Amount of Scholarship: $8,500
Number of Awards: 17
Deadline: not given
Education Level: college juniors and seniors and graduate students
Eligibility: Applicant must major in an engineering or physical sciences program at a participating college or university, plan to pursue research after graduating, and be a U.S. citizen.

The Foundation Background and History and the Scholarship Program links lead to more general information about this scholarship program. Click the Scholarship Guidelines link at the very bottom of the page to find the eligibility requirements. This link also lists the participating universities. Note that you cannot apply directly for this scholarship; a faculty member at your school must nominate you (you can encourage a professor or advisor to visit the site and consider you for nomination, however). Explore the rest of the site to learn more about the activities that Astronaut Scholars participate in and the benefits they receive.

Barry M. Goldwater Scholarship

Sponsor: Barry M. Goldwater Scholarship and Excellence in Education Foundation
Web Site: http://www.act.org/goldwater
Amount of Scholarship: up to $7,500 (renewable for two years)
Number of Awards: 300
Deadline: February 1
Education Level: college sophomores and juniors
Eligibility: Applicant must plan to pursue a career in engineering, mathematics, or the natural sciences; be a full-time student at an accredited two-year or four-year college; have a grade average of at least a B; be ranked in the top 25 percent of the class; and be a U.S. citizen or permanent resident.

Follow the Bulletin of Information link to learn more about the scholarship program, including its purpose, eligibility requirements, nomination procedures, and selection criteria. Examples, but not a comprehensive list, of acceptable undergraduate majors and career objectives are also listed on this page. Note that you can't apply directly for this prestigious scholarship; your college must nominate you. To find the name of the scholarship contact at your college, click the Faculty Representatives link, click your state on the map, and then locate your college in the list. Nomination materials are also available at the Web site.

Also see the following scholarships:

- AISE Steel Foundation Scholarships: Chapter 14, "Unions and Professional Associations" section
- AISES A. T. Anderson Memorial Scholarship: Chapter 9, "Native American" section
- Burlington Northern Santa Fe Foundation Scholarship: Chapter 9, "Native American" section
- Development Fund for Black Students in Science and Technology Scholarship: Chapter 12, "African-American" section
- Dr. Vicki L. Schechtman Scholarship: Chapter 12, "Female" section
- Maryland Science and Technology Scholarship: Chapter 15, "Maryland" section
- New Economy Technology Scholarship: Chapter 15, "Pennsylvania" section
- NTA Science Scholarship Award: Chapter 9, "All Minorities" section
- San Diego County Scholarship: Chapter 15, "California" section
- SPE Foundation Scholarships: Chapter 6, "Engineering" section
- SPE GCS Scholarship: Chapter 6, "Engineering" section
- UNCF/Merck Undergraduate Science Research Scholarship Awards: Chapter 6, "Biology" section

Social Work

See the following scholarship:

- Indian Health Service Scholarship: Chapter 9, "Native American" section

Sociology

See the following scholarship:

- National Pathfinder Scholarship: Chapter 12, "Female" section

Space Sciences

ISGC Scholarships and Fellowships

Sponsor: Idaho Space Grant Consortium (ISGC)

Web Site: http://ivc.uidaho.edu/isgc/
fellow.html
Amount of Scholarship: $1,000 to $6,000
Number of Awards: not given
Deadline: March 1
Education Level: college undergraduates and
graduate students
Eligibility: Applicant must study an astronautics- or space sciences-related field at an ISGC member college or university, have a minimum 3.0 GPA, and be a U.S. citizen.

The goals of this program are outlined on the Web page. At the undergraduate level, the program recruits students interested in studying space sciences within the larger fields of math, science, education, and engineering by awarding $1,000 scholarships. Fellowships of $6,000 go to graduate students conducting research in the space or aerospace sciences. Women, minorities, and students with disabilities are encouraged to apply for all awards. To be eligible, you must attend an Idaho Space Grant Consortium member school, all of which are listed on the Web page. Click the appropriate Applications link to find detailed eligibility requirements for awards at your educational level, plus application instructions and a link to the scholarship application in Word format.

NASA/TSGC Undergraduate Scholarship

Sponsor: NASA/Texas Space Grant Consortium (TSGC)
Web Site: http://www.tsgc.utexas.edu/grants
Amount of Scholarship: $500
Number of Awards: not given
Deadline: March 10
Education Level: college sophomores and juniors
Eligibility: Applicant must demonstrate interest in space-related education and research, be a full-time student at a participating Texas college, and be a U.S. citizen.

This page provides details on the amount of the award and eligibility requirements. Note that underrepresented students are particularly encouraged to apply. Participating universities are listed at the bottom of the page, along with the faculty representative at each college whom you can contact if you have further questions. Follow the link to the application form to download a PDF copy of the application form. If you follow the link to the main grants page under Applications & Questions, you will find a list of past scholarship recipients and a link to the electronic eligibility verification form that you must submit if you receive a scholarship. You will also find links to pages that provide more information about TSGC and the participating universities.

Rocky Mountain NASA Space Grant Consortium Scholarships and Fellowships

Sponsor: Rocky Mountain NASA Space Grant Consortium
Web Site: http://www.rmc.sdl.usu.edu/rocky/
rm_grad.html
Amount of Scholarship: varies
Number of Awards: not given
Deadline: varies
Education Level: college undergraduates and graduate students
Eligibility: Applicant must enroll in a space-related program at a participating college or university.

The top half of this Web page briefly describes the graduate fellowship available under this program, including the names of participating universities and the required components of the application package. Click the name of each university to link to a page that describes the fields in the space sciences that you can study under the fellowship at that school, current projects that the Rocky Mountain NASA Space Grant Consortium is conducting there, and the name of the faculty representative whom you can contact with further questions. Click the Application Form link to open an application that you can fill out inside your Web browser and then print. If you are an undergraduate student, scroll down the page until you see the Undergraduate Scholarships section. This brief paragraph gives an overview of the scholarship and the items that you must submit with your application package, as well as an address you can contact for more information. Follow the Application From for Undergraduate Scholarships link to find an application that you can fill out inside your Web browser and then print with your responses.

USRA Scholarship

Sponsor: Universities Space Research Association (USRA)
Web Site: http://www.usra.edu/scholarships/overview.html
Amount of Scholarship: $500
Number of Awards: not given
Deadline: May 1
Education Level: college sophomores and juniors
Eligibility: Applicant must demonstrate an interest in space research or education, major in a field in the physical sciences or engineering, and be a U.S. citizen.

Read the Purpose, Eligibility, and Criteria sections of the scholarship's Web page to determine if you would make a good candidate for this award. Follow the instructions under Application Procedure to find out how to apply. PDF versions of the application and recommendation forms are linked to the bottom of the page.

Also see the following scholarships:

- Dr. Vicki L. Schechtman Scholarship: Chapter 12, "Female" section
- LaSPACE Undergraduate Student Scholarship: Chapter 6, "Aerospace Sciences and Engineering" section

Speech

See the following scholarship:

- Roberta Thumin Scholarship: Chapter 6, "Communications" section

Speech Language Pathology and Hearing Audiology

See the following scholarship:

- AMBUCS Scholarships: Chapter 6, "Occupational and Physical Therapy" section

Study Abroad

AIFS International Scholarships

Sponsor: American Institute for Foreign Study (AIFS)
Web Site: http://www.aifs.com/java/US/aifscol/index.htm
Amount of Scholarship: $500 to $1,000
Number of Awards: not given
Deadline: varies
Education Level: college undergraduates
Eligibility: Applicant must be admitted to an AIFS study abroad program, be currently enrolled in college, and have a minimum 3.0 GPA.

To find information about available scholarships, click the Scholarships link in the bar at the top of the page. This program offers $500 scholarships for summer study abroad and $1,000 scholarships for semester study abroad. There are two special scholarships: one for minority students, and one for students attending a college in Georgia's public university system. To learn more about these programs and find their applications, click on their respective links at the top of the page. Or keep reading to find out about the general scholarships, including eligibility requirements, selection criteria, application procedures, and a list of study abroad programs where scholarships may be used. You will also find a link to the PDF application form. To learn more about AIFS's study abroad programs and find out how to enroll, explore the buttons in the bar at the top of the page. You can also submit an electronic inquiry form to request more information.

Ambassadorial Scholarships

Sponsor: Rotary International
Web Site: http://www.rotary.org/programs/amb_scho
Amount of Scholarship: $10,000 to $23,000
Number of Awards: 1,300
Deadline: varies
Education Level: college sophomores and juniors and graduate students
Eligibility: Applicant must be proficient in the language of the proposed host country, have completed at least two years of college-level coursework, and be a citizen of a country in which there are Rotary clubs.

This is one of the most prestigious study abroad scholarship programs available for undergraduate students. Competition is tough, but the rewards are high. The scholarship's main page describes the history, purpose, and benefits of the program, as well as the three types of scholarships available. Scholarships can fund between three months and three years of study abroad, with the most common scholarship awarding $23,000 for one full year of study in another country. Follow the menu links to learn more. The Eligibility Requirements page describes who may apply for Ambassadorial Scholarships; note that students from most countries, including the United States, are eligible. Students with disabilities are

especially encouraged to apply. Be sure to explore the other links before applying, so that you are thoroughly familiar with the program. To find application forms, instructions, a scholarship leaflet, and a FAQ, follow the Ambassadorial Scholarship Forms link. Note that you must apply through your local Rotary club and that you should start application procedures more than a year in advance of when you would like to start studying abroad. You will find a link to a list of Rotary clubs in the FAQ, or contact the scholarships or study abroad office at your college.

Bridging Scholarships for Study in Japan

Sponsor: Association of Teachers of Japanese Bridging Clearinghouse for Study Abroad in Japan
Web Site: http://www.Colorado.EDU/ealld/atj/Bridging/scholarships.html
Amount of Scholarship: $2,500 to $4,000
Number of Awards: 30
Deadline: April 3
Education Level: college undergraduates
Eligibility: Applicant must be accepted in a study abroad program in Japan, attend a four-year college, and be a U.S. citizen.

Read through the scholarship description to understand the purpose and conditions of this award. Note that students majoring in any field are eligible to apply. The Instructions for Applicants section of the page lists all of the documents that must be included with the application package. This section also links to text and PDF copies of the application form.

IES Scholarships

Sponsor: Institute for the International Education of Students (IES)
Web Site: http://www.iesabroad.org/info/finaid.html

Amount of Scholarship: $500 to half tuition
Number of Awards: not given
Deadline: April 1 and October 15
Education Level: college undergraduates
Eligibility: Applicant must be admitted to an IES study abroad program, attend a four-year college, and have a minimum 3.3 GPA.

This page describes the 13 scholarships available to students participating in IES study abroad programs. First, explore the rest of the IES Web site to learn about the 22 study abroad programs available through IES and to apply for admittance. Use the links in the bar at the top of the page and the menus at the bottom of the page to get around. Once you find study abroad programs that you are interested in, take a look at the list of available scholarships to see if any awards are available for your field of study or for the city where you want to study. The link for each scholarship leads to a detailed description of the award amount, the eligibility requirements, and the required application materials for that award. You may apply for more than one scholarship, if you qualify. The scholarship's information page describes the general procedures for applying for all scholarships and answers to common questions.

IIE Study Abroad Grants

Sponsor: Institute of International Education (IIE)
Web Site: http://www.iie.org/southern/sagrant.htm
Amount of Scholarship: $500 to $2,000
Number of Awards: 26
Deadline: March 16
Education Level: college undergraduates and graduate students
Eligibility: Applicant must be accepted into a study abroad program, attend a southern U.S. college or university that participates in IIE's

Educational Associates Program, and be a U.S. citizen or permanent resident.

This page describes the seven different study abroad grants available to students of participating colleges from IIE. One scholarship is unrestricted, two are awarded for study in a business-related field, one is awarded for study in India, one goes to South Carolina students, one goes to North Carolina students, and one goes to Texas students. To find out if these grants are available at your college, contact your school's study abroad office. The Web page also lists application requirements and conditions of accepting a scholarship. Note that applications for study in non-Western countries are encouraged. Follow the link at the bottom of the page to download an application form in PDF format.

International Study Programs Scholarship

Sponsor: Council on International Educational Exchange
Web Site: http://www.ciee.org/study/scholarships/isp.htm
Amount of Scholarship: $1,000
Number of Awards: not given
Deadline: April 1 and October 26
Education Level: college undergraduates
Eligibility: Applicant must apply to a Council Study Center study abroad program and attend an Academic Consortium member college.

This page describes eligibility requirements and application procedures for this scholarship program and provides a link to a PDF version of the application form. To learn more about Council Study Center study abroad programs and how to apply for admittance to them, follow the Council Study Centers link on the left side of the page. To find out which colleges are Academic Consortium members, go to the

Council-ISP Main Menu and click the Academic Consortium link.

Millennium Scholars

Sponsor: Millennium Society
Web Site: http://millenniumsociety.org/scholars_program.html
Amount of Scholarship: not given
Number of Awards: not given
Deadline: none
Education Level: college undergraduates
Eligibility: Applicant must be accepted to an accredited undergraduate college outside his or her home country, demonstrate financial need, and be between the ages of 17 and 25.

Read through this Web page to learn about the purpose of this scholarship, eligibility requirements, selection criteria, and application review process. Click the Scholarship Recipients link at the top of the page to find a list of scholarship winners from all around the world, which will give you an idea of the amounts awarded and the colleges where scholarships are used. Note that scholarships are available for students from all countries, not just the U.S. Click the Application Form link to find an electronic application that you can submit online and a link to an alternative printable application form.

Monbusho Scholarship

Sponsor: Government of Japan
Web Site: http://www.embjapan.org/la/jicc/japanesestud.htm
Amount of Scholarship: full tuition
Number of Awards: not given
Deadline: not given
Education Level: college undergraduates
Eligibility: Applicant must study Japanese language, culture, or a closely related field at a U.S. college; be proficient in the Japanese language; be between the ages of 18 and 30; and be a U.S. citizen.

First, read the Qualifications section of the Web page to make certain that you qualify for this scholarship for study in Japan. The Scholarship Benefits section of the page details the components of the award. The Japanese Studies Program section describes the course of study that participants undergo. Go to Application Procedure to find out how to prepare and submit an application. Note that you must submit your application to your regional Monbusho Coordinator. Go to Contact the Monbusho Coordinator to find the address, phone number, and e-mail address of the Monbusho Coordinator in your area of the country.

National Security Education Program Undergraduate Scholarship

Sponsor: National Security Education Board and Institute of International Education
Web Site: http://www.iie.org/nsep
Amount of Scholarship: $2,500 to $8,000
Number of Awards: not given
Deadline: February 7
Education Level: college undergraduates
Eligibility: Applicant must be accepted to an eligible study abroad program, attend a U.S. two-year or four-year college, and be a U.S. citizen.

The Program Overview on the main Web page describes in detail what the National Security Education Program is and why it was created. The scholarship must be applied to study abroad programs in countries and fields of study deemed critical for U.S. national security. These requirements, along with foreign language and service requirements, are described in more detail in the Outline of Requirements section of the site. The Application Guide section lists eligibility requirements, award amounts, study abroad program options, selection criteria, and application instructions. There is also a link to an electronic application form. Read the Frequently Asked Questions page to find the answers to the most common questions about this program. Be sure to explore the other links on the site to discover more valuable information that may help you with preparing your application.

Robert B. Bailey III Scholarship

Sponsor: Council on International Educational Exchange
Web Site: http://www.ciee.org/study/scholarships/bailey.htm
Amount of Scholarship: $500
Number of Awards: not given
Deadline: April 1 and October 26
Education Level: college undergraduates
Eligibility: Applicant must apply to a Council Study Center or University Direct Enrollment Service study abroad program, be a member of an underrepresented group, and be a U.S. citizen.

This page describes the scholarship's eligibility requirements and application process and provides a link to a PDF version of the application form. To learn more about Council Study Center and University Direct Enrollment Service study programs and how to apply for admittance to them, follow the links on the left side of the page.

Also see the following scholarship:

• Zeta Phi Beta Scholarships and Fellowships: Chapter 12, "Female" section

Technical Communication

ACM SIGDOC Undergraduate Scholarship

Sponsor: Association of Computing Machinery Special Interest Group in Documentation (ACM SIGDOC)

Web Site: http://www.acm.org/sigdoc/Scholarship.html
Amount of Scholarship: $500
Number of Awards: 1
Deadline: February 20
Education Level: college sophomores and juniors
Eligibility: Applicant must enroll as a full-time student in an established degree program in technical or professional communication.

The sponsor of this scholarship is dedicated to furthering the technical communication profession, and the scholarship is intended to assist a student in an established degree program in technical or professional communication. As such, those studying journalism, computer programming, broadcasting, or creative writing are not eligible. Scholarship winners must join ACM SIGDOC before they can accept their awards. These eligibility requirements and others are outlined on the scholarship's Web page. If you choose to apply, you will find a Word version of the application form linked to the bottom of the page, as well as a list of the other items that you will need to submit in your application package. Also explore the SIGDOC Home Page to learn more about this group and its objectives.

STC Scholarship

Sponsor: Society for Technical Communication (STC)
Web Site: http://www.stc-va.org/scholarships.html
Amount of Scholarship: $2,500
Number of Awards: 14
Deadline: February 7
Education Level: college sophomores, juniors, and seniors and graduate students
Eligibility: Applicant must study technical communication and be a full-time student.

Under this program, seven scholarships go to undergraduates and seven go to graduate students who are studying the communication of information about technical subjects. Read the background of the scholarship, its purpose, and the eligibility requirements on the scholarship's Web page. If you feel like you are a good match, contact the address at the bottom of the page to request an application.

Also see the following scholarship:

• Vaughan/NAHWW Scholarship: Chapter 6, "Journalism" section

Telecommunications

See the following scholarships:

• Jim Bourque Scholarship: Chapter 9, "Native American" section
• New Economy Technology Scholarship: Chapter 15, "Pennsylvania" section

Textile Science and Fiber Arts

HGA and Dendel Scholarships

Sponsor: The Handweavers Guild of America, Inc. (HGA)
Web Site: http://www.weavespindye.org/html/hgaschol.html
Amount of Scholarship: varies
Number of Awards: not given
Deadline: March 15
Education Level: college undergraduates and graduate students
Eligibility: Applicant must study the fiber arts at a U.S. or Canadian college or university.

The two scholarships awarded under this program are intended for students of fiber-related fields. HGA Scholarships are awarded only for

tuition, but Dendel Scholarships can also pay for supplies, travel, and other education-related expenses. The HGA and Dendel Scholarship Regulations page describes exactly how to submit an application package. If you decide to apply, print out a copy of the application and the slide sheet by following the links at the bottom of the page.

Thread Committee Excellence in Manufacturing Scholarship

Sponsor: American Textile Manufacturers Institute
Web Site: http://www.atmi.org/Publications/tcschool.html
Amount of Scholarship: $2,500 (renewable for four years)
Number of Awards: not given
Deadline: February 19
Education Level: high school seniors
Eligibility: Applicant must enroll in a textile science program or related discipline at a participating college and have a minimum 3.0 GPA.

To use this scholarship, you must attend one of the six colleges listed on the scholarship's Web page. This page also outlines the eligibility and application requirements for the award and provides a link to a PDF version of the application form. The scholarship is awarded every other year, so check that the competition is open before applying.

Theater

See the following scholarship:

• Roberta Thumin Scholarship: Chapter 6, "Communications" section

Travel and Tourism

ASTA Scholarships

Sponsor: American Society of Travel Agents (ASTA) Foundation
Web Site: http://www.astanet.com/www/asta/pub/car/scholarships2.htmlx
Amount of Scholarship: $2,000 to $3,000
Number of Awards: 27
Deadline: varies
Education Level: college undergraduates and graduate students
Eligibility: Applicant must enroll in travel and tourism courses at a two-year college, four-year college, or university and have a minimum 2.5 GPA.

This page describes the 15 travel and tourism scholarships available from the ASTA Foundation. The top of the page lists all the of the supporting materials that must be submitted when applying for any of the scholarships. Beneath that are brief descriptions of the scholarships organized by educational level, along with each award's essay requirements. Many awards specify residency requirements, and one is intended only for children of employees of the travel industry. Make a note of all of the scholarships for which you are qualified to apply. Click the Apply Now! link at the bottom of the page to access the application form, which you can fill out in your Web browser and then print. Be sure to check the boxes beside the names of the scholarships for which you want to apply.

IATAN Ronald A. Santana Memorial Foundation Scholarship

Sponsor: International Airlines Travel Agent Network (IATAN) Ronald A. Santana Memorial Foundation

Web Site: http://www.iatan.org/mnuFnd.htm
Amount of Scholarship: $500 to $2,500
Number of Awards: 4
Deadline: April 15
Education Level: college undergraduates
Eligibility: Applicant must enroll in a travel and tourism program or a related discipline, be at least 17 years old, and be a U.S. resident.

To learn more about the scholarships available and the eligibility requirements, click the IATAN Foundation Scholarships link on the right side of the page. Four awards are given out: one $2,500 award, two $1,000 awards, and one $500 award. You will also find past winner biographies and essays on this page, which you can use as models for your own application. Return to the main page and click the Application Forms link to download the application in either PDF or Microsoft Word format.

National Tourism Foundation Scholarships

Sponsor: National Tourism Foundation
Web Site: http://www.ntaonline.com/www/member/about_nta/departmental/national_tourism_foundation/education/general_scholarship_info.html
Amount of Scholarship: $500 to $5,000
Number of Awards: 30
Deadline: April 17
Education Level: college sophomores and juniors
Eligibility: Applicant must enroll as a full-time student in a travel and tourism-related degree program at a two-year or four-year college in North America.

This page describes the 7 general scholarships and the 23 state-specific scholarships awarded by the National Tourism Foundation. The top of the page goes over the general details, including award benefits, eligibility requirements, and application requirements. Beneath that is a list of all of the scholarships, along with their amounts and specific eligibility requirements. Following that, you will find a list of essay topics that you can address in your application. At the very top of the page is a link to the application form in PDF format. You have to check a box beside each scholarship for which you want to be considered. You can apply for as many scholarships as you like, but you can only receive one award.

Turfgrass and Golf Course Management

GSCAA Scholars

Sponsor: Golf Course Superintendents Association of America (GSCAA) Foundation
Web Site: http://www.gcsaa.org/career/pursuing/scholarships/schlrap.html
Amount of Scholarship: $500 to $3,500
Number of Awards: not given
Deadline: June 1
Education Level: college sophomores and juniors
Eligibility: Applicant must have completed the first year of an accredited program related to golf course management and be a member of GCSAA.

This competition recognizes outstanding students who plan a career in golf course management or a related field with five different scholarships. The first-place winner receives a $3,500 scholarship, the second- and third-place winners receive $2,500 scholarships, and the other scholars receive awards of between $1,500 and $2,500. Merit Scholars also receive $500 awards. A special scholarship, the Ambassador Award, is designated for international students. All four of the required application forms are available on the scholarship's Web site. All forms are designed to be filled out inside the Web browser and then printed, although plain text versions of the recommendation forms are also available if your recommenders do not have Internet access. Be sure to read and follow the instructions at the bottom of the scholarship page, which tell you how to complete and submit the application forms.

NYSTA Scholarship

Sponsor: New York State Turfgrass Association (NYSTA)
Web Site: http://www.nysta.org/nysta/scholarships_awards/index.htm
Amount of Scholarship: not given
Number of Awards: not given
Deadline: October 1
Education Level: college sophomores and juniors
Eligibility: Applicant must major in turfgrass management or a closely related subject and be a member of NYSTA.

While you do have to be a member of NYSTA to apply for this scholarship, you don't have to be a resident of New York (preference is given to New York residents, though). Follow the Membership link on the left side of the page to learn how to become a member of NYSTA. You must also major in turfgrass management or in a closely related field like agriculture, landscape architecture, soil science, or horticulture and take all the turfgrass courses available at your college. To get a copy of the application, contact the address given at the bottom of the page.

Scotts Company Scholars

Sponsor: Scotts Company and Golf Course Superintendents Association of America (GCSAA) Foundation
Web Site: http://www.gcsaa.org/career/pursuing/scholarships/scttspro.html
Amount of Scholarship: $500 to $2,500
Number of Awards: 7
Deadline: March 1

Education Level: high school seniors and college undergraduates

Eligibility: Applicant must plan to pursue a career in the green industry and major in a green-related field at a two-year or four-year college.

Academic programs that support green industry careers, and thus are eligible for study under the scholarship, include turfgrass management, agronomy, crop science, and horticulture. Find more information about such programs by exploring the Career Center on GCSAA's Web site (go to http://www.gcsaa.org/career/careersh.html). The five finalists in this scholarship program receive a $500 award and qualify for a summer internship; follow the Available Internships link on the Career Center page to learn more. After successfully completing the internship, the finalists compete for two $2,500 scholarships. The selection criteria are spelled out on the scholarship's Web page and include cultural diversity, so minorities, students with disabilities, women, and students from diverse cultural and socioeconomic backgrounds have better chances of winning. The application form is designed to be filled out inside your Web browser, but it must then be printed and mailed to the scholarship submission address.

Veterinary Medicine and Technology

See the following scholarships:

- Frank and Elizabeth Spencer Scholarship: Chapter 15, "North Carolina" section
- Michigan Farm Bureau Scholarships: Chapter 14, "Employer and Profession" section
- New York State Regents Professional Opportunity Scholarship: Chapter 15, "New York" section

Vocational and Technical Education

California-Hawaii Elks Association Scholarship for Vocational Education

Sponsor: California-Hawaii Elks Association
Web Site: http://www.cheo.org/docs/vocapps.htm
Amount of Scholarship: $1,000 (renewable for two years)
Number of Awards: not given
Deadline: not given
Education Level: high school seniors
Eligibility: Applicant must enroll in an accredited vocational program and be a resident of California or Hawaii.

Here you will find a very brief description of this scholarship and its eligibility requirements. If you want to apply, you can download a Microsoft Word version of the application form from the Web page.

Iowa Vocational-Technical Tuition Grant

Sponsor: Iowa College Student Aid Commission
Web Site: http://www.state.ia.us/government/icsac/grants.html
#IowaVocationalTechnicalTuitionGrants
Amount of Scholarship: $600 per year (awarded over two years)
Number of Awards: not given
Deadline: April 21
Education Level: college undergraduates
Eligibility: Applicant must enroll as a full-time student in a career education or career option course that lasts at least 12 weeks, demonstrate financial need, be an Iowa resident, and be a U.S. citizen or permanent resident.

This program awards need-based grants to students enrolled in vocational-technical or career option programs at community colleges. Read the eligibility requirements to see if you fit the description. If so, follow the directions under How to Apply to apply for a grant.

Also see the following scholarships:

- AAL Vocational/Technical School Scholarship: Chapter 11, "Lutheran" section
- APWU Vocational Scholarship: Chapter 14, "Unions and Professional Associations" section

GRADUATE SCHOOL SCHOLARSHIPS

This chapter lists fellowships intended for graduate study in specific academic disciplines. Students in master's programs, doctoral programs, and professional business, law, and medical schools will all find sources of funding here. Fellowships are categorized by field of study, and at the end of each section you will find cross references to relevant awards listed in other chapters of this book.

Another good place to look for graduate school funding is your own academic department. Look up the name of your university in Chapter 16, "College-Specific Scholarships," to find Web sites that list departmental scholarships and fellowships for graduate students at that school. The other chapters also list more general graduate-level scholarships awarded on the basis of organization membership, ethnicity, religious affiliation, gender, military service, family affiliation, or residency, so don't neglect reading through those chapters to find additional funding that you might be eligible to receive.

Accounting

AAHCPA Graduate Scholarship

Sponsor: American Association of Certified Public Accountants (AAHCPA)
Web Site: http://www.aahcpa.org/grad.htm
Amount of Scholarship: not given
Number of Awards: not given
Deadline: September 15
Education Level: college seniors and graduate students

Eligibility: Applicant must enroll in a graduate accounting program or the last year of a five-year accounting program, have a minimum 3.0 GPA, and be Hispanic.

This page describes the eligibility requirements and selection criteria for the graduate-level scholarship awarded by AAHCPA. It also lists all of the documents that must be included in the application package. Click the link at the bottom of the page to open the application form, which you can fill out inside your Web browser and then print with your answers already typed in. (Even though this looks like an electronic form, you cannot submit it online.)

AICPA John L. Carey Scholarship

Sponsor: American Institute of Certified Public Accountants (AICPA)
Web Site: http://www.aicpa.org/members/div/career/edu/jlcs.htm
Amount of Scholarship: $5,000 (renewable for two years)
Number of Awards: 5
Deadline: April 1
Education Level: graduate students
Eligibility: Applicant must enroll in an accredited graduate program in accounting that will enable him or her to sit for the CPA Examination, and hold a bachelor's degree in a liberal arts subject from an accredited U.S. college.

This page gives an overview of the scholarship program, including eligibility requirements and selection criteria. There is also a link to the application form in PDF format; the form contains detailed instructions for submitting an application.

Also see the following scholarships:

- Account for Your Future Scholarship: Chapter 6, "Accounting" section
- AICPA Scholarship for Minority Accounting Students: Chapter 6, "Accounting" section
- Institute of Management Accountants National Scholarships: Chapter 6, "Accounting" section
- Minorities in Government Finance Scholarship: Chapter 9, "All Minorities" section
- NAFOA Student Scholarship: Chapter 9, "Native American" section
- Robert Kaufman Memorial Scholarship: Chapter 6, "Accounting" section
- Virginia BPW Foundation Scholarships: Chapter 15, "Virginia" section

Acupuncture

See the following scholarship:

- New York State Regents Professional Opportunity Scholarship: Chapter 15, "New York" section

Advertising, Marketing, and Public Relations

See the following scholarship:

- Jessica Savitch Scholarship: Chapter 6, "Communications" section

Aerospace Sciences and Engineering

AIAA Foundation Graduate Awards

Sponsor: American Institute of Aeronautics and Astronautics (AIAA) Foundation

Web Site: http://www.aiaa.org/information/student/scholarship/grad.html
Amount of Scholarship: $5,000
Number of Awards: 10
Deadline: January 31
Education Level: graduate students
Eligibility: Applicant must have an approved thesis or research project in an eligible technical area, have completed at least one year of graduate work in a related technical course of study, be a full-time student at an accredited university, have a minimum 3.0 GPA, and be a student member of AIAA.

The Objective section of the Web page describes the purpose of this awards program and the qualifications sought in applicants. More detailed applicant qualifications are listed in the Eligibility section of the page. The Selection Criteria selection lists the required components of the application package and explains how they are used to select recipients of the award. To find out what technical areas are eligible for consideration, scroll down to the Areas of Specialization section of the page, which describes the seven different kinds of awards available under this program. Note that the Willy Z. Sadeh Graduate Award in Space Engineering and Space Sciences is described in more detail on a separate page; just follow the link to access it. You have to indicate the appropriate field of specialization on your application if you choose to apply for one of these awards. Because two of the awards are for study in any specialty field for which there is a Technical Committee, you should also visit the AIAA Technical Activities page to find out what these fields are; you will find a link to this page under the Member Activities heading on the left-hand side of the page. From the scholarship information page, you can also open a text version of the application form, which you may use to apply for any of the awards. Follow the Student link under the Membership heading on the left-hand side of the page to find information about becoming a student member of AIAA and an online membership application form.

Amelia Earhart Fellowship Awards for Women

Sponsor: Zonta International (ZI) Foundation
Web Site: http://www.zonta.org/programs/descriptions.htm
Amount of Scholarship: $6,000
Number of Awards: not given
Deadline: November 1
Education Level: graduate students
Eligibility: Applicant must enroll in a graduate degree program in aerospace sciences or engineering, hold a bachelor's degree in an aerospace-related field, and be female.

This fellowship program is described briefly at the top of the page, directly under the ZI Program Descriptions heading. To get more details about eligibility requirements and selection criteria, open the PDF application form. There is also an e-mail address that you can contact for more information about the fellowship.

LaSPACE Fellowship

Sponsor: Louisiana Space Consortium
Web Site: http://phacts.phys.lsu.edu
Amount of Scholarship: $17,500 to $20,000 (renewable for up to five years)
Number of Awards: 1 to 3
Deadline: February 4
Education Level: college seniors and graduate students
Eligibility: Applicant must enroll as a full-time student in an aerospace- or space-related graduate program at a LaSPACE member university and be a U.S. citizen.

Click the LaSPACE Fellowship link to learn about this fellowship, which awards a $17,500

stipend to a master's students and a $20,000 stipend to doctoral students. The fellowship information is divided into several sections. First, read the General Information section to learn about the background and purpose of the program. The LaSPACE Graduate Fellowship Program section describes the objectives of the fellowship, eligibility requirements, award details, and other important information about the fellowship itself. The next two sections describe the procedures for submitting applications and the proper formatting of application packages. You will also find a list of LaSPACE member universities, along with on-campus faculty contacts for the fellowship program, and Microsoft Word and PDF versions of all the forms you need to submit in the application package.

NASA Graduate Student Researchers Program Fellowship

Sponsor: National Aeronautics and Space Administration (NASA)
Web Site: http://education.nasa.gov/gsrp
Amount of Scholarship: up to $22,000 (renewable for three years)
Number of Awards: not given
Deadline: February 1
Education Level: college seniors and graduate students
Eligibility: Applicant must enroll as a full-time student in an aerospace- or space-related graduate program in engineering, mathematics, or science at an accredited U.S. university and be a U.S. citizen.

This page describes NASA's graduate fellowship program. Explore the links to learn more about NASA and about the program. The General Policies & Procedures page provides details on proposal submission deadlines, selection criteria, eligibility requirements, and the conditions of accepting the fellowship. Note that minorities, women, and students with disabilities are particularly encouraged to apply. Read the Preparation of Proposal page to find out how to assemble your application package. The Disciplines at NASA Centers link is helpful for finding out which specific fields of study are acceptable for the program. At the bottom of the main page, you can download a copy of the Proposal Submission Form in either PDF or Microsoft Word format.

OSGC Graduate Fellowship

Sponsor: Ohio Space Grant Consortium (OSGC)
Web Site: http://www.oai.org/OSGC/page/Fellowship.html
Amount of Scholarship: full tuition and a stipend of $14,000 to $18,000
Number of Awards: not given
Deadline: January 31
Education Level: graduate students
Eligibility: Applicant must enroll in an aerospace-related graduate degree program at a participating OSGC university and be a U.S. citizen.

This program provides fellowships of full tuition plus $14,000 for master's students or $18,000 for doctoral students. The Web page provides an overview of the fellowship program, a list of past winners, and links to all of the forms that you will need to apply. First, find out if you attend an eligible university by clicking the OSGC Universities link. Then, download the PDF version of the Graduate Fellowship Brochure to learn more about the program, including application instructions, selection criteria, eligibility requirements, and conditions of accepting the fellowship. Note that members of underrepresented groups are particularly encouraged to apply. If you decide to apply, you can download PDF copies of the

Application Form and Recommendation Form from the site, as well.

Also see the following scholarships:

- AFCEA Ralph W. Shrader Scholarship: Chapter 7, "Communications Engineering and Technology" section
- Donald K. "Deke" Slayton Memorial Scholarship: Chapter 6, "Aerospace Sciences and Engineering" section
- GEM Fellowships: Chapter 9, "All Minorities" section
- Hertz Foundation Fellowship: Chapter 7, "Sciences" section
- ISGC Scholarships and Fellowships: Chapter 6, "Space Sciences" section
- Montana Space Grant Consortium Scholarships and Fellowships: Chapter 6, "Aerospace Sciences and Engineering" section
- NASA Nebraska Space Grant and EPSCoR Programs Scholarships and Fellowships: Chapter 6, "Aerospace Sciences and Engineering" section
- National Defense Science and Engineering Graduate Fellowship: Chapter 7, "Sciences" section
- NPSC Graduate Fellowships in the Physical Sciences: Chapter 7, "Sciences" section
- NSF Graduate Research Fellowships: Chapter 7, "Sciences" section
- VSGC Scholarships and Fellowships: Chapter 6, "Aerospace Sciences and Engineering" section

Agriculture

See the following scholarships:

- FFGC Scholarships: Chapter 15, "Florida" section
- Garden Club of Georgia Scholarships: Chapter 15, "Georgia" section

- National Council of State Garden Clubs Scholarship: Chapter 6, "Horticulture" section
- North Carolina Tomato Growers Scholarship: Chapter 15, "North Carolina" section

Anthropology and Archaeology

See the following scholarships:

- Andrew W. Mellon Fellowship in Humanistic Studies: Chapter 7, "Humanities" section
- AWIS Graduate Awards: Chapter 12, "Female" section
- International Predissertation Fellowships: Chapter 7, "Social Sciences" section
- Jacob Javits Fellowship: Chapter 7, "Humanities" section
- NSF Graduate Research Fellowship: Chapter 7, "Sciences" section

Architecture

See the following scholarships:

- Garden Club of Georgia Scholarships: Chapter 15, "Georgia" section
- New York State Regents Professional Opportunity Scholarship: Chapter 15, "New York" section

Art and Art History

Swann Foundation Fellowship

Sponsor: The Swann Foundation
Web Site: http://lcweb.loc.gov/rr/print/swann/swann_foundation.html#fellow

Amount of Scholarship: $15,000
Number of Awards: 1
Deadline: February 15
Education Level: graduate students
Eligibility: Applicant must be researching the field of caricature and cartoon and be enrolled in an MA or PhD program at a North American university.

This fellowship is intended to assist scholarly research in the field of caricature and cartoon. The Web page briefly describes the fellowship, the eligibility requirements, and the conditions of accepting the award. A contact address from which you can request a printed application form is also given, or you can link to text and WordPerfect versions of the application online. One of the conditions of the fellowship is a two-week residency at the Library of Congress; at the bottom of the Web page you will find more information about the Library of Congress's cartoon and caricature collection.

Also see the following scholarships:

- Andrew W. Mellon Fellowship in Humanistic Studies: Chapter 7, "Humanities" section
- Jacob Javits Fellowship: Chapter 7, "Humanities" section

Atmospheric Sciences

See the following scholarships:

- AMS Scholarships: Chapter 6, "Atmospheric Sciences" section
- NASA Graduate Student Researchers Program Fellowship: Chapter 7, "Aerospace Sciences and Engineering" section
- NPSC Graduate Fellowships in the Physical Sciences: Chapter 7, "Sciences" section
- NSF Graduate Research Fellowship: Chapter 7, "Sciences" section

Aviation

See the following scholarships:

- AIAA Foundation Graduate Awards: Chapter 7, "Aerospace Sciences and Engineering" section
- NASA Nebraska Space Grant and EPSCoR Programs Scholarships and Fellowships: Chapter 6, "Aerospace Sciences and Engineering" section

Biology

Howard Hughes Medical Institute Predoctoral Fellowship in Biological Sciences

Sponsor: Howard Hughes Medical Institute
Web Site: http://www4.nas.edu/osep/fo.nsf/web/hhmi_predoctoral
Amount of Scholarship: $31,000 (renewable for five years)
Number of Awards: 400
Deadline: November 9
Education Level: college seniors and first-year graduate students
Eligibility: Applicant must enroll as a full-time student in a doctoral degree program in an eligible field in the biological sciences.

On this page you will find information about eligible fields of study, eligibility requirements, location of study, the fellowship term, stipends and allowances, selection criteria, conditions of accepting the award, and the application process for this fellowship program. You will also find a lot of information about the fellowship's sponsor. To download a PDF copy of the application form or request a printed application, follow the appropriate links at the bottom of the page.

Jennifer Robinson Memorial Scholarship

Sponsor: Arctic Institute of North America
Web Site: http://www.ucalgary.ca/aina/scholar/scholar.html#robinson
Amount of Scholarship: $5,000
Number of Awards: 1
Deadline: January 7
Education Level: graduate students
Eligibility: Applicant must study northern biology.

Here you will find a very brief description of the scholarship and instructions for preparing an application package. You don't have to submit an official application form for this scholarship. If you have additional questions, contact the address, telephone number, or e-mail address listed underneath the scholarship description.

Robert D. Watkins Minority Graduate Fellowship

Sponsor: American Society for Microbiology (ASM)
Web Site: http://www.asm.org/edusrc/edu23c.htm
Amount of Scholarship: $15,000 (awarded for three years)
Number of Awards: not given
Deadline: May 1
Education Level: doctoral students
Eligibility: Applicant must have completed the first year of a microbiology Ph.D. program at an accredited U.S. university, be a student member of ASM, be a member of a minority

group, and be a U.S. citizen or permanent resident.

This fellowship awards stipends to minority students pursing the Ph.D. in microbiology. Eligible minority groups include African-Americans, Hispanics, Native Americans, and Pacific Islanders. Scroll down the Web page to read brief descriptions of the fellowship program, including information about funding, eligibility requirements, and selection criteria. At the bottom of the page are links to all pages of the application form, which you must print out from your Web browser.

Also see the following scholarships:

- GEM Fellowships: Chapter 9, "All Minorities" section
- Hertz Foundation Fellowship: Chapter 7, "Sciences" section
- NASA Graduate Student Researchers Program Fellowship: Chapter 7, "Aerospace Sciences and Engineering" section
- National Council of State Garden Clubs Scholarship: Chapter 6, "Horticulture" section
- National Defense Science and Engineering Graduate Fellowship: Chapter 7, "Sciences" section
- NPSC Graduate Fellowships in the Physical Sciences: Chapter 7, "Sciences" section
- NSF Graduate Research Fellowship: Chapter 7, "Sciences" section

Botany

See the following scholarships:

- FFGC Scholarships: Chapter 15, "Florida" section

- Garden Club of Georgia Scholarships: Chapter 15, "Georgia" section
- National Council of State Garden Clubs Scholarship: Chapter 6, "Horticulture" section
- NSF Graduate Research Fellowship: Chapter 7, "Sciences" section

Business

Avis Scholarship

Sponsor: American Society of Travel Agents Scholarship Foundation
Web Site: http://www.astanet.com/www/asta/pub/car/scholarships1.htmlx
Amount of Scholarship: $2,000 (renewable for three years)
Number of Awards: not given
Deadline: July 28
Education Level: college undergraduates and graduate students
Eligibility: Applicant must enroll in an accredited undergraduate or graduate program in business, hold a bachelor's degree in travel and tourism or have a minimum of two years of full-time experience in the travel industry, be currently employed in the travel industry, and have a minimum 3.0 GPA.

Scroll all the way to the bottom of the page to find information about this scholarship, which is intended for travel industry professionals who want to earn a business degree. You will find a brief description of the scholarship and a list of materials that must be submitted in the application package. Click the Apply Now! link if you would like to apply for the scholarship. This opens an application form that you can fill out inside your Web browser and then print out with your answers. Be sure to check the box beside "Avis" to indicate which scholarship you are applying for.

Consortium for Graduate Study in Management Fellowship

Sponsor: Consortium for Graduate Study in Management
Web Site: http://www.cgsm.org
Amount of Scholarship: not given
Number of Awards: 250
Deadline: January 15
Education Level: Master of Business Administration (MBA) students
Eligibility: Applicant must enroll as a full-time student in an MBA program at a member university and be a member of a minority group.

The opening page of this Web site provides more information about the fellowship sponsor. To learn more about the fellowship program for minority MBA students, click the Apply button at the very top of the page. This program enables you to apply for admission to up to six business schools that are members of the Consortium for Graduate Study in Management and to apply for a fellowship at the same time. All minorities except Asian-Americans are eligible to apply. The Apply page provides an application timeline and links to application forms in various formats for printing. You can also add your name to the mailing list to receive more information about the program. The links under the Questions heading on the left side of the page should answer most of your questions about the fellowship. Under the Contact heading, you will see links to faculty liaisons and interviewers at each member institution that you may need to get in touch with if you decide to apply. To find out which schools are members of the consortium, click the Schools button at the top of the page. Exploring the other buttons will help you learn more about the fellowship program, its sponsor, and its benefits.

DDS Anniversary Scholarship

Sponsor: Donovan Data Systems, Inc. (DDS)
Web Site: http://www.donovandata.com/scholarship
Amount of Scholarship: full tuition
Number of Awards: not given
Deadline: April 30
Education Level: graduate students
Eligibility: Applicant must enroll in a graduate business program at an eligible business school in Europe.

This scholarship pays one year's tuition at an eligible business school for a student who wants to enter a career in advertising, marketing, or communications. The award is given to a British, German, or French student attending a selected school in North America and to an American or Canadian student attending a selected school in Europe in alternate years, so to be eligible, you must apply during the correct year and plan to attend one of the selected business schools. The eligible business schools for North American students are listed at the bottom of the scholarship's Web page. Be sure to read the Policy Statement, available on the Web site in PDF format, to understand how the scholarship works and the application procedures. You can then download the Cover Statement and Application forms, both in PDF format, if you choose to apply.

Jacki Tuckfield Memorial Graduate Business Administration Scholarship

Sponsor: Dade Community Foundation
Web Site: http://www.jackituckfield.org
Amount of Scholarship: $1,000
Number of Awards: not given

Deadline: April 7
Education Level: graduate students
Eligibility: Applicant must enroll as a full-time student in a graduate business degree program at a Florida university, plan to pursue a professional career in south Florida, be African-American, be a resident of south Florida, and be a U.S. citizen.

Follow the links at the top of the Web page to learn more about this scholarship program. The Scholarship Requirements link describes the eligibility requirements, application requirements, and deadlines. Click the Application Form link to access a copy of the application in PDF format.

National Restaurant Association Graduate Degree Scholarship

Sponsor: National Restaurant Association Educational Foundation
Web Site: http://www.edfound.org/NewASP/careers/scholarshp/careers_graddegree.htm
Amount of Scholarship: $5,000
Number of Awards: not given
Deadline: May 1
Education Level: graduate students
Eligibility: Applicant must enroll in a business-related graduate degree program and have at least 1,000 hours of hospitality or restaurant work experience.

This page very briefly describes the scholarship program and provides a list of materials that you must submit with your application to be considered. Click the link at the left of the page to download the scholarship application in PDF format, which gives a lot more information about the program.

NSHMBA Scholarship

Sponsor: National Society of Hispanic MBA (NSHMBA)

Web Site: http://www.nshmba.org/scholarshipinfo.asp
Amount of Scholarship: $2,000 to $10,000
Number of Awards: not given
Deadline: July 15
Education Level: master's students
Eligibility: Applicant must enroll in a master's degree program in business or management, have a minimum 3.0 GPA, be Hispanic, and be a U.S. citizen or permanent resident.

This page provides an overview of the scholarship program, including the scholarship's goals, eligibility requirements, selection criteria, and application procedures. At the top of the page are links to PDF and Microsoft Word versions of the application form that you can download and print.

State Farm Companies Foundation Doctoral Dissertation Awards

Sponsor: State Farm Companies Foundation
Web Site: http://www.statefarm.com/foundati/doctoral.htm
Amount of Scholarship: $10,000
Number of Awards: 3
Deadline: March 31
Education Level: doctoral students
Eligibility: Applicant must have completed a major portion of the doctoral program, be writing a dissertation related to insurance and risk management or business, and be a U.S. citizen.

Here you will find an overview of this dissertation award program. Be sure to read the eligibility requirements, the categories of awards, and the selection criteria to make certain that you would be a good candidate for the award. Look under the Applications heading for a link to a PDF version of the application form, which you can print out.

Also see the following scholarships:

- AICPA Scholarship for Minority Accounting Students: Chapter 6, "Accounting" section
- Atlas Shrugged Essay Contest: Chapter 6, "Business" section
- Economics Doctoral Research Fellowship: Chapter 7, "Economics and Finance" section
- Indian Health Service Scholarship: Chapter 9, "Native American" section
- Minorities in Government Finance Scholarship: Chapter 9, "All Minorities" section
- NAFOA Student Scholarship: Chapter 9, "Native American" section
- Pathfinder Historians Scholarship: Chapter 7, "History" section
- Public Employee Retirement Research and Administration Scholarship: Chapter 7, "Economics and Finance" section
- Public Investor Scholarship: Chapter 7, "Economics and Finance" section

Chemistry

See the following scholarships:

- AWIS Graduate Awards: Chapter 12, "Female" section
- Cooperative Research Fellowship: Chapter 9, "All Minorities" section
- GEM Fellowships: Chapter 9, "All Minorities" section
- Graduate Research Program for Women Fellowship: Chapter 12, "Female" section
- Hertz Foundation Fellowship: Chapter 7, "Sciences" section
- Lucent Florida Universities Fellowship: Chapter 15, "Florida" section

- NASA Graduate Student Researchers Program Fellowship: Chapter 7, "Aerospace Sciences and Engineering" section
- National Defense Science and Engineering Graduate Fellowship: Chapter 7, "Sciences" section
- National Pathfinder Scholarship: Chapter 12, "Female" section
- NPSC Graduate Fellowships in the Physical Sciences: Chapter 7, "Sciences" section
- NSF Graduate Research Fellowship: Chapter 7, "Sciences" section
- Xerox Technical Minority Scholarship: Chapter 9, "All Minorities" section

Chiropractic Medicine

See the following scholarships:

- Arkansas Health Education Grant: Chapter 15, "Arkansas" section
- New York State Regents Professional Opportunity Scholarship: Chapter 15, "New York" section

City Planning and Land Management

See the following scholarships:

- FFGC Scholarships: Chapter 15, "Florida" section
- Garden Club of Georgia Scholarships: Chapter 15, "Georgia" section
- National Council of State Garden Clubs Scholarship: Chapter 6, "Horticulture" section

- NSF Graduate Research Fellowship: Chapter 7, "Sciences" section

Classics

See the following scholarships:

- Andrew W. Mellon Fellowship in Humanistic Studies: Chapter 7, "Humanities" section
- Jacob Javits Fellowship: Chapter 7, "Humanities" section

Clinical Laboratory Science

See the following scholarship:

- Alpha Mu Tau Fraternity Scholarships: Chapter 6, "Clinical Laboratory Science" section

Communications

See the following scholarships:

- ARRL Foundation Scholarships: Chapter 8, "Amateur Radio" section
- Jacob Javits Fellowship: Chapter 7, "Humanities" section
- Jessica Savitch Scholarship: Chapter 6, "Communications" section

Communications Engineering and Technology

AFCEA Fellowship

Sponsor: Air Force Communications and Electronics Association (AFCEA)

Web Site: http://www.afcea.org/awards/scholarships.htm#fellow
Amount of Scholarship: $25,000
Number of Awards: not given
Deadline: February 1
Education Level: doctoral students
Eligibility: Applicant must enroll in a doctoral program in communications engineering, computer science, electrical engineering, electronic engineering, mathematics, or physics at an accredited U.S. university, and be a U.S. citizen.

You won't find a lot of information about this fellowship at the Web site, just enough to tell you if you are qualified. If you are interested in applying, contact the address or phone number given for more information. Applications for the next award year are usually available on the Web site after November 1.

AFCEA Ralph W. Shrader Scholarship

Sponsor: Air Force Communications and Electronics Association (AFCEA)
Web Site: http://www.afcea.org/awards/scholarships.htm#shrader
Amount of Scholarship: $3,000
Number of Awards: not given
Deadline: February 1
Education Level: master's students
Eligibility: Applicant must enroll in a master's program in aerospace engineering, communications engineering, communications technology, computer engineering, computer science, electrical engineering, electronics, information management, mathematics, or physics at a U.S. university, and be a U.S. citizen.

You won't find a lot of information about this scholarship at the Web site, just enough to tell you if you are qualified. At least one award is reserved for a female or minority applicant who meets all of the eligibility requirements. If you decide to apply, print out a PDF version of the application from the Web site. Applications for the next award year are usually available after November 1.

AT&T Labs Fellowship

Sponsor: AT&T Labs
Web Site: http://www.research.att.com/academic
Amount of Scholarship: full tuition and a monthly stipend of $1,400 (renewable for up to six years)
Number of Awards: not given
Deadline: January 15
Education Level: doctoral students
Eligibility: Applicant must enroll in a doctoral program in a communications- or computer-related field, and either be female or a member of a minority group.

To find information about this fellowship program, click the Special Programs and Fellowships link in the left frame, and then click the AT&T Labs Fellowship Program link. This page describes all the benefits of the fellowship. You can apply for the fellowship right on the Web. Be sure to follow all of the instructions exactly to make certain that your application is processed properly and that all of the supporting materials are received.

Also see the following scholarships:

- ARRL Foundation Scholarships: Chapter 8, "Amateur Radio" section
- Cooperative Research Fellowship: Chapter 9, "All Minorities" section
- Graduate Research Program for Women Fellowship: Chapter 12, "Female" section

Computer Science and Engineering

See the following scholarships:

- AFCEA Fellowship: Chapter 7, "Communications Engineering and Technology" section
- AFCEA Ralph W. Shrader Scholarship: Chapter 7, "Communications Engineering and Technology" section
- AT&T Labs Fellowship: Chapter 7, "Communications Engineering and Technology" section
- AWIS Graduate Awards: Chapter 12, "Female" section
- Cooperative Research Fellowship: Chapter 9, "All Minorities" section
- Department of Energy Computational Science Graduate Fellowship: Chapter 7, "Sciences" section
- Gates Millennium Scholars: Chapter 9, "All Minorities" section
- GEM Fellowships: Chapter 9, "All Minorities" section
- Graduate Research Program for Women Fellowship: Chapter 12, "Female" section
- Hertz Foundation Fellowship: Chapter 7, "Sciences" section
- Lucent Florida Universities Fellowship: Chapter 15, "Florida" section
- NASA Graduate Student Researchers Program Fellowship: Chapter 7, "Aerospace Sciences and Engineering" section
- National Defense Science and Engineering Graduate Fellowship: Chapter 7, "Sciences" section
- NPSC Graduate Fellowships in the Physical Sciences: Chapter 7, "Sciences" section
- NSBE Scholarships: Chapter 9, "African-American" section
- NSF Graduate Research Fellowship: Chapter 7, "Sciences" section

- Richard E. Merwin Student Scholarship: Chapter 6, "Computer Science and Engineering" section
- Society of Women Engineers Scholarships: Chapter 12, "Female" section
- Upsilon Pi Epsilon Student Award for Excellence: Chapter 6, "Computer Science and Engineering" section
- Xerox Technical Minority Scholarship: Chapter 9, "All Minorities" section

Construction

See the following scholarship:

- AGC Scholarships: Chapter 6, "Construction" section

Creative Writing

See the following scholarship:

- Jacob Javits Fellowship: Chapter 7, "Humanities" section

Criminal Justice

See the following scholarship:

- ASC Gene Carte Student Paper Competition: Chapter 6, "Criminal Justice" section

Demography

See the following scholarships:

- AWIS Graduate Awards: Chapter 12, "Female" section

- International Predissertation Fellowships: Chapter 7, "Social Sciences" section
- NSF Graduate Research Fellowship: Chapter 7, "Sciences" section

Dentistry and Dental Hygiene

AADS/Warner-Lambert Oral Hygiene Preventive Dentistry Scholarship

Sponsor: American Association of Dental Schools (AADS) and Warner-Lambert Company
Web Site: http://www.aads.jhu.edu/Awards/1999%20Awards/Student_Awards/Preventive_dentistry.htm
Amount of Scholarship: $2,500
Number of Awards: 12
Deadline: December 10
Education Level: dental school students
Eligibility: Applicant must enroll as a full-time student at a U.S. dental school, demonstrate an interest in preventive dentistry, and belong to AADS.

This page provides a brief overview of the scholarship program. It outlines eligibility requirements and the application process and provides a link to an application form that you can print out from your Web browser. To find out how to become a member of AADS, follow the link under the Eligibility section.

Dr. and Mrs. Gerald M. Kramer Scholarship for Excellence

Sponsor: American Academy of Periodontology Foundation

Web Site: http://www.perio.org/foundation/kramer.html
Amount of Scholarship: $10,000
Number of Awards: 1
Deadline: May 15
Education Level: graduate students
Eligibility: Applicant must be enrolled in the third year of an accredited periodontal graduate program at a U.S. or Canadian university.

This page is basically a FAQ (frequently asked questions) for the scholarship program. It tells you the basics about eligible requirements, selection criteria, and the nomination process. The PDF application form, which is linked to the scholarship's Web page, provides a lot more information about the objectives of the scholarship and application requirements.

Hellenic American Dental Society Scholarship

Sponsor: Hellenic American Dental Society
Web Site: http://www.hads.com/html/scholarship.html
Amount of Scholarship: not given
Number of Awards: not given
Deadline: December 15
Education Level: dental school students
Eligibility: Applicant must enroll in an accredited U.S. dental school, be of Hellenic descent, and demonstrate financial need.

This page simply lists the eligibility requirements for the scholarship and provides a text version of the application form for printing. You can also download the application form in Microsoft Word format.

Also see the following scholarships:

• ADHA Institute for Oral Health Scholarships: Chapter 6, "Dentistry and Dental Hygiene" section

• Arkansas Health Education Grant: Chapter 15, "Arkansas" section
• Martin Luther King, Jr. Physician & Dentist Scholarship: Chapter 15, "New Jersey" section
• New York State Regents Health Care Opportunity Scholarship: Chapter 15, "New York" section
• Professional School Scholarship: Chapter 15, "Maryland" section

Design

See the following scholarships:

• ASID Scholarships: Chapter 6, "Design" section
• IDSA Scholarships: Chapter 6, "Design" section

Economics and Finance

Daniel B. Goldberg Scholarship

Sponsor: Government Finance Officers Association
Web Site: http://www.gfoa.org
Amount of Scholarship: $3,500
Number of Awards: 1
Deadline: February 4
Education Level: master's students
Eligibility: Applicant must enroll as a full-time student in a graduate program in preparation for a career in local or state government finance, hold a bachelor's degree, and be a U.S. or Canadian citizen or permanent resident.

To find information about this scholarship, click the Scholarships link under the Services section and scroll down until you see the scholarship's name under Available Scholarships. Click the Forms link in the left frame to find a copy of the application. Scroll down until you see the Scholarships section and click the Daniel B. Goldberg Scholarship link to view the application form in PDF format. The application form provides a lot more information about eligibility requirements and judging criteria.

Economics Doctoral Research Fellowship

Sponsor: Consortium of Universities of the Washington Metropolitan Area and the Economic Club of Washington
Web Site: http://www.consortium.org/econ-g95.htm
Amount of Scholarship: $10,000
Number of Awards: 1
Deadline: March 31
Education Level: doctoral students
Eligibility: Applicant must enroll in a doctoral program in economics, business, finance, or international trade at a Consortium university.

This fellowship is intended to help fund dissertation research for doctoral students in economics-related subjects. Read the eligibility requirements to make sure you qualify. Follow the Consortium Institution link to find out if your university is a member of the sponsoring consortium. To apply for the fellowship, follow the instructions under the Application Procedures. You don't need to submit an official application form in order to apply.

Predissertation Fellowship in Applied Economics

Sponsor: Social Science Research Council (SSRC)
Web Site: http://www.ssrc.org/paefell.htm#dis
Amount of Scholarship: not given
Number of Awards: 20 to 25

Deadline: February 3
Education Level: doctoral students
Eligibility: Applicant must enroll as a full-time student in a doctoral program in economics or a related field and have completed the required coursework and qualifying examinations for the Ph.D.

Read the description on this page to find out who is eligible for the fellowship and what kind of research and other activities the fellowship money may be used to support. This page also describes the qualifications of a successful applicant. You will find a link to a list of past fellows and their dissertation topics at the end of the fellowship description. Click the link on the left-hand side of the Web page to download the application form in PDF format. Note that applicants who have attended an SSRC Summer Workshop in Applied Economics are given preference; learn more about this program by following the appropriate link on the left side of the page.

Public Employee Retirement Research and Administration Scholarship

Sponsor: Government Finance Officers Association and ICMA Retirement Corporation
Web Site: http://www.gfoa.org
Amount of Scholarship: $3,500
Number of Awards: 1
Deadline: February 4
Education Level: graduate students
Eligibility: Applicant must enroll in a graduate program in business administration, finance, public administration, or social sciences; plan to pursue a career in state or local government with a focus on public-sector retirement benefits; hold a bachelor's degree; and be a U.S. or Canadian citizen or permanent resident.

To find information about this scholarship, click the Scholarships link under the Services section and scroll down until you see the scholarship's name listed under Available Scholarships. Click the Forms link in the left frame to find a copy of the application. Scroll down until you see the Scholarships section, then click the Public Employee Retirement Research Scholarship link to view the application form in PDF format. The application provides a lot more information about eligibility requirements and judging criteria.

Public Investor Scholarship

Sponsor: Government Finance Officers Association and Fidelity Investments Public Sector Services Company
Web Site: http://www.gfoa.org
Amount of Scholarship: $3,000
Number of Awards: 1
Deadline: February 4
Education Level: master's students
Eligibility: Applicant must enroll in a graduate program in finance, public administration, business administration, or social sciences; hold a bachelor's degree; and be a U.S. or Canadian citizen or permanent resident.

To find information about this scholarship, click the Scholarships link under the Services section and scroll down until you see the scholarship's name listed under Available Scholarships. Click the Forms link in the left frame to find a copy of the application. Scroll down until you see the Scholarships section, then click the Public Investor Scholarship link to view the application form in PDF format. The application provides a lot more information about eligibility requirements and judging criteria.

Also see the following scholarships:

- AICPA Scholarship for Minority Accounting Students: Chapter 6, "Accounting" section
- AWIS Graduate Awards: Chapter 12, "Female" section
- Graduate Foreign Affairs Fellowship: Chapter 7, "International Studies" section
- Institute of Management Accountants National Scholarships: Chapter 6, "Accounting" section
- International Predissertation Fellowships: Chapter 7, "Social Sciences" section
- Jacob Javits Fellowship: Chapter 7, "Humanities" section
- Karla Scherer Foundation Scholarship: Chapter 6, "Economics and Finance" section
- Minorities in Government Finance Scholarship: Chapter 9, "All Minorities" section
- NAFOA Student Scholarship: Chapter 9, "Native American" section
- NSF Graduate Research Fellowship: Chapter 7, "Sciences" section

Education

AASA Graduate Student Scholarship

Sponsor: American Association of School Administrators (AASA)
Web Site: http://www.aasa.org/Programs/program9.htm
Amount of Scholarship: $2,000
Number of Awards: 6
Deadline: September 1
Education Level: graduate students
Eligibility: Applicant must enroll in a graduate program in educational administration and intend to pursue a career in public school superintendence.

This Web page provides a very brief description of the scholarship. The chairs of their educational administration departments must nominate candidates, and applications can be obtained from them. Get more information about the scholarship by contacting the address, phone number, or e-mail address given on the Web page.

FAME Student Scholarship

Sponsor: Florida Association for Media in Education (FAME)
Web Site: http://sun3.firn.edu/webfiles/others/fame/award.htm#scholarship
Amount of Scholarship: not given
Number of Awards: not given
Deadline: not given
Education Level: graduate students
Eligibility: Applicant must enroll in a education media program at a Florida university, have a minimum 3.0 GPA, and be a Florida resident.

This page describes the purpose, eligibility, and conditions of this scholarship for educational media graduate students in Florida. At the end of the description, you will find a link to a PDF copy of the application form that you can download.

HOPE Teacher Scholarship

Sponsor: Georgia State Finance Commission
Web Site: http://www.gsfc.org/hope/ttoc.htm
Amount of Scholarship: $10,000 (awarded over five years)
Number of Awards: not given
Deadline: none
Education Level: graduate students
Eligibility: Applicant must enroll in an advanced degree teacher education program in a critical teacher shortage field at an eligible Georgia university, be a Georgia resident, and be a U.S. citizen or permanent resident.

Scroll down to the bottom half of the Web page to find the HOPE Teacher Scholarship information. This program helps teachers obtain master's and doctoral degrees in exchange for agreeing to teach in critical shortage disciplines. First, read the Eligibility Requirements section to make sure that you qualify and that you are willing to comply with all the conditions of the scholarship. Also follow the Eligible Institutions and Critical Shortage Fields link to find out if the field you want to study and the university where you want to study it qualify for the program. Scroll down to the bottom of the scholarship's Web page and click the Promissory Notes link to find printable copies of the scholarship regulations and the service agreement (or promissory note) that you will have to sign if you accept the scholarship; this tells you exactly what your commitment will be. If you decide to apply, the Application Process page tells you how to get started.

James Madison Fellowship

Sponsor: James Madison Memorial Fellowship Foundation
Web Site: http://www.jamesmadison.com
Amount of Scholarship: up to $24,000 (awarded over two to five years)
Number of Awards: 53
Deadline: March 1
Education Level: college seniors and master's students
Eligibility: Applicant must enroll in a Master of Arts program in history or political science, a Master of Arts in Teaching program concentrating on American Constitutional history or American government, a Master of Education program concentrating on American history or government, or a Master of Arts or Master of Science program in education concentrating on American history or government at a U.S. university; already be or plan to become a teacher of American history, American government, or social studies at the secondary school level; hold a bachelor's degree; and be a U.S. citizen.

To learn more about this prestigious fellowship program, explore the links on the left of the introductory page. The Chairman's Welcome and About the Foundation links provide some background on the program. The Types of Fellowships page tells you about the two kinds of fellowships available: Junior Fellowships for recent college graduates and Senior Fellowships for experienced teachers. It also gives details on what fields of study are applicable for the fellowship and the summer institute component of the program. To find out if you are qualified to apply and what the conditions of accepting the fellowship are, go to the Requirements page. This page also provides short biographies of past recipients. The Questions & Answers page should answer your most common questions about the fellowship. Click the Faculty Reps link to find names and contact numbers of faculty representatives for the fellowship at different universities; the representative at the university you plan to attend can answer your questions and help you with the application procedures. To download the complete application package, click Application Deadline; you will have to fill out a short electronic form before you will be allowed to download the application materials.

Maley/FTE Technology Teacher Scholarship

Sponsor: Foundation for Technology Education (FTE)
Web Site: http://www.iteawww.org/I3c.html
Amount of Scholarship: $1,000
Number of Awards: not given
Deadline: December 1
Education Level: graduate students
Eligibility: Applicant must be a technology teacher at any grade level who is beginning or continuing graduate study, and be a member of the International Technology Education Association (ITEA).

This page describes the selection criteria and eligibility requirements for this scholarship for technology teachers. You do not have to submit an official application form for this scholarship; rather, you must assemble an application package as instructed in the Application and Deadline section of the Web page. Applicants must belong to ITEA. To learn more about membership and get a copy of the membership application, follow the Membership link at the bottom of the page. You can enclose your membership application with your scholarship application package.

Spencer Foundation Dissertation Fellowship

Sponsor: The Spencer Foundation
Web Site: http://www.spencer.org/fellows/index.htm
Amount of Scholarship: $20,000
Number of Awards: 30 to 35
Deadline: October 20
Education Level: doctoral students
Eligibility: Applicant must be writing a dissertation concerning education, be enrolled in a doctoral program at a U.S. university, and have completed all predissertation requirements.

This page provides an overview of the fellowship program, including its objectives and background. To learn more, explore the links on the left side of the page. The General Information page provides details about fellowship goals, eligibility requirements, conditions of accepting the award, and application deadlines. The Frequently Asked Questions page may provide answers to many of your questions about the program. To download an application form, click Fellowship Application Download. The other links lead to announcements and other information of interest to students who have received the fellowship.

Young Educators Committee Scholarship

Sponsor: United Teachers of Dade (UTD)
Web Site: http://www.utofd.com/yecschol.html
Amount of Scholarship: $1,000
Number of Awards: 4
Deadline: February 11
Education Level: graduate students
Eligibility: Applicant must enroll in a graduate education program and be a member of UTD.

This page briefly describes the eligibility requirements and application procedure for this scholarship. Follow the link at the bottom of the page to open a printable copy of the application form. To learn more about joining UTD, go to http://www.utofd.com/Membersh.html. You must be working as an education professional in Dade County, Florida, to become a member.

Also see the following scholarships:

- Gates Millennium Scholars: Chapter 9, "All Minorities" section
- Jewish Foundation for Education of Women Scholarships: Chapter 15, "New York" section
- KHEAA Teacher Scholarship: Chapter 6, "Education" section
- Maryland HOPE Teacher Scholarship: Chapter 6, "Education" section
- Martin Luther King, Jr. Memorial Scholarship: Chapter 6, "Education" section
- Minority Masters Fellowship: Chapter 9, "All Minorities" section
- NSF/STEMTEC Teaching Scholars: Chapter 6, "Education" section
- Tennessee Teaching Scholars: Chapter 6, "Education" section
- Underwood-Smith Teacher Scholarship: Chapter 6, "Education" section
- Zeta Phi Beta Scholarships and Fellowships: Chapter 12, "Female" section

Electronics

SRC Graduate Fellowships

Sponsor: Semiconductor Research Corporation (SRC)
Web Site: http://www.src.org/students/felowshp/gfpprog.dgw
Amount of Scholarship: one-half to full tuition plus a monthly stipend of $710 to $1,420
Number of Awards: not given
Deadline: February 3
Education Level: doctoral students
Eligibility: Applicant must enroll in a doctoral program in microelectronics under the guidance of an SRC-sponsored faculty member at a participating university, and be a U.S. or Canadian citizen or permanent resident.

This page provides an overview of the fellowship program and links to more information. First, follow the Eligibility link to find out if you qualify. The Support Level link describes the different kinds of general fellowships available and their award amounts. You can learn more about the 10 named fellowships by following their links from the fellowship's main page. Go to How to Apply to learn how to obtain an application form. Then read the Application Instructions, which tell you how to put together an application package and link to downloadable application materials in PDF format. Be sure to indicate which specific fellowships you are applying for by checking the appropriate boxes on the application form.

SRC Master's Scholarship

Sponsor: Semiconductor Research Corporation (SRC)
Web Site: http://www.src.org/students/felowshp/masters.dgw

Amount of Scholarship: $14,000 per year and a monthly stipend of $1,400 (awarded over two years)

Number of Awards: not given

Deadline: February 3

Education Level: master's students

Eligibility: Applicant must enroll in a master's degree program in microelectronics under the guidance of an SRC-sponsored faculty member at a participating university, either be female or a member of a minority group, and be a U.S. or Canadian citizen or permanent resident.

Here you will find information about the scholarship program for female, African-American, Hispanic, and Native American master's students of microelectronics. To find out if you qualify for the scholarship, click the Eligibility link. Go to the Support Level page to learn about the fellowship award amounts and what they may be used for. The How to Apply and Application Instructions pages tell you where to obtain application materials and how to put together and submit an application package. The Application Instructions section also provides links to downloadable application forms and to a list of participating universities where the fellowship may be used.

Also see the following scholarships:

- AFCEA Ralph W. Shrader Scholarship: Chapter 7, "Communications Engineering and Technology" section
- ARRL Foundation Scholarships: Chapter 8, "Amateur Radio" section

Energy

Fusion Energy Sciences Fellowship

Sponsor: U.S. Department of Energy Office of Fusion Energy and Oak Ridge Institute for Science and Education

Web Site: http://www.orau.gov/orise/edu/uggrad/fesfelhome.htm

Amount of Scholarship: full tuition and a $15,600 stipend (renewable for three years)

Number of Awards: not given

Deadline: last Monday in January

Education Level: college seniors and first-year graduate students

Eligibility: Applicant must enroll as a full-time student in a doctoral program in fusion science or engineering at a participating university; hold a bachelor's degree in engineering, the physical sciences, mathematics, or a related discipline; and be a U.S. citizen or permanent resident.

Start by reading the Introduction to the Program and the Program at a Glance pages to get an overview of this fellowship program, its objectives, and other basic facts. Then, visit the Fellowship Obligations and Benefits pages to find all the details on the fellowship. The Participating Universities link provides a list of schools where the fellowship may be used, including faculty contacts at each university. The Practicum Sites link lists the laboratories where fellows may complete the practicum requirement of the fellowship. If you decide to apply, go to the Application Procedures page to see the eligibility requirements and find out how the selection process works. You can download all application materials in Microsoft Word, WordPerfect, or PDF format on the Application Materials page, as well as find instructions for completing the application forms. Follow the links at the very bottom of the fellowship's main page to learn more about the program's sponsors.

WiNUP Scholarships

Sponsor: Women's International Network of Utility Professionals (WiNUP)

Web Site: http://www.winup.org/sch.htm

Amount of Scholarship: $400 to $2,000
Number of Awards: 3
Deadline: not given
Education Level: graduate students
Eligibility: Applicant must enroll in an advanced degree program related to the study of electrical energy.

This page briefly describes the three scholarships available for graduate students in electrical energy: one for $2,000, one for $1,000, and one for $400. Only the $400 scholarship is restricted to WiNUP members. Click the Scholarship Application link at the bottom of the page to open a text version of the application form that you can print from your Web browser.

Also see the following scholarship:

- NSF Graduate Research Fellowship: Chapter 7, "Sciences" section

Engineering

Arthur S. Tuttle Memorial National Scholarship

Sponsor: American Society of Civil Engineers (ASCE)
Web Site: http://www.asce.org/peta/ed/app_tut.html
Amount of Scholarship: $3,000 to $5,000
Number of Awards: not given
Deadline: February 11
Education Level: master's students
Eligibility: Applicant must enroll in an accredited master's program in civil engineering and be a member of ASCE.

This page describes the eligibility requirements, selection criteria, and application procedures for this scholarship for civil engineering mas-

ter's students. At the bottom of the page, you will find the application form in text format and a link to a PDF version of the form. Click the Membership button on the left side of the Web page to learn about joining ASCE and find an online membership application; you must be a member of ASCE to apply for the scholarship.

ASME Graduate Teaching Fellowship

Sponsor: American Society of Mechanical Engineers (ASME)
Web Site: http://www.asme.org/educate/aid/fellow.htm
Amount of Scholarship: $5,000 per year (awarded for two years)
Number of Awards: not given
Deadline: October 20
Education Level: doctoral students
Eligibility: Applicant must be a doctoral student in mechanical engineering, hold a master's degree or pass a qualifying exam, hold a bachelor's degree from an ABET-accredited engineering program, demonstrate interest in teaching as a career, have a lecture-responsibility teaching commitment from his or her academic department, teach at least one lecture class during the term, be a student member of ASME, and be a U.S. citizen or permanent resident.

According to the description on the fellowship's Web page, this program is intended to encourage more mechanical engineering students, particularly women and minorities, to pursue the doctorate in mechanical engineering and pursue engineering education as a career. Most of the Web page details the strict eligibility requirements for this fellowship. If you qualify, you can download a copy of the application form in PDF format by following a link on the page. You can also access the ASME

Student Membership Application if you are not yet a member of ASME.

Yanmar/SAE Scholarship

Sponsor: Yanmar Diesel America Corporation and Society of Automotive Engineers (SAE) Foundation
Web Site: http://www.sae.org/students/yanmar.htm
Amount of Scholarship: $2,000 (awarded over two years)
Number of Awards: 1
Deadline: April 1
Education Level: college seniors and graduate students
Eligibility: Applicant must enroll in an engineering program studying the conservation of energy in transportation, agriculture, construction, or power generation; and be a U.S., Canadian, or Mexican citizen.

The Web page briefly describes the eligibility requirements, selection criteria, and corporate sponsor of this scholarship. You can link to an application form at the bottom of the page. Although you can fill out the application in your Web browser, you cannot submit it electronically. Instead, you must print it out complete with your responses and mail it in to the address given, along with all of the requested supporting documents.

Also see the following scholarships:

- AFCEA Fellowship: Chapter 7, "Communications Engineering and Technology" section
- AFCEA Ralph W. Shrader Scholarship: Chapter 7, "Communications Engineering and Technology" section
- AGC Scholarships: Chapter 6, "Construction" section
- AISES A. T. Anderson Memorial Scholarship: Chapter 9, "Native American" section

- ARRL Foundation Scholarships: Chapter 8, "Amateur Radio" section
- ASME Auxiliary Scholarships: Chapter 6, "Engineering" section
- ASNE Scholarships: Chapter 6, "Engineering" section
- Astronaut Scholarship: Chapter 6, "Sciences" section
- AWIS Graduate Awards: Chapter 12, "Female" section
- Cooperative Research Fellowship: Chapter 9, "All Minorities" section
- Department of Energy Computational Science Graduate Fellowship: Chapter 7, "Sciences" section
- Gates Millennium Scholars: Chapter 9, "All Minorities" section
- GEM Fellowships: Chapter 9, "All Minorities" section
- Graduate Research Program for Women Fellowship: Chapter 12, "Female" section
- Hertz Foundation Fellowship: Chapter 7, "Sciences" section
- IIE Scholarships: Chapter 6, "Engineering" section
- Lucent Florida Universities Fellowship: Chapter 15, "Florida" section
- NASA Graduate Student Researchers Program Fellowship: Chapter 7, "Aerospace Sciences and Engineering" section
- National Defense Science and Engineering Graduate Fellowship: Chapter 7, "Sciences" section
- NPSC Graduate Fellowships in the Physical Sciences: Chapter 7, "Sciences" section
- NSBE Scholarships: Chapter 9, "African-American" section
- NSF Graduate Research Fellowship: Chapter 7, "Sciences" section
- SME Scholarships: Chapter 6, "Engineering" section
- Society of Women Engineers Scholarships: Chapter 12, "Female" section

- SPE Foundation Scholarships: Chapter 6, "Engineering" section
- Winston Churchill Foundation Scholarship: Chapter 7, "Study Abroad" section
- Xerox Technical Minority Scholarship: Chapter 9, "All Minorities" section

English and Comparative Literature

See the following scholarships:

- Andrew W. Mellon Fellowship in Humanistic Studies: Chapter 7, "Humanities" section
- Jacob Javits Fellowship: Chapter 7, "Humanities" section

Environmental Studies

Canadian Water Resources Association Scholarship

Sponsor: Canadian Water Resources Association
Web Site: http://www.cwra.org/scholar/scholarshipframe1.html
Amount of Scholarship: $1,250 (Canadian)
Number of Awards: 4
Deadline: March 1
Education Level: graduate students
Eligibility: Applicant must study the applied, natural, or social sciences aspects of water resources, be a full-time student at a Canadian university, and be a Canadian citizen.

This scholarship is intended for students researching all aspects of water resources, as described in the introduction on the scholarship's Web page. Click the More About the Scholarship Program link to get the details. This page

lists the eligibility requirements and tells you how to obtain an application form and submit the application package. You will also find a link to a sample application form that you can use to start preparing your application right away.

Earl Renshaw Memorial Scholarship

Sponsor: Furbearers Unlimited, Inc.
Web Site: http://www.furbearers.org/Scholarship.htm
Amount of Scholarship: $500 to $1,000
Number of Awards: 1 to 2
Deadline: July 1
Education Level: graduate students
Eligibility: Applicant must study wildlife management.

This page provides only a few details about the scholarship program. There is also a link to a text version of the scholarship application, which you can print out from your Web browser.

Environmental Public Policy and Conflict Resolution Fellowship

Sponsor: Morris K. Udall Foundation
Web Site: http://udallfoundation.org/p_fellowships.htm
Amount of Scholarship: $24,000
Number of Awards: 2
Deadline: January 15
Education Level: doctoral students
Eligibility: Applicant must be researching environmental public policy or environmental conflict resolution, be in the final writing year of his or her Ph.D. work, and be a U.S. citizen or permanent resident.

Here you will find a brief overview of the fellowship and a list of past recipients. Click the Application Guidelines link to find out how to apply. This page also describes the purpose of the fellowship, the qualifications that the sponsor is looking for in fellowship applicants, and the conditions of accepting the fellowship. Finally, it tells you how to obtain an application and how to submit the form.

IAGLR-C.S. Mott Scholarship

Sponsor: International Association for Great Lakes Research (IAGLR)
Web Site: http://www.iaglr.org/as/iaglrmottapp.html
Amount of Scholarship: $5,000
Number of Awards: 2
Deadline: February 29
Education Level: graduate students
Eligibility: Applicant must be conducting large lakes research and be a full-time student in a MS or Ph.D. program at an accredited university.

On this page you will learn about the purpose of this scholarship, the eligibility requirements, the judging criteria, and the conditions of accepting the award. You will also find a list of all of the documents that make up the application package. An official application form is not required.

Switzer Environmental Fellowship

Sponsor: Switzer Environmental Programs
Web Site: http://www.switzernetwork.org/HTMLSrc/Fellowships.html
Amount of Scholarship: not given
Number of Awards: 20
Deadline: not given
Education Level: graduate students

Eligibility: Applicant must study a field related to improving the quality of the natural environment and be a resident of either New England or California.

While not a lot of information is given about the actual fellowship award, this page does describe what the sponsor is looking for in fellowship applicants, so you can better decide if you will make a good candidate for the award. The page also provides some information about the application process and gives contact information for learning more, depending on which region you live in. To read about the background of the program, click the Home link at the bottom of the page, then click Switzer Environmental Programs.

Also see the following scholarships:

- AISES A. T. Anderson Memorial Scholarship: Chapter 9, "Native American" section
- FFGC Scholarships: Chapter 15, "Florida" section
- Garden Club of Georgia Scholarships: Chapter 15, "Georgia" section
- Georgia Water and Pollution Control Association Scholarships: Chapter 14, "Unions and Professional Associations" section
- James L. Goodwin Memorial Scholarship: Chapter 6, "Environmental Studies" section
- NASA Graduate Student Researchers Program Fellowship: Chapter 7, "Aerospace Sciences and Engineering" section
- National Council of State Garden Clubs Scholarship: Chapter 6, "Horticulture" section
- NEHA/AAS Scholarship: Chapter 6, "Health Care" section
- NPSC Graduate Fellowships in the Physical Sciences: Chapter 7, "Sciences" section
- NSF Graduate Research Fellowship: Chapter 7, "Sciences" section
- Paul W. Rodgers Scholarship: Chapter 6, "Environmental Studies" section

Family and Consumer Sciences

Kappa Omicron Nu Fellowships

Sponsor: Kappa Omicron Nu
Web Site: http://www.kon.org/grants.html
Amount of Scholarship: $2,000
Number of Awards: 5
Deadline: April 1
Education Level: graduate students
Eligibility: Applicant must enroll in a family and consumer sciences program and be a member of Kappa Omicron Nu.

Two separate fellowship programs are available: a master's program, which awards two fellowships; and a doctoral program, which awards three fellowships. The selection criteria and application procedures for both programs are described on this page. Open a printable application form for each fellowship by following the link at the end of the fellowship description. To find out what the necessary qualifications for joining Kappa Omicron Nu are and how to become a member, click the Kappa Omicron Nu Member link at the top of the page.

Film and Television

See the following scholarships:

- David J. Clark Memorial Scholarship Grant: Chapter 6, "Film and Television" section
- Jacob Javits Fellowship: Chapter 7, "Humanities" section
- Jessica Savitch Scholarship: Chapter 6, "Communications" section
- Kodak Scholarship: Chapter 6, "Film and Television" section

- NHFA Entertainment Industry Scholarship: Chapter 9, "Hispanic" section

Food Science and Nutrition

See the following scholarships:

- ADA Scholarships: Chapter 6, "Food Science and Nutrition" section
- IFT Scholarships: Chapter 6, "Food Science and Nutrition" section
- School Food Service Foundation Scholarships: Chapter 14, "Employer and Profession" section

Geography

William A. Fischer Memorial Scholarship

Sponsor: American Society for Photogrammetry and Remote Sensing (ASPRS)
Web Site: http://www.asprs.org/membership.html
Amount of Scholarship: $2,000
Number of Awards: 1
Deadline: December 1
Education Level: graduate students
Eligibility: Applicant must study remote sensing at an accredited university and be a member of ASPRS.

To find the scholarship information, click the Awards and Scholarships link, then click the name of the scholarship in the list of awards. There you will find a description of the goals of this scholarship for students of remote sensing, as well as information on who is eligible to apply, how to submit an application, and how the application is evaluated. To find the application form, return to the top of the page and click the Application Instructions link, which tells you how to complete the application. Then follow the Application Forms link to open the application in PDF format. To find out how to become a member of ASPRS, click the Individual Membership link on the left side of the page.

Also see the following scholarships:

- ACSM Scholarships: Chapter 6, "Geography" section
- AWIS Graduate Awards: Chapter 12, "Female" section
- International Predissertation Fellowship: Chapter 7, "Social Sciences" section
- Jacob Javits Fellowship: Chapter 7, "Humanities" section
- NSF Graduate Research Fellowship: Chapter 7, "Sciences" section
- Robert E. Altenhofen Memorial Scholarship: Chapter 6, "Geography" section

Geosciences

AAPG Foundation Grant-in-Aid

Sponsor: American Association of Petroleum Geologists (AAPG) Foundation
Web Site: http://www.aapg.org/foundation/gia/about.html
Amount of Scholarship: $2,000
Number of Awards: around 150
Deadline: January 31
Education Level: graduate students
Eligibility: Applicant must enroll in a graduate program in the geosciences and perform research related to petroleum and energy-

minerals resources and related environmental geology issues.

This page describes this grant program, including the basis for awarding grants and how grants may be used. Note that grants can only be used for thesis or dissertation research; they cannot be used for tuition or living expenses. Click the How to Apply link on the left-hand side of the Web page to find instructions for filling out an application for a grant. Follow the Application link to open the application form in PDF format.

AGI Minority Geoscience Scholarship

Sponsor: American Geological Institute (AGI)
Web Site: http://www.agiweb.org/ehr/mgsftp.html
Amount of Scholarship: not given
Number of Awards: not given
Deadline: not given
Education Level: college undergraduates and graduate students
Eligibility: Applicant must major in a geoscience field, be a full-time student at an accredited college or university, be a member of a minority group, and be a U.S. citizen.

The top of the Web page outlines the eligibility requirements for this scholarship. Note that only undergraduates who are already participating in the AGI Minority Scholarship Program are eligible to apply for an undergraduate scholarship; new applications are not being accepted at the time of this writing. Keep watching this page, because applications may reopen to undergraduates in future years. At the graduate level, however, any qualified students may apply, whether they have previously received a scholarship or not. Eligible minorities include

African-Americans, Hispanics, Native Americans, Alaskan Natives, Hawaiian Natives, and Samoans. Applicable majors include geology, geophysics, geochemistry, hydrology, meteorology, physical oceanography, planetary geology, or earth sciences education. You will find instructions for submitting an application underneath the Application Procedures heading. A text version of the application form that you can print out is provided at the bottom of the page.

GSA Graduate Student Research Grants

Sponsor: Geological Society of America (GSA)
Web Site: http://www.geosociety.org/profdev/grants/gradgrants.htm
Amount of Scholarship: varies
Number of Awards: around 200
Deadline: February 1
Education Level: graduate students
Eligibility: Applicant must enroll in a graduate program in the earth sciences at a North American or Central American university.

This page gives an overview of the grant program and tells you how to apply. To learn more about what grants are available, link to the Information About GSA Grants Program page, which tells you what kinds of grants are available. Specialized and division grants are awarded only for research in specific subdisciplines of the earth sciences, and the section grants are limited to students in particular geographic regions, as detailed in their descriptions. The Tips for Student Applications page provides valuable help with preparing a successful application. Go to the Policies and Procedures page to get all the facts about eligibility, guidelines for using grants, and submitting applications. Note that women, minorities, and

students with disabilities are particularly encouraged to apply. If you decide to apply, click the Forms link to find copies of all of the required application forms in PDF format.

Also see the following scholarships:

- AWIS Graduate Awards: Chapter 12, "Female" section
- GEM Fellowships: Chapter 9, "All Minorities" section
- Hertz Foundation Fellowship: Chapter 7, "Sciences" section
- NASA Graduate Student Researchers Program Fellowship: Chapter 7, "Aerospace Sciences and Engineering" section
- National Defense Science and Engineering Graduate Fellowship: Chapter 7, "Sciences" section
- NPSC Graduate Fellowships in the Physical Sciences: Chapter 7, "Sciences" section
- NSF Graduate Research Fellowship: Chapter 7, "Sciences" section
- SEG Foundation Scholarships: Chapter 6, "Geosciences" section

Gerontology

AARP Andrus Foundation Graduate Scholarships in Gerontology

Sponsor: Association for Gerontology in Higher Education and American Association of Retired Persons (AARP) Andrus Foundation
Web Site: http://www.aghe.org/scholfell.htm
Amount of Scholarship: $7,000 to $15,000
Number of Awards: 8
Deadline: February 4

Education Level: graduate students
Eligibility: Applicant must enroll as a full-time student in a graduate program in gerontology or aging studies at an accredited U.S. university and plan to work in the field of aging.

This scholarship information page starts out with a brief description of the goal of the program, followed by an overview of the different awards available for master's and doctoral students. Three fellowships of $15,000 each are available for doctoral students, and five fellowships of $7,000 each are awarded to master's students. Two of the master's fellowships are reserved for terminal master's students. Keep reading to find out what the eligibility requirements, application procedures, and selection criteria are. At the bottom of the page you will find a checklist of all items that must be included in the application package and links to printable copies of the application and nomination forms.

Government and Public Service

See the following scholarship:

- Public Service Scholarship: Chapter 6, "Government and Public Service" section

Health Care

See the following scholarships:

- ACMPE Scholarships: Chapter 6, "Health Care" section
- Congressional Black Caucus Spouses Scholarship: Chapter 15 "Alabama" section
- Hays Medical Center Scholarships: Chapter 6, "Health Care" section

- Indian Health Service Scholarship: Chapter 9, "Native American" section
- NEHA/AAS Scholarship: Chapter 6, "Health Care" section
- Secretary's Award for Innovations in Health: Chapter 6, "Health Care" section
- Zeta Phi Beta Scholarships and Fellowships: Chapter 12, "Female" section

Heating, Refrigeration, and Air Conditioning

See the following scholarship:

- ASHRAE Scholarships: Chapter 6, "Heating, Refrigeration, and Air Conditioning" section

Historic Preservation

See the following scholarship:

- Garden Club of Georgia Scholarships: Chapter 15, "Georgia" section

History

Life Members' Fellowship in Electrical History

Sponsor: Institute of Electrical and Electronics Engineers (IEEE) History Center
Web Site: http://www.ieee.org/organizations/history_center/general_info/programs_and_projects/fellowship/fellowship.html
Number of Awards: 1

Amount of Scholarship: $15,000
Deadline: February 1
Education Level: graduate students
Eligibility: Applicant must study the history of electrical science and technology, hold a bachelor's degree, and be a full-time student at an accredited university.

This Web page provides a brief overview of the fellowship and the eligibility requirements. Beneath that are a link to the fellowship application in printable text format and instructions for completing the application.

Pathfinder Historians Scholarship

Sponsor: Pathfinder Historians
Web Site: http://www.pathfinder.org/index.html
Amount of Scholarship: not given
Number of Awards: not given
Deadline: January 15
Education Level: graduate students
Eligibility: Applicant must intend to research the legacy of enslavement and retribution in the United States and be a U.S. citizen.

The main page of the Web site describes the organization's purpose and its reasons for awarding scholarships. As you can see from this description, scholarships and fellowships go to graduate students in history, business, law, journalism, and political science fields researching the history of slavery in the United States, particularly slaves of African descent. To learn more, click the Our Purpose link. If you would like to apply for a scholarship to support this goal, click the Scholarships & Fellowships link. Preference is given to students who apply using the electronic form on this page. Unfortunately, the Web page does not describe the

scholarship program in depth, so you may want to contact the mailing address listed on the main page for more information before applying.

Sir John A. Macdonald Graduate Fellowship in Canadian History

Sponsor: Ontario Ministry of Training, Colleges, and Universities
Web Site: http://osap.gov.on.ca/NOT_SECURE/MAC.htm
Amount of Scholarship: $8,500 Canadian (renewable for three years)
Number of Awards: 1
Deadline: March 20
Education Level: graduate students
Eligibility: Applicant must enroll as a full-time student in a graduate program in Canadian history at an Ontario university, hold an Honours Bachelor of Arts degree from an Ontario university, have at least a B+ GPA, be a resident of Ontario, and be a Canadian citizen.

All of the information about this scholarship published on the Web site is in PDF format, so you will need the Adobe Acrobat Reader to access it. For general information and instructions on submitting an application, follow the Instructions link. Click the Application Form link to view and print the fellowship application.

Also see the following scholarships:

• Andrew W. Mellon Fellowship in Humanistic Studies: Chapter 7, "Humanities" section
• AWIS Graduate Awards: Chapter 12, "Female" section
• International Predissertation Fellowship: Chapter 7, "Social Sciences" section

- Jacob Javits Fellowship: Chapter 7, "Humanities" section
- James Madison Fellowship: Chapter 7, "Education" section
- NSF Graduate Research Fellowship: Chapter 7, "Sciences" section

Horticulture

American Iris Society Scholarship

Sponsor: American Iris Society
Web Site: http://www.www4.net/dwarfiris.soc/AIS-SC.htm
Amount of Scholarship: $2,000
Number of Awards: 1
Deadline: March 1
Education Level: graduate students
Eligibility: Applicant must be studying the Iridaceae at a U.S. or Canadian university and be a U.S. or Canadian citizen.

This scholarship is awarded only to students conducting researching on the Iridaceae. The description on the scholarship's Web page tells you exactly what kinds of research the sponsor is soliciting. It also tells you how to put together and submit an application package and where to send it. There is no official application form for this scholarship.

Also see the following scholarships:

- Bedding Plants Foundation Scholarships: Chapter 6, "Horticulture" section
- FFGC Scholarships: Chapter 15, "Florida" section
- Garden Club of Georgia Scholarships: Chapter 15, "Georgia" section

- Katharine M. Grosscup Scholarships: Chapter 6, "Horticulture" section
- National Council of State Garden Clubs Scholarship: Chapter 6, "Horticulture" section
- North Carolina Tomato Growers Scholarship: Chapter 15, "North Carolina" section
- NSF Graduate Research Fellowship: Chapter 7, "Sciences" section
- Sidney B. Meadows Scholarship: Chapter 6, "Horticulture" section"

Humanities

Andrew W. Mellon Fellowship in Humanistic Studies

Sponsor: Andrew W. Mellon Foundation
Web Site: http://www.woodrow.org/mellon
Amount of Scholarship: full tuition and a $14,750 stipend
Number of Awards: 85
Deadline: December 21
Education Level: college seniors
Eligibility: Applicant must enroll as a full-time student in a doctoral program in an eligible field of study in the humanities at an accredited U.S. or Canadian university and be a U.S. citizen or permanent resident.

This Web page describes this very prestigious fellowship for graduate students in the humanities. First, you should learn more about the fellowship's sponsor by following the link to the Andrew W. Mellon Foundation. The fellowship's Web page describes the overall goals of the program. Follow the link to The Award on the left-hand side of the page to find out about eligibility requirements, application guidelines, and the selection process. This page also provides a list of eligible humanities disciplines that you can use the fellowship to study. Request an application form by following the link to the electronic application request form under the Requesting an Application section. This section also links to a list of Mellon campus representatives; you should enlist the help of your college's or university's campus representative to help you prepare an application package for this very competitive fellowship.

ISI Weaver Fellowship

Sponsor: Intercollegiate Studies Institute (ISI)
Web Site: http://www.isi.org/programs/fellowships/weaver.asp
Amount of Scholarship: full tuition and a $5,000 stipend
Number of Awards: not given
Deadline: February 15
Education Level: college seniors and graduate students
Eligibility: Applicant must pursue a graduate degree for the purpose of teaching at the college level in the liberal arts or social sciences, receive *The Intercollegiate Review,* and be a U.S. citizen.

Read the introduction to the fellowship's Web page to learn more about the purpose of the fellowship and the kind of student the fellowship is intended to aid. Scroll down the page to find an outline of all the materials that must be included in the application package. A toll-free phone number and e-mail address are given at the bottom of the page, if you require more information. To learn more about receiving *The Intercollegiate Review,* click the Publications link in the bar at the bottom of the page. You should also explore the rest of the links to learn more about ISI purposes and

programs, which is one of the fellowship's eligibility requirements.

Jacob Javits Fellowship

Sponsor: U.S. Department of Education
Web Site: http://www.ed.gov/offices/OPE/OHEP/iegps/javits.html
Amount of Scholarship: $25,500 (awarded over two years)
Number of Awards: around 43
Deadline: November 29
Education Level: college seniors and first-year graduate students
Eligibility: Applicant must enroll in a Master of Fine Arts (MFA) or doctoral program in an eligible field of study in the arts, humanities, or social sciences at an accredited U.S. university, and be a U.S. citizen or permanent resident.

This page provides an overview of this extremely prestigious fellowship program and its eligibility requirements, as well as instructions for applying. The bulk of the fellowship awards go to students in the humanities, but 20 percent of the awards are reserved for students of the arts and 20 percent for students of the social sciences. You can download a copy of the complete application package in either PDF or Microsoft Word format by following the links at the bottom of the Web page. The application package contains more detailed information about the fellowship, including a list of eligible fields of study, the conditions of accepting the award, a description of the application review process, and detailed application instructions.

Also see the following scholarships:

- International Dissertation Field Research Fellowship: Chapter 7, "Study Abroad" section

• Jewish Foundation for Education of Women Scholarships: Chapter 15, "New York" section

Insurance

See the following scholarship:

• State Farm Companies Foundation Doctoral Dissertation Awards: Chapter 7, "Business" section

International Studies

Graduate Foreign Affairs Fellowship

Sponsor: U.S. Department of State
Web Site: http://www.woodrow.org/public-policy/gfaf
Amount of Scholarship: full tuition (awarded for two years)
Number of Awards: not given
Deadline: February 28
Education Level: first-year master's students
Eligibility: Applicant must enroll as a full-time student in a two-year master's program of relevance to the U.S. Foreign Service at a U.S. university, have a minimum 3.2 GPA, and be a U.S. citizen.

This fellowship recruits graduate students into serving in the U.S. Foreign Service. The Goal section of the page describes the objectives of the program and eligible fields of study. The rest of the page provides details on eligibility requirements, selection criteria, benefits of the award, and the service requirement. Eligible fields of study include international affairs, public policy and administration, or relevant academic fields, as detailed in this section. (Note that women, minorities, and students with financial need are particularly encouraged to apply.) You will also find some background information on the U.S. Foreign Service. At the bottom of the page, follow a link to an electronic form that you can fill out and submit to request that an application package be mailed to you.

NSEP Graduate International Fellowship

Sponsor: National Security Education Program (NSEP)
Web Site: http://www.aed.org/nsep
Amount of Scholarship: $2,000 per semester for domestic study and $10,000 per semester for study abroad (awarded for up to six semesters)
Number of Awards: not given
Deadline: January 15
Education Level: graduate students
Eligibility: Applicant must enroll in a graduate program at an accredited U.S. university in an eligible field of area or cultural studies, including study of a foreign language, and be a U.S. citizen.

This fellowship encourages cultural, language, and area study of regions that are important to U.S. national security but that are less frequently studied by U.S. students. This Web page details the goals of the fellowship, describes generally what an eligible program of study is, and lists the selection criteria. Note that this is a service scholarship; details of the service requirement are also provided on the Web page. At the bottom of the page you will find links to profiles of past fellows, frequently asked questions about the fellowship program, and an e-mail address that you may use to ask questions. You can also download the application form and guidelines in PDF format. The application form includes a list of areas of the world and fields of study that are critical to national security and thus eligible for study under the fellowship.

Also see the following scholarships:

- Andrew W. Mellon Fellowship in Humanistic Studies: Chapter 7, "Humanities" section
- International Predissertation Fellowship: Chapter 7, "Social Sciences" section
- Jacob Javits Fellowship: Chapter 7, "Humanities" section
- NSF Graduate Research Fellowship: Chapter 7, "Sciences" section

Jewish Studies

Maurice and Marilyn Cohen Fund for Doctoral Dissertation Fellowships in Jewish Studies

Sponsor: National Foundation for Jewish Culture
Web Site: http://www.jewishculture.org/scholarship/doctoralgrants.htm
Amount of Scholarship: $7,000 to $10,000
Number of Awards: 12
Deadline: January 3
Education Level: doctoral students
Eligibility: Applicant must enroll in a doctoral program in Jewish studies, have completed all requirements for the Ph.D. except the dissertation, have proficiency in a Jewish language, and be a U.S. citizen or permanent resident.

This page just gives a brief description of the fellowship's eligibility requirements and application procedures. For more details, link to the application form page, which provides information on the goals of the fellowship program and selection criteria, as well as application instructions.

Journalism

Stoody-West Fellowship

Sponsor: United Methodist Communications
Web Site: http://www.umcom.org/scholarships
Amount of Scholarship: $6,000
Number of Awards: 2
Deadline: March 15
Education Level: graduate students
Eligibility: Applicant must enroll in a graduate program in journalism at an accredited U.S. university, plan to enter the field of religious journalism, and be a Christian.

To access the information and application for this scholarship, click the Stoody-West Fellowship link. You will need to have Adobe Acrobat Reader installed to read the file. The first page of the application form lists the eligibility requirements, and the last page lists the selection criteria.

Also see the following scholarships:

- Jessica Savitch Scholarship: Chapter 6, "Communications" section
- Johnson F. Hammond, MD Memorial Scholarship: Chapter 7, "Medicine" section
- Pathfinder Historians Scholarship: Chapter 7, "History" section

• Vaughan/NAHWW Scholarship: Chapter 6, "Journalism" section

Landscape Architecture and Design

See the following scholarships:

• FFGC Scholarships: Chapter 15, "Florida" section
• Garden Club of Georgia Scholarships: Chapter 15, "Georgia" section
• National Council of State Garden Clubs Scholarship: Chapter 6, "Horticulture" section
• New York State Regents Professional Opportunity Scholarship: Chapter 15, "New York" section

Languages and Linguistics

See the following scholarships:

• Andrew W. Mellon Fellowship in Humanistic Studies: Chapter 7, "Humanities" section
• AWIS Graduate Awards: Chapter 12, "Female" section
• Graduate Foreign Affairs Fellowship: Chapter 7, "International Studies" section
• Jacob Javits Fellowship: Chapter 7, "Humanities" section
• Minority Masters Fellowship: Chapter 9, "All Minorities" section
• NSEP Graduate International Fellowship: Chapter 7, "International Studies" section
• NSF Graduate Research Fellowship: Chapter 7, "Sciences" section

Law

AALL James F. Connolly Congressional Information Service Scholarship

Sponsor: American Association of Law Libraries (AALL)
Web Site: http://www.aallnet.org/services/sch_connolly.asp
Amount of Scholarship: $3,000
Number of Awards: 1
Deadline: April 1
Education Level: law school students
Eligibility: Applicant must enroll in an accredited law degree program, hold a degree in library science, and be a law librarian.

The short description of the scholarship indicates that it is intended for a law librarian who would like to pursue a law degree. If you fit this description, click the link at the bottom of the page to download the application form in PDF format.

C. Clyde Ferguson Law Scholarship

Sponsor: New Jersey Higher Education Student Assistance Authority
Web Site: http://www.state.nj.us/treasury/osa/grants/cfergindex.html
Amount of Scholarship: varies
Number of Awards: not given
Deadline: not given
Education Level: law school students
Eligibility: Applicant must enroll as a full-time student in an eligible New Jersey law school, be a member of a minority group or a disadvantaged student, be a New Jersey resident, and be a former or current Educational Opportunity Fund (EOG) grant recipient or meet EOF grant eligibility requirements.

The Eligibility section of the Web site describes the eligibility requirements for this scholarship, including a list of law schools in New Jersey where the scholarship may be used. To learn more about the EOF requirement, click the EOF link under Other Grants (on the right-hand side of the page). Click the Application link to find out how to obtain an application form (the form is not available on the Web site).

Mercer County Bar Association Scholarship

Sponsor: Mercer County Bar Association
Web Site: http://www.mercerbar.com
Amount of Scholarship: not given
Number of Awards: 3
Deadline: April 1
Education Level: law school students
Eligibility: Applicant must enroll in an accredited law school, demonstrate financial need, and be a resident of Mercer County.

Here you will find a brief description of the three scholarships available from the Mercer County Bar Association. If you would like to apply, go to the Contact MCBA page to request a scholarship application over the Internet.

Nelson Mandela Scholarship

Sponsor: National Black Law Students Association (NBLSA)
Web Site: http://www.nblsa.org/ m_scholr.htm
Amount of Scholarship: $500
Number of Awards: 6
Deadline: February 15
Education Level: law school students
Eligibility: Applicant must enroll in a U.S. law school, be a member of a NBLSA chapter, and be African-American.

This page briefly describes the scholarship, including the award's purpose, eligibility requirements, proposal topic, and required documents for the application. To obtain a copy of the application in PDF format, click the Application Form link at the bottom of the page.

Sandy Brown Scholarship

Sponsor: National Black Law Students Association (NBLSA)
Web Site: http://www.nblsa.org/ s_brown.htm
Amount of Scholarship: $500
Number of Awards: 2
Deadline: February 15
Education Level: law school students
Eligibility: Applicant must be a second- or third-year law student, be a member of NBLSA, and be African-American.

This is actually an essay contest. You will find the current essay topic on the Web page, along with instructions for submitting an application. To obtain a copy of the application form in PDF format, click the link at the bottom of the page.

Also see the following scholarships:

- AALL Educational Scholarships: Chapter 7, "Library and Information Science" section
- ABA Doctoral Dissertation Fellowship in Law and Social Science: Chapter 7, "Social Sciences" section
- George A. Strait Minority Stipend: Chapter 7, "Library and Information Science" section
- New York State Regents Professional Opportunity Scholarship: Chapter 15, "New York" section
- Pathfinder Historians Scholarships: Chapter 7, "History" section
- Professional School Scholarship: Chapter 15, "Maryland" section

Library and Information Science

AALL Educational Scholarships

Sponsor: American Association of Law Libraries (AALL)
Web Site: http://www.aallnet.org/services/sch_edu.asp
Amount of Scholarship: not given
Number of Awards: not given
Deadline: April 1
Education Level: gradate students
Eligibility: Applicant must enroll in an accredited library and information science program with an emphasis on law librarianship, or hold a library science degree and enroll in a related graduate degree program or in law school.

This page describes the five different scholarships available for law library students and provides application forms for each scholarship. Each award differs in the kind of graduate degree it supports: one goes to law school graduates earning a library science degree; one goes to college graduates earning a library science degree; one goes to library school graduates earning a law degree; one goes to library school graduates earning a graduate degree in a field other than the law; and one goes to law librarians for continuing education. Each award also has different eligibility requirements, listed underneath the name of the scholarship. All awards support current and future law librarians, though. Note that members of AALL are given preference for all of the scholarships, and one scholarship is restricted to members only (to learn how to become a member, click Join AALL at the top of the page). Choose the scholarship for which you would like to apply and click the Application link underneath the scholarship description to download a PDF copy of the application form.

ALA Scholarships

Sponsor: American Library Association (ALA)
Web Site: http://www.ala.org/work/awards/scholars.html
Amount of Scholarship: $1,000 to $6,000
Number of Awards: 68
Deadline: April 1
Education Level: graduate students
Eligibility: Applicant must enroll in an ALA-accredited library and information science program.

Here you will find information about all of the scholarships offered by ALA. First, click the Scholarship Descriptions link to find a list of available awards, with their specific award amounts. Make a list of all the scholarships for which you want to apply and note which group each scholarship belongs to; each group has different eligibility requirements that you must meet. Group 1 scholarships include three general awards, three awards for current library employees, and one award for a student specializing in library youth services; all awards in this group are for $3,000. The Group 2 scholarship of $2,500 is for a student preparing to become a school library media specialist. The two Group 3 scholarships of $6,000 each go to students pursuing degrees in children's librarianship. The Group 4 scholarship is for a student with disabilities, and the four Group 5 scholarships are for minority students; all of these awards are $2,500 each. The Group 6 scholarship of $1,000 requires membership in ALA. Finally, the Group 7 scholarships of $5,000 each also go to minority students. While you can apply for as many scholarships as you like, you can only receive one. You must check the appropriate boxes on the application form for all of the scholarships for which you want to be considered, and you have to follow special instructions if you are applying for more than one group of scholarships, as detailed in the Application Instructions at the top of the page. Open and print the application checklist, application form, and reference form by following the links at the top of the page.

Alaska Library Association Scholarship

Sponsor: Alaska Library Association
Web Site: http://www.alaska.net/~akla/scholar.html
Amount of Scholarship: $2,000
Number of Awards: 1
Deadline: January 15
Education Level: graduate students
Eligibility: Applicant must enroll as a full-time student in an accredited library and information science program, hold a bachelor's degree from an accredited college, and be a resident of Alaska.

This is a service scholarship that requires recipients to commit to work in an Alaskan library after graduation, as detailed in the Eligibility section of the scholarship's Web page. The rest of the page describes the purpose of the scholarship program and the criteria used to select winners. Note that preference is given to Alaskan Native applicants. If you want to apply, contact the mailing address or phone number at the bottom of the page.

Beta Phi Mu Scholarships

Sponsor: Beta Phi Mu
Web Site: http://www.beta-phi-mu.org/scholarship.html

Amount of Scholarship: $750 to $3,000
Number of Awards: not given
Deadline: March 15
Education Level: graduate students
Eligibility: Applicant must enroll in a library and information science program.

This page describes the six scholarships and fellowships offered by Beta Phi Mu. Each scholarship description lists that award's eligibility requirements and application requirements. Click the Application Form link under the scholarship's description to open a printable application form for that award. Although you can fill out the application form inside your Web browser, you must print it out and mail it in; you cannot submit it online. You will also find sample letters of recommendation for those scholarships that require them.

George A. Strait Minority Stipend

Sponsor: American Association of Law Libraries
Web Site: http://www.aallnet.org/services/sch_strait.asp
Amount of Scholarship: $3,500
Number of Awards: not given
Deadline: April 1
Education Level: master's students and law school students
Eligibility: Applicant must enroll in an accredited library and information science program or law school, have law librarianship experience, be a member of a minority group, and demonstrate financial need.

This page provides a brief description of this stipend for minority library science and law students. If you meet the eligibility requirements, you can download a PDF version of the application form by following the link on the Web page.

ISI Information Science Doctoral Dissertation Proposal Scholarship

Sponsor: Institute for Scientific Information (ISI) and American Society for Information Science Information Science Education Committee
Web Site: http://www.asis.org/awards/dscholarisi.htm
Amount of Scholarship: $1,500
Number of Awards: 1
Deadline: July 1
Education Level: doctoral students
Eligibility: Applicant must enroll in a doctoral program in information science, have completed all coursework for the Ph.D., and have a dissertation proposal accepted.

This page provides all of the details about this scholarship for information science doctoral students. First, read the Guidelines, which go over award amounts, the purpose of the award, and eligibility requirements. The Nomination Information section of the page tells you how to submit a nomination for the scholarship and how scholarship recipients are chosen. You don't have to submit an official application form to apply.

Louise Jane Moses—Agnes Davis Memorial Scholarship

Sponsor: California Librarians Black Caucus, Greater Los Angeles Chapter
Web Site: http://www.clbc.org/scholar.html
Amount of Scholarship: not given
Number of Awards: not given

Deadline: fall
Education Level: graduate students
Eligibility: Applicant must enroll in an accredited library and information science program at a California university, be a resident of California, and be African-American.

This page very briefly describes the scholarship program, with information on the award's purpose and eligibility requirements. It also provides the mailing address that you can write to for an application form (the application is not available on the Web site).

MASL Scholarship

Sponsor: Maine Association of School Libraries (MASL)
Web Site: http://www.maslibraries.org/_Organization/Scholarship_Information/scholarship_information.html
Amount of Scholarship: not given
Number of Awards: not given
Deadline: May 1
Education Level: graduate students
Eligibility: Applicant must enroll in a library and information science or educational media program at a Maine university and be a member of MASL.

This page briefly describes the scholarship and its eligibility requirements. Click the Application Form link to find a copy of the application form that you can print out from your Web browser. You can mail the application package to the address given on the scholarship's Web page.

NCLA Scholarships

Sponsor: North Carolina Library Association (NCLA)

Web Site: http://www.mindspring.com/~ncla /scholarships/schoregs.htm
Amount of Scholarship: $1,000
Number of Awards: 2
Deadline: May 15
Education Level: graduate students
Eligibility: Applicant must enroll in a library and information science program, hold a bachelor's degree, and be a North Carolina resident.

This page briefly describes the two scholarships available and lists the eligibility requirements and selection criteria for each. One is a general award, and the other goes to students of children and young adult librarianship. (A student loan is also available.) Click the Applications link at the bottom of the page to open a printable text application, and click the References link to open the recommendation form that you will also need to submit.

NJLA Scholarships

Sponsor: New Jersey Library Association (NJLA)
Web Site: http://www.njla.org/scholarships
Amount of Scholarship: $400 to full tuition
Number of Awards: not given
Deadline: February 11
Education Level: graduate students
Eligibility: Applicant must enroll in an accredited library science program, demonstrate financial need, and be a New Jersey resident.

Here you will find a list of the nine scholarships available under this program and their eligibility requirements, including one full-tuition scholarship for public librarianship. Scholarship applications are not available online, so you must contact the mailing address, phone number, or e-mail address listed at the bottom of the page to obtain application materials.

REFORMA Scholarship

Sponsor: REFORMA—National Association to Promote Library Services to the Spanish Speaking
Web Site: http://clnet.ucr.edu/library/ reforma/schinfo.html
Amount of Scholarship: $2,000
Number of Awards: not given
Deadline: May 15
Education Level: college seniors and graduate students
Eligibility: Applicant must enroll in a library and information science program, speak Spanish, and be a U.S. citizen or permanent resident.

This Web page gives all the details for the REFORMA Scholarship program, including the purpose of the award, eligibility requirements, and application procedures. There is also a link to the official application form in PDF format.

Sheila Suen Lai Scholarship of Library and Information Science

Sponsor: Chinese American Librarians Association (CALA)
Web Site: http://www.cala-web.org
Amount of Scholarship: $500
Number of Awards: 1
Deadline: February 1
Education Level: graduate students
Eligibility: Applicant must enroll as a full-time student in an accredited library and information science program at a North American university, and be of Chinese descent.

To find information about this scholarship, click the Scholarships link in the left frame, then click the name of the scholarship. Follow the Annual Announcement link to find all the details about the scholarship program. The Application Guidelines page tells you how to prepare and submit your application package. You will also find links to the Application Form and the Reference Form, which you will need to submit in your application package.

SLA Scholarships

Sponsor: Special Libraries Association (SLA)
Web Site: http://www.sla.org/membership/hpschol.html
Amount of Scholarship: $1,000 to $6,000
Number of Awards: 7
Deadline: October 31
Education Level: college seniors and graduate students
Eligibility: Applicant must enroll in an accredited library and information science program, show an interest in special librarianship, and demonstrate financial need.

Here you will find descriptions of the master's, Ph.D., and postgraduate scholarships available from SLA. Each scholarship listing provides details on award amounts, eligibility requirements, and application instructions. There are two scholarships for master's students, two for doctoral students, and one for postgraduate study. The master's scholarships include a general award and an award for minority students; both awards are $6,000. The two Ph.D. scholarships of $1,000 each require membership in SLA. (To find out how to become a member of SLA, click the Join SLA Now link on the left-hand side of the page.) At the bottom of the page are links to text versions of all scholarship applications and instructions for completing the applications. Be sure to print the correct application form for the scholarship for which you want to apply.

Also see the following scholarships:

- ASCLA Century Scholarship: Chapter 10, "Any Disability" section
- Gates Millennium Scholars: Chapter 9, "All Minorities" section

Logistics

See the following scholarship:

- Logistics Scholarship: Chapter 6, "Logistics" section

Marine Science

See the following scholarships:

- AMS Scholarships: Chapter 6, "Atmospheric Sciences" section
- FFGC Scholarships: Chapter 15, "Florida" section
- NASA Graduate Student Researchers Program Fellowship: Chapter 7, "Aerospace Sciences and Engineering" section
- National Defense Science and Engineering Graduate Fellowship: Chapter 7, "Sciences" section
- NSF Graduate Research Fellowship: Chapter 7, "Sciences" section

Materials Science and Metallurgy

See the following scholarships:

- Cooperative Research Fellowship: Chapter 9, "All Minorities" section
- FEF Scholarships: Chapter 6, "Materials Science and Metallurgy" section
- GEM Fellowships: Chapter 9, "All Minorities" section

- Graduate Research Program for Women Fellowship: Chapter 12, "Female" section
- Hertz Foundation Fellowship: Chapter 7, "Sciences" section
- Lucent Florida Universities Fellowship: Chapter 15, "Florida" section
- NASA Graduate Student Researchers Program Fellowship: Chapter 7, "Aerospace Sciences and Engineering" section
- National Defense Science and Engineering Graduate Fellowship: Chapter 7, "Sciences" section
- NSBE Scholarships: Chapter 9, "African-American" section
- NPSC Graduate Fellowships in the Physical Sciences: Chapter 7, "Sciences" section
- NSF Graduate Research Fellowship: Chapter 7, "Sciences" section
- TMS Outstanding Student Papers Contest: Chapter 6, "Materials Science and Metallurgy" section
- TMS Student Scholarships: Chapter 6, "Materials Science and Metallurgy" section
- Xerox Technical Minority Scholarship: Chapter 9, "All Minorities" section

- Department of Energy Computational Science Graduate Fellowship: Chapter 7, "Sciences" section
- GEM Fellowships: Chapter 9, "All Minorities" section
- Graduate Research Program for Women Fellowship: Chapter 12, "Female" section
- Hertz Foundation Fellowship: Chapter 7, "Sciences" section
- Minority Masters Fellowship: Chapter 9, "All Minorities" section
- NASA Graduate Student Researchers Program Fellowship: Chapter 7, "Aerospace Sciences and Engineering" section
- National Defense Science and Engineering Graduate Fellowship: Chapter 7, "Sciences" section
- NPSC Graduate Fellowships in the Physical Sciences: Chapter 7, "Sciences" section
- NSF Graduate Research Fellowship: Chapter 7, "Sciences" section
- Virginia BPW Foundation Scholarships: Chapter 15, "Virginia" section
- Winston Churchill Foundation Scholarship: Chapter 7, "Study Abroad" section

Mathematics

See the following scholarships:

- AFCEA Fellowship: Chapter 7, "Communications Engineering and Technology" section
- AFCEA Ralph W. Shrader Scholarship: Chapter 7, "Communications Engineering and Technology" section
- AISES A. T. Anderson Memorial Scholarship: Chapter 9, "Native American" section
- AWIS Graduate Awards: Chapter 12, "Female" section
- Cooperative Research Fellowship: Chapter 9, "All Minorities" section

Medicine

Arthur N. Wilson, MD Scholarship

Sponsor: American Medical Association Foundation
Web Site: http://www.ama-assn.org/med-sci/erf/educ007.htm
Amount of Scholarship: $3,000
Number of Awards: 1
Deadline: January 31
Education Level: medical school students

Eligibility: Applicant must enroll in medical school and have graduated from a high school in southeast Alaska.

This page briefly describes the scholarship for medical students from southeast Alaska. It also tells you how to put together an application package and where to send your application. You do not have to submit an official application form for this scholarship.

CAPS Scholarships

Sponsor: Chinese American Physicians Society (CAPS)
Web Site: http://www.caps-ca.org
Amount of Scholarship: $1,000
Number of Awards: 8 to 10
Deadline: first Friday in October
Education Level: medical school students
Eligibility: Applicant must enroll in medical school.

The home page for this site tells you about the goals of CAPS, which can be helpful in preparing application materials. To learn about the scholarship, follow the Scholarship link in the left frame. There are two different scholarships, one for Chinese-American medical students from the San Francisco Bay area and one for all medical students regardless of ethnicity or residency. The Web page describes the two scholarships and the selection criteria and tells you how to obtain an application form. Applications are not available on the Web site, but there is an e-mail address you can write to with further questions.

International Medical Student Studies Scholarship

Sponsor: American Medical Association Foundation
Web Site: http://www.ama-assn.org/med-sci/erf/educate.htm

Amount of Scholarship: $1,000
Number of Awards: 1
Deadline: September 24 and January 14
Education Level: medical school students
Eligibility: Applicant must enroll in a U.S. medical school and plan to participate in a study abroad program.

This page briefly describes the scholarship and the goals for the program. It also includes a list of all the materials that must be submitted in the application package and the address where the package can be sent. You do not have to submit an official form to apply for this scholarship.

Jerry L. Pettis Memorial Scholarship

Sponsor: American Medical Association (AMA) Foundation
Web Site: http://www.ama-assn.org/med-sci/erf/educ005.htm
Amount of Scholarship: $2,500
Number of Awards: 1
Deadline: January 31
Education Level: junior and senior medical school students
Eligibility: Applicant must enroll in an AMA-approved medical school.

The dean of your medical school must nominate you for this scholarship. The Web page explains the nomination process and tells you what materials must be included in the application package and where the application should be sent.

Johnson F. Hammond, MD Memorial Scholarship

Sponsor: American Medical Association (AMA) Foundation

Web Site: http://www.ama-assn.org/med-sci/erf/educ004.htm
Amount of Scholarship: $3,000
Number of Awards: 1
Deadline: January 31
Education Level: medical school students
Eligibility: Applicant must enroll in an AMA-approved medical school and demonstrate an interest in a career in medical journalism.

The dean of your medical school must nominate you for this scholarship. The Web page explains the eligibility requirements for the scholarship and the nomination process. It also tells you what materials must be included in the application package and where the application should be sent.

National Health Service Corps Scholarship

Sponsor: U.S. Department of Health and Human Services and National Health Service Corps
Web Site: http://www.bphc.hrsa.dhhs.gov/nhsc/Pages/about_nhsc/3B1_nhscschol.htm
Amount of Scholarship: full tuition
Number of Awards: 350
Deadline: not given
Education Level: college undergraduates, graduate students, and medical school students
Eligibility: Applicant must enroll in an allopathic or osteopathic medicine, family nurse practitioner, nurse-midwifery, or physician assistant program at an accredited U.S. college or university and be a U.S. citizen.

The National Health Service Corps is a large service scholarship program that entices students to enter needed health professions and serve in health shortage areas throughout the United States in exchange for scholarship money. You must complete a residency program in a designated area and fulfill a service

commitment after graduating if you accept the scholarship. This page provides a brief overview of the program. Click the Q&A link under NNHSC Scholarships in the left frame for more details. Follow the Click Here to Request More Info link at the bottom of the scholarship's information page to send an electronic form that requests that a program packet be mailed to you.

Sherry R. Arnstein Minority Student Scholarship

Sponsor: American Association of Colleges of Osteopathic Medicine (AACOM)
Web Site: http://www.aacom.org
Amount of Scholarship: $2,000
Number of Awards: not given
Deadline: March 27
Education Level: college seniors and first-, second-, and third-year medical school students
Eligibility: Applicant must enroll in a AACOM member college of osteopathic medicine and be a member of a minority group.

To find information about this scholarship, click the Prospective Students button on the left-hand side of the page and click the Scholarships link. Then click the name of the scholarship for your educational level. If you are already enrolled in medical school, follow the Sherry R. Arnstein Minority Student Scholarship link. If you have been accepted to medical school but haven't yet started, follow the Sherry R. Arnstein New Student Minority Student Scholarship link. Each page briefly describes the eligibility requirements for the scholarship and lists topics for the essay that you must submit with your application. You can also print out a copy of the cover sheet that must be enclosed with your application package.

University of North Carolina Board of Governors Medical School Scholarship

Sponsor: University of North Carolina Board of Governors and North Carolina State Educational Assistance Authority
Web Site: http://www.ncseaa.edu/bgms.html
Amount of Scholarship: full tuition and a $5,000 stipend (renewable for up to four years)
Number of Awards: 20
Deadline: not given
Education Level: medical school students
Eligibility: Applicant must enroll in a North Carolina medical school, be a North Carolina resident, and be a member of a minority group or an economically disadvantaged student.

This page describes the history and nomination process of this program, which is designed to encourage more minority students in North Carolina to attend medical school. It also provides details about the award and how the scholarship may be renewed. To apply for the scholarship, you must apply for financial aid at the North Carolina medical school you want to attend; the financial aid office can also provide more information about the scholarship program. The four eligible North Carolina medical schools where you can use the scholarship are listed in the History section of the page.

Also see the following scholarships:

- ACSM Graduate Scholarship: Chapter 7, "Sports Science and Administration" section
- AISES A. T. Anderson Memorial Scholarship: Chapter 9, "Native American" section
- Arkansas Health Education Grant: Chapter 15, "Arkansas" section
- Congressional Black Caucus Spouses Scholarship: Chapter 15, "Alabama" section
- Indian Health Service Scholarship: Chapter 9, "Native American" section
- Martin Luther King, Jr. Physician & Dentist Scholarship: Chapter 15, "New Jersey" section
- New York State Regents Health Care Opportunity Scholarship: Chapter 15, "New York" section
- Professional School Scholarship: Chapter 15, "Maryland" section
- Rock Sleyster, MD Memorial Scholarship: Chapter 7, "Psychology and Psychiatry" section
- Zeta Phi Beta Scholarships and Fellowships: Chapter 12, "Female" section

Music and Music History

See the following scholarships:

- Andrew W. Mellon Fellowship in Humanistic Studies: Chapter 7, "Humanities" section
- Jacob Javits Fellowship: Chapter 7, "Humanities" section
- NHFA Entertainment Industry Scholarship: Chapter 9, "Hispanic" section

Neuroscience

See the following scholarship:

- APA Minority Fellowships: Chapter 7, "Psychology" section

Northern Studies

Lorraine Allison Scholarship

Sponsor: Arctic Institute of North America (AINA)

Web Site: http://www.ucalgary.ca/aina/scholar/scholar.html#allison
Amount of Scholarship: $2,000 (Canadian)
Number of Awards: not given
Deadline: January 7
Education Level: graduate students
Eligibility: Applicant must study any field related to northern issues at a Canadian university.

Here you will find a very brief description of the scholarship, the selection criteria, and instructions for preparing an application package. There is no formal application for this scholarship. If you have additional questions, contact the address, telephone number, or e-mail address listed underneath the scholarship description.

Also see the following scholarship:

• Jennifer Robinson Memorial Scholarship: Chapter 7, "Biology" section

Nursing

ANA Ethnic/Racial Minority Fellowships

Sponsor: American Nurses Association (ANA)
Web Site: http://www.nursingworld.org/emfp
Amount of Scholarship: $11,748 to $14,686 per year (renewable for three to five years)
Number of Awards: not given
Deadline: January 15
Education Level: doctoral students
Eligibility: Applicant must enroll in an eligible doctoral psychiatric or mental health nursing program, hold a master's degree in psychiatric or mental health nursing or a related field, be a Registered Nurse, be a member of ANA, be

a member of a minority group, and be a U.S. citizen or permanent resident.

First, click the About EMFP link to learn more about the Ethnic/Racial Minority Fellowship Program. Then click Types of Fellowship Programs Offered and Basic Criteria to find out if there is a fellowship that fits your needs and if you are eligible to apply. Two fellowships are available: one for doctoral study in psychiatric and mental health nursing and one for study of mental health issues affecting minority populations This page also describes the selection criteria and answers other common questions about the fellowship program. The other links, especially the About Current Fellows link, will help you better understand the program and the kinds of applicants the sponsor is looking for. If you decide to apply, follow the Online Application link, which leads to PDF copies of the application form and the applicant evaluation form. If you are not yet a member of ANA, click the Join ANA link at the bottom of the fellowship's main Web page to find an online membership application.

Doctoral Degree Scholarship in Cancer Nursing

Sponsor: American Cancer Society, Inc. Extramural Grants Program
Web Site: http://www.cancer.org/research/grants/health_grants/types_of_health_grants.html
Amount of Scholarship: $8,000 per year (renewable for four years)
Number of Awards: not given
Deadline: December 15
Education Level: doctoral students
Eligibility: Applicant must enroll as a full-time student in a doctoral nursing program specializing in cancer nursing and have a current license to practice as a registered nurse.

You will find a brief description of this scholarship under the Health Professional Training Grants section of the Web page. Click the Get Grant Applications and Instructions Online link to find copies of the application forms, instructions, and policies in both Microsoft Word and PDF format. The Policies page describes the mission of the scholarship's sponsor and gives a lot more information about the program, including eligibility requirements, selection criteria, and details about the award amount and conditions.

March of Dimes Nursing Scholarship

Sponsor: March of Dimes
Web Site: http://www.modimes.org/ Programs2/ProfEd/schip_announ.htm
Amount of Scholarship: $5,000
Number of Awards: 4
Deadline: January 31
Education Level: graduate students
Eligibility: Applicant must be a Registered Nurse (RN); be a member of the American College of Nurse-Midwives, the Association of Women's Health, Obstetric, and Neonatal Nurses, or the National Association of Neonatal Nurses; and enroll in a maternal-child nursing program.

This page briefly describes the scholarship program, including the program's goals and eligibility requirements. Follow the Nursing Scholarship Application link to obtain a printable application form, along with detailed application instructions.

Master's Degree Scholarship in Cancer Nursing

Sponsor: American Cancer Society, Inc. Extramural Grants Program

Web Site: http://www.cancer.org/research/ grants/health_grants/ types_of_health_grants.html
Amount of Scholarship: $8,000 per year (renewable for two years)
Number of Awards: not given
Deadline: December 15
Education Level: master's students
Eligibility: Applicant must enroll in a master's nursing program specializing in cancer nursing and have a current license to practice as a registered nurse.

You will find a brief description of this scholarship under the Health Professional Training Grants section of the Web page. Click the Get Grant Applications and Instructions Online link to find copies of the application forms, instructions, and policies in both Microsoft Word and PDF format. The Policies page describes the mission of the scholarship's sponsor and gives a lot more information about the scholarship program, including eligibility requirements, selection criteria, and details about the award amount and conditions.

North Carolina Nurse Scholar's Program Master's Scholarship

Sponsor: North Carolina State Educational Assistance Authority
Web Site: http://www.ncseaa.edu/mnsp.html
Amount of Scholarship: $6,000 per year (renewable for two years)
Number of Awards: not given
Deadline: early May
Education Level: master's students
Eligibility: Applicant must enroll in a master's nursing program at a participating North Carolina university, have earned a minimum 3.2 GPA in an accredited bachelor's degree pro-

gram in nursing, be a North Carolina resident, and be a U.S. citizen.

This page briefly describes the goals and history of this program and provides details about eligibility requirements, selection criteria, the application process, and the service commitment that scholarship recipients must make. A list of participating North Carolina universities where the scholarship may be used is also provided. Click the Apply Here link at the bottom of the page to access the application instructions and all required forms in Microsoft Word format.

Also see the following scholarships:

- AORN Foundation Scholarship: Chapter 6, "Nursing" section
- Hays Medical Center Scholarships: Chapter 6, "Health Care" section
- Indian Health Service Scholarship: Chapter 9, "Native American" section
- National Health Service Corps Scholarship: Chapter 7, "Medicine" section
- New York State Regents Professional Opportunity Scholarship: Chapter 15, "New York" section
- Professional School Scholarship: Chapter 15, "Maryland" section
- Scott & White Nursing Scholarships: Chapter 6, "Nursing" section

Occupational Health and Safety

See the following scholarship:

- KSHN Educational Scholarships: Chapter 6, "Occupational Health and Safety" section

Occupational and Physical Therapy

See the following scholarships:

- AMBUCS Scholarships: Chapter 6, "Occupational and Physical Therapy" section
- AOTF Scholarships: Chapter 6, "Occupational and Physical Therapy" section
- Indian Health Service Scholarship: Chapter 9, "Native American" section
- New York State Regents Professional Opportunity Scholarship: Chapter 15, "New York" section

Operations Research

See the following scholarships:

- Cooperative Research Fellowship: Chapter 9, "All Minorities" section
- Graduate Research Program for Women Fellowship: Chapter 12, "Female" section
- Lucent Florida Universities Fellowship: Chapter 15, "Florida" section

Optics and Optometry

Brazelton Memorial Award

Sponsor: Low Vision Section of the American Academy of Optometry
Web Site: http://www.aaopt.org/Awards/brazelton.html
Amount of Scholarship: $500
Number of Awards: 1
Deadline: September 1
Education Level: graduate students

Eligibility: Applicant must enroll in a graduate optometry program.

This competition awards an outstanding student paper on low vision. The Web page details the criteria under which submitted papers are judged and tells you how to submit your own entry in the contest.

Corning Scholarships

Sponsor: American Optometric Foundation and Corning, Inc.
Web Site: http://www.ezell.org/Awards/corning_scholarships.html
Amount of Scholarship: $2,000 to $4,000
Number of Awards: 2
Deadline: May 1
Education Level: third-year optometry students
Eligibility: Applicant must enroll in an accredited optometry program.

Your school must nominate you for this scholarship. First prize is $4,000 and second prize is $2,000. The Web page describes the purpose of the award, basic eligibility requirements, and the nomination process. You can also print an official nomination form from the site. Under the Criteria section, you will find instructions for assembling an application package and a list of acceptable application essay topics.

Julius F. Neumueller Award in Optics

Sponsor: American Academy of Optometry
Web Site: http://www.aaopt.org/Awards/neumueller.html
Amount of Scholarship: $500
Number of Awards: 1
Deadline: September 1
Education Level: doctoral students
Eligibility: Applicant must enroll in a doctoral program in optometry.

This essay contest rewards the best paper on optics. Specific essay topics that are acceptable for entering into the contest are listed on the Web page. You will also find a brief description of the application process and a mailing address where essays may be sent.

William C. Ezell Fellowship

Sponsor: American Optometrics Foundation
Web Site: http://www.ezell.org/Awards/EzellFelInfo.html
Amount of Scholarship: $8,000 (renewable for three years)
Number of Awards: not given
Deadline: March 15
Education Level: graduate students
Eligibility: Applicant must enroll as a full-time student in a graduate program in vision science or a related field.

On this page you'll find all the facts about the fellowship, including the program's purpose and history, the eligibility requirements, how to obtain application forms, how applications are reviewed, and conditions of accepting a fellowship. You can also print out copies of the application and confidential evaluation forms from the site.

Also see the following scholarships:

- Arkansas Health Education Grant: Chapter 15, "Arkansas" section
- Indian Health Service Scholarship: Chapter 9, "Native American" section
- Lucent Florida Universities Fellowship: Chapter 15, "Florida" section
- National Defense Science and Engineering Graduate Fellowship: Chapter 7, "Sciences" section
- New York State Regents Professional Opportunity Scholarship: Chapter 15, "New York" section

- NSF Graduate Research Fellowship: Chapter 7, "Sciences" section
- Raymond Davis Scholarship: Chapter 6, "Optics" section
- SPIE Scholarships: Chapter 6, "Optics" section

Pharmacy and Pharmacology

Fellowship for Advanced Predoctoral Training in Pharmaceutics

Sponsor: Pharmaceutical Research and Manufacturers of America Foundation
Web Site: http://www.phrmaf.org/program/predoc.pharmaceut.html
Amount of Scholarship: $12,000 per year
Number of Awards: not given
Deadline: September 15
Education Level: doctoral students
Eligibility: Applicant must enroll as a full-time student in a Ph.D. program in pharmaceutics at an accredited U.S. school of pharmacy; have completed the bulk of the pre-thesis requirements; hold a B.S., M.S., or Pharm.D. degree in pharmacy; and be a U.S. citizen or permanent resident.

This Web page describes the goals of the fellowship and the eligibility requirements in great detail, which should help you decide if you will make a good candidate for the award. You must submit your application through your academic department, as described in the Applications section of the page. This section also lists all of the documentation that must be included in the application package. The required Information Summary Form can be downloaded in either Microsoft Word or PDF

format by following the appropriate links. Finally, you will find details of the fellowship awards and requirements.

Fellowship for Advanced Predoctoral Training in Pharmacology and Toxicology

Sponsor: Pharmaceutical Research and Manufacturers of America Foundation
Web Site: http://www.phrmaf.org/program/predoc.pharm.tox.html
Amount of Scholarship: $12,000 per year
Number of Awards: not given
Deadline: September 15
Education Level: doctoral students
Eligibility: Applicant must enroll as a full-time student in a PhD program in pharmacology or toxicology at an accredited U.S. school of medicine, pharmacy, dentistry, or veterinary medicine; have completed the bulk of the pre-thesis requirements; and be a U.S. citizen or permanent resident.

This Web page describes the goals of the fellowship and the eligibility requirements in great detail, which should help you decide if you will make a good candidate for the award. You must submit your application through your academic department, as described in the Applications section of the page. This section also lists all of the documentation that must be included in the application package. The required Information Summary Form can be downloaded in either Microsoft Word or PDF format by following the appropriate links in this section. Finally, you will find details of the fellowship awards and requirements.

Also see the following scholarships:

- Indian Health Service Scholarship: Chapter 9, "Native American" section
- National Pathfinder Scholarship: Chapter 12, "Female" section

- Professional School Scholarship: Chapter 15, "Maryland" section

Philosophy

See the following scholarships:

- Andrew W. Mellon Fellowship in Humanistic Studies: Chapter 7, "Humanities" section
- AWIS Graduate Awards: Chapter 12, "Female" section
- Jacob Javits Fellowship: Chapter 7, "Humanities" section
- NSF Graduate Research Fellowship: Chapter 7, "Sciences" section

Physician Assistant

Breitman-Dorn Endowed Research Fellowship

Sponsor: Physician Assistant Foundation
Web Site: http://www.aapa.org/breitman.html
Amount of Scholarship: $3,000
Number of Awards: 1
Deadline: January 31
Education Level: doctoral students
Eligibility: Applicant must enroll in a doctoral physician assistant program.

This page briefly describes the fellowship, including for what purposes funds may be used, how applicants are judged, and the responsibilities of fellowship recipients. At the bottom of the page are instructions for obtaining the application form by phone or fax.

Also see the following scholarships:

- National Health Service Corps Scholarship: Chapter 7, "Medicine" section
- Physician Assistant Foundation Annual Scholarship: Chapter 6, "Physician Assistant" section

Physiology

Porter Physiology Development Program Minority Fellowship in Physiology

Sponsor: American Physiological Society
Web Site: http://www.faseb.org/aps/educatn/porter2.htm
Amount of Scholarship: $15,000
Number of Awards: not given
Deadline: January 15
Education Level: graduate students
Eligibility: Applicant must enroll as a full-time student in a doctoral program in physiology, be a member of a minority group, and be a U.S. citizen or permanent resident.

This page describes the background of this fellowship program, which should help you prepare a more targeted application package. It also provides an overview of the eligibility requirements, conditions of accepting the award, and selection criteria. Eligible minorities who may apply for the fellowship are African-Americans, Hispanics, Native Americans, Alaskan Natives, and Pacific Islanders. Click the Application Forms link at the bottom of the page to open a text version of the application form in your Web browser, which you can then print out.

Physics

See the following scholarships:

- AFCEA Fellowship: Chapter 7, "Communications Engineering and Technology" section
- AFCEA Ralph W. Shrader Scholarship: Chapter 7, "Communications Engineering and Technology" section
- AWIS Graduate Awards: Chapter 12, "Female" section
- Cooperative Research Fellowship: Chapter 9, "All Minorities" section
- GEM Fellowships: Chapter 9, "All Minorities" section
- Graduate Research Program for Women Fellowship: Chapter 12, "Female" section
- Hertz Foundation Fellowship: Chapter 7, "Sciences" section
- Lucent Florida Universities Fellowship: Chapter 15, "Florida" section
- NASA Graduate Student Researchers Program Fellowship: Chapter 7, "Aerospace Sciences and Engineering" section
- National Defense Science and Engineering Graduate Fellowship: Chapter 7, "Sciences" section
- NPSC Graduate Fellowships in the Physical Sciences: Chapter 7, "Sciences" section
- NSBE Scholarships: Chapter 9, "African-American" section
- NSF Graduate Research Fellowship: Chapter 7, "Sciences" section
- Xerox Technical Minority Scholarship: Chapter 9, "All Minorities" section

Podiatry

See the following scholarships:

- Arkansas Health Education Grant: Chapter 15, "Arkansas" section
- Indian Health Service Scholarship: Chapter 9, "Native American" section
- New York State Regents Professional Opportunity Scholarship: Chapter 15, "New York" section

Political Science

See the following scholarships:

- AWIS Graduate Awards: Chapter 12, "Female" section
- Graduate Foreign Affairs Fellowship: Chapter 7, "International Studies" section
- International Predissertation Fellowship: Chapter 7, "Social Sciences" section
- Jacob Javits Fellowship: Chapter 7, "Humanities" section
- James Madison Fellowship: Chapter 7, "Education" section
- Minorities in Government Finance Scholarship: Chapter 9, "All Minorities" section
- NSF Graduate Research Fellowship: Chapter 7, "Sciences" section
- Pathfinder Historians Scholarships: Chapter 7, "History" section

Project Management

See the following scholarships:

- AACE International Scholarship: Chapter 6, "Project Management" section
- Robert J. Yourzak Scholarship Award: Chapter 6, "Project Management" section

Psychology and Psychiatry

APA Minority Fellowships

Sponsor: American Psychological Association (APA)
Web Site: http://www.apa.org/mfp/homepage.html
Amount of Scholarship: varies
Number of Awards: not given
Deadline: January 15
Education Level: graduate students
Eligibility: Applicant must enroll as a full-time student in an accredited doctoral program in psychology, be a member of a minority group, and be a U.S. citizen or permanent resident.

This Web site describes the five fellowship programs available for African-American, Hispanic, Native American, Alaskan Native, Pacific Islander, and Asian-American students from the APA. Each fellowship targets a different subdiscipline: clinical psychology; substance abuse treatment and prevention; research psychology; HIV/AIDS research; and neuroscience. First, read the Welcome and History pages to understand the background of the fellowship program. The different fellowships are described in more detail on the Psychology Programs and Neuroscience Programs pages, where you will find an overview of each fellowship, a list of the specific eligibility requirements for that award, and answers to frequently asked questions. Once you have decided for which fellowship you want to apply, go to the Application Forms page to download the correct application form for that fellowship. You can only apply for one fellowship.

NASP-ERT Minority Scholarship

Sponsor: National Association of School Psychologists (NASP)

Web Site: http://www.naspweb.org/about_nasp/minority.html
Amount of Scholarship: $5,000 (renewable for three years)
Number of Awards: 1
Deadline: February 1
Education Level: graduate students
Eligibility: Applicant must enroll in an accredited specialist program in school psychology at a U.S. university (doctoral students are not eligible), plan to become a practicing school psychologist, have a minimum 3.0 GPA, be a member of a minority group, and be a U.S. citizen.

Don't be fooled by the solicitation for donations to the scholarship fund at the top of the Web page. Just keep scrolling down to locate information about the scholarship for applicants. There you will find a brief statement of the goal of the scholarship, a list of eligibility requirements, and instructions for submitting an application. There is also contact information for requesting an application form; applications are not available through the Web site.

Rock Sleyster, MD Memorial Scholarship

Sponsor: American Medical Association (AMA) Foundation
Web Site: http://www.ama-assn.org/med-sci/erf/educ006.htm
Amount of Scholarship: $2,500
Number of Awards: 20
Deadline: May 1
Education Level: third-year medical students
Eligibility: Applicant must enroll in a U.S. or Canadian medical school, specialize in psychiatry, and be a U.S. citizen.

This page provides a brief overview of this scholarship program and describes how the nomination process works. Students cannot apply directly for the scholarship, but must be nominated by their medical schools. A list of supporting materials that must be included with the nomination is also given. Scroll to the bottom of the page to find contact information where you can get more information about the scholarship and send application materials.

Also see the following scholarships:

- AWIS Graduate Awards: Chapter 12, "Female" section
- Indian Health Service Scholarship: Chapter 9, "Native American" section
- International Predissertation Fellowship: Chapter 7, "Social Sciences" section
- Jacob Javits Fellowship: Chapter 7, "Humanities" section
- NASA Graduate Student Researchers Program Fellowship: Chapter 7, "Aerospace Sciences and Engineering" section
- National Pathfinder Scholarship: Chapter 12, "Female" section
- New York State Regents Professional Opportunity Scholarship: Chapter 15, "New York" section
- NSF Graduate Research Fellowship: Chapter 7, "Sciences" section
- United States Army Health Professions Scholarships: Chapter 13, "Army and Army ROTC" section
- Zeta Phi Beta Scholarships and Fellowships: Chapter 12, "Female" section

Public Policy and Administration

See the following scholarships:

- Environmental Public Policy and Conflict Resolution Fellowship: Chapter 7, "Environmental Studies" section

- Graduate Foreign Affairs Fellowship: Chapter 7, "International Studies" section
- Jacob Javits Fellowship: Chapter 7, "Humanities" section
- Minorities in Government Finance Scholarship: Chapter 9, "All Minorities" section
- Public Employee Retirement Research and Administration Scholarship: Chapter 7, "Economics and Finance" section
- Public Investor Scholarship: Chapter 7, "Economics and Finance" section

Real Estate

See the following scholarship:

- George M. Brooker Collegiate Scholarship for Minorities: Chapter 6, "Real Estate" section

Religious Studies

FTE Dissertation Fellowship

Sponsor: Fund for Theological Education, Inc. (FTE)
Web Site: http://www.thefund.org/programs/ fellowships/dissertation/index.html
Amount of Scholarship: $15,000
Number of Awards: 10
Deadline: not given
Education Level: doctoral students
Eligibility: Applicant must enroll as a full-time student in the final year of a Ph.D. or Th.D. program, be African-American, and be a U.S. citizen.

First, read the objectives and eligibility requirements of this fellowship program to determine if you would make a good applicant. The Benefits section of the Web page describes the monetary and other benefits of becoming an FTE Fellow. If you would like to apply, contact the e-mail address given at the bottom of the page for further information about the program.

FTE Doctoral Fellowship

Sponsor: Fund for Theological Education, Inc. (FTE)
Web Site: http://www.thefund.org/programs/fellowships/doctoral/index.html
Amount of Scholarship: $15,000 (renewable for two years)
Number of Awards: 15
Deadline: not given
Education Level: first-year graduate students
Eligibility: Applicant must enroll in a Ph.D. or Th.D. program, be African-American, and be a U.S. citizen.

First, read the objectives and eligibility requirements of this fellowship program to determine if you would make a good applicant. The Benefits section of the Web page describes the monetary and other benefits of becoming an FTE Fellow. If you would like to apply, contact the e-mail address given at the bottom of the page for further information about the program.

FTE Ministry Fellowship

Sponsor: Fund for Theological Education, Inc. (FTE)
Web Site: http://www.thefund.org/programs/fellowships/ministry/index.html
Amount of Scholarship: $5,000
Number of Awards: 40
Deadline: not given
Education Level: first-year master's students

Eligibility: Applicant must enroll in a Master of Divinity program at an accredited seminary and be a U.S. or Canadian citizen.

First, read the objectives and eligibility requirements of this fellowship program to determine if you would make a good applicant. The Benefits section of the Web page describes the monetary and other benefits of becoming an FTE Fellow. If you would like to apply, contact the e-mail address given at the bottom of the page for further information about the program.

FTE North American Doctoral Fellowship

Sponsor: Fund for Theological Education, Inc. (FTE)
Web Site: http://www.thefund.org/programs/fellowships/doctoral/northamerican.html
Amount of Scholarship: $7,500
Number of Awards: not given
Deadline: not given
Education Level: doctoral students
Eligibility: Applicant must enroll as a full-time student in a Ph.D. or Th.D. program, be a member of a minority group, and be a U.S. or Canadian citizen or permanent resident.

First, read the objectives and eligibility requirements of this fellowship program to determine if you would make a good applicant. The Benefits section of the Web page describes the monetary and other benefits of becoming an FTE Fellow. If you would like to apply, contact the e-mail address given at the bottom of the page for further information about the program.

Also see the following scholarships:

• Andrew W. Mellon Fellowship in Humanistic Studies: Chapter 7, "Humanities" section

- Chattanooga Christian Community Foundation Scholarships: Chapter 15, "Tennessee" section
- Herbert W. and Corrine Chilstrom Scholarship: Chapter 11, "Lutheran" section
- Homeland Ministries Scholarships: Chapter 11, "Christian Church (Disciples of Christ)" section
- Jacob Javits Fellowship: Chapter 7, "Humanities" section
- Order of the Eastern Star Scholarships: Chapter 15, "California" section

Respiratory Therapy

Education Recognition Awards for Postgraduate Students

Sponsor: American Respiratory Care Foundation
Web Site: http://www.aarc.org/arcf/post.html
Amount of Scholarship: $1,500
Number of Awards: 2
Deadline: June 30
Education Level: graduate students
Eligibility: Applicant must enroll in an advanced degree program in respiratory therapy at an accredited university, hold a bachelor's degree in respiratory therapy, and have a minimum 3.0 GPA.

This page describes the two scholarships available for graduate students in respiratory therapy, which are exactly the same except for their names. Click the scholarship links to find a brief description of each award, as well as a list of eligibility requirements and documents that must be included in the application package. To find the application form, click the Return link at the bottom of the scholarship's description page. Then follow the link to the application form at the top of the page.

Sciences

Department of Energy Computational Science Graduate Fellowship

Sponsor: U.S. Department of Energy (DOE) Office of Science and Office of Defense Programs
Web Site: http://www.krellinst.org/CSGF
Amount of Scholarship: full tuition and a monthly stipend of $1,800 (renewable for four years)
Number of Awards: not given
Deadline: January 26
Education Level: first- and second-year graduate students
Eligibility: Applicant must enroll as a full-time student in a doctoral program in computer, engineering, life, mathematical, or physical sciences and be a U.S. citizen or permanent resident.

This fellowship is intended to encourage students to prepare for careers in computational science. To get an idea of what the computational science field encompasses, click the About the Program link. This page also provides links to information about the benefits, obligations, and eligibility requirements of the fellowship. Return to the main Web page and follow the Fellows link to find a list of current fellows and their universities and fields of study. The fellowship requires a three-month practicum at a DOE research laboratory; find a list of sites where your practicum might be hosted by following the DOE Practicum Host Sites link. If you decide to apply for the fellowship, click the Application link. There you will find both the application forms and the program description, which provides a lot of valuable information about the program's objectives and how applicants are evaluated. It also lists faculty contacts for the fellowship at various universities.

Hertz Foundation Fellowship

Sponsor: Fannie and John Hertz Foundation
Web Site: http://www.hertzfoundation.org
Amount of Scholarship: full tuition and a stipend of $25,000 (renewable for five years)
Number of Awards: not given
Deadline: November 5
Education Level: college seniors and graduate students
Eligibility: Applicant must enroll in a doctoral program in an eligible field of study in the applied physical sciences at a participating university, have a minimum 3.75 GPA during the last two years of undergraduate work, and be a U.S. citizen or permanent resident.

This fellowship for study of the physical sciences is considered to be among the most prestigious graduate fellowships. The Web site tells you all about the program. To learn about the sponsor, click the History link. Then follow the Awards link to find out what the benefits of the fellowship are. The Eligibility page details the eligibility requirements that applicants must meet, including the personal character qualities that the sponsor is looking for in potential applicants. To find out what fields of study are eligible, click the Fields link on the left-hand side of the page and follow the Schools link to learn at which universities you can use the fel-

lowship. The Commitment link describes the moral commitment that recipients of the fellowship must make. Go to the Application page to access the electronic application, which you can submit over the Internet. You will also need to have professors submit reference reports for you; they can do so from the References page. If you have further questions, the Contact link tells you how to contact the foundation.

National Defense Science and Engineering Graduate Fellowship

Sponsor: United States Army, Navy, and Air Force and American Society for Engineering Education
Web Site: http://www.asee.org/ndseg
Amount of Scholarship: $18,500 to $20,500
Number of Awards: 100 to 150
Deadline: January 19
Education Level: graduate students
Eligibility: Applicant must enroll in a graduate program in science or engineering at a U.S. university, hold a bachelor's degree, and be a U.S. citizen.

To learn all the details of this fellowship program, click the About the Program link. There you will find the goals of the program, a list of eligible fields of study, eligibility requirements, selection criteria, details and conditions of the award, and links to all of the required application materials. Note that minorities, women, and students with disabilities are particularly encouraged to apply. If you decide to apply, follow the link to the Application Instructions from the fellowship's main page. This page provides detailed instructions for filling out the application materials, as well as other useful information about your chances for winning, assembling and mailing your application package, and answers to frequently asked questions.

NPSC Graduate Fellowship in the Physical Sciences

Sponsor: National Physical Science Consortium (NPSC)
Web Site: http://www.npsc.org
Amount of Scholarship: full tuition and a stipend of $12,500 to $15,000 per year (renewable for six years)
Number of Awards: not given
Deadline: November 5
Education Level: college seniors and terminal master's degree students
Eligibility: Applicant must enroll as a full-time student in a doctoral program in the physical sciences at a participating university, have a minimum 3.0 GPA, and be a U.S. citizen.

This page provides an overview of this graduate fellowship program for students of the physical sciences, including a list of broad fields of study for which the fellowship might be used. Click the History of the National Physical Science Consortium link to learn about the fellowship's sponsor and the background of the program. The Unique Features of the NPSC Program and the Tuition, Fees, Stipend, and Summer Employment links describe all of the monetary and other benefits of the fellowship. The Renewable page describes the requirements for renewing the fellowship, while the Conditions of the Award page details other requirements that recipients must meet. Go to the Eligibility Requirements page to find out if you are qualified to apply for the fellowship, and follow the Selection Based On link to find out what qualifications are most important in selecting fellowship recipients. Note that applications

from minorities and female students are given preference. To learn which universities fellowship recipients can attend, follow the Signatory Institute Members link. The Disciplines Used by NPSC Sponsoring Employers link will help you determine what specific fields of study in the physical sciences the fellowship program seeks. If you have any more questions about the program, check the Frequently Asked Questions page. The rest of the fellowship's main Web page gives instructions for completing the online application and provides links to all of the required application forms.

NSF Graduate Research Fellowship

Sponsor: National Science Foundation (NSF)
Web Site: http://www.ehr.nsf.gov/EHR/DGE/grf.htm
Amount of Scholarship: $25,500
Number of Awards: 900
Deadline: November 4
Education Level: college seniors and first-year graduate students
Eligibility: Applicant must enroll in a graduate program in the sciences, mathematics, or engineering and be a U.S. citizen or permanent resident.

This fellowship goes to graduate students in science, mathematics, and engineering fields. Several awards are reserved for female students of computer and information science and engineering, as outlined in the Description section of the Web page. The Eligibility section will tell you if you are eligible to apply for this fellowship. Look under How to Apply to find out how you can submit an application electronically, download one off the Internet, and order printed application materials. The Graduate Research Fellowship Program Announcement, linked at the end of the page, contains much more detailed information about eligibility, selection criteria, and application procedures, and it lists all eligible fields of study. The other links at the bottom of the page may also be useful for learning more about the program's background and objectives.

UNCF/MERCK Graduate Science Research Dissertation Fellowship

Sponsor: United Negro College Fund (UNCF) and the Merck Company Foundation
Web Site: http://www.uncf.org/merck/programs/grad.htm
Amount of Scholarship: $30,000
Number of Awards: 12
Deadline: January 31
Education Level: doctoral students
Eligibility: Applicant must enroll as a full-time student in a doctoral program in the life or physical sciences, be within one to three years of completing dissertation research, be African-American, and be a U.S. citizen or permanent resident.

On this page you will find details about the fellowship, including award amounts, eligibility requirements, and application deadlines. For more detailed information, click the Application Details link at the top of the page. There you will learn about the purpose of the fellowship, award amounts, and selection criteria. Then follow the Application Procedures link to find instructions for putting together and submitting an application package. At the bottom of that page you will find a link to an electronic form that you can fill out to request application brochures and forms be sent to you through the mail.

Also see the following scholarships:

- AISES A. T. Anderson Memorial Scholarship: Chapter 9, "Native American" section
- Astronaut Scholarship: Chapter 6, "Sciences" section
- AWIS Graduate Awards: Chapter 12, "Female" section
- Gates Millennium Scholars: Chapter 9, "All Minorities" section
- GEM Fellowships: Chapter 9, "All Minorities" section
- Minority Masters Fellowship: Chapter 9, "All Minorities" section
- NASA Graduate Student Researchers Program Fellowship: Chapter 7, "Aerospace Sciences and Engineering" section
- Winston Churchill Foundation Scholarship: Chapter 7, "Study Abroad" section

Social Sciences

ABA Doctoral Dissertation Fellowship in Law and Social Science

Sponsor: American Bar Association (ABA)
Web Site: http://www.abf-sociolegal.org/pre.html
Amount of Scholarship: $15,000 (renewable for two years)
Number of Awards: not given
Deadline: February 1
Education Level: doctoral students
Eligibility: Applicant must enroll in a doctoral program in the social sciences, be researching the general area of socio-legal studies, and have completed all of the Ph.D. requirements except the dissertation.

The first section of this page describes the purpose of this fellowship program. Following that are the eligibility requirements. Note that minority students are particularly encouraged to apply. The rest of the Web page describes the amounts of the fellowship award, the tenure of the fellowship, and conditions that recipients must meet, including spending the fellowship time in residence at the ABA. At the end of the page is an overview of the application process, which describes the materials that must be enclosed in the application package and where to send submissions. You do not have to submit an official application form in order to apply.

International Predissertation Fellowships

Sponsor: Social Science Research Council, American Council of Learned Societies, and the Ford Foundation
Web Site: http://www.ssrc.org/ipfpfell.htm
Amount of Scholarship: full tuition and a monthly stipend of $1,800
Number of Awards: not given
Deadline: varies
Education Level: doctoral students
Eligibility: Applicant must enroll in a social sciences program at a participating university and prepare for dissertation research in a developing region of the world.

Here you will find all the details on this fellowship aimed at enticing talented graduate students into teaching and research careers oriented to the developing world. First, read the description of the fellowship's objectives to find out if you would make a good candidate. Then check the eligibility requirements and award restrictions to learn if the fellowship fits your needs. At the bottom of the page you will find a link to a list of participating universities and the contact information for the faculty representative on each campus whom you can contact for more information and application materials. Follow the Detailed Literature link to find more details about the goals and background of the fellowship program, the types of fellowships awarded, the application process, and administration of the fellowship program. There is also a link to a frequently asked questions page, which should answer your most common questions about the fellowship program, including a list of eligible fields of study within the social sciences and a list of criteria used to evaluate applicants. On the left-hand side of the page are links to lists of past fellows and their field reports, which might give you a better idea of what kinds of candidates the program is looking for and what kind of work you will do under the fellowship. If you do decide to apply, click the Writing Proposals link at the top of the page to get some helpful tips for writing your fellowship proposal.

Also see the following scholarships:

- AWIS Graduate Awards: Chapter 12, "Female" section
- International Dissertation Field Research Fellowship: Chapter 7, "Study Abroad" section
- ISI Weaver Fellowship: Chapter 7, "Humanities" section
- NASA Graduate Student Researchers Program Fellowship: Chapter 7, "Aerospace Sciences and Engineering" section
- NSF Graduate Research Fellowship: Chapter 7, "Sciences" section
- Public Employee Retirement Research and Administration Scholarship: Chapter 7, "Economics and Finance" section
- Public Investor Scholarship: Chapter 7, "Economics and Finance" section

Social Work

Master's Training Grants in Clinical Oncology Social Work

Sponsor: American Cancer Society, Inc. Extramural Grants Program

Web Site: http://www.cancer.org/research/grants/health_grants/types_of_health_grants.html
Amount of Scholarship: $8,000 to $12,000
Number of Awards: not given
Deadline: October 1
Education Level: master's students
Eligibility: Applicant must enroll in a master's social work program and demonstrate an interest in providing psychosocial services to persons with cancer and their families.

You will find a brief description of this grant under the Health Professional Training Grants section of the Web page. Click the Get Grant Applications Online link to find copies of the application forms, instructions, and policies in both Microsoft Word and PDF format. The Policies page describes the mission of the scholarship's sponsor and gives a lot more information about the scholarship program.

Also see the following scholarships:

- Indian Health Service Scholarship: Chapter 9, "Native American" section
- Jewish Foundation for Education of Women Scholarships: Chapter 15, "New York" section
- Zeta Phi Beta Scholarships and Fellowships: Chapter 12, "Female" section

Sociology

ASA Minority Fellowship

Sponsor: American Sociological Association
Web Site: http://www.asanet.org/student/mfp.html
Amount of Scholarship: full tuition and a stipend of $14,688
Number of Awards: not given
Deadline: December 31

Education Level: college seniors and graduate students
Eligibility: Applicant must enroll in a doctoral program in sociology, be a member of a minority group, and be a U.S. citizen or permanent resident.

On this page you will learn briefly what the goals of the fellowship program and the requirements you must meet before applying. Eligible minority groups include African-Americans, Hispanics, Asian-Americans, Native Americans, Alaskan Natives, and Pacific Islanders. Following that are the 10 most-asked questions about the fellowships, which provides basic information about eligibility, selection criteria, financial support, and fellowship terms. At the bottom of the page is the mailing address where you can request application forms.

Also see the following scholarships:

- AWIS Graduate Awards: Chapter 12, "Female" section
- Graduate Foreign Affairs Fellowship: Chapter 7, "International Studies" section
- International Predissertation Fellowship: Chapter 7, "Social Sciences" section
- Jacob Javits Fellowship: Chapter 7, "Humanities" section
- National Pathfinder Scholarship: Chapter 12, "Female" section
- NSF Graduate Research Fellowship: Chapter 7, "Sciences" section

Space Sciences

Massachusetts Space Grant Consortium Graduate Fellowship

Sponsor: Massachusetts Space Grant Consortium

Web Site: http://www.mit.edu:8001/activities/masgc/fellowship.html
Amount of Scholarship: full tuition and a stipend
Number of Awards: not given
Deadline: February 18
Education Level: first-year graduate students
Eligibility: Applicant must enroll in a space sciences or engineering program at a member university and be a U.S. citizen.

Not many details about this fellowship are given on the Web page, just the bare facts about eligibility requirements and the items that must be included in the application package. There is also a list of participating Massachusetts universities where the fellowship may be used. Follow the link at the bottom of the page to find application and evaluation forms that you can print from your Web browser.

NASA/TSGC Graduate Fellowship

Sponsor: NASA/Texas Space Grant Consortium (TSGC)
Web Site: http://www.tsgc.utexas.edu/grants
Amount of Scholarship: $5,000 (renewable for three years)
Number of Awards: not given
Deadline: February 18
Education Level: graduate students
Eligibility: Applicant must enroll as a full-time student in a graduate program in space sciences or engineering at a participating Texas university, have received full financial support from the university, and be a U.S. citizen.

This Web page provides details on the amount of the fellowship, its duration, its eligibility requirements, and the criteria used to select recipients. Note that minority and female students are particularly encouraged to apply. Participating universities are listed at the bottom of the page, along with the name of the faculty representative at each university whom you can contact if you have further questions. Follow the link to the application form to download a PDF copy of the form. If you go to the main grants page at http://www.tsgc.utexas.edu/grants, you will find a link to a list of past fellowship recipients and a link to the electronic eligibility verification form that you must submit if you receive a fellowship. You will also find links to pages that provide more information about TSGC and the participating universities.

Also see the following scholarships:

- AIAA Foundation Graduate Awards: Chapter 7, "Aerospace Sciences and Engineering" section
- Hertz Foundation Fellowship: Chapter 7, "Sciences" section
- ISGC Scholarships and Fellowships: Chapter 6, "Space Sciences" section
- LaSPACE Fellowship: Chapter 7, "Aerospace Sciences and Engineering"
- NASA Graduate Student Researchers Program Fellowship: Chapter 7, "Aerospace Sciences and Engineering" section
- NPSC Graduate Fellowships in the Physical Sciences: Chapter 7, "Sciences" section
- NSF Graduate Research Fellowship: Chapter 7, "Sciences" section
- Rocky Mountain NASA Space Grant Consortium Scholarships and Fellowships: Chapter 6, "Space Sciences" section

Speech

See the following scholarships:

- Andrew W. Mellon Fellowship in Humanistic Studies: Chapter 7, "Humanities" section

- Jacob Javits Fellowship: Chapter 7, "Humanities" section

Speech Language Pathology and Hearing Audiology

Sertoma International Communicative Disorders Scholarship

Sponsor: Sertoma International
Web Site: http://www.sertoma.org/Scholarships/default.htm
Amount of Scholarship: $2,500
Number of Awards: 30
Deadline: March 31
Education Level: master's students
Eligibility: Applicant must enroll as a full-time student in a graduate program in speech pathology and audiology at a North American university, have a minimum 3.2 GPA, and be a U.S., Canadian, or Mexican citizen or permanent resident.

Look for a brief description of this scholarship at the top of the right frame. Click the Scholarship Applications link in the left frame to find the application in PDF format, as well as instructions for completing and submitting the application form. The instructions page also provides more details about the scholarship, including the award's purpose and eligibility requirements.

Also see the following scholarships:

- AMBUCS Scholarships: Chapter 6, "Occupational and Physical Therapy" section
- New York State Regents Professional Opportunity Scholarship: Chapter 15, "New York" section

Sports Science and Administration

ACSM Graduate Scholarship

Sponsor: American College of Sports Medicine (ACSM)
Web Site: http://acsm.org/scholarships.html
Amount of Scholarship: $1,500 (renewable for four years)
Number of Awards: not given
Deadline: January 21
Education Level: graduate and medical school students
Eligibility: Applicant must enroll as a full-time student in a Ph.D. or M.D. program in exercise science, sports medicine, or a related field and be female or a member of a minority group.

The General Information section of this Web page describes the purpose of this scholarship program and the details of the award. If you would like to apply, you can download the application form in PDF format. The application gives more information about eligibility requirements, as well as complete instructions for putting together an application package. Note that eligible minority groups for this scholarship include African-Americans, Hispanics, Native Americans, Alaskan Natives, Asian-Americans, and Pacific Islanders.

Dorothy Harris Endowed Scholarship

Sponsor: Women's Sports Foundation
Web Site: http://www.womenssportsfoundation.org/templates/grants/grant/featured.html?record=3
Amount of Scholarship: $1,500
Number of Awards: not given
Deadline: December 8
Education Level: graduate students

Eligibility: Applicant must enroll as a full-time student in a graduate program in physical education, sports management, sports psychology, or sports sociology; and be female.

First, read the History of the Program section of the Web page to understand this scholarship's background and goals, which will affect how you present your application. Underneath that are the Guidelines and Application for the scholarship, which will tell you if you are eligible and how to apply. You can also download a PDF copy of the application form for printing and filling out.

Also see the following scholarship:

• NCAA Scholarships: Chapter 8, "Athletics" section

Statistics

Gertrude Cox Scholarship

Sponsor: American Statistical Association Committee on Women in Statistics and the Caucus for Women in Statistics
Web Site: http://www.amstat.org/awards/cox-scholarship.html
Amount of Scholarship: $1,000
Number of Awards: 1
Deadline: April 30
Education Level: graduate students
Eligibility: Applicant must enroll as a full-time student in a graduate statistics program, be female, and be a U.S. or Canadian citizen or permanent resident.

This page provides just the facts about this scholarship, including the eligibility requirements and scholarship's purpose. You will find links to PDF copies of the application form at the bottom of the page.

Also see the following scholarships:

• Cooperative Research Fellowship: Chapter 9, "All Minorities" section
• GEM Fellowships: Chapter 9, "All Minorities" section
• Graduate Research Program for Women Fellowship: Chapter 12, "Female" section
• Lucent Florida Universities Fellowship: Chapter 15, "Florida" section
• NSF Graduate Research Fellowship: Chapter 7, "Sciences" section

Study Abroad

British Marshall Scholarship

Sponsor: British Parliament
Web Site: http://www.britishcouncil-usa.org/usabms.htm
Amount of Scholarship: full tuition and a stipend (awarded for two years)
Number of Awards: 40
Deadline: October 12
Education Level: graduate students
Eligibility: Applicant must hold a bachelor's degree from an accredited U.S. university, have a minimum 3.7 GPA, and be a U.S. citizen.

For more information about this prestigious scholarship that supports study in Britain leading to a graduate degree, click the General Information link. That page describes the history of the scholarship, the length and objectives of the award, and the characteristics of a successful candidate. Follow the Information About the Competition link to learn specifics about next year's competition, including the scholarship's benefits, eligibility requirements, required application materials, and selection process. Under the Timetable section, you will find a link to a site where you can access application materials, as well as detailed application instructions and rules. Underneath that is contact information for each region of the U.S.; you must submit your application to the appropriate British Consulate General for the region where you live. If you return to the main page, you will find links to related sites, which will give you more information and insight into the scholarship. This should help you immensely when preparing your application for this prestigious program.

DAAD Scholarships for Study and Research in Germany

Sponsor: DAAD German Academic Exchange Service
Web Site: http://www.daad.org/frg_all.htm
Amount of Scholarship: varies
Number of Awards: not given
Deadline: varies
Education Level: graduate students
Eligibility: Applicant must enroll in a full-time graduate program and have a good command of the German language.

First, click the appropriate link to find information about the scholarships available for you. For instance, U.S. and Canadian citizens studying at universities in their home countries should click the first link, while international students at universities in the U.S. and Canada should click the second link. If neither of these applies to you, click the third link. Then follow the links to learn about the different kinds of grants that are available. Grants range from one month to one year in duration and are awarded to students in all fields. Some special grants are available solely for students of German studies. The Upcoming Deadlines link tells you when application materials are due for each kind of grant. To find general information about the scholarship program as a whole, click the FAQ link in the upper-right corner of the Web page.

Follow the Contact link to find contact information where you can request application materials.

Fulbright Fellowship

Sponsor: U.S. State Department Bureau of Educational and Cultural Affairs, J. William Fulbright Scholarship Board, and the United States Information Agency
Web Site: http://e.usia.gov/education/fulbright
Amount of Scholarship: varies
Number of Awards: not given
Deadline: October 25
Education Level: college seniors and graduate students
Eligibility: Applicant must hold a Bachelor of Arts degree or the equivalent, have sufficient proficiency in the language of the host country, and be a U.S. citizen.

The Fulbright Fellowship is one of the most prestigious awards available for graduate students who want to study abroad. This page provides a brief overview of the program's goals and history and gives you access to much more information. Prospective applicants should click the Students link on the left-hand side of the page to obtain more information about qualifying and applying for Fulbright Fellowships. (The other links are worth exploring for the background information on the program that they provide.) Then find the link to the type of fellowship you want to apply for; most readers will be interested in the Fulbright Student Program for U.S. Citizens link. This page provides an overview of the Fulbright program for graduate students, describes the type of grants available, and lists the factors affecting selection. There is even a link to helpful information about planning and financing study abroad. Follow the How to Apply link to find eligibility and health requirements, details on the application procedure, and a list of participating countries. Go to the Frequently Asked Questions page for answers to the most common questions about the program. Return to the main page and follow the Grant Summaries by Country link to find summaries of available fellowships for each participating country, including details on language requirements, the type of applicant sought for that grant, preferred fields of study, visa requirements, living conditions, and other basic facts. Explore the remaining links on the main page to find more information that will be helpful in preparing an application, including a list of information sessions for applicants and statistics that demonstrate the competitiveness of the program.

George J. Mitchell Scholarship

Sponsor: Government of Ireland, British Government, and U.S.-Ireland Alliance
Web Site: http://www.us-irelandalliance.org/mitchell/index.html
Amount of Scholarship: full tuition and a stipend of $11,000
Number of Awards: 12
Deadline: October 15
Education Level: graduate students
Eligibility: Applicant must be between the ages of 18 and 30, hold a bachelor's degree, and be a U.S. citizen.

To get an overview of this scholarship program, follow the Announcing the Inaugural George J. Mitchell Scholars link. This scholarship program funds postgraduate study at universities in the Republic of Ireland and Northern Ireland. The Regulations and Eligibility link describes the award conditions, application procedures, and selection criteria. Go to the Institutions of Higher Education link to find out where you can study and in what fields of study you may pursue. Follow the Procedures for Application link to learn what the eligibility re-

quirements are and how to submit an application. Applications for the next school year are available on the Web site after March.

International Dissertation Field Research Fellowship

Sponsor: Social Science Research Council and Andrew W. Mellon Foundation
Web Site: http://www.ssrc.org/idrffell.htm
Amount of Scholarship: up to $17,000
Number of Awards: 50
Deadline: November 15
Education Level: doctoral students
Eligibility: Applicant must be enrolled as a full-time student in a doctoral program in the social sciences or humanities at a U.S. university, have completed all of the requirements for the Ph.D. but the fieldwork component, and need to conduct field research in any area of the world outside the U.S.

This fellowship supports doctoral students' field research outside the United States; it cannot be used for any other purpose. The Web page describes the scope and objectives of the fellowship program, eligibility requirements, selection criteria, and conditions of accepting the fellowship. You can download an application form in PDF format by following the link at the very bottom of the page. The links on the left side of the fellowship's main Web page provide useful information about the program, including the field reports of past recipients and the background of the program.

Luce Scholars

Sponsor: Henry Luce Foundation
Web Site: http://www.hluce.org/3scholfm.html
Amount of Scholarship: not given
Number of Awards: 18
Deadline: not given

Education Level: college seniors and graduate students

Eligibility: Applicant must hold a bachelor's degree, be younger than the age of 29, and be a U.S. citizen.

This prestigious scholarship program enables graduate students in any field but Asian studies to study in Asia. The Web page describes the purpose of the scholarship and provides links to further information. First, read the Program Description to better understand what the award is, what qualities the sponsor is looking for in a successful applicant, and how the nomination process works. The Frequently Asked Questions page should answer any remaining questions that you have. You will also find a list of participating universities that can nominate students for participation in the program, as well as the names of campus contacts at each school. You must contact one of these campus representatives to obtain application materials; you cannot apply directly for the scholarship.

Rhodes Scholarship

Sponsor: The Rhodes Trust
Web Site: http://www.rhodesscholar.org
Amount of Scholarship: full tuition and a stipend (awarded for three years)
Number of Awards: 32
Deadline: October 8
Education Level: graduate students
Eligibility: Applicant must hold a bachelor's degree, be between the ages of 18 and 24, and be a U.S. citizen.

This Web site will help you learn all about one of the most prestigious and competitive scholarships for graduate students studying abroad. This scholarship supports study at Oxford University in England, as described on the Scholarship Information page. This page also provides a history of the scholarship

program, describes Oxford's approach to learning, and gives details about the application process, including selection criteria, eligibility requirements, and helpful tips for preparing the application. And there is a list of degrees and fields of study available at Oxford. The Regulations of Application page will help you with the application process. On that page you will find a link to a downloadable sample copy of the application form, as well as all the regulations pertaining to eligibility, selection, and choosing a course of study. The FAQ— Should I Apply? page will be particularly helpful if you are having trouble determining whether the Rhodes Scholarship will meet your educational goals, whether you will be happy living at Oxford, and whether you will make a good candidate for the scholarship. You should also look at the Recent Scholars page to see if your qualifications are similar to the qualifications of past recipients. If you do decide to apply, you will need to obtain application materials from and the official representative at your college; click the University Representatives button to open a database that you can search to find the name, mailing address, and e-mail address of the representative at your school.

Winston Churchill Foundation Scholarship

Sponsor: Winston Churchill Foundation
Web Site: http://members.aol.com/churchillf
Amount of Scholarship: full tuition and a stipend of $7,500 to $9,000 (awarded for one year)
Number of Awards: not given
Deadline: November 15
Education Level: graduate students
Eligibility: Applicant must be enrolled in a graduate program in engineering, mathematics, or science at a participating U.S. university;

hold a bachelor's degree from a U.S. college; be between the ages of 19 and 26; and be a U.S. citizen.

This scholarship enables American students to study engineering, mathematics, or science at Cambridge University in England. The opening page provides some information about the scholarship's sponsor. Click the Winston Churchill Scholarship link underneath that to learn more about the scholarship itself. You will find details about the subjects you can study under the scholarship, the value of the award, eligibility requirements, selection criteria, application procedures, and obligations of accepting a scholarship. At the end of the page is a link to the application form in Microsoft Word format. Beneath that is a list of participating universities; you can obtain more information about the scholarship and official application forms from the Churchill Foundation representative at your school.

Also see the following scholarships:

- Ambassadorial Scholarships: Chapter 6, "Study Abroad" section
- DDS Anniversary Scholarship: Chapter 7, "Business" section
- IIE Study Abroad Grants: Chapter 6, "Study Abroad" section
- International Medical Student Studies Scholarship: Chapter 7, "Medicine" section
- NSEP Graduate International Fellowship: Chapter 7, "International Studies" section
- Zeta Phi Beta Scholarships and Fellowships: Chapter 12, "Female" section

Taxation

See the following scholarships:

- Account for Your Future Scholarship: Chapter 6, "Accounting" section

- AICPA Scholarship for Minority Accounting Students: Chapter 6, "Accounting" section

Technical Communication

See the following scholarships:

- STC Scholarship: Chapter 6, "Technical Communication" scholarship
- Vaughan/NAHWW Scholarship: Chapter 6, "Journalism" section

Theater

See the following scholarships:

- Jacob Javits Fellowship: Chapter 7, "Humanities" section
- NHFA Entertainment Industry Scholarship: Chapter 9, "Hispanic" section

Travel and Tourism

See the following scholarship:

- ASTA Scholarships: Chapter 6, "Travel and Tourism" section

Turfgrass and Golf Course Management

GCSAA Watson Fellowship

Sponsor: Golf Course Superintendents Association of America (GCSAA) and The Toro Company

Web Site: http://www.gcsaa.org/career/pursuing/scholarships/watson.html
Amount of Scholarship: not given
Number of Awards: not given
Deadline: October 1
Education Level: graduate students
Eligibility: Applicant must enroll in a graduate program in turfgrass science or golf course management and plan to pursue a career in research, instruction, or extension in a university setting.

This page describes the goal of the fellowship, the selection criteria, and the eligibility requirements. It also tells you how to apply for the fellowship and lists all of the required documents for the application package. Follow the Application Form link to find an application form that you can complete inside your Web browser and then print out with your responses.

Veterinary Medicine

Veterinary Education Scholarship

Sponsor: New Hampshire Postsecondary Education Commission
Web Site: http://www.state.nh.us/postsecondary/vcp.html
Amount of Scholarship: not given
Number of Awards: not given
Deadline: not given
Education Level: Doctor of Veterinary Medicine students
Eligibility: Applicant must enroll in a veterinary medicine program at Tufts University or Cornell University and be a New Hampshire resident.

This scholarship is intended to give New Hampshire residents the opportunity to study veterinary medicine at an out-of-state university, since the University of New Hampshire does not offer a degree in veterinary medicine. The Web page does not provide many details about the scholarship, but you can fill out and submit the electronic form at the bottom of the page to request more information and an application form.

Also see the following scholarships:

• Arkansas Health Education Grant: Chapter 15, "Arkansas" section
• New York State Regents Professional Opportunity Scholarship: Chapter 15, "New York" section

Waste Management

Civilian Radioactive Waste Management Fellowship

Sponsor: U.S. Department of Energy Office of Civilian Radioactive Waste Management and Oak Ridge Institute for Science and Education
Web Site: http://www.orau.gov/orise/edu/uggrad/civfel1.htm
Amount of Scholarship: $14,400 (renewable for four years)
Number of Awards: not given
Deadline: last Monday in January
Education Level: college seniors and first-year graduate students
Eligibility: Applicant must enroll as a full-time student in a graduate program related to the management of nuclear and radioactive waste at a participating university; hold a bachelor's degree in the physical sciences, life sciences, mathematics, or engineering; and be a U.S. citizen or permanent resident.

This page provides the bare details about this fellowship for graduate students in earth science, engineering, materials science, and radioactive science who would like to research the management of nuclear waste. Click the How to Apply button to find a more complete description of the program and an application form in PDF format. This information sheet also lists all of the participating universities, as well as program objectives, eligibility requirements, selection criteria, and fellowship obligations.

Water Supply

NAWC Scholarship

Sponsor: National Association of Water Companies (NAWC)
Web Site: http://www.nawc.org/scholarship.html
Amount of Scholarship: $5,000

Number of Awards: 1
Deadline: April 1
Education Level: college seniors and master's students
Eligibility: Applicant must enroll in a master's program in biology, business, chemistry, engineering, or a similar field; plan to pursue a career in the public water-supply business; and be a U.S. citizen.

This page gives the basic facts about this scholarship program, including the award's purpose, eligibility requirements, and application instructions. You will find the electronic application form at the bottom of the page, which you can fill out and submit online.

Women's Studies

See the following scholarship:

• Andrew W. Mellon Fellowship in Humanistic Studies: Chapter 7, "Humanities" section

EXTRACURRICULAR ACTIVITY SCHOLARSHIPS

This chapter lists scholarships related to activities and interests outside of the classroom. Many scholarships described in this chapter go to student members of honor societies, civic groups, sororities and fraternities, and afterschool clubs. Others reward students with athletic or artistic talents (if you are an athlete or artist, be sure to check your college's listing in Chapter 16 to find school-specific scholarships that you can compete for as well). Some scholarships go to students with special hobbies, such as ham radio or bowling. Also included in this chapter are scholarships for students with afterschool jobs.

Be sure to skim through all the categories in this chapter to find all of the scholarships that you qualify for. Related scholarships listed in other chapters are cross-referenced at the end of each category.

Amateur Radio

ARRL Foundation Scholarships

Sponsor: American Radio Relay League (ARRL) Foundation
Web Site: http://www.arrl.org/arrlf/scholgen.html
Amount of Scholarship: $500 to $5,000
Number of Awards: not given
Deadline: February 1
Education Level: high school seniors, college undergraduates, and graduate students

Eligibility: Applicant must hold an amateur radio license.

This Web page describes the 30 scholarships that ARRL awards to ham radio enthusiasts each year. Each scholarship description lists the name of the scholarship, the amount of the award, the number of awards given out, the minimum amateur radio license required, and other requirements such as residency, field of study, grade point average, or college. Most of these scholarships have residency requirements, and many are intended only for electronics, engineering, or communications majors. You must also be a member of ARRL to apply for some scholarships; download a membership application by clicking the Join ARRL button in the top left-hand corner of the page. You can use one application form to apply for all the scholarships for which you are eligible; just be sure to list the names of those scholarships in the correct place on the form. A text version of the application form that you can print from your Web browser is linked at the top of the page.

Athletics

Charles M. Rowson, Jr. Memorial Scholarship

Sponsor: Orlando Runners Club (ORC)
Web Site: http://www.orlandorunnersclub.org/orcweb/scholar.html
Amount of Scholarship: $1,000

Number of Awards: 4
Deadline: April 12
Education Level: high school seniors
Eligibility: Applicant must have participated in high school track or cross country and attend high school in Orange County or Seminole County, Florida.

This site provides details of a scholarship for Orlando-area runners, including a list of eligibility requirements and a list of items that must be included in the application package. Click the ORC Scholarship Application link to find a text version of the application form that you can print from your Web browser. You will also find a link to the scholarship committee chairperson's e-mail address, which you can write to if you need more information about the scholarship.

Hooked on Sports Scholarship

Sponsor: Footaction USA
Web Site: http://www.footaction.com/scholarships.html
Amount of Scholarship: $1,000 to $10,000
Number of Awards: 84
Deadline: January 15
Education Level: high school seniors
Eligibility: Applicant must be a student athlete and be a U.S. resident.

As the Web page explains, the purpose of this scholarship is to reward graduating high school seniors who excel in both academics and athletics. Eighty-four awards are given out each year under this program: 80 for $1,000, 2 for $2,500, 1 for $5,000, and 1 for $10,000. Click the Official Rules link for details of eligibility requirements and selection criteria. Follow the Apply link to find application instructions and an application form in PDF format. You will also find links to other online scholarship information and general tips for applying for scholarships on this site.

Junior Olympic Program Committee/National Gymnastics Foundation Scholarship for Men

Sponsor: USA Gymnastics Junior Olympic Program Committee and National Gymnastics Foundation
Web Site: http://www.usa-gymnastics.org/men/scholarship.html
Amount of Scholarship: not given
Number of Awards: not given
Deadline: April 15
Education Level: college undergraduates
Eligibility: Applicant must be an elite-level gymnast, be male, and be a U.S. citizen.

This page describes the history and purpose of this scholarship program. It also briefly lists the eligibility requirements for the award. To learn more, follow the Scholarship Guidelines link, which provides more details about the scholarship's purpose, eligibility requirements, application instructions, and conditions for renewing the scholarship. Click the Get the Application link to find a printable text copy of the application form.

Linda Riddle/SGMA Endowed Scholarship

Sponsor: Women's Sports Foundation
Web Site: http://www.womenssportsfoundation.org/templates/grants/grant/featured.html?record=8
Amount of Scholarship: $1,500
Number of Awards: not given

Deadline: December 8
Education Level: high school seniors
Eligibility: Applicant must be a student athlete, be a full-time student, be female, and be a U.S. citizen or permanent resident.

First, read the History of the Program to understand this scholarship's goals, which may affect how you present your application. Underneath that are the Guidelines and Application for the scholarship, which tell you if you are eligible and how to apply. You can also download a PDF copy of the application form for printing and filling out.

Mervyn's California/Women's Sports Foundation College Scholarship

Sponsor: Women's Sports Foundation and Mervyn's California
Web Site: http://www.womenssportsfoundation.org/templates/grants/grant/featured.html?record=10
Amount of Scholarship: $1,000 to $10,000
Number of Awards: 281
Deadline: spring
Education Level: high school seniors
Eligibility: Applicant must be a student athlete, be a full-time student, be female, and be a U.S. citizen or permanent resident.

This scholarship program gives away a total of 281 awards: 267 awards of $1,000 each to residents of the fourteen states where Mervyn's California has stores; 10 awards of $1,000 each to residents of other states; 1 award of $5,000 to an athlete who has overcome barriers to athletic participation; 1 award of $5,000 to an athlete who has coached other youth or adults; 1 award of $5,000 to an athlete who has helped promote athletics in her community; and 1

$10,000 scholarship to an athlete who has participated in interscholastic activities and community service and who plans to pursue a sports-related career. First, read the History of the Program to understand this scholarship's goals, which may affect how you present your application. This section also lists the criteria for selecting the scholarship winners. Underneath that are the Guidelines and Application for the scholarship, which tell you if you are eligible and how to apply. You can also download a PDF copy of the application form for printing and filling out.

NCAA Scholarships

Sponsor: National Collegiate Athletic Association (NCAA)
Web Site: http://www.ncaa.org/about/scholarships.html
Amount of Scholarship: $3,000 to $12,500
Number of Awards: not given
Deadline: varies
Education Level: high school students, college undergraduates, and graduate students
Eligibility: Applicant must either be a student-athlete at an NCAA member institution or study an eligible sports-related field.

This page provides an overview of NCAA's scholarship program. To find NCAA scholarships for your sport, click the Sponsorships link at the top of the page; then search for colleges that sponsor your sport to obtain the contact information for athletic scholarships given at that school. Follow the Eligibility link to find out if you meet the eligibility requirements to be an NCAA student-athlete and can thus receive scholarships. The rest of the page describes the five named scholarships administered by the NCAA, which all support either the final year of undergraduate study or graduate study. Note the specific eligibility requirements for each scholarship. Two awards, the Postgraduate Scholarship and the Walter Byers Postgraduate Scholarship, go to student-athletes to support graduate education in any field. The Ethnic Minority and Women's Enhancement Scholarship is awarded to minority and female students for graduate study of a sports administration-related field. The Freedom Forum-NCAA Foundation Sports Journalism Scholarship assists a journalism major who wants to pursue a career in sports journalism in the final year of undergraduate study. And the Degree Completion scholarship goes to student-athletes who require financial assistance with completing college. If any of these scholarships interest you, click the link at the bottom of the page to find the e-mail address of the contact person who can answer your questions about the scholarships and provide application materials.

New Mexico Athletic Scholarship

Sponsor: New Mexico Commission on Higher Education
Web Site: http://www.nmche.org/financialaid/athlete.html
Amount of Scholarship: varies
Number of Awards: not given
Deadline: varies
Education Level: high school seniors, college undergraduates, and graduate students
Eligibility: Applicant must attend a public postsecondary institution in New Mexico.

This page doesn't provide much information about athletic scholarships available at New Mexico's public colleges, but it should be enough to get you started. If you are interested in applying for a scholarship, contact the ath-

letic department or the financial aid office at the college you want to attend.

Northshore Youth Soccer Association Scholarship

Sponsor: Northshore Youth Soccer Association (NYSA)
Web Site: http://www.northshoresoccer.org
Amount of Scholarship: $500
Number of Awards: 2
Deadline: April 14
Education Level: high school seniors
Eligibility: Applicant must have participated in the NYSA soccer program for at least one year.

This scholarship goes to soccer players in the Northshore area of Washington state. On the Web page you will find a brief overview of the scholarship and a text copy of the application form that you can print from your Web browser, fill out, and send to the address given.

Also see the following scholarships:

- Terry Fox Humanitarian Award: Chapter 15, "Canada" section
- "Will to Win" Asthma Athlete Scholarship: Chapter 10, "Asthma" section

Aviation

Kolstad College Scholarship Grant

Sponsor: Soaring Society of America (SSA)
Web Site: http://home.rmi.net/~mid/klsthmpg.htm
Amount of Scholarship: $1,250
Number of Awards: 1 to 2

Deadline: October 1
Education Level: high school students and college undergraduates
Eligibility: Applicant must be a soaring pilot, earn a Silver Badge or a Century Award, and be between the ages of 14 and 21.

This page describes all the awards available to soaring pilots, including the annual scholarship. First, click the Annual College Scholarship Grant link to find information about the scholarship, including an address for submitting applications and a link to SSA's Web site, where you can learn more about the scholarship's sponsor. Return to the top of the page and follow the Century Awards and SSA Silver Badge links to learn more about obtaining one of these awards, which is a prerequisite for applying for the scholarship. If you qualify, click the Application for Scholarship link to find a text version of the application form, which you can print out from your Web browser.

Bowling

Charles (Bud) Fridlin Scholarship

Sponsor: Indiana Bowling Association (IBA)
Web Site: http://www.in.net/iba/buds.htm
Amount of Scholarship: not given
Number of Awards: 9
Deadline: February 1
Education Level: high school seniors
Eligibility: Applicant must bowl in a sanctioned league and attend an Indiana high school.

One member of each of the nine districts of IBA wins this scholarship for young bowlers. The Web page provides details about eligibility requirements and the application process.

Check the Forms Distribution section of the Web page to find out how to obtain an application form; application materials are not available on the Web site. To find a mailing address, phone number, and e-mail address that you can contact for more information about this scholarship, go to http://www.in.net/iba/scholar.htm.

Evan S. (Red) Stuart Memorial Scholarship

Sponsor: Indiana Bowling Association
Web Site: http://www.in.net/iba/reds.htm
Amount of Scholarship: $1,000 (renewable for four years)
Number of Awards: 1
Deadline: February 1
Education Level: high school seniors
Eligibility: Applicant must be a member of the Young American Bowling Alliance, have amateur status in all athletics, enroll in a bachelor's degree program at an Indiana college or enroll in an associate's degree program in bowling center management or lane maintenance at an Indiana community college, and be male.

This Web page details the eligibility requirements and conditions of this scholarship for male bowlers. The application instructions are listed at the bottom of the page. Be sure to follow them exactly, or your application won't be considered. Click the Scholarships Page link under the Application Procedures section of the page to find a mailing address, phone number, and e-mail address that you can contact with questions about the scholarship.

Pennsylvania State Bowling Association Scholarship

Sponsor: Pennsylvania State Bowling Association

Web Site: http://www.psbabowl.org/
Scholarships/scholarship_program.htm
Amount of Scholarship: $1,000
Number of Awards: 4
Deadline: January 31
Education Level: high school seniors
Eligibility: Applicant must participate in an organized bowling program and have a minimum 2.0 GPA.

This Web page provides a brief overview of the scholarship program's history and goals and lists eligibility requirements. Note that you don't have to be a resident of Pennsylvania to apply. The application form is available on the Web site in four different formats: PDF, Microsoft Word, WordPerfect, and text.

Clubs

AMA/Charles H. Grant Scholarship

Sponsor: Academy of Model Aeronautics (AMA)
Web Site: http://www.modelaircraft.org/
Edu-scholarship/Scholarship.htm
Amount of Scholarship: not given
Number of Awards: not given
Deadline: April 30
Education Level: high school seniors
Eligibility: Applicant must have been a member of AMA for the last three years and enroll in a college degree or certificate program.

Four scholarships are awarded to model airplane enthusiasts under this program. The Web page describes the different scholarships, as well as the eligibility requirements and the criteria used to select recipients. Links to all of the forms you will need to apply for any of the scholarships, all in PDF format, are provided

at the bottom of the page. Be sure to download and print all of the required parts of the application.

FBLA-PBL Scholarships

Sponsor: Future Business Leaders of America-Phi Beta Lambda, Inc. (FBLA-PBL)
Web Site: http://www.fbla-pbl.org/
progs.htm#schol
Amount of Scholarship: varies
Number of Awards: not given
Deadline: April 15
Education Level: high school students, college undergraduates, and graduate students
Eligibility: Applicant must be a member of FBLA or PBL and enroll in a two-year or four-year college or a graduate school.

This Web page lists the six different scholarships available exclusively for FBLA-PBL members, as well as several more general awards that FBLA-PBL members would be well qualified to apply for. Each scholarship description tells you who sponsors the award, how much the scholarship is for, specific eligibility requirements for that award, the application deadline, and how to apply. There are three general scholarships: one $500 award and one $1,000 award for FBLA members graduating from high school; and one $500 award for PBL members already enrolled in college or graduate school. Johnson & Wales University offers several scholarships ranging from $500 to $10,000 to FBLA members who elect to attend that university. In addition, a number of competitive events for FBLA-PBL members give out cash prizes; learn more about these events by clicking the Competitive Events link under that award's description. One of these contests, ServiStar's Tools for Tomorrow, is open to all high school students enrolled in vocational education classes and awards prizes ranging from $100 to $1,000. You must apply for each scholarship separately, following the instructions listed under the scholarship's description. No application forms are available on the Web site.

FCC and 4-H Scholarship

Sponsor: Farm Credit Corporation (FCC)
Web Site: http://www.fcc-sca.ca/english/OurCommunity/workforce/4H.html
Amount of Scholarship: $1,000 (Canadian)
Number of Awards: 16
Deadline: March 31
Education Level: high school students
Eligibility: Applicant must have been a member of 4-H for at least two years, be at least 16 years old, and be a Canadian resident.

This Web page provides a lot of information about 4-H in Canada, the scholarship's sponsor, and the scholarship's objectives. To find out if you qualify for the scholarship and how to submit an application, scroll down to the How to Apply section of the page. This section also describes the rules of preparing and submitting a community service project proposal, which is a required part of the scholarship application. At the bottom of the page you will find an address where you can submit your application, as well as a link to a list of FCC offices that you can contact with questions about the scholarship program.

Key Club International Scholarships

Sponsor: Kiwanis International Foundation
Web Site: http://www.keyclub.org/resources_opportunities.html
Amount of Scholarship: $500 to full tuition
Number of Awards: not given
Deadline: varies
Education Level: high school seniors

Eligibility: Applicant must be a member of Key Club International, have a minimum 3.0 GPA, and enroll in a two-year or four-year college.

On this Web page you can learn about the 12 different scholarships for members of Key Club International. The general eligibility requirements for all scholarships are listed at the top of the page, along with an introduction to the scholarship program. A table beneath that provides the facts about award amounts and application deadlines for each scholarship. Click the scholarship's name to learn the specifics about that award, including detailed eligibility and application requirements. Five scholarships, with award amounts ranging from $500 to $4,000, are open to all qualifying Key Club International members. The Who's Who Scholarship of $500 is reserved for Key Club leaders. The Ag-Bag International Scholarship of $1,000 goes to members studying agriculture. The Sigma Phi Epsilon Balanced Man Scholarship of $2,500 is restricted to male members with athletic and community service experience. And three scholarships can only be used at specific colleges: the Arizona State University Scholarship, which awards full tuition and a $1,500 stipend; the DePauw University Scholarship, which awards $14,720 per year; and the Wabash College Scholarships, which consists of four awards of three-fourths tuition and eight awards of one-half tuition for male Key Club International members. You can use the Key Club International common scholarship application to apply for all of the scholarships except the college-specific ones. A PDF version of this application form is linked to the bottom of the page. If you want to apply for one of the college-specific scholarships, follow the link under that particular scholarship's description to find out how.

National Beta Club Scholarship

Sponsor: National Beta Club
Web Site: http://betaclub.org/jho/scholarship.html
Amount of Scholarship: $1,000 to $15,000
Number of Awards: 208
Deadline: December 10
Education Level: high school seniors
Eligibility: Applicant must be an active member of National Beta Club.

Here you'll find a general overview of the scholarship program for National Beta Club members, including some information on eligibility requirements, selection criteria, and test score requirements. You will also find links to tips for preparing a successful scholarship application and answers to frequently asked questions about the scholarship program. Candidates must be nominated by their local Beta Club chapters, so if you want to apply, you must obtain application materials from your Beta Club sponsor. To learn more about National Beta Club, click the Home button in the upper left-hand corner of the page.

National FFA Scholarships

Sponsor: Future Farmers of America (FFA)
Web Site: http://www.ffa.org/activities/index.html
Amount of Scholarship: varies
Number of Awards: around 1,700
Deadline: February 15
Education Level: high school seniors and college undergraduates
Eligibility: Applicant must be a member of FFA and enroll in a two-year or four-year college.

To find information about FFA Scholarships, click the Scholarships Program link in the left-hand frame. There you will find a PDF version of FFA's scholarship booklet, which explains the general eligibility requirements, selection criteria, and how to apply for all of the scholarships available under the program, and provides descriptions of the 328 different scholarships for FFA members. You might want to print out all the pages of this booklet to keep as a reference when completing the scholarship application. Each scholarship description tells you who sponsors the award, outlines the specific eligibility requirements for that scholarship, describes how many awards are available and how much they are, and gives specific application instructions if they differ from the general application procedures. The average scholarship awarded under this program is $1,000, but some awards are as high as $10,000 or more. Note that many scholarships are restricted to students planning to study agriculture or a related field in college or to members of farming families. Some scholarships also specify residency requirements or the colleges that recipients must attend. A few awards are reserved for disabled and minority students, as well. So, be sure to read the eligibility requirements for all scholarships carefully and write down the names of all of the awards that you are eligible to receive. You can apply for all of the scholarships for which you are eligible using just one application form. You have three different choices for how to apply. You can download the application form in either PDF or Microsoft Excel format, print it out, complete it, and mail it in. Or you can complete and submit an electronic version of the application. Links to all three versions of the application form are given at the very top of the scholarship program's Web page. Be sure to circle the correct numbers for all of the scholarships that you are applying for on the application form. While you can apply for as many scholarships as you like, you can only receive one scholarship as a graduating high school senior and one scholarship as a college undergraduate.

Serteen Scholarship

Sponsor: Sertoma Foundation
Web Site: http://www.sertoma.org/ Scholarships/default.htm
Amount of Scholarship: $1,000
Number of Awards: 4
Deadline: April 1
Education Level: high school seniors
Eligibility: Applicant must be a member of Sertoma International.

To find information about this scholarship, scroll to the bottom of the Web page. The short paragraph describes the eligibility requirements for the award. To receive more information about the scholarship, follow the instructions given at the very bottom of the page for requesting application materials by mail. Explore the links in the left frame to learn more about Sertoma International and its activities.

Sertoma Collegiate Scholarship

Sponsor: Sertoma International
Web Site: http://www.sertoma.org/ Scholarships/default.htm
Amount of Scholarship: $1,000
Number of Awards: 4
Deadline: April 1
Education Level: college undergraduates
Eligibility: Applicant must be a member of Sertoma Collegiate Club.

To find information about this scholarship, scroll to the very bottom of the Web page. The short paragraph describes the selection criteria

for the award. To receive more information about the scholarship, follow the instructions given at the bottom of the page for requesting application materials by mail. Explore the links in the left frame to learn more about Sertoma International and its activities.

Also see the following scholarships:

- Astrid G. Cates/Myrtle Beinhauer Scholarships: Chapter 14, "Clubs and Community Organizations" section
- DECUS Merit Scholarship: Chapter 14, "Clubs and Community Organizations" section
- Pennsylvania Youth Foundation Scholarships: Chapter 14, "Clubs and Community Organizations" section

Community Service

Bonner Scholars

Sponsor: The Bonner Foundation
Web Site: http://www.bonner.org/foundation /BSP/aboutbsp.htm
Amount of Scholarship: $4,000 per year (renewable for four years)
Number of Awards: 1,500
Deadline: not given
Education Level: high school seniors
Eligibility: Applicant must participate in community service, enroll at a participating college, and demonstrate financial need.

This Web page describes the purpose of the scholarship program and provides links to more information for potential applicants. The Goals and History pages go over the background and objectives of the program in more depth. The Extended Description page lists the details of the award, including eligibility requirements and the conditions of accepting the scholarship. Click the Participating Colleges & Universities link to find out which schools participate in the program. Get more information about the scholarship program by contacting the admissions office at the college where you plan to apply for admission; toll-free phone numbers for the admissions offices at all of the participating schools are also listed on the page.

Golden Key Service Award

Sponsor: Golden Key National Honor Society
Web Site: http://gknhs.gsu.edu/scholar/service/index.html
Amount of Scholarship: $250
Number of Awards: 1
Deadline: not given
Education Level: college undergraduates
Eligibility: Applicant must be a member of Golden Key National Honor Society, and have completed a community service project.

This award program rewards a Golden Key member for outstanding community service. In addition to the $250 award, the winner's chapter also receives $250 and the winner's favorite charity receives $500. On the Web page you will find the rules for the contest and a list of materials that must be included in the application package. You can download the application form in PDF format by following the given link. You will have to enter your name and e-mail address in an electronic form and select the two pages of the Service Award Application from the list under Scholarships & Awards Applications in order to download the forms.

Outstanding Young Volunteer of the Year Award

Sponsor: Ladies Auxiliary of the Veterans of Foreign Wars
Web Site: http://www.ladiesauxvfw.com/outstand.html
Amount of Scholarship: $1,000
Number of Awards: 2
Deadline: varies
Education Level: high school students
Eligibility: Applicant must participate in volunteer community service, be sponsored by an Auxiliary in the same state, be between the ages of 12 and 15, and be a U.S. citizen.

This page provides all the facts about this scholarship, including eligibility requirements, selection criteria, how to apply, and how applications are judged. At the bottom of the page is a link to the entry form that you can fill out and submit online.

President's Student Service Scholarship

Sponsor: Corporation for National Service and Citizens' Scholarship Foundation of America
Web Site: http://www.student-service-awards.org/scholarship.html
Amount of Scholarship: $1,000
Number of Awards: not given
Deadline: not given
Education Level: high school juniors and seniors
Eligibility: Applicant must have performed at least 100 hours of community service within the past year, attend high school in the U.S., and enroll in an accredited U.S. college.

Under this scholarship program, each high school in the country can nominate one student to receive a scholarship for an outstanding community service contribution. The Web page provides details about eligibility, the selection process, and how the nomination process works. Scholarship Certification Forms are available on the Web site after January of each year; this form must be completed and submitted by the applicant's high school principal.

Prudential Spirit of Community Award

Sponsor: Prudential Insurance Company of American and National Association of Secondary School Principals
Web Site: http://www.prudential.com/community/spirit/awards/cmsaz1000.html
Amount of Scholarship: $1,000 to $5,000
Number of Awards: 60
Deadline: October 29
Education Level: grades 5 through 12
Eligibility: Applicant must have participated in a volunteer activity within the past year and be a U.S. resident.

This program recognizes exemplary community service by middle school and high school students. Two winners from each state, Puerto Rico, and the District of Columbia receive $1,000 each. The 10 national honorees receive $5,000 each. The Web page tells you how the selection process works, who is eligible to apply, and what qualifications are used to select winners. If you would like to apply, follow the link at the very bottom of the page to download an application form.

Take Action Award

Sponsor: react Magazine and the New World Foundation
Web Site: http://www.react.com/take_action/awards.html
Amount of Scholarship: $250 to $20,000
Number of Awards: 25
Deadline: December 10
Education Level: high school students

Eligibility: Applicant must be active in a community service project, be between the ages of 12 and 18, and be a U.S. resident.

Under this program, the 5 first-place winners receive $20,000 scholarships and a trip to New York City, the 10 second-place winners receive $1,000 scholarships, and the 10 runners-up receive $250 scholarships. In addition, one application receives a $5,000 scholarship and $5,000 worth of computer equipment for using online technologies to support his or her cause; follow the Take Action/AOL Innovator Award link to learn more about this particular scholarship. To find out more about the main scholarship program, go to the FAQ page, where you'll find answers to the most commonly asked questions. The Past Winners link provides detailed biographies of scholarship recipients, which will help you determine if you would make a good candidate. You will also find tips from previous winners on how to get involved in your community and a list of organizations and causes that you can join. Click on the Application link to open a page that details the selection criteria and application instructions, as well as a link to additional rules. It also provides a text application form that you can print.

Also see the following scholarships:

- Canada Trust Scholarship for Outstanding Community Leadership: Chapter 15, "Canada" section
- LIFE Unsung Hero Scholarship: Chapter 15, "Florida" section

Fraternities and Sororities

Alpha Phi Delta Scholarships

Sponsor: Alpha Phi Delta Foundation
Web Site: http://www.apd.org/scholarships/index.html

Amount of Scholarship: $750 to $2,400
Number of Awards: 20
Deadline: May 15
Education Level: college undergraduates
Eligibility: Applicant must be a member of Alpha Phi Delta fraternity or the relative or friend of a member.

Alpha Phi Delta gives out 20 different scholarships each year to its members: 16 awards of $750 each; 1 award of $1,000; 1 award of $1,400; 1 award of $1,600; and 1 award of $2,400. The scholarship program's Web page provides a list of all available scholarships and links to the application form in PDF format.

Delta Delta Delta Scholarships

Sponsor: Delta Delta Delta Foundation
Web Site: http://www.tridelta.org/foundation/fschol.htm
Amount of Scholarship: $500 to $3,000
Number of Awards: not given
Deadline: varies
Education Level: college sophomores, juniors, and seniors and graduate students
Eligibility: Applicant must be a member of Delta Delta Delta sorority.

The Tri Delta scholarship program includes one undergraduate scholarship with awards ranging from $500 to $1,500 and six graduate fellowships of $3,000 each. Both programs are briefly described on the Web page, with a link to the application form in PDF format at the end of each description. The application forms also provide more details about eligibility requirements and selection criteria, as well as instructions for submitting the application.

Delta Gamma Foundation Scholarships

Sponsor: Delta Gamma Foundation
Web Site: http://www.deltagamma.org/found/scholar.htm

Amount of Scholarship: $1,000 to $2,500
Number of Awards: 141
Deadline: April 1
Education Level: college undergraduates and graduate students
Eligibility: Applicant must be a member of Delta Gamma sorority.

The Delta Gamma sorority offers $1,000 scholarships for undergraduate study, $2,500 fellowships for graduate study, and higher education loans of $1,000 to $2,000. All of these programs are briefly described on the Web page. You can download scholarship and fellowship applications in either PDF or Microsoft Word format by following a link at the bottom of the page and then choosing the correct form from the list that appears.

National Order of Omega Scholarships and Fellowships

Sponsor: National Order of Omega
Web Site: http://www.orderofomega.com/scholfel/scholarship_fellowship.htm
Amount of Scholarship: $100 to $1,000
Number of Awards: 103
Deadline: October
Education Level: college juniors and seniors and graduate students
Eligibility: Applicant must be a member of a chapter of the National Order of Omega (undergraduates) or be employed advising Greek Life or Order of Omega (graduate students).

This Web site describes all of the undergraduate scholarships and graduate fellowships available from the National Order of Omega for its members. First, click the General Information link to learn more about what awards are available, how to become eligible for them, and how to apply. There are three different graduate fellowships: one $1,000 award for doctoral students; one $750 award for master's students, and one $500 award for graduate assistants. The National Order of Omega also gives away 100 undergraduate scholarships total: 50 awards of $500 each and 50 honorable mentions of $100 each. The Scholarship Criteria and Sample Application page provides more detailed information about the undergraduate scholarship program, including examples of all the items required for application that you can use as a model when putting together your application package. The Fellowship Criteria and Sample Application does the same for the graduate fellowships.

Phi Kappa Tau Scholarships

Sponsor: Phi Kappa Tau Foundation
Web Site: http://www.phikappatau.org/ fraternity/chaptersvcs/scholarship/ scholarship.asp
Amount of Scholarship: $500 to $5,000
Number of Awards: 41
Deadline: varies
Education Level: college undergraduates and graduate students
Eligibility: Applicant must be a member of Phi Kappa Tau fraternity.

This Web page lists the five different scholarships available to members of Phi Kappa Tau members, along with the number of awards given out for each scholarship and the amounts of those awards. At the top of the page is a link to the scholarship application in PDF format that you can download. The application form also provides a lot more information about eligibility requirements, selection criteria, and the scholarship program in general.

Triangle Fraternity Education Foundation Scholarships

Sponsor: Triangle Fraternity Education Foundation, Inc.

Web Site: http://www.tuff.gatech.edu/ triangle.html
Amount of Scholarship: $2,500 to $3,000
Number of Awards: not given
Deadline: May 1
Education Level: college sophomores and juniors
Eligibility: Applicant must be an active member of Triangle Fraternity, enroll in a degree program at a four-year college, have completed at least two full years of college, and demonstrate financial need.

The Web page describes the need-based scholarship and student loan program that Triangle Fraternity offers to members. The Eligibility section of the page lists the eligibility requirements. Look in the Scholarships section for descriptions of the two scholarships offered under the program: one for $3,000, and one for $2,500. Preference for the larger scholarship is given to students of engineering and the hard sciences. You will also find a description of the loan program on the Web page. Scroll to the bottom of the page to find a scholarship and loan application in PDF format. You can use the same form to apply for either scholarships or loans.

Also see the following scholarship:

- Zeta Phi Beta Scholarships and Fellowships: Chapter 12, "Female" section

Golf

Gloria Fecht Memorial Scholarship

Sponsor: Women's Southern California Golf Association

Web Site: http://www.womensgolf.org/wscga/scholar/#scholar3
Amount of Scholarship: $1,000 to $3,000 (renewable for four years)
Number of Awards: 20 to 30
Deadline: March 1
Education Level: high school seniors
Eligibility: Applicant must be an amateur golfer, be female, enroll at an accredited four-year U.S. college, and reside in Southern California.

This Web page first tells you about the history of the scholarship program and lists past winners. Scroll down to the Application Information section to find out if you are eligible, learn how recipients are selected, and download an application form in PDF format.

MasterCard Graduate Scholarship Award

Sponsor: MasterCard International and College Golf Foundation
Web Site: http://chili.collegesportsnews.com/cgf/
MASTERCARD_SCHOLARSHIP_P1.htm
Amount of Scholarship: $1,000
Number of Awards: 6
Deadline: February 15
Education Level: graduate students
Eligibility: Applicant must have earned a varsity collegiate golf letter in NCAA Division I, II, or III, hold a bachelor's degree, and have a minimum 3.0 GPA.

This page provides a brief listing of the eligibility requirements and required application materials for this scholarship for college golfers who plan to attend graduate school. Click the link at the bottom of the page to open a text version of the application form that you can print from your browser.

Southern Texas PGA Foundation Scholarship

Sponsor: Southern Texas Professional Golfers' Association (PGA) Foundation
Web Site: http://www.stpga.com/stpgaf/jrgolf03.htm
Amount of Scholarship: $1,000 to $3,000
Number of Awards: 8
Deadline: April 1
Education Level: high school seniors and college undergraduates
Eligibility: Applicant must have an interest in golf, be a full-time student, have a minimum 2.5 GPA, demonstrate financial need, and live in the geographic boundaries of the Southern Texas PGA Section.

This page describes the purpose of the scholarship program, eligibility requirements for applying for the scholarship, and selection criteria used to pick the winners. It also provides details about the awards given out under the program. Four different scholarships are available: two general scholarships for $2,500 that are renewable for up to four years; one Nicholas Battle Scholarship for $3,000; three Tommy Aycock Scholarships for $1,000; and two Jack Harden Scholarships for $2,500. The latter two scholarships specify the southern Texas counties that applicants must reside in, while the former two are open to all residents of the region. To apply, follow the link to the application form, which you can print out from your Web browser.

Honor Societies

Golden Key Graduate Scholar Award

Sponsor: Golden Key National Honor Society
Web Site: http://gknhs.gsu.edu/scholar/gradschl.html

Amount of Scholarship: $10,000
Number of Awards: 11
Deadline: January 15
Education Level: college seniors and graduate students
Eligibility: Applicant must be a lifetime member of Golden Key National Honor Society, attend a college or be a recent alumnus (within five years) of a college with an active chapter of Golden Key National Honor Society, hold a bachelor's degree, enroll as a full-time student in a graduate program at an accredited university, and be a U.S. or Canadian resident.

This page describes the graduate scholarship available for members of the Golden Key National Honor Society. You will find a list of eligibility requirements, a list of materials that must be included in the application package, and a description of the selection criteria and selection process. Download the application form in PDF format by following the link under the Application Packet section of the page. You must then enter your name and e-mail address in an electronic form and select the two pages of the Scholar Award Application from the list under Scholarships & Awards Applications in order to download the forms. To learn more about the Golden Key National Honor Society, click the Home link on the left-hand side of the Web page.

Golden Key Student Scholastic Showcase

Sponsor: Golden Key National Honor Society
Web Site: http://gknhs.gsu.edu/scholar/showcase/index.html
Amount of Scholarship: $1,000
Number of Awards: 4
Deadline: March 1
Education Level: college undergraduates

Eligibility: Applicant must be a member of Golden Key National Honor Society.

This program rewards the scholarly work of Golden Key members. The four applicants with the best research receive $1,000 scholarships and present their research at the Golden Key International Convention. Be sure to read the purpose and rules of the contest carefully to make certain that your entry will be competitive. If you decide to apply, download a copy of the Student Scholastic Showcase application, which is linked to the Rules section of the Web page. You will have to enter your name and e-mail address in an electronic form and select the Student Scholastic Showcase Application from the list under Scholarships & Awards Applications to download the form. To learn more about the Golden Key National Honor Society, click the Home link on the left-hand side of the Web page.

Guistwhite Scholars

Sponsor: Phi Theta Kappa International Honor Society
Web Site: http://www.ptk.org/schol/guistwhite.htm
Amount of Scholarship: $1,000 to $5,000
Number of Awards: 20
Deadline: not given
Education Level: second-year community college students
Eligibility: Applicant must be a member of Phi Theta Kappa International Honor Society and plan to transfer to a bachelor's degree program at a four-year college.

Phi Theta Kappa is the honor society of two-year colleges. This scholarship program helps members pursue bachelor's degrees, as described on the Web page. Ten $5,000 scholarships and ten $1,000 scholarships are given out each year under the program. On the Web page, read about the kinds of awards available and their eligibility requirements, and link to a list of past recipients. Find a directory of college-specific scholarships offered exclusively to transfer students who are Phi Theta Kappa members by clicking the Scholarship Directory link on the left-hand side of the page. You will also find additional scholarship and college resources chosen especially for members transferring to four-year colleges on the Web site. To learn more about Phi Theta Kappa, explore the buttons at the very top of the Web page.

National Honor Society Scholarship

Sponsor: National Association of Secondary School Principals and National Honor Society
Web Site: http://www.nassp.org/scholarships/schol_nhs.htm
Amount of Scholarship: $1,000
Number of Awards: 250
Deadline: November
Education Level: high school seniors
Eligibility: Applicant must be a member of the National Honor Society.

This page briefly describes the scholarship program for National Honor Society members, including the criteria for which scholarship recipients are chosen. Your National Honor Society chapter must nominate you in order for you to be considered for the award.

Also see the following scholarships:

- Golden Key Art International Showcase: Chapter 8, "Visual Arts" section
- Golden Key Literary Achievement Award: Chapter 8, "Writing" section
- Golden Key Performing Arts Showcase: Chapter 8, "Performing Arts" section
- Golden Key Service Award: Chapter 8, "Community Service" section

Horseback Riding

AMHI Scholarships

Sponsor: American Morgan Horse Institute, Inc. (AMHI)
Web Site: http://www.morganhorse.com/yp_cash.html
Amount of Scholarship: varies
Number of Awards: not given
Deadline: varies
Education Level: high school seniors and college undergraduates
Eligibility: Applicant must demonstrate achievement with Morgan horses.

AMHI supports six different scholarships, all of which are described on this Web page. The eligibility requirements and selection criteria for each scholarship are listed. You can apply for most of the scholarships online at fastweb.com, or you can order printed application forms by following the instructions at the very bottom of the page.

AQHA National Female Equestrian Award

Sponsor: Women's Sports Foundation and American Quarter Horse Association (AQHA)
Web Site: http://www.womenssportsfoundation.org/templates/grants/grant/featured.html?record=1
Amount of Scholarship: $2,000
Number of Awards: 1

Deadline: not given
Education Level: all
Eligibility: Applicant must be an equestrian with national ranking and be female.

First, read the History of the Program to understand this scholarship's goals, which may affect how you present your application. Underneath that are the Guidelines and Application for the scholarship, which tell you if you are eligible and how to apply.

Performing Arts

"Duke" Demay Jazz Scholarship

Sponsor: Alabama Jazz and Blues Federation
Web Site: http://www.ajbf.com/demay.htm
Amount of Scholarship: $500
Number of Awards: 1
Deadline: not given
Education Level: college undergraduates
Eligibility: Applicant must study jazz at a college in Alabama or Georgia.

This Web page provides a little information about the history of the scholarship and a list of past winners. Scroll to the bottom of the page to find instructions for submitting an audition tape or CD.

Golden Key Performing Arts Showcase

Sponsor: Golden Key National Honor Society
Web Site: http://gknhs.gsu.edu/scholar/performing/index.html
Amount of Scholarship: $1,000
Number of Awards: 6
Deadline: March 1

Education Level: college undergraduates
Eligibility: Applicant must be a member of Golden Key National Honor Society.

As described on this Web page, the Golden Key National Honor Society awards one $1,000 scholarship to a talented member in each of six performing arts categories: dance; drama; filmmaking; instrumental performance; original musical composition; and vocal performance. The rules for submitting an entry are listed on the Web page. If you decide to apply, download a copy of the application form, which is linked to the Rules section of the Web page. You must enter your name and e-mail address in an electronic form and select the Performing Arts Showcase Application from the list under Scholarships & Awards Applications in order to download the form.

Kristen Pfaff Memorial Scholarship

Sponsor: Kristen Pfaff Scholarship Fund
Web Site: http://www.buffalomusic.org/community/Kristen_Pfaff.html
Amount of Scholarship: $1,000
Number of Awards: 1
Deadline: November 1
Education Level: Open to all.
Eligibility: Applicant must be active in the arts and be a U.S. resident.

This Web page provides a short history of this scholarship program and tells you how to submit an application. It also describes the application process; finalists are asked to submit artwork samples as slides, recordings, or videos. At the bottom of the page is a text copy of the application form that you can print from inside your Web browser.

Madison Jazz Society Scholarship

Sponsor: Madison Jazz Society
Web Site: http://www.madisonjazz.com/scholarshipinfo.html
Amount of Scholarship: $1,000
Number of Awards: not given
Deadline: March 20
Education Level: high school seniors
Eligibility: Applicant must demonstrate an interest in jazz, plan to study music at an accredited college, and be a Wisconsin resident.

This page briefly describes the scholarship program. To learn more, click the College Scholarship Application Form link, which provides more detail about the eligibility requirements and tells you how to prepare and submit audition tapes. Print this page to obtain a copy of the application form.

Also see the following scholarships:

- Archibald Rutledge Scholarship: Chapter 15, "South Carolina" section
- Distinguished Scholar Award: Chapter 15, "Maryland" section
- Jewish Foundation for Education of Women Scholarships: Chapter 15, "New York" section
- Montana Bandmasters Association Scholarship: Chapter 6, "Music" section

Scouting

American Legion Eagle Scout of the Year Scholarship

Sponsor: American Legion Posts
Web Site: http://www.legion.org/educasst.htm
Amount of Scholarship: $2,500 to $10,000 (awarded over four years)
Number of Awards: 4
Deadline: March 1
Education Level: high school students
Eligibility: Applicant must be a Registered Scout who has reached the rank of Eagle and enroll at an accredited U.S. college.

To find the description of this award, scroll down the Web page until you see the scholarship's name. Under the program, one $10,000 and three $2,500 scholarships are given to Eagle Scouts nominated by their Posts. The description also provides a link to a PDF copy of the application form.

Elks' Eagle Scout Scholarship

Sponsor: Elks National Foundation
Web Site: http://www.elks.org/enf/eaglescout00.cfm
Amount of Scholarship: $4,000 to $8,000 (awarded over four years)
Number of Awards: 8
Deadline: February 28
Education Level: high school seniors
Eligibility: Applicant must be a Registered Scout who has reached the rank of Eagle, have a minimum SAT I score of 1090 or ACT score of 26, and demonstrate financial need.

This program awards four $4,000 scholarships and four $8,000 scholarships to Eagle Scouts. You must get an application form through the Boy Scouts, which also processes applications and selects scholarship recipients. The Web page briefly describes the scholarship and the eligibility requirements, lists the past year's recipients, and tells you how to obtain application materials.

Gold Award Scholarships

Sponsor: Elks National Foundation
Web Site: http://www.elks.org/enf/goldawards.cfm
Amount of Scholarship: $6,000 (awarded over four years)
Number of Awards: 8
Deadline: not given
Education Level: high school seniors
Eligibility: Applicant must be a Girl Scout who has won the Gold Award.

This Web page briefly describes the scholarships available for girls who have won the highest ranking in Girl Scouting—the Gold Award. One applicant from each Girl Scout Service Area receives a scholarship. The criteria used to choose the winners are also listed on the page. You can't obtain application materials on the Web site. Instead, get application forms and other information through your Girl Scout troop.

Also see the following scholarship:

• Eagle Scout Scholarships: Chapter 11, "Judaism" section

Visual Arts

Fearless Eye Photo Contest

Sponsor: GRIP Publications
Web Site: http://www.gripvision.com/money.html
Amount of Scholarship: $250
Number of Awards: not given
Deadline: none
Education Level: Open to all.
Eligibility: Open to all.

To find information about this scholarship, click the Photo Award button on the left-hand side of the page. There you will find the basic facts about the contest, enough to tell you how to enter. The contest rewards "outrageous" works of photojournalism, art illustration, or cartooning. To enter, send your samples to the e-mail address given, or mail them to the postal address listed at the top of the page.

Golden Key Art International Showcase

Sponsor: Golden Key National Honor Society
Web Site: http://gknhs.gsu.edu/scholar/artcontest/index.html
Amount of Scholarship: $100 to $1,000
Number of Awards: 66
Deadline: April 1
Education Level: college undergraduates
Eligibility: Applicant must be a member of Golden Key National Honor Society.

This art contest awards one $1,000 scholarship in each of six categories to first-place winners and up to ten $100 scholarships in each category to the runners-up. Visual arts categories include painting, drawing, photography, sculpture, computer-generated art, set design, graphic design and illustration, applied art, printmaking, and mixed media. First, follow the Art Guidelines link to find out what the rules for this contest are. This page also tells you how to prepare an art sample and how to submit an application. If you still have questions about the contest, go to the Art FAQ page to try to find an answer. You will also find past contest winners listed on the Web site, along with their winning artwork samples; looking at these should help you choose an appropriate art sample to enter in the contest. If you decide to apply, click the Art Application link. You will have to enter your name and e-mail address in an electronic form and select Art International Application from the list under Scholarships & Awards Applications in order to download the PDF application form.

Imation Computer Arts Scholarship

Sponsor: Imation Corporation, National Art Education Association, and the American Association of School Administrators
Web Site: http://www.imation.com/about/ scholarship/content/0,1011,152,00.html
Amount of Scholarship: $1,000
Number of Awards: 25
Deadline: not given
Education Level: high school students
Eligibility: Open to all.

This program awards scholarships for the best original computer-generated art creations. The Web page tells you the contest rules and how the judging process works. If you want to enter, your school must request an entry packet from Imation. You can't receive an application yourself. So ask your art teacher, computer instructor, or guidance counselor to visit the Web page, where they will find a toll-free phone number they can use to request entry packets. The artwork of past winners is also published on the Web site; you should look them over to make certain that your creations are competitive.

Rhythm & Hues Computer Graphics Scholarship

Sponsor: Rhythm & Hues Studios
Web Site: http://www.rhythm.com/recruiting /scholarship/index.shtml
Amount of Scholarship: $1,000

Number of Awards: 5
Deadline: June 1
Education Level: college undergraduates and graduate students
Eligibility: Applicant must be a full-time student at an accredited college or university.

This program awards scholarship prizes to computer graphic artists in three categories: computer modeling, computer character animation, and digital cinematography. Before you apply, read the Background section of the Web page to understand who the scholarship sponsor is and why scholarship was established. Beneath that, you'll find information on eligibility, instructions for formatting and submitting entries, and other important details. You don't have to submit an official application form for this contest, but if you have questions, you can contact the e-mail address or phone number given at the very bottom of the page.

Scholastic Art and Writing Awards

Sponsor: Scholastic, Inc. and Alliance for Young Artists & Writers, Inc.
Web Site: http://www.scholastic.com/ artandwriting/index.htm
Amount of Scholarship: not given
Number of Awards: 1,000
Deadline: not given
Education Level: grades 7 through 12
Eligibility: Applicant must attend secondary school in the U.S. or Canada.

This is one of the largest and oldest art and writing contests for students, and it receives over 250,000 entries each year. Scholarship prizes are awarded in 16 visual art categories and 9 writing categories. To learn more, click the About the Scholastic Awards link on the contest's Web page. You will also find a gallery of works by previous winners, which will help you determine what makes a winning entry. To obtain an entry form, go to the How to Enter page, select whether you want to enter the art contest or the writing contest, and enter your zip code into the space provided; then, click the OK button. You will also find a Student Forum on the Web site, where you can post your art- and writing-related comments and read what others have to say.

Young American Creative Patriotic Art Award

Sponsor: Ladies Auxiliary to the Veterans of Foreign Wars
Web Site: http://www.ladiesauxvfw.com/ypatart.html
Amount of Scholarship: $500 to $3,000
Number of Awards: 5
Deadline: varies
Education Level: grades 9 through 12
Eligibility: Applicant must attend high school in the same state as their sponsoring Auxiliary.

Five prizes are given out in this art contest, ranging from $500 to $3,000. The Web page provides the contest rules, which tell you how to submit your artwork. You will also find ex- amples of winning artwork, which you can use to help you prepare a competitive entry. To find a copy of the entry form, which you must submit with your artwork, click the link at the very bottom of the page.

Also see the following scholarships:

- Archibald Rutledge Scholarship: Chapter 15, "South Carolina" section
- HGA and Dendel Scholarships: Chapter 6, "Textile Science and Fiber Arts" section
- Kristen Pfaff Memorial Scholarship: Chapter 8, "Performing Arts" section

Work

BILO John Rohaley Scholarship

Sponsor: BILO
Web Site: http://www.scholarshipprograms.org/johnrohaley.html
Amount of Scholarship: $2,000
Number of Awards: 3
Deadline: February 1
Education Level: high school seniors and col- lege freshmen, sophomores, and juniors
Eligibility: Applicant must be a current BILO associate with at least one full year of employ- ment working an average of 15 hours a week, be a full-time student at a two-year or four- year college, and study a field related to the food retail industry.

The scholarship's Web page outline the quali- fications required to apply for the award, in- cluding acceptable programs of study, and the selection criteria. If you decide to apply, down- load and print all the application forms and instructions in PDF format by following the links at the bottom of the page.

Burger King/McLamore North American Scholarship

Sponsor: Burger King and Trust to Reach Ed- ucation Excellence
Web Site: http://www.nassp.org/scholarships/bk_scholarship.htm
Amount of Scholarship: $1,000
Number of Awards: 269
Deadline: January 31
Education Level: high school seniors
Eligibility: Applicant must work part-time and have a grade average of at least a B.

This page simply consists of a poster for the scholarship, which tells you the bare details about eligibility requirements. Note that you don't have to work at Burger King to be eligible to apply; any part-time employment qualifies. To get more information and obtain application materials, contact the e-mail address listed at the bottom of the Web page.

Chick-fil-A Scholarship

Sponsor: Chick-fil-A, Inc.
Web Site: http://www.eatmorechicken.com/scholar_info.html
Amount of Scholarship: $1,000
Number of Awards: not given
Deadline: not given
Education Level: high school seniors and college undergraduates
Eligibility: Applicant must be an employee of Chick-fil-A and enroll in an accredited two-year or four-year college.

This Web page provides a little background on the scholarship and tells you how to qualify. You don't have to submit an official application form to apply for this award; just follow the instructions for putting together an application package given on the Web page.

Eisenhower-Evans Scholarship

Sponsor: Western Golf Association
Web Site: http://www.golfhousecolorado.org/scholar
Amount of Scholarship: full tuition (renewable for four years)
Number of Awards: not given
Deadline: not given
Education Level: high school seniors
Eligibility: Applicant must be a caddie, rank in the upper quarter of his or her graduating high school class, and demonstrate financial need.

This is a scholarship for golf caddies. If you win, you receive full tuition at the University of Colorado and housing in the Eisenhower-

Evans Chapter House. See the Web page to find out what qualifications you must meet to be an eligible caddie. The page also tells you how to obtain an application and how to put together an application package.

New York Tri-State BMOA McDonald's Scholarship

Sponsor: New York Tri-State Black McDonald's Owner/Operator Association (BMOA)
Web Site: http://us.nu-net.com/mcdonalds
Amount of Scholarship: $1,000 to $5,000
Number of Awards: 40
Deadline: March 1
Education Level: high school seniors and college undergraduates
Eligibility: Applicant must be a McDonald's employee, be African-American, and live in Connecticut, New Jersey, or New York.

You can find more general information about the scholarship and its sponsor by following the Introduction to BMOA link. Click the Tri-State BMOA Scholarship Program Guidelines link to find the eligibility requirements, selection criteria, and application instructions. You will also find a link to the application form. Note that although it appears that you can fill out this form online, you must print it out from your Web browser and mail it in; you cannot submit it over the Internet.

Undergraduate Merit Scholarship for College Students

Sponsor: National Restaurant Association Educational Foundation
Web Site: http://www.edfound.org/NewASP/careers/scholarshp/careers_undergrad.htm
Amount of Scholarship: $1,000
Number of Awards: not given
Deadline: November 1, March 1, and July 1
Education Level: college undergraduates

Eligibility: Applicant must have a minimum of 750 hours of work experience in the restaurant and hospitality industry, have completed at least one term of a food service-related program at a two-year or four-year college, have a minimum 2.75 GPA, and be a U.S. citizen or permanent resident.

This page briefly describes the eligibility requirements for this scholarship. You can also download the application form in PDF format, which provides more information about the program, including application requirements and selection criteria.

Undergraduate Merit Scholarship for High School Seniors

Sponsor: National Restaurant Association Educational Foundation
Web Site: http://www.edfound.org/NewASP/careers/scholarshp/careers_undergrad.htm
Amount of Scholarship: $2,000
Number of Awards: not given
Deadline: May 1
Education Level: high school seniors
Eligibility: Applicant must have a minimum of 250 hours of work experience in food service, enroll in a food service-related program at a two-year or four-year college, have a minimum 2.75 GPA, and be a U.S. citizen or permanent resident.

This page briefly describes the eligibility requirements for this scholarship. You can also download the application form in PDF format, which provides more information about the program, including application requirements and selection criteria.

Wal-Mart Associate Scholarship

Sponsor: Wal-Mart Stores, Inc.
Web Site: http://compedge.wal-mart.com/wa_scholar.html
Amount of Scholarship: $1,000
Number of Awards: not given
Deadline: March 1
Education Level: high school seniors
Eligibility: Applicant must be an employee of Wal-Mart Stores, Inc. or the child of an employee who is not eligible for a Walton Foundation Scholarship.

This Web page provides a brief description of the scholarship, outlining the eligibility requirements and the judging criteria. You can't apply for the scholarship online. Instead, obtain an application form from your personnel manager.

Wal-Mart Distribution Center Scholarship

Sponsor: Wal-Mart Stores, Inc.
Web Site: http://compedge.wal-mart.com/dc_scholar.html
Amount of Scholarship: $2,500 (renewable for four years)
Number of Awards: 2
Deadline: May 1
Education Level: high school seniors and college undergraduates
Eligibility: Applicant must have worked at least 1,000 hours in a Wal-Mart Distribution Center and enroll in an accredited two-year or four-year college.

This Web page just provides a brief paragraph describing the scholarship program. If you qualify, contact your personnel manager to obtain application materials.

Also see the following scholarship:

- AHF Scholarships: Chapter 6, "Hotel and Restaurant Management" section

Writing

Been There, Done That Contest

Sponsor: The Princeton Review and Time Magazine
Web Site: http://www.review.com/college
Amount of Scholarship: $1,000
Number of Awards: 3
Deadline: May 1
Education Level: high school students
Eligibility: Applicant must be a North American resident.

Look for the contest link and click it to find information about this contest. To enter the contest, you must submit an essay, poem, song, or comic strip on the topic given. Using the sample entry form on the Web page as a guide, submit your entry to either the e-mail address or the postal address given.

Golden Key Literary Achievement Award

Sponsor: Golden Key National Honor Society
Web Site: http://gknhs.gsu.edu/scholar/literary/index.html
Amount of Scholarship: $1,000
Number of Awards: 4
Deadline: April 1
Education Level: college undergraduates
Eligibility: Applicant must be a member of Golden Key National Honor Society.

This art contest awards one $1,000 scholarship in each of four writing categories: fiction; non-fiction; poetry; and news/feature writing. The Web page describes the purpose of the contest and the rules for preparing and submitting an entry. If you decide to apply, you can download the application form in PDF format by following the link under the Rules section of the page. You must enter your name and e-mail address in the electronic form that opens and select Literary Award Application from the list under Scholarships & Awards Applications in order to download the form.

Gonzo Journalist Challenge

Sponsor: GRIP Publications
Web Site: http://www.gripvision.com/money.html
Amount of Scholarship: $250
Number of Awards: not given
Deadline: none
Education Level: All
Eligibility: Open to all.

To find information about this scholarship, click the Gonzo Award button on the left-hand side of the page. There you will find the basic facts about the contest, enough to tell you how to enter. The contest rewards the best journalism or writing samples, including creative writing, on any topic. To enter, send your samples to the e-mail address given, or mail them to the postal address listed at the top of the page.

Lambda Iota Tau Scholarship

Sponsor: Lambda Iota Tau
Web Site: http://www.bsu.edu/english/lit/schol.html
Amount of Scholarship: $1,000
Number of Awards: 2

Deadline: May 31
Education Level: college undergraduates
Eligibility: Applicant must be a member of Lambda Iota Tau.

Lambda Iota Tau is the national honor society for literature. Members may apply for scholarships by submitting an application package, including an essay or piece of creative writing, as described on the scholarship's Web page. You don't need to submit an official application form to apply. The selection criteria are also listed on the Web page.

"Let's Get Creative!" Scholarship

Sponsor: FreSch!
Web Site: http://www.freschinfo.com/creative2000intro.phtml
Amount of Scholarship: $100 to $1,000
Number of Awards: 5
Deadline: June 1
Education Level: high school seniors, college undergraduates, and graduate students
Eligibility: Applicant must attend an accredited college or university in the U.S. or Canada, and be a U.S. or Canadian citizen or permanent resident.

This scholarship rewards the best short fiction, with a first prize of $1,000, a second prize of $250, and three third prizes of $100 each. You can read stories by past winners on the Web site to find out what makes a winning entry in this contest. Also be sure to read and understand the contest rules so that you will submit a competitive entry. Beneath the rules you'll find instructions for submitting your entry either through the mail or online, with links to a printable application form and an electronic application form. The rules state that mailed applications are preferred because the electronic application form can introduce formatting errors, so you should follow this suggestion and mail in your entry to give it the best chance of winning.

Original Poetry and Literature Scholarship

Sponsor: OPALS
Web Site: http://geocities.com/opals_1
Amount of Scholarship: $1,000
Number of Awards: 1
Deadline: March 1
Education Level: high school juniors and seniors
Eligibility: Open to all.

For this scholarship contest, the best poem receives the award. Be sure to read the Scholarship Information page to understand eligibility requirements and how to submit your entry. You don't need to turn in an official application form for this scholarship. You should also read the Our Organization page to understand who the scholarship sponsors are and why they began the scholarship program.

Also see the following scholarships:

- Archibald Rutledge Scholarship: Chapter 15, "South Carolina" section
- Scholastic Art and Writing Awards: Chapter 8, "Visual Arts" section

SCHOLARSHIPS FOR MEMBERS OF MINORITY AND ETHNIC GROUPS

This chapter guides you to scholarships set aside exclusively for members of minority and ethnic groups. These scholarship programs are usually established to help even the playing field and bring members of underrepresented groups into particular careers. The minority groups targeted by the scholarships listed in the "All Minorities" category generally include African-Americans, Hispanics, Native Americans, Alaskan Natives, Pacific Islanders, and sometimes Asian-Americans, but you should still read the eligibility requirements carefully to make certain that you qualify before applying.

This chapter also includes scholarships restricted to particular ethnic groups, such as Armenian, Hellenic, and Portuguese students. And it lists scholarships for gay, lesbian, bisexual, and transsexual students. At the end of each section, you'll find cross references to scholarships in other chapters of this book that are also restricted to specific minorities or ethnic groups. Don't forget to look up your college or university in Chapter 16 to find scholarships for minorities offered only to students at your school.

All Minorities

Cooperative Research Fellowship

Sponsor: Lucent Technologies Foundation
Web Site: http://www.bell-labs.com/fellowships/CRFP
Amount of Scholarship: full tuition and $17,000 stipend (renewable for four years)

Number of Awards: not given
Deadline: December 20
Education Level: college seniors and first-year graduate students
Eligibility: Applicant must be a member of a minority group, enroll as a full-time student in an eligible science or engineering doctoral program at an approved university, and be a U.S. citizen or permanent resident.

This fellowship program is designed to entice more underrepresented minorities—African-Americans, Native Americans, and Hispanics—into the sciences. The main fellowship page lists the science and engineering disciplines for which the fellowship may be used and provides an overview of the program. Click the buttons on the left-hand side of the page to learn more. The History page provides important background information on the fellowship program that you can use when preparing an application. The Mentors page describes the mentoring aspect of the fellowship. Read about the qualifications and accomplishments of past recipients by following the Fellows link. The News page publishes events and announcements. If you would like to apply for the fellowship, click the Apply button. The Apply page describes the eligibility requirements, selection criteria, and application requirements, and links to a page where you can download the application form in Microsoft Word, PDF, or PostScript format.

Ford Foundation Dissertation Fellowship for Minorities

Sponsor: Ford Foundation and National Research Council of the National Academies

Web Site: http://www4.nas.edu/osep/fo.nsf/web/forddiss?OpenDocument
Amount of Scholarship: $21,500
Number of Awards: 29
Deadline: November 12
Education Level: doctoral students
Eligibility: Applicant must be a member of a minority group, enroll in a doctoral program in an eligible field of study at an accredited U.S. university, have completed all requirements for the degree excepted for writing the dissertation, plan to pursue a career in teaching and research, and be a U.S. citizen.

This fellowship is intended to help minority students complete the dissertation for the Ph.D. or Sc.D. degree, as described in the introduction on the fellowship's Web page. The introduction also goes over the criteria used to select fellowship recipients. To find out if you qualify, look under the Eligibility section. African-Americans, Mexican-Americans, Puerto Ricans, Native Americans, Alaskan Natives, and Pacific Islanders are all eligible to apply. Following this section, you'll find information about eligible fields of study and verification of doctoral candidacy. Then read about the benefits of the fellowship, how applicants are evaluated and selected, and the conditions of accepting the award. Click the Download link to complete the application form online, or click the Request link to request that a printed copy of the application form be mailed to you. A list of fields that are eligible for study under the fellowship is given at the very bottom of the page. Essentially, all academic fields of study are eligible, but professional and practice-oriented programs are not.

Ford Foundation Pre-Doctoral Fellowship for Minorities

Sponsor: Ford Foundation and National Research Council of the National Academies

Web Site: http://www4.nas.edu/osep/fo.nsf/web/fordpredoc?OpenDocument
Amount of Scholarship: $21,500 (renewable for three years)
Number of Awards: 50
Deadline: November 12
Education Level: college seniors and graduate students
Eligibility: Applicant must be a member of a minority group, enroll as a full-time student in a doctoral program in an eligible field of study at an accredited U.S. university, plan to pursue a career in teaching and research, and be a U.S. citizen.

This fellowship is intended to help minority students complete the Ph.D. or Sc.D. degree, as described in the introduction on the fellowship's Web page. The introduction also goes over the criteria used to select fellowship recipients. To find out if you qualify, look under the Eligibility section. African-Americans, Mexican-Americans, Puerto Ricans, Native Americans, Alaskan Natives, and Pacific Islanders are all eligible to apply. Following this section, you'll find information about eligible fields of study and test score requirements. Then read about the benefits of the fellowship, how applicants are evaluated and selected, the conditions of accepting the award, and the documents required for the application package. Click the Download link to complete the application form online, or click the Request link to request that a printed copy of the application form be mailed to you. A list of fields that are eligible for study under the fellowship is given at the very end of the page. Essentially, all academic fields of study are eligible, but professional and practice-oriented programs are not. Terminal master's, fine arts, education, and joint degree programs are also not eligible.

Gates Millennium Scholars

Sponsor: Bill and Melinda Gates Foundation, United Negro College Fund, American Indian

College Fund, Hispanic College Fund, and Asian Pacific American Advisory Committee
Web Site: http://www.gmsp.org
Amount of Scholarship: not given
Number of Awards: not given
Deadline: March 15
Education Level: college undergraduates and graduate students
Eligibility: Applicant must be a member of a minority group, enroll as a full-time student in an accredited college or an eligible graduate program, have a minimum 3.3 GPA, demonstrate financial need, and be a U.S. citizen or permanent resident.

First, read the About GMS page to learn more about this financial aid program, including the goals of the program and the eligibility requirements. African-Americans, Native Americans, Alaskan Natives, Asian-Pacific Americans, and Hispanics are all eligible to apply. This page also lists all of the eligible graduate fields of study (any undergraduate major is eligible). The News page publishes announcements about the program and provides links to sites where you can get additional information. You cannot apply directly for this scholarship. You must be nominated, as described on the Nomination Materials page. All the forms needed to nominate a student are also linked to this page.

GEM Fellowships

Sponsor: National Consortium for Graduate Degrees for Minorities in Engineering and Science, Inc. (GEM)
Web Site: http://www.nd.edu/~gem
Amount of Scholarship: $6,000 to $14,400 per year
Number of Awards: over 200
Deadline: December 1
Education Level: college seniors and graduate students

Eligibility: Applicant must be a member of a minority group, enroll in an master's program in engineering or a doctoral program in engineering or the natural sciences at a GEM member university, have a minimum 2.8 GPA (master's students) or 3.0 GPA (doctoral students), and be a U.S. citizen.

Three different fellowships are available under this program: one for the Master of Science degree in engineering, one for the Ph.D. in engineering, and one for the Ph.D. in a science field. African-Americans, Native Americans, and Hispanics are eligible to apply for all of the fellowships. Click on the link to the fellowship you are interested in at the bottom of the page to read a short paragraph describing the objectives and benefits of that fellowship. The eligibility requirements and award amounts differ for each fellowship, so be sure you understand the specifics for the fellowship for which you want to apply. You will find a link to a page that lists GEM member universities where the fellowship may be used on this page, as well. Go to the Application Information page to find details about eligibility requirements, award conditions and amounts, and application procedures. The Frequently Asked Questions for Prospective Fellows page will answer your most common questions about the program, including a list of engineering and science disciplines that are eligible for support. Finally, you can download the application form in PDF format or complete it online. Explore the links on the left side of the page to learn more about GEM, the fellowship's sponsor.

Jackie Robinson Foundation Scholarship

Sponsor: Jackie Robinson Foundation
Web Site: http://www.jackierobinson.org
Amount of Scholarship: $6,000 per year (awarded over four years)

Number of Awards: not given
Deadline: April 1
Education Level: high school seniors
Eligibility: Applicant must be a member of a minority group, enroll in an accredited four-year college, demonstrate financial need, and be a U.S. citizen.

To learn more about this award, click The Scholarship Program link on the left-hand side of the Web page. This page describes the benefits of winning a scholarship, the eligibility requirements, and the application deadlines. Follow the link at the bottom of the page to find an application form that you can print from within your Web browser. Follow the other links on the left-hand side of the main Web page to learn more about the scholarship's sponsor and contact the sponsor via e-mail.

Minorities in Government Finance Scholarship

Sponsor: Government Finance Officers Association
Web Site: http://www.gfoa.org
Amount of Scholarship: $3,500
Number of Awards: 1
Deadline: February 12
Education Level: college juniors and seniors and graduate students
Eligibility: Applicant must be a member of a minority group; enroll in a finance or related program; plan to pursue a career in state or local government finance; and be a U.S. or Canadian citizen or permanent resident.

To find information about this scholarship, click the Scholarships link under the Services section and scroll down until you see the scholarship listing under Available Scholarships. Click the Forms link in the left frame to locate a copy of the application. Scroll down until you see the Scholarships section, and click the Mi-

norities in Gov't Finance Scholarship link to open the application form in PDF format. The application provides a lot more information about eligibility requirements and judging criteria, and it includes a list of eligible fields of study. African-Americans, Hispanics, Native Americans, Alaskan Natives, Asian-Americans, and Pacific Islanders can all apply for the scholarship.

Minority Masters Fellowship

Sponsor: Arkansas Department of Higher Education
Web Site: http://www.adhe.arknet.edu/finance/mmasters.html
Amount of Scholarship: $7,500
Number of Awards: not given
Deadline: June 1
Education Level: master's students
Eligibility: Applicant must be a member of a minority group; enroll as a full-time student in a master's program in mathematics, the sciences, or foreign languages; have a minimum 2.75 GPA; hold a bachelor's degree; be an Arkansas resident; and be a U.S. citizen or permanent resident.

This is a service scholarship that provides support for African-American, Asian-American, and Hispanic students to obtain master's degrees in exchange for agreeing to teach in an Arkansas public school. The Web page describes the service commitment and eligibility requirements. To obtain an application, call the toll-free phone number listed at the bottom of the page.

Minority Undergraduate Retention Grant

Sponsor: State of Wisconsin Higher Educational Aids Board

Web Site: http://heab.state.wi.us/programs.html
Amount of Scholarship: $250 to $2,500 (renewable for four years)
Number of Awards: not given
Deadline: not given
Education Level: college undergraduates
Eligibility: Applicant must be a member of a minority group, enroll in a four-year or technical college in Wisconsin, and be a Wisconsin resident.

Scroll down the Web page until you see the Minority Undergraduate Retention Grant listing to find information about this financial aid program for minorities who live in Wisconsin. Eligible minority groups include African-Americans, Native Americans, Hispanics, and Southeast Asians. You don't directly submit an application form for this award. Instead, you must submit the FAFSA, which the state of Wisconsin uses to award state financial aid to all eligible students. The financial aid office at your college must also nominate you for the award, so talk to your financial aid officer if you have further questions about qualifying for the grant. The nomination form can be downloaded in Microsoft Word format from the Web site.

Morris Scholarship

Sponsor: The Morris Scholarship Fund, Inc.
Web Site: http://www.assoc-mgmt.com/users/morris/morris.html
Amount of Scholarship: not given
Number of Awards: not given
Deadline: February 1
Education Level: high school seniors and college undergraduates
Eligibility: Applicant must be a member of a minority group, have a minimum 2.5 GPA, and either be an Iowa resident or attend an Iowa college.

The first paragraph of this Web page describes the goals and selection criteria for the scholarship. Note that Iowa residents attending college in the state are given preference, but you don't have to be an Iowa resident to apply. Follow the link at the bottom of the page to download a PDF copy of the application form. To request more information about the scholarship via e-mail and get a printed application form, follow the Information link instead.

NTA Science Scholarship Award

Sponsor: National Technical Association (NTA)
Web Site: http://www.ntaonline.org/science.htm
Amount of Scholarship: $500 to $5,000
Number of Awards: not given
Deadline: January 31
Education Level: high school seniors and college freshmen
Eligibility: Applicant must be the member of a minority group, major in a science or technology field, and be a U.S. citizen.

The Program Goals section of the scholarship's Web page outlines why the scholarship was created and which science fields it supports. The Program Objectives section describes the kind of applicant the sponsor is looking for. The Eligibility section details the eligibility requirements for the award. African-Americans, Asian-Americans, Hispanics, Native Americans, and Pacific Islanders are all eligible to apply. Click the Download Application link at the very bottom of the page to download a Microsoft Word copy of the application form.

Page Education Foundation Scholarship

Sponsor: Page Education Foundation
Web Site: http://www.page-ed.org/mechanics.html

Amount of Scholarship: $750 to $2,000 (renewable)
Number of Awards: around 390
Deadline: May 1
Education Level: college undergraduates
Eligibility: Applicant must be a member of a minority group, enroll as a full-time student at a two-year or four-year college in Minnesota, and demonstrate financial need.

This Web page describes the history and purpose of this scholarship for minority students in Minnesota and outlines the community service condition of winning the award. The links at the bottom of the page tell you how to apply for a scholarship and answer students' most frequently asked questions about the program.

Rosewood Family Scholarship

Sponsor: Florida Department of Education
Web Site: http://www.firn.edu/doe/bin00065/99apps.htm
Amount of Scholarship: up to $4,000 (renewable)
Number of Awards: 25
Deadline: April 1
Education Level: high school seniors and college undergraduates
Eligibility: Applicant must be a member of a minority group, be a descendant of a Rosewood family, and enroll as a full-time student in a public two-year or four-year college in Florida.

To find information about this scholarship, click its link in the list of scholarship and loan programs on the Web page. This opens the scholarship brochure and application form in PDF format, so you will need Adobe Acrobat Reader to view it. The form details the eligibility requirements, conditions for renewing the scholarship, and other terms of the scholarship. Note that you don't have to be a resident of Florida to apply, but you do have to attend a public college in Florida to receive the award.

Xerox Technical Minority Scholarship

Sponsor: Xerox
Web Site: http://www.xerox.com/go/xrx/about_xerox/AX.jsp
Amount of Scholarship: $4,000 to $5,000
Number of Awards: not given
Deadline: September 15
Education Level: college undergraduates and graduate students
Eligibility: Applicant must be a member of a minority group; be a full-time student; major in chemistry, engineering, information management, materials science, or physics; and be a U.S. citizen or permanent resident.

This scholarship awards up to $4,000 a year to undergraduate students and up to $5,000 a year to graduate students in an effort to recruit minorities like African-Americans, Asian-Americans, Pacific Islanders, Native Americans, Alaskan Natives, and Hispanics into the technical sciences. To find the scholarship's Web page, follow the Working at Xerox link, click College Recruiting, and then click Technical Minority Scholarship Program under Related Links. Applicants must have a stellar academic record and meet all of the requirements listed under We'll Consider Students Who Are. If you would like to apply, scroll down to Ready to Apply?, where you will see links to the cover letter, application form, and sample résumé. The cover letter and application form are in Microsoft Word format, and the sample résumé is in PDF format; it is included only to show you how to format your résumé, which you must submit with the application package.

Also see the following scholarships:

- ACS Scholarships: Chapter 6, "Chemistry" section
- ACSM Graduate Scholarship: Chapter 7, "Sports Science and Administration" section
- Actuarial Scholarships for Minority Students: Chapter 6, "Actuarial Science" section
- AGI Minority Geoscience Scholarship: Chapter 7, "Geosciences" section
- AHF Scholarships: Chapter 6, "Hotel and Restaurant Management" section
- AICPA Scholarship for Minority Accounting Students: Chapter 6, "Accounting" section
- AIFS International Scholarships: Chapter 6, "Study Abroad" section
- ALA Scholarships: Chapter 7, "Library and Information Science" section
- AMS Scholarships: Chapter 6, "Atmospheric Sciences" section
- ANA Ethnic/Racial Minority Fellowships: Chapter 7, "Nursing" section
- APA Minority Fellowships: Chapter 7, "Psychology" section
- ASA Minority Fellowship: Chapter 7, "Sociology" section
- AT&T Labs Fellowship: Chapter 7, "Communications Engineering and Technology" section
- C. Clyde Ferguson Law Scholarship: Chapter 7, "Law" section
- Charles E. Price Scholarship Award: Chapter 6, "Engineering" section
- Consortium for Graduate Study in Management Fellowship: Chapter 7, "Business" section
- Forum for Concerns of Minorities Scholarship: Chapter 6, "Clinical Laboratory Science" section
- Foundation for Exceptional Children Scholarship: Chapter 10, "Any Disability" section
- Freshman/Sophomore Minority Grant: Chapter 6, "Education" section
- FTE North American Doctoral Fellowship: Chapter 7, "Religious Studies" section
- George A. Strait Minority Stipend: Chapter 7, "Library and Information Science" section
- George M. Brooker Collegiate Scholarship for Minorities: Chapter 6, "Real Estate" section
- IIE Scholarships: Chapter 6, "Engineering" section
- Jimmy A. Young Memorial Education Recognition Award: Chapter 6, "Respiratory Therapy" section
- Leonard M. Perryman Communications Scholarship: Chapter 6, "Communications" section
- Martin Luther King, Jr. Memorial Scholarship: Chapter 6, "Education" section
- Martin Luther King, Jr. Physician & Dentist Scholarship: Chapter 15, "New Jersey" section
- Microsoft National Technical Scholarships: Chapter 6, "Computer Science and Engineering" section
- Minority Teacher Incentive Grant: Chapter 6, "Education" section
- Minority Teachers of Illinois Scholarship: Chapter 6, "Education" section
- Minority Teachers Scholarship: Chapter 6, "Education" section
- Minority Teaching Fellows: Chapter 6, "Education" section
- NACME Scholarships: Chapter 6, "Engineering" section
- NASP-ERT Minority Scholarship: Chapter 7, "Psychology" section
- NCAA Scholarships: Chapter 8, "Athletics" section
- NPC Scholarship: Chapter 6, "Journalism" section
- NSMH Scholarships: Chapter 6, "Hotel and Restaurant Management" section
- OCECS Scholarship: Chapter 15, "Oregon" section
- Porter Physiology Development Program Minority Fellowship in Physiology: Chapter 7, "Physiology" section

- Robert D. Watkins Minority Graduate Fellowship: Chapter 7, "Miocrobiology" section
- Sherry R. Arnstein Minority Student Scholarship: Chapter 7, "Medicine" section
- SLA Scholarships: Chapter 7, "Library and Information Science" section
- Society of Women Engineers Scholarships: Chapter 12, "Female" section
- SRC Master's Scholarship: Chapter 7, "Electronics" section
- Synod of the Covenant Ethnic Scholarships: Chapter 11, "Presbyterian" section
- University of North Carolina Board of Governors Medical School Scholarship: Chapter 7, "Medicine" section

African-Americans

Development Fund for Black Students in Science and Technology Scholarship

Sponsor: Development Fund for Black Students in Science and Technology
Web Site: http://ourworld.compuserve.com/homepages/dlhinson/dfb_sch.htm
Amount of Scholarship: $2,000 (renewable for four years)
Number of Awards: not given
Deadline: June 15
Education Level: college undergraduates
Eligibility: Applicant must be African-American; enroll as a full-time student at a prequalified Historically Black College or University; major in a science, engineering, or another technical field; and be a U.S. citizen or permanent resident.

This page describes the process of selecting applicants for this scholarship program, the qualifications that applicants must posses, and the criteria used to evaluate applicants. To apply, you must be nominated and screened through your college, and you can only obtain applications through your school's financial aid office. Prequalified colleges are listed at the bottom of the scholarship's Web page. You might find it helpful to link to the sponsor's Main Page to learn more about this scholarship fund and what it is trying to accomplish.

McDonald's African-American Heritage Scholarships

Sponsor: McDonald's New York Tri-State Owners and Operators
Web Site: http://www.archingintoeducation.com/heritage.html
Amount of Scholarship: $1,000 to $5,000
Number of Awards: not given
Deadline: March 1
Education Level: high school seniors
Eligibility: Applicant must be African-American and be a resident of New York, New Jersey, or Connecticut.

In addition to the general $1,000 scholarships given out under this program, two $5,000 scholarships are awarded, one to the applicant with the most outstanding academic achievements and the other to the applicant who best demonstrates a commitment to community service. The Web page doesn't provide many details about the scholarship, but it does link to a downloadable application form in PDF format.

McDonald's UNCF Tri-State Scholarship

Sponsor: McDonald's New York Tri-State Owners and Operators and United Negro College Fund (UNCF)
Web Site: http://www.archingintoeducation.com/uncf.html

Amount of Scholarship: $20,000 (awarded over four years)
Number of Awards: 3
Deadline: March 1
Education Level: high school seniors
Eligibility: Applicant must be African-American; enroll in a UNCF college; and be a resident of Fairfield County, Connecticut, New Jersey, or New York.

On the scholarship's Web page you'll find a brief description of the award and a list of UNCF member colleges where the scholarship can be used. There is also a link to a PDF copy of the application form, which you can download and print.

McKnight Doctoral Fellowship

Sponsor: Florida Education Fund
Web Site: http://www.fl-educ-fd.org/mdf.html
Amount of Scholarship: $16,000 (renewable for five years)
Number of Awards: 25
Deadline: January 15
Education Level: doctoral students
Eligibility: Applicant must be African-American, enroll in a doctoral program in an eligible field of study at a participating Florida university, hold a bachelor's degree, and be a U.S. citizen.

As described on the scholarship's Web page, this fellowship is intended to increase the number of African-American Ph.D. students in crucial fields of study at Florida universities. Scroll down the page to find a list of participating Florida universities and eligible fields of study for which the fellowship may be used. The only fields not covered by the fellowship are professional degree programs (like law and medical programs) and education programs. Any doctoral degree program in the arts, sciences,

mathematics, business, or engineering disciplines is eligible. The Web page also lists the other eligibility requirements for the fellowship. At the bottom of the page you'll find a link to a page where you can download the application forms in Microsoft Word, WordPerfect, and PDF formats.

NSBE Scholarships

Sponsor: National Society of Black Engineers (NSBE)
Web Site: http://www.nsbe.org/scholarships
Amount of Scholarship: $1,500 to $3,000
Number of Awards: not given
Deadline: varies by scholarship
Education Level: college undergraduates and graduate students
Eligibility: Applicant must be African-American and be a member of NSBE.

NSBE offers nine different scholarships to African-American students in engineering and other technical academic programs. To learn about each scholarship, follow the links on the left side of the page, or simply scroll down the page (note that the Delta Airlines Scholarship is described on a separate Web page). Each scholarship listing describes the award's specific mission, eligibility requirements, amount, and application procedures. Each scholarship is different, so read the descriptions carefully and select only those scholarships for which you are best qualified. For example, some scholarships set a minimum GPA or educational level for applicants. While most of the scholarships are intended for all engineering students, others go to students of specific technical subjects, including computer science, chemical engineering, electrical engineering, mechanical engineering, optical engineering, physics, materials science, and information technology. Make a note of the scholarships for which you want to apply. Then click the Download Forms link on the left side of the page, scroll down to the Scholarships and Competitions section, and download the application forms for those scholarships, which are in Microsoft Word format (you must be a registered member of NSBE to get these forms off the Web site). You can get more information or request printed copies of application forms by contacting the phone number or e-mail address listed at the very bottom of the scholarship's Web page. To find out how to become a member of NSBE, follow the Membership link at the top of the same page.

Project Excellence Scholarships

Sponsor: Project Excellence, Inc.
Web Site: http://www.project-excellence.com
Amount of Scholarship: $4,000 to full tuition
Number of Awards: over 600
Deadline: February 11
Education Level: high school seniors
Eligibility: Applicant must be African-American; enroll in an accredited college; have a minimum 2.0 GPA; attend high school in the Washington, DC, metropolitan area; and be a U.S. citizen or permanent resident.

Visit this Web site to find information about scholarships given out by Project Excellence to African-American students from Washington, DC, and the nearby Maryland and Virginia suburbs. The Remarks By Mr. Rowan link tells you about the history and goals of the scholarship program. Click The Program link to find all the details about eligibility requirements, nomination procedures, application deadlines, available awards, and the judging process. Two kinds of scholarships are awarded under this program: Partnership Awards, which cover full tuition at a partner college; and Scholarship Awards, which range from $4,000 to $10,000 and can be used at any accredited college. Ten different Scholarship Awards are available. The

Program page also provides a list of partner schools where Partnership Awards may be used. Your high school must nominate you for this award; you can't apply for it directly. Nomination forms and other required application forms are available for download from The Program page. The FAQ page should answer most of your remaining questions about the scholarship program. You should explore the rest of the links to learn more about the sponsors of the various scholarships and about Scholarship Day, when many scholarships are given out.

Ron Brown Scholars

Sponsor: CAP Charitable Foundation
Web Site: http://www.ronbrown.org
Amount of Scholarship: $10,000 (renewable for four years)
Number of Awards: 10
Deadline: January 9
Education Level: high school seniors
Eligibility: Applicant must be African-American, enroll as a full-time student at a four-year college, and demonstrate financial need.

Follow the links on the Web page to learn all about this scholarship program for African-American students. The Program History and the Message From the Director links describe the history of the scholarship, the goals of the program, and the kind of applicant the sponsor is seeking. The Pre-Professional Internships page goes over the internship component of the program, and the Community Service link explains the community service component. Go to The Selection Process page to learn how applicants are selected and what qualities the sponsors are looking for in applicants. The Statistical Information link tells you which colleges Ron Brown Scholars attend and what their average SAT I scores are. If you still have questions about the scholarship program, perhaps the Frequently Asked Questions page will answer them. If you decide on the basis of all this that you would make a good candidate, follow the Application Procedure link to learn how to apply for the scholarship. The Application link opens a page where you can download the application in one of four formats: PDF, RTF, HTML, and text. Finally, if you win a scholarship, the Scholar Network section of the site will help you get in touch with your fellow Ron Brown Scholars and take advantage of all the benefits of the program.

Sachs Foundation Scholarship

Sponsor: Sachs Foundation
Web Site: http://www.frii.com/~sachs
Amount of Scholarship: $4,000 (renewable)
Number of Awards: 50
Deadline: March 1
Education Level: high school seniors
Eligibility: Applicant must be African-American, demonstrate financial need, and be a Colorado resident.

The average grant awarded under this program is $4,000 per year. The Web site tells you everything you need to know to apply. The eligibility requirements are listed on the main page of the site. The Information link describes application procedures, selection criteria, award amounts, conditions for renewing the scholarship, and graduate awards that are available to scholarship winners. To apply, open and print the Application Form and Financial Statement, which are both linked to the main page. Note that you cannot submit these forms online.

UNCF Scholarships

Sponsor: United Negro College Fund (UNCF)
Web Site: http://www.uncf.org/programs
Amount of Scholarship: not given

Number of Awards: not given
Deadline: December
Education Level: high school seniors and college undergraduates
Eligibility: Applicant must be African-American, attend a UNCF member college, have a minimum 2.5 GPA, and demonstrate financial need.

This Web site describes the UNCF scholarship program, which encompasses more than 400 different scholarships. A few scholarships are listed on the Web page to give you an idea of what kinds of awards are available and what their eligibility requirements are, which can include residency requirements, fields of study, academic achievements, and financial need. To be eligible, you must attend a UNCF member college; follow the Member Colleges/Universities link to find a list of these schools. The financial aid office at your school must nominate you for a UNCF scholarship, so the first step in applying is to contact your financial aid officer to learn about your college's nomination procedures. You can also download application forms for some scholarships from the Web site.

Also see the following scholarships:

- Army ROTC Scholarship for Historically Black Colleges and Universities: Chapter 13, "Army and Army ROTC" section
- FTE Dissertation Fellowship: Chapter 7, "Religious Studies" section
- FTE Doctoral Fellowship: Chapter 7, "Religious Studies" section
- Homeland Ministries Scholarships: Chapter 11, "Christian Church (Disciples of Christ)" section
- Jacki Tuckfield Memorial Graduate Business Administration Scholarship: Chapter 7, "Business" section
- Louise Jane Moses-Agnes Davis Memorial Scholarship: Chapter 7, "Library and Information Science" section

- Minority Teacher/Special Education Scholarship: Chapter 6, "Education" section
- Nelson Mandela Scholarship: Chapter 7, "Law" section
- New York Tri-State BMOA McDonald's Scholarship: Chapter 8, "Work" section
- RMHC and College Fund/UNCF Scholarship: Chapter 6, "Health Care" section
- Sandy Brown Scholarship: Chapter 7, "Law" section
- UNCF/Merck Graduate Science Research Dissertation Fellowship: Chapter 7, "Sciences" section
- UNCF/Merck Undergraduate Science Research Scholarship Awards: Chapter 6, "Biology" section
- Yes You Can (Y.Y.C.) Scholarship: Chapter 15, "Washington" section

Armenian

Armenian Professional Society of the Bay Area Scholarship

Sponsor: Armenian Professional Society of the Bay Area
Web Site: http://www.sfbay-aps.org
Amount of Scholarship: not given
Number of Awards: not given
Deadline: November 15
Education Level: college sophomores, juniors, and seniors and graduate students
Eligibility: Applicant must demonstrate substantial involvement in Armenian affairs, enroll as a full-time student at an accredited four-year college, and have a minimum 3.2 GPA.

To find information about this scholarship, click the Scholarships button in the left frame. Follow the Scholarship Policy and Guidelines link to locate the eligibility requirements and

instructions for submitting an application. Note that preference is given to Armenian Studies students, students who plan to teach in Armenian schools, and students of the arts. Click the Scholarship Application Form link to open a text application form that you can print from within your Web browser.

Mousa Ler Association of California Scholarship

Sponsor: Mousa Ler Association of California
Web Site: http://www.mousaler.org/scholarship
Amount of Scholarship: $500
Number of Awards: 2
Deadline: April 15
Education Level: college sophomores and juniors
Eligibility: Applicant must be of Musa Daghian descent, enroll in a bachelor's degree program at an accredited U.S. college, and have a minimum 3.0 GPA.

This Web page briefly outlines the eligibility requirements, selection criteria, and other details of this scholarship. Click the link at the bottom of the page to open an application form that you can print from within your Web browser.

Asian-American

KASF Scholarship

Sponsor: Korean American Scholarship Foundation (KASF)
Web Site: http://www.kasf.org/scholarship.html
Amount of Scholarship: not given
Number of Awards: not given
Deadline: varies

Education Level: college undergraduates and graduate students

Eligibility: Applicant must be Korean-American and be a full-time student.

First, click the KASF Qualifications link to find out if you qualify to apply for a scholarship. If you do, follow the KASF Regions and Deadlines link to find the contact information for the KASF office in your region and the deadlines for submitting applications to that regional office. You can also download the application and recommendation forms in Microsoft Word or PDF format.

Also see the following scholarships:

- Angelfire Scholarship: Chapter 13, "Veterans" section
- CAPS Scholarships: Chapter 7, "Medicine" section
- Homeland Ministries Scholarships: Chapter 11, "Christian Church (Disciples of Christ)" section
- Sheila Suen Lai Scholarship for Library and Information Science: Chapter 7, "Library and Information Science" section

Gay and Lesbian

Audra M. Edwards Scholarship

Sponsor: Audra M. Edwards Scholarship Fund and Peacock Productions, Inc.
Web Site: http://www.gaypdx.com/peacock/scholarship.shtm
Amount of Scholarship: not given
Number of Awards: not given
Deadline: May 1
Education Level: college undergraduates
Eligibility: Applicant must either be gay, lesbian, bisexual, or transgender or be the child of a gay, lesbian, bisexual, or transgender person; enroll in a four-year or two-year college; demonstrate financial need; and be a resident of Oregon or southwest Washington.

The Web page briefly describes the scholarship's eligibility requirements. If you would like to apply, you can either fill out an electronic form to request a printed copy of the application form via e-mail, or you can download and print the application yourself.

GSBA, Pride, and INBA Scholarships

Sponsor: Greater Seattle Business Association (GSBA), Pride Foundation, and Inland Northwest Business Alliance (INBA)
Web Site: http://www.the-gsba.org/scholarship/scholarship.html
Amount of Scholarship: $3,500
Number of Awards: not given
Deadline: February 18
Education Level: high school seniors and college undergraduates
Eligibility: Applicant must demonstrate leadership potential in the sexual minority community and be a resident of Washington, Oregon, Idaho, Montana, or Alaska.

This page briefly describes the scholarship program and its sponsors. Several scholarships are available, with differing eligibility requirements, but you can apply for all of them with one application. Click the Applications link at the top of the page to find an application form, as well as instructions for submitting the application online and for providing supplemental materials.

LEAGUE Foundation Academic Scholarship

Sponsor: LEAGUE Foundation
Web Site: http://www.league-att.org/foundation/fscholarships.html

Amount of Scholarship: $1,500
Number of Awards: not given
Deadline: March 17
Education Level: high school seniors
Eligibility: Applicant must identify as a gay, lesbian, bisexual, or transgender person; enroll as a full-time student at an accredited two-year or four-year college; and have a minimum 3.0 GPA.

This Web page describes the eligibility requirements and selection criteria for the scholarship. Obtain application materials by writing the postal address given at the bottom of the page.

Legacy's Lesbian Leadership Scholarship

Sponsor: An Uncommon Legacy Foundation, Inc.
Web Site: http://www.uncommonlegacy.org/scholguidelines.html
Amount of Scholarship: $1,000
Number of Awards: not given
Deadline: May 1
Education Level: college undergraduates and graduate students
Eligibility: Applicant must be a lesbian, be a full-time student at an accredited U.S. college or university, have a minimum 3.0 GPA, and demonstrate financial need.

On this page, you'll find an overview of the eligibility requirements and the selection criteria for the scholarship, as well as a list of documents required for the application package. Look at the bottom of the page for a link to the application form in PDF format.

Markowski-Leach Scholarship

Sponsor: San Francisco Foundation
Web Site: http://www.sfsu.edu/~finaid/scholarships/mls.htm

Amount of Scholarship: $1,250
Number of Awards: not given
Deadline: April 14
Education Level: college sophomores, juniors, and seniors and graduate students
Eligibility: Applicant must be gay or lesbian; enroll as a full-time student at San Francisco State University, Stanford University, or the University of California at Berkeley; and have a minimum 2.5 GPA.

On this Web page you'll find an overview of the scholarship's purpose and application process, and a list of the eligibility requirements for the award. The printable application form follows the eligibility requirements. At the bottom of the page are the names of scholarship contacts on each of the participating college campuses whom you can contact for more information about the award.

Minnesota Gay/Lesbian/ Bisexual/Transgender Scholarships

Sponsor: Minnesota Gay/Lesbian/Bisexual/Transgender Educational Fund
Web Site: http://www.scc.net/~t-bonham/EDFUND.HTM
Amount of Scholarship: $500 to $1,000
Number of Awards: not given
Deadline: April 1
Education Level: high school seniors, college undergraduates, and graduate students
Eligibility: Applicant must be gay, lesbian, bisexual, or transgender, enroll in a postsecondary educational program, and either be a Minnesota resident or attend a Minnesota school.

This Web page describes the purpose of this scholarship program and gives links to all of the information and forms you'll need. First, click the General Info About These Awards link to find the eligibility requirements and other details you need to know before you apply. Go to the Award Descriptions page to read about the 10 different scholarships available under the program, including the kinds of applicants who are given preference for each award; this information will help you tailor your application to make you more competitive for a particular award. Two scholarships are restricted to students at the College of St. Catherine, and two scholarships are limited to Lutheran applicants. You'll find other valuable information on the Web site as well, including more information about the scholarships' sponsor, a list of previous winners, and links to other scholarships for gay, lesbian, bisexual, and transgender students. When you are ready to apply, you can either print the application form page-by-page or as one long document. Don't forget to print the Application Materials Checklist, which will help you make sure that your application package is complete.

Pat Hoban Memorial Scholarship

Sponsor: Fourth Tuesday
Web Site: http://www.lambda.net/~4thtues/Schol.html
Amount of Scholarship: $1,000
Number of Awards: 1
Deadline: May 31
Education Level: college undergraduates and graduate students
Eligibility: Applicant must be a lesbian, live in the Atlanta area, and need to attend a higher education institution to further her professional skills.

This Web page provides a brief description of the scholarship. If you qualify, you can print a copy of the application form from the site.

PFLAG Scholarship

Sponsor: Parents, Families, and Friends of Lesbians and Gays (PFLAG), New Orleans Chapter
Web Site: http://pflagnola.homepage.com/scholarinfo1.htm
Amount of Scholarship: $1,000
Number of Awards: 20
Deadline: February 1
Education Level: high school seniors and college undergraduates
Eligibility: Applicant must be gay, lesbian, bisexual, or transgender; enroll in a postsecondary institution; be at least 17 years old; and be a Louisiana resident.

Here you'll find an overview of the scholarship program, including its purpose, eligibility requirements, conditions of accepting a scholarship, selection criteria, and instructions for submitting an application. Request an application form online by filling out the Scholarship Packet Request Form.

Regional EAGLE Scholarship

Sponsor: Regional Employee Association for Gays and Lesbians (EAGLE) Scholarship Fund
Web Site: http://www.eaglefund.org/ scholarship/services.htm *Site down*
Amount of Scholarship: $1,000
Number of Awards: not given
Deadline: May 1 and October 1
Education Level: high school seniors and college undergraduates
Eligibility: Applicant must be gay, lesbian, bisexual, or transgender or work on civil rights issues for sexual minorities; enroll in an ac-

credited undergraduate institution; and either live in or attend school in the region served by the Regional EAGLE Scholarship Fund.

First, read the Overview of the scholarship program to learn what the eligibility requirements are, including what states are included in the scholarship region and what kinds of applicants are given preference for an award. The Providing Monies/Amount page tells you a little more about the kinds of applicants the scholarship sponsor is looking for, as well as award amounts. Follow the Selection Criteria link to learn about the criteria used to judge applicants. If you would like to apply, click the Scholarship Application link to open a printable version of the application form.

Robbie Kirkland Annual Memorial Scholarships

Sponsor: Gay, Lesbian, and Straight Education Network, Cleveland Chapter
Web Site: http://www.geocities.com/WestHollywood/9600/kirklandschol.htm
Amount of Scholarship: $250 to $1,000
Number of Awards: 3
Deadline: varies
Education Level: high school students and college undergraduates
Eligibility: Applicant must be gay, lesbian, bisexual, or transgender or an active supporter of the sexual minority community; enroll in an accredited postsecondary institution; be between the ages of 16 and 21; and be a resident of northeast Ohio.

This page provides information about the annual scholarship and the essay contest, which also awards cash prizes. First, read over the scholarship description, eligibility requirements, and selection criteria to find out if you are eligible to apply for the $1,000 scholarship. A link to the Scholarship Application Form is provided at the end of the scholarship description. Information about the essay contest, which is open to all high school and college students, is given at the bottom of the page. First prize is $250 and second prize is $150. You will find the essay topic for both high school students and college students published on the Web page, as well as the contest application form.

Also see the following scholarship:

• NGLTF Messenger-Anderson Journalism Scholarship: Chapter 6, "Journalism" section

Haitian

See the following scholarship:

• Nicaraguan and Haitian Scholarship: Chapter 15, "Florida" section

Hellenic

Hellenic Times Scholarship

Sponsor: Hellenic Times Scholarship Fund
Web Site: http://www.htsfund.org/guidelines.html
Amount of Scholarship: not given
Number of Awards: not given
Deadline: February 12
Education Level: college undergraduates and graduate students
Eligibility: Applicant must be of Greek descent, enroll in an accredited college or university, and be between the ages of 17 and 30.

This Web page provides a brief outline of the scholarship details, including the eligibility requirements. To apply, click the Scholarship Application link on the left-hand side of the page. You can fill out the application inside your Web browser, but you must print it out and mail it in; you can't submit the application online.

Also see the following scholarship:

• Hellenic American Dental Society Scholarship: Chapter 7, "Dentistry and Dental Hygiene" section

Hispanic

Hispanic American Commitment to Education Resources Scholarship

Sponsor: Ronald McDonald House Charities and McDonald's Corporation
Web Site: http://www.rmhc.com/charities/us/scholarships/hacer/index.html
Amount of Scholarship: $1,000
Number of Awards: not given
Deadline: February 1
Education Level: high school seniors
Eligibility: Applicant must be Hispanic, live in a participating area, enroll as a full-time student in a two-year or four-year college, and be a U.S. citizen or permanent resident.

This Web page gives an overview of the scholarship and a list of cities that participate in the program. If you are eligible to apply, you can either download the application form in PDF format by following the link on the right side of the page or obtain a printed application by following the instructions at the bottom of the page. The application form also provides more detailed information about the scholarship and how to qualify.

Hispanic College Fund Scholarship

Sponsor: Hispanic College Fund, Inc.
Web Site: http://hispanicfund.org/hcf-scholar.html
Amount of Scholarship: not given
Number of Awards: 140
Deadline: April 15
Education Level: college undergraduates
Eligibility: Applicant must be Hispanic, be a full-time student, have a minimum 3.0 GPA, plan to pursue a career in business, demonstrate financial need, and be a U.S. citizen.

This scholarship is intended to help disadvantaged Hispanic students pursue careers in business. To qualify, you must major in a business-related curriculum, such as accounting, architecture, communications, computer science, economics, engineering, human resources, finance, information technology, international business, management, marketing, multimedia production, or psychology. The Eligibility Criteria page tells you more about these requirements. You can download a copy of the scholarship application form in either PDF or Word format (an electronic version is in development). Be sure to click the buttons at the bottom of the page to explore the rest of the Web site and learn more about this financial aid program for Hispanic students.

HSF College Retention/General Scholarship

Sponsor: Hispanic Scholarship Fund (HSF)
Web Site: http://www.hsf.net/scholarship/CollegeRetention.html
Amount of Scholarship: $1,000 to $2,500
Number of Awards: not given
Deadline: October 15
Education Level: college undergraduates and graduate students

Eligibility: Applicant must be Hispanic, enroll as a full-time student at an accredited U.S. two-year or four-year college or graduate school, have earned at least 15 college credits, have a minimum 2.7 GPA, and be a U.S. citizen or permanent resident.

The Web page tells you what the eligibility requirements and selection criteria are for this scholarship program designed to help Hispanic college students stay in school. Click the General Program Application link at the very bottom of the page to obtain a copy of the application form. You should also follow the Suggestions & Tips link to find helpful information on preparing your application and with locating other scholarships for Hispanic students.

HSF Community College Transfer Scholarship

Sponsor: Hispanic Scholarship Fund (HSF)
Web Site: http://www.hsf.net/scholarship/CCTProgram.html
Amount of Scholarship: $2,500
Number of Awards: 600
Deadline: March 31
Education Level: community college students
Eligibility: Applicant must be Hispanic, be enrolled as a full-time student at a community college in a participating area, plan to transfer from a community college to a four-year college, have a minimum 3.0 GPA, and be a U.S. citizen or permanent resident.

The Web page tells you what the eligibility requirements and selection criteria are for this scholarship program that helps Hispanic students transfer from community college to a four-year degree program. A list of participating areas is given on the page, so make sure you attend community college in one of those places before applying. If you want an application form, call the toll-free phone number or send a message to the e-mail address given at the bottom of the Web page. You should also take a look at the Suggestions & Tips page to find helpful information on preparing your application and with locating other scholarships for Hispanic students.

HSF High School Scholarship

Sponsor: Hispanic Scholarship Fund (HSF)
Web Site: http://www.hsf.net/scholarship/highschool.html
Amount of Scholarship: not given
Number of Awards: not given
Deadline: March 31
Education Level: high school seniors
Eligibility: Applicant must be Hispanic, attend high school in a participating area, have a minimum 3.0 GPA, enroll as a full-time student at an accredited four-year college, and be a U.S. citizen or permanent resident.

The Web page tells you what the eligibility requirements and selection criteria are for this scholarship program for graduating high school seniors. A list of participating areas is given on the page, so make sure you attend high school in one of those places before applying. If you want an application form, call the toll-free phone number or send a message to the e-mail address given at the bottom of the Web page. You should also take a look at the Suggestions & Tips page to find helpful information on preparing your application and with locating other scholarships for Hispanic students.

José Marti Scholarship Challenge Grant

Sponsor: Florida Department of Education
Web Site: http://www.firn.edu/doe/bin00065/99apps.htm
Amount of Scholarship: not given

Number of Awards: not given
Deadline: April 1
Education Level: high school seniors and graduate students
Eligibility: Applicant must be of Spanish descent, enroll in a degree program at a Florida college or university, have a minimum 3.0 GPA, demonstrate financial need, and be a U.S. citizen or permanent resident.

To find information about this scholarship and an application form, click the name of the scholarship in the list given. This opens a PDF file, so you will need Adobe Acrobat Reader to access it. The PDF file tells you what the eligibility requirements for the scholarship are. Note that although graduate students are eligible to apply, preference is given to graduating high school students, who will be funded for all four years of undergraduate study if they meet the conditions listed on the application form.

Latin American Educational Foundation Scholarship

Sponsor: Latin American Educational Foundation
Web Site: http://theedge.com/laef/scholarships.htm
Amount of Scholarship: not given
Number of Awards: not given
Deadline: February 15
Education Level: high school seniors, college undergraduates, and graduate students
Eligibility: Applicant must be Hispanic or be actively involved in the Hispanic community, enroll in an accredited two-year or four-year college or university, have a minimum 2.5 GPA, and be a Colorado resident.

On this page, you'll find an overview of the scholarship's goals, eligibility requirements, selection criteria, and application instructions. A text version of the application form is given at the bottom of the Web page, or you can download a Microsoft Word version of the form by following the appropriate link.

NHFA Entertainment Industry Scholarship

Sponsor: National Hispanic Foundation for the Arts (NHFA)
Web Site: http://hispanicfund.org/nhfa.html
Amount of Scholarship: not given
Number of Awards: not given
Deadline: April 15
Education Level: graduate students
Eligibility: Applicant must be Hispanic, enroll as a full-time student in an entertainment-related graduate program at a participating university, have a minimum 3.0 GPA, demonstrate financial need, and be a U.S. citizen.

This page describes in detail the eligibility requirements for this scholarship. Take particular note of the list of eligible universities and fields of study. Also note that students who can demonstrate special talent in the arts are given the closest consideration. To apply, click the NHFA Scholarship Application link at the bottom of the page, which links to a PDF copy of the application form.

Also see the following scholarships:

- AAHCPA Graduate Scholarship: Chapter 7, "Accounting" section
- AAHCPA Undergraduate Scholarship: Chapter 6, "Accounting" section
- Hispanic Education Endowment Fund General Scholarships: Chapter 15, "California" section
- Joel Garcia Memorial Scholarship: Chapter 6, "Journalism" section

- Minority Teacher/Special Education Scholarship: Chapter 6, "Education" section
- NSHMBA Scholarship: Chapter 7, "Business" section

Native American

AISES A.T. Anderson Memorial Scholarship

Sponsor: American Indian Science and Engineering Society (AISES)
Web Site: http://www.aises.org/scholarships/#ATAnderson
Amount of Scholarship: $1,000 to $2,000
Number of Awards: not given
Deadline: June 15
Education Level: college undergraduates and graduate students
Eligibility: Applicant must be Native American or Alaskan Native, be a member of AISES, enroll as a full-time student at an accredited two-year or four-year college or graduate school, major in an eligible field of study, and have a minimum 2.0 GPA.

This scholarship program awards $1,000 scholarships to undergraduate students and $2,000 scholarships to graduate students. First, click the Scholarship Criteria link to find out what the eligibility requirements and application procedures are. This page also provides a list of appropriate majors that can be studied under the scholarship. Follow the Download Applications link to obtain a copy of the scholarship application in PDF format. If you are not yet a member of AISES, return to the main page and click the Membership Application link.

Burlington Northern Santa Fe Foundation Scholarship

Sponsor: Burlington Northern Santa Fe Foundation
Web Site: http://www.aises.org/scholarships/#BNSF
Amount of Scholarship: $1,000 to $2,500 (renewable for four years)
Number of Awards: 5
Deadline: April 15
Education Level: high school seniors
Eligibility: Applicant must be Native American, enroll in an accredited four-year college in an eligible field of study, have a minimum 2.0 GPA, and reside in a state serviced by Burlington Northern and Santa Fe Pacific Corporation.

First, read the brief overview of the scholarship to determine if you live in an eligible state and can thus apply for the scholarship. If you can, go ahead and follow the link at the bottom of the page to download a copy of the application form in PDF format. The application form provides a lot more information about eligibility requirements, including a list of majors that can be studied under the scholarship.

Cherokee National Higher Education Scholarships

Sponsor: Cherokee National Higher Education Department
Web Site: http://www.cherokee.org/Higher%20Ed.asp
Amount of Scholarship: not given
Number of Awards: 500 to 550
Deadline: varies
Education Level: high school seniors, college undergraduates, and graduate students
Eligibility: Applicant must be a member of the Cherokee Nation or the United Keetoowah

Band of Cherokee Indians; enroll in an associate's, bachelor's, or graduate degree program; and demonstrate financial need.

This Web page gives a history of the general scholarship program for Cherokee students and describes four special scholarships available under the program. Learn more about these special scholarships by contacting the Higher Education Department directly, as instructed on the Web page. Keep reading to learn about the general scholarships available for undergraduate and graduate students including eligibility criteria. At the end of each scholarship description you'll find a link to an e-mail address that you can write to request an application form.

Chickasaw Nation Department of Education Scholarships

Sponsor: Chickasaw Nation Department of Education
Web Site: http://www.chickasaw.com/
~cnation/education/reference/index.htm
Amount of Scholarship: not given
Number of Awards: not given
Deadline: varies
Education Level: high school seniors, college undergraduates, and graduate students
Eligibility: Applicant must be a citizen of the Chickasaw Nation or demonstrate Chickasaw lineage, and enroll at an accredited U.S. institution of higher education.

This program gives out 14 different scholarships to members of the Chickasaw Nation. Read about each scholarship by clicking its name in the list on the Web page. Each scholarship program differs greatly in objectives, eligibility requirements, and application procedures, so be sure to read the details care-

fully before you apply. Many scholarships specify a field of study, and three are restricted to students at Murray State University in Oklahoma. You must apply for each scholarship separately. Printable application forms and instructions for completing them are linked to each scholarship's information page. You can also read about the Chickasaw Nation's educational loan program on this Web site.

Indian Health Service Scholarship

Sponsor: Indian Health Service
Web Site: http://www.ihs.gov/
JobsCareerDevelop/DHPS/SP/SBTOC3.asp
Amount of Scholarship: not given
Number of Awards: not given
Deadline: April 15
Education Level: college undergraduates and graduate students
Eligibility: Applicant must be Native American or Alaskan Native and enroll in a health professions, medicine, or dentistry program.

To learn about what scholarships are available under this program and their eligibility requirements, click the Scholarships Available link in the graphical menu. Each number describes a different scholarship program. Program 103p is for students preparing to enter a nursing, medical technology, pharmacy, dietetics, social work, physical therapy, or accounting program, while program 103 is for pre-medicine and pre-dentistry students. Program 104 is a service scholarship for more than 30 disciplines in the health professions, which are listed along with eligible degrees on the page. Note that all scholarship winners are expected to work in their fields in the Native American community. For more information about any of these programs and to find out how to apply, contact your region's scholarship coordinator (follow the Scholarship Coordinators link to get a list). Scholarship winners will also find a lot of valuable information on this site, including copies of forms they need and a newsletter for program participants.

Indian Student Assistance Grant

Sponsor: State of Wisconsin Higher Educational Aids Board
Web Site: http://heab.state.wi.us/programs.html
Amount of Scholarship: $250 to $1,100 (renewable for five years)
Number of Awards: not given
Deadline: not given
Education Level: college undergraduates and graduate students
Eligibility: Applicant must be at least 25 percent Native American; enroll in a four-year college, graduate school, or technical college in Wisconsin; and be a Wisconsin resident.

Scroll down the Web page until you see the Indian Student Assistance Grant listing to find information about this financial aid program for Native Americans who live in Wisconsin. To apply for this grant, you must complete and submit the FAFSA, which the state of Wisconsin uses to award state financial aid to all eligible students. You must also file the Indian Student Grant Application, which you can download as a Microsoft Word document from the Web site.

Jim Bourque Scholarship

Sponsor: Arctic Institute of North America
Web Site: http://www.ucalgary.ca/aina/scholar/scholar.html#bourque
Amount of Scholarship: $1,000 (Canadian)
Number of Awards: 1
Deadline: July 15

Education Level: college undergraduates
Eligibility: Applicant must be a Canadian Aborigine and enroll in a higher education program in education, environmental studies, telecommunications, or traditional knowledge.

The brief description on the Web page indicates who is eligible for this scholarship and what items must be submitted in the application package. Application forms are not available on the site, so contact the address, phone number, or e-mail address listed to obtain one.

Minnesota Indian Scholarship

Sponsor: State of Minnesota
Web Site: http://www.mheso.state.mn.us
Amount of Scholarship: $1,850
Number of Awards: not given
Deadline: none
Education Level: college undergraduates and graduate students
Eligibility: Applicant must be at least 25 percent Native American; be a member of a federally recognized tribe; enroll in a vocational school, four-year college, or graduate school in Minnesota; demonstrate financial need; and be a Minnesota resident.

To find the scholarship information, click the Students & Parents link, then follow the Scholarships link. This Web page outlines the basic facts regarding this grant program, including eligibility requirements. You cannot apply for the grant directly. Instead, you must apply for financial aid with the federal government, Minnesota government, and your tribal agency. If you need help with this, contact your local tribal education office, your college's financial aid office, or the address or phone number given on the Web site.

NAFOA Student Scholarship

Sponsor: Native American Finance Officers Association (NAFOA)

Web Site: http://nafoa.org/scholarshipfunds/student
Amount of Scholarship: $2,000
Number of Awards: not given
Deadline: not given
Education Level: college juniors and seniors and graduate students
Eligibility: Applicant must be a member a federally recognized Native American tribe; declare a major in or enroll in an MBA program in accounting, business administration, finance, or management; and have a minimum 2.8 GPA.

The mission and goals outlined at the top of the page describe what NAFOA is trying to accomplish by awarding this scholarship; reading these over can help you tailor your application to make yourself a better candidate for the award. The bottom of the page lists the eligibility requirements and tells you exactly what you need to submit with the application package. At the very bottom of the page, you'll find a link to a printable copy of the application that you can mail to the contact address given.

Seminole and Miccosukee Indian Scholarship

Sponsor: Florida Department of Education
Web Site: http://www.firn.edu/doe/bin00065/99apps.htm
Amount of Scholarship: not given
Number of Awards: not given
Deadline: April 1
Education Level: college undergraduates and graduate students
Eligibility: Applicant must be a member of either the Seminole Tribe of Florida or the Miccosukee Tribe of Indians of Florida; enroll in a degree program at a Florida community college, college, or university; demonstrate financial need; and be a Florida resident.

To find information about this scholarship, click the name of the scholarship in the list given. This opens a PDF file, so you will need Adobe Acrobat Reader to access it. The PDF file tells you what the eligibility requirements for the scholarship are, and it provides an application form you can print. You must submit the completed application to the appropriate tribal higher education committee listed at the top of the form.

State Aid to Native Americans

Sponsor: New York State Higher Education Services Corporation and New York State Education Department
Web Site: http://www.hesc.com/aid.html
Amount of Scholarship: $1,750
Number of Awards: not given
Deadline: May 20, July 15, and December 31
Education Level: college undergraduates
Eligibility: Applicant must either be the enrolled member of or the child of an enrolled member of a New York Native American tribe, enroll in a two-year or four-year college in New York, and be a New York resident.

This page just provides the basic facts about this aid program for Native Americans in New York, including a rundown of the eligibility requirements and available awards. To get more information and an application form, write to the postal address given at the very bottom of the page.

Also see the following scholarships:

- EPA Tribal Lands Environmental Science Scholarship: Chapter 6, "Environmental Studies" section
- Morris K. Udall Foundation Undergraduate Scholarships: Chapter 6, "Environmental Studies" section
- Truman D. Picard Scholarship: Chapter 6, "Environmental Studies" section

New American

Paul & Daisy Soros Fellowship for New Americans

Sponsor: Paul & Daisy Soros Fellowships for New Americans Program
Web Site: http://www.pdsoros.org
Amount of Scholarship: one-half tuition and a $20,000 stipend (renewable for two years)
Number of Awards: 30
Deadline: November 30
Education Level: college seniors and first- and second-year graduate students
Eligibility: Applicant must hold a bachelor's degree; enroll in a graduate degree program at an accredited U.S. university; be younger than the age of 30; and be a resident alien, have been naturalized as a U.S. citizen, or be the child of two parents who were both naturalized citizens.

The main page of this site describes the purpose of the fellowship program and the type of applicant that the program seeks. Explore the links to learn more. The Requirements link describes the eligibility requirements and the selection criteria. This page also lists the application requirements and process, the benefits of the award, and the responsibilities of accepting the award. The Current Fellows page provides biographies of past recipients, which you will probably find helpful in deciding whether you will be a successful applicant. If you wish to apply, go to the Application Forms page to print the application instructions and all of the required forms. The News page posts important announcements and deadlines, so if you do apply, you should revisit this page often.

Nicaraguan

See the following scholarship:

• Nicaraguan and Haitian Scholarship: Chapter 15, "Florida" section

Portuguese

Portuguese Heritage Scholarships

Sponsor: Portuguese Heritage Scholarship Foundation
Web Site: http://www.vivaportugal.com/phsf/index.htm
Amount of Scholarship: $1,000 to $8,000
Number of Awards: not given
Deadline: January 15
Education Level: high school seniors and college undergraduates
Eligibility: Applicant must be of Portuguese-American ancestry, enroll as a full-time student in a four-year college, and be a U.S. citizen or permanent resident.

To learn more about this scholarship, explore the links on the left-hand side of the page. There you can read about the history and goals of the scholarship's sponsor. Click the Scholarships link to find a list of the seven scholarships available, along with a brief description of the award amounts, eligibility requirements, and selection criteria for each scholarship. All but one of the scholarships are $8,000 awards distributed over four years. The only exception is the Leonette Leal Feliciano Memorial Award, which is a one-time grant of $1,000. Click the

Criteria link to find a list of the eligibility requirements and renewal conditions for all of the scholarships. The Applying for Scholarship page tells you generally how to obtain an application form and submit it. You can also obtain the application form from the Web site in either text or Microsoft Word format by clicking the Application link.

SCHOLARSHIPS FOR STUDENTS WITH DISABILITIES AND MEDICAL CONDITIONS

In this chapter you'll find scholarships on the Web for students with disabilities or with particular medical conditions. Not many scholarships are given out in this area, but if you do have a disability, it's worth applying for as many of these awards as you can find. Many scholarships listed in other chapters of this book, while not specifically targeted to students with disabilities, still give preference to those students. Be sure to read about awards in other categories that interest you, and look for scholarship programs that particularly target students with disabilities. Finally, don't neglect searching for financial aid at your school. Look up your college or university in Chapter 16 to find out if it offers scholarships to disabled students enrolled there—many do. Also, contact the disability services office at your school to find out about financial aid opportunities and other services that you can take advantage of.

Any Disability

ASCLA Century Scholarship

Sponsor: Association of Specialized and Cooperative Library Agencies (ASCLA) and American Library Association
Web Site: http://www.ala.org/ascla/centuryscholarship.html
Amount of Scholarship: $2,500
Number of Awards: 1
Deadline: April 1
Education Level: graduate students

Eligibility: Applicant must have a disability, enroll in a library and information science program, demonstrate financial need, and be a U.S. or Canadian citizen.

This scholarship is intended to recruit people with disabilities into the library profession. This Web page provides a general overview of the scholarship. To read the specific eligibility and application requirements, click the link at the end of the scholarship description. You will also find links to printable application and reference forms. Be sure to check the appropriate box beside ASCLA Century Scholarship on the application form when you apply.

Bank of America ADA Abilities Scholarship

Sponsor: Bank of America
Web Site: http://www.scholarshipprograms.org/bankofamerica.html
Amount of Scholarship: varies
Number of Awards: not given
Deadline: February 15
Education Level: high school seniors and college undergraduates
Eligibility: Applicant must meet the definition of disabled as defined by the Americans with Disabilities Act; be a full-time student; reside in a state where Bank of America has retail locations; major in business, computer science, or finance; plan to pursue a career in the financial services industry; have a minimum 3.0 GPA; and be a U.S. citizen.

The eligibility requirements for this scholarship are strict. Read them over carefully and be sure you qualify before going further, particularly the residency requirements (you can also look up your state in Chapter 15 to quickly find out if you are eligible for the scholarship). If you keep scrolling down the page, you'll see a paragraph describing the purpose of the scholarship, which should be helpful in preparing your application. The entire application package can be downloaded and printed from the Web site in PDF format. The first form, Eligibility Criteria & Instructions, is required reading; it describes the eligibility requirements in much more detail and provides instructions for completing the rest of the forms. Note that you will have to print and fill out different application forms depending on your educational level, so be sure to follow the instructions to the letter, or your application will be rejected.

Foundation for Exceptional Children Scholarship Awards

Sponsor: Foundation for Exceptional Children
Web Site: http://www.cec.sped.org/fd/scholapp.htm
Amount of Scholarship: not given
Number of Awards: 6
Deadline: February 1
Education Level: high school seniors
Eligibility: Applicant must be disabled, enroll as a full-time student in a two-year or four-year college, and demonstrate financial need.

Six different scholarships are given out under this program. Two are general awards for all disabled students. Two of the awards are restricted to members of minority groups like African-Americans, Hispanics, Native Americans, and Asians. The other three reward students with particular talents. All of these require-

ments are explained on the Web page, along with instructions for how to apply for any of the awards and a text copy of the application form that you can print from within your Web browser.

Asthma

Award of Excellence Asthma Scholarship

Sponsor: Associates to the American Academy of Allergy, Asthma, and Immunology
Web Site: http://www.aaaai.org/professional/associates/asthmascholarship/default.stm
Amount of Scholarship: $1,000
Number of Awards: 10
Deadline: February 1
Education Level: high school seniors
Eligibility: Applicant must have asthma, enroll in an accredited two-year or four-year college, and be a U.S. citizen.

Two different scholarships are given out under this program, with a total of 10 awards of $1,000 each. The eligibility requirements and application procedures for both scholarships are exactly the same, and they are described on the Web page. The page also provides a toll-free phone number that you can call to obtain application forms.

"Will to Win" Asthma Athlete Scholarship

Sponsor: Schering/Key
Web Site: http://www.thriveonline.com/health/asthma/teens/info.scholarships.html
Amount of Scholarship: up to $10,000

Number of Awards: 10
Deadline: April 30
Education Level: high school seniors
Eligibility: Applicant must have asthma, and be a student athlete.

To learn more about this scholarship, click the Scholarship Details link. This page outlines the purpose of the scholarship, the eligibility requirements, and the documents that must be included in your application package. Application materials aren't available on the Web site, but you can call the toll-free phone number at the end of the scholarship description to receive more information and an application form.

Cancer

American Cancer Society College Scholarship

Sponsor: American Cancer Society
Web Site: http://www2.cancer.org/state/fl/scholarship.htm
Amount of Scholarship: $2,000
Number of Awards: around 30
Deadline: April 10
Education Level: high school seniors
Eligibility: Applicant must have been diagnosed with cancer before the age of 21, enroll in an accredited two-year or four-year Florida college, be under the age of 21, be a Florida resident, and be a U.S. citizen.

This page goes over the goals and selection criteria of this scholarship program for students who have survived criteria. Click the View College Scholarship Criteria link to get the basic facts regarding the scholarship, including eligibility requirements and a list of documents that must be enclosed in the application pack-

age. The Web page also provides a toll-free phone number that you can call to obtain an application form. You cannot download application materials from the Web site.

Hearing-Impaired

Hearing and Visually Handicapped Student Grant

Sponsor: State of Wisconsin Higher Educational Aids Board
Web Site: http://heab.state.wi.us/programs.html
Amount of Scholarship: $250 to $1,800 (renewable for five years)
Number of Awards: not given
Deadline: not given
Education Level: high school seniors, college undergraduates, and graduate students
Eligibility: Applicant must have a severe hearing or visual impairment, be a Wisconsin resident, and demonstrate financial need.

To find a brief description of this grant program, scroll down the Web page until you see the award's name. As the instructions state, you must file both the FAFSA and the Handicapped Student Grant Application in order to be considered for the award. You can download the Handicapped Student Grant Application in Microsoft Word format from the Web site. If you need help with submitting the FAFSA, return to Chapter 1 of this book.

Scholarship for Hearing-Impaired Students

Sponsor: Sertoma International
Web Site: http://www.sertoma.org/Scholarships/default.htm

Amount of Scholarship: $1,000 (renewable for four years)
Number of Awards: 20
Deadline: May 1
Education Level: high school seniors and college undergraduates
Eligibility: Applicant must have a documented hearing loss, have a minimum 3.2 GPA, and enroll as a full-time student in a bachelor's degree program at a four-year college in the U.S. or Canada.

Scroll down the right frame of the Web page to find a brief description of this scholarship program for hearing-impaired students. To locate the application form, click the Scholarship Applications link in the left frame, where you can download the Hearing Loss Scholarship application in PDF format. Be sure to read the instructions for completing the application form, which also tells you more about the scholarship's sponsor, eligibility requirements, selection criteria, and other facts you need to know before applying.

William C. Stokoe Scholarship

Sponsor: National Association of the Deaf
Web Site: http://nad.policy.net/proactive/newsroom/release.vtml?id=17251
Amount of Scholarship: $2,000
Number of Awards: not given
Deadline: March 15
Education Level: graduate students
Eligibility: Applicant must be deaf, hold a bachelor's degree, and enroll in a master's or doctoral program in a field related to sign language or the deaf community.

On this Web page, you'll find all the facts about this graduate scholarship for hearing-impaired students, including an overview of the eligibility requirements, the evaluation criteria, and the project that the winner will have to complete. Obtain an application form by writing to the postal address given at the bottom of the page. Application materials are not available for downloading from the Web site.

Hemophilia

Hemophilia Health Services Memorial Scholarship

Sponsor: Hemophilia Health Services
Web Site: http://www.hemophiliahealth.com/scholarship/scholarpg.html
Amount of Scholarship: $500 to $1,000
Number of Awards: not given
Deadline: May 1
Education Level: high school seniors, college undergraduates, and graduate students
Eligibility: Applicant must have hemophilia or von Willebrand disease and enroll as a full-time student in an accredited two-year college, four-year college, or graduate school.

The Web page goes over everything you need to know about the scholarship, including the program's history, eligibility requirements, application procedures, selection criteria, and responsibilities of recipients. Click the Request an Application link at the very bottom of the page. This opens an electronic form that you can fill out and submit to request that printed application materials be mailed to you. You'll also find links to lists of past winners at the bottom of the Web page.

Physically Challenged

ChairScholars Scholarships

Sponsor: ChairScholars Foundation, Inc.
Web Site: http://www.chairscholars.org

Amount of Scholarship: $3,000 to full-tuition
Number of Awards: not given
Deadline: not given
Education Level: high school seniors and college freshmen
Eligibility: Applicant must be confined to a wheelchair or have some other serious physical challenge, and demonstrate financial need.

First, click the About Us link on the right-hand side of the page to read more about the sponsor of scholarships for students with severe physical challenges and the scholarship program itself. Two different scholarships are awarded under the umbrella of this program: a $3,000 national scholarship open to students throughout the United States; and a local scholarship restricted to students in the Tampa Bay, Florida, area, which awards full tuition at any college in Florida. If you would like to apply for either scholarship, click the Apply For Scholarship tab. This page goes over the eligibility requirements and tells you how to obtain application forms. The rest of the Web site publishes news related to the scholarship program and a list of past recipients

Spina Bifida

SBAA Scholarship

Sponsor: Spina Bifida Association of America (SBAA)
Web Site: http://www.sbaa.org/html/sbaa_scholarships.html
Amount of Scholarship: not given
Number of Awards: not given
Deadline: April 1
Education Level: high school seniors and college undergraduates

Eligibility: Applicant must have spina bifida and enroll in a two-year or four-year college.

Click the More Information link at the bottom of the Web page to find all the details regarding this scholarship program, including eligibility requirements and selection criteria. Follow the Application link to open an application form that you can print from within your Web browser.

Visually Impaired

ACB Scholarships

Sponsor: American Council of the Blind (ACB)
Web Site: http://www.acb.org/Resources/assistance.html/#educational
Amount of Scholarship: $500 to $2,500
Number of Awards: 18
Deadline: March 1
Education Level: high school seniors, college undergraduates, and graduate students
Eligibility: Applicant must be legally blind and enroll in a two-year college, four-year college, or graduate school.

Fifteen different scholarships are awarded under this program to legally blind students. All available scholarships are listed on the Web page, along with each award's amount and specific eligibility requirements, if there are any. Some scholarships do state residency requirements or specific fields of study, so be sure to make a note of those awards for which you are eligible to apply. In addition to a specific named scholarship, every winner receives a general cash scholarship of $1,000. A copy of the application form is provided on the Web site for your reference, but if you want to apply, you must write to the address given to request an official application form. Nothing else will be accepted.

American Foundation for the Blind Scholarships

Sponsor: American Foundation for the Blind
Web Site: http://www.afb.org/ scholdetail.html
Amount of Scholarship: $500 to $2,500
Number of Awards: 11
Deadline: April 30
Education Level: college undergraduates and graduate students
Eligibility: Applicant must be legally blind and be a U.S. citizen or permanent resident.

The seven scholarships available from this scholarship program for visually impaired students are described on this Web page. For each scholarship listed, you'll find out what the award amounts, specific eligibility requirements, and application requirements are. Some awards specify fields of study or educational level. The average award is $1,000. To request an application package, including application forms for all of the scholarships, contact the postal address, e-mail address, or phone number given at the bottom of the Web page. You can't obtain application forms on the Web site.

National Federation of the Blind Scholarships

Sponsor: National Federation of the Blind
Web Site: http://www.nfb.org/schlpg00.htm
Amount of Scholarship: $3,000 to $21,000
Number of Awards: 30
Deadline: March 31
Education Level: high school seniors, college undergraduates, and graduate students
Eligibility: Applicant must be legally blind and enroll as a full-time student in a postsecondary course of study in the U.S.

Fourteen different scholarships are awarded under this program to legally blind students. The average award is $3,000. Some scholarships specify particular fields of study or other restrictions, but many are open to all blind students. At the bottom of the page, you'll find general information about applying for all scholarships, as well as the criteria used to select the winners. A copy of the application form used to apply for all scholarships awarded under the program is provided at the very bottom of the Web page.

Also see the following scholarship:

- Hearing and Visually Handicapped Student Grant: Chapter 10, "Hearing Impaired" section

RELIGIOUS AFFILIATION SCHOLARSHIPS

In this chapter you'll find scholarships that require applicants to practice a particular religion. Cross references to related scholarships in other chapters are listed at the end of each applicable section. In addition to these awards, you will likely track down more scholarships for members of your religion through your local church. Also, many private colleges and universities are affiliated with a particular denomination, such as Catholicism, Lutheranism, or United Methodism. If you choose to attend one of these schools, not only will you find a familiar, spiritual environment, but you are also likely to locate scholarship money reserved for members of your church.

attend a public college or technical school and $500 grants to attend a private, Catholic college. Application materials are not available on the Web site, but you can order them by sending an e-mail message to the address listed at the bottom of the Web page, or by calling the toll-free phone number given. To find out more about joining the Catholic Aid Association, click the Membership button on the left-hand side of the page. Membership is open to practicing Catholics in Minnesota, Wisconsin, North Dakota, South Dakota, and Iowa.

Catholic

Catholic Aid Association College Tuition Scholarship

Sponsor: Catholic Aid Association
Web Site: http://www.catholicaid.com/SCHOLARSHIPS_12921.html
Amount of Scholarship: $300 to $500
Number of Awards: not given
Deadline: February 15
Education Level: high school seniors and college freshmen
Eligibility: Applicant must have been a member of the Catholic Aid Association for at least two years and enroll in a degree program at an accredited two-year or four-year college.

Under this program, eligible Catholic Aid Association members can receive $300 grants to

Christian Church (Disciples of Christ)

Homeland Ministries Scholarships

Sponsor: Center for Leadership and Ministry
Web Site: http://www.homeland.org/leadership/scholarship/guidelines.shtml
Amount of Scholarship: not given
Number of Awards: not given
Deadline: March 15
Education Level: college undergraduates and graduate students
Eligibility: Applicant must be a member of the Christian Church (Disciples of Christ), plan to prepare for the ordained ministry, enroll as a full-time student at an accredited college or seminary, have a grade average of at least a C+, and demonstrate financial need.

Seven different scholarships are given out under this program. These scholarships and their specific eligibility requirements are described on the Web page immediately following the list of general eligibility requirements for all scholarships. There are two general seminary scholarships: one for all seminary students, and one for first-year seminary students. One scholarship is reserved Asian-American ministerial students, one is reserved for African-American ministerial students, one goes only to female seminary students, and one goes to ministers' wives. Finally, one scholarship goes to seminary or graduate ministerial students at the University of Chicago, Union Theological Seminary, Vanderbilt University, or Yale University. These service scholarships require all recipients to serve in a professional ministry after graduation, or the scholarship must be repaid. Contact the e-mail or postal address listed at the very bottom of the page to obtain application materials.

Christianity

Foundation for College Christian Leaders Scholarship

Sponsor: Foundation for College Christian Leaders
Web Site: http://collegechristianleader.com/default.asp
Amount of Scholarship: not given
Number of Awards: not given
Deadline: April
Education Level: high school seniors and college undergraduates

Eligibility: Applicant must demonstrate Christian leadership, have a minimum 3.0 GPA, and demonstrate financial need.

First, click the Read All About It link on the Web page to learn more about this scholarship program for Christian students. If you meet all the requirements listed on that page, return to the main page and click the Application link to find an application form that you can submit online. You will also have to fill out and mail in the Leadership Assessment form, available for printing from the Web site, and mail financial documents and transcripts as instructed on the site.

Also see the following scholarship:

• Chattanooga Christian Community Foundation Scholarships: Chapter 15, "Tennessee" section

Judaism

Eagle Scout Scholarships

Sponsor: National Jewish Committee on Scouting, Boy Scouts of America
Web Site: http://shamash.org/scouts/awards/eagle.html
Amount of Scholarship: $500 to $1,000
Number of Awards: 4
Deadline: December 31
Education Level: high school seniors
Eligibility: Applicant must be an active member of a synagogue who has received the Ner Tamid religious emblem; and be a registered, active member of a Boy Scout troop, Varsity Scout team, or Explorer Post who has received the Eagle Scout award.

Two different scholarships are given out under this program: the Frank L. Weil Memorial Eagle Scout Scholarship awards $1,000 to the first-place winner and $500 each to the two second-place winners; and the Chester M. Vernon Memorial Eagle Scout Scholarship gives out one $1,000 award every other year. The eligibility requirements, selection criteria, and application procedures for both scholarships are the same, as detailed on the Web page.

Lessans Family Scholarship

Sponsor: Central Scholarship Bureau and Jewish Community Federation of Baltimore
Web Site: http://www.centralsb.org/lessan.htm
Amount of Scholarship: not given
Number of Awards: not given
Deadline: April 1
Education Level: college undergraduates
Eligibility: Applicant must be Jewish, enroll at an accredited two-year or four-year college, have a minimum 3.0 GPA, have applied for a Central Scholarship Bureau interest-free loan, and demonstrate financial need.

This Web page goes over the eligibility requirements for this scholarship. At the bottom of the page you'll find links to the required application and budget forms in PDF format.

Lutheran

AAL Adult Scholarship

Sponsor: Aid Association for Lutherans (AAL)
Web Site: http://www.aal.org/AAL/benefits/vssp.html

Amount of Scholarship: $250 to $500 (renewable)
Number of Awards: 100
Deadline: January 31
Education Level: college undergraduates
Eligibility: Applicant must be an AAL benefit member, be 25 years old or older, and be pursuing a first associate's or bachelor's degree.

This scholarship is intended for adult students going to college for the first time. If you meet the eligibility requirements listed on the Web page, click the Scholarship Application Request link and fill out the electronic form to request that an application form be mailed to you. Follow the Become an AAL Member link on the left side of the page to learn more about joining AAL.

AAL All-College Scholarship

Sponsor: Aid Association for Lutherans (AAL)
Web Site: http://www.aal.org/AAL/benefits/vssp.html
Amount of Scholarship: $500 (renewable for four years)
Number of Awards: not given
Deadline: January 31
Education Level: high school seniors
Eligibility: Applicant must be an AAL benefit member and enroll in a bachelor's degree program at any accredited U.S. college.

The Web page lists the eligibility requirements and selection criteria for this general scholarship for AAL members. If you would like to apply, click the AAL Scholarship Request link, and fill out and submit the electronic form to request that a printed application form be mailed to you. Follow the Become an AAL Member link on the left side of the page to learn more about joining AAL.

AAL Lutheran Campus Scholarship

Sponsor: Aid Association for Lutherans (AAL)
Web Site: http://www.aal.org/AAL/benefits/vssp.html
Amount of Scholarship: $200 to $1,000 (renewable)
Number of Awards: over 1,600
Deadline: varies by school
Education Level: high school seniors and college undergraduates
Eligibility: Applicant must be an AAL benefit member and enroll at a participating Lutheran college, university, or Bible institute.

This scholarship goes to AAL members who attend Lutheran colleges and universities. Click the List of Participating Schools link to find out where the scholarship can be used. You can e-mail AAL at the link given at the bottom of the page for more information, or contact the financial aid office at your school. Follow the Become an AAL Member link on the left side of the page to learn more about joining AAL.

AAL Vocational/Technical School Scholarship

Sponsor: Aid Association for Lutherans (AAL)
Web Site: http://www.aal.org/AAL/benefits/vssp.html
Amount of Scholarship: $500 (renewable for two years)
Number of Awards: 100
Deadline: January 31
Education Level: high school seniors
Eligibility: Applicant must be an AAL benefit member and enroll in an accredited vocational or technical program or community college.

This scholarship is intended for students pursuing vocational diplomas and associate's degrees. If you meet the eligibility requirements listed on the Web page, click the AAL Scholarship Request link and submit the electronic form to request that an application form be mailed to you. Follow the Become an AAL Member link on the left side of the page to learn more about joining AAL.

Herbert W. and Corrine Chilstrom Scholarship

Sponsor: Women of the Evangelical Lutheran Church of America (ELCA)
Web Site: http://www.elca.org/wo/scholhcc.html
Amount of Scholarship: not given
Number of Awards: not given
Deadline: February 15
Education Level: master's students
Eligibility: Applicant must be a member of the Evangelical Lutheran Church of America, enroll in a Master of Divinity program at an ELCA seminary, be female, have experienced an interruption of at least five years in education since college graduation, and be a U.S. citizen.

This Web page briefly describes the purpose, eligibility requirements, and application guidelines for this scholarship. Get an application form by clicking the Request for Scholarship Application Form link on the left-hand side of the page. Fill out and submit the electronic form that opens to request that application materials be mailed to you. To learn more about the Women of the ELCA's general scholarship program, click the Scholarships Program link.

Lutheran College Scholarships

Sponsor: Lutheran Brotherhood
Web Site: http://www.luthbro.com/institutions/programs/lcs.html

Amount of Scholarship: $800 to $1,500 (renewable)
Number of Awards: not given
Deadline: varies by school
Education Level: high school seniors and college sophomores
Eligibility: Applicant must be Lutheran and enroll as a full-time student at a Lutheran college.

Three different scholarships are awarded under this program: senior college scholarships, which go to graduating high school seniors who enroll at a four-year Lutheran college; junior college scholarships, which go to graduating high school seniors who enroll at a Lutheran junior college or Bible school; and junior college graduate awards, which go to graduates of Lutheran junior colleges or Bible schools who transfer to a four-year Lutheran college. Follow the appropriate links on the Web page to learn more about each award. The award amounts for all three scholarships are the same. You don't have to be a member of Lutheran Brotherhood to apply for these scholarships, but members receive a grant of $1,500, while nonmembers only get $800. To learn more about Lutheran Brotherhood and about becoming a member, explore the links at the top of the page, particularly the Members and About Us links. Follow the How to Apply link to find out how to apply for any of the scholarships and to find a list of financial aid offices at Lutheran colleges, junior colleges, and Bible schools, along with their contact information.

Scholarships for Lutheran Women

Sponsor: Women of the Evangelical Lutheran Church of America (ELCA)

Web Site: http://www.elca.org/wo/schollay.html
Amount of Scholarship: not given
Number of Awards: not given
Deadline: February 15
Education Level: college undergraduates and graduate students
Eligibility: Applicant must be a member of the Evangelical Lutheran Church in American, be female, be at least 21 years old, have experienced an interruption of at least two years in education since high school, study for a career other than a church-related profession, and be a U.S. citizen.

This page lists the five scholarships awarded to Lutheran women under this program, including each scholarship's specific eligibility requirements. Following that are the eligibility requirements you must meet to apply for any of the awards. Get an application form by clicking the Request for Scholarship Application Form link on the left-hand side of the page. Fill out and submit the electronic form on the page that opens to request that application materials be mailed to you. To learn more about the Women of the ELCA's general scholarship program, click the Scholarships Program link.

Also see the following scholarship:

• Minnesota Gay/Lesbian/Bisexual/Transgender Scholarships: Chapter 9, "Gay and Lesbian" section

Presbyterian

First Presbyterian Church Scholarships

Sponsor: First Presbyterian Church of Tulsa, Oklahoma

Web Site: http://www.firstchurchtulsa.org/schoprog.html
Amount of Scholarship: $500 to $2,000 (renewable)
Number of Awards: not given
Deadline: June 1
Education Level: college undergraduates and graduate students
Eligibility: Applicant must be a member of the Presbyterian Church (U.S.A.); enroll at an accredited college, university, or seminary; and have a grade average of at least a C.

Eight different scholarships are awarded under this program to members of the Presbyterian Church. For each scholarship, you'll find a brief description of the eligibility requirements, applicant preferences, and selection criteria. Note that you don't have to be a member of the First Presbyterian Church of Tulsa to apply for most scholarships, but preference for all awards is given to members. At the bottom of the Web page you'll find application instructions and a link to a printable application form.

Synod of the Covenant Ethnic Scholarships

Sponsor: The Synod of the Covenant
Web Site: http://www.synodofcovenant.org/ceca/scholarship.html
Amount of Scholarship: $400 to $2,000 (renewable for five years)
Number of Awards: not given
Deadline: February 1 and August 15
Education Level: college undergraduates and master's students
Eligibility: Applicant must be Presbyterian and be a member of a minority group.

Three different grants are awarded under this program: one grant of $600 to $800 for full-time students; one grant of $400 for part-time students; and one grant of $1,500 to $2,000 for

theological master's students attending Presbyterian seminaries. Following the descriptions of the different grants, you'll find instructions for completing and submitting an application package. You can also download a copy of the application form in Microsoft Word format by clicking the link at the very bottom of the Web page.

United Methodist

United Methodist Scholarships

Sponsor: General Board of Higher Education and Ministry of the United Methodist Church
Web Site: http://www.gbhem.org/gbhem/scholar.html
Amount of Scholarship: not given
Number of Awards: not given
Deadline: varies
Education Level: high school seniors, college undergraduates, and graduate students
Eligibility: Applicant must have been a member of the United Methodist Church for at least one year, enroll as a full-time student at an accredited higher education institution in the U.S., and be a U.S. citizen or permanent resident.

Five different scholarships are described on this Web page, but these aren't the only scholarships awarded by the United Methodist Church to its members. To order a complete list, call, fax, or write the United Methodist Scholarship Office; contact information is given at the bottom of the page. For each scholarship described here, you'll find an overview of eligibility requirements, award amounts, and application procedures. There are three undergraduate scholarships and two graduate scholarships. Students must attend a United Methodist-affiliated college or university to be eligible to receive all but one of these scholarships.

Also see the following scholarships:

- Leonard M. Perryman Communications Scholarship: Chapter 6, "Communications" section
- Stoody-West Fellowship: Chapter 7, "Journalism" section

GENDER-BASED SCHOLARSHIPS

This chapter describes scholarships reserved exclusively for either male or female students. Actually, far more scholarships are available just for women than just for men. These programs attempt to even the playing field and entice female students into careers or fields of study where they are underrepresented. As always, relevant scholarships found elsewhere in this book are cross-referenced at the end of each section. When you finish looking over these awards, check with your college's or university's financial aid office for gender-related scholarships offered by your school, particularly scholarships for women. Look up your school in Chapter 16 to find the address of its financial aid or scholarships office's Web site.

Female

America's Junior Miss Scholarships

Sponsor: America's Junior Miss Program
Web Site: http://www.ajm.org
Amount of Scholarship: $700 to full tuition (renewable for four years)
Number of Awards: not given
Deadline: not given
Education Level: high school sophomores and juniors
Eligibility: Applicant must be female, have never been married, be a legal resident of the district and state she represents, and be a U.S. citizen.

One unique kind of scholarship program for female students is the pageant, which typically awards scholarships as prizes. America's Junior Miss is the oldest and largest such pageant for high school seniors in the United States. Learn all about this program by clicking the Overview link at the top of the main Web page. The Overview page tells you the history of the pageant, how the pageant is conducted on the local, state, and national levels, and how contestants are judged. Click the Scholarships link to find out what kinds of scholarships are available, which colleges offer them, and how much they are worth. Over 200 colleges and universities offer scholarships to America's Junior Miss participants. These scholarships are available to the winners and runners-up of both the national and state contests, so even if you don't win the crown, you still stand a good chance of receiving a scholarship. In addition, the contest awards 33 general scholarship prizes of between $1,000 and $40,000 to the winner, runners-up, finalists, and for scholastic, artistic, athletic, and other achievements, as detailed on the Awards page. If you are interested in participating, click the How to Apply link, which explains how to obtain application materials from your state's chairperson. The State Program page provides a list of the chairpersons in all states, along with their contact information, so you can easily start the application procedure. You'll also find a schedule of pageant events and profiles of past winners on the Web site.

AWC-DC Scholarship

Sponsor: Association for Women in Communications (AWC), Washington, DC, chapter
Web Site: http://www.awic-dc.org/text/scholar_app.shtml
Amount of Scholarship: $1,000
Number of Awards: 1

Deadline: March 17
Education Level: college sophomores and juniors
Eligibility: Applicant must be female; study advertising, communications, graphic arts, journalism, public relations, or a related field at a Washington, DC, area college; and have a minimum 3.0 GPA.

This Web site does not tell you much about the scholarship, aside from outlining the stringent eligibility and application requirements. Besides the eligibility requirements listed above, you will also need work experience in communications and a well-rounded list of extracurricular activities to be competitive for this scholarship. If you meet all of the requirements listed, you should definitely apply, as competition is probably limited. Probably the fastest way to apply is to fill out the electronic form on the same page and submit it over the Internet. If you like, though, you can print out a PDF copy of the application and mail it in the old-fashioned way.

AWIS Graduate Awards

Sponsor: Association for Women in Science (AWIS) Educational Foundation
Web Site: http://www.awis.org/html/ed_foundation.html#graduate
Amount of Scholarship: not given
Number of Awards: 5 to 10
Deadline: January 19
Education Level: doctoral students
Eligibility: Applicant must be female and enroll in a Ph.D. program in the behavioral, engineering, life, physical, or social sciences.

AWIS gives between 5 and 10 graduate awards each year. Four named fellowships have specific requirements, as described in the first paragraph of the scholarship information. One of these awards is reserved for a student who interrupted her education to raise a family. The page also briefly describes the general eligibility requirements, selection criteria, and how to apply for all fellowships given out under the program. Follow the Letter From Educational Foundation link to get a list of science fields that are eligible for study under the fellowships. The Instructions link tells you how to prepare an application package. You will also find links to text versions of the application form and the reference form.

Betty Rendel Scholarship

Sponsor: National Federation of Republican Women (NFRW)
Web Site: http://www.nfrw.org/programs/scholarships.htm
Amount of Scholarship: $1,000
Number of Awards: 1
Deadline: August 4
Education Level: college juniors and seniors
Eligibility: Applicant must be female, be a member of NFRW, and study a politics-related field. This scholarship is awarded to a female student who intends to pursue a career in politics, and who shows that commitment by majoring in a related subject like political science, government, or economics. If you fit the bill, you can download a copy of the application in either Microsoft Word or PDF format from the Web site. You must submit the application package to your State Federation President, who must sign your application for it to be accepted by the scholarship committee.

BPW Scholarship

Sponsor: Business and Professional Women/USA (BPW) Foundation

Web Site: http://www.bpwusa.org/content/
BPWFoundation/Scholarships/
Alumnae_Section/
Scholarship_Alumnae_Association.htm
Amount of Scholarship: not given
Number of Awards: 226
Deadline: April 15
Education Level: college undergraduates and graduate students
Eligibility: Applicant must be female, be 25 years old or older, enroll at an accredited higher education institution in the U.S., demonstrate financial need, and be a U.S. citizen.

BPW awards scholarships to adult women returning to higher education. The Web site lists the eligibility requirements for this grant program and gives a brief overview of the program. Note that you must graduate within one to two years of the date you receive the grant to be eligible. Click the Application link on the left-hand side of the page to find a printable application form and instructions for completing it.

Dr. Vicki L. Schechtman Scholarship

Sponsor: Association for Women in Science Educational Foundation
Web Site: http://www.awis.org/html/
ed_foundation.html#undergraduate
Amount of Scholarship: $1,000
Number of Awards: 1
Deadline: mid-January
Education Level: high school seniors and college freshmen
Eligibility: Applicant must be female, enroll in a degree program in the sciences, have a minimum 3.0 GPA, and be a U.S. citizen.

The top half of this Web page describes the scholarship available for undergraduate students. A brief outline goes over eligibility requirements, selection criteria, and application instructions. Beneath the description are links to all of the application materials, including a letter about the scholarship, application instructions, the summary form, and the reference form. The Instructions page also lists the exact science majors that are eligible for study under the scholarship.

Graduate Research Program for Women Fellowship

Sponsor: Lucent Technologies Foundation and Bell Laboratories
Web Site: http://www.bell-labs.com/
fellowships/GRPW/
Amount of Scholarship: full tuition and a $17,000 stipend
Number of Awards: not given
Deadline: December 20
Education Level: college seniors and first-year graduate students
Eligibility: Applicant must be female, enroll as a full-time student in an eligible science or engineering doctoral program at an approved university, and be a U.S. citizen or permanent resident.

This fellowship supports women pursuing doctoral degrees in the sciences and engineering. Eligible fields of study are listed on the fellowship program's main Web page. This page also provides a good overview of the program. To learn more, follow the links on the left-hand side of the page. The History page describes the program's background and objectives, while the Mentors page describes the mentoring aspect of the fellowship. Go to the Fellows page to read about past recipients. The News page publishes important announcements for applicants and current fellows. Click the Apply button to learn about eligibility and application requirements, and to find downloadable copies of the application form in PDF, Microsoft Word, and PostScript formats.

Jeannette Rankin Foundation Scholarship

Sponsor: Jeannette Rankin Foundation
Web Site: http://www.wmst.unt.edu/jrf/
Amount of Scholarship: not given
Number of Awards: 25
Deadline: March 1
Education Level: college undergraduates
Eligibility: Applicant must be female, be at least 35 years old, and enroll at a four-year college or vocational/technical program.

This Web site provides a brief overview of the scholarship program and links to many more details. You can read about the history of the foundation and biographies of previous scholarship winners. If you would like to apply, click the How to Apply for a JRF Award link. This page lists the eligibility requirements and provides links to application instructions, a printable application form, and a printable letter of recommendation form. Finally, you can explore links to other financial aid and scholarship sites from here.

Mary Rubin and Benjamin M. Rubin Scholarship

Sponsor: Central Scholarship Bureau and Jewish Community Federation of Baltimore
Web Site: http://www.centralsb.org/maryrubin.htm
Amount of Scholarship: $500 to $3,500
Number of Awards: not given
Deadline: March 1
Education Level: college sophomores, juniors, and seniors and graduate students

Eligibility: Applicant must be female, enroll at an accredited institution of higher education, have a minimum 3.0 GPA, and demonstrate financial need.

This Web page provides all the facts you need to know about this scholarship. Check under the Guidelines section for a rundown of the financial qualifications you must meet to be eligible. The rest of the page tells you how scholarships are awarded and how to put together and submit an application package. You'll find links to the required application and budget forms in PDF format at the bottom of the page.

Miss America Scholarships

Sponsor: Miss America Organization
Web Site: http://www.missamerica.org/index.html
Amount of Scholarship: not given
Number of Awards: not given
Deadline: not given
Education Level: college undergraduates and graduate students
Eligibility: Applicant must be female.

This Web site provides all the information you need about the Miss America pageant, including a history of the pageant, biographies of contestants, judging criteria, and the latest news. Click the Scholarships link at the bottom of the page to learn what scholarships are available to contestants. In addition to these scholarships awarded by the national program, the local and state programs also give out scholarship money to participants. Twenty-five different scholarships are awarded out in all. Each scholarship is described in detail, with facts about the amount of the award, what qualifications are required, how the recipient is selected, and how the funds may be used. Some scholarships specify particular fields of study, such as medicine, teacher education, and performing arts. If you would like to compete, click the Become a Contestant link, where you will find Web site and e-mail addresses for the Miss America program in your state, as well as a list of important dates you need to be aware of. Your state's Miss America program can help you enter a local pageant and get started on your way to becoming Miss America.

National Pathfinder Scholarship

Sponsor: National Federation of Republican Women (NFRW)
Web Site: http://www.nfrw.org/programs/scholarships.htm
Amount of Scholarship: $2,000
Number of Awards: 2
Deadline: February 14
Education Level: college sophomores, juniors, and seniors and graduate students
Eligibility: Applicant must be female, be a member of NFRW, and study a substance abuse-related field.

This scholarship is given to women who intend to pursue careers in the prevention of drug and alcohol abuse. Therefore, to qualify, you must be enrolled in an undergraduate or graduate program that is related to substance abuse studies and plan a career in chemical, biological, or medical research or in addiction counseling. Since these requirements are rather open ended, it is up to you to prove that you best deserve the scholarship. You can download and print a copy of the application form in either PDF or Microsoft Word format from the site. You must then submit the application package to your State Federation President, who must sign your application for it to be accepted.

Pennsylvania's Outstanding Young Woman Scholarships

Sponsor: Pennsylvania's Outstanding Young Woman Program

Web Site: http://www.1usa.com/youngwoman
Amount of Scholarship: $400 to $6,400
Number of Awards: not given
Deadline: not given
Education Level: high school juniors
Eligibility: Applicant must be female, have never been married, have no children, be a Pennsylvania resident, and be a U.S. citizen.

This Web page provides an overview of this scholarship pageant and a list of winners. Click the How to Become a Contestant link to find eligibility requirements and a list of local, regional, and state programs, along with their locations and dates. You can enter the contest online by following a link on this page. In addition to scholarship prizes awarded by the pageant's scholarship fund, described in the pageant overview on the main Web page, 12 local colleges give scholarships to contestants. Follow the Participating College/University Scholarships and Other Awards link from the main page to find a list of these.

Royal Neighbors of America Scholarships

Sponsor: Royal Neighbors of America (RNA)
Web Site: http://royalneighbors.com/belong/benefits.htm#scholarship
Amount of Scholarship: $500 to $2,500 (renewable for four years)
Number of Awards: 26
Deadline: January 1
Education Level: high school seniors and college undergraduates
Eligibility: Applicant must be female, be a member of RNA or have a qualifying RNA benefit certificate, and enroll at a four-year college.

Three different scholarships are available under this program to RNA members. Ten Traditional

Scholarships of $2,000 each go to graduating high school students who have a qualifying RNA benefit certificate. Fifteen Nontraditional Scholarships of $500 for part-time study or $1,000 for full-time study are available for RNA members who are at least 23 years old and are returning to college after a break in their education. Finally, the Marie Kirkland Scholarship of $2,500 is awarded to the most qualified student drawn from the applicant pool for both the Traditional and Nontraditional Scholarships. The details of all three scholarships are given on the Web page, along with a link to the electronic application form, which you can submit over the Internet. Be sure to select the correct name of the scholarship for which you are applying when you complete the form.

Society of Women Engineers Scholarships

Sponsor: Society of Women Engineers (SWE)
Web Site: http://www.swe.org/SWE/
StudentServices/Scholarship/brochure.htm
Amount of Scholarship: $200 to $5,000
Number of Awards: 90
Deadline: February 1 (undergraduate and graduate students); May 15 (high school seniors)
Education Level: high school seniors, college undergraduates, and graduate students
Eligibility: Applicant must be female and study computer science or engineering.

The Society of Women Engineers offers 90 scholarships, giving out over $150,000 each year. All female engineering and computer science students should take advantage of this lucrative scholarship program. To be eligible, you must be enrolled in an academic program accredited by the Accreditation Board of Engineering and Technology (ABET) or a SWE-approved college; find lists of such programs at http://www.abet.org/accreditation/

accredit.htm and by following the SWE-Approved Schools link on the scholarship's Web page. The scholarship Web page lists the 33 major scholarship programs offered by SWE at each educational level, along with award amounts, number of awards, and specific eligibility requirements for each. Most scholarships are open to all computer science and engineering students, although you will also find scholarships for specific engineering disciplines, including aeronautical, aerospace, astronautical, automotive, chemical, civil, electrical, industrial, manufacturing, materials, mechanical, and petroleum engineering. Some scholarships are restricted only to members of minority groups. A special category of reentry scholarships is limited to women who have been out of the engineering job market and out of school for at least two years and who plan to reenter the engineering field. You can download a common application form for all SWE scholarships in either Microsoft Word or PDF format from the Web page or obtain a copy from the Dean of Engineering at your school. Use the same form to apply for all of the SWE scholarships that you are eligible for at your educational level (entering freshman, undergraduate, graduate, or reentry); simply check the scholarship category for which you want to be considered at the top of the application form.

Third Wave Scholarship

Sponsor: Third Wave Foundation
Web Site: http://www.feminist.com/
3wsch.htm
Amount of Scholarship: $1,000 to $5,000
Number of Awards: not given
Deadline: April 1 and October 1
Education Level: high school seniors, college undergraduates, and graduate students
Eligibility: Applicant must be female; be under the age of 30; enroll at an accredited two-year

college, four-year college, or university; and demonstrate financial need.

This scholarship program is open to all women who meet the eligibility requirements listed above. In addition, applicants must be involved as activists, artists, or cultural workers working on civil rights issues like homophobia, sexism, and racism, as described on the scholarship's Web site. If you decide that you would make a good candidate, print and complete the text application provided on the Web page, and mail it to the address given. Follow the link at the end of the application form to learn more about the scholarship's sponsor.

Zeta Phi Beta Scholarships and Fellowships

Sponsor: Zeta Phi Beta Sorority, Inc. National Educational Foundation
Web Site: http://www.zpb1920.org/nefforms.htm
Amount of Scholarship: $500 to $2,500
Number of Awards: not given
Deadline: February 1
Education Level: high school seniors, college undergraduates, and graduate students
Eligibility: Applicant must be female and be a full-time student.

Eight different scholarships and fellowships are awarded to female students under this program. Six are open to all women, regardless of whether they belong to Zeta Phi Beta Sorority. A general graduate fellowship of $2,500 goes to women in master's, doctoral, professional, and postdoctoral programs. A general undergraduate scholarship of $500 to $1,000 is open to graduating high school seniors and all college undergraduates. There is also a fellowship for study abroad, one for study of medicine or the health sciences, one for study of counseling, and one for study of education. These four

awards are all open to both undergraduate and graduate students, and award amounts range from $500 to $1,000. Two awards are restricted to members of Zeta Phi Beta sorority. These include one fellowship for general graduate study and one fellowship for study of social work at the graduate level. Both of these awards also range between $500 and $1,000. General procedures for applying for all scholarships are given at the bottom of the Web page, along with a link to the application form in PDF format.

Also see the following scholarships:

- ACSM Graduate Scholarship: Chapter 7, "Sports Science and Administration" section
- Amelia Earhart Fellowship Awards for Women: Chapter 7, "Aerospace Sciences and Engineering" section
- American Legion Auxiliary Memorial Scholarship: Chapter 14, "Military Personnel and Veterans" section
- AQHA National Female Equestrian Award: Chapter 8, "Horseback Riding" section
- AT&T Labs Fellowship: Chapter 7, "Communications Engineering and Technology" section
- Dorothy Harris Endowed Scholarship: Chapter 7, "Sports Science and Administration" section
- Gertrude Cox Scholarship: Chapter 7, "Statistics" section
- Gloria Fecht Memorial Scholarship: Chapter 8, "Golf" section
- Herbert W. and Corrine Chilstrom Scholarship: Chapter 11, "Lutheran" section
- Homeland Ministries Scholarships: Chapter 11, "Christian Church (Disciples of Christ)" section
- IIE Scholarships: Chapter 6, "Engineering" section
- Jewish Foundation for Education of Women Scholarships: Chapter 15, "New York" section

- Karla Scherer Foundation Scholarship: Chapter 6, "Economics and Finance" section
- Linda Riddle/SGMA Endowed Scholarship: Chapter 8, "Athletics" section
- Microsoft National Technical Scholarships: Chapter 6, "Computer Science and Engineering" section
- Microsoft Women's Technical Scholarship: Chapter 6, "Computer Science and Engineering" section
- Nancy Lorraine Jensen Memorial Scholarship: Chapter 14, "Clubs and Community Organizations" section
- NCAA Scholarships: Chapter 8, "Athletics" section
- NSF Graduate Research Fellowship: Chapter 7, "Sciences" section
- OCECS Scholarship: Chapter 15, "Oregon" section
- Pat Nixon Scholarship: Chapter 15, "California" section
- Scholarships for Lutheran Women: Chapter 11, "Lutheran" section
- SRC Master's Scholarship: Chapter 7, "Electronics" section
- Virginia BPW Foundation Scholarships: Chapter 15, "Virginia" section
- WAI Scholarships: Chapter 6, "Aviation" section
- Zonta International Foundation Jane M. Klausman Women in Business Scholarship: Chapter 6, "Business" section

Male

See the following scholarships:

- Evan S. (Red) Stuart Memorial Scholarship: Chapter 8, "Bowling" section
- Junior Olympic Program Committee/National Gymnastics Foundation Scholarship for Men: Chapter 8, "Athletics" section
- Key Club International Scholarships: Chapter 8, "Clubs" section

MILITARY SERVICE SCHOLARSHIPS

In this chapter you'll find scholarships and grants for students who are currently serving in the military, who commit to serving in the military after graduation, and who are veterans. Besides these awards, members of the military, students who serve in the Reserve and the National Guard, and veterans of all branches of the Armed Forces are entitled to many educational benefits, such as the Montgomery GI Bill and other tuition assistance programs. A good site to read all about these benefits and find out how to join up is http://www.myfuture.com/milops/mil_whatme.html. Veterans can learn about educational benefits that they can take advantage of at the U.S. Department of Veteran Affairs Web site at http://www.gibill.va.gov. If you are the dependent of a member of the Armed Forces or a veteran, you'll find more scholarships in the "Military Personnel and Veterans" section of Chapter 14, "Family Affiliation Scholarships."

All Branches

AFCEA General Emmett Paige Scholarship

Sponsor: Armed Forces Communications and Electronics Association (AFCEA) Educational Foundation
Web Site: http://www.afcea.org/awards/scholarships.htm#paige
Amount of Scholarship: $2,000
Number of Awards: not given
Deadline: March 1

Education Level: college freshmen (veterans only), sophomores, and juniors
Eligibility: Applicant must be on active duty in the uniformed military services, a veteran, or the spouse or dependent of a member of the military or a veteran; attend a four-year U.S. college; study aerospace engineering, computer science, computer engineering, electrical engineering, electronics, mathematics, or physics; have a minimum 3.4 GPA; and be a U.S. citizen.

You won't find a lot of information about this scholarship on the Web page—just enough to determine if you qualify. If you do, you can either download the PDF version of the application or find out how to request an application directly from the sponsor. Be sure to check the box for the General Emmett Paige Scholarship at the top of the application form; you are only allowed to apply for one AFCEA-sponsored scholarship. You will also have to provide evidence of your status as a member of the Armed Forces, as a veteran, or as the spouse or dependent of an active or veteran member of the military.

AFCEA ROTC Scholarship

Sponsor: Armed Forces Communications and Electronics Association (AFCEA) Educational Foundation
Web Site: http://www.afcea.org/awards/scholarships.htm#rotc
Amount of Scholarship: $2,000
Number of Awards: not given
Deadline: April 1
Education Level: college sophomores and juniors

Eligibility: Applicant must be a member of ROTC; attend a four-year U.S. college; study aerospace engineering, computer science, computer engineering, electrical engineering, electronics, mathematics, or physics; have a minimum 3.4 GPA; and be a U.S. citizen.

You won't find a lot of information about this scholarship—just enough to determine if you qualify. If you do, you can download the PDF version of the application form from the Web page. Be sure to check the box for the ROTC Scholarship at the top of the application; you are only allowed to apply for one AFCEA-sponsored scholarship. Because this scholarship has different requirements than the others served by this application form, you must be especially careful to follow the directions and fill out all required parts of the application. A professor of military science, naval science, or aerospace studies at your school must nominate you for the scholarship, and your ROTC commander must endorse and submit your application.

North Georgia College ROTC Grant

Sponsor: Georgia Student Finance Commission
Web Site: http://www.hope.gsfc.org
Amount of Scholarship: $1,500
Number of Awards: around 260
Deadline: not given
Education Level: high school seniors and college undergraduates
Eligibility: Applicant must be a Georgia resident; enroll as a full-time student at North Georgia College and State University and enroll in the ROTC program there; and be a U.S. citizen or permanent resident.

To find information about this scholarship, click the State Grants link in the bar at the top

of the Web page, follow the Program Information link, and then click the name of the scholarship in the list that opens. There you'll find details about the program's objective, eligibility requirements, and application procedures. Contact the address or toll-free phone number given at the bottom of the page to request an application.

Also see the following scholarship:

- Air Force Enlisted Personnel Commissioning Scholarships: Chapter 13, "Air Force and Air Force ROTC" section

Air Force and Air Force ROTC

Air Force Enlisted Personnel Commissioning Scholarships

Sponsor: Air Force Reserve Officers Training Corps (AFROTC)
Web Site: http://www.afoats.af.mil/ Opportunities/Enlisted/af-enlisted.htm
Amount of Scholarship: up to $15,000
Number of Awards: not given
Deadline: varies
Education Level: college undergraduates
Eligibility: Applicant must be an active-duty, enlisted member of the Air Force.

AFROTC offers four college programs that enable enlisted personnel to receive a college education while earning an officer's commission. All four programs are described on this Web page. For three of these programs, participants receive scholarships of up to $15,000, along with a stipend or active duty pay and a textbook allowance. While the fourth program doesn't offer scholarships, participants may receive an incentive of up to $3,000 each year.

These benefits, the eligibility requirements, deadlines, academic majors you can study, and the lengths of the programs are listed on the Web page. You will also find copies of the application forms that you need, although you should contact your base education office for one-on-one counseling before deciding whether to apply. If you currently serve in the Army, Navy, Marines, or another branch of the Armed Forces, you may also qualify for one of these programs; follow the link on the Web page to learn more and find application instructions.

Air Force ROTC In-College Scholarships

Sponsor: Air Force Reserve Officers Training Corps (AFROTC)
Web Site: http://www.afoats.af.mil/ Opportunities/College/college.htm
Amount of Scholarship: up to $15,000
Number of Awards: not given
Deadline: not given
Education Level: college freshmen and sophomores
Eligibility: Applicant hold an AFROTC Professional Officer Course (POC) allocation (two-year scholarship) or successfully compete for an allocation (three-year scholarship); have a minimum 2.65 GPA; and meet weight, fitness, medical, age, citizenship, and test score requirements.

In addition to scholarships for graduating high school students, AFROTC offers two- and three-year scholarships to students who are already enrolled in college. This Web page describes the scholarship program, and it gives a rundown of the eligibility requirements. To apply, you must contact your college's AFROTC unit; application materials are not available through the Web site. Many colleges also offer school-specific scholarships to students who

participate in AFROTC, which can help pay for room and board and additional fees. Click the College Subsidy list to find a list of such schools.

Air Force ROTC Scholarship

Sponsor: Air Force Reserve Officers Training Corps (AFROTC)
Web Site: http://www.afoats.af.mil/ Opportunities/Highschool/high.htm
Amount of Scholarship: full tuition and a monthly stipend
Number of Awards: 2,300
Deadline: December 1
Education Level: high school seniors
Eligibility: Applicant must join AFROTC, have a minimum 2.5 GPA, have a minimum ACT score of 24 or a minimum SAT I score of 1100, have a high school class standing in the top 40 percent, complete the applicant fitness test, be at least 17 years old, not be a single parent, and be a U.S. citizen.

All of the ROTC programs offer full-tuition scholarships to qualified participants, so if you are interested in pursuing a military career after college, you should definitely look into the benefits of joining ROTC. In exchange for scholarship money, you must make a commitment to serve as an officer in the Armed Forces for a specified number of years after graduating. You must also join your college's ROTC unit, so make sure that the schools you're interested in offer the programs you want before applying. On this Web site, you can learn about scholarships for members of Air Force ROTC. The site tells you what the eligibility requirements are, including specifics about the test score and physical fitness requirements. You'll also learn what academic majors you can study under the scholarship; on your application, you must specify up to three academic majors from this list that you would be willing to pursue.

You can learn about the Air Force Officer Qualification Test (AFOQT), which you must take if you win a scholarship in order to activate it. Finally, you'll discover how the application and selection process works, and find an electronic form that you can submit to request application materials. Be sure to use the Ask a Question electronic form on the site if you have additional questions about the program.

Pre-Health and Armed Forces Health Professions Scholarships

Sponsor: Air Force Reserve Officers Training Corps (AFROTC)
Web Site: http://www.afoats.af.mil/ Opportunities/College/PREHLTH.html
Amount of Scholarship: $15,000 to full tuition
Number of Awards: not given
Deadline: June 15
Education Level: college freshmen and sophomores
Eligibility: Applicant must join AFROTC, be a full-time student, plan to study medicine, and have a minimum 3.65 GPA (three-year scholarship) or 3.5 GPA (two-year scholarship).

This scholarship program is for pre-med students in the Air Force ROTC. One scholarship funds two years of undergraduate study, and the other funds three years. Read the description on the Web page carefully, as there are more eligibility requirements than can be outlined here. After graduating and being accepted into an accredited medical school, you become eligible for the Medical School Scholarship, also described on this page. Pre-Health Scholarship recipients are guaranteed sponsorship if accepted into an accredited medical school prior to commissioning. To receive more information about both of these programs, contact your local AFROTC unit or the mailing address given at the bottom of the page. A toll-free phone number is also listed for Medical School Scholarship inquiries.

Army and Army ROTC

Army ROTC Scholarships

Sponsor: United States Army Cadet Command Headquarters
Web Site: http://www-rotc.monroe.army.mil/ scholarships/fouryear
Amount of Scholarship: up to $16,000
Number of Awards: not given
Deadline: November 15
Education Level: high school seniors and college freshmen and sophomores
Eligibility: Applicant must join Army ROTC at a participating four-year college, have a minimum 2.5 GPA, have a minimum SAT I score of 920 or ACT score of 19, meet physical fitness requirements, be at least 17 years old, and be a U.S. citizen.

On this Web site you'll find all the information you need about the four-year scholarship for students who join the Army ROTC and earn a commission as an officer in the Army, Army Reserve, or National Guard while getting a college education. First, follow the Army ROTC Four-Year Scholarship Program link to get an overview of the program. This page also tells you how to start the application process by contacting the Army Professor of Military Science (PMS) at each college where you plan to apply. (A limited number of two- and three-year scholarships are also available for students already enrolled in college; contact your campus's PMS to learn more.) Next, you should check out the List of Schools With ROTC Programs to find out which colleges you can attend under the scholarship. The other links on the site tell you about the eligibility requirements, the desired qualities that are sought in applicants, the application process, the obligations of accepting a scholarship, and the criteria used to select recipients. Be sure to read all of these pages over carefully to find out if you qualify and are willing to make the commitment required. If you'd like to compete for a scholarship, click the Apply for 4 Year Scholarship link to find electronic application forms that you can fill out and submit online. The Web site also provides information about two specialty programs, the Nurse Program and the Scholarship Program for the Historically Black College/University, which are described separately in this section.

Army ROTC Nurse Scholarships

Sponsor: Army Reserve Officers Training Corps (AROTC)
Web Site: http://147.248.154.207/ information/site2/scholar3.html
Amount of Scholarship: full tuition
Number of Awards: not given
Deadline: November 15
Education Level: high school seniors and college undergraduates
Eligibility: Applicant must join AROTC, enroll in a nursing program at a Partnership in Nursing Education (PNE) college, have a minimum 2.5 GPA, have a minimum SAT I score of 920 or ACT score of 19, meet physical fitness requirements, be at least 17 years old, and be a U.S. citizen.

This is a special type of the Army ROTC Four-Year Scholarship for nursing students. You can apply for the four-year scholarship online by following the link on this page; be sure to follow the instructions to indicate that you are competing for a nursing scholarship. Among the application materials is a list of PNE schools, so you can find out where you can use the scholarship. There is also a link to more information about the Nurse Program. Two- and three-year nursing scholarships are available for students who have already started college. For more information about these, contact your campus ROTC recruiter. Be sure to explore the rest of the site if you are still considering joining ROTC and want to learn more.

Army ROTC Scholarship for Historically Black Colleges and Universities

Sponsor: Army Reserve Officers Training Corps (AROTC)
Web Site: http://147.248.154.207/ information/site2/scholar4.html
Amount of Scholarship: full tuition
Number of Awards: not given
Deadline: November 15
Education Level: high school seniors
Eligibility: Applicant must join AROTC, enroll at a participating Historically Black College or University, have a minimum 2.5 GPA, have a minimum SAT I score of 920 or ACT score of 19, meet physical fitness requirements, be at least 17 years old, and be a U.S. citizen.

This is a special type of the Army ROTC Four-Year Scholarship for students who want to attend a Historically Black College or University (HBCU). You apply for the scholarship in the same way you would for a general Army ROTC Four-Year Scholarship, except your first college choice must be a HBCU. You will find instructions for applying on the Web page, along with a link the electronic application form for the four-year scholarship. But first check the list of HBCUs by following the appropriate link given on the page, to make sure that the college you want to attend is eligible. If you'd like more information about Army ROTC in general, follow the link at the bottom of the page.

Green to Gold Scholarships

Sponsor: United States Army Cadet Command Headquarters
Web Site: http://www-rotc.monroe.army.mil/scholarships/green
Amount of Scholarship: full tuition and a monthly stipend of $150
Number of Awards: not given
Deadline: not given
Education Level: high school graduates, and college freshmen and sophomores
Eligibility: Applicant must be an enlisted member of the Army who has served at least two years on active duty, be allowed to voluntary request discharge from active duty, and join Army ROTC at a four-year college.

This program awards two-, three-, and four-year scholarships to enlisted personnel in the U.S. Army, as described on the main page of the program's Web site. The kind of scholarship you receive depends on how many college credits you have previously completed. The award carries many benefits in addition to the full-tuition scholarship, including training for an officer's commission in the ROTC. Follow the Options link to read more about the different kinds of scholarships available and the benefits of receiving an award. Follow the Obligations link to find out what the service requirements of accepting a scholarship are. The Early Discharge page tells you how to obtain an early discharge in order to take advantage of the scholarship program. Finally, the Frequently Asked Questions page answers the most common questions about the program, including which colleges offer Army ROTC programs. To find scholarship applications and related documents in PDF format, click the Back to Scholarship Information link at the very bottom of the page, and then follow the Scholarship Document Site link.

United States Army Health Professions Scholarships

Sponsor: Walter Reed Army Medical Center, Psychology Department
Web Site: http://www.wramc.amedd.army.mil/departments/psychology/hpsp.htm
Amount of Scholarship: full tuition and a monthly stipend
Number of Awards: not given
Deadline: not given
Education Level: doctoral students
Eligibility: Applicant must be commissioned as an officer in the United States Army Reserve, enroll as a full-time student in an accredited doctoral clinical or counseling psychology program at a U.S. university, and be a U.S. citizen.

This page describes the United States Army's two- and three-year scholarship programs for psychology doctoral students. In exchange for the scholarship, you must commit to serve in the Army Reserve during your schooling and to active service after you receive your degree. The page lists the eligibility requirements for the scholarship, the benefits provided by the Army to scholarship recipients, and the requirements that recipients are expected to fulfill in return. Find out how to obtain application forms and whom to contact for more information under the Application Procedures section of the page.

National Guard

Educational Assistance Program for the Pennsylvania National Guard

Sponsor: Pennsylvania Higher Education Assistance Agency and the Pennsylvania Department of Military and Veterans Affairs

Web Site: http://www.pheaa.org/students/sg5.shtml
Amount of Scholarship: up to $2,412
Number of Awards: not given
Deadline: not given
Education Level: college undergraduates
Eligibility: Applicant must commit to serve in the Pennsylvania National Guard, be a Pennsylvania resident, and enroll at an approved Pennsylvania institution of higher education.

This program awards grants to Pennsylvania residents who commit to serve in the National Guard, usually for a period of six years. As the Web page explains, grants can pay up to two-thirds of the tuition at a Pennsylvania state college or university. The page also goes over the eligibility requirements and briefly describes the service commitment that recipients must make. To get more information and find out how to apply, call the phone number given at the end of the grant description.

Georgia Military College State Service Scholarship

Sponsor: Georgia Student Finance Commission
Web Site: http://www.hope.gsfc.org
Amount of Scholarship: full tuition
Number of Awards: 33
Deadline: February 1
Education Level: high school seniors
Eligibility: Applicant must be a Georgia resident, have a minimum 2.5 GPA, have a minimum SAT I score of 800, enroll as a full-time student at Georgia Military College, and be a U.S. citizen or permanent resident.

To find information about this scholarship, click the State Grants link in the bar at the top of the Web page, follow the Program Information link, and then click the name of the scholarship in the list that opens. There you'll

find details about the program's objective, eligibility requirements, and application procedures. Contact the address or toll-free phone number given at the bottom of the page to request an application. Note that you must commit to serving two years in the Georgia National Guard if you accept the scholarship.

Illinois National Guard Grant

Sponsor: Illinois Student Assistance Commission
Web Site: http://www.isac1.org/ilaid/specgt.html#inggp
Amount of Scholarship: full tuition (renewable for four years)
Number of Awards: not given
Deadline: September 15
Education Level: college undergraduates and graduate students
Eligibility: Applicant must have completed one full year of service in the Illinois National Guard, be an enlisted person or any company grade officer up to the rank of captain, and enroll at an approved community college or public college or university in Illinois.

This Web page briefly outlines the eligibility requirements for this grant for members of the Illinois National Guard. It also tells you how to obtain application forms and how to submit them, and when the application deadlines are.

Indiana National Guard Supplemental Grant

Sponsor: State Student Assistance Commission of Indiana (SSACI)
Web Site: http://www.ai.org/ssaci/ngsg.htm
Amount of Scholarship: full tuition
Number of Awards: not given
Deadline: March 1
Education Level: college undergraduates

Eligibility: Applicant must be in active drilling status in the Indiana Air and Army National Guard, and enroll in an associate's or bachelor's degree program at a state-funded college in Indiana.

On this Web page you'll learn about the grant program for members of the National Guard in Indiana. The page goes over eligibility requirements, National Guard eligibility, and application procedures. You must file the FAFSA to be considered for the grant; you'll find instructions for completing and submitting the FAFSA in Chapter 1 of this book. If you have further questions, contact your unit commander, your school's financial aid office, or SSACI directly, as indicated at the bottom of the Web page.

North Georgia College Military Scholarship

Sponsor: Georgia Student Finance Commission
Web Site: http://www.hope.gsfc.org
Amount of Scholarship: full tuition
Number of Awards: 33
Deadline: January 3
Education Level: high school seniors
Eligibility: Applicant must be a Georgia resident, have a minimum 3.0 GPA, have a minimum SAT I score of 1010, enroll as a full-time student at North Georgia College and State University, meet National Guard physical and mental standards, and be a U.S. citizen or permanent resident.

To find information about this scholarship, click the State Grants link in the bar at the top of the Web page, follow the Program Information link, and then click the name of the scholarship in the list that opens. There, you'll find details about the program's objective, eligibility requirements, and application proce-

dures. Contact the address or toll-free phone number given at the bottom of the page to request an application. Note that you must commit to serving four years in the Georgia National Guard if you accept the scholarship.

Navy ROTC

Four-Year Navy Nurse Scholarship

Sponsor: Navy Reserve Officers Training Corps (NROTC)
Web Site: http://www.cnet.navy.mil/nrotc/nrotc.htm
Amount of Scholarship: full tuition and a monthly stipend of $200
Number of Awards: not given
Deadline: January 31
Education Level: high school seniors
Eligibility: Applicant must join NROTC, enroll in a nursing program at a certified NROTC college, have a minimum SAT I score of 530 Verbal and 520 Math or a minimum ACT score of 22, meet physical fitness requirements, be at least 17 years old, and be a U.S. citizen.

To find information about this scholarship, click the Applying for an NROTC Scholarship link in the left frame, and then follow the 4-Year Navy Nurse link. There is not a lot of information there, though—just a brief paragraph describing the scholarship and telling you how to get more information. To find out where you can use the scholarship, click the Colleges and Universities link in the left-hand frame. This opens a list of all colleges with NROTC programs; colleges that have a nursing program are marked with the letter 'N'. As the Navy Nurse Scholarship is a four-year scholarship, you should also read the information under How to Apply for an NROTC 4-Year Scholarship, which outlines the steps for applying. To find this information, return to the Applying for an NROTC Scholarship page and click the appropriate link at the top of the page. You will also find a copy of the application questionnaire that you can download under this section.

Four-Year Scholarship Marine Option

Sponsor: Navy Reserve Officers Training Corps (NROTC)
Web Site: http://www.cnet.navy.mil/nrotc/nrotc.htm
Amount of Scholarship: full tuition and a monthly stipend of $200
Number of Awards: not given
Deadline: January 31
Education Level: high school seniors
Eligibility: Applicant must join NROTC, enroll at a certified NROTC college, have a minimum SAT I score of 1000, meet physical fitness requirements, be at least 17 years old, and be a U.S. citizen.

To find information about this scholarship, click the Applying for an NROTC Scholarship link in the left frame, and then follow the 4-Year Scholarship Marine Option link. This describes the four-year scholarship for participants in NROTC who go on to earn a commission as an officer in the U.S. Marine Corps. The eligibility requirements are almost the same as for the Four-Year Scholarship Navy Option, so you should also read that information on the same page (this scholarship is described in more detail later in this section). If you would like to apply, return to the top of the page and click the How to Apply for an NROTC 4-Year Scholarship link, which takes you to an outline of the application process. You will also find a link to the application ques-

tionnaire, which you can download. It's a good idea to learn more about NROTC before applying. Do so by exploring the links in the left-hand frame, particularly the About NROTC, Program Mission, History of NROTC, and Career Options links. The College and Universities link provides a list of colleges with on-campus NROTC programs, which will be helpful when deciding where to apply. After you apply, you can check the status of your application by following that link in the left-hand frame.

Four-Year Scholarship Navy Option

Sponsor: Navy Reserve Officers Training Corps (NROTC)
Web Site: http://www.cnet.navy.mil/nrotc/nrotc.htm
Amount of Scholarship: full tuition and a monthly stipend of $200
Number of Awards: not given
Deadline: January 31
Education Level: high school seniors
Eligibility: Applicant must join NROTC, enroll at a certified NROTC college, have a minimum SAT I score of 530 Verbal and 520 Math or a minimum ACT score of 22, meet physical fitness requirements, be at least 17 years old, and be a U.S. citizen.

To find information about this scholarship, click the Applying for an NROTC Scholarship link in the left frame, then follow the 4-Year Scholarship Navy Option link. This describes the basic four-year scholarship for participants in NROTC who go on to earn a commission as an officer in the U.S. Navy, including the eligibility requirements. If you would like to apply, return to the top of the page and click the How to Apply for an NROTC 4-Year Scholarship link, which takes you to an outline of the application process. You will also find a link to the application questionnaire that you can download in this section of the page. It's a good idea to learn more about NROTC before applying. Do so by exploring the links in the left-hand frame, particularly the About NROTC, Program Mission, History of NROTC, and Career Options links. The College and Universities link provides a list of colleges with on-campus NROTC programs, which will be helpful when deciding where to apply. After you apply, you can check the status of your application by following that link in the left-hand frame.

Two-Year Navy ROTC Scholarship

Sponsor: Navy Reserve Officers Training Corps (NROTC)
Web Site: http://www.cnet.navy.mil/nrotc/nrotc.htm
Amount of Scholarship: full tuition and a monthly stipend of $200
Number of Awards: not given
Deadline: not given
Education Level: college sophomores
Eligibility: Applicant must join NROTC.

To find information about this scholarship, click the Applying for an NROTC Scholarship link in the left frame, then follow the 2-Year Scholarship link. There is not a lot of information there, though—just a brief paragraph describing the scholarship and telling you how to get more information. If you want to apply, you must contact your college's NROTC unit. A list of such units, along with links to their Web sites, is linked to the scholarship description, or you can call the toll-free phone number given for more information.

Veterans

Angelfire Scholarship

Sponsor: Datatel Scholars Foundation
Web Site: http://www.datatel.com/scholars_foundation/index.html
Amount of Scholarship: $700 to $2,000
Number of Awards: 1
Deadline: February 15 (deadlines may vary at different institutions)
Education Level: college undergraduates and graduate students
Eligibility: Applicant must be a Vietnam veteran or the spouse or child of a Vietnam veteran or refugee from Vietnam, Cambodia, or Laos who entered the U.S. between 1964 and 1975; attend a college or university that is a Datatel client site or work at a Datatel non-education site; and take at least six credit hours per semester.

The Angelfire Scholarship is awarded under the Datatel Scholars program, described in Chapter 5. Except for the additional requirement of Vietnam veteran status, the eligibility requirements are exactly the same for the two scholarships. To verify that your school or company is a Datatel client, ask your financial aid officer, or contact the Foundation directly using the address, phone number, or e-mail address given on the Contact the Foundation page. If you attend a Datatel client school, you must apply through your school's scholarship or financial aid office; you cannot apply directly through the Web site. Likewise, if you work for a Datatel client, you must apply for the scholarship through your human resources department or CEO's office. The How to Apply link describes the process of getting nominated by your school or employer. Be sure to read the application instructions, which tell you what additional eligibility requirements you must meet and what additional materials you must submit to compete for the Angelfire Scholarship. A PDF copy of the application form is also linked to this page, which you can print out for your reference, but your school or employer will have official printed copies of the application to use for your final submission.

Illinois Veteran Grant

Sponsor: Illinois Student Assistance Commission
Web Site: http://www.isac1.org/ilaid/specgt.html#ivggp
Amount of Scholarship: full tuition
Number of Awards: not given
Deadline: none
Education Level: college undergraduates and graduate students
Eligibility: Applicant must have served at least one full year of full-time active duty in the U.S. Armed Forces and received an honorable discharge, be an Illinois resident, return to Illinois within six months of discharge, and enroll at an approved community college or public college or university in Illinois.

On the Web site you'll find a brief overview of this grant program for veterans from Illinois, a list of eligibility requirements, and instructions for applying for a grant. Grant applications are not available online, but you can obtain them from Department of Veteran Affairs' field offices and from your school's financial aid office. Once you receive a grant, you don't need to reapply to continue getting financial aid during the entirety of your education.

Persian Gulf Veterans Tuition Award

Sponsor: New York State Higher Education Services Corporation
Web Site: http://www.hesc.com/persiangulf.html
Amount of Scholarship: $500 to $1,000 per semester
Number of Awards: not given
Deadline: September 1
Education Level: college undergraduates and graduate students
Eligibility: Applicant must have served in the U.S. Armed Forces in the hostilities in the Persian Gulf; have been discharged under other than dishonorable conditions; be a resident of New York state; and attend an approved vocational training program, undergraduate college, or graduate school in New York state.

This program awards grants of $500 per semester for part-time study and $1,000 per semester for full-time study to Persian Gulf veterans. The Web page gives all the details on the grant, including how much you can receive, for how long, and for what kinds of study. The page also lists the eligibility requirements. Note that you must apply for federal financial aid by filing the FAFSA in order to be eligible for the grant. The Web page tells you what other forms you need to file to be considered, how to establish eligibility, and whom to contact for more information.

State Grant for Veterans

Sponsor: Pennsylvania Higher Education Assistance Agency
Web Site: http://www.pheaa.org/students/sg3.shtml
Amount of Scholarship: $800 to $3,100

Number of Awards: not given
Deadline: May 1 and August 1
Education Level: college undergraduates
Eligibility: Applicant must have engaged in active service with the U.S. Army, Navy, Air Force, Marines, or Coast Guard, or have been a cadet or midshipman at one of the service academies but have been released under honorable conditions; have not been incarcerated; enroll at an approved two-year or four-year college; and be a Pennsylvania resident.

This Web page gives an overview of Pennsylvania's grant program for veterans, along with the eligibility requirements and requirements for approved colleges. To apply for the program, you must fill out and submit the FAFSA. Chapter 1 gives instructions for filing this application form for federal financial aid. You will also find a brief description of the state's grant program for children of Pennsylvania residents who were reported missing in action or who were prisoners of war. If you qualify, scroll down to the POW-MIA Program section of the page to learn more. You apply for these grants in the same way that you would apply for state grants for veterans—by filing the FAFSA. The Web page also gives information on federal and veterans' financial aid programs that you might qualify for and toll-free phone numbers that you can call to get more information about state grants and student loans.

Vietnam Veterans' Scholarship

Sponsor: State of New Mexico Commission on Higher Education and New Mexico Veterans' Service Commission
Web Site: http://www.nmche.org/financialaid/veterans.html
Amount of Scholarship: full tuition
Number of Awards: not given
Deadline: varies

Education Level: college undergraduates and master's students
Eligibility: Applicant must be a Vietnam veteran; be a New Mexico resident; and attend a public or selected private, nonprofit college or university in New Mexico.

This Web page gives you the facts on this scholarship for Vietnam veterans who live in New Mexico. You'll find out what the scholarship is, how much you get, and whether you are eligible. To apply, contact the New Mexico Veterans' Service Commission by calling the phone number given on the page, or see a financial aid officer at your school.

Vietnam Veterans Tuition Award

Sponsor: New York State Higher Education Services Corporation
Web Site: http://www.hesc.com/persiangulf.html
Amount of Scholarship: $500 to $1,000 per semester
Number of Awards: not given
Deadline: September 1
Education Level: college undergraduates and graduate students
Eligibility: Applicant must have served in the U.S. Armed Forces in Indochina between December 22, 1961, and May 7, 1975; have been discharged under other than dishonorable conditions; be a resident of New York state; and attend an approved vocational training program, undergraduate college, or graduate school in New York state.

This program awards grants of $500 per semester for part-time study and $1,000 per semester for full-time study to Vietnam veterans. The Web page gives all the details on the grant, including how much you can receive, for how long, and for what kinds of study. The page also lists the eligibility requirements. Note that you must apply for federal financial aid by filing the FAFSA in order to be eligible for the grant. The Web page tells you what other forms you need to file to be considered, how to establish eligibility, and whom to contact for more information.

Also see the following scholarship:

- AFCEA General Emmett Paige Scholarship: Chapter 13, "All Branches" section

FAMILY AFFILIATION SCHOLARSHIPS

For the scholarships in this chapter, it doesn't matter who you are, but who you are related to. Eligibility for most of these awards depends on your parents—what they do for a living, the organizations they belong to, whether they served in the military, and even where they bank. You can qualify for some awards listed in this chapter through your grandparents, spouse, or other relatives as well. Before looking over these scholarships, sit down with your parents and make a list of their associations: professions, employers, clubs, community organizations, unions, professional associations, military service, service as a public safety officer, sororities and fraternities, and anything else they can think of. Then browse through the awards listed here and keep an eye out during your other searches for additional scholarships that you qualify for based on these associations. (Appropriate scholarships listed in other chapters are cross-referenced at the end of each applicable section.) Don't forget about where your parents went to college. If you're willing to attend the same school, you may qualify for legacy scholarships. The admissions or financial aid office at that school can tell you more.

Clubs and Community Organizations

Astrid G. Cates/Myrtle Beinhauer Scholarships

Sponsor: Sons of Norway Foundation
Web Site: http://www.sofn.com
Amount of Scholarship: $500 to $3,000
Number of Awards: 7
Deadline: March 1
Education Level: high school seniors and college undergraduates
Eligibility: Applicant must be a member, the child of a member, or the grandchild of a member of Sons of Norway and demonstrate financial need.

To find information about this scholarship, click the Foundation link on the left side of the page, then follow the Scholarships and Grants link. You will need to install Adobe Acrobat Reader to access this information. This brochure describes the two scholarships, which are offered in tandem. The Astrid G. Cates Scholarship ranges between $500 and $750; one award is given to one member in each of the six districts. The most deserving applicant receives the Myrtle Beinhauer Scholarship of $3,000. To find out more about the Sons of Norway, return to the main page and explore the links in the bar at the bottom of the Web page. Note that you don't need to be of Norwegian descent to join the Sons of Norway.

DECUS Merit Scholarship

Sponsor: Digital Equipment Computer Users Society (DECUS)
Web Site: http://www.decus.org/Scholarship.html
Amount of Scholarship: $1,000 (renewable for four years)
Number of Awards: not given
Deadline: not given
Education Level: high school seniors

Eligibility: Applicant must be a member or the child of a member of DECUS, enroll as a full-time student at a four-year college in the U.S., and be a U.S. citizen.

This Web page describes the scholarship program for DECUS members and their children. Scholarship recipients are chosen through the National Merit Scholarship competition. If you become a National Merit Semifinalist and you meet the eligibility requirements for this award, you should notify the sponsor as described on the Web page so you can be considered for the award. The page also lists the conditions of accepting the scholarship.

Elks Legacy Award

Sponsor: The Elks National Foundation
Web Site: http://www.elks.org/enf/legacy.cfm
Amount of Scholarship: $1,000
Number of Awards: 500
Deadline: December 1
Education Level: high school seniors
Eligibility: Applicant must be the child of an Elk who has been a member in good standing for at least two years and enroll at an accredited U.S. college.

Here you will find answers to all of the most common questions about the Elks' largest scholarship program for children of members. You will find out if you are eligible to apply for an award, who you compete against, how applications are judged, how to apply, and how awards may be used. You will also find contact information if you have further questions and a link to the application form in PDF format. At the bottom of the page is a list of the number of awards given to students in each state, so you can get a better idea of what the competition is like where you live.

Emergency Educational Fund Grant

Sponsor: The Elks National Foundation
Web Site: http://www.elks.org/enf/eefgrants.cfm
Amount of Scholarship: not given
Number of Awards: not given
Deadline: December 31
Education Level: college undergraduates
Eligibility: Applicant must be the child of a deceased Elk or an Elk who is totally incapacitated, enroll as a full-time student at a U.S. college, be unmarried, be under the age of 23, and demonstrate financial need.

This Web page describes the educational grant program offered by the Elks for students with great financial need. Read over this information to learn what the eligibility requirements are, how the amount of the grant is determined, how to obtain application materials, and where to submit applications. Application forms are not available online. Instead, you must obtain an application from the Lodge where your parent was a member.

John H. Strong Scholarship

Sponsor: SIL International and Wycliffe Bible Translators USA
Web Site: http://www.sil.org/ched/jhs.html
Amount of Scholarship: not given
Number of Awards: not given
Deadline: April 1
Education Level: high school seniors and college undergraduates
Eligibility: Applicant must be the child of an active member of SIL International, enroll as a full-time student at a two-year or four-year college, and be under the age of 25.

SIL International is a Christian service organization that studies, develops, and documents the world's lesser-known languages. This Web page briefly describes the scholarship available for children of SIL International members, including a list of the eligibility requirements. Click the JHS Application Form link to download the application in PDF format.

Nancy Lorraine Jensen Memorial Scholarship

Sponsor: Sons of Norway Foundation
Web Site: http://www.sofn.com
Amount of Scholarship: half tuition to full tuition (renewable for four years)
Number of Awards: not given
Deadline: March 1
Education Level: college freshmen, sophomores, and juniors
Eligibility: Applicant must be a member or the daughter or granddaughter of a member of the Sons of Norway or be an employee or daughter or granddaughter of an employee of NASA/ Goddard Space Flight Center in Maryland; be a full-time student; have completed at least one term of undergraduate study; major in chemical engineering, chemistry, electrical engineering, mechanical engineering, or physics; have an SAT I score of at least 1200 or an ACT score of at least 26; be female; be between the ages of 17 and 35; and be a U.S. citizen.

To find information about this scholarship, click the Foundation link on the left side of the page, then follow the Scholarships and Grants link. This scholarship supports female students of chemistry, physics, and engineering. To learn more, scroll down the page until you find a link to the scholarship, then click it to open the informational brochure and application form in PDF format. The eligibility requirements are strict, so be sure that you meet them all before you decide to apply. The application form also describes the selection criteria and the additional materials that you must submit with your application package.

Pennsylvania Youth Foundation Scholarships

Sponsor: Educational Endowment Fund of the Pennsylvania Youth Foundation
Web Site: http://www.grandlodge.net/pyf/ scholar/list/index.html
Amount of Scholarship: varies
Number of Awards: not given
Deadline: March 15
Education Level: high school seniors and college undergraduates
Eligibility: Applicant must be a child, stepchild, grandchild, sibling, or dependent of a member, living or deceased, of a Pennsylvania Masonic lodge, or be a member of a Pennsylvania Masonic-related youth group.

This page describes the scholarships available to the dependents of members of the Pennsylvania Grand Lodge, Knights Templar, Scottish Rite, and other Masonic lodges in Pennsylvania and to members of Pennsylvania Masonic-related youth groups, such as Job's Daughters, Rainbow Girls, and DeMolays. Fifty-four scholarships and two loans are awarded under this program. Their descriptions are grouped by category on the page, with the newest awards listed at the top of the page. Click on a scholarship's link to find facts about it, including its sponsor, the amount awarded, eligibility requirements, application deadline, and whom to contact for more information. To apply for any of the scholarships, click the Application link at the very top of the page, then download the PDF copy of the application. You will automatically be considered for all of the awards for which you are eligible. Also look at the Helpful Tips page to find tips for preparing a successful scholarship application. The other buttons provide useful information about the scholarship program's sponsor, Pennsylvania Masonic lodges, and Pennsylvania Masonic-related youth groups.

Employer and Profession

AFSA Scholarships

Sponsor: American Foreign Service Association (AFSA), Association of American Foreign Service Women (AAFSW), and Diplomatic and Consular Officers, Retired (DACOR)
Web Site: http://www.afsa.org/mbr/scholar.html
Amount of Scholarship: $500 to $2,500
Number of Awards: not given
Deadline: February 6
Education Level: high school seniors and college undergraduates
Eligibility: Applicant must be the dependent of an American Foreign Service employee (active, retired, or deceased) who has served at least one year abroad.

Three different scholarships are awarded under this program: a Financial Aid Award, which is based on financial need; a Merit Award, which is based on academic accomplishments; and an Art Merit Award, which is based on artistic accomplishments. The Financial Aid Award ranges from $500 to $2,500 per year. The Merit Award is $1,000 and is given to 20 graduating high school seniors each year. The Art Merit Award honors students who excel in the visual arts, dance, music, drama, or creative writing; one award of $1,000 is given each year. To qualify for a Merit Award, your parent must belong to AFSA or AAFSW, in addition to being an employee of the American Foreign Service. All three scholarships are described on the Web site, along with their eligibility requirements

and general details about the scholarship program. You can either download application materials from the Web site or fill out an electronic form to request that an application package be mailed to you—just follow the appropriate links.

ARA Scholarship

Sponsor: Automotive Recyclers Association (ARA) Scholarship Foundation
Web Site: http://www.geocities.com/Athens/Troy/8781/
Amount of Scholarship: not given
Number of Awards: not given
Deadline: March 15
Education Level: high school seniors and college undergraduates
Eligibility: Applicant must be the child of a current employee of a Direct Member of ARA, enroll as a full-time student in a post-high school educational program, and have a minimum 3.0 GPA.

On this page you'll find a list of the eligibility requirements for this scholarship, as well as links to a list of application deadlines and to application instructions. Request application forms by writing the address given for the ARA Scholarship Foundation at the bottom of each Web page. If you have questions about the program, contact the ARA Scholarship Advisor, whose mailing and e-mail addresses are also given at the bottom of each page.

ASBA Educational Foundation Scholarship

Sponsor: Arkansas School Boards Association (ASBA) Educational Foundation
Web Site: http://www.arsba.org/scholarship.html
Amount of Scholarship: $500
Number of Awards: 5

Deadline: April 1
Education Level: high school seniors
Eligibility: Applicant must be the child of an Arkansas school board member and enroll at a two-year or four-year college in Arkansas.

This Web page provides a list of eligibility requirements and judging criteria for this scholarship for children of Arkansas school board members. A list of past winners of the award follows. Scroll to the bottom of the page to locate the link to the printable scholarship application form.

Beverage Industry Scholarship

Sponsor: Christermon Foundation
Web Site: http://www.christermon.com/scholarship.html
Amount of Scholarship: $1,000 to $5,000
Number of Awards: not given
Deadline: February 1
Education Level: high school seniors and community college transfer students
Eligibility: Applicant must be the child, grandchild, or legal dependent of the proprietor or employee of a business holding a valid California liquor license.

If your parent, grandparent, or guardian works at or owns a business holding a California liquor license, then you are eligible to compete for this scholarship. Such businesses include restaurants, hotels, grocery stores, drug stores, convenience store, wineries, breweries, and airlines. If you would like to apply, you must submit an electronic application online. Printed application forms are not accepted. Be sure to choose the correct application form for your educational level, either a graduating high school senior or a second-year community college student preparing to transfer to a four-year college.

FEEA Scholarship

Sponsor: Federal Employee Education and Assistance (FEEA) Fund and Blue Cross and Blue Shield Association
Web Site: http://www.fpmi.com/FEEA/Scholarships.html
Amount of Scholarship: $300 to $1,500
Number of Awards: not given
Deadline: May
Education Level: high school seniors, college undergraduates, and graduate students
Eligibility: Applicant must be a current civilian federal or postal employee or the child or spouse of an employee; enroll at an accredited two-year college, four-year college, or graduate school; and have a minimum 3.0 GPA.

If you are the dependent of a federal or postal employee, you must be a full-time student to qualify for this scholarship. Current federal employees who want a scholarship may attend school part-time. The Web page describes the other eligibility requirements and the selection criteria and provides a mailing address that you can write to request an application form. You will also find information about the FEEA student loan program on this page.

Horace Mann Scholarship

Sponsor: Horace Mann
Web Site: http://www.horacemann.com/html/edprograms/escholar.html
Amount of Scholarship: $1,000 to $20,000 (awarded over four years)
Number of Awards: 16
Deadline: not given
Education Level: high school seniors
Eligibility: Applicant must be the dependent of a U.S. public education employee, have a grade average of at least a B, and have a minimum SAT I score of 1100 or a minimum ACT score of 23.

Click the HM Scholarship link on the left-hand side of the Web page to find information about this scholarship program, which gives scholarships to children of employees of the U.S. public education system. The top applicant receives a four-year $20,000 scholarship. In addition, 5 applicants receive four-year $4,000 scholarships, and 10 applicants receive $1,000 scholarships. The Web page lists the past winners and goes over the eligibility requirements. Applications for the next school year are available on the Web site after September 1.

John F. Condon Memorial Scholarship

Sponsor: Hanscom Federal Credit Union
Web Site: http://hfcu.org/about/scholarship.html
Amount of Scholarship: $1,000
Number of Awards: 3
Deadline: March 31
Education Level: high school seniors
Eligibility: Applicant must be a member of Hanscom Federal Credit Union and enroll at an accredited two-year or four-year college.

On this Web page you'll read about the scholarship for members of Hanscom Federal Credit Union in Massachusetts. For you to become a member, one of your parents, grandparents, or siblings must work for one of the federal agencies or organizations listed on the Who May Join page at http://hfcu.org/about/eligibility.html and also belong to the Hanscom Federal Credit Union. You have to become a member of the credit union by December 31 of the year before you apply for the scholarship in order to be eligible, as well. The scholarship's Web page describes these eligibility requirements as well as other requirements of applying for the scholarship. A link to an electronic application form that you can submit over the Internet is provided at the bottom of the page.

Michigan Farm Bureau Scholarships

Sponsor: Michigan Farm Bureau
Web Site: http://www.fb.com/mifb/scholar.htm
Amount of Scholarship: $1,500 to $3,000
Number of Awards: 2
Deadline: December 1
Education Level: college freshmen, sophomores, and juniors
Eligibility: Applicant must be from a Michigan Farm Bureau family or be a member of the Michigan Farm Bureau if married or over the age of 21; attend Michigan State University; major in agriculture, agriculture technology, or veterinary medicine; have a 2.6 GPA; and demonstrate financial need.

Two scholarships are given out under this program: one for $1,500 and one for $3,000. The $1,500 scholarship is for a student in the agriculture technology program, and the $3,000 scholarship is for a student in the agriculture and natural resources or veterinary medicine program. Read the eligibility requirements for each scholarship carefully; they are strict, and not many students will qualify. If you are eligible, request an application form by calling the toll-free phone number or by sending an e-mail message to the address given at the bottom of the Web page.

Rich Vogler Memorial Scholarship

Sponsor: Rich Vogler Memorial Scholarship Fund
Web Site: http://www.richvoglerscholarship.org/
Amount of Scholarship: $1,000
Number of Awards: not given
Deadline: not given

Education Level: high school seniors, college undergraduates, and graduate students

Eligibility: Applicant must have an immediate family member who is affiliated with auto racing, and must reside in the U.S.

The main Web page provides an overview of the history and purpose of this scholarship. To learn more, follow the Rich Vogler History and Scholarship Recipients links on the left-hand side of the page. If you would like to apply, click the How to Apply link. This page provides a postal address and an e-mail address that you can write to request an application form. Scholarships can be used for any form of postsecondary study; the only qualification is that an immediate family member of yours must work in the auto racing industry in some way.

Roofing Industry Scholarship

Sponsor: National Roofing Contractors Association (NCRA)

Web Site: http://nrca.net/about/nrf/ris.asp

Amount of Scholarship: $1,000 (renewable for four years)

Number of Awards: not given

Deadline: not given

Education Level: high school seniors and college undergraduates

Eligibility: Applicant must be the employee of an NCRA-contractor member, the immediate family member of an employee of an NCRA-contractor member, or the immediate family member of an NCRA-contractor member; and enroll as a full-time student at an accredited vocational-technical school, two-year college, or four-year college.

Here you'll find a brief description of the scholarship, including eligibility requirements and renewal conditions. To obtain an application form, contact the toll-free phone number, e-mail address, or postal address given at the bottom of the page.

School Food Service Foundation Scholarships

Sponsor: School Food Service Foundation

Web Site: http://www.asfsa.org

Amount of Scholarship: $1,000

Number of Awards: not given

Deadline: April 1 and April 15

Education Level: college undergraduates and graduate students

Eligibility: Applicant must be a school food service employee or the dependant of a school food service employee.

Three scholarships are available under this program. The Tony's/Schwan's Scholarship goes to members of American School Food Service Association (ASFSA) members and their dependents who are pursuing a degree in school food service and nutrition. The Professional Growth Scholarship helps ASFSA members attain graduate degrees in school food service and child nutrition. And the Heinz Scholarship is open to all school food service employees and their dependents, regardless of whether they belong to ASFSA. Be sure that you meet all the eligibility requirements listed on the application forms for the scholarship for which you want to apply. You will find PDF versions of application forms for all three scholarships at the bottom of the page.

State Farm Companies Foundation Scholarship

Sponsor: State Farm Companies Foundation

Web Site: http://www.statefarm.com/foundati/foundsch.htm

Amount of Scholarship: not given
Number of Awards: 100
Deadline: not given
Education Level: high school seniors
Eligibility: Applicant must be the dependent of a State Farm agent, employee, or retiree.

This scholarship is awarded based on National Merit Scholarship status, so to qualify, you must take the PSAT as a junior in high school and qualify as a National Merit Scholarship finalist. Get more information by contacting the address, phone number, or e-mail address given on the Web page. Your high school guidance office can also answer your questions about the PSAT and the National Merit Scholarship.

Syncrude Higher Education Award

Sponsor: Syncrude Canada Ltd.
Web Site: http://home.the-wire.com/CKB/syncrude.html
Amount of Scholarship: $1,800 (Canadian)
Number of Awards: not given
Deadline: September 29
Education Level: high school seniors, college undergraduates, and graduate students
Eligibility: Applicant must be the dependent of an employee or retired employee of Syncrude Canada Ltd. or Northwards Development Ltd.; enroll as a full-time student at a Canadian college, university, or community college or at an accredited foreign university; and be under the age of 25.

You will need to install Adobe Acrobat Reader to access the information about this scholarship. First, read the Scholarship Program Brochure to make sure that you qualify. If you do, the New Applicant Guide tells you how to ap-

ply. You can also download and print all four pages of the application form from the Web site. The Web site provides links to the renewal application form and instructions for past recipients of the scholarship, as well.

Walton Foundation Scholarship

Sponsor: Wal-Mart Stores, Inc.
Web Site: http://compedge.wal-mart.com/wf_scholar.html
Amount of Scholarship: $6,000 (awarded over four years)
Number of Awards: 100
Deadline: March 1
Education Level: high school seniors
Eligibility: Applicant must be the child of a Wal-Mart Stores, Inc. associate who has been employed full-time for at least one year, and enroll at a four-year college.

Here you'll find a brief overview of this scholarship for dependents of Wal-Mart employees. The Web page tells you if you are eligible to apply and the criteria for which recipients are selected. If you would like to apply, ask your parent to pick up an application form from their location's personnel office. Application materials are not available on the Web site.

Wendell Milliman Scholarship

Sponsor: Milliman & Robertson, Inc.
Web Site: http://www.collegeplan.org/cpnow/pnwguide/onlineaps/wmonap.htm
Amount of Scholarship: $5,000
Number of Awards: 1
Deadline: February 29
Education Level: high school seniors and college undergraduates
Eligibility: Applicant must be the dependent of a non-shareholder employee of Milliman &

Robertson; enroll as a full-time student at a U.S. college; and major in actuarial science, business, computer science, economics, finance, health sciences, or mathematics.

This Web page simply describes the scholarship's eligibility requirements and the items that must be included up the application package, the bulk of which must be submitted through the mail. It also contains an electronic version of the basic scholarship application form that interested students can submit online. If you have any questions about the application submission process, contact the address, phone number, or e-mail address given at the bottom of the page.

WSSC Scholarship

Sponsor: Washington Suburban Sanitary Commission (WSSC)
Web Site: http://www.wssc.dst.md.us/info/scholar/eligibility.html
Amount of Scholarship: not given
Number of Awards: not given
Deadline: March 31
Education Level: high school seniors and college undergraduates
Eligibility: Applicant must be the dependent of a WSSC employee who is currently enrolled in the WSSC Scholarship Fund and enroll at an accredited vocational-technical school, two-year college, or four-year college.

Here you will find a brief rundown of the eligibility requirements for this scholarship. Click the Application link to locate downloadable copies of the application form in Microsoft Word format, PDF, and Rich Text Format. This page also tells you how to submit the application and gives more information about eligibility requirements and selection criteria.

Also see the following scholarships:

- AHF Scholarships: Chapter 6, "Hotel and Restaurant Management" section
- Arizona Chapter Dependent Scholarship: Chapter 14, "Unions and Professional Associations" section
- ASTA Scholarships: Chapter 6, "Travel and Tourism" section
- Chattanooga Christian Community Foundation Scholarships: Chapter 15, "Tennessee" section
- Nancy Lorraine Jensen Memorial Scholarship: Chapter 14, "Clubs and Community Organizations" section
- Wal-Mart Associate Scholarship: Chapter 8, "Work" section

Military Personnel and Veterans

American Legion Auxiliary Memorial Scholarship

Sponsor: American Legion Auxiliary
Web Site: http://www.michalaux.org/memorial_scholarships.htm
Amount of Scholarship: $500
Number of Awards: not given
Deadline: March 15
Education Level: high school seniors and college undergraduates
Eligibility: Applicant must be the daughter, granddaughter, or great-granddaughter of an honorably discharged or deceased veteran; attend a Michigan college; be female; be between the ages of 16 and 21; and be a Michigan resident.

The eligibility requirements for this scholarship are complex, so carefully read the Web page to determine if you qualify. Pay particular attention to the paragraph describing which relatives of which veterans are eligible to apply. This page also details the criteria used to select scholarship winners and provides a list of documents that must accompany the application form. Scroll to the bottom of the page to find a copy of the application form that you can print out.

American Legion Auxiliary Scholarship for Non-Traditional Students

Sponsor: American Legion Auxiliary
Web Site: http://www.michalaux.org/memorial_scholarships.htm
Amount of Scholarship: $500 (renewable for two years)
Number of Awards: not given
Deadline: March 15
Education Level: high school seniors and college undergraduates
Eligibility: Applicant must be the dependent or descendant of a veteran; be a nontraditional student returning to college after an interruption in education, a student over the age of 22 attending college for the first time, or a student over the age of 22 attending vocational or trade school; and attend school in Michigan.

Here you will find an overview of the eligibility requirements for this scholarship for nontraditional students, as well as the criteria used to select the winners. Scroll to the bottom of the page to find a copy of the application form that you can print out.

AMF/AFSA Scholarship

Sponsor: Airmen Memorial Foundation (AMF) and Air Force Sergeants Association (AFSA)
Web Site: http://www.amf.org/scholarship.html
Amount of Scholarship: $500 to $3,000

Number of Awards: around 50
Deadline: not given
Education Level: high school seniors and college undergraduates
Eligibility: Applicant must be the dependent child of an enlisted member of the Air Force on active duty, serving in the ANG/AFRES, or retired; attend an accredited two-year college, four-year college, or trade or technical school; and be unmarried.

A brief description of the scholarship program is given on this Web page. If you want to know more and get an application form, write to the mailing address given at the bottom of the page. Be sure to enclose a self-addressed, stamped envelope as instructed.

Brewer Scholarship

Sponsor: American Legion of Michigan
Web Site: http://michiganlegion.org/scholarships.htm
Amount of Scholarship: not given
Number of Awards: not given
Deadline: February 1
Education Level: high school seniors
Eligibility: Applicant must be the child of a veteran, enroll at an accredited college, and be a Michigan resident.

This scholarship is described at the top of the Web page. There you'll see the eligibility requirements, selection criteria, and a list of documents that must accompany the application form. Click the name of the scholarship at the beginning of the description to open a printable application form.

Chief Master Sergeants of the Air Force Scholarship

Sponsor: Airmen Memorial Foundation (AMF)

Web Site: http://www.amf.org/cmsaf.htm
Amount of Scholarship: up to $3,000
Number of Awards: around 10
Deadline: not given
Education Level: high school seniors and college undergraduates
Eligibility: Applicant must be the dependent child of an enlisted member of the Air Force; attend an accredited two-year college, four-year college, or trade or technical school; and be unmarried.

Recipients for this scholarship are selected from among the applicants for the AMF/AFSA Scholarship, described previously in this section. You apply for both scholarships together. Applicants can submit additional materials that they feel should be taken into consideration by the scholarship committee, if they like. The kinds of additional materials that would be welcome are listed on the scholarship's Web page.

Children of Deceased Military and State Police Personnel Scholarship

Sponsor: State of New Mexico Commission on Higher Education and New Mexico Veterans Service Commission
Web Site: http://www.nmche.org/financialaid/milipolice.html
Amount of Scholarship: full tuition and a $300 stipend
Number of Awards: not given
Deadline: not given
Education Level: high school seniors, college undergraduates, and graduate students
Eligibility: Applicant must be the child of a member of the military, member of the New Mexico National Guard, or member of the New Mexico State Police who was killed in the line of duty; attend a public college or university in New Mexico; and be between the ages of 16 and 26.

This Web page provides a brief overview of the grant program. You'll learn what the eligibility requirements are and how to obtain application materials. If you have questions, contact the New Mexico Veterans Service Commission at the phone number given or see your financial aid officer.

Educational Benefits for Children of Deceased Veterans and Others

Sponsor: Delaware Higher Education Commission
Web Site: http://www.doe.state.de.us/high-ed/vets.htm
Amount of Scholarship: full tuition (renewable for four years)
Number of Awards: not given
Deadline: three weeks before classes begin
Education Level: high school seniors, college undergraduates, and graduate students
Eligibility: Applicant must be the child of a military veteran or state police officer who died in the line of duty, was a prisoner of war, or was declared missing in action; enroll at a state-supported postsecondary institution; be between the ages of 16 and 24; and be a Delaware resident.

This Web page gives just the facts about the eligibility requirements, award amounts, and application deadline for this grant program. Application materials are not provided on the Web site. To learn more, contact your guidance counselor or financial aid officer, or click the Contact Us link at the bottom of the Web page to send an e-mail message to the Delaware Higher Education Commission.

Edward T. Conroy Memorial Scholarship

Sponsor: Maryland Higher Education Commission
Web Site: http://www.mhec.state.md.us/SSA/introduction.htm
Amount of Scholarship: up to full tuition
Number of Awards: not given
Deadline: July 15
Education Level: high school seniors and college undergraduates
Eligibility: Applicant must be the child of a veteran, a state public safety officer, or a local public safety officer who was a Maryland resident and who was killed or disabled in the line of duty or who was a prisoner of war; and enroll for at least six credits per semester at a Maryland college or private career school.

To find information about this scholarship, click the Program Description link on the left side of the page, and then click the name of the scholarship in the list of awards that opens. Be sure to read the paragraph under How Do I Qualify? carefully, as it tells you exactly what the eligibility requirements are. These requirements are more complicated than can be described here. For example, spouses of deceased public safety officers and disabled public safety officers may qualify for a scholarship. The scholarship description also tells you how much you can receive and what forms you need to submit to apply. Application forms are not available on the Web site at the time of this writing. To find out how to contact the Maryland State Scholarship Administration office and order an application, click the Online Applications link on the left side of the page.

First Marine Division Association Scholarship

Sponsor: First Marine Division Association
Web Site: http://users.erols.com/oldbreed/1MarDiv%20OBNSchol.html
Amount of Scholarship: $1,500 (renewable for four years)
Number of Awards: not given
Deadline: not given
Education Level: college undergraduates
Eligibility: Applicant must be the dependent of a deceased or permanently disabled honorably discharged veteran with the First Marine Division and enroll as a full-time student at an accredited four-year college or technical trade school.

Look on this Web page for an overview of the scholarship program, including eligibility requirements and details about the award. You must contact the First Marine Division Association directly to obtain an application form. Find contact information by clicking the Home link at the bottom of the Web page.

General Henry H. Arnold Education Grant

Sponsor: Air Force Aid Society
Web Site: http://www.afas.org/Afasedu.htm
Amount of Scholarship: $1,500
Number of Awards: not given
Deadline: March
Education Level: high school seniors and college undergraduates
Eligibility: Applicant must be the child of an active duty, retired, or deceased Air Force member or the spouse of an active duty or deceased Air Force member; enroll as a full-time student at an accredited college or vocational or trade school; and have a minimum 2.0 GPA.

On this page you'll find an overview of this grant program for children and spouses of members of the Air Force. Follow the links at the bottom of the page to learn more. The Eligibility link describes the eligibility requirements in more detail, while the Deadline link tells you when applications are due. The Grant Application Procedures page gives instructions for submitting an application. Finally, you will find links to the application form in both PDF and text formats.

Marine Corps Scholarships

Sponsor: Marine Corps Scholarship Foundation, Inc.
Web Site: http://www.marine-scholars.org
Amount of Scholarship: not given
Number of Awards: 1,100
Deadline: April 1
Education Level: high school seniors and college undergraduates
Eligibility: Applicant must be the child of a current or former U.S. Marine, attend an accredited undergraduate institution, and demonstrate financial need.

This Web page provides a general overview of the Marine Corps Scholarship Foundation's program. Scroll down to the list of links to find information about the awards themselves. First, go to the Scholarship Eligibility Requirements and Application Request page to find out if you qualify to apply. This page also tells you how to request an application form via e-mail. To find out what awards are available, return to the main page and follow the Memorial Scholarships and Honorary Scholarships links. These pages just list the names of the 196 different awards given out by the program, although additional information is given for a few. The eligibility requirements for all of the scholarships are the same. Finally, you should explore the

other links to learn amore about the sponsor of the scholarship program.

MG James Ursano Scholarship

Sponsor: Army Emergency Relief
Web Site: http://www.aerhq.org/MGJames.htm
Amount of Scholarship: $600 to $1,700 (renewable for four years)
Number of Awards: not given
Deadline: March 1
Education Level: high school seniors and college undergraduates
Eligibility: Applicant must be the dependent of an active duty, retired, or deceased member of the U.S. Armed Forces; be registered in the Defense Eligibility Enrollment Reporting System; enroll as a full-time student at an accredited postsecondary educational institution; be unmarried; be under the age of 22; and be a U.S. citizen or permanent resident.

This page lists the eligibility requirements and other requirements for this scholarship and tells you how to obtain application materials. Click the Continued link at the bottom of the page to read about award amounts, how the award may be used, and other important details. You can obtain application forms on the Web site between November 1 and March 1, or you can write the postal address given to request that an application form be mailed to you.

Missing in Action/Killed in Action Dependents' Scholarship

Sponsor: Arkansas Department of Higher Education
Web Site: http://www.adhe.arknet.edu/finance/miakia.html
Amount of Scholarship: not given
Number of Awards: not given

Deadline: not given
Education Level: high school seniors, college undergraduates, and graduate students
Eligibility: Applicant must be the dependent of an Arkansas citizen who was a prisoner of war, missing in action, killed in action, or killed on ordnance delivery during active military duty after January 1, 1960; and enroll as a full-time student at a state-supported college or university.

Be sure to read the eligibility requirements for this scholarship carefully, as they are strict. Note that only students who didn't receive an undergraduate degree in Arkansas are eligible to pursue a professional graduate degree under the scholarship. The Web page also tells you what items you must submit along with the application form. Obtain an application by calling the toll-free phone number provided at the bottom of the page.

Navy League Scholarships

Sponsor: Navy League National Scholarship Foundation
Web Site: http://www.navyleague.org/youth/applicat.htm
Amount of Scholarship: not given
Number of Awards: not given
Deadline: March 17
Education Level: high school seniors
Eligibility: Applicant must be the dependant or direct descendant of a person who served in a U.S. sea service, enroll at an accredited four-year college, have a minimum 3.0 GPA, demonstrate financial need, be under the age of twenty-five, and be a U.S. citizen.

If you are the dependent of a current or former member of the Navy, Marine Corps, Coast Guard, or Merchant Marines, you are eligible to apply for this scholarship program. This Web page provides a lot of helpful information,

so be sure to read it carefully. You'll find out what the eligibility requirements for the scholarship are, when the application deadline is, what supporting documents you need to submit, and helpful hints for making your application the best possible. Follow the link at the bottom of the page to find a printable application form. You only need to submit this one application form to apply for all scholarships offered by the Navy League, although the Web site doesn't tell you what scholarships are available or how much the different awards are.

Nurses, Physical Therapists, and Respiratory Therapists Scholarship

Sponsor: American Legion Auxiliary
Web Site: http://www.michalaux.org/nurse_app.htm
Amount of Scholarship: $500
Number of Awards: not given
Deadline: March 15
Education Level: college undergraduates
Eligibility: Applicant must the relative of a veteran; be a Michigan resident; and enroll in a nursing, physical therapy, or respiratory therapy program at a Michigan college.

The eligibility requirements for this scholarship are complex, so carefully read the Web page to determine if you qualify. Pay particular attention to the paragraph describing which relatives of which veterans are eligible to apply. This page also describes the criteria used to select scholarship winners. Scroll to the bottom of the page to find a copy of the application form that you can print out.

Ohio War Orphans Scholarship

Sponsor: Ohio Board of Regents
Web Site: http://www.regents.state.oh.us/sgs/sgsprogs.html

Amount of Scholarship: not given
Number of Awards: not given
Deadline: July 1
Education Level: high school seniors and college undergraduates
Eligibility: Applicant must be the child of a deceased or severely disabled Ohio veteran, enroll as a full-time student at an eligible two-year or four-year college in Ohio, be under the age of 21, and be an Ohio resident.

To find a description of this scholarship, scroll down the Web page until you see the scholarship's name. This brief paragraph tells you what the eligibility requirements are and where you can obtain application forms. If you have further questions, return to the top of the Web page to find a toll-free phone number that you can call.

Regents Award for Child of Veteran

Sponsor: New York State Higher Education Services Corporation
Web Site: http://www.hesc.com/cv.html
Amount of Scholarship: $450
Number of Awards: not given
Deadline: May 1
Education Level: high school seniors and college undergraduates
Eligibility: Applicant must be the child of a veteran from New York state who is deceased, disabled, missing in action, or was a prisoner of war; enroll at a college in New York state; and be a New York resident.

Read the description of this award over carefully to determine if you are eligible. The Web page describes exactly which veterans qualify. If you are eligible, you must apply for the award by filing the FAFSA (return to Chapter 1 for

instructions on how to do this), and then apply for state financial aid. You will have to submit a Child of Veteran Award Supplement form along with your state financial aid application to be considered for the award. You can obtain all forms that you need by contacting the mailing address or toll-free phone number given at the bottom of the Web page.

Scholarship for Children of Deceased and Disabled Veterans

Sponsor: Florida Department of Education, Bureau of Student Financial Assistance State Programs
Web Site: http://www.firn.edu/doe/bin00065/99apps.htm
Amount of Scholarship: full tuition (renewable for four years)
Number of Awards: not given
Deadline: April 1
Education Level: high school seniors and college undergraduates
Eligibility: Applicant must be the dependent child of a Florida veteran who died in action, is disabled, is missing in action, or was a prisoner of war; enroll as a full-time student at an eligible two-year or four-year college in Florida; not have previously received a bachelor's degree; be between the ages of 16 and 22; and be a Florida resident.

To find the scholarship information, click the name of the scholarship in the list of awards on the Web page. You will need to have Adobe Acrobat Reader to read this information. This PDF file tells you everything you need to know about the award, including the specific conditions that you must meet in order to be eligible. You'll also find out how to renew the scholarship, at which institutions the money may be used, and other important details. A copy of the application form that you can print out is given at the end of the file.

Scholarship for Orphans of Veterans

Sponsor: New Hampshire Postsecondary Education Commission
Web Site: http://www.state.nh.us/postsecondary/wos.html
Amount of Scholarship: up to full tuition
Number of Awards: not given
Deadline: not given
Education Level: high school seniors and college undergraduates
Eligibility: Applicant must be the child of a veteran from New Hampshire who died in World War I, World War II, the Korean conflict, or the Vietnam conflict; enroll at a two-year or four-year college; be between the ages of 16 and 25; and be a New Hampshire resident.

This program provides scholarships for orphans of veterans to attend any two-year or four-year college. In addition, these students are eligible for full-tuition scholarships at public two-year and four-year colleges in the state of New Hampshire, which are all listed on the Web page. Not many other details about the scholarship program are given, though. To get more information or an application form, fill out the electronic form at the bottom of the Web page.

Seabee Memorial Scholarship Association Scholarship

Sponsor: Seabee Memorial Scholarship Association, Inc.
Web Site: http://www.seabee.org/scholarships.html

Amount of Scholarship: not given
Number of Awards: not given
Deadline: April 15
Education Level: high school seniors and college undergraduates
Eligibility: Applicant must be the child or grandchild of a regular, reserve, retired, or deceased officer or enlisted member who served with the Naval Construction Force or Navy Civil Engineer Corps; and enroll at a four-year college.

To find information and an application form for this scholarship program, click the Application link. The application form provides some details about eligibility requirements and selection criteria, as well as instructions for filling out the application itself. You will need Adobe Acrobat Reader to download the application materials, or you can submit an electronic form to request that an application packet be mailed to you.

TROA Scholarship

Sponsor: TROA Scholarship Fund
Web Site: https://www.troa.org/Education/ScholarshipFund.asp
Amount of Scholarship: $500 to $3,000
Number of Awards: 300
Deadline: not given
Education Level: high school seniors and college undergraduates
Eligibility: Applicant must be the dependent child of a member of the uniformed services, enroll as a full-time student at an accredited four-year college or technical institution in the U.S., have a minimum 3.0 GPA, be unmarried, and be under the age of 24.

This educational assistance program awards grants and interest-free loans to children of members of the military. You can read about both kinds of financial aid on the Web page. You must apply for a loan in order to be considered for a grant. Note the special eligibility requirements for children of officers—their parents must be members of TROA, if they are eligible. (They can become members by following the Join TROA link on the left-hand side of the page.) Children of enlisted personnel are also eligible to apply. Follow the Scholarship Fund Frequently Asked Questions link at the bottom of the page to find answers to the most common questions about the financial aid program. Check the Web site after November 8 for online application forms.

United Daughters of the Confederacy Scholarships

Sponsor: United Daughters of the Confederacy
Web Site: http://www.hqudc.org/scholarship.html
Amount of Scholarship: not given
Number of Awards: not given
Deadline: February 15
Education Level: high school seniors, college undergraduates, and graduate students
Eligibility: Applicant must be the lineal descendant of a Confederate soldier and have a minimum 3.0 GPA.

This page describes the scholarship program for descendants of Confederate soldiers. Note that you must provide certified proof of your ancestor's Confederate military service and the line of descent from your ancestor. Instructions for how to do this and the appropriate forms are linked to the Web page, in the section describing the required documents that must be submitted with the application. The Web site also lists the general eligibility requirements for all scholarships awarded under the program, the names and specific eligibility requirements (if any) for the 30 different scholarships given

out each year, and instructions for submitting an application package. Note that some scholarships specify residency, gender, or field of study requirements, and some can only be used at specified colleges. The majority of the scholarships are intended for college undergraduates, but three are set aside for graduate students in specified fields.

Vietnam Veterans Survivor Grant

Sponsor: Missouri Department of Higher Education
Web Site: http://www.mocbhe.gov/mostars/scholar2.htm#Vietnam
Amount of Scholarship: up to full tuition
Number of Awards: not given
Deadline: none
Education Level: high school seniors and college undergraduates
Eligibility: Applicant must be the child or spouse of a Vietnam veteran whose death was attributed to exposure to toxic chemicals during the Vietnam conflict, enroll as a full-time student at a participating Missouri college, not pursue a degree in theology or divinity, be a Missouri resident, and be a U.S. citizen or permanent resident.

Here you will find a list of the eligibility requirements that you must meet to qualify for this grant and instructions for proving your eligibility. The Web page also tells you how much grant money you can receive under the program and provides a toll-free phone number that you can call to request an application form. Although there is no deadline for this program, you should apply early before funds run out.

Virginia Division Scholarships

Sponsor: United Daughters of the Confederacy, Virginia Division

Web Site: http://users.erols.com/va-udc/scholarships.html
Amount of Scholarship: not given
Number of Awards: 14
Deadline: June 1
Education Level: high school seniors, college undergraduates, and graduate students
Eligibility: Applicant must be the lineal descendant of a Confederate soldier, enroll at a Virginia college or university, have a minimum 3.0 GPA, demonstrate financial need, and be a Virginia resident.

To apply for these scholarships, you must meet all of the eligibility and application requirements for the general United Daughters of the Confederacy scholarship program, as well as live in and attend school in Virginia. Check the United Daughters of the Confederacy Scholarships description, listed earlier in this section, for information on applying for the general scholarships. On this Web page you'll find information about the Virginia Division's 14 different scholarships. Read about these awards by following the Tuition and Part-Tuition Scholarships and Virginia Division Gift Scholarships links at the bottom of the Web page. Note that many awards have specific requirements, such as the college or university you must attend, the field you must study, or the gender of the awardee. For general information regarding eligibility, applications, and renewal of awards, read the Rules Governing Applications and Awards, the Qualifications, and the Other Information pages. If you meet all of the qualifications, fill out the electronic format the bottom of the main page to request that application materials be mailed to you.

Wilson Scholarship

Sponsor: American Legion of Michigan
Web Site: http://michiganlegion.org/scholarships.htm

Amount of Scholarship: not given
Number of Awards: not given
Deadline: February 1
Education Level: high school seniors
Eligibility: Applicant must be the child of a veteran, enroll at an accredited college in Michigan, have a minimum 2.5 GPA, and be a Michigan resident.

This scholarship is described at the bottom of the Web page, after the description of the Brewer Scholarship. There you'll see the eligibility requirements, selection criteria, and a list of documents that must accompany the application form. Click the name of the scholarship at the beginning of the description to open a printable application form.

Also see the following scholarships:

- AFCEA General Emmett Paige Scholarship: Chapter 13, "All Branches" section
- Angelfire Scholarship: Chapter 13, "Veterans" section
- State Grant for Veterans: Chapter 13, "Veterans" section

Public Safety Officers

American Federation of Police and Concerned Citizens/National Association of Chiefs of Police Scholarship

Sponsor: American Federation of Police and Concerned Citizens and National Association of Chiefs of Police
Web Site: http://www.aphf.org/aphf.nsf/htmlmedia/scholarship_program.html
Amount of Scholarship: $1,000
Number of Awards: 50
Deadline: not given

Education Level: high school seniors, college undergraduates, and graduate students

Eligibility: Applicant must be the relative of a police officer killed in the line of duty or a law enforcement officer who has been injured or disabled and enroll at an approved college, university, or vocational school.

Here you will find a brief description of the scholarship program, which outlines the eligibility requirements and how the awards may be used. Look under the Procedure section to find contact information for ordering application materials.

Deceased or Disabled Public Safety Officer Grant

Sponsor: Oregon Student Assistance Commission

Web Site: http://www.osac.state.or.us/disabled_officers.html

Amount of Scholarship: up to full tuition (renewable for four years)

Number of Awards: not given

Deadline: varies

Education Level: high school seniors and college undergraduates

Eligibility: Applicant must be the child of a public safety officer in Oregon who was killed or disabled in the line of duty, enroll as a full-time student at a two-year or four-year college in Oregon, demonstrate financial need, and be an Oregon resident.

This Web page gives all the facts about the grant program, including the kinds of public safety officers whose children are eligible to apply. You'll also find out what the amount of the grant is and what forms you need to file. To get more information and application forms, write to the address given under For More Information . . . at the bottom of the page.

Dependent Children Scholarship

Sponsor: Tennessee Student Assistance Corporation (TSAC)

Web Site: http://www.state.tn.us/tsac/grants.htm#Dependent

Amount of Scholarship: not given

Number of Awards: not given

Deadline: not given

Education Level: high school seniors and college undergraduates

Eligibility: Applicant must be a dependant child of a law enforcement officer, firefighter, or emergency medical technician who was killed or disabled in the line of duty; enroll as a full-time student at a two-year or four-year college; and be a Tennessee resident.

This Web page only gives a brief paragraph describing the scholarship, but you should be able to determine if you qualify. To get more information, scroll to the bottom of the page and click the TSAC Home button. This opens TSAC's main Web page, where you will find links to e-mail addresses and phone numbers that you can contact to request application materials.

Grant for Dependents of Correctional Officers

Sponsor: Illinois Student Assistance Commission

Web Site: http://www.isac1.org/ilaid/specgt.html#gpdco

Amount of Scholarship: not given

Number of Awards: not given

Deadline: not given

Education Level: high school seniors and college undergraduates

Eligibility: Applicant must be the spouse or child of a State of Illinois Department of Corrections officer killed or disabled in the line of duty, enroll at an approved two-year or four-year college in Illinois, and be a U.S. citizen or permanent resident.

This section of the Web page goes over the eligibility requirements for this grant for dependents of correctional officers who were killed or disabled in the line of duty. If you meet the qualifications listed, check under How to Apply to find out where to obtain application materials.

Grant for Dependants of Police or Fire Officers

Sponsor: Illinois Student Assistance Commission

Web Site: http://www.isac1.org/ilaid/specgt.html#pofosgp

Amount of Scholarship: not given

Number of Awards: not given

Deadline: not given

Education Level: high school seniors and college undergraduates

Eligibility: Applicant must be the spouse or child of an Illinois police or fire officer killed or disabled in the line of duty, enroll at an approved two-year or four-year college in Illinois, and be a U.S. citizen or permanent resident.

This section of the Web page goes over the eligibility requirements for this grant for dependants of police and fire officers who are killed or disabled in the line of duty. If you meet the qualifications, check under How to Apply to find out where to obtain application materials.

Law Enforcement Officers' Dependants Scholarship

Sponsor: Arkansas Department of Higher Education

Web Site: http://www.adhe.arknet.edu/finance/lawenforcement.html

Amount of Scholarship: full tuition (renewable for four years)

Number of Awards: not given

Deadline: not given

Education Level: high school seniors, college undergraduates, and graduate students

Eligibility: Applicant must be the dependant of a law enforcement officer or other state employee who was killed or permanently disabled in the line of duty and who was a resident of Arkansas, and enroll as a full-time student at a state-supported college or university.

This Web page lists all of the state employees whose dependants are eligible to apply for a scholarship if they are killed or disabled in the line of duty. This list includes not only law enforcement officers and firefighters, but also certain Highway and Transportation Department employees, state forestry and park employees, and public school teachers. The page also provides details on where the award may be used and how to qualify as a dependant child or spouse. Obtain an application by calling the toll-free phone number given at the bottom of the page.

Law Enforcement Personnel Dependants Grant

Sponsor: Georgia Student Finance Commission

Web Site: http://www.hope.gsfc.org

Amount of Scholarship: $2,000

Number of Awards: 35

Deadline: last day of registration for the school term

Education Level: high school seniors and college undergraduates

Eligibility: Applicant must be the dependant child of a Georgia law enforcement officer, firefighter, or prison guard who was permanently disabled or killed in the line of duty, enroll as a full-time student at an eligible college or technical institute in Georgia, be a Georgia resident, and be a U.S. citizen or permanent resident.

To find information about this grant, click State Grants in the bar at the top of the page, then click the Program Information link, and finally click the name of the grant in the list that opens. There you'll find a rundown of the eligibility requirements and application requirements. Contact the address or phone number at the bottom of the Web page to order application materials.

Memorial Scholarship for Families of Deceased Police Officers and Firefighters

Sponsor: New York State Higher Education Services Corporation
Web Site: http://www.hesc.com/memorial.html
Amount of Scholarship: up to full tuition (renewable for four years)
Number of Awards: not given
Deadline: May 1
Education Level: high school seniors and college undergraduates
Eligibility: Applicant must be the child or spouse of a New York police officer, firefighter, or volunteer firefighter who was killed in the line of duty, enroll as a full-time student at an approved college in New York state, and be a New York resident.

This scholarship is given in addition to the $450 grant received through the Regents Award for Child of Correction Officer program, described later in this section. The Web page tells you what the eligibility requirements are and how to apply for the scholarship. You can obtain any forms you need by contacting the mailing address or toll-free phone number at the bottom of the Web page.

Ohio Safety Officers College Memorial Scholarship

Sponsor: Ohio Board of Regents
Web Site: http://www.regents.state.oh.us/sgs/sgsprogs.html
Amount of Scholarship: up to full tuition
Number of Awards: not given
Deadline: not given
Education Level: high school seniors, college undergraduates, and graduate students
Eligibility: Applicant must be the child or spouse of an Ohio police officer, firefighter, or other safety officer who was killed in the line of duty and enroll at a participating postsecondary institution in Ohio.

To find a description of this scholarship, scroll down the Web page until you see the scholarship's name. This brief paragraph tells you what the eligibility requirements are and where you can obtain application forms. If you have further questions, return to the top of the Web page to find a toll-free phone number that you can call.

Postsecondary Educational Gratuity

Sponsor: Pennsylvania Higher Education Assistance Agency
Web Site: http://www.pheaa.org/students/s5.html
Amount of Scholarship: full tuition
Number of Awards: not given
Deadline: not given
Education Level: high school seniors and college undergraduates

Eligibility: Applicant must be the child of a police officer, firefighter, rescue or ambulance squad member, correction employee, or National Guard member who died in the line of duty; enroll at a publicly funded two-year or four-year college in Pennsylvania; be younger than the age of 25; and be a Pennsylvania resident.

This Web page goes over the eligibility requirements for this grant for children of Pennsylvania public safety officers who died in the line of duty. If you qualify and have not already received an application form, you can request an application by contacting the address or phone number listed at the bottom of the Web page.

Public Safety Memorial Grant

Sponsor: Georgia Student Finance Commission
Web Site: http://www.hope.gsfc.org
Amount of Scholarship: full tuition
Number of Awards: 35
Deadline: last day of registration for the school term
Education Level: high school seniors and college undergraduates
Eligibility: Applicant must be the dependant child of a Georgia public safety officer who was permanently disabled or killed in the line of duty; enroll as a full-time student at an eligible college or technical institute in Georgia; be a Georgia resident; and be a U.S. citizen or permanent resident.

To find information about this grant, click State Grants in the bar at the top of the page, then click the Program Information link, and finally click the name of the grant in the list that opens. There you'll find a rundown of the eli-gibility requirements and application requirements. Check the list of kinds of public safety officers whose children are eligible for the grant to make certain that you qualify. Contact the address or phone number at the bottom of the Web page to obtain application materials.

Public Service Survivor Grant

Sponsor: Missouri Department of Higher Education
Web Site: http://www.mocbhe.gov/mostars/scholar2.htm#Survivor
Amount of Scholarship: up to full tuition
Number of Awards: not given
Deadline: none
Education Level: high school seniors and college undergraduates
Eligibility: Applicant must be the child or spouse of a Missouri public safety officer or Department of Transportation employee who was killed or permanently disabled in the line of duty, enroll as a full-time student at a participating Missouri college, not pursue a degree in theology or divinity, be a Missouri resident, and be a U.S. citizen or permanent resident.

Here you will find a list of the eligibility requirements that you must meet to qualify for this grant. The Web page also tells you how much grant money you can receive under the program and provides a toll-free phone number that you can call to request an application form. Although there is no deadline for this program, you should apply early before funds run out.

Regents Award for Child of Correction Officer

Sponsor: New York State Higher Education Services Corporation

Web Site: http://www.hesc.com/ra.html
Amount of Scholarship: $450 (renewable for four years)
Number of Awards: not given
Deadline: May 1
Education Level: high school seniors and college undergraduates
Eligibility: Applicant must be the child of a correction officer who was killed while serving at a New York state correctional facility, enroll as a full-time student at an approved college in New York state, and be a New York resident.

The Web page for this grant program tells you what the eligibility requirements are and what forms you need to submit to apply. Obtain any forms you need by contacting the mailing address or toll-free phone number given at the bottom of the Web page.

Safety Officers' Survivor Grant

Sponsor: Minnesota Higher Education Services Office
Web Site: http://www.mheso.state.mn.us
Amount of Scholarship: up to full tuition
Number of Awards: not given
Deadline: not given
Education Level: high school seniors and college undergraduates
Eligibility: Applicant must be the dependant child or spouse of a Minnesota public safety officer killed in the line of duty on or after January 1, 1973; enroll as a full-time student at a two-year or four-year college in Minnesota; and not already have a bachelor's degree or have completed four years of college coursework.

To find information about this grant, click the Students & Parents link, then the Grants link, then the name of the grant. There you'll find information about this grant program for surviving dependents of Minnesota public safety officers, including the eligibility requirements and the amount of the grant. If you want to receive a grant, you must follow the application process described on the Web site; you don't actually have to submit an application form.

Survivor Tuition Benefits

Sponsor: New Jersey Higher Education Student Assistance Authority
Web Site: http://www.state.nj.us/treasury/osa/scholar/survivor_eligiblity.html
Amount of Scholarship: up to full tuition
Number of Awards: not given
Deadline: October 1 and March 1
Education Level: high school seniors and college undergraduates
Eligibility: Applicant must be the spouse or child of a New Jersey emergency service employee or law enforcement officer killed in the line of duty, enroll at an approved two-year or four-year college in New Jersey, and be a New Jersey resident.

This Web page describes the requirements for qualifying for this benefits program for dependents of New Jersey public safety officers killed in the line of duty. The Amounts and Deadline links at the top of the page provide additional information about the amount of the grant and the application deadline. To receive more information and application instructions, click the Contact Us button on the left-hand side of the page and contact the appropriate e-mail address, mailing address, or phone number.

Utah Highway Patrol Association Scholarship

Sponsor: Utah Highway Patrol Association
Web Site: http://www.uhp.state.ut.us/uhpa/scholarships.html
Amount of Scholarship: $500 (renewable)

Number of Awards: not given
Deadline: April 30
Education Level: high school seniors and college undergraduates
Eligibility: Applicant must be the child of a member of the Utah Highway Patrol Association, enroll as a full-time student at a four-year college in Utah, have a minimum 3.0 GPA, and be a Utah resident.

The eligibility requirements for this scholarship are listed under the Rules for Participation section of the Web page. The Rules for the Awarding of a Scholarship describes the conditions of accepting a scholarship and other important details. A downloadable copy of the application form in PDF format is linked at the top of the page.

W. H. "Howie" McClennan Scholarship

Sponsor: International Association of Fire Fighters
Web Site: http://www.iaff.org/iaff/Education_Resources/w_h_howie.html
Amount of Scholarship: not given
Number of Awards: not given
Deadline: February 1
Education Level: high school seniors and college undergraduates
Eligibility: Applicant must be the child of a firefighter killed in the line of duty, enroll at an accredited two-year or four-year college, have a minimum 2.0 GPA, and demonstrate financial need.

This Web page gives all the facts about this scholarship program for children of firefighters who were killed in the line of duty. You'll find out what the purpose of the scholarship program is, how the application process works, what materials you'll need to include in your application package, where and for what pur-

pose you can use the scholarship money, and what the selection criteria are. At the bottom of the page, you'll find links to the scholarship rules (which repeats the information given on the Web page, but in printer-friendly form) and the application form, both in PDF format.

Also see the following scholarships:

- Children of Deceased Military and State Police Personnel Scholarship: Chapter 14, "Military Personnel and Veterans" section
- Educational Benefits for Children of Deceased Veterans and Others: Chapter 14, "Military Personnel and Veterans" section
- Edward T. Conroy Memorial Scholarship: Chapter 14, "Military Personnel and Veterans" section

Unions and Professional Associations

AFSCME Council 62 Scholarship

Sponsor: American Federation of State, County, and Municipal Employees (AFSCME) Council 62
Web Site: http://www.afscmeindiana.org/scholars.htm
Amount of Scholarship: $500
Number of Awards: 6
Deadline: April 15
Education Level: high school seniors
Eligibility: Applicant must be the child or grandchild of an AFSCME member in good standing, enroll at an accredited two-year or four-year college, and have a minimum 2.0 GPA.

This Web page provides a brief overview of the scholarship program for the children of public employees in Indiana, including a list of eligibility requirements and selection criteria. At the bottom of the page you'll find a link to the application form in PDF format that you can print, fill out, and mail in.

AFSCME Family Scholarship

Sponsor: American Federation of State, County, and Municipal Employees (AFSCME)
Web Site: http://www.afscme.org/about/scholarf.htm
Amount of Scholarship: $2,000 (renewable for four years)
Number of Awards: 10
Deadline: December 31
Education Level: high school seniors
Eligibility: Applicant must be the dependent child or grandchild of a member of AFSCME, and enroll as a full-time student at an accredited four-year college.

The first part of this Web page describes the purpose of the scholarship program, important information if you decide to apply. Scroll down to find details about eligibility, selection criteria, and application instructions. Links to all three of the required application forms are provided at the bottom of the page. You will need to print these forms from within your Web browser, and then complete them and mail them to the address provided.

AFSCME Union Plus Credit Card Scholarship

Sponsor: American Federation of State, County, and Municipal Employees (AFSCME) Advantage
Web Site: http://www.afscme.org/about/aa-scho.htm
Amount of Scholarship: $500 to $4,000
Number of Awards: not given
Deadline: January 31

Education Level: high school seniors and college undergraduates
Eligibility: Applicant must be a member of AFSCME or the spouse or dependent child of a member and enroll at an accredited college, community college, or trade or technical school.

You will find all the facts you need to know about the scholarship on the Web page, including who is eligible, how to apply, when applications are due, and the criteria used to select award recipients. A downloadable copy of the application form in PDF format is linked at the top of the Web page, and a toll-free phone number that you can call with questions is provided at the bottom.

AISE Steel Foundation Scholarships

Sponsor: Association of Iron and Steel Engineers (AISE) Steel Foundation
Web Site: http://www.steelfoundation.org/scholarships/scholrequire.htm
Amount of Scholarship: $500 to $3,000 (renewable for four years)
Number of Awards: not given
Deadline: not given
Education Level: high school seniors and college undergraduates
Eligibility: Applicant must be the child of a member of AISE, enroll at an accredited four-year college and be a U.S. or Canadian citizen or permanent resident.

The AISE Steel Foundation awards 13 different scholarships each year under its scholarship program for children of members. The Web page provides general information about the scholarship program, including contact information for questions about any of the scholarships. Click the links at the top of the page to learn the specifics about each award given out under the program, including eligibility requirements (if any) and instructions for obtaining application forms. One award, the National Merit Scholarship, requires that students take the PSAT and become National Merit semifinalists to qualify. Some scholarships have residency requirements. For example, one award—the David H. Samson Canadian Scholarship—is earmarked solely for Canadian students. Others are restricted to children of members of particular districts of AISE, such as the Canton District Section Scholarship, the Chicago District Section Scholarship, the Ohio Valley District Section Scholarship, and the Pittsburgh District Section Scholarship. Many awards require or prefer that applicants study engineering, the sciences, metallurgy, or another field related to iron and steel production while in college. Four scholarships are restricted to use at specific colleges: Carnegie Mellon University; the Rose Hulman Institute of Technology; the Massachusetts Institute of Technology; and the University of Pennsylvania. You must apply for each scholarship for which you are eligible separately, according to the instructions given under the scholarship's description on the Web page. The application forms for some, but not all, of the awards are available for downloading from the Web site; just follow the links under the names of the scholarships to find them.

APWU Vocational Scholarship

Sponsor: American Postal Workers Union (APWU)
Web Site: http://www.apwu.org/vocational.htm
Amount of Scholarship: $1,000 (renewable for three years)
Number of Awards: not given
Deadline: March 1
Education Level: high school seniors

Eligibility: Applicant must be the child or grandchild of an active or deceased member of APWU and attend an accredited vocational school or a vocational program at a community college.

This Web page describes the eligibility requirements and application procedures for the scholarship, and provides a checklist of documents that must be included with the application form. To obtain more information and an application form, contact the phone number or mailing address listed at the bottom of the Web page.

Arizona Chapter Dependent Scholarship

Sponsor: American Society of Travel Agents (ASTA) Scholarship Foundation
Web Site: http://www.astanet.com/www/asta/pub/car/scholarships1.htmlx
Amount of Scholarship: $1,500
Number of Awards: 1
Deadline: July 28
Education Level: community college sophomores and college juniors and seniors
Eligibility: Applicant must be the dependant of an ASTA Arizona Chapter Active or Active Associate member or an employee of an Arizona ASTA member agency, and enroll at a two-year or four-year college in Arizona.

Scroll to the Non-Travel Majors section at the very bottom of the Web page to find information about this scholarship, which is intended for dependants of the Arizona Chapter of ASTA. There you will see a brief description of the scholarship and a list of materials that must be included in the application package. Go down to the bottom of the Web page and click the Apply Now! link if you would like to apply for the scholarship. This opens an application form that you can fill out inside your

Web browser and then print out with your answers. Be sure to check the box beside Arizona Dependent to indicate which scholarship you are applying for.

COMTO National Scholarships

Sponsor: Conference of Minority Transportation Officials (COMTO)
Web Site: http://www.comto.com/scholar.htm
Amount of Scholarship: $1,500
Number of Awards: 2
Deadline: April 28
Education Level: high school seniors and college undergraduates
Eligibility: Applicant must be the child of a COMTO member, be an active COMTO member for at least one year, or be a student of a transportation-related discipline.

Two scholarships are awarded under this program. One is reserved for a COMTO member who is currently enrolled or has been accepted to college. The other is reserved for the child of a COMTO member or for a student who plans to study a transportation-related field. The Web page doesn't tell you much about the scholarship program, but you will find contact information for ordering application forms.

CTA Scholarships

Sponsor: California Teachers Association (CTA)
Web Site: http://www.cta.org/inside_cta/training/hr_scholarship.html
Amount of Scholarship: $2,000
Number of Awards: 33
Deadline: February 15
Education Level: high school seniors, college undergraduates, and graduate students
Eligibility: Applicant must be the dependent child of an active, retired, or deceased member

of CTA, an active member of CTA, or a member of the Student California Teachers Association (SCTA) and enroll at an accredited institution of higher education.

Three different scholarships are given out under this program. The largest is the CTA Scholarship for Dependent Children, which gives 25 $2,000 awards to dependents of CTA members. Five $2,000 scholarships are available for members of CTA. Finally, three L. Gordon Bittle Memorial Scholarships, also worth $2,000 each, go to members of SCTA who plan to pursue a career in public education. For each award you'll find a list of the eligibility requirements and a list of past recipients on the Web page. Go to the bottom of the page to find general instructions for obtaining application forms for any of these scholarships.

E. C. Halbeck Memorial Scholarship

Sponsor: American Postal Workers Union (APWU)
Web Site: http://www.apwu.org/hallbeckrules.htm
Amount of Scholarship: $1,000 (renewable for four years)
Number of Awards: 5
Deadline: March 1
Education Level: high school seniors
Eligibility: Applicant must be the child or grandchild of an active or deceased member of APWU and enroll as a full-time student at an accredited two-year or four-year college.

The Web page first provides a rundown of the rules and regulations governing the scholarship program, which will tell you if you are eligible to apply and how to submit an application. Following that is a checklist of all materials that must be included in the application package. Five different awards are given out, one to an applicant in each region of the country; the regions are listed on the Web page. Finally, you will find out what the judging criteria are and whom to contact for more information and to request application forms. Applications are not available on the Web site.

GCSAA Legacy Award

Sponsor: Golf Course Superintendents Association of America (GCSAA) Foundation and Novartis
Web Site: http://www.gcsaa.org/career/pursuing/scholarships/legpro.html
Amount of Scholarship: $1,500
Number of Awards: 10
Deadline: April 15
Education Level: high school seniors, college undergraduates, and graduate students
Eligibility: Applicant must be the child or grandchild of a currently active or deceased GCSAA member for five or more years, enroll as a full-time student at an accredited institution of higher education, and study a field unrelated to golf course management.

On this Web page you'll find a brief overview of the scholarship program, a list of eligibility requirements, a list of selection criteria, and instructions for applying. Follow the Legacy Award Application link at the top of the page to open an application form that you can fill out inside your Web browser and then print with all of your answers already typed in; you can't submit this form electronically, though. A link to a list of past winners, along with their biographies, is also provided at the top of the page.

Georgia Water and Pollution Control Association Scholarships

Sponsor: Georgia Water and Pollution Control Association, Inc. (GW&PCA)

Web Site: http://www.gwpca.org/scholarship.htm
Amount of Scholarship: $1,000 to $1,500
Number of Awards: 5
Deadline: June 15
Education Level: high school seniors, college undergraduates, and graduate students
Eligibility: Applicant must be a member or the child of a member of GW&PCA or study environmental engineering, water resources, water quality, or a related field, and enroll at an accredited two-year college, four-year college, graduate school, or technical training school.

GW&PCA maintains three different scholarships, all of which are described in detail on this Web page. You'll find a brief overview of the scholarship program and the selection criteria for all scholarships at the top of the page. Scroll down to read about each of the scholarships available, including eligibility requirements for each. The General Scholarship of $1,000 can be used at any institute of higher education; three of these awards are given out each year. The William J. Greene, Jr. Scholarship of $1,500 is restricted to use at Georgia Institute of Technology. The Philip R. Karr, III Scholarship is the only award given under this program that does not require applicants to be related to a member of GW&PCA; this $1,500 scholarship goes to students of environmental engineering, water resources, or a related field. (Note that the other scholarships don't specify a field of study.) At the bottom of the Web page, you'll find a printable text application form for all three scholarships. Be sure to check the names of the scholarships for which you are applying.

IFPTE Scholarship

Sponsor: International Federation of Professional and Technical Engineers (IFPTE)

Web Site: http://www.ifpte.org/scholarship.html
Amount of Scholarship: $1,500
Number of Awards: 3
Deadline: March 14
Education Level: high school seniors
Eligibility: Applicant must be the child or grandchild of an IFPTE member and enroll at an accredited two-year or four-year college.

Under this program, three awards are given out each year: one to a relative of a federal sector employee; one to a relative of a private sector employee; and one to a relative of a public sector employee. The Web page provides a lot of general information about the scholarship, including the eligibility requirements, application requirements, selection criteria, and details about the application process. Click the Official Entry Form link at the top of the page to find a printable text copy of the application form.

Jerry Clark Memorial Scholarship

Sponsor: American Federation of State, County, and Municipal Employees (AFSCME)
Web Site: http://www.afscme.org/about/scholarj.htm
Amount of Scholarship: $10,000 (awarded over two years)
Number of Awards: 1
Deadline: July 1
Education Level: college sophomores
Eligibility: Applicant must be the dependent of an AFSCME member, be a full-time student, major in political science, and have a minimum 3.0 GPA.

Check under the Scholarship Information section of the Web page for the eligibility requirements for this award. The Application

Instructions section describes how to prepare and submit an application package. Print out both required application forms by following the links at the bottom of the page.

NASE Scholarships

Sponsor: National Association for the Self-Employed (NASE)
Web Site: http://www.nase.org/2000benefits/personal/nase_scholarship_program.htm
Amount of Scholarship: $4,000 to $12,000
Number of Awards: 23
Deadline: April 28 (Future Entrepreneur of the Year Scholarship) and May 29 (General Scholarships)
Education Level: high school seniors and college undergraduates
Eligibility: Applicant must be the dependent child of a NASE member in good standing, enroll as a full-time student at a two-year or four-year college, have a minimum 3.0 GPA, and be between the ages of 16 and 24.

This scholarship program awards two different scholarships. Twenty-two General Scholarships of $4,000 each are available to children of NASE members. The Future Entrepreneur of the Year Scholarship provides one award of $12,000 to a child of a NASE member who aspires to own his or her own business; learn more about the history and objectives of this award by clicking the Future Entrepreneur of the Year Scholarship link on the Web page. At the bottom of this page is a link to the application form for both scholarships in PDF format, which you can download and print out. The application also provides a lot more information about both scholarships, including details of eligibility, selection criteria, and application procedures.

Richard F. Walsh/Alfred W. DiTolla/Harold P. Spivak Scholarship

Sponsor: International Alliance of Theatrical Stage Employees and Moving Picture Technicians, Artists, and Allied Crafts of the United States and Canada (IATSE)
Web Site: http://www.iatse.lm.com/schol.html
Amount of Scholarship: $1,750 (renewable for four years)
Number of Awards: 2
Deadline: December 31
Education Level: high school seniors
Eligibility: Applicant must be the child of a member of IATSE and enroll at an accredited four-year college.

First, click the Information About the Scholarship link to read the details of this scholarship program. This page lists the eligibility requirements, describes the awards, and tells you how to submit an application package. Return to the main page and click the Application for the Scholarship link to find an electronic form that you can submit over the Internet to request an application form (this is not the actual application form). There is also a link to a list of past scholarship winners, including biographies of these winners. Studying these can help you figure out what kinds of applicants the scholarship sponsor is looking for.

Robert G. Porter Scholarship

Sponsor: American Federation of Teachers (AFT)
Web Site: http://www.aft.org/scholarships/porter/index.html
Amount of Scholarship: $8,000 (awarded over four years)

Number of Awards: not given
Deadline: March 31
Education Level: high school seniors
Eligibility: Applicant must be the dependent of a member of AFT and plan to pursue a career in education, health care, government service, or labor.

This Web page describes the history and purpose of the scholarship program. Download an application form by following the link at the bottom of the page. Be sure to select the $8,000 Scholarship application. The application form also describes the eligibility requirements in more detail.

UTD Scholarship

Sponsor: United Teachers of Dade (UTD)
Web Site: http://www.utofd.com/utdschol.html
Amount of Scholarship: $500 (renewable for four years)
Number of Awards: 6
Deadline: May 30
Education Level: high school seniors
Eligibility: Applicant must be the child of a UTD member of at least three years who contributes the major share of the family income, and graduate from a Florida public high school.

Six awards are given out under this scholarship program: four awards for the children of teachers; one award for the child of an office employee; and one award for the child of a paraprofessional. To learn more about the scholarship, click the UTD Scholarship Policy link at the bottom of the page, which provides details about eligibility requirements, selection criteria, and renewal conditions. Access printable text copies of the required application form and confidential reference form by following the appropriate links at the bottom of the page.

Also see the following scholarships:

- Martin Luther King, Jr. Memorial Scholarship: Chapter 6, "Education" section
- NSA Scholarships: Chapter 6, "Accounting" section
- School Food Service Foundation Scholarships: Chapter 14, "Employer and Profession" section

Other

GreenPoint Achievers Scholarship

Sponsor: GreenPoint Foundation and Citizens' Scholarship Foundation of America, Inc.
Web Site: http://www.greenpoint.com/internet/community/scholar.cfm
Amount of Scholarship: $2,500 (renewable for four years)

Number of Awards: not given
Deadline: March 1
Education Level: high school seniors
Eligibility: Applicant must be a depositor or the dependent of a depositor at GreenPoint Bank; enroll as a full-time student at an accredited two-year college, four-year college, or vocational school; have a minimum 3.0 GPA; and have a minimum SAT I score of 1000.

This Web page gives a thorough overview of the scholarship for depositors at GreenPoint Bank in Minnesota and their dependents. If you fit this description, be sure to read the entire page to learn about eligibility requirements, selection criteria, the amount of the awards, and how scholarships may be used. At the bottom of the page you'll find a mailing address and a phone number that you can contact for more information and to request an application form. GreenPoint Bank is not the only bank that offers scholarships to members and their dependents. Check with your parents' banks, credit unions, insurance companies, and other companies that provide financial services to find out if they offer similar scholarship programs.

RESIDENCE-SPECIFIC SCHOLARSHIPS

This chapter lists regional scholarships, which require applicants to live in a particular region, state, county, or city. You will also find need-based grants and merit awards offered by state governments. Only state scholarship programs that publish information on the Web are listed here, but all states give some form of financial aid to its residents. Take advantage of these programs, as they represent a large chunk of available financial aid dollars. Usually, all you need to do to apply for state financial aid is to submit the Free Application for Federal Student Aid (FAFSA); Chapter 1 of this book tells you how. Some states require applicants to file additional forms, though, so pay attention to the application instructions on the Web site and follow them exactly when applying for aid from your state.

Another good source of state aid is from the public college and university system in your state. If you attend one of these schools, you will qualify for reduced in-state tuition, and you may also be eligible for merit scholarships offered only to state residents. Look up the names of all the state colleges and universities you are considering attending in Chapter 16 to find the addresses of their online financial aid offices, where you can learn more about such awards.

Alabama

Congressional Black Caucus Spouses Scholarships

Sponsor: Congressional Black Caucus (CBC) Spouses

Web Site: http://www.cbcfnet.org/programs/#Spouses
Amount of Scholarship: not given
Number of Awards: not given
Deadline: September 15 and May 15
Education Level: high school seniors, college undergraduates, and graduate students
Eligibility: Applicant must reside in or attend school in a Congressional district represented by an African-American member of Congress, enroll as a full-time student at an accredited institution of higher education, and have a minimum 2.5 GPA.

Two scholarships are available under this program. The first is a general scholarship for all students who meet the eligibility requirements listed above. The second is the CBC Spouses Cheerios Brand Health Initiative Scholarship, which goes to students who meet those requirements and are studying a health-related field; the Web page tells you what the additional requirements for this second scholarship are. If you would like to apply for either scholarship, print out the application from the Web site. You must submit the application directly to the Local Scholarship Selection Committee for the Congressional district where you live; a list of all the committees with their mailing addresses is linked to the Web page. Note that you don't have to be African-American to be eligible to apply; you only have to live or attend school in a Congressional district served by an African-American representative. At the time of this writing, these districts were located in Alabama, California, the District of Columbia, Florida, Georgia, Illinois, Indiana, Louisiana, Maryland, Michigan, Mississippi, Missouri, New Jersey, New York, North Carolina, Ohio, Pennsylvania, South Carolina, Tennessee, Texas,

Virginia, and the Virgin Islands. But be sure to check the current list before applying, as it may change in the next election.

Also see the following scholarships:

- "Duke" Demay Jazz Scholarship: Chapter 8, "Performing Arts" section
- Mercedes-Benz U.S. International/SAE Scholarship: Chapter 6, "Engineering" section
- Sidney B. Meadows Scholarship: Chapter 6, "Horticulture" section
- State Funeral Director Associations Scholarships: Chapter 6, "Funeral Service and Mortuary Science" section

Alaska

University of Alaska Scholars Award

Sponsor: University of Alaska Statewide System
Web Site: http://www.alaska.edu/scholars/index.html
Amount of Scholarship: full tuition (awarded for four years)
Number of Awards: not given
Deadline: not given
Education Level: high school juniors
Eligibility: Applicant must attend a participating high school in Alaska, rank in the top 10 percent of the high school class, and enroll as a full-time student at a University of Alaska campus.

This scholarship program encourages Alaska high school students to attend college in-state. Scroll to the bottom of the Web page to find links to additional information about the program. First, click the Program Booklet link to read about the purpose of the award, the eli-

gibility requirements, the conditions for maintaining the scholarship, how to get nominated, and other details. The Questions & Answers page answers the most frequently asked questions about the program. You can't apply directly for the scholarship. Instead, your high school must select nominees according to the criteria set by each school. If you are nominated, you'll receive a Reservation Form that you must complete and return to hold your scholarship. If you have remaining questions about this program, click the Email Us or Call Us links at the bottom of the Web page to contact the scholarship sponsor directly.

Also see the following scholarships:

- Alaska Library Association Scholarship: Chapter 7, "Library and Information Science" section
- Arthur N. Wilson, MD Scholarship: Chapter 7, "Medicine" section
- GSBA, Pride, and INBA Scholarships: Chapter 9, "Gay and Lesbian" section

Arizona

See the following scholarships:

- Arizona Chapter Dependent Scholarship: Chapter 14, "Unions and Professional Associations" section
- Bank of America ADA Abilities Scholarship: Chapter 10, "Any Disability" section
- Burlington Northern Santa Fe Foundation Scholarship: Chapter 9, "Native American" section
- Hispanic American Commitment to Education Resources Scholarship: Chapter 9, "Hispanic" section
- HSF Community College Transfer Scholarship: Chapter 9, "Hispanic" section

- Regional EAGLE Scholarship: Chapter 9, "Gay and Lesbian" section
- State Funeral Director Associations Scholarships: Chapter 6, "Funeral Service and Mortuary Science" section

Arkansas

Arkansas Academic Challenge Scholarship

Sponsor: Arkansas Department of Higher Education
Web Site: http://www.adhe.arknet.edu/finance/archalangescholar.html
Amount of Scholarship: $2,500 (renewable for four years)
Number of Awards: not given
Deadline: October 1
Education Level: high school seniors
Eligibility: Applicant must attend high school in Arkansas, meet minimum academic and financial need standards, enroll as a full-time student at a public four-year college in Arkansas, and be a U.S. citizen or permanent resident.

All Arkansas high school students are encouraged to apply for this scholarship. You won't receive a scholarship unless you meet the academic and financial need prerequisites listed on the Web page, though. If you decide to apply, you can get an application form from your high school guidance office. The Web page tells what documents you must submit with the application to prove your eligibility.

Arkansas Governor's Scholars

Sponsor: Arkansas Department of Higher Education

Web Site: http://www.adhe.arknet.edu/finance/governorscholars.html
Amount of Scholarship: $4,000 to full tuition (renewable for four years)
Number of Awards: 100
Deadline: March 1
Education Level: high school seniors
Eligibility: Applicant must attend high school in Arkansas, have a minimum 3.6 GPA or have minimum ACT score of 27 or have a minimum SAT I score of 1100, and enroll as a full-time student at an approved college in Arkansas.

This scholarship program encourages outstanding Arkansas high school students to continue their education in the state. As described on the Web page, the scholarship is reserved for students with the highest academic qualifications. Actually, two scholarships are awarded under the program. The Governor's Scholar award of $4,000 per year goes to students who meet the academic requirements listed above. Those students with exceptional academic qualifications—a minimum ACT score of 32 or a minimum SAT I score of 1410—receive the Governor's Distinguished Scholars award, which pays full tuition and room and board at any Arkansas college. You apply for both scholarships together. You can get application forms from your high school's guidance office.

Arkansas Health Education Grant

Sponsor: Arkansas Department of Higher Education
Web Site: http://www.adhe.arknet.edu/finance/ahegp.htm
Amount of Scholarship: $5,000
Number of Awards: not given
Deadline: not given
Education Level: medical school students
Eligibility: Applicant must be an Arkansas resident, enroll as a full-time student in an eligible

professional medical program at a participating out-of-state university, and be a U.S. citizen or permanent resident.

This program supports Arkansas residents studying medicine who want to attend school out-of-state. A list of eligible fields of study is provided on the main page. To learn more, follow the Information link. The Rules and Regulations page describes the eligibility requirements for the grant program. The Participating Institutions page gives a list of eligible universities for each medical field. You will also find links to the application form and to the Affidavit for Arkansas Residency Certification that you must submit with your application; both are in PDF format.

Arkansas Student Assistance Grant

Sponsor: Arkansas Department of Higher Education
Web Site: http://www.adhe.arknet.edu/finance/asag.html
Amount of Scholarship: $100 to $600
Number of Awards: not given
Deadline: not given
Education Level: high school seniors, college undergraduates, and graduate students
Eligibility: Applicant must be an Arkansas resident and be a full-time student.

This grant goes only to the applicants with the highest financial need. Filing the FAFSA automatically puts you in consideration for the grant. The colleges themselves allocate the grant funds, so see a financial aid officer at your school if you have further questions.

Second Effort Scholarship

Sponsor: Arkansas Department of Higher Education

Web Site: http://www.adhe.arknet.edu/finance/secondeffort.html
Amount of Scholarship: $1,000 (renewable for four years)
Number of Awards: 10
Deadline: not given
Education Level: GED recipients
Eligibility: Applicant must be an Arkansas resident, not have graduated from high school, take the Arkansas High School Diploma test, enroll at a four-year college, and be either at least 18 years old or a member of a high school class that has graduated.

As explained on the Web page, this scholarship program was established to encourage those students who successfully pass the Arkansas High School Diploma test to enroll in a bachelor's degree program. The scholarship is automatically awarded to the students who achieved the 10 highest scores on the test during the previous year. You don't have to apply for it. The Web page provides the details about the scholarship, including eligibility requirements and the conditions for renewing the scholarship.

Student Advantage Scholarship

Sponsor: Arkansas Student Loan Authority
Web Site: http://www.asla.state.ar.us/giveaway_old/index.html
Amount of Scholarship: $250
Number of Awards: 10
Deadline: April 15
Education Level: high school seniors and college undergraduates
Eligibility: Applicant must either be an Arkansas resident or an out-of-state student attending college in Arkansas, and enroll at a two-year college, four-year college, or technical or trade school.

This contest awards 10 scholarships to applicants who are randomly drawn from the entire pool of entries, so you should definitely enter if you meet the eligibility requirements listed on the Web page. Entering the contest is easy; simply fill out and submit the online Entry Form linked to the contest's Web page.

Also see the following scholarships:

- Arkansas Environmental Federation Scholarship: Chapter 6, "Environmental Studies" section
- ASBA Educational Foundation Scholarship: Chapter 14, "Employer and Profession" section
- Bank of America ADA Abilities Scholarship: Chapter 10, "Any Disability" section
- Freshman/Sophomore Minority Grant: Chapter 6, "Education" section
- Law Enforcement Officers' Dependents Scholarship: Chapter 14, "Public Safety Officers" section
- Minority Masters Fellowship: Chapter 9, "All Minorities" section
- Minority Teachers Scholarship: Chapter 6, "Education" section
- Missing in Action/Killed in Action Dependents' Scholarship: Chapter 14, "Military Personnel and Veterans" section
- Sidney B. Meadows Scholarship: Chapter 6, "Horticulture" section
- State Funeral Director Associations Scholarships: Chapter 6, "Funeral Service and Mortuary Science" section

California

California Masonic Foundation Scholarships

Sponsor: California Masonic Foundation (CMF)
Web Site: http://www.mhcsf.org/foundation

Amount of Scholarship: $500 to $10,000
Number of Awards: not given
Deadline: March 15
Education Level: high school seniors
Eligibility: Applicant must be a California resident, enroll as a full-time student at an accredited two-year or four-year college, have a minimum 3.0 GPA, demonstrate financial need, and be a U.S. citizen.

This scholarship program gives out 40 different scholarships to graduating high school students in California. First, download the Scholarship Manual in PDF format by clicking the link at the bottom of the Web page. This manual lists all scholarships awarded by Masonic-related organizations of California, including their specific eligibility requirements. The Frequently Asked Questions page answers the most common questions about the scholarship program, so it would be a good second stop. Then go to the CMF Scholarship Application page to find a copy of the application form and instructions for completing it. When you submit an application, you will automatically be considered for all scholarships for which you qualify. Applications for the next school year are only available on the Web site after September 1. You will also find a list of the previous year's winners on the site.

Hispanic Education Endowment Fund General Scholarships

Sponsor: Hispanic Education Endowment Fund of the Orange County Community Foundation
Web Site: http://www.oc-communityfoundation.org/HEEFoptions.html
Amount of Scholarship: $500 to $2,500
Number of Awards: 103
Deadline: February 22

Education Level: high school juniors and seniors, college undergraduates, and law students
Eligibility: Applicant must attend school in Orange County, be Hispanic, and demonstrate financial need.

First, click the General Information Relating to Application link to learn the facts about this scholarship program. Six different scholarships are available under this program; they are listed on the General Information page, along with the eligibility requirements and application instructions for all scholarships. Return to the main page and click the Additional Information Relating to Application link to find more details about each scholarship, including specific requirements, award amounts, and application procedures. One scholarship is for community college students planning to transfer to a four-year degree program, one is reserved for California State University Fullerton students, and one is set aside for law students. The others are general scholarships for high school juniors and seniors. Be sure to only apply for the scholarships for which you are eligible.

MEF Donor-Advised Scholarships

Sponsor: Marin Education Fund (MEF)
Web Site: http://www.mefund.org/donoradv.html
Amount of Scholarship: not given
Number of Awards: not given
Deadline: not given
Education Level: high school seniors and college undergraduates
Eligibility: Applicant must be a resident of Marin or Sonoma County and enroll at a two-year or four-year college.

MEF currently administers six donor-advised scholarships, which you can read about on this Web page. The eligibility requirements and other conditions of each scholarship vary greatly. If you are interested in learning more about any of them or obtaining application forms, click the Contact MEF link to find contact information.

MEF Undergraduate and Fifth Year Teaching Credential Grant

Sponsor: Marin Education Fund (MEF)
Web Site: http://www.mefund.org/undergraduate.html
Amount of Scholarship: $800 to $2,000
Number of Awards: not given
Deadline: not given
Education Level: college undergraduates
Eligibility: Applicant must be a resident of Marin County, enroll in a four-year degree program or a fifth-year teaching credential program, demonstrate financial need, and be a U.S. citizen or permanent resident.

On this Web page, you'll find all the details about the grant program for undergraduates who live in Marin County, California. The page lists the eligibility requirements, selection criteria, and award amounts. If you qualify, click the Contact MEF link at the bottom of the page to request an application. You can also pick up applications at the college choice and financial aid workshops given by MEF; click the Workshops link to learn more about these programs.

Order of the Eastern Star Scholarships

Sponsor: Order of the Eastern Star Grand Chapter of California
Web Site: http://www.oescal.org/index.html
Amount of Scholarship: not given
Number of Awards: not given
Deadline: April 1
Education Level: high school seniors, college undergraduates, and graduate students

Eligibility: Applicant must be a California resident, have a minimum 3.0 GPA, and be a U.S. resident.

To find the scholarship information, click the Scholarships button in the left frame. Two kinds of scholarships are available: academic scholarships for students at colleges, universities, community colleges, and trade schools; and religious scholarships for students at seminaries and theological schools. Both kinds have the same basic eligibility requirements and application instructions, as described on the Web page. Religious scholarships are only awarded to college graduates attending graduate school in California, however; undergraduates aren't eligible. Click the buttons at the top of the page to download PDF versions of the application forms for each scholarship.

Pat Nixon Scholarship

Sponsor: Orange County Federation of Republican Women
Web Site: http://ocfrw.cfrw.org/scholarships.html
Amount of Scholarship: not given
Number of Awards: not given
Deadline: not given
Education Level: college undergraduates and graduate students
Eligibility: Applicant must be a resident of Orange County, be female, be a registered Republican voter, and be at least 25 years old.

This Web page provides some background on the scholarship and lists the eligibility requirements. If you qualify, scroll to the bottom of the page to find an electronic application form, which you can fill out and submit right away.

San Diego County Scholarship

Sponsor: Armed Forces Communications and Electronics Association, San Diego Chapter

Web Site: http://www.afcea-sd.org/education.html
Amount of Scholarship: $2,000 (renewable for four years)
Number of Awards: 1
Deadline: end of April
Education Level: high school seniors and college undergraduates
Eligibility: Applicant must be a resident of San Diego County; attend college in San Diego County; major in computer science, engineering, math, or the natural sciences; and be a U.S. citizen.

This scholarship is briefly described at the top of the Educational Events and Programs Web page. To learn more, follow the link to eligibility criteria and additional information. First, check the eligibility requirements to make certain that you qualify. Under Student Requirements, you'll find a list of all the documents that you must include in the application package. The criteria for selecting scholarship winners and for renewing the scholarship are listed beneath that. If you decide to apply, return to he first page and follow the Applications link. You can then print out a copy of the application form using the Print function of your Web browser.

San Diego Foundation Scholarships

Sponsor: San Diego Foundation
Web Site: http://www.sdcf.org/scholarships
Amount of Scholarship: $500 to $7,500
Number of Awards: 95
Deadline: March 2
Education Level: high school seniors, college undergraduates, and graduate students
Eligibility: Applicant must be a resident of San Diego County; have a grade average of at least a B; enroll as a full-time student at an accredited two-year college, four-year college, gradu-

ate school, or trade school; demonstrate financial need; and be a U.S. citizen or permanent resident.

The first part of this Web page provides a lot of helpful but general information about applying for scholarships and financial aid. Scroll down to the San Diego Foundation's Scholarship Program section to find details about the 12 scholarships offered to San Diego County residents under this program. First, you'll see a list of general eligibility requirements for all scholarships and answers to other commonly asked questions about the program. Following that, you'll find instructions for completing the foundation's common application, which enables you to apply for all of the scholarships for which you are eligible with one form. A list of all the available scholarships follows, noting their eligibility requirements, award amounts, and the number of awards given. Make a note of the scholarships you qualify for, as you must indicate these on the application. You will also find a list of additional scholarships that you can apply for separately; contact the San Diego Foundation for more information about these. While a copy of the common application is provided at the bottom of the page, it appears to be out of date. A safer course would be to call or write the foundation to request the latest application form; contact information is given at the very bottom of the page.

Scholarship Foundation of Santa Barbara Scholarship

Sponsor: Scholarship Foundation of Santa Barbara
Web Site: http://www.sbscholarship.org
Amount of Scholarship: not given
Number of Awards: not given
Deadline: last business day of January
Education Level: high school seniors

Eligibility: Applicant must have attended grades 11 through 12 in Santa Barbara County and graduated from a Santa Barbara County high school; have a minimum 2.0 GPA; and enroll as a full-time student at an approved two-year college, four-year college, or vocational school.

This Web page describes the mission of the scholarship program, which may be helpful in preparing your application. To find out if you are eligible, how recipients are selected, and how to request an application, click the Applicant Info button on the left-hand side of the page. This page also provides information about the foundation's student loan program. The Recipient Info page gives details about renewing your award if you win one.

Veterans Foundation for Monterey County Scholarship

Sponsor: Veterans Foundation for Monterey County
Web Site: http://www.anawalt.com/vf/scholarships.html
Amount of Scholarship: $500
Number of Awards: not given
Deadline: November 15 and March 15
Education Level: high school seniors, college undergraduates, and graduate students
Eligibility: Applicant must be a resident of Monterey County, demonstrate outstanding voluntary service, and be a U.S. citizen or permanent resident.

This scholarship program awards scholarships to Monterey County residents for use at all educational levels, from grade school through university. The Web page describes the eligibility requirements that you must meet to be considered for a scholarship, as well as the selection criteria. You don't have to be related to a veteran to apply for an award, but relatives of veterans are given preference, as are students who attend school in Monterey County. You'll find an electronic version of the application form that you can submit online and a PDF version that you can download and print out linked at the bottom of the Web page.

Virginia Smith Scholarship

Sponsor: Virginia Smith Scholarship Trust and Merced County Board of Education
Web Site: http://www.merced.k12.ca.us/smith/smith.html
Amount of Scholarship: not given
Number of Awards: not given
Deadline: May 1
Education Level: college juniors and seniors and graduate students
Eligibility: Applicant must have attended at least three years at a public high school in Merced, have a minimum 2.8 GPA, enroll as a full-time student at an accredited college or university in California, and demonstrate financial need.

This Web page provides a brief history of the scholarship and a rundown of the eligibility requirements. You can also follow a link to open the application form in PDF format, which provides a lot more details about eligibility, selection criteria, and the awards.

Also see the following scholarships:

- Bank of America ADA Abilities Scholarship: Chapter 10, "Any Disability" section
- Beverage Industry Scholarship: Chapter 14, "Employer and Profession" section
- Burlington Northern Santa Fe Foundation Scholarship: Chapter 9, "Native American" section
- California Farm Bureau Scholarship: Chapter 6, "Agriculture" section
- California-Hawaii Elks Association Scholarship for Vocational Education: Chapter 6,

"Vocational and Technical Education" section
- CAPS Scholarships: Chapter 7, "Medicine" section
- CAR Scholarships: Chapter 6, "Real Estate" section
- Congressional Black Caucus Spouses Scholarships: Chapter 15, "Alabama" section
- CTA Scholarships: Chapter 14, "Unions and Professional Associations" section
- Gloria Fecht Memorial Scholarship: Chapter 8, "Golf" section
- Hispanic American Commitment to Education Resources Scholarship: Chapter 9, "Hispanic" section
- HSF Community College Transfer Scholarship: Chapter 9, "Hispanic" section
- HSF High School Scholarship: Chapter 9, "Hispanic" section
- Joel Garcia Memorial Scholarship: Chapter 6, "Journalism" section
- Louise Jane Moses–Agnes Davis Memorial Scholarship: Chapter 7, "Library and Information Science" section
- Martin Luther King, Jr. Memorial Scholarship: Chapter 6, "Education" section
- State Funeral Director Associations Scholarships: Chapter 6, "Funeral Service and Mortuary Science" section
- Switzer Environmental Fellowship: Chapter 7, "Environmental Studies" section

Canada

AGF Financial Life Skills Scholarship

Sponsor: AGF
Web Site: http://www.agf.com/menus/index00frame.cfm?section=2&subsection=10
Amount of Scholarship: $2,080 (Canadian)

Number of Awards: 40
Deadline: May 26
Education Level: high school seniors
Eligibility: Applicant must be a Canadian resident, have a 75 percent GPA, and enroll as a full-time student at a Canadian college.

Scroll down the Web page until you see the AGF Financial Life Skills Scholarship description to find a brief overview of the scholarship. Click the link to learn details about eligibility, where the scholarship can be used, and how to apply. A link to a PDF version of the application form is provided at the bottom of this page. Forty awards in all are given out under the program: 10 to applicants from British Columbia, the Northwest Territories, and the Yukon; 10 to applicants from Alberta, Saskatchewan, and Manitoba; 10 to applicants from Ontario; and 10 to applicants from Quebec and Atlantic Canada.

APEGBC Entrance Scholarships

Sponsor: Association of Professional Engineers and Geoscientists of British Columbia (APEGBC)
Web Site: http://www.apeg.bc.ca/outreach/apeg.htm
Amount of Scholarship: $1,000 to $2,500 (Canadian)
Number of Awards: not given
Deadline: June 30
Education Level: high school seniors
Eligibility: Applicant must study engineering or geoscience at a Canadian college.

This program awards two scholarships. University Entrance Scholarships of $2,500 go to students entering a degree program at Simon Fraser University, the University of British Columbia, or the University of Victoria. Engineering Transfer Entrance Scholarships of $1,000 go to students entering an engineering

transfer program at any college in Canada. This Web page gives a general overview of both scholarships, including selection criteria. To learn more details about each scholarship and find all the forms you need to apply, click the link to the scholarship's name at the bottom of the Web page.

As Prime Minister Award

Sponsor: Magna for Canada Scholarship Fund and The Fair Enterprise Institute
Web Site: http://www.magnaforcanada.com
Amount of Scholarship: $500 to $20,000 (Canadian)
Number of Awards: 61
Deadline: June 5
Education Level: college undergraduates and graduate students
Eligibility: Applicant must enroll as a full-time student at an accredited Canadian college or university.

First, click the As Prime Minister Awards Program link to learn all about this essay contest for Canadian students. To find out what the eligibility requirements are, what the essay question is, how to apply, and other important details, click the How to Enter link on the left-hand side of the page. You can also submit your application online from this link. The Prizes link tells you what you might win: 50 semifinalists receive $500; 10 finalists receive $10,000 and paid four-month internships at Magna International; and the winner receives $20,000 and a one-year paid internship. All semifinalists and finalists also receive a free, weeklong trip to Toronto for Judging Week; the Events link tells you what you will experience on this trip. Explore the other links to learn about the judges and the scholarship sponsors. Finally, you can see a list of past winners and even read their essays. A Resource Centre lists links to other sites of interest, including many scholarship sites.

Canada Trust Scholarship for Outstanding Community Leadership

Sponsor: Canada Trust
Web Site: http://www.canadatrust.com/corporate/sponsorship/scholar/intro.html
Amount of Scholarship: $500 (Canadian) to full tuition
Number of Awards: 80
Deadline: November 1
Education Level: high school seniors
Eligibility: Applicant must attend high school in Canada, demonstrate outstanding community leadership, and enroll at an accredited four-year college in Canada.

This Web page gives an overview of the mission of this scholarship program. Under the program, 20 Canadian students receive full tuition and a yearly stipend of $3,500 for living expenses. Sixty runners-up receive a Certificate of Merit and $500. Click the What You Can Win button for more details about these awards. The Eligibility Criteria link tells you what qualifications you need to apply. Follow the How to Apply link to find a text version of the application that you can print from inside your Web browser, along with a list of documents that you must submit with the application. The Selection Process, Other Rules, and FAQs pages also give valuable information about the scholarship that will be helpful in preparing your application.

Canadian Merit Scholarships

Sponsor: Canadian Merit Scholarship Foundation (CMSF)
Web Site: http://www.yorku.ca/org/cmsf

Amount of Scholarship: $500 to full tuition (renewable for four years)
Number of Awards: 150
Deadline: November
Education Level: high school seniors
Eligibility: Applicant must attend an accredited high school in Canada and enroll at a four-year college in Canada.

The opening page of this Web site gives an overview of the scholarship program. Learn more by clicking the Our History link on the left-hand side of the page. The Eligibility page lists the eligibility requirements, tells you how to apply, and goes over the selection process. Four different awards are given out under this program, although you apply for all in the same way. The CMS National Awards include tuition up to $4,000 plus a yearly stipend of $4,000 to $5,000 for living expenses, but it can only be used at participating Canadian colleges, which are listed under its description on the Awards page. The CMSF Regional Award is a one-time scholarship of between $1,000 and $2,500, and the CMSF Provincial Award is a one-time scholarship of between $500 and $1,000. These awards go to runners-up for the CMSF National Award. Both can be used at any Canadian college. Finally, the Morehead Award enables Canadian students to attend the University of North Carolina at Chapel Hill on a full-tuition scholarship. You will automatically be considered for all four awards when you submit an application. Click the Application & Flysheet link to download the application form and instructions in PDF format.

Garfield Weston Merit Scholarships for Colleges

Sponsor: W. Garfield Weston Foundation
Web Site: http://www.sheridanc.on.ca/gwmsc
Amount of Scholarship: $500 to $4,000 (Canadian)

Number of Awards: 56
Deadline: February 25
Education Level: high school seniors
Eligibility: Applicant must be a Canadian citizen or permanent resident and enroll as a full-time student in a two-year or three-year program at a community college in Canada.

The opening Web page tells you what the goals are for this scholarship program. Click the Awards link to learn about the three different scholarships available. The National Award provides up to 15 scholarships of between $2,500 and $4,000 for two or three years of study at participating community colleges throughout Canada (a list of participating colleges is linked to the page). The Regional Award gives 21 scholarships worth $1,000 each for student at any accredited community college of applied arts in Ontario. And the Provincial Award gives 20 $500 scholarships for study at any accredited college of applied arts in Ontario. Follow the Eligibility link to find out if you qualify to apply for these awards. The Criteria page tells you what qualities are sought in successful applicants. Click the Apply link to download an application form in PDF format. The Interviews and Calendar pages give further details about the selection process. Finally, read about the scholarship's sponsor on the About GWMSC page.

Leonard Foundation Scholarship

Sponsor: Leonard Foundation
Web Site: http://www.leonardfnd.org
Amount of Scholarship: $1,000 to $1,500 (Canadian)
Number of Awards: 140
Deadline: March 15
Education Level: college undergraduates and professional degree students

Eligibility: Applicant must be a Canadian citizen or permanent resident, enroll as a full-time student at a college or university in Canada, and demonstrate financial need.

You should first click the What Is the Leonard Foundation? link to read about the history and goals of the scholarship's sponsor. Then go to the Criteria page to find out if you are eligible to apply. This page also tells you which applicants receive preferential consideration for the award. Return to the main page to find a link to the downloadable application form in PDF format. You must forward your application through a nominator; a list of these nominators, along with their addresses, phone numbers, and e-mail addresses, is linked to the main Web page.

Ontario Graduate Scholarship

Sponsor: Ontario Ministry of Training, Colleges, and Universities
Web Site: http://osap.gov.on.ca/not_secure/OGS.htm
Amount of Scholarship: $7,906 to $11,859 (Canadian)
Number of Awards: 1,300
Deadline: November 16
Education Level: graduate students
Eligibility: Applicant must enroll as a full-time student in a master's or doctoral program at an Ontario university, have a grade average of at least an A−, and be a Canadian citizen or permanent resident or have entered Canada on a student visa.

To get an overview of this scholarship program, click the Information and Instructions link. You will need to install Adobe Acrobat Reader before you can read this brochure. The brochure describes the purpose of the program, the number of awards given out, the eligibility requirements, and the application instructions. Note that 60 of the 1,300 scholarships awarded each year are reserved for foreign students entering Canada on a student visa. Return to the main Web page and click the Frequently Asked Questions link to find answers to questions not covered in the brochure. A link to the application form in PDF format is also provided.

SSHRC Doctoral Fellowships

Sponsor: Social Sciences and Humanities Research Council of Canada (SSHRC)
Web Site: http://www.sshrc.ca/english/programinfo/fellguide/p-info-docs.htm
Amount of Scholarship: $16,620 to $22,620 (Canadian)
Number of Awards: not given
Deadline: varies
Education Level: doctoral students
Eligibility: Applicant must be a Canadian citizen or permanent resident, enroll in either a full-time Ph.D. program or an LL.M. degree program with the intention of pursuing an academic career, and have completed either a master's degree or one year of doctoral study.

The three fellowships and three supplemental grants available under this program are described in the table at the top of the Web page. Following that are general details on eligibility, evaluation criteria, and the competition process. Apply for the general Doctoral Fellowships by submitting Application Form 701, which is linked to the table at the top of the page; you have the option of applying online or downloading a PDF copy of the form. The most outstanding applicants are automatically considered for the other two fellowships, which supplement the Doctoral Fellowship. If you would like to compete for one of the supple-

mental grants listed in the table, be sure to fill out the application as instructed on the Web page.

Terry Fox Humanitarian Award

Sponsor: Terry Fox Humanitarian Award Program
Web Site: http://www.terryfox.org/English/eng.html
Amount of Scholarship: $2,500 to $4,000 Canadian (renewable for four years)
Number of Awards: 20
Deadline: February 1
Education Level: high school seniors and college undergraduates
Eligibility: Applicant must be a Canadian citizen, enroll at a four-year college in Canada, participate in sports, and be under the age of 25.

First, click The Program button to read about the history, objective, and amount of this scholarship. Go to the Applications page to find a list of eligibility requirements and a link to the application form in PDF format. You should also read the Recipients page to learn what kinds of applicants the scholarship sponsor seeks and get a better idea of whether you would make a good candidate.

Also see the following scholarships:

- Buffalo Sabres Alumni Association Scholarship: Chapter 15, "New York" section
- Canadian Water Resources Association Scholarship: Chapter 7, "Environmental Studies" section
- FCC and 4-H Scholarship: Chapter 8, "Clubs" section
- Lorraine Allison Scholarship: Chapter 7, "Northern Studies" section

- Sir John A. Macdonald Graduate Fellowship in Canadian History: Chapter 7, "History" section
- SWANA BC Pacific Chapter Scholarship: Chapter 6, "Environmental Studies" section

Colorado

See the following scholarships:

- Burlington Northern Santa Fe Foundation Scholarship: Chapter 9, "Native American" section
- Careers in Agriculture Scholarship: Chapter 6, "Agriculture" section
- Hispanic American Commitment to Education Resources Scholarship: Chapter 9, "Hispanic" section
- Latin American Educational Foundation Scholarship: Chapter 9, "Hispanic" section
- Regional EAGLE Scholarship: Chapter 9, "Gay and Lesbian" section
- Sachs Foundation Scholarship: Chapter 9, "African-American" section

Connecticut

American Savings Bank Scholarship

Sponsor: American Savings Bank Foundation, Inc.
Web Site: http://www.americansavingsbank.com/found.asp
Amount of Scholarship: not given
Number of Awards: not given
Deadline: March 30

Education Level: high school seniors and college undergraduates
Eligibility: Applicant must be a resident of American Savings Bank's 45-town service territory in Connecticut, have a minimum 2.5 GPA, and enroll at a two-year or four-year college.

Click the Complete Scholarship Guidelines link to learn all the details about this scholarship, including eligibility requirements and selection criteria. To find out if you live in American Savings Bank's service area, click the 45-Town Service Area link, which opens a list of all eligible Connecticut towns. You will also find a link to the application form in PDF format.

Ellington Community Scholarship

Sponsor: Ellington Community Scholarship Association
Web Site: http://www.libsys.com/schol.htm
Amount of Scholarship: not given
Number of Awards: not given
Deadline: April 30
Education Level: high school seniors
Eligibility: Applicant must live in Ellington, Connecticut; graduate from a public high school or vocational school; and enroll at a two-year college, four-year college, technical school, trade school, or business school.

The top of this Web page describes the selection criteria and eligibility requirements for the scholarship. Scroll to the bottom of the page to find an electronic application form, which you can submit online.

McDonald's Golden Arches Scholarships

Sponsor: McDonald's New York Tri-State Owners and Operators

Web Site: http://
www.archingintoeducation.com/
golden_arches.html
Amount of Scholarship: $1,000 to $5,000
Number of Awards: not given
Deadline: March 8
Education Level: high school seniors
Eligibility: Applicant must reside in Connect-
icut, New Jersey, or New York and enroll at a
four-year college.

Three scholarships are awarded under this program. Most winning students receive the
$1,000 general scholarship. The applicant with
the most outstanding academic achievements
gets the $5,000 McDonald's Big Mac Valedic-
torian Award. The applicant who best demonstrates a commitment to community service
receives the $5,000 McDonald's Community
Service Award. Download the application form
in PDF format by clicking the link at the bottom of the Web page.

Also see the following scholarships:

- Hispanic American Commitment to Educa-
  tion Resources Scholarship: Chapter 9,
  "Hispanic" section
- James L. Goodwin Memorial Scholarship:
  Chapter 6, "Environmental Studies" section
- Jessica Savitch Scholarship: Chapter 6,
  "Communications" section
- McDonald's African American Heritage
  Scholarship: Chapter 9, "African-American"
  section
- McDonald's UNCF Tri-State Scholarship:
  Chapter 9, "African-American" section
- New York Tri-State BMOA McDonald's
  Scholarship: Chapter 8, "Work" section
- Roberta Thumin Scholarship: Chapter 6,
  "Communications" section
- State Funeral Director Associations Scholar-
  ships: Chapter 6, "Funeral Service and Mor-
  tuary Science" section

- Switzer Environmental Fellowship: Chapter
  7, "Environmental Studies" section

Delaware

B. Bradford Barnes Memorial Scholarship

Sponsor: Delaware Higher Education Commis-
sion
Web Site: http://www.doe.state.de.us/
high-ed/barnes.htm
Amount of Scholarship: full tuition (renewa-
ble for four years)
Number of Awards: 1
Deadline: February 4
Education Level: high school seniors
Eligibility: Applicant must be a Delaware res-
ident, rank in the upper 25 percent of the high
school class, have a minimum SAT I score of
1200, and enroll as a full-time student at the
University of Delaware.

This merit scholarship pays tuition, fees, and
room and board at the University of Delaware
for one Delaware student each year. You will
find the bare facts about the scholarship on this
Web page. Click the Additional Information
link to get more details about the purpose of
the award, the eligibility requirements, and the
renewal conditions. Click the Common Merit
Application link to open a printable application
form for all merit scholarships given by the
Delaware Higher Education Commission. Be
sure to check the box beside the name of the
scholarship for which you are applying on this
form. You will also need to print out the High
School Senior Academic Report, which is
linked to the scholarship's Web page. The Ap-

plication Checklist for High School Students will help you keep track of all the papers that you must submit in your application package.

Diamond State Scholarship

Sponsor: Delaware Higher Education Commission
Web Site: http://www.doe.state.de.us/high-ed/diamond.htm
Amount of Scholarship: $1,250 (renewable for four years)
Number of Awards: 50
Deadline: March 31
Education Level: high school seniors
Eligibility: Applicant must be a Delaware resident, rank in the upper 25 percent of the high school class, have a minimum SAT I score of 1200 or an ACT score of 27, and enroll as a full-time student at an accredited four-year college.

You will find the just the facts about the scholarship on this Web page. Click the Additional Information link to get more details about the purpose of the award, the eligibility requirements, and the renewal conditions. Click the Common Merit Application link to open a printable application form for all merit scholarships given by the Delaware Higher Education Commission. Be sure to check the box beside the name of the scholarship for which you are applying on this form. You will also need to print the High School Senior Academic Report, which is linked to the scholarship's Web page. The Application Checklist for High School Students will help you keep track of all the papers that you must submit in your application package.

Governor's Workforce Development Grant

Sponsor: Delaware Higher Education Commission
Web Site: http://www.doe.state.de.us/high-ed/governor.htm
Amount of Scholarship: $1,500
Number of Awards: not given
Deadline: not given
Education Level: college undergraduates
Eligibility: Applicant must be a Delaware resident or work in Delaware; be employed on a part-time or temporary basis, be employed by an independently owned business with fewer than one hundred employees, or be self-employed; enroll as a part-time student at a participating college or community college; demonstrate financial need; and be over the age of 18.

This program provides a grant for workers in Delaware to attend an educational program as a part-time student. You must meet all of the stringent eligibility requirements listed on the Web page in order to apply. A link to the grant application is given at the bottom of the page. The application form also lists all the schools that you may attend under the grant program.

Herman M. Holloway, Sr. Memorial Scholarship

Sponsor: Delaware Higher Education Commission
Web Site: http://www.doe.state.de.us/high-ed/holloway.htm
Amount of Scholarship: full tuition (renewable for four years)
Number of Awards: 1
Deadline: March 10
Education Level: high school seniors
Eligibility: Applicant must be a Delaware resident, rank in the upper 25 percent of the high school class, have a minimum 3.25 GPA, have a minimum SAT I score of 850 or an ACT score of 20, enroll as a full-time student at Delaware State University, and demonstrate financial need.

This merit scholarship pays all of the tuition, fees, and room and board charges at Delaware State University for one student each year. You will find the bare facts about the scholarship on this Web page. Click the Additional Information link to get more details about the purpose of the award, the eligibility requirements, and the renewal conditions. Click the Common Merit Application link to open a printable application form for all merit scholarships given by the Delaware Higher Education Commission. Be sure to check the box beside the name of the scholarship for which you are applying on this form. You will also need to print out the High School Senior Academic Report, which is linked to the scholarship's Web page. The Application Checklist for High School Students will help you keep track of all the papers that you must submit in your application package.

Long & Foster Scholarship

Sponsor: Long & Foster Realtors
Web Site: http://www.longandfoster.com/scholarship
Amount of Scholarship: $1,000
Number of Awards: 60
Deadline: March 1
Education Level: high school seniors
Eligibility: Applicant must live in the Long & Foster service area, have a minimum 3.0 GPA, enroll at a four-year college, demonstrate financial need, and be a U.S. citizen.

First, click the Scholarship Program Details link to find all the details about the scholarship program, including its purpose and the criteria used to select recipients. Applicants must live in the Long & Foster service area, which includes parts of Delaware, Maryland, Pennsylvania, Virginia, and Washington, DC, as described in the Scope section of the page. If you qualify, return to the main page and click the Application Instructions and Form link to open a printable version of the application.

MBNA Delaware Scholars

Sponsor: MBNA
Web Site: http://www.mbnainternational.com/a_sch_delaware.html
Amount of Scholarship: $500 to $7,500 (renewable for four years)
Number of Awards: not given
Deadline: December 11
Education Level: high school seniors
Eligibility: Applicant must be a Delaware resident, have a minimum 2.5 GPA, have a minimum SAT I score of 900 or ACT score of 19, enroll as a full-time student at an accredited four-year college in Delaware or in the University of Delaware's Parallel Program, demonstrate financial need, and be a U.S. citizen or permanent resident.

In addition to a scholarship, winners of this award also receive advising, summer internships, and part-time employment opportunities. The Web page goes over all the facts you need to know, including program benefits, eligibility requirements, how to obtain application materials, selection criteria, and renewal conditions. The Frequently Asked Questions page answers the most common questions about the scholarship. The Important Dates page tells you when applications are due and when other important steps in the application process occur. Although application materials aren't available on the Web site, you can easily obtain an application form from your high school guidance office or by calling the MBNA Scholars Program at the phone number given on the scholarship's main Web page.

Robert C. Byrd Honors Scholarship

Sponsor: Delaware Higher Education Commission

Web Site: http://www.doe.state.de.us/high-ed/byrd.htm

Amount of Scholarship: $1,500 (renewable for four years)

Number of Awards: 15

Deadline: March 31

Education Level: high school seniors and GED recipients

Eligibility: Applicant must be a Delaware resident, rank in the upper 25 percent of the high school class or score at least 300 on the GED, have a minimum SAT I score of 1200 or an ACT score of 27, enroll at least half-time at an accredited higher education program that lasts at least one year, and be a U.S. citizen or permanent resident.

You will find the facts about the scholarship on this Web page. Click the Additional Information link to get more details about the purpose of the award, the eligibility requirements, and the renewal conditions. Click the Common Merit Application link to open a printable application form for all merit scholarships given by the Delaware Higher Education Commission. Be sure to check the box beside the name of the scholarship for which you are applying on this form. You will also need to print out the High School Senior Academic Report, which is linked to the scholarship's Web page. The Application Checklist for High School Students will help you keep track of all the papers that you must submit in your application package.

Scholarship Incentive

Sponsor: Delaware Higher Education Commission

Web Site: http://www.doe.state.de.us/high-ed/scip.htm

Amount of Scholarship: $700 to $2,220

Number of Awards: not given

Deadline: April 15

Education Level: high school seniors, college undergraduates, and graduate students

Eligibility: Applicant must be a Delaware resident, have a minimum 2.5 GPA, enroll as a full-time student at an accredited two-year or four-year college in Delaware or Pennsylvania or enroll as a full-time student in a graduate degree program at an accredited out-of-state or private university if your major is not offered at a public university in Delaware, and demonstrate financial need.

This Web page describes Delaware's educational grant program, and it will help you figure out whether you will qualify for a state grant. Find additional information about the program and eligibility by following the link at the bottom of the page. You don't need to file a separate application for this grant, just the FAFSA.

Also see the following scholarship:

• Educational Benefits for Children of Deceased Veterans and Others: Chapter 14, "Military Personnel and Veterans" section

District of Columbia

See the following scholarships:

• AWC-DC Scholarship: Chapter 12, "Female" section
• Bank of America ADA Abilities Scholarship: Chapter 10, "Any Disability" section
• Congressional Black Caucus Spouses Scholarships: Chapter 15, "Alabama" section
• Long & Foster Scholarship: Chapter 15, "Delaware" section

- Project Excellence Scholarships: Chapter 9, "African-American" section

Florida

FFGC Scholarships

Sponsor: Florida Federation of Garden Clubs (FFGC)
Web Site: http://www.ffgc.org/index1.htm
Amount of Scholarship: $1,500 to $3,000
Number of Awards: 10
Deadline: May 1
Education Level: high school seniors, college undergraduates, and graduate students
Eligibility: Applicant must be a Florida resident, study a horticulture-related field at a Florida college, and have a grade average of at least a B.

Scroll down through the top frame until you see a link to FFGC Scholarships. Clicking this link opens a page describing the scholarships offered to Florida residents. There are 10 scholarships in all, each with specific eligibility requirements and award amounts. Make a note of the scholarships for which you are eligible to apply. There are two application forms: one for all undergraduate and graduate school scholarships; and one for scholarships for graduating high school seniors. Be sure to print the correct application form for the scholarships for which you are applying. Scroll to the bottom of the page to learn how to prepare your application package and what the selection criteria are.

Florida Bright Futures Scholarships

Sponsor: Florida Department of Education
Web Site: http://www.firn.edu/doe/bin00072/home0072.htm

Amount of Scholarship: $1,040 to $2,834
Number of Awards: not given
Deadline: not given
Education Level: high school seniors
Eligibility: Applicant must earn a Florida standard high school diploma or its equivalent, meet minimum academic standards, and enroll at an eligible two-year or four-year college in Florida.

Florida's academic scholarship program awards three different scholarships. Each award has its own eligibility requirements, award amounts, and duration. First, read the Bright Futures Facts page to learn how much you can receive for each kind of scholarship. The Eligible Colleges and Schools link lists the colleges where you can use the scholarship. If you've never applied for the scholarship program before, click the First-Time Applicants link to find out how to apply, what the prerequisites are, and other important details. The Academic Requirements page describes the academic and other requirements for the three different scholarships. You apply by submitting the Student Authorization Form, which you can download from the Web site on the How Do I Apply? page. Renewal applicants, high school guidance counselors, and financial aid officers will also find information about the program on the site.

Florida College Student of the Year Award

Sponsor: *Florida Leader* Magazine, SunTrust Education Loans, and Publix Super Markets, Inc.
Web Site: http://www.floridaleader.com/soty
Amount of Scholarship: not given
Number of Awards: 20
Deadline: February 1
Education Level: college undergraduates and graduate students

Eligibility: Applicant must be currently enrolled at a Florida community college, college, university, vocational school, technical school, or business school; have a minimum 3.25 GPA; and have completed at least 30 credit hours of college coursework.

This page provides an overview of the history of this scholarship program; knowing these details can help you prepare a better application package. Follow the Are You Eligible? link to find out if you qualify to compete for the scholarship and to learn how to apply. Click the How You Can Apply link to download the application form in PDF format; you must first fill out and submit a short electronic form before you can access the actual application. The Q&A page gives answers to the most commonly asked questions about the scholarship. You should also explore the other links to learn even more about the scholarship program, its sponsors, and past winners.

LIFE Unsung Hero Scholarship

Sponsor: Leaders in Furthering Education (LIFE)
Web Site: http://www.life-edu.org/scholarships.html
Amount of Scholarship: $10,000
Number of Awards: not given
Deadline: December 1
Education Level: high school students
Eligibility: Applicant must attend high school in Palm Beach County, volunteer at least 30 hours per month, and have participated in volunteer community service for at least two years.

This scholarship rewards outstanding community service. To learn what kinds of high school volunteers the scholarship sponsor is looking for, read the Selection Criteria section of the Web page. You will also find information about putting together an application package and the conditions for keeping the scholarship. At the bottom of the page are links to both pages of the application form in PDF format.

Lucent Florida Universities Fellowship

Sponsor: Lucent Technologies and the State of Florida
Web Site: http://www.bell-labs.com/fellowships/LFFP
Amount of Scholarship: full tuition and $15,000 stipend
Number of Awards: not given
Deadline: not given
Education Level: college seniors
Eligibility: Applicant must enroll in an eligible graduate program at a participating Florida state university and be a U.S. citizen or permanent resident.

This program supports graduate students in science and engineering fields who attend public universities in Florida. Eligible fields of study are listed on the fellowship's main Web page, along with a complete description of the program. Click the History button on the left-hand side of the page to learn more details about the program's background and sponsor. Clicking the Apply button takes you to a page describing the eligibility requirements, the documents required for the application package, and a list of participating Florida universities. This page also links to the application form in Microsoft Word and PDF formats.

Nicaraguan and Haitian Scholarship

Sponsor: Florida Department of Education
Web Site: http://www.firn.edu/doe/bin00065/99apps.htm
Amount of Scholarship: $5,000

Number of Awards: 2
Deadline: July 1
Education Level: college undergraduates and graduate students
Eligibility: Applicant must be a Florida resident, enroll at a state university in Florida, have a minimum 3.0 GPA, and be either Nicaraguan or Haitian.

To find information about this scholarship and an application form, click the Nicaraguan and Haitian Scholarship link in the list of awards on the Web page. The file is in PDF format, so you will need to install Adobe Acrobat Reader before you can open it. One scholarship is given each year to a Nicaraguan student and one to a Haitian student. The application form tells you more about the eligibility requirements and selection criteria.

Public Education and Citizenship Committee's Scholarship

Sponsor: Grand Lodge of Florida
Web Site: http://www.glflamason.org/scholarship.html
Amount of Scholarship: $500
Number of Awards: 10
Deadline: February 15
Education Level: high school seniors
Eligibility: Applicant must graduate from a Florida high school and enroll at a public two-year or four-year college in Florida.

This Web page lists the eligibility and application requirements for the scholarship. Follow the instructions under the Rules/Deadline section of the page to request an application form.

Robert C. Byrd Honors Scholarship

Sponsor: Florida Department of Education
Web Site: http://www.firn.edu/doe/bin00065/99apps.htm

Amount of Scholarship: $5,000
Number of Awards: 2
Deadline: July 1
Education Level: high school seniors
Eligibility: Applicant must be a Florida resident, enroll as a full-time student in a postsecondary educational program lasting at least one year, and be a U.S. citizen or permanent resident.

To find information about this scholarship and an application form, click the Robert C. Byrd Honors Scholarship link in the list of awards on the Web page. The file is in PDF format, so you will need to install Adobe Acrobat Reader before you can open it. The application form tells you more about the eligibility requirements and selection criteria so you can better determine if you would make a good candidate.

SIRS/FAME Intellectual Freedom Student Scholarship

Sponsor: Florida Association for Media in Education (FAME)
Web Site: http://sun3.firn.edu/webfiles/others/fame/sirs.htm#student
Amount of Scholarship: $100 to $1,000
Number of Awards: 2
Deadline: February 15
Education Level: high school seniors
Eligibility: Applicant must graduate from a Florida high school.

The winner of this essay contest receives a $1,000 award, and the runner-up gets $500. The Web page tells you what the eligibility requirements are, what the essay topic is, and the criteria used to judge essays. You will also find a text application form that you can print from inside your Web browser.

Southern Scholarship

Sponsor: Southern Scholarship Foundation (SSF)

Web Site: http://www.scholarships.org/ssf
Amount of Scholarship: not given
Number of Awards: not given
Deadline: November 1, January 1, and March 1
Education Level: high school seniors and community college transfer students
Eligibility: Applicant must enroll at a participating college in Florida, have a minimum 3.0 high school GPA or a minimum 2.85 community college GPA, and demonstrate financial need.

This scholarship is a bit different. Instead of giving you money for tuition, it provides a rent-free room in a completely furnished home near one of the four participating Florida colleges. These colleges are Florida A&M University, Florida State University, the University of Florida, and Bethune-Cookman College. To learn more about this unique program, click the What Is the SSF? link in the upper right corner of the Web page. There you can read about the sponsor, how the program works, and what the selection criteria are. To better determine if you should apply and whether you meet the eligibility requirements, follow the Is SSF For Me? link. Go to the Application page to download an application form in PDF format.

West Palm Beach Kiwanis Foundation, Inc. Scholarship

Sponsor: Kiwanis Club of West Palm Beach Foundation
Web Site: http://gb.gopbi.com/servlets/SiteServlet/wpbkiwanisclub/Kiwanis_Scholarship_.html
Amount of Scholarship: not given
Number of Awards: not given
Deadline: April 15
Education Level: high school seniors
Eligibility: Applicant must attend high school and live in the West Palm Beach area, have a minimum 3.0 GPA, enroll at a two-year or four-year college, and demonstrate financial need.

This Web page lists the eligibility requirements for the scholarship, including a precise definition of where you must live and attend high school in order to qualify. Click the link at the bottom of the page to find out how to obtain an application form.

Also see the following scholarships:

- American Cancer Society College Scholarship: Chapter 10, "Cancer" section
- Bank of America ADA Abilities Scholarship: Chapter 10, "Any Disability" section
- ChairScholars Scholarships: Chapter 10, "Physically Challenged" section
- Congressional Black Caucus Spouses Scholarships: Chapter 15, "Alabama" section
- FAME Student Scholarship: Chapter 7, "Education" section
- Florida Engineering Society Scholarships: Chapter 6, "Engineering" section
- Hispanic American Commitment to Education Resources Scholarship: Chapter 9, "Hispanic" section
- HSF Community College Transfer Scholarship: Chapter 9, "Hispanic" section
- HSF High School Scholarship: Chapter 9, "Hispanic" section
- Jacki Tuckfield Memorial Graduate Business Administration Scholarship: Chapter 7, "Business" section
- José Marti Scholarship Challenge Grant: Chapter 9, "Hispanic" section
- Rosewood Family Scholarship: Chapter 9, "All Minorities" section
- Seminole and Miccosukee Indian Scholarship: Chapter 9, "Native American" section
- Scholarship for Children of Deceased and Disabled Veterans: Chapter 14, "Military Personnel and Veterans" section
- Sidney B. Meadows Scholarship: Chapter 6, "Horticulture" section

- State Funeral Director Associations Scholarships: Chapter 6, "Funeral Service and Mortuary Science" section
- UTD Scholarships: Chapter 14, "Unions and Professional Associations" section
- Young Educators Committee Scholarship: Chapter 7, "Education" section

Georgia

Garden Club of Georgia Scholarships

Sponsor: The Garden Club of Georgia, Inc.
Web Site: http://www.uga.edu/gardenclub/Scholar.html
Amount of Scholarship: $1,250 to $5,000
Number of Awards: 9
Deadline: March 1
Education Level: college juniors and seniors and graduate students
Eligibility: Applicant must be a Georgia resident and major in a garden-related subject at a Georgia college.

Nine Garden Club Scholarships are awarded each year to Georgia college students who are studying a field related to gardening, such as horticulture, floriculture, landscape design, conservation, forestry, botany, agronomy, plant pathology, environmental control, city planning, land management, or a similar subject. One scholarship is also available to students of historic preservation, decorative arts, or historic architecture. To receive an application packet and more detailed information, contact the address, phone number, or e-mail address given on the Web page. Before requesting an application packet, look over the list of past winners. Notice that the average GPA of schol-arship winners is over 3.7—make sure you can compete at this level.

Georgia Tuition Equalization Grant

Sponsor: Georgia Student Finance Commission
Web Site: http://www.hope.gsfc.org
Amount of Scholarship: $1,000
Number of Awards: not given
Deadline: varies by school
Education Level: college undergraduates
Eligibility: Applicant must be a Georgia resident, enroll as a full-time student at a private four-year college in Georgia, and be a U.S. citizen or permanent resident.

To find information about this grant, click the State Grants link in the bar at the top of the Web page, follow the Program Information link, and then click the name of the grant in the list that opens. There, you'll find all the facts, including the program's objective, the eligibility requirements, and the application procedures. You can obtain a copy of the required Georgia Tuition Equalization Grant form from the financial aid office at your school. Scroll to the bottom of the page to find a list of private Georgia colleges and out-of-state schools that you may attend using the grant.

Governor's Scholarship

Sponsor: Georgia Student Finance Commission
Web Site: http://www.hope.gsfc.org
Amount of Scholarship: $1,575 (renewable for four years)
Number of Awards: around 3,000
Deadline: not given
Education Level: high school seniors
Eligibility: Applicant must be a Georgia resident; be named a Georgia Scholar, valedicto-

rian, salutatorian, or STAR student at an eligible Georgia high school; enroll as a full-time student at an eligible college in Georgia; and be a U.S. citizen or permanent resident.

To find information about this scholarship, click the State Grants link in the bar at the top of the Web page, follow the Program Information link, and then click the name of the scholarship in the list that opens. There you'll find details about the program's objective, eligibility requirements, and application procedures. A copy of the Governor's Scholarship Application form is automatically mailed to each qualifying candidate.

Robert C. Byrd Honors Scholarship

Sponsor: Georgia Student Finance Commission
Web Site: http://www.hope.gsfc.org
Amount of Scholarship: $1,500
Number of Awards: around 600
Deadline: not given
Education Level: high school seniors
Eligibility: Applicant must graduate from a Georgia high school and enroll at an eligible postsecondary institution.

To find information about this scholarship, click the State Grants link in the bar at the top of the Web page, follow the Program Information link, and click the name of the scholarship in the list that opens. There you can read about the program's objective, eligibility requirements, and application procedures. You can get a copy of the Robert C. Byrd Honors Scholarship application form from your high school's guidance office.

Also see the following scholarships:

- Bank of America ADA Abilities Scholarship: Chapter 10, "Any Disability" section
- Charles McDaniel Teacher Scholarship: Chapter 6, "Education" section
- Congressional Black Caucus Spouses Scholarships: Chapter 15, "Alabama" section
- "Duke" Demay Jazz Scholarship: Chapter 8, "Performing Arts" section
- Georgia Military College State Service Scholarship: Chapter 13, "National Guard" section
- Georgia Trust for Historic Preservation Scholarship: Chapter 6, "Historic Preservation" section
- Georgia Water and Pollution Control Association Scholarships: Chapter 14, "Unions and Professional Associations" section
- HOPE Teacher Scholarship: Chapter 7, "Education" section
- Law Enforcement Personnel Dependents Grant: Chapter 14, "Public Safety Officers" section
- North Georgia College Military Scholarship: Chapter 13, "National Guard" section
- North Georgia College ROTC Grant: Chapter 13, "All Branches" section
- Pat Hoban Memorial Scholarship: Chapter 9, "Gay and Lesbian" section
- Public Safety Memorial Grant: Chapter 14, "Public Safety Officers" section
- Sidney B. Meadows Scholarship: Chapter 6, "Horticulture" section
- State Funeral Director Associations Scholarships: Chapter 6, "Funeral Service and Mortuary Science" section

Hawaii

See the following scholarship:

- California-Hawaii Elks Association Scholarship for Vocational Education: Chapter 6,

"Vocational and Technical Education" section

Idaho

Magic Valley Dairy Days Scholarship

Sponsor: Wendell Chamber of Commerce
Web Site: http://www.wendell-idchamber.org/schola.htm
Amount of Scholarship: not given
Number of Awards: not given
Deadline: June 15
Education Level: high school seniors
Eligibility: Applicant must reside in Wendell, Idaho, and enroll at a two-year college, four-year college, or vocational school in Idaho.

Here you will find a brief description of the scholarship, including the selection criteria. A text copy of the application form that you can print out is given at the bottom of the Web page.

Also see the following scholarships:

* Bank of America ADA Abilities Scholarship: Chapter 10, "Any Disability" section
* Careers in Agriculture Scholarship: Chapter 6, "Agriculture" section
* GSBA, Pride, and INBA Scholarships: Chapter 9, "Gay and Lesbian" section
* Larry Wimer Memorial Scholarship: Chapter 6, "Environmental Science" section
* Regional EAGLE Scholarship: Chapter 9, "Gay and Lesbian" section
* State Funeral Director Associations Scholarships: Chapter 6, "Funeral Service and Mortuary Science" section

Illinois

Bonus Incentive Grant

Sponsor: Illinois Student Assistance Commission
Web Site: http://www.isac1.org/ilaid/specgt.html#big
Amount of Scholarship: varies
Number of Awards: not given
Deadline: May 30
Education Level: high school seniors and college undergraduates
Eligibility: Applicant must use the proceeds of an Illinois College Savings Bond to pay for educational expenses at an approved two-year or four-year college in Illinois, and not enroll in a divinity program.

If you decide to take advantage of this bonus grant, read the eligibility requirements on the Web page carefully, as there are a lot of conditions. Contact your college's financial aid or registrar's office for application forms.

Illinois Incentive for Access Grant

Sponsor: Illinois Student Assistance Commission
Web Site: http://www.isac1.org/ilaid/specgt.html#iiap
Amount of Scholarship: $500
Number of Awards: not given
Deadline: not given
Education Level: college freshmen
Eligibility: Applicant must be an Illinois resident, enroll at a participating college, have an Estimated Family Contribution of zero, and be a U.S. citizen or permanent resident.

This grant is intended for very needy students and is awarded only to students who receive an Estimated Family Contribution (EFC) of zero when they file the FAFSA. Follow the instructions given on the Web page when completing the FAFSA to make certain that you will be considered for the grant. Note that grants received under this program can be used for any education-related expenses, not only for tuition and fees.

Merit Recognition Scholarship

Sponsor: Illinois Student Assistance Commission

Web Site: http://www.isac1.org/ilaid/schols.html#MRSP

Amount of Scholarship: $1,000

Number of Awards: not given

Deadline: not given

Education Level: high school seniors

Eligibility: Applicant must be an Illinois resident, attend high school in Illinois, rank in the top 5 percent of the high school class, enroll at an approved two-year or four-year college in Illinois, and be a U.S. citizen or permanent resident.

Here you will find a list of the eligibility requirements for this scholarship. But you don't have to apply for the award. If you are ranked in the top 5 percent of your high school class, you will automatically be considered.

Monetary Award

Sponsor: Illinois Student Assistance Commission

Web Site: http://www.isac1.org/ilaid/map.html

Amount of Scholarship: up to $4,530

Number of Awards: not given

Deadline: not given

Education Level: high school seniors and college undergraduates

Eligibility: Applicant must be an Illinois resident, enroll at an approved two-year or four-year college in Illinois, demonstrate financial need, and be a U.S. citizen or permanent resident.

The Monetary Award Program (MAP) is Illinois's major educational grant program. The Web page provides a list of the eligibility requirements, information about the application process, and restrictions on how the grant may be used. You must submit the FAFSA to be considered for this grant; no other application form is necessary.

Robert C. Byrd Honors Scholarship

Sponsor: Illinois Student Assistance Commission

Web Site: http://www.isac1.org/ilaid/schols.html#RCBHSP

Amount of Scholarship: $1,500 (renewable for four years)

Number of Awards: not given

Deadline: January 15

Education Level: high school seniors

Eligibility: Applicant must be an Illinois resident, graduate from an Illinois high school or achieve a minimum GED test score, enroll as a full-time student at an accredited two-year or four-year college, and be a U.S. citizen or permanent resident.

Here you will find a list of eligibility requirements for this merit scholarship and a list of requirements you must meet to renew the scholarship if you win one. Check under the How to Apply section to find out where you can get an application form. The Selection Process describes the criteria used to select the scholarship's winners.

Also see the following scholarships:

- Bank of America ADA Abilities Scholarship: Chapter 10, "Any Disability" section
- Congressional Black Caucus Spouses Scholarships: Chapter 15, "Alabama" section
- David A. DeBolt Teacher Shortage Scholarship: Chapter 6, "Education" section
- Grant for Dependents of Correctional Officers: Chapter 14, "Public Safety Officers" section
- Grant for Dependents of Police or Fire Officers: Chapter 14, "Public Safety Officers" section
- Hispanic American Commitment to Education Resources Scholarship: Chapter 9, "Hispanic" section
- HSF Community College Transfer Scholarship: Chapter 9, "Hispanic" section
- HSF High School Scholarship: Chapter 9, "Hispanic" section
- Illinois National Guard Grant: Chapter 13, "National Guard" section
- Illinois Veteran Grant: Chapter 13, "Veterans" section
- Minority Teachers of Illinois (MTI) Scholarship: Chapter 6, "Education" section
- State Funeral Director Associations Scholarships: Chapter 6, "Funeral Service and Mortuary Science" section

Indiana

Art Bender Scholarship

Sponsor: American Society for Quality, Indianapolis Section
Web Site: http://www.indyasq.org/misc/awards/benderscholarship.html
Amount of Scholarship: $500
Number of Awards: not given
Deadline: not given

Education Level: high school seniors, college undergraduates, and graduate students
Eligibility: Applicant must be an Indiana resident, attend college in Indiana, study a quality profession-related field, demonstrate financial need, and be a U.S. citizen.

This Web page provides an overview and history of the scholarship. Follow the link under the Information Sheet section to open a page that explains the purpose of the scholarship and lists the eligibility requirements, selection criteria, and other rules governing the competition. Return to the first page and click the link at the top to access an online application form.

Boone County Community Foundation Scholarships

Sponsor: Boone County Community Foundation
Web Site: http://www.bccn.boone.in.us/cf/scholarships.html
Amount of Scholarship: not given
Number of Awards: not given
Deadline: varies
Education Level: high school seniors
Eligibility: Applicant must be a resident of Boone County and enroll as a full-time student at a postsecondary institution.

The Boone County Community Foundation administers 26 different scholarships for high school students living in Boone County, Indiana. At the top of this Web page you'll find links to the application form and the recommendation form for all scholarships in PDF format. Following that is a table listing the names of all of the available scholarships and the geographic preference for each award. Click the name of a scholarship to read its details, including eligibility requirements, preferences, and requirements for the application. The requirements for each award differ greatly. Some scholarships specify a field of study, achievements in athletics or community service, or graduation from a particular Boone County high school. Make a note of all the scholarships for which you are eligible, as you must write their names at the top of the application form. The remainder of the Web page tells you about application deadlines and conditions for renewing multiyear scholarships.

Hoosier Scholar Award

Sponsor: State Student Assistance Commission of Indiana
Web Site: http://www.ai.org/ssaci/hsa.html
Amount of Scholarship: $500
Number of Awards: not given
Deadline: not given
Education Level: high school seniors
Eligibility: Applicant must be an Indiana resident, attend an approved high school in Indiana, rank in the top 20 percent of the high school graduating class, and enroll as a full-time student at an eligible college in Indiana.

This page simply lists the eligibility requirements for this merit award. You don't apply directly for the scholarship. If you qualify, your high school will nominate you for an award.

Indiana Higher Education Grant

Sponsor: State Student Assistance Commission of Indiana
Web Site: http://www.ai.org/ssaci/hea.html
Amount of Scholarship: not given
Number of Awards: not given
Deadline: March 1
Education Level: high school seniors and college undergraduates
Eligibility: Applicant must be an Indiana resident, enroll as a full-time student at an eligible two-year or four-year college, and demonstrate financial need.

This in Indiana's largest educational grant program. To be considered for the grant, you must file the FAFSA, as instructed on the Web page. The page also lists the eligibility requirements for the grant.

Robert C. Byrd Honors Scholarship

Sponsor: State Student Assistance Commission of Indiana
Web Site: http://www.ai.org/ssaci/robert.html
Amount of Scholarship: $1,500 (renewable for four years)
Number of Awards: not given
Deadline: April 24
Education Level: high school seniors and GED recipients
Eligibility: Applicant must be an Indiana resident, have a minimum SAT I score of 1300 or a minimum ACT score of 31 or have earned an average standard core of 65 or higher on the GED, and enroll as a full-time student at an institution of higher education in the U.S.

The Web page lists the eligibility requirements and other facts about the scholarship. You can obtain an application form from your high school's guidance office or by contacting the address, phone number, or e-mail address given on the Web page.

Twenty-First Century Scholars

Sponsor: State Student Assistance Commission of Indiana, Indiana Career and Postsecondary Advancement Center, Indiana Commission for Higher Education, and Indiana Department of Education
Web Site: http://scholars.indiana.edu
Amount of Scholarship: up to full tuition (renewable for four years)
Number of Awards: not given

Deadline: June 30
Education Level: eighth-grade students
Eligibility: Applicant must be an Indiana resident, be eligible for free or reduced-price lunches under the national school lunch program or free or reduced textbooks under the textbook assistance program, fulfill the Twenty-First Century Scholars pledge, and enroll at an Indiana college after high school graduation.

The opening Web page explains the goals of this ambitious scholarship program. Click the Step Up to the Pledge link to read the pledge that you must commit to in eighth grade in order to be eligible. You must promise to graduate from an Indiana high school with a GPA of at least 2.0, not to use any illegal drugs or commit any crime, meet all the prerequisites for college admission, and apply for college and financial aid as a high school senior. Follow the Information link in the bar at the top of the page to learn more about the program. The Twenty-First Century Scholars Fact Sheet tells you why the program was established, how to apply, and the specific conditions that you must fulfill to remain eligible for a scholarship. The Information section also provides an explanation of the pledge, answers to frequently asked questions about the program, and a list of colleges in Indiana you can attend under the scholarship. Return to the main page and click the How to Apply link to open a PDF copy of the application form; you can also send an e-mail request for a printed application through this page. The rest of the Web site provides valuable information for students participating in the program, including news, updates, and forms for high school seniors claiming a scholarship.

Also see the following scholarships:

- AFSCME Council 62 Scholarship: Chapter 14, "Unions and Professional Organizations" section

- Charles (Bud) Fridlin Scholarship: Chapter 8, "Bowling" section
- Congressional Black Caucus Spouses Scholarships: Chapter 15, "Alabama" section
- David J. Clark Memorial Scholarship Grant: Chapter 6, "Film and Television" section
- Evan S. (Red) Stuart Memorial Scholarship: Chapter 8, "Bowling" section
- Hispanic American Commitment to Education Resources Scholarship: Chapter 9, "Hispanic" section
- Indiana National Guard Supplemental Grant: Chapter 13, "National Guard" section
- Minority Teacher/Special Education Scholarship: Chapter 6, "Education" section
- State Funeral Director Associations Scholarships: Chapter 6, "Funeral Service and Mortuary Science" section
- State Student Assistance Commission of Indiana Nursing Scholarship: Chapter 6, "Nursing" section

Iowa

Carver Scholars

Sponsor: Roy J. Carver Charitable Trust
Web Site: http://www.carvertrust.org/grants/s-scholar.htm
Amount of Scholarship: $3,800 to $7,600
Number of Awards: not given
Deadline: not given
Education Level: college sophomores
Eligibility: Applicant must have graduated from an Iowa high school, enroll as a full-time student at a participating four-year college in Iowa, have a minimum 2.8 GPA, and be a U.S. citizen.

This Web page describes the eligibility requirements and other details of this scholarship for students who have had to overcome significant obstacles in obtaining a college education. Pay special attention to the Selection Criteria section, which will help you determine if you would make a good candidate. You must apply directly to your college's financial aid office. Participating colleges are listed at the bottom of the Web page, along with phone numbers you can call with general questions about the program.

IEC Scholarship

Sponsor: Iowa Energy Center (IEC)
Web Site: http://www.energy.iastate.edu/about/grantloan/scholarship.htm
Amount of Scholarship: $500 to $2,250
Number of Awards: 6
Deadline: not given
Education Level: grades 9 through 12
Eligibility: Applicant must enter an energy-related project in the Iowa State University Science and Technology Fair.

Six awards total are given out in this contest: three in the category of energy efficiency and three in the category of renewable energy. The first-place winners receive $2,000, the second-place winners get $1,000, and the third-place winners get $500 to be used at the colleges of their choice. If winners elect to attend college or community college in Iowa, they receive an additional $250. This Web page describes the projects of past winners and other details about the scholarship. An e-mail address is given if you have further questions. To learn more about the fair itself, click the Iowa State University Science and Technology Fair link.

Iowa Grant

Sponsor: Iowa College Student Aid Commission
Web Site: http://www.state.ia.us/government/icsac/grants.html#IowaGrants

Amount of Scholarship: $1,000 (renewable for four years)
Number of Awards: not given
Deadline: none
Education Level: high school seniors and college undergraduates
Eligibility: Applicant must be an Iowa resident, enroll at an eligible two-year or four-year college in Iowa, demonstrate financial need, and be a U.S. citizen or permanent resident.

This section of the Web page describes Iowa's need-based grant program for college students, including the eligibility requirements. You will be automatically considered for the grant when you file the FAFSA. Be sure to submit your application for financial aid as soon as possible after January 1 to take advantage of limited funds.

Iowa Tuition Grant

Sponsor: Iowa College Student Aid Commission
Web Site: http://www.state.ia.us/government/icsac/grants.html#IowaTuitionGrants
Amount of Scholarship: $3,150 (renewable for four years)
Number of Awards: not given
Deadline: April 21
Education Level: high school seniors and college undergraduates
Eligibility: Applicant must be an Iowa resident, enroll at an eligible private four-year college in Iowa, and be a U.S. citizen or permanent resident.

This section of the Web page describes Iowa's tuition equalization program for students attending private colleges in Iowa, including the eligibility requirements. You will be automatically considered of the grant when you file the FAFSA, as long as you list an eligible college on the form.

Robert C. Byrd Honors Scholarship

Sponsor: Iowa College Student Aid Commission

Web Site: http://www.state.ia.us/government/icsac/grants.html#ByrdScholarships

Amount of Scholarship: $1,110 (renewable for four years)

Number of Awards: not given

Deadline: April 15

Education Level: high school seniors

Eligibility: Applicant must be an Iowa resident and enroll at an institution of higher education.

Here you will find a list of eligibility requirements for this merit scholarship for Iowa high school students. You can obtain an application form from your high school's guidance office.

State of Iowa Scholarship

Sponsor: Iowa College Student Aid Commission

Web Site: http://www.state.ia.us/government/icsac/grants.html#StateOfIowaScholarships

Amount of Scholarship: $410

Number of Awards: not given

Deadline: November 1

Education Level: high school seniors

Eligibility: Applicant must attend high school in Iowa and rank in the top 15 percent of the high school class.

Here you will find a list of eligibility requirements for this merit scholarship for Iowa high school students. You can obtain an application form from your high school's guidance office. Be sure to follow the instructions under How to Apply to receive proper consideration for the award.

Also see the following scholarships:

- Bank of America ADA Abilities Scholarship: Chapter 10, "Any Disability" section
- Careers in Agriculture Scholarship: Chapter 6, "Agriculture" section
- Catholic Aid Association College Tuition Scholarship: Chapter 11, "Catholic" section
- Iowa Vocational-Technical Tuition Grant: Chapter 6, "Vocational and Technical Education" section
- Morris Scholarship: Chapter 9, "All Minorities" section
- Regional EAGLE Scholarship: Chapter 9, "Gay and Lesbian" section
- State Funeral Director Associations Scholarships: Chapter 6, "Funeral Service and Mortuary Science" section

Kansas

State Scholarship

Sponsor: Kansas Board of Regents

Web Site: http://www.kansasregents.org/academic_affairs/financial/state.html

Amount of Scholarship: $1,000 (renewable for four years)

Number of Awards: not given

Deadline: May 1

Education Level: high school seniors

Eligibility: Applicant must be a Kansas resident and demonstrate financial need.

The top of this Web page describes how to qualify for State Scholar designation, which is a prerequisite for the scholarship. State Scholar designation is based on a combination of ACT scores and GPA. Keep reading to learn about the purpose of the scholarship, the academic criteria for the current year's State Scholars, the award amount, the application deadline, and conditions for renewing the scholarship. To apply, you must submit both the FAFSA and the Kansas financial aid application, which you can obtain from high school guidance and college financial aid offices.

Also see the following scholarships:

- Bank of America ADA Abilities Scholarship: Chapter 10, "Any Disability" section
- Burlington Northern Santa Fe Foundation Scholarship: Chapter 9, "Native American" section
- Careers in Agriculture Scholarship: Chapter 6, "Agriculture" section
- Hays Medical Center Scholarships: Chapter 6, "Health Care" section
- KBOR Nursing Scholarship: Chapter 6, "Nursing" section
- State Funeral Director Associations Scholarships: Chapter 6, "Funeral Service and Mortuary Science" section

Kentucky

College Access Program Grant

Sponsor: Kentucky Higher Education Assistance Authority
Web Site: http://www.kheaa.com/prog_cap.html
Amount of Scholarship: up to $1,100
Number of Awards: not given
Deadline: not given
Education Level: high school seniors and college undergraduates
Eligibility: Applicant must be a Kentucky resident, enroll at a two-year college, four-year college, or technical college, and demonstrate financial need.

This Web page briefly describes Kentucky's educational grant program, including how much financial need a student must have to qualify and how much a qualified student may receive. You will be automatically considered for the grant when you file the FAFSA. A link to the online version of the FAFSA is also given on the page.

Kentucky Educational Excellence Scholarship

Sponsor: Kentucky Higher Education Assistance Authority
Web Site: http://www.kheaa.com/kees.html
Amount of Scholarship: varies
Number of Awards: not given
Deadline: not given
Education Level: high school students
Eligibility: Applicant must graduate from an eligible Kentucky high school, have a minimum 2.5 GPA, and enroll at an accredited two-year or four-year college in Kentucky.

The Frequently Asked Questions section of this Web page should answer your questions about qualifying for the scholarship and how you can use the scholarship money if you do win one. The amount of the scholarship varies depending on the GPA you maintain during high school, as explained in the Frequently Asked Questions. Follow the KEES Authorized Curriculum link to find out what courses you must take during high school to remain eligible for the scholarship. Good ACT or SAT I scores can qualify you for a supplemental scholarship, as well. The bonuses for ACT scores are explained in the Frequently Asked Questions, and a link to a SAT to ACT Conversion Table is provided so you can figure out what the equivalent SAT I scores are. You don't have to apply for the scholarship. If you meet the minimum GPA and curriculum requirements, your high school will automatically nominate you for an award.

Kentucky Tuition Grant

Sponsor: Kentucky Higher Education Assistance Authority
Web Site: http://www.kheaa.com/prog_ktg.html
Amount of Scholarship: $50 to $1,500
Number of Awards: not given
Deadline: not given
Education Level: high school seniors and college undergraduates
Eligibility: Applicant must be a Kentucky resident; enroll as a full-time student at an accredited private two-year or four-year college in Kentucky; not pursue a degree in divinity, theology, or religious education; and demonstrate financial need.

This Web page briefly describes Kentucky's tuition equalization grant program for students who attend private colleges in the state. You will be automatically considered for the grant when you file the FAFSA. A link to the online version of the FAFSA is also given on the Web page.

Also see the following scholarships:

- David J. Clark Memorial Scholarship Grant: Chapter 6, "Film and Television" section
- KHEAA Teacher Scholarship: Chapter 6, "Education" section
- KSCPA College Scholarship: Chapter 6, "Accounting" section
- KSCPA High School Scholarship: Chapter 6, "Accounting" section
- KSHN Educational Scholarships: Chapter 6, "Occupational Health and Safety" section
- Sidney B. Meadows Scholarship: Chapter 6, "Horticulture" section
- State Funeral Director Associations Scholarships: Chapter 6, "Funeral Service and Mortuary Science" section

Louisiana

Leveraging Educational Assistance Partnership Grant

Sponsor: Louisiana Office of Student Financial Assistance
Web Site: http://www.osfa.state.la.us/schgrt3.htm
Amount of Scholarship: $200 to $2,000 per year
Number of Awards: around 3,000
Deadline: not given
Education Level: high school seniors and college undergraduates
Eligibility: Applicant must be a Louisiana resident; enroll as a full-time student at an eligible two-year college, four-year college, or technical college in Louisiana; have a minimum 2.0 GPA, a minimum ACT score of 20, or a minimum score of 45 on the GED; demonstrate substantial financial need; and be a U.S. citizen or permanent resident.

This Web page lists all of the eligibility requirements of this need-based grant and the conditions for maintaining a grant once you have received one. Grant funds are distributed through college financial aid offices, so contact your financial aid officer if you want to be considered for a grant.

Rockefeller State Wildlife Scholarship

Sponsor: Louisiana Office of Student Financial Assistance
Web Site: http://www.osfa.state.la.us/schgrt4.htm
Amount of Scholarship: $1,000 per year (awarded over five years of undergraduate study and two years of graduate study)

Number of Awards: 30
Deadline: July 1
Education Level: college undergraduates and graduate students
Eligibility: Applicant must be a Louisiana resident; enroll as a full-time student at a Louisiana college or university; major in forestry, wildlife, or marine science; have completed at least 24 college credit hours; have a minimum 2.5 GPA; and be a U.S. citizen or permanent resident.

Be sure to read all the information on this page carefully to make certain that you meet the restrictive eligibility requirements. Note that if you don't fulfill all the requirements for maintaining eligibility, you must pay the scholarship money back with interest. You can download the application form in PDF format from the Web page, as well.

Tuition Opportunity Program for Students (TOPS) Scholarships

Sponsor: Louisiana Office of Student Financial Assistance
Web Site: http://www.osfa.state.la.us/schgrt6.htm
Amount of Scholarship: full tuition plus a stipend of up to $800
Number of Awards: not given
Deadline: April 15
Education Level: high school seniors
Eligibility: Applicant must graduate from a Louisiana high school, be a Louisiana resident, have a minimum 2.5 GPA, have a minimum ACT score of 19 or the equivalent SAT I score, and attend an eligible college in Louisiana.

Click the TOPS Frequently Asked Questions link to learn about this scholarship program. Five different awards are given under the program, each with its own eligibility require-ments, amounts, and renewal conditions. The TOPS Matrix page lists the GPA, test score, and other requirements for each award. The TOPS Core Curricula page lists the high school courses that you must take to qualify for all awards. Most of the awards are academic scholarships, but one is designated for students who plan to work as public school teachers in the state. To apply, you must submit the FAFSA and list the name of the Louisiana college you plan to attend on the form.

Also see the following scholarships:

• Congressional Black Caucus Spouses Scholarships: Chapter 15, "Alabama" section
• PFLAG Scholarship: Chapter 9, "Gay and Lesbian" section
• Sidney B. Meadows Scholarship: Chapter 6, "Horticulture" section
• State Funeral Director Associations Scholarships: Chapter 6, "Funeral Service and Mortuary Science" section

Maine

Maine Community Foundation Scholarships

Sponsor: Maine Community Foundation
Web Site: http://www.mainecf.org/scholar.html
Amount of Scholarship: not given
Number of Awards: not given
Deadline: varies
Education Level: high school seniors, college undergraduates, and graduate students
Eligibility: Applicant must be a Maine resident.

Maine Community Foundation is one of the largest sources of scholarship money in the state, offering 146 different scholarships for higher education. On the Web site, you can browse through the statewide awards by educational level and the regional awards by county. For each scholarship, you'll find a brief description of the award and the eligibility requirements, the name of the contact, the application deadline, and a downloadable application form in PDF format or instructions on how to obtain an application. Each scholarship has its own eligibility requirements, selection process, and application deadlines, so pay careful attention to the information given and follow instructions exactly.

Maine Student Incentive Scholarship

Sponsor: Finance Authority of Maine
Web Site: http://www.famemaine.com/msisp.htm
Amount of Scholarship: $500 to $1,250
Number of Awards: not given
Deadline: April 15
Education Level: high school seniors and college undergraduates
Eligibility: Applicant must be a Maine resident, attend an accredited two-year or four-year college in Maine or in a state that has a reciprocity agreement with Maine, and demonstrate financial need.

This Web page describes Maine's educational grant program. Read about eligibility requirements, award amounts, and applying for a grant. You will be automatically considered for a grant if you file the FAFSA.

MBNA Maine Scholars

Sponsor: MBNA
Web Site: http://www.mbnainternational.com/a_sch_maine.html
Amount of Scholarship: $500 to $6,500 (renewable for four years)
Number of Awards: not given
Deadline: December 11
Education Level: high school seniors
Eligibility: Applicant must live in an eligible area in Maine, have a minimum 2.5 GPA, have a minimum SAT I score of 900 or ACT score of 19, enroll as a full-time student at an accredited four-year college in Maine, demonstrate financial need, and be a U.S. citizen or permanent resident.

In addition to a scholarship, winners of this award also receive advising, summer internships, and part-time employment opportunities. The Web page goes over all the facts you need to know, including program benefits, eligibility requirements, how to obtain application materials, selection criteria, and renewal conditions. The Eligibility section lists the towns and counties in Maine where you must live in order to qualify. The Frequently Asked Questions page answers the most common questions about the scholarship. The Important Dates page tells you when applications are due and when other important steps in the application process occur. Although application materials aren't available on the Web site, you can easily obtain an application form from your high school guidance office or by calling the MBNA Scholars Program at the phone number given on the scholarship's main Web page.

MES Foundation Scholarships

Sponsor: MES Foundation
Web Site: http://www.mesfoundation.com
Amount of Scholarship: $150 to $2,500
Number of Awards: 46
Deadline: varies
Education Level: high school seniors, college undergraduates, and graduate students
Eligibility: Applicant must be a Maine resident.

You can learn about and apply for the six different scholarships administered by the MES Foundation through this Web site. Click the MES Online Scholarship Center link to access the scholarship information. There you will find brief descriptions of each scholarship; click the scholarship's name to learn details of eligibility requirements, award amounts, and application requirements. You can apply for any of the scholarships online by clicking the Begin Online Application Process link at the end of the scholarship's description. Since the application instructions and deadlines vary for each scholarship, you must be especially careful to fulfill all the requirements for the awards for which you are applying in order to receive proper consideration.

Robert C. Byrd Honors Scholarship

Sponsor: Finance Authority of Maine
Web Site: http://www.famemaine.com/edu/index.html
Amount of Scholarship: $1,500 (renewable for four years)
Number of Awards: not given
Deadline: April 15
Education Level: high school seniors
Eligibility: Applicant must attend high school in Maine and enroll at an eligible postsecondary institution.

To find information about this merit scholarship for high school seniors with high academic achievements, click the Maine Scholarships button in the left frame, then scroll to the bottom of the right frame. There you will see a short paragraph describing the award. As the paragraph explains, you can get application forms from your high school's guidance office. A contact phone number is also given for further questions and to request an application.

Also see the following scholarships:

- MASL Scholarship: Chapter 7, "Library and Information Science" section
- State Funeral Director Associations Scholarships: Chapter 6, "Funeral Service and Mortuary Science" section
- Switzer Environmental Fellowship: Chapter 7, "Environmental Studies" section

Maryland

Delegate Scholarship

Sponsor: Maryland Higher Education Commission and Maryland State Scholarship Administration (SSA)
Web Site: http://www.mhec.state.md.us/SSA/introduction.htm
Amount of Scholarship: $200
Number of Awards: not given
Deadline: March 1
Education Level: high school seniors, college undergraduates, and graduate students
Eligibility: Applicant must be a Maryland resident, and enroll at a two-year or four-year college or graduate school in Maryland.

To find information about this scholarship, click the Program Description link in the left frame, scroll down the list until you find the name of the scholarship, and then click it. You will see an overview of the scholarship, including the applicant qualifications and application instructions. Each of the Maryland delegates establish their own eligibility requirements and application procedures for the scholarship, so you should call or write the delegates in your legislative district to find out exactly how to apply. You can also contact the State Scholarship Administration directly with questions; click the Email SSA link in the left frame to send an e-mail message to the State Scholarship Administration.

Distinguished Scholar Award

Sponsor: Maryland Higher Education Commission and Maryland State Scholarship Administration

Web Site: http://www.mhec.state.md.us/SSA/introduction.htm

Amount of Scholarship: $3,000 (renewable for four years)

Number of Awards: not given

Deadline: not given

Education Level: high school juniors

Eligibility: Applicant must be a Maryland resident and enroll as a full-time student at a Maryland college.

To find information about this scholarship, click the Program Description link in the left frame, scroll down the list until you find the name of the scholarship, and then click it. You can qualify for this scholarship in three ways: become a National Merit Scholarship finalist; be nominated by your high school for excellence in the performing arts; or have a minimum 3.7 GPA in academic subjects. Applications are available from your high school's guidance office.

Educational Assistance Grant

Sponsor: Maryland Higher Education Commission and Maryland State Scholarship Administration

Web Site: http://www.mhec.state.md.us/SSA/introduction.htm

Amount of Scholarship: $200 to $3,000 (renewable for four years)

Number of Awards: not given

Deadline: March 1

Education Level: high school seniors and college undergraduates

Eligibility: Applicant must be a Maryland resident, enroll as a full-time student at a two-year or four-year college in Maryland, and demonstrate financial need.

To find information about this state educational grant, click the Program Description link in the left frame, scroll down the list until you find the name of the scholarship, and then click it. You will automatically be considered for the grant if you submit the FAFSA.

Guaranteed Access (GA) Grant

Sponsor: Maryland Higher Education Commission and Maryland State Scholarship Administration

Web Site: http://www.mhec.state.md.us/SSA/introduction.htm

Amount of Scholarship: $8,400 (renewable for four years)

Number of Awards: not given

Deadline: March 1

Education Level: high school seniors and college undergraduates

Eligibility: Applicant must be a Maryland resident, graduate from a Maryland high school, have a minimum 2.5 GPA, enroll as a full-time student at a two-year or four-year college in Maryland, be under the age of 22, and have an annual total family income below 130 percent of the federal poverty level.

To find information about this grant, click the Program Description link in the left frame, scroll down the list until you find the name of the scholarship, and then click it. To apply for this scholarship, you must file the FAFSA and submit the GA Grant Application. You can get this application from your high school guidance counselor. Alternatively, click the Online Applications link in the left frame to find contact information for the Maryland State Scholarship Administration, from whom you can order applications (application materials were not available on the Web site at the time of this writing).

Jack F. Tolbert Memorial Grant

Sponsor: Maryland Higher Education Commission and Maryland State Scholarship Administration
Web Site: http://www.mhec.state.md.us/SSA/introduction.htm
Amount of Scholarship: $200 to $1,500
Number of Awards: not given
Deadline: not given
Education Level: career school students
Eligibility: Applicant must be a Maryland resident, enroll at an approved private career school in Maryland for at least 18 clock hours a week, and demonstrate financial need.

To find information about this grant, click the Program Description link in the left frame, scroll down the list until you find the name of the grant, and then click it. You must apply directly to the financial aid office of the career school you want to attend and file the FAFSA in order to be considered for the grant.

Maryland HOPE Scholarship

Sponsor: Maryland Higher Education Commission and Maryland State Scholarship Administration
Web Site: http://www.mhec.state.md.us/SSA/introduction.htm
Amount of Scholarship: $1,000 to $3,000 (renewable for four years)
Number of Awards: not given
Deadline: March 1
Education Level: high school seniors
Eligibility: Applicant must be a Maryland resident, have a minimum 3.0 GPA, enroll as a full-time student in an eligible degree program at a two-year or four-year college in Maryland, and demonstrate financial need.

To find information about this scholarship, click the Program Description link in the left frame, scroll down the list until you find the name of the scholarship, and then click it. You will see an overview of the scholarship, including the program's goal, eligibility requirements, application instructions, and a list of eligible degree programs that you can study under the award. Note that this is a service scholarship; you must commit to one year of employment in Maryland for each year that you received scholarship money. To apply, you must submit the FAFSA and the Maryland HOPE Scholarship Programs application, which you can obtain from your school's financial aid office or guidance office, or by contacting the State Scholarship Administration directly. Click the Online Applications link in the left frame to find a phone number that you can call to order application forms; presently, no applications are available on the Web.

Maryland Science and Technology Scholarship

Sponsor: Maryland Higher Education Commission and Maryland State Scholarship Administration
Web Site: http://www.mhec.state.md.us/SSA/introduction.htm
Amount of Scholarship: $1,000 to $3,000
Number of Awards: not given
Deadline: March 1
Education Level: high school seniors
Eligibility: Applicant must be a Maryland resident, enroll as a full-time student at a two-year or four-year Maryland college, major in an eligible subject in the sciences or technology, and have a minimum 3.0 GPA.

To find information about this scholarship, click the Program Description link in the left frame, scroll down the list until you find the name of the scholarship, and then click it. You will see an overview of the scholarship, including the program's goals, eligibility requirements, application instructions, and a list of eligible majors and colleges. To apply, you must submit the HOPE Scholarship application, which you can obtain from your guidance counselor or by contacting the State Scholarship Administration directly. Click the Online Applications link in the left frame to find a phone number that you can call to order application forms; presently, no applications are available on the Web.

Part-Time Grant

Sponsor: Maryland Higher Education Commission and Maryland State Scholarship Administration
Web Site: http://www.mhec.state.md.us/SSA/introduction.htm
Amount of Scholarship: $200 to $1,000 (renewable for eight years)
Number of Awards: not given
Deadline: not given
Education Level: college undergraduates
Eligibility: Applicant must be a Maryland resident, enroll at a Maryland college for between 6 and 11 credit hours each semester, and demonstrate financial need.

To find information about this grant, click the Program Description link in the left frame, scroll down the list until you find the name of the grant, and then click it. You must apply directly to the financial aid office of the career school you want to attend and file the FAFSA in order to be considered for the grant.

Professional School Scholarship

Sponsor: Maryland Higher Education Commission and Maryland State Scholarship Administration
Web Site: http://www.mhec.state.md.us/SSA/introduction.htm
Amount of Scholarship: $200 to $1,000 (renewable for four years)

Number of Awards: not given
Deadline: March 1
Education Level: college undergraduates and graduate students
Eligibility: Applicant must be a Maryland resident; enroll as a full-time student in an undergraduate nursing or pharmacy program or in a graduate dentistry, law, medical, nursing, or pharmacy program; and demonstrate financial need.

To find information about this scholarship, click the Program Description link in the left frame, scroll down the list until you find the name of the scholarship, and then click it. You will see an overview of the scholarship, including the program's goals, eligibility requirements, and application instructions. To apply, you must submit the FAFSA and the Professional School Scholarship application, which you can obtain from your school's financial aid office or by contacting the State Scholarship Administration directly. Click the Online Applications link in the left frame to find a phone number that you can call to order application forms; presently, no applications are available on the Web.

Senatorial Scholarship

Sponsor: Maryland Higher Education Commission and Maryland State Scholarship Administration (SSA)
Web Site: http://www.mhec.state.md.us/SSA/introduction.htm
Amount of Scholarship: $200 to $2,000
Number of Awards: not given
Deadline: March 1
Education Level: high school seniors, college undergraduates, and graduate students
Eligibility: Applicant must be a Maryland resident, enroll at a two-year or four-year college or graduate school in Maryland, and demonstrate financial need.

To find information about this scholarship, click the Program Description link in the left frame, scroll down the list until you find the name of the scholarship, and then click it. You will see an overview of the scholarship, including the applicant qualifications and application instructions. Each of the Maryland senators establishes their own application procedures for the scholarship, so you should write your senator directly to find out exactly how to apply. You can also contact the State Scholarship Administration with questions; click the Email SSA link in the left frame to send an e-mail message to the State Scholarship Administration.

Also see the following scholarships:

- Bank of America ADA Abilities Scholarship: Chapter 10, "Any Disability" section
- Child Care Provider Scholarship: Chapter 6, "Education" section
- Congressional Black Caucus Spouses Scholarships: Chapter 15, "Alabama" section
- Distinguished Scholar Teacher Education Scholarship: Chapter 6, "Education" section
- Edward T. Conroy Memorial Scholarship: Chapter 14, "Military Personnel and Veterans" section
- Hispanic American Commitment to Education Resources Scholarship: Chapter 9, "Hispanic" section
- Long & Foster Scholarship: Chapter 15, "Delaware" section
- MACPA Scholarship: Chapter 6, "Accounting" section
- Maryland HOPE Teacher Scholarship: Chapter 6, "Education" section
- Maryland Physical and Occupational Therapists and Assistants Grant: Chapter 6, "Occupational and Physical Therapy" section
- Maryland State Nursing Scholarship and Living Expenses Grant: Chapter 6, "Nursing" section

- Project Excellence Scholarships: Chapter 9, "African-American" section
- Sharon Christa McAuliffe Memorial Teacher Education Award: Chapter 6, "Education" section
- Sidney B. Meadows Scholarship: Chapter 6, "Horticulture" section
- State Funeral Director Associations Scholarships: Chapter 6, "Funeral Service and Mortuary Science" section

Massachusetts

City of Boston Scholarship

Sponsor: City of Boston
Web Site: http://www.cityofboston.com/scholarship/program.asp
Amount of Scholarship: not given
Number of Awards: not given
Deadline: April 1
Education Level: high school seniors
Eligibility: Applicant must have been a legal resident of Boston for at least two years and enroll as a full-time student at an accredited two-year or four-year college in Massachusetts.

Here you will find a rundown of all the facts about the scholarship, including the eligibility requirements, the documents required in the application package, the selection criteria, and where to write to request an application. Application materials are not available on the Web site.

Also see the following scholarships:

- Hispanic American Commitment to Education Resources Scholarship: Chapter 9, "Hispanic" section
- Switzer Environmental Fellowship: Chapter 7, "Environmental Studies" section

Michigan

Adult Part-Time Grant

Sponsor: State of Michigan Office of Scholarship and Grants
Web Site: http://www.MI-StudentAid.org/parentsandstudents/highbeyond/cbprogs/aptg.html
Amount of Scholarship: $600 (renewable for two years)
Number of Awards: not given
Deadline: not given
Education Level: college undergraduates
Eligibility: Applicant must be a Michigan resident; have been out of high school for at least two years or have earned the GED; enroll as a part-time student in an undergraduate program lasting at least nine months at a participating two-year or four-year college in Michigan, excluding theology and divinity programs; demonstrate financial need; and be a U.S. citizen or permanent resident.

Here you will find an overview of the eligibility requirements for this grant for adult college students. You must file the FAFSA to be considered for the grant; a link to the electronic FAFSA is provided under the Application Procedures section of the Web page. You may also have to complete additional forms, so check with your school's financial aid office to find out what is required. A link to a list of participating Michigan colleges is also given on the Web page.

Community Foundation of Greater Rochester Scholarships

Sponsor: Community Foundation of Greater Rochester
Web Site: http://www.cfound.org/sch_main.html
Amount of Scholarship: $500 to $2,500
Number of Awards: not given
Deadline: February 1
Education Level: high school seniors
Eligibility: Applicant must reside in the greater Rochester area.

In the general description of the scholarship program at the top of the page, you'll find details about selection criteria and the application process. Beneath that, you will find links to the application forms and instructions in PDF format, as well as a list of all the items that must be included in the application package. Click the Descriptions link to download a list of the 14 available scholarships, along with their eligibility requirements and award amounts. Make a note of the scholarships for which you are the most qualified; you are only allowed to apply for two awards, which you must indicate on the application form.

Grand Rapids Foundation Scholarships

Sponsor: Grand Rapids Foundation
Web Site: http://www.grfoundation.org/scholarships.html
Amount of Scholarship: not given
Number of Awards: not given
Deadline: varies
Education Level: high school seniors, college undergraduates, and graduate students
Eligibility: Applicant must reside in the Grand Rapids area.

The Grand Rapids Foundation offers 25 different scholarships. All of the awards are described at the bottom of the Web page. Check eligibility requirements carefully and note the awards that you qualify for. You must apply for each scholarship separately. PDF copies of the application forms for some scholarships are available for downloading from the Web site, but you will have to request the other applications directly as instructed in the scholarship's descriptions.

Lenawee County Education Foundation Scholarships

Sponsor: Lenawee County Education Foundation
Web Site: http://scholarships.lisd.k12.mi.us
Amount of Scholarship: not given
Number of Awards: not given
Deadline: March
Education Level: high school seniors and college undergraduates
Eligibility: Applicant must graduate from a Lenawee County high school or be a resident of Lenawee County.

Here you will find descriptions of the 56 different scholarships offered to Lenawee County residents. Scholarships are categorized by the field the applicant must plan to study in order to qualify: sciences; health care; teacher education; business; vocational-technical; and miscellaneous. For each scholarship, you'll find a short description of eligibility requirements, selection criteria, and goals, as well as a link to a downloadable application form in PDF format. You must apply separately for each scholarship.

Michigan Competitive Scholarship

Sponsor: State of Michigan Office of Scholarship and Grants
Web Site: http://www.MI-StudentAid.org/aboutus/MOSG/mcsp.html
Amount of Scholarship: not given
Number of Awards: around 30,000
Deadline: February 21 (entering freshmen) and March 21 (upperclassmen)
Education Level: high school seniors and college undergraduates

Eligibility: Applicant must be a Michigan resident; have a minimum 2.0 GPA; achieve a qualifying score on the ACT; enroll at an approved two-year or four-year college in Michigan; not pursue a degree in theology, divinity, or religious education; demonstrate financial need; and be a U.S. citizen or permanent resident.

Here you will find a rundown of all the eligibility requirements for this scholarship. You must file the FAFSA to be considered for the award; a link to the electronic FAFSA is provided under the Application Procedure section. At the bottom of the page, you'll find a list of colleges in Michigan where you can use the scholarship.

Michigan Educational Opportunity Grant

Sponsor: State of Michigan Office of Scholarship and Grants
Web Site: http://www.MI-StudentAid.org/parentsandstudents/highbeyond/cbprogs/meog.html
Amount of Scholarship: $1,000 (renewable for up to five years)
Number of Awards: not given
Deadline: not given
Education Level: high school seniors and college undergraduates
Eligibility: Applicant must be a Michigan resident; enroll in an undergraduate program lasting at least nine months at a participating public two-year or four-year college in Michigan, excluding theology and divinity programs; demonstrate financial need; and be a U.S. citizen or permanent resident.

Here you will find a list of all the eligibility requirements for this grant. You must file the FAFSA to be considered; a link to the electronic FAFSA is given under the Application Procedure section of the Web page. You may also have to complete additional forms, so check with your school's financial aid office to find out what is required. A link to a list of participating Michigan colleges is also provided on the Web page.

Michigan Tuition Grant

Sponsor: State of Michigan Office of Scholarship and Grants
Web Site: http://www.MI-StudentAid.org/aboutus/MOSG/mtgp.html
Amount of Scholarship: not given
Number of Awards: around 30,000
Deadline: February 21 (entering freshmen) and March 21 (upperclassmen)
Education Level: high school seniors and college undergraduates
Eligibility: Applicant must be a Michigan resident; enroll at an approved private college in Michigan; not pursue a degree in theology, divinity, or religious education; demonstrate financial need; and be a U.S. citizen or permanent resident.

This page gives find an overview of all the eligibility requirements for this tuition equalization scholarship for students attending private colleges in Michigan. You must file the FAFSA to be considered for the scholarship; a link to the electronic FAFSA is given under the Application Procedures section of the Web page. At the bottom of the page, you'll find a list of private colleges in Michigan where you can use the scholarship.

Newaygo County Scholarships

Sponsor: Fremont Area Foundation
Web Site: http://www.tfaf.org/pages/3.html
Amount of Scholarship: $250 to $2,000
Number of Awards: not given
Deadline: not given

Education Level: high school seniors
Eligibility: Applicant must attend high school in Newaygo County.

Thirty-four different scholarships are available under this program. Scholarships descriptions are categorized by eligible high school and are linked to the top of the Web page. Be sure to check the eligibility requirements carefully and make a note of all awards for which you want to apply. Return to the main page to find links to the application form and financial questionnaire for all scholarships. To complete the application, fill out the form in your Web browser, click the Create Printable Application button, and then use the Print function of your browser to print the results for mailing. You can apply for as many scholarships as you want using the same application form; just follow the instructions under Application Process on the main Web page.

Robert C. Byrd Honors Scholarship

Sponsor: State of Michigan Office of Scholarship and Grants
Web Site: http://www.MI-StudentAid.org/aboutus/MOSG/byrd.html
Amount of Scholarship: not given
Number of Awards: not given
Deadline: not given
Education Level: high school seniors
Eligibility: Applicant must be a Michigan resident, enroll as a full-time student at an approved postsecondary institution, and be a U.S. citizen or permanent resident.

Here you will find a rundown of all the eligibility requirements for this merit scholarship. You don't apply for the scholarship. Instead, you must be nominated by your high school principal, as described in the Application Procedures section of the page.

Also see the following scholarships:

- American Legion Auxiliary Memorial Scholarship: Chapter 14, "Military Personnel and Veterans" section
- American Legion Auxiliary Scholarship for Non-Traditional Students: Chapter 14, "Military Personnel and Veterans" section
- Brewer Scholarship: Chapter 14, "Military Personnel and Veterans" section
- Careers in Agriculture Scholarship: Chapter 6, "Agriculture" section
- Congressional Black Caucus Spouses Scholarships: Chapter 15, "Alabama" section
- Michigan Farm Bureau Scholarships: Chapter 14, "Employer and Profession" section
- Nurses, Physical Therapists, and Respiratory Therapists Scholarship: Chapter 14, "Military Personnel and Veterans" section
- State Funeral Director Associations Scholarships: Chapter 6, "Funeral Service and Mortuary Science" section
- Wilson Scholarship: Chapter 14, "Military Personnel and Veterans" section

Minnesota

Minnesota Academic Excellence Scholarship

Sponsor: Minnesota Higher Education Services Office
Web Site: http://www.mheso.state.mn.us
Amount of Scholarship: up to full tuition (renewable for four years)
Number of Awards: not given
Deadline: not given
Education Level: high school seniors
Eligibility: Applicant must enroll as a full-time student in a nonsectarian bachelor's degree program at a college in Minnesota.

To find information about this scholarship, click the Students & Parents link, then follow the Scholarships link. This scholarship rewards students who have demonstrated outstanding academic achievement, as described on the Web page. The page also tells you who is eligible for the scholarship and how much money you can get. Contact the financial aid officer at the college you want to attend if you are interested in applying for this scholarship.

Minnesota Masonic Foundation Public School Scholarship

Sponsor: Minnesota Masonic Foundation, Inc.
Web Site: http://www.mn-mason.org/ scholars.html
Amount of Scholarship: not given
Number of Awards: not given
Deadline: varies
Education Level: high school seniors
Eligibility: Applicant must graduate from a Minnesota public high school.

This scholarship is sponsored through participating Masonic Lodges in Minnesota, so if you want to be considered, you must apply through your local Lodge. While a generic application form is provided on the Web page, some Lodges may require you to complete their application forms, so be sure to find out what the precise application procedures are before submitting an application. Application deadlines vary between Lodges, as well. The Web page also tells you about the purpose of the scholarship and the topic of the essay that you must include with your application.

Minnesota State Grant

Sponsor: Minnesota Higher Education Services Office
Web Site: http://www.mheso.state.mn.us

Amount of Scholarship: $100 to $7,089 (renewable for four years)
Number of Awards: not given
Deadline: not given
Education Level: high school seniors and college undergraduates
Eligibility: Applicant must be a Minnesota resident, enroll for at least three credits at an eligible two-year or four-year college in Minnesota, be over the age of 17, and demonstrate financial need.

To find information about this grant, click the Students & Parents link, then follow the Grants link. This Web page explains everything you need to know about Minnesota's educational grant program for low- to moderate-income students. You'll find out how the amount of the award is determined, how much financial need you must have to qualify, who is eligible, and how you can renew the grant in future years. You will automatically be considered for a Minnesota State Grant when you file the FAFSA; you don't have to do anything else.

Robert C. Byrd Scholarship

Sponsor: Minnesota Higher Education Services Office
Web Site: http://www.mheso.state.mn.us
Amount of Scholarship: $1,500 (renewable for four years)
Number of Awards: 119
Deadline: early March
Education Level: high school seniors
Eligibility: Applicant must be a Minnesota resident and attend any accredited postsecondary institution in the U.S.

To find information about this scholarship, click the Students & Parents links, then follow the Scholarships link. On this Web page you can learn who is eligible for this scholarship program, how many awards are given out each year, how much money you can get, and what the application process is. Your high school principal must nominate you for this award, so if you are interested in applying, contact your principal or guidance counselor to find out what you need to do.

Also see the following scholarships:

- Burlington Northern Santa Fe Foundation Scholarship: Chapter 9, "Native American" section
- Careers in Agriculture Scholarship: Chapter 6, "Agriculture" section
- Catholic Aid Association College Tuition Scholarship: Chapter 11, "Catholic" section
- Minnesota Gay/Lesbian/Bisexual/Transgender Scholarships: Chapter 9, "Gay and Lesbian" section
- Minnesota Indian Scholarship: Chapter 9, "Native American" section
- Page Education Foundation Scholarship: Chapter 9, "All Minorities" section
- Regional EAGLE Scholarship: Chapter 9, "Gay and Lesbian" section
- Safety Officers' Survivor Grant: Chapter 14, "Public Safety Officers" section
- State Funeral Director Associations Scholarships: Chapter 6, "Funeral Service and Mortuary Science" section

Mississippi

See the following scholarships:

- Congressional Black Caucus Spouses Scholarships: Chapter 15, "Alabama" section
- Sidney B. Meadows Scholarship: Chapter 6, "Horticulture" section
- State Funeral Director Associations Scholarships: Chapter 6, "Funeral Service and Mortuary Science" section

Missouri

Charles Gallagher Student Financial Assistance Grant

Sponsor: Missouri Department of Higher Education Student Assistance Division
Web Site: http://www.mocbhe.gov/mostars/scholar2.htm#Gallagher
Amount of Scholarship: up to $1,500
Number of Awards: not given
Deadline: April 1
Education Level: high school seniors and college undergraduates
Eligibility: Applicant must be a Missouri resident, enroll as a full-time student at a participating four-year college in Missouri, not already hold a bachelor's degree, not pursue a degree in theology or divinity, demonstrate financial need, and be a U.S. citizen or permanent resident.

This is Missouri's need-based educational grant program. The Web page tells you how to become eligible for the grant and how much you can receive. You will automatically be considered for the grant when you file the FAFSA. To find a list of participating Missouri colleges where you can use the grant, scroll to the top of the page and click the State Student Financial Assistance Programs Eligible Schools List link. Contact information for asking further questions about this grant is provided at the very bottom of the page.

Greater Kansas City Community Foundation Scholarships

Sponsor: Greater Kansas City Community Foundation
Web Site: http://www.gkccf.org
Amount of Scholarship: not given
Number of Awards: 350

Deadline: varies
Education Level: high school seniors, college undergraduates, and graduate students
Eligibility: Applicant must reside or attend school in the greater Kansas City area.

This page lists the 60 scholarships sponsored by the foundation for college- and graduate-level study. Scroll down to the Undergraduate and Graduate sections of the Web page to find applicable scholarships. Click on the link to any scholarship to read about the award's objectives, eligibility requirements, amount, and application deadline. You'll also find a contact address you can write to request additional information and application materials. You must apply for each scholarship separately, but if you have any general questions about the program, you can contact the Scholarships Coordinator at the e-mail address given at the top of the page.

Higher Education Academic Scholarship

Sponsor: Missouri Department of Higher Education Student Assistance Division
Web Site: http://www.mocbhe.gov/mostars/scholar2.htm#Bright
Amount of Scholarship: $2,000
Number of Awards: not given
Deadline: July 31
Education Level: high school seniors
Eligibility: Applicant must be a Missouri resident, enroll as a full-time student at an approved two-year or four-year college in Missouri, have an ACT or SAT I score in the top 3 percent of all Missouri students, not pursue a degree in theology or divinity, and be a U.S. citizen or permanent resident.

This section of the Web page tells you what the eligibility requirements for this merit scholarship are and provides a toll-free phone number you can call to find out what the qualifying ACT and SAT I scores for that year are. Also find out how to qualify for the scholarship if you were home-schooled. If you qualify, you can obtain application materials from your high school guidance counselor or college financial aid officer. To find a list of participating Missouri colleges where you can use the scholarship, scroll to the top of the page and click the State Student Financial Assistance Programs Eligible Schools List link.

Marguerite Ross Barnett Memorial Scholarship

Sponsor: Missouri Department of Higher Education Student Assistance Division
Web Site: http://www.mocbhe.gov/mostars/scholar2.htm#Ross
Amount of Scholarship: not given
Number of Awards: not given
Deadline: April 1
Education Level: college undergraduates
Eligibility: Applicant must be a Missouri resident, enroll as a part-time student at a participating postsecondary school in Missouri, be employed at least 20 hours a week, not pursue a degree in theology or divinity, demonstrate financial need, and be a U.S. citizen or permanent resident.

This section of the Web page gives the details about this scholarship for Missouri residents who are working their way through college. You'll learn what the eligibility requirements are, how much you can receive, and how you can apply for the scholarship. A toll-free phone number that you can call to request application materials is also provided. To find a list of participating Missouri colleges where you can use the scholarship, scroll to the top of the page and click the State Student Financial Assistance Programs Eligible Schools List link.

Missouri College Guarantee Scholarship

Sponsor: Missouri Department of Higher Education Student Assistance Division
Web Site: http://www.mocbhe.gov/mostars/scholar2.htm#Guarantee
Amount of Scholarship: not given
Number of Awards: not given
Deadline: April 1
Education Level: high school seniors and college undergraduates
Eligibility: Applicant must be a Missouri resident, enroll as a full-time student at a participating two-year or four-year college in Missouri, have a minimum 2.5 GPA, have a minimum ACT score of 20 or a minimum SAT I score of 950, not pursue a degree in theology or divinity, demonstrate financial need, and be a U.S. citizen or permanent resident.

This scholarship is awarded based on both financial need and academic achievement. The section of the Web page describing the scholarship lists the eligibility requirements and other details. You will be automatically considered for the scholarship when you file the FAFSA. To find a list of participating Missouri colleges where you can use the scholarship, scroll to the top of the page and click the State Student Financial Assistance Programs Eligible Schools List link. Contact information for asking further questions about this scholarship is provided at the very bottom of the page.

Missouri Department of Agriculture Scholarship

Sponsor: Missouri Department of Agriculture
Web Site: http://www.mda.state.mo.us/a5a.htm
Amount of Scholarship: $250 to $500
Number of Awards: 22
Deadline: March 3

Education Level: high school seniors

Eligibility: Applicant must be a Missouri resident, major in agriculture or family and consumer sciences at a preapproved two-year or four-year college in Missouri, and receive income from a family farm.

Missouri's state department of agriculture offers financial aid to Missouri residents from rural backgrounds who plan to study agriculture. Fourteen scholarship winners who attend a four-year college receive $500 scholarships, and eight winners who attend a two-year college receive $250 scholarships. If you meet all the eligibility requirements, download and print the PDF application form linked to the Web page. The application also lists participating Missouri colleges where the scholarship money may be used, along with the agricultural programs they offer.

Also see the following scholarships:

- Bank of America ADA Abilities Scholarship: Chapter 10, "Any Disability" section
- Congressional Black Caucus Spouses Scholarships: Chapter 15, "Alabama" section
- Public Service Survivor Grant: Chapter 14, "Public Safety Officers" section
- Sidney B. Meadows Scholarship: Chapter 6, "Horticulture" section
- State Funeral Director Associations Scholarships: Chapter 6, "Funeral Service and Mortuary Science" section
- Vietnam Veterans Survivor Grant: Chapter 14, "Military Personnel and Veterans" section

Montana

Baker Grant

Sponsor: Montana Guaranteed Student Loan Program

Web Site: http://www.mgslp.state.mt.us/mtap.html

Amount of Scholarship: $500

Number of Awards: not given

Deadline: not given

Education Level: high school seniors and college undergraduates

Eligibility: Applicant must be a Montana resident, enroll as a full-time student at an eligible two-year or four-year college in Montana, be pursuing a first degree or certificate, have $2,500 or more from earned income from the previous year, and demonstrate financial need.

This grant is intended to reward students who work to help pay their college costs. The Web page describes the purpose of the grant, the eligibility requirements, and the application procedures. You will automatically be considered for the grant when you file the FAFSA. A list of eligible colleges where the grant may be used is given at the bottom of the page.

Also see the following scholarships:

- Burlington Northern Santa Fe Foundation Scholarship: Chapter 9, "Native American" section
- Careers in Agriculture Scholarship: Chapter 6, "Agriculture" section
- GSBA, Pride, and INBA Scholarships: Chapter 9, "Gay and Lesbian" section
- Montana Bandmasters Association Scholarship: Chapter 6, "Music" section
- Regional EAGLE Scholarship: Chapter 9, "Gay and Lesbian" section
- State Funeral Director Associations Scholarships: Chapter 6, "Funeral Service and Mortuary Science" section

Nebraska

See the following scholarships:

- Careers in Agriculture Scholarship: Chapter 6, "Agriculture" section
- Regional EAGLE Scholarship: Chapter 9, "Gay and Lesbian" section
- State Funeral Director Associations Scholarships: Chapter 6, "Funeral Service and Mortuary Science" section

Nevada

Millennium Scholarship

Sponsor: Office of the State Treasurer
Web Site: http://millennium.state.nv.us
Amount of Scholarship: $40 to $80 per credit hour (renewable for eight years)
Number of Awards: not given
Deadline: not given
Education Level: high school seniors
Eligibility: Applicant must have been a Nevada resident for at least two years, graduate from a Nevada high school, have a minimum 3.0 GPA, pass all areas of the Nevada High School Proficiency Examination, and enroll at a public two-year or four-year college in Nevada.

To get an overview of this scholarship, click the General Information link. Then, follow the Fact Sheet link to learn all the details about qualifying for the scholarship, where and how you can use the award, and how to keep the scholarship in successive years. The bottom of this page provides contact information for the Millennium Scholarship Office and for admissions and financial aid offices at all eligible Nevada colleges. You will automatically receive the scholarship if you meet all the prerequisites;

contact your guidance counselor if you need to know more.

Also see the following scholarships:

- Bank of America ADA Abilities Scholarship: Chapter 10, "Any Disability" section
- Hispanic American Commitment to Education Resources Scholarship: Chapter 9, "Hispanic" section

New Hampshire

New Hampshire Career Incentive Grant

Sponsor: New Hampshire Postsecondary Education Commission
Web Site: http://www.state.nh.us/postsecondary/cip.html
Amount of Scholarship: not given
Number of Awards: not given
Deadline: December 15 and June 1
Education Level: college sophomores, juniors, and seniors and graduate students
Eligibility: Applicant must enroll in a degree program in a career shortage area at a New Hampshire four-year college or graduate school and have a minimum 3.0 GPA.

For this service scholarship, students receive money in exchange for studying a field that has been named a career shortage area in New Hampshire. Career shortage areas are determined on a biennial basis, and the current fields are listed on the Web page, along with the eligibility requirements and other details of the scholarship. If you are interested in applying, fill out and submit the electronic form at the bottom of the Web page, and application materials will be mailed to you.

New Hampshire Charitable Foundation Scholarships

Sponsor: New Hampshire Charitable Foundation
Web Site: http://www.nhcf.org
Amount of Scholarship: not given
Number of Awards: not given
Deadline: varies
Education Level: high school seniors, college undergraduates, and graduate students
Eligibility: Applicant must be a New Hampshire resident.

The opening page describes the mission of this large scholarship sponsor. To learn more about the scholarships that are available under the program, click the Student Scholarships and Loans button in the left frame. First, click the Understand link to find an overview of the program as a whole. Then follow the Learn link to read a rundown of the application and selection process; this information will help you prepare a better application package. Finally, follow the Discover link to open a list of the twenty scholarships available under the program. These scholarships are categorized by geographical region. Click on the link beneath each scholarship's description to open a PDF file with a longer description and an application form. You must apply for each scholarship separately. Note that some, but not all, of these scholarships require an application fee.

New Hampshire Incentive Grant

Sponsor: New Hampshire Postsecondary Education Commission
Web Site: http://www.state.nh.us/postsecondary/nhip.html
Amount of Scholarship: not given
Number of Awards: not given

Deadline: May 1
Education Level: high school seniors and college undergraduates
Eligibility: Applicant must be a New Hampshire resident, enroll as a full-time student at an accredited postsecondary institution in New England, and have a minimum 2.0 GPA.

This Web page describes New Hampshire's educational grant program, including the eligibility requirements. You will automatically be considered for the grant if you file the FAFSA. To receive more information about the grant program, fill out and submit the electronic form at the bottom of the page.

Robert C. Byrd Scholarship

Sponsor: New Hampshire Postsecondary Education Commission
Web Site: http://www.state.nh.us/postsecondary/rcbs.html
Amount of Scholarship: not given
Number of Awards: not given
Deadline: May 1
Education Level: high school seniors
Eligibility: Applicant must be a New Hampshire resident, enroll as a full-time student at an accredited postsecondary institution, and be a U.S. citizen or permanent resident.

Here you will find a brief description of a merit scholarship for New Hampshire students. Call the telephone number listed at the bottom of the page to request more information and an application.

Also see the following scholarships:

- Scholarship for Orphans of Veterans: Chapter 14, "Military Personnel and Veterans" section
- State Funeral Director Associations Scholarships: Chapter 6, "Funeral Service and Mortuary Science" section

- Switzer Environmental Fellowship: Chapter 7, "Environmental Studies" section
- Veterinary Education Scholarship: Chapter 7, "Veterinary Medicine" section

New Jersey

Edward J. Bloustein Distinguished Scholars

Sponsor: New Jersey Education Student Assistance Authority
Web Site: http://www.state.nj.us/treasury/osa/scholar/bloustein_desc.html
Amount of Scholarship: $1,000 (renewable for five years)
Number of Awards: not given
Deadline: not given
Education Level: high school seniors
Eligibility: Applicant must attend a New Jersey high school; either rank in the top 10 percent of the high school class and have a minimum SAT I score of 1260 or rank first, second, or third in the high school class; and enroll at an approved two-year or four-year college in New Jersey.

The Description page of this scholarship's Web site gives a brief overview of the award. Click the Amounts and Payments links to find out the amount of the scholarship and its duration. Go to the Criteria page to learn what the eligibility criteria are. The Application page describes the application process. You don't apply directly for this scholarship; rather, your high school will nominate you for the award if you meet the eligibility criteria by the end of your junior year.

Martin Luther King, Jr. Physician & Dentist Scholarship

Sponsor: New Jersey Education Student Assistance Authority
Web Site: http://www.state.nj.us/treasury/osa/grants/mlkindex.html
Amount of Scholarship: not given
Number of Awards: not given
Deadline: not given
Education Level: college seniors
Eligibility: Applicant must have been a New Jersey resident for at least two years, enroll as a full-time student in a program leading to a medical degree at the University of Medicine and Dentistry in New Jersey, and be a member of a minority group.

The Eligibility page of this scholarship's Web site gives a brief overview of the requirements applicants must meet. Click the Benefits link to find out what the scholarship amounts are. The Application link tells you how to obtain an application form.

NJPSA Student Scholarship

Sponsor: New Jersey Principals and Supervisors Association (NJPSA)
Web Site: http://www.njpsa.org/docs/scholarships.htm
Amount of Scholarship: $1,000
Number of Awards: 9
Deadline: April 30
Education Level: high school seniors
Eligibility: Applicant must attend high school in New Jersey.

This Web page gives the details of the scholarship, including eligibility requirements and the application process. A link to the scholarship application is provided at the bottom of the page. Because each high school can only nominate one student for the award, you should ask your guidance counselor or principal how the nomination procedure works at your school.

Tuition Aid Grant

Sponsor: New Jersey Education Student Assistance Authority
Web Site: http://www.state.nj.us/treasury/osa/grants/tagelig.html
Amount of Scholarship: $844 to $6,674
Number of Awards: not given
Deadline: October 1, March 1, and June 1
Education Level: high school seniors and college undergraduates
Eligibility: Applicant must be a New Jersey resident, enroll as a full-time student at an approved two-year or four-year college in New Jersey, not have previously received an associate's or bachelor's degree, demonstrate financial need, and be a U.S. citizen or permanent resident.

The Eligibility page of this grant program's Web site lists the requirements you must meet to qualify for the grant. Click the Award Amounts link to find out the amount of the grant. The Deadline link tells you when you must file the FAFSA in order to be considered for the award.

Urban Scholars

Sponsor: New Jersey Education Student Assistance Authority
Web Site: http://www.state.nj.us/treasury/osa/scholar/urban_desc.html
Amount of Scholarship: $1,000 (renewable for five years)
Number of Awards: not given

Deadline: not given
Education Level: high school seniors
Eligibility: Applicant must attend high school in New Jersey's urban and economically distressed areas, rank in the top 10 percent of the high school class, have a minimum 3.0 GPA, and enroll at an approved two-year or four-year college in New Jersey.

The Description page of this scholarship's Web site gives a brief overview of the award. Click the Amounts and Payments links to find out the amount of the scholarship and its duration. Go to the Criteria page to learn what the eligibility criteria are. The Application page describes the application process. You don't apply directly for this scholarship; rather, your high school will nominate you for the award if you meet the eligibility criteria by the end of your junior year.

Also see the following scholarships:

- C. Clyde Ferguson Law Scholarship: Chapter 7, "Law" section
- Congressional Black Caucus Spouses Scholarships: Chapter 15, "Alabama" section
- Hispanic American Commitment to Education Resources Scholarship: Chapter 9, "Hispanic" section
- Jessica Savitch Scholarship: Chapter 6, "Communications" section
- McDonald's African American Heritage Scholarship: Chapter 9, "African-American" section
- McDonald's Golden Arches Scholarships: Chapter 15, "Connecticut" section
- McDonald's UNCF Tri-State Scholarship: Chapter 9, "African American" section
- Mercer County Bar Association Scholarship: Chapter 7, "Law" section
- New York Tri-State BMOA McDonald's Scholarship: Chapter 8, "Work" section

- NJLA Scholarships: Chapter 7, "Library and Information Science" section
- NJSCPA Accounting Manuscript Contest: Chapter 6, "Accounting" section
- NJSCPA College Scholarship: Chapter 6, "Accounting" section
- NJSCPA High School Scholarship: Chapter 6, "Accounting" section
- Roberta Thumin Scholarship: Chapter 6, "Communications" section
- State Funeral Director Associations Scholarships: Chapter 6, "Funeral Service and Mortuary Science" section
- Survivor Tuition Benefits: Chapter 14, "Public Safety Officers" section

New Mexico

Competitive Scholarship

Sponsor: New Mexico Commission on Higher Education
Web Site: http://www.nmche.org/financialaid/competitive.html
Amount of Scholarship: $200 and in-state tuition
Number of Awards: not given
Deadline: varies
Education Level: high school seniors
Eligibility: Applicant must enroll at a public college in New Mexico, not be a New Mexico resident, and meet academic standards.

This page doesn't provide much information about the scholarship program that offers in-state tuition to out-of-state students who attend a public college in New Mexico, but you should find enough details to get started. To learn more, contact the financial aid office at the college you want to attend.

Excel Staffing Companies Endowment for Excellence in Continuing Education Scholarship

Sponsor: Albuquerque Community Foundation and Excel Staffing Companies
Web Site: http://www.swcp.com/albcfdn/forms/excel.htm
Amount of Scholarship: $1,000
Number of Awards: 2 to 4
Deadline: July 1
Education Level: college undergraduates and graduate students
Eligibility: Applicant must be an Albuquerque area resident, enroll in a degree or professional certification program, work at least 30 hours a week, have a minimum 3.0 GPA, be at least 21 years old, and demonstrate financial need.

This Web page goes over the purpose of this scholarship for students who are working their way through college. It also lists the eligibility requirements. A text application form that you can print out is provided at the bottom of the page.

Graduate Scholarship

Sponsor: New Mexico Commission on Higher Education
Web Site: http://www.nmche.org/financialaid/gradshol.html
Amount of Scholarship: $7,500
Number of Awards: not given
Deadline: varies
Education Level: college seniors and graduate students
Eligibility: Applicant must be a New Mexico resident and enroll at a public university in New Mexico.

This Web page goes over the facts about the scholarship, including award amounts and eligibility requirements. Note that minorities, particularly Native Americans and women, are especially encouraged to apply. In addition, preference is given to applicants studying the fields listed under the Who Is Eligible? section. You must file the FAFSA to be considered for this scholarship. Contact the Dean of Graduate Studies at the university you want to attend to learn more.

Legislative Endowment Scholarship

Sponsor: New Mexico Commission on Higher Education
Web Site: http://www.nmche.org/financialaid/legislative.html
Amount of Scholarship: $1,000 to $2,500
Number of Awards: not given
Deadline: varies
Education Level: high school seniors and college undergraduates
Eligibility: Applicant must be a New Mexico resident and enroll at a public two-year or four-year college in New Mexico.

Here you will find details about New Mexico's educational grant program, including eligibility requirements and the amounts of the grants. You must file the FAFSA to be considered for the grant. To learn more, contact the financial aid office at the college you want to attend.

Lottery Success Scholarship

Sponsor: New Mexico Commission on Higher Education
Web Site: http://www.nmche.org/financialaid/lotto.html
Amount of Scholarship: full tuition (renewable for four years)
Number of Awards: not given

Deadline: varies
Education Level: high school seniors
Eligibility: Applicant must be a New Mexico resident, graduate from a New Mexico high school or obtain a New Mexico GED, enroll as a full-time student at an eligible public college in New Mexico, and earn a minimum 2.5 GPA during the first semester of college.

This Web page goes over the facts about the scholarship, including award amounts and eligibility requirements. You cannot receive a scholarship until you complete your first semester of college and prove your eligibility. To learn more, contact the financial aid office at the college you want to attend.

New Mexico Manufactured Housing Scholarship

Sponsor: Albuquerque Community Foundation
Web Site: http://www.swcp.com/albcfdn/forms/housing.htm
Amount of Scholarship: $750
Number of Awards: 1
Deadline: March 24
Education Level: high school seniors
Eligibility: Applicant must graduate from an Albuquerque high school, have a minimum 2.5 GPA, enroll at a two-year or four-year college in New Mexico, and live in mobile or manufactured housing.

This Web page simply consists of a text copy of the application form for the scholarship, which you can print from within your Web browser. Be sure to follow the instructions given at the bottom of the page to ensure that your application will be properly considered.

New Mexico Scholars

Sponsor: New Mexico Commission on Higher Education

Web Site: http://www.nmche.org/ financialaid/scholars.html
Amount of Scholarship: full tuition (renewable for four years)
Number of Awards: not given
Deadline: varies
Education Level: high school seniors and college undergraduates
Eligibility: Applicant must be a New Mexico resident, enroll at an eligible college in New Mexico, rank in the top 5 percent of the high school class, have a minimum ACT score of 25, and demonstrate financial need.

This Web page goes over the facts about the scholarship, including award amounts and eligibility requirements. Look under the What Is It? section to find a list of private New Mexico colleges where the scholarship may be used (all public colleges in New Mexico are eligible). You must apply for the scholarship through the financial aid office of the college you want to attend.

Student Choice Grant

Sponsor: New Mexico Commission on Higher Education
Web Site: http://www.nmche.org/ financialaid/choice.html
Amount of Scholarship: not given
Number of Awards: not given
Deadline: varies
Education Level: high school seniors and college undergraduates
Eligibility: Applicant must be a New Mexico resident and enroll at an eligible private college in New Mexico.

This Web page goes over the facts about the grant, including award amounts and eligibility requirements. Look under the What Is It? section to find a list of private New Mexico colleges where the scholarship may be used. You

must file the FAFSA to be considered for this grant. Contact the financial aid office at the college you want to attend if you want to know more.

Student Incentive Grant

Sponsor: New Mexico Commission on Higher Education
Web Site: http://www.nmche.org/ financialaid/incentive.html
Amount of Scholarship: $200 to $2,500
Number of Awards: not given
Deadline: varies
Education Level: high school seniors and college undergraduates
Eligibility: Applicant must be a New Mexico resident, enroll at an eligible college in New Mexico, and demonstrate financial need.

This Web page goes over the facts about the grant, including award amounts and eligibility requirements. You must file the FAFSA to be considered for this grant. Contact the financial aid office at the college you want to attend if you want to learn more.

Sussman-Miller Education Assistance Scholarship

Sponsor: Albuquerque Community Foundation and Sussman-Miller Education Assistance Fund
Web Site: http://www.swcp.com/albcfdn/ forms/sussman.htm
Amount of Scholarship: not given
Number of Awards: not given
Deadline: April 20 (high school seniors) and July 7 (undergraduates)
Education Level: high school seniors and college undergraduates
Eligibility: Applicant must be a New Mexico resident, enroll as a full-time student at an accredited U.S. college, have a minimum 3.0 GPA

(high school seniors) or 2.5 GPA (undergraduates), demonstrate financial need, and be a U.S. citizen or permanent resident.

This page provides instructions for applying for this scholarship and links to all of the required forms. Note that the application forms and instructions are different depending on whether you are a graduating high school senior or you are already enrolled in college, so be sure to complete the correct application for your educational level. You will also find a list of eligibility requirements for each educational level on the application forms.

Three Percent Scholarship

Sponsor: New Mexico Commission on Higher Education
Web Site: http://www.nmche.org/financialaid/three.html
Amount of Scholarship: full tuition
Number of Awards: not given
Deadline: varies
Education Level: high school seniors and college undergraduates
Eligibility: Applicant must be a New Mexico resident and enroll at a public college in New Mexico.

This Web page goes over the facts about the scholarship, including award amounts and eligibility requirements. You must apply for this scholarship through the financial aid office of the college you want to attend.

Also see the following scholarships:

- Bank of America ADA Abilities Scholarship: Chapter 10, "Any Disability" section
- Burlington Northern Santa Fe Foundation Scholarship: Chapter 9, "Native American" section
- Children of Deceased Military and State Police Personnel Scholarship: Chapter 14, "Military Personnel and Veterans" section

- Hispanic American Commitment to Education Resources Scholarship: Chapter 9, "Hispanic" section
- HSF Community College Transfer Scholarship: Chapter 9, "Hispanic" section
- HSF High School Scholarship: Chapter 9, "Hispanic" section
- New Mexico Athletic Scholarship: Chapter 8, "Athletics" section
- Regional EAGLE Scholarship: Chapter 9, "Gay and Lesbian" section
- Vietnam Veterans' Scholarship: Chapter 13, "Veterans" section

New York

Aid for Part-Time Study

Sponsor: New York State Regents and New York State Higher Education Services Corporation
Web Site: http://www.hesc.com/apts.html
Amount of Scholarship: $2,000
Number of Awards: not given
Deadline: not given
Education Level: college undergraduates
Eligibility: Applicant must be a New York resident, enroll as a part-time student at an eligible college in New York state, have a grade average of at least a C, demonstrate financial need, and be a U.S. citizen or permanent resident.

The Web page describes the eligibility requirements and selection criteria for this scholarship, including specifics about eligible income limits and part-time student status. You must apply for the grant through your school's financial aid office, which also provides application forms.

Buffalo Sabres Alumni Association Scholarship

Sponsor: Buffalo Sabres Alumni Association
Web Site: http://www.sabresalumni.com/rules.html
Amount of Scholarship: not given
Number of Awards: not given
Deadline: June 12
Education Level: high school seniors
Eligibility: Applicant must be a resident of western New York or southern Ontario, have a minimum 2.5 GPA, and enroll as a full-time student at an accredited college in the U.S. or Canada.

On this Web page, you will find a rundown of the eligibility requirements, judging criteria, application instructions, and other details about the scholarship. If you qualify, click the Application link at the top of the page to open a text copy of the application form that you can print from inside your Web browser.

Chautauqua County Scholarships

Sponsor: Chautauqua Region Community Foundation
Web Site: http://www.ccy.org/scholarships.html
Amount of Scholarship: varies
Number of Awards: not given
Deadline: June 1
Education Level: high school seniors, college undergraduates, and graduate students
Eligibility: Applicant must either attend high school or be a resident of Chautauqua County or the surrounding region.

Here you will find descriptions of the 160 different scholarships offered to Chautauqua County high school students, categorized by high school. Some scholarships are also open to students in Cattaraugus and Warren Counties. You will also find information about scholarships not administered by the foundation, which are open to students all across the state or across the country. Each scholarship description presents just the facts, including eligibility requirements, number of awards, award amounts, scholarship duration, deadline, and contact. You will find a link to a printable text application form at the end of each page. You have to submit a separate application to the correct contact for each scholarship for which you are applying.

Jewish Foundation for Education of Women Scholarships

Sponsor: Jewish Foundation for Education of Women
Web Site: http://www.jfew.org/index.html
Amount of Scholarship: $5,000 (renewable)
Number of Awards: not given
Deadline: not given
Education Level: high school seniors, college undergraduates, and graduate students
Eligibility: Applicant must be female and live within 50 miles of New York City.

First, read the History page to learn about the background of the foundation and its scholarship program. The Programs page describes the five different scholarship programs: one for education majors; one for performing arts students; one for doctoral students in the humanities; one for disadvantaged teenagers; and one for social work students. Each award must be used at a New York college or university specified in the award description. The Awards link tells you about the award amounts and other details. Follow the Eligibility/How to Apply link to find general eligibility requirements for all scholarships and instructions for obtaining application forms. The Contact Information link gives a mailing address and an e-mail address that you can write to request applications.

New York State Primary Care Service Corps Scholarship

Sponsor: New York State Department of Health
Web Site: http://www.hesc.com/speprog.html
Amount of Scholarship: $7,500 to $15,000
Number of Awards: not given
Deadline: early February
Education Level: college juniors and seniors
Eligibility: Applicant must be a New York resident and enroll in an approved program in midwifery, nurse practitioner, or physician assistant at a U.S. university.

Scroll down the page until you see the name of the scholarship. This section of the Web page briefly describes the scholarship program, including eligibility requirements. It also outlines the service commitment that you must make if you accept the award. Contact the address, phone number, or e-mail address given to get more information.

New York State Regents Health Care Opportunity Scholarship

Sponsor: New York State Regents and New York State Higher Education Services Corporation
Web Site: http://www.hesc.com/nyshealthcare.html
Amount of Scholarship: $1,000 to 10,000 (renewable for four years)
Number of Awards: not given
Deadline: not given

Education Level: dental and medical school students
Eligibility: Applicant must be a New York resident, enroll as a full-time student at an approved New York medical or dental school, and be a U.S. citizen or permanent resident.

Here you can learn about this service scholarship for medical and dental school students. The Web page describes the eligibility requirements and selection criteria, as well as the service obligation that scholarship recipients must fulfill. Note that economically disadvantaged students and members of minority groups are given preference in receiving the award. Check under the heading How to Apply to find out how to request an application form.

New York State Regents Professional Opportunity Scholarship

Sponsor: New York State Regents and New York State Education Department
Web Site: http://www.hesc.com/professional.html
Amount of Scholarship: $1,000 to $5,000 (renewable for four to five years)
Number of Awards: not given
Deadline: not given
Education Level: college undergraduates and graduate students
Eligibility: Applicant must be a New York resident and enroll as a full-time in an approved degree program at a college or university in New York.

This scholarship program is intended to encourage New York residents to pursue a career in a needed profession. Consult the list of programs at the top of the page to ensure that the program and degree you want to enter are eligible for the scholarship. Awards are given first to economically disadvantaged students who are members of a minority group that is historically underrepresented in the profession. Next, historically underrepresented minority students who don't have financial need are considered. Then, the award is given to students who enrolled in or graduated from one of the state-sponsored opportunity programs listed. Note that if you accept this scholarship, you must work in that profession in New York state for one year for each year that you received the scholarship. Request a scholarship application by contacting the address given at the bottom of the page.

New York State Scholarship for Academic Excellence

Sponsor: New York State Regents and New York State Higher Education Services Corporation
Web Site: http://www.hesc.com/academicexcellence.html
Amount of Scholarship: $500 to $1,500 (renewable for five years)
Number of Awards: 8,000
Deadline: May 1
Education Level: high school seniors
Eligibility: Applicant must be a New York resident, enroll as a full-time student at an eligible college in New York state, and be a U.S. citizen or permanent resident.

Under this program, 2,000 $1,500 scholarships are awarded to the top graduating seniors at all high schools in the state, and 6,000 $500 scholarships go to other outstanding high school graduates. The Web page explains the eligibility requirements, duration, and notification procedure. Contact your high school guidance counselor if you want to apply for this award.

Robert C. Byrd Honors Scholarship

Sponsor: New York State Regents and New York State Higher Education Services Corporation
Web Site: http://www.hesc.com/byrd.html
Amount of Scholarship: $1,500 (renewable for four years)
Number of Awards: 8,000
Deadline: May 1
Education Level: high school seniors
Eligibility: Applicant must be a New York resident, graduate from a New York high school or receive a GED, achieve minimum academic standards, and enroll at an institution of higher education.

This federally funded merit scholarship goes to academically talented high school graduates. The Web page explains the eligibility requirements and other details of the scholarship. Contact your high school guidance counselor if you want to apply for this award.

Tuition Assistance Program Grant

Sponsor: New York State Regents and New York State Higher Education Services Corporation
Web Site: http://www.hesc.com/tap.html
Amount of Scholarship: $100 to $4,125
Number of Awards: 8,000
Deadline: May 1
Education Level: high school seniors and college undergraduates
Eligibility: Applicant must be a New York resident, enroll as a full-time student at an approved college in New York, demonstrate financial need, and be a U.S. citizen or permanent resident.

Here you will find all the facts about New York's educational grant program, including details on eligibility, financial need requirements, and award amounts. You have to file the FAFSA to apply for the grant. Be sure to follow the instructions under the How Do I Apply? section of the page, or you won't be considered.

Also see the following scholarships:

- Congressional Black Caucus Spouses Scholarships: Chapter 15, "Alabama" section
- Excellence in Accounting Scholarship: Chapter 6, "Accounting" section
- Hispanic American Commitment to Education Resources Scholarship: Chapter 9, "Hispanic" section
- HSF Community College Transfer Scholarship: Chapter 9, "Hispanic" section
- Jessica Savitch Scholarship: Chapter 6, "Communications" section
- McDonald's African American Heritage Scholarship: Chapter 9, "African-American" section
- McDonald's Golden Arches Scholarships: Chapter 15, "Connecticut" section
- McDonald's UNCF Tri-State Scholarship: Chapter 9, "African-American" section
- Memorial Scholarship for Families of Deceased Police Officers and Firefighters: Chapter 14, "Public Safety Officers" section
- New York Tri-State BMOA McDonald's Scholarship: Chapter 8, "Work" section
- Persian Gulf Veterans Tuition Award: Chapter 13, "Veterans" section
- Regents Award for Child of Correction Officer: Chapter 14, "Public Safety Officers" section
- Regents Award for Child of Veteran: Chapter 14, "Military Personnel and Veterans" section
- Roberta Thumin Scholarship: Chapter 6, "Communications" section
- State Aid to Native Americans: Chapter 9, "Native American" section
- State Funeral Director Associations Scholarships: Chapter 6, "Funeral Service and Mortuary Science" section
- Vietnam Veterans Tuition Award: Chapter 13, "Veterans" section

North Carolina

Aubrey Lee Brooks Scholarship

Sponsor: North Carolina State Education Assistance Authority
Web Site: http://www.ncseaa.edu/brooks.html
Amount of Scholarship: $3,500 (renewable for four years)
Number of Awards: 17
Deadline: not given
Education Level: high school seniors
Eligibility: Applicant must attend high school in Alamance, Bertie, Caswell, Durham, Forsyth, Granville, Guilford, Orange, Person, Rockingham, Stokes, Surry, Swain, or Warren Counties; and enroll at a participating college.

Here you will find information about the history of the scholarship program and the award itself. The scholarship is only available to students attending North Carolina State University, the University of North Carolina at Chapel Hill, and the University of North Carolina at Greensboro. You can obtain an application form from your high school's guidance office.

C. M. and M. D. Suther Scholarship

Sponsor: North Carolina State Education Assistance Authority
Web Site: http://www.ncseaa.edu/suther.html
Amount of Scholarship: $875
Number of Awards: 16

Deadline: not given
Education Level: high school seniors and college undergraduates
Eligibility: Applicant must be a North Carolina resident, enroll as a full-time student at a University of North Carolina (UNC) campus, and demonstrate financial need.

Here you will find information about the history of the scholarship program and the award itself. You do not apply directly for the scholarship. Instead, the financial aid office at each UNC campus chooses the recipient. If you'd like more information, see your financial aid officer.

Dr. A. P. and Frances Dickson Scholarship

Sponsor: North Carolina State Education Assistance Authority
Web Site: http://www.ncseaa.edu/dickson.html
Amount of Scholarship: $800 (renewable)
Number of Awards: 16
Deadline: not given
Education Level: high school seniors
Eligibility: Applicant must be a resident of Hoke County, enroll as a full-time student at a University of North Carolina campus, and demonstrate financial need.

Here you will find information about the history of the scholarship program and the award itself. You can only apply for the scholarship through the financial aid office at your college.

Dr. Wade H. Atkinson Scholarship

Sponsor: North Carolina State Education Assistance Authority
Web Site: http://www.ncseaa.edu/atkinson.html

Amount of Scholarship: $1,400 (renewable)
Number of Awards: 3
Deadline: not given
Education Level: high school seniors
Eligibility: Applicant must have been a resident of Johnston County for at least two years, enroll as a full-time student at a participating college, and demonstrate financial need.

Here you will find information about the history of the scholarship program and the award itself. The scholarship is only available to students attending North Carolina State University, the University of North Carolina at Chapel Hill, and the University of North Carolina at Greensboro. Apply for the scholarship through the financial aid office at your college.

Frank and Elizabeth Spencer Scholarship

Sponsor: North Carolina Cooperative Extension
Web Site: http://cleveland.ces.state.nc.us/pubs/spencer/app.html
Amount of Scholarship: not given
Number of Awards: not given
Deadline: April 15
Education Level: college undergraduates
Eligibility: Applicant must be a resident of Cleveland or Gaston County and enroll in a degree program in agriculture, home economics, or pre-veterinary medicine.

This scholarship goes to students who plan to pursue a degree in agriculture or a closely related field. According to the scholarship's Web page, not just any academic program will qualify; students enrolled in two-year programs at community colleges and technical institutes are not eligible. The page details what the scholarship committee is looking for in applicants. Priority is given to members of 4-H, Future Homemakers of America (FHA), and Future

Farmers of America (FFA). You can print out the application form directly from this page, as well.

Governor James G. Martin College Scholarship

Sponsor: North Carolina State Education Assistance Authority and Public Service Company of North Carolina, Inc.
Web Site: http://www.ncseaa.edu/martin.html
Amount of Scholarship: $1,000 (renewable for five years)
Number of Awards: 5
Deadline: April 12
Education Level: high school seniors
Eligibility: Applicant must be a North Carolina resident, enroll as a full-time student at a four-year college in North Carolina, and be a U.S. citizen.

Here you will find information about the history of the scholarship program and the award itself, including eligibility requirements. You can obtain application forms from the financial aid office at your college.

Jagannathan Scholarship

Sponsor: North Carolina State Education Assistance Authority
Web Site: http://www.ncseaa.edu/jagannathan.html
Amount of Scholarship: $3,500 (renewable for four years)
Number of Awards: not given
Deadline: February 26
Education Level: high school seniors
Eligibility: Applicant must be a resident of North Carolina, enroll as a full-time student at a University of North Carolina campus, and demonstrate financial need.

Here you will find information about the history of the scholarship program and the award itself. Note that preference for the award is given to children of employees of Tolaram Polymers, Cookson Fibers, and related companies. You can obtain an application form from the financial aid office at the college you plan to attend or from the personnel director of your parent's employer, if applicable.

James Lee Love Scholarship

Sponsor: North Carolina State Education Assistance Authority
Web Site: http://www.ncseaa.edu/love.html
Amount of Scholarship: $2,700
Number of Awards: 16
Deadline: not given
Education Level: high school seniors and college undergraduates
Eligibility: Applicant must be a North Carolina resident, enroll as a full-time student at a University of North Carolina (UNC) campus, and demonstrate financial need.

Here you will find information about the history of the scholarship program and the award itself. You do not apply directly for the scholarship. Instead, the financial aid office at each UNC campus chooses the recipient. If you'd like more information, see your financial aid officer.

North Carolina Sheriff's Association Undergraduate Criminal Justice Scholarship

Sponsor: North Carolina State Education Assistance Authority and North Carolina Sheriff's Association
Web Site: http://www.ncseaa.edu/justice.html
Amount of Scholarship: $2,000

Number of Awards: 10
Deadline: not given
Education Level: high school seniors and college undergraduates
Eligibility: Applicant must be a North Carolina resident, enroll as a full-time student at a University of North Carolina (UNC) campus, and major in criminal justice.

Here you will find information about the history of the scholarship program and the award itself. Note that first preference is given to children of law enforcement officers. You do not apply directly for the scholarship. Instead, the financial aid office at each UNC campus with a criminal justice degree program chooses the recipient. If you'd like more information, see your financial aid officer.

North Carolina Student Incentive Grant

Sponsor: College Foundation, Inc. and North Carolina State Education Assistance Authority
Web Site: http://www.cfnc.org/html/need.asp
Amount of Scholarship: not given
Number of Awards: not given
Deadline: March 15
Education Level: high school seniors and college undergraduates
Eligibility: Applicant must be a North Carolina resident, enroll as a full-time student at a postsecondary institution in North Carolina, not enroll in a program designed primarily for career preparation in a religious vocation, demonstrate financial need, and be a U.S. citizen.

Click the name of the scholarship in the list to find more information. The information page gives the facts about North Carolina's educational grant program, including a list of eligibility requirements and a definition of substantial financial need that successful applicants must meet. You must file the FAFSA to be considered for the grant. Follow the instructions under the What Are the Application Procedures? section of the page to make certain that your application is properly considered.

North Carolina Tomato Growers Scholarship

Sponsor: North Carolina Tomato Growers Education Foundation
Web Site: http://www.agr.state.nc.us/markets/commodit/horticul/tomatoes/foundation.htm
Amount of Scholarship: $500 (renewable)
Number of Awards: not given
Deadline: June 20
Education Level: college undergraduates and graduate students
Eligibility: Applicant must be a North Carolina resident and commit to a career in agribusiness or horticulture.

This scholarship is designed to promote the North Carolina tomato industry, as outlined in the mission statement at the top of the page. Read the scholarship guidelines to determine if you qualify. Most importantly, you must demonstrate a sincere commitment to a career in horticulture or agribusiness, which you must show in your answers to application questions. To apply, follow the link at the bottom of the page and print out a copy of the text application form that opens; the application address is listed at the top of the page.

Robert C. Byrd Honors Scholarship

Sponsor: North Carolina Department of Public Instruction

Web Site: http://www.dpi.state.nc.us/scholarships/robcbyrd.htm
Amount of Scholarship: $1,500 (renewable for four years)
Number of Awards: 160
Deadline: first Monday in February
Education Level: high school seniors
Eligibility: Applicant must be a North Carolina resident, graduate from a North Carolina high school, have a minimum 3.0 GPA, have a minimum SAT I score of 900, and enroll as a full-time student at an accredited institution of higher education.

This Web page explains the eligibility requirements and renewal conditions for this merit scholarship. You can obtain application forms from your high school's guidance office.

Ruth Jewell Memorial Scholarship

Sponsor: North Carolina State Education Assistance Authority and Folk, Round, and Square Dance Federation of North Carolina
Web Site: http://www.ncseaa.edu/rjms.html
Amount of Scholarship: $2,000
Number of Awards: 1 to 2
Deadline: not given
Education Level: high school seniors and college undergraduates
Eligibility: Applicant must be a North Carolina resident, enroll as a full-time student at a University of North Carolina campus, and demonstrate financial need.

Here you will find information about the history of the scholarship program and the award itself. Note that first preference for the scholarship is for dance majors. You do not apply directly for the award. Instead, the financial aid office chooses the recipient. If you'd like more information, see your financial aid officer.

State Contractual Scholarship

Sponsor: North Carolina State Education Assistance Authority
Web Site: http://www.ncseaa.edu/scsf.html
Amount of Scholarship: not given
Number of Awards: not given
Deadline: not given
Education Level: high school seniors and college undergraduates
Eligibility: Applicant must be a North Carolina resident, enroll at an eligible private two-year or four-year college in North Carolina, have not previously received a bachelor's degree, not enroll in a program of study designed primarily for career preparation in a religious vocation, and demonstrate financial need.

Here you will find information about the history of the scholarship program and the award itself, including eligibility requirements and the scholarship's value. You can only apply through the financial aid office at your college. Ask your financial aid officer about the State Contractual Scholarship Fund if you want to know more.

Thomas Holmes Carrow Scholarship

Sponsor: North Carolina State Education Assistance Authority
Web Site: http://www.ncseaa.edu/brooks.html
Amount of Scholarship: $3,800 (renewable for four years)
Number of Awards: 4
Deadline: not given
Education Level: high school seniors
Eligibility: Applicant must graduate from East Carteret High School or West Carteret High School and enroll as a full-time student at a University of North Carolina campus.

Here you will find information about the history of the scholarship program and the award itself. You must complete a nomination form, available in your high school's guidance office, in order to be considered for the scholarship.

Turrentine Scholarship

Sponsor: North Carolina State Education Assistance Authority and William Holt and Ella (Rea) Turrentine Memorial Educational Foundation
Web Site: http://www.ncseaa.edu/turrentine.html
Amount of Scholarship: $200 to $2,100
Number of Awards: not given
Deadline: not given
Education Level: high school seniors
Eligibility: Applicant must be a resident of Alamance County, enroll as a full-time student at a participating college, and demonstrate financial need.

Here you will find information about the history of the scholarship program and the award itself. The scholarship is only available to students attending North Carolina State University, the University of North Carolina at Chapel Hill, and the University of North Carolina at Greensboro. Apply for the scholarship through the financial aid office at your college.

Also see the following scholarships:

- Bank of America ADA Abilities Scholarship: Chapter 10, "Any Disability" section
- Congressional Black Caucus Spouses Scholarships: Chapter 15, "Alabama" section
- NCLA Scholarships: Chapter 7, "Library and Information Science" section
- North Carolina Nurse Scholars: Chapter 6, "Nursing" section
- North Carolina Nurse Scholars Program Master's Scholarship: Chapter 7, "Nursing" section
- North Carolina Teaching Fellows: Chapter 6, "Education" section
- Sidney B. Meadows Scholarship: Chapter 6, "Horticulture" section
- State Funeral Director Associations Scholarships: Chapter 6, "Funeral Service and Mortuary Science" section
- University of North Carolina Board of Governors Medical School Scholarship: Chapter 7, "Medicine" section

North Dakota

See the following scholarships:

- Burlington Northern Santa Fe Foundation Scholarship: Chapter 9, "Native American" section
- Careers in Agriculture Scholarship: Chapter 6, "Agriculture" section
- Catholic Aid Association College Tuition Scholarship: Chapter 11, "Catholic" section
- Hispanic American Commitment to Education Resources Scholarship: Chapter 9, "Hispanic" section
- Regional EAGLE Scholarship: Chapter 9, "Gay and Lesbian" section

Ohio

Canton Lincoln High School Alumni Scholarship

Sponsor: Canton Lincoln High School Alumni Association (CLHSAA)
Web Site: http://www.speedynet.net/lincoln/scholar.htm
Amount of Scholarship: not given
Number of Awards: around 40
Deadline: March 15
Education Level: high school seniors, college undergraduates, and graduate students

Eligibility: Applicant must have attended Canton Lincoln Junior or Senior High School or be the child, grandchild, great-grandchild, or spouse of an attendee who is a paid member of CLHSAA.

This Web page tells you about the scholarship program, including how you can qualify for an award and how many awards you can win. Click the Application link at the top of the page to find an application form that you can print from your Web browser.

CSP Scholarships

Sponsor: Cleveland Scholarship Programs, Inc. (CSP)
Web Site: http://www.cspohio.org/scholar/index.html
Amount of Scholarship: varies
Number of Awards: not given
Deadline: varies
Education Level: high school seniors, college undergraduates, and master's students
Eligibility: Applicant must be a resident of Cuyahoga, Lake, Geauga, Summit, Portage, Medina, Lorain, Ashtabula, Mahoning, Stark, or Trumbull Counties or attend a high school with CSP advisory services.

CSP administers 15 different scholarships for Ohio residents. You will find a brief description of each scholarship on this Web page. Click on the links under the descriptions to get more details about any scholarship. Awards are available for graduating high school seniors, adults returning to college, community college transfer students, and students returning to school to obtain teacher certification. Each scholarship's eligibility requirements are unique, so make certain that you only apply for those awards for which you are truly qualified. You can download the application form for most scholarships by clicking the Application link

underneath the scholarship's description. To learn about the others, you should contact CSP directly; a contact phone number and e-mail address are provided on the left-hand side of the page. You can also learn about CSP's Resource Center on the Web site, where you can search for scholarships offered by outside organizations.

MBNA Cleveland Scholars

Sponsor: MBNA
Web Site: http://www.mbnainternational.com/a_sch_ohio.html
Amount of Scholarship: $500 to $7,500 (renewable for four years)
Number of Awards: not given
Deadline: December 11
Education Level: high school seniors
Eligibility: Applicant must graduate from a Cleveland area high school, reside in Cleveland, have a minimum 2.5 GPA, have a minimum SAT I score of 900 or ACT score of 19, enroll as a full-time student at an accredited four-year college in Ohio, demonstrate financial need, and be a U.S. citizen or permanent resident.

In addition to a scholarship, winners of this award also receive advising, summer internships, and part-time employment opportunities. The Web page goes over all the facts you need to know, including program benefits, eligibility requirements, how to obtain application materials, selection criteria, and renewal conditions. The Frequently Asked questions page answers the most common questions about the award. The Important Dates page tells you when applications are due and when other important steps in the application process occur. Although application materials aren't available on the Web site, you can easily obtain an application form from your high school guidance office or by calling the MBNA

Scholars Program at the phone number given on the scholarship's main Web page.

Ohio Academic Scholarship

Sponsor: Ohio Board of Regents
Web Site: http://www.regents.state.oh.us/sgs/sgsprogs.html
Amount of Scholarship: $2,000 (renewable for four years)
Number of Awards: not given
Deadline: not given
Education Level: high school seniors
Eligibility: Applicant must be an Ohio resident and enroll as a full-time student at a college in Ohio.

Each year at least one student graduating from each Ohio high school receives this scholarship. To find information about the scholarship, scroll down the Web page until you see its name. The brief paragraph that follows describes the amount of the award, how to qualify, and how to apply through your high school's guidance office.

Ohio Instructional Grant

Sponsor: Ohio Board of Regents
Web Site: http://www.regents.state.oh.us/sgs/sgsprogs.html
Amount of Scholarship: $156 to $4,644
Number of Awards: not given
Deadline: October 1
Education Level: high school seniors and college undergraduates
Eligibility: Applicant must be an Ohio resident, enroll as a full-time student at a two-year or four-year college, and demonstrate financial need.

To find information about this grant, scroll down the Web page until you see the grant's name. The brief paragraph that follows describes the amount of the grant, how to qualify,

and how to apply. You will automatically be considered for this grant when you file the FAFSA.

Ohio Student Choice Grant

Sponsor: Ohio Board of Regents
Web Site: http://www.regents.state.oh.us/sgs/sgsprogs.html
Amount of Scholarship: $960
Number of Awards: not given
Deadline: not given
Education Level: high school seniors and college undergraduates
Eligibility: Applicant must be an Ohio resident and enroll as a full-time student at a private college in Ohio.

To find information about this grant, scroll down the Web page until you see the grant's name. The brief paragraph that follows describes the amount of the grant, how to qualify, and how to apply. You will automatically be considered for this grant when you apply for financial aid from your college.

Ohio Twelfth-Grade Proficiency Tests Scholarship

Sponsor: Ohio Board of Regents
Web Site: http://www.regents.state.oh.us/sgs/sgsprogs.html
Amount of Scholarship: $500
Number of Awards: not given
Deadline: not given
Education Level: high school seniors
Eligibility: Applicant must be an Ohio resident, pass all five sections of the Ohio twelfth-grade proficiency tests, and enroll at a college in Ohio.

To find information about the scholarship, scroll down the Web page until you see its name. The brief paragraph that follows describes the amount of the scholarship and how to qualify. You don't apply directly for the scholarship. If you qualify, you will receive a scholarship voucher that you can give to the financial aid office at the college you attend.

Part-Time Student Instructional Grant

Sponsor: Ohio Board of Regents
Web Site: http://www.regents.state.oh.us/sgs/sgsprogs.html
Amount of Scholarship: not given
Number of Awards: not given
Deadline: not given
Education Level: college undergraduates
Eligibility: Applicant must be an Ohio resident, enroll as a part-time student at an eligible college in Ohio, and demonstrate financial need.

To find information about this grant, scroll down the Web page until you see the grant's name. The brief paragraph that follows describes the amount of the grant, how to qualify, and how to apply. If you would like to apply for this grant, you should contact the financial aid office at your school.

PNC Bank Big 33 Academic Scholarship

Sponsor: PNC Bank Corporation
Web Site: http://www.eduloans.pncbank.com/pncbankscholarship.html
Amount of Scholarship: $1,000
Number of Awards: 10
Deadline: February 1
Education Level: high school seniors
Eligibility: Applicant must attend high school in Ohio or Pennsylvania.

This page doesn't give much information about the scholarship, but the description of the criteria used to select scholarship recipients should help you decide whether to apply. Ten awards are given out in all—five to applicants from Ohio and five to applicants from Pennsylvania. If you are interested, you can obtain an application form from your high school guidance counselor. Application materials are not available on the Web site.

Regents Graduate/Professional Fellowship

Sponsor: Ohio Board of Regents
Web Site: http://www.regents.state.oh.us/sgs/sgsprogs.html
Amount of Scholarship: $3,500 (renewable for two years)
Number of Awards: not given
Deadline: not given
Education Level: college seniors
Eligibility: Applicant must have earned a bachelor's degree from a college in Ohio, enroll as a full-time student at a graduate or professional school in Ohio, and demonstrate financial need.

To find information about this fellowship, scroll down the Web page until you see its name. The brief paragraph that follows describes the amount of the fellowship, how to qualify, and how to apply. Your college must nominate you for the fellowship, so contact your school's financial aid office to find out how to enter the nomination process. Generally, one student from each undergraduate college in Ohio receives a fellowship each year.

Robert C. Byrd Honors Scholarship

Sponsor: Ohio Board of Regents
Web Site: http://www.regents.state.oh.us/sgs/sgsprogs.html
Amount of Scholarship: not given
Number of Awards: not given

Deadline: second Friday in March
Education Level: high school seniors
Eligibility: Applicant must graduate from an Ohio high school.

To find information about the scholarship, scroll down the Web page until you see its name. The brief paragraph that follows describes the amount of the scholarship, how to qualify, and how to apply. Obtain application forms from your high school guidance counselor.

Also see the following scholarships:

- Congressional Black Caucus Spouses Scholarships: Chapter 15, "Alabama" section
- David J. Clark Memorial Scholarship Grant: Chapter 6, "Film and Television" section
- Ohio Safety Officers College Memorial Scholarship: Chapter 14, "Public Safety Officers" section
- Ohio War Orphans Scholarship: Chapter 14, "Military Personnel and Veterans" section
- State Funeral Director Associations Scholarships: Chapter 6, "Funeral Service and Mortuary Science" section

Oklahoma

See the following scholarships:

- Bank of America ADA Abilities Scholarship: Chapter 10, "Any Disability" section
- Burlington Northern Santa Fe Foundation Scholarship: Chapter 9, "Native American" section
- Hispanic American Commitment to Education Resources Scholarship: Chapter 9, "Hispanic" section
- Sidney B. Meadows Scholarship: Chapter 6, "Horticulture" section

- State Funeral Director Associations Scholarships: Chapter 6, "Funeral Service and Mortuary Science" section

Oregon

Independence Essay Competition

Sponsor: Cascade Polity Institute
Web Site: http://www.cascadepolicy.org/essay/entry00.htm
Amount of Scholarship: $1,000
Number of Awards: 5
Deadline: March 15
Education Level: high school students
Eligibility: Applicant must attend an Oregon high school.

You can download the entry guidelines for this essay contest for Oregon high school students in either PDF or HTML format. The guidelines give the essay topic, provide a list of suggested readings, and list the contest rules. There is even a link to a page of essay-writing tips. You can also review the essays written by past winners of the contests. If you choose to enter, you can either mail in your essay or submit it via e-mail; the addresses are given on the Guidelines page. You don't have to send an official application form with your essay, but you do have to include a cover sheet, as directed in the guidelines.

OCECS Scholarship

Sponsor: Oregon University System and Intel Corporation
Web Site: http://www.ous.edu/ocecs/OCECS2000SchAp.html
Amount of Scholarship: $2,500 (renewable for up to three years)

Number of Awards: 18
Deadline: March 1
Education Level: high school seniors
Eligibility: Applicant must be an Oregon resident, attend an Oregon University System college, and major in engineering or computer science.

Winners of this scholarship not only receive money for college, but also summer internships at Intel or in campus programs. Eighteen scholarships total are available, with six designated for female students and six designated for underrepresented populations. Eligible colleges where the scholarship can be used are listed at the bottom of the Web page. After reading over the eligibility requirements, download a PDF copy of the application form by following the link at the bottom of the Web page.

Oregon Need Grant

Sponsor: Oregon Student Assistance Commission
Web Site: http://www.osac.state.or.us/ong.html
Amount of Scholarship: $342 to $2,932
Number of Awards: not given
Deadline: not given
Education Level: high school seniors and college undergraduates
Eligibility: Applicant must be an Oregon resident; enroll as a full-time student at a two-year or four-year college in Oregon; not enroll in a course of study leading to a degree in theology, divinity, or religious education; and demonstrate financial need.

This Web page describes Oregon's educational grant program, including the eligibility requirements. You will automatically be considered for the grant when you file the FAFSA. While no application deadline is given, you should file as soon as possible after January 1 to take advantage of available funds. The Eligibility Table page, linked at the bottom of the main page, provides information about eligibility that will give you a better idea of whether you will qualify for a grant. The Awards Amounts page will help you figure out how much of a grant you can receive, depending on where you go to college.

Oregon Student Assistance Commission Scholarships and Grants

Sponsor: Oregon Student Assistance Commission (OSAC), Oregon Community Foundation, US Bank, and Wells Fargo Bank
Web Site: http://www.osac.state.or.us/scholarships_section.html
Amount of Scholarship: not given
Number of Awards: not given
Deadline: March 1
Education Level: high school seniors, college undergraduates, and graduate students
Eligibility: Applicant must be an Oregon resident.

Here you can learn about the 164 scholarships that OSAC administers for Oregon residents. First, click the Student link to find instructions for applying for financial aid and scholarships. Then follow the Scholarship Programs link to find a listing of all of the available scholarships. Each listing quickly tells you whether high school seniors, undergraduates, or graduate students can apply for the scholarship and what the specific eligibility requirements are. Make a note of each award you'd like to apply for, including the scholarship's code number. Then return to the main page and click the Apply On-line link to find an electronic application form that you can use to apply for any of these scholarships. You'll also find a link to the application in PDF format, but it is recommended that you use the electronic form instead since it's faster and there is less chance of making errors. Finally, after you apply, you can click the Awarding Status link to find out where the scholarship committees are in the process of considering scholarship applications. The links at the bottom of the page take you to more information about the state's financial aid programs and applying for outside scholarships.

Students in Charge Scholarship

Sponsor: First Tech Credit Union
Web Site: http://www.1sttech.com/sic
Amount of Scholarship: $500 to $1,000
Number of Awards: 3
Deadline: April 14
Education Level: high school seniors
Eligibility: Applicant must be a member or eligible for membership of First Tech Credit Union in Beaverton, Oregon.

You will find information about the scholarship on the right-hand side of the page. (The rest of the page gives over credit union services for student members.) Three awards in all are given out each year: two $500 scholarships and one $1,000 scholarship. Click the link following the scholarship description to download the application form.

Also see the following scholarships:

- Audra M. Edwards Scholarship: Chapter 9, "Gay and Lesbian" section
- Bank of America ADA Abilities Scholarship: Chapter 10, "Any Disability" section
- Burlington Northern Santa Fe Foundation Scholarship: Chapter 9, "Native American" section
- Careers in Agriculture Scholarship: Chapter 6, "Agriculture" section
- Deceased or Disabled Public Safety Officer Grant: Chapter 14, "Public Safety Officers" section

- GSBA, Pride, and INBA Scholarships: Chapter 9, "Gay and Lesbian" section
- Larry Wimer Memorial Scholarship: Chapter 6, "Environmental Studies" section
- Oregon Barbers and Hairdressers Grant: Chapter 6, "Cosmetology" section
- Oregon Nurserymen's Foundation Scholarships: Chapter 6, "Horticulture" section
- Oregon Realtors Scholarship: Chapter 6, "Real Estate" section
- Regional EAGLE Scholarship: Chapter 9, "Gay and Lesbian" section
- State Funeral Director Associations Scholarships: Chapter 6, "Funeral Service and Mortuary Science" section

Pennsylvania

Health Professions Scholarship

Sponsor: Memorial Hospital of Bedford County Foundation
Web Site: http://www.bedford.org/fndtn.htm
Amount of Scholarship: $6,000 (renewable for up to four years)
Number of Awards: 1
Deadline: not given
Education Level: college undergraduates
Eligibility: Applicant must be a resident of Bedford County and enroll in a health professions program.

This page describes the scholarship program's eligibility requirements and selection criteria. Note that scholarship winners are guaranteed a job at Bedford Memorial Hospital if a suitable position is open when the student graduates. Hospital employees can also apply. If you have more questions or would like an application, link to the Feedback page to send an e-mail message.

Lawrence Conservation District Scholarship

Sponsor: Lawrence Conservation District
Web Site: http://www.pathway.net/lawcon/scholar.html
Amount of Scholarship: $500
Number of Awards: 2
Deadline: December 31
Education Level: college undergraduates
Eligibility: Applicant must be a resident of Lawrence County and major in agriculture, conservation, environmental resource management, or education in one of these fields at a U.S. college.

This scholarship is intended to support environmental and agricultural education. The eligibility requirements are spelled out at the top of the scholarship's Web page. Beneath that, you will find a text copy of the application form, which you can print out from within your Web browser. Be sure to attach all of the additional documents listed at the end of the form. Before using this form, make certain that it is the correct application for the current school year; contact the scholarship sponsor if you have questions. To learn more about Lawrence Conservation District and its mission, follow the link to the home page at the very bottom of the page.

New Economy Technology Scholarships

Sponsor: Pennsylvania Higher Education Assistance Authority and the Pennsylvania Department of Education
Web Site: http://www.pheaa.org/students/s2.shtml
Amount of Scholarship: $1,000 to $3,000
Number of Awards: not given
Deadline: December 31
Education Level: college sophomores

Eligibility: Applicant must be a Pennsylvania resident, have graduated from a Pennsylvania high school, study science or technology at a Pennsylvania college, and have a minimum 3.0 GPA.

This is a service scholarship designed to attract Pennsylvania students into studying science and technology fields and then working in-state. Be sure to read the scholarship description to understand the conditions and goals of the grant program. There are two separate awards, one for college students and one for community college students. The specific eligibility requirements, scholarship conditions, and award amounts for each are described on this page. Underneath that, you will find instructions for applying for either scholarship. Follow the link at the bottom of the page to find the application form and list of approved fields of study in PDF format, as well as a printable scholarship brochure (you have to scroll down to the Forms section of the page).

Pennsbury Scholarship Foundation Scholarship

Sponsor: Pennsbury Scholarship Foundation
Web Site: http://members.aol.com/pennsbury1
Amount of Scholarship: $1,000 to $4,000
Number of Awards: around 40
Deadline: April 15
Education Level: high school seniors and college undergraduates
Eligibility: Applicant must have graduated from Pennsbury High School and enroll at a two-year college, four-year college, or trade school.

First, follow the links under About the Foundation to learn more about the scholarships' sponsor and its mission. Then read about the awards themselves by exploring the links under

Our Scholarships. Click the Application Form link to find information about the eligibility requirements and selection criteria, a description of the award, and details about the application and payment procedures. Note that each award is one-half scholarship and one-half loan with a 0 percent interest rate that you'll have to repay. This page also links to the application form, essay topics, and instructions for submitting an application package. Return to the main page and click the Selection Criteria link to find out exactly what qualities the scholarship sponsor is looking for in applicants. The Grants Awarded page gives information about the number and amount of scholarships awarded in past years, which can give you a good idea of how much you'll get and how much competition you'll face. You will also find valuable information about selecting a college and searching for outside scholarships on this site.

Pennsylvania State Grant

Sponsor: Pennsylvania Higher Education Assistance Authority
Web Site: http://www.pheaa.org/students/sg1.shtml
Amount of Scholarship: $300 to $3,100
Number of Awards: not given
Deadline: May 1
Education Level: high school seniors and college undergraduates
Eligibility: Applicant must be a Pennsylvania resident, enroll on at least a half-time basis at an approved two-year or four-year college, and demonstrate financial need.

This Web page describes Pennsylvania's educational grant program, including eligibility requirements. The Estimated Awards link tells you how much of a grant you can expect to receive for your family's income level. The Frequently Asked Questions page answers the most common questions about the grant program. If you want more information about the program or need to order an application form, click the Request Information or an Application link and submit the electronic form. You can also check on the status of an application that you've already filed by clicking the Request State Grant Application Status link.

Also see the following scholarships:

- Congressional Black Caucus Spouses Scholarships: Chapter 15, "Alabama" section
- Educational Assistance Program for the Pennsylvania National Guard: Chapter 13, "National Guard" section
- Hispanic American Commitment to Education Resources Scholarship: Chapter 9, "Hispanic" section
- Long & Foster Scholarship: Chapter 15, "Delaware" section
- Pennsylvania Youth Foundation Scholarships: Chapter 14, "Clubs and Community Organizations" section
- PNC Bank Big 33 Academic Scholarship: Chapter 15, "Ohio" section
- Postsecondary Educational Gratuity: Chapter 14, "Public Safety Officers" section
- State Funeral Director Associations Scholarships: Chapter 6, "Funeral Service and Mortuary Science" section
- State Grant for Veterans: Chapter 13, "Veterans" section
- Washington Crossing Foundation Scholarship: Chapter 6, "Government and Public Service" section

Rhode Island

See the following scholarship:

- Switzer Environmental Fellowship: Chapter 7, "Environmental Studies" section

South Carolina

Archibald Rutledge Scholarship

Sponsor: South Carolina Department of Education
Web Site: http://www.state.sc.us/sde/students/sch-ship.htm#ARCHIBALD RUTLEDGE SCHOLARSHIP
Amount of Scholarship: $5,000
Number of Awards: 4
Deadline: not given
Education Level: high school seniors
Eligibility: Applicant must be a South Carolina resident, enroll at a South Carolina college; and be talented in music, drama, visual arts, or creative writing.

This program awards one $5,000 scholarship to an artistically talented student in four categories: visual arts, music, drama, and creative writing. The Web page briefly describes the eligibility requirements and tells you how to enter the competition and how your application is judged. You can obtain the application form from your high school guidance counselor, or contact the e-mail address or phone number listed at the end of the scholarship description.

Byrnes Scholarship

Sponsor: Byrnes Foundation
Web Site: http://www.byrnesscholars.org
Amount of Scholarship: not given
Number of Awards: not given
Deadline: February 15
Education Level: high school seniors
Eligibility: Applicant must be a South Carolina resident, have lost one or both parents by death, enroll at a four-year college, and demonstrate financial need.

First, click The Byrnes Foundation Scholarships link to learn more about the scholarships. On the page that opens, you will find a link to the eligibility requirements and other conditions. You can request an application form by e-mail or download the form in either Microsoft Word or RTF format from the page, as well. Before you apply, be sure to explore the other links on the Web site. These pages will tell you about the history of the scholarship program, its purpose, and past recipients, which should help you prepare a more effective application.

Kittie M. Fairey Scholarship

Sponsor: Kittie Moss Fairey Educational Fund and Wachovia Bank
Web Site: http://www.scholarshipprograms.org/kittiefairey.html
Amount of Scholarship: one-half tuition (renewable for four years)
Number of Awards: not given
Deadline: January 15
Education Level: high school seniors
Eligibility: Applicant must be a South Carolina resident, attend a South Carolina high school, have a minimum 3.0 GPA, have a minimum SAT I Score of 1000, enroll as a full-time student at an accredited four-year college in South Carolina, and demonstrate financial need.

This Web page provides a list of the eligibility requirements for the scholarship and links to all of the application forms and instructions in PDF format. Be sure to read the Instructions and Eligibility Information page first to more fully understand the eligibility requirements and how to submit an application package.

LIFE Scholarship

Sponsor: South Carolina Commission on Higher Education Division of Student Services

Web Site: http://www.che400.state.sc.us/web/Student/LIFE/LIFE%20home.html
Amount of Scholarship: not given
Number of Awards: not given
Deadline: not given
Education Level: high school seniors and undergraduate transfer students
Eligibility: Applicant must be a South Carolina resident, enroll as a full-time student in a degree program at an eligible two-year or four-year college in South Carolina, have a minimum 3.0 GPA, achieve minimum academic and test scores requirements, and be a U.S. citizen or permanent resident.

This program awards $2,000 scholarships to students at four-year colleges and $1,000 scholarships to students at two-year colleges. First, click the General Eligibility Requirements link to find out how to qualify for a scholarship. If you are a graduating high school senior, be sure to click the Initial Eligibility Requirements link at the bottom of the page to find out what academic and test score prerequisites you must achieve while in high school. If you are transferring to an eligible college from another undergraduate institution and would like to apply for a scholarship, click the Transfer Student Eligibility link to find out what minimum standards you must meet. You will also find a link to a page describing how you can renew the scholarship if you win one. Return to the main page and click the Question and Answer link to find answers to the most common questions about the scholarship program. Follow the Contact LIFE Program link to find out whom to contact if you require more information. The Statistics page gives interesting facts about how many students at each eligible college received a scholarship and how much money total was awarded at each school. You must apply for the scholarship through the financial aid office of the college you plan to attend.

Robert C. Byrd Honors Scholarship

Sponsor: South Carolina Department of Education
Web Site: http://www.state.sc.us/sde/students/sch-ship.htm
Amount of Scholarship: $1,500 (renewable for four years)
Number of Awards: not given
Deadline: not given
Education Level: high school seniors
Eligibility: Applicant must be a South Carolina resident and enroll at a postsecondary institution in the U.S.

Click on the scholarship's name to find more information about it. This Web page just gives the facts about this merit scholarship for South Carolina students. If you would like to apply, obtain an application form from your high school guidance counselor.

South Carolina Tuition Grant

Sponsor: South Carolina Higher Education Tuition Grants Commission
Web Site: http://www.state.sc.us/tuitiongrants
Amount of Scholarship: not given
Number of Awards: not given
Deadline: June 30
Education Level: high school seniors and college undergraduates
Eligibility: Applicant must be a South Carolina resident; graduate in the upper 75 percent of the high school class, score at least a 900 on the SAT I, or score at least a 19 on the ACT; enroll as a full-time student at a participating

private college in South Carolina; and demonstrate financial need.

First, click the Frequently Asked Questions link to learn the facts about this tuition equalization program for South Carolina students attending private colleges in the state, including how to qualify. You will automatically be considered for the grant when you file the FAFSA if you meet all of the eligibility requirements. A list of participating colleges and the phone numbers of their financial aid offices is given at the bottom of this page. If you return to the main page, you will find a link to a list of Web sites for participating colleges, as well.

Also see the following scholarships:

- Bank of America ADA Abilities Scholarship: Chapter 10, "Any Disability" section
- Congressional Black Caucus Spouses Scholarships: Chapter 15, "Alabama" section
- SCHPA Scholarship: Chapter 6, "Heating, Refrigeration, and Air Conditioning" section
- Sidney B. Meadows Scholarship: Chapter 6, "Horticulture" section

South Dakota

See the following scholarships:

- Burlington Northern Santa Fe Foundation Scholarship: Chapter 9, "Native American" section
- Careers in Agriculture Scholarship: Chapter 6, "Agriculture" section
- Catholic Aid Association College Tuition Scholarship: Chapter 11, "Catholic" section
- Regional EAGLE Scholarship: Chapter 9, "Gay and Lesbian" section

Tennessee

Chattanooga Christian Community Foundation Scholarships

Sponsor: Chattanooga Christian Community Foundation
Web Site: http://www.cccfdn.org/scholar.htm
Amount of Scholarship: not given
Number of Awards: not given
Deadline: varies
Education Level: high school seniors and master's students
Eligibility: Applicant must be from the greater Chattanooga area and be Christian.

Three scholarships are available under this program. Each has different eligibility requirements, so make certain that you meet the qualifications before applying. The Dora Macllelan Brown Seminary Scholarship goes to Chattanooga residents who are seeking a Master of Divinity or Master of Theology degree at an approved seminary. If you are interested in this scholarship, click the buttons underneath the short description to read the guidelines and access an application form. The Timothy Scholarship goes to children of ministry leaders in Chattanooga and supports post-high school education. If you would like to learn more about this scholarship, click the Instructions and Application buttons underneath its description. Finally, the Paul B. Carter Scholarship is intended only for graduates of Chattanooga Christian School who will attend Covenant College. You can find more information about the scholarships and a phone number to contact for more information by clicking the Information button underneath the scholarship's description.

Christa McAuliffe Scholarship

Sponsor: Tennessee Student Assistance Corporation (TSAC)
Web Site: http://www.state.tn.us/tsac/grants.htm#Christa
Amount of Scholarship: $1,000
Number of Awards: not given
Deadline: April 1
Education Level: college juniors
Eligibility: Applicant must attend college in Tennessee and plan to pursue a career in teaching in Tennessee.

Here you will find a brief description of the scholarship for teacher education students in Tennessee. You can obtain application forms directly from TSAC. Click the TSAC Home button at the bottom of the Web page to find links to phone numbers and e-mail addresses for TSAC.

Ned McWherter Scholars

Sponsor: Tennessee Student Assistance Corporation (TSAC)
Web Site: http://www.state.tn.us/tsac/grants.htm#Ned
Amount of Scholarship: $6,000
Number of Awards: not given
Deadline: February 15
Education Level: high school seniors and college undergraduates
Eligibility: Applicant must be a Tennessee resident, have graduated from a Tennessee high school, have a GPA and ACT or SAT I score in the top 5 percent nationally, and enroll at a Tennessee college.

Here you will find a brief description of the scholarship, including eligibility requirements. You can obtain application forms from your high school's guidance office or directly from TSAC. Click the TSAC Home button at the bottom of the Web page to find links to phone numbers and e-mail addresses for TSAC.

Robert C. Byrd Honors Scholarship

Sponsor: Tennessee Student Assistance Corporation (TSAC)
Web Site: http://www.state.tn.us/tsac/grants.htm#Robert
Amount of Scholarship: $6,000
Number of Awards: not given
Deadline: March 1
Education Level: high school seniors
Eligibility: Applicant must be a Tennessee resident; have a 3.5 GPA, a GED score of 57, or a combination of a 3.0 GPA and an ACT score of 24; and enroll at a Tennessee college.

Here you will find a brief description of the scholarship, including eligibility requirements. You can obtain application forms from your high school's guidance office or directly from TSAC. Click the TSAC Home button at the bottom of the Web page to find links to phone numbers and e-mail addresses for TSAC.

Tennessee Student Assistance Award

Sponsor: Tennessee Student Assistance Corporation (TSAC)
Web Site: http://www.state.tn.us/tsac/grants.htm#Tennessee
Amount of Scholarship: up to full tuition
Number of Awards: not given
Deadline: May 1
Education Level: high school seniors and college undergraduates
Eligibility: Applicant must be a Tennessee resident, enroll at an eligible postsecondary insti-

tution in Tennessee, and demonstrate financial need.

Here you will find a brief description of Tennessee's educational grant for needy students. You will automatically be considered for the grant when you file the FAFSA.

Also see the following scholarships:

- Bank of America ADA Abilities Scholarship: Chapter 10, "Any Disability" section
- Congressional Black Caucus Spouses Scholarships: Chapter 15, "Alabama" section
- Dependent Children Scholarship: Chapter 14, "Public Safety Officers" section
- Minority Teaching Fellows: Chapter 6, "Education" section
- Sidney B. Meadows Scholarship: Chapter 6, "Horticulture" section
- State Funeral Director Associations Scholarships: Chapter 6, "Funeral Service and Mortuary Science" section
- Tennessee Teaching Scholars: Chapter 6, "Education" section

Texas

Opportunity Scholarship

Sponsor: Houston Livestock Show and Rodeo
Web Site: http://www.hlsr.com/opportunity.html
Amount of Scholarship: $10,000 (renewable for four years)
Number of Awards: 100
Deadline: April 1
Education Level: high school seniors
Eligibility: Applicant must be a Texas resident; graduate from specified school districts within Harris, Brazoria, Chambers, Fort Bend, Galveston, Liberty, Montgomery, and Waller Counties; rank in the upper 50 percent of the high

school class; pass the TAAS Mastery/Exit Level exam; have a minimum SAT I score of 800 or a minimum ACT score of 18; enroll at a four-year college in Texas; and be a U.S. citizen.

Under this program, 44 $10,000 scholarships are designated for students graduating from the Houston Independent School District, while the remaining awards go to applicants from the other participating school districts. The Web page explains the eligibility requirements, selection criteria, application requirements, and how to request an application by phone or e-mail. A complete list of participating school districts is also given, so you can make certain that you meet the residency requirement.

Scholarship for Early High School Graduates

Sponsor: Texas Higher Education Coordinating Board Student Services Division
Web Site: http://www.thecb.state.tx.us/divisions/student/ehs/ehs.htm
Amount of Scholarship: $1,000
Number of Awards: not given
Deadline: not given
Education Level: high school seniors
Eligibility: Applicant must be a Texas resident, have attended a public high school in Texas, complete the requirements for high school graduation in at least 36 consecutive months, and enroll at a public college in Texas or any private college that agrees to provide a matching scholarship.

This Web page describes the eligibility requirements for the scholarship and tells you how to apply. You must have an official at your high school send a certification letter attesting to your successful completion of high school in less than 36 months to the Texas Higher Education Coordinating Board in order to be considered. A link to a sample certification letter is provided on the Web page. You'll also find a link to a Frequently Asked Questions page and contact information if you have further questions about the program.

TEXAS Grant

Sponsor: Texas Higher Education Coordinating Board Student Services Division
Web Site: http://www.thecb.state.tx.us/divisions/student/TEXAS.htm
Amount of Scholarship: $940 to $2,400 (renewable for six years)
Number of Awards: not given
Deadline: varies
Education Level: high school seniors and college undergraduates
Eligibility: Applicant must be a Texas resident, graduate from a Texas high school, complete the recommended or advanced high school curriculum, enroll at least three-quarter time at a two-year or four-year college in Texas, and demonstrate financial need.

Here you will find all the facts about Texas's educational grant program, including a rundown of the eligibility requirements, award amounts, and renewal conditions. You will also find a link to a page explaining the recommended and advanced high school curriculum, so you can make certain to meet that prerequisite. You must apply for this grant through the financial aid office at your college.

Also see the following scholarships:

- Bank of America ADA Abilities Scholarship: Chapter 10, "Any Disability" section
- Congressional Black Caucus Spouses Scholarships: Chapter 15, "Alabama" section
- HSF Community College Transfer Scholarship: Chapter 9, "Hispanic" section
- HSF High School Scholarship: Chapter 9, "Hispanic" section

- Sidney B. Meadows Scholarship: Chapter 6, "Horticulture" section
- Southern Texas PGA Foundation Scholarship: Chapter 8, "Golf" section
- State Funeral Director Associations Scholarships: Chapter 6, "Funeral Service and Mortuary Science" section
- Teach for Texas Conditional Grant: Chapter 6, "Education" section
- TH&MA Educational Foundation Scholarships: Chapter 6, "Hotel and Restaurant Management" section

Utah

See the following scholarships:

- Careers in Agriculture Scholarship: Chapter 6, "Agriculture" section
- Regional EAGLE Scholarship: Chapter 9, "Gay and Lesbian" section
- Utah Highway Patrol Association Scholarship: Chapter 14, "Public Safety Officers" section

Vermont

Vermont State Grants

Sponsor: Vermont Student Assistance Corporation (VSAC)
Web Site: http://www.vsac.org/html/pw_pay1.htm#grants
Amount of Scholarship: not given
Number of Awards: not given
Deadline: not given
Education Level: high school seniors and college undergraduates

Eligibility: Applicant must be a Vermont resident and enroll at a two-year or four-year college.

Two different educational grants are awarded by the state of Vermont: Incentive Grants for full-time undergraduate students, and Part-Time Grants for part-time undergraduate students. The Web page tells you a little about the program, including how to apply, and it provides a link to the electronic application form that you can submit online. Click the Continued link at the bottom of the page to find more information about financial aid for Vermont residents, including how to order a booklet of scholarships for Vermonters.

Also see the following scholarships:

- State Funeral Director Associations Scholarships: Chapter 6, "Funeral Service and Mortuary Science" section
- Switzer Environmental Fellowship: Chapter 7, "Environmental Studies" section

Virgin Islands

Also see the following scholarships:

- Congressional Black Caucus Spouses Scholarships: Chapter 15, "Alabama" section

Virginia

Lee-Jackson Scholarship

Sponsor: Lee-Jackson Foundation of Charlottesville, Virginia

Web Site: http://hermes.bitlink.com/leejackson
Amount of Scholarship: $1,000 to $3,000
Number of Awards: 24
Deadline: not given
Education Level: high school juniors and seniors
Eligibility: Applicant must be a Virginia resident, attend high school in Virginia, and enroll at an accredited four-year college or the transfer program of an accredited community college in the U.S.

This program award scholarships for the best essays commemorating Generals Lee and Jackson, as described on the Web page. Click The Essay link to find essay topic suggestions. Beneath that, you will find details on the amount of the scholarship, eligibility requirements, and how to apply. Twenty-four scholarships are awarded in all, divided among the eight high school regions in Virginia. The 15 third-place winners receive $1,000, the 8 second-place winners receive $2,000, and the 1 grand place winner receives $3,000. You'll find a link to the application form at the very bottom of the page.

Virginia BPW Foundation Scholarships

Sponsor: Virginia Business and Professional Women (BPW) Foundation
Web Site: http://bpwva.advocate.net/foundation.htm#scholarships
Amount of Scholarship: $100 to $1,000
Number of Awards: not given
Deadline: April 1
Education Level: high school seniors, college undergraduates, and graduate students
Eligibility: Applicant must enroll at a Virginia college or university and be a Virginia resident.

Three different scholarships are described on this Web page. The Nettie Tucker Yowell Scholarship is awarded to Virginia high school seniors, and both men and women are eligible to apply for it. The Buena M. Chesshir Memorial Women's Educational Scholarship goes to women 25 years of age or older to help them further their education. The Women in Science and Technology Scholarship is college juniors and seniors and graduate students who are studying mathematics or actuarial science. You can download a PDF copy of the application form for each scholarship from the Web site. Be sure to only apply for scholarships for which you are qualified.

Also see the following scholarships:

- Bank of America ADA Abilities Scholarship: Chapter 10, "Any Disability" section
- Congressional Black Caucus Spouses Scholarships: Chapter 15, "Alabama" section
- Long & Foster Scholarship: Chapter 15, "Delaware" section
- NSA Scholarships: Chapter 6, "Accounting" section
- Project Excellence Scholarships: Chapter 9, "African American" section
- RMA Scholarship: Chapter 6, "Retailing" section
- Sidney B. Meadows Scholarship: Chapter 6, "Horticulture" section
- State Funeral Director Associations Scholarships: Chapter 6, "Funeral Service and Mortuary Science" section
- Virginia Division Scholarships: Chapter 14, "Military Personnel and Veterans" section
- VSCLS Scholarship: Chapter 6, "Clinical Laboratory Science" section
- VSGC Scholarships and Fellowships: Chapter 6, "Aerospace Sciences and Engineering" section

Washington

Anne D. Maloof Scholarship

Sponsor: College Planning Network
Web Site: http://www.collegeplan.org/cpnow/pnwguide/onlineaps/msonap.htm
Amount of Scholarship: $3,000
Number of Awards: not given
Deadline: March 31
Education Level: high school seniors, college undergraduates, and graduate students
Eligibility: Applicant must be a resident of Snohomish, Island, King, Kitsap, Jefferson, Pierce, or Thurston Counties; enroll at a public two-year college, four-year college, or graduate school in the U.S; and demonstrate financial need.

At the top of this Web page, you'll find a list of eligibility requirements and a list of documents that you must submit to apply for the scholarship. Scroll to the bottom of the page to find an electronic application that you can submit online.

College Planning Network Scholarship

Sponsor: College Planning Network
Web Site: http://www.collegeplan.org/cpnow/pnwguide/onlineaps/cpnonap.htm
Amount of Scholarship: $1,000
Number of Awards: 1
Deadline: March 31
Education Level: high school juniors
Eligibility: Applicant must be a Washington resident, have a GPA between 2.5 and 3.5, and enroll at a two-year or four-year college in Washington, Oregon, Idaho, or Alaska.

At the top of this Web page, you'll find a list of eligibility requirements and a list of documents that you must submit to apply for the scholarship. Scroll to the bottom of the page to find an electronic application that you can submit online.

Dick Larsen Scholarship

Sponsor: The Seattle Foundation and the Washington News Council
Web Site: http://www.collegeplan.org/cpnow/pnwguide/onlineaps/dlsonap.htm
Amount of Scholarship: $2,000
Number of Awards: 1
Deadline: May 1
Education Level: high school seniors and college undergraduates
Eligibility: Applicant must graduate from a Washington high school, enroll at a public four-year college in Washington, commit to a career in communications, and demonstrate financial need.

The top of this Web page provides an overview of the scholarship program, including its purpose and the eligibility requirements. Scroll to the bottom of the page to find an electronic application that you can submit online. Be sure to follow the instructions given beneath the electronic application for sending in the required supplemental materials by mail, or your application won't be considered.

Edmund F. Maxwell Foundation Scholarship

Sponsor: Edmund F. Maxwell Foundation
Web Site: http://www.maxwell.org
Amount of Scholarship: $3,500 (renewable)
Number of Awards: not given
Deadline: April 30
Education Level: high school seniors

Eligibility: Applicant must be a resident of western Washington, enroll at an accredited private college, have a minimum SAT I score of 1200, and demonstrate financial need.

First, click the Scholarship link to read about the award amounts and the type of applicant that the sponsor is seeking. The Guidelines link tells you about the eligibility requirements, the requirements for the application package, and other important details. If you decide to apply, click the links to the Application and Financial Aid Worksheet to open the forms in printable text format. You will also find links to a renewal application form and to a list of scholarship recipients on this Web site.

Educational Opportunity Grant

Sponsor: Washington Higher Education Coordinating Board
Web Site: http://www.hecb.wa.gov/paying/aidprograms.html
Amount of Scholarship: $2,500 (renewable for one year)
Number of Awards: not given
Deadline: March 31 to August 31
Education Level: college sophomores
Eligibility: Applicant must be a "placebound" Washington resident living in a designated county in the state; have completed the first two years of college or an Associate of Arts degree; enroll at an eligible four-year college in Washington; not enroll in religious, seminarian, or theological studies; and demonstrate financial need.

To learn about this state-sponsored grant program, scroll down the Web page until you see the name of the grant. The short paragraph that follows describes the award amount, the eligibility requirements, and how the award may be used. Click the link at the end of the description to find a copy of the application form in PDF format. The application provides a lot more information about the grant, including a definition of the "placebound" requirement, a list of designated counties, and a list of eligible four-year colleges you can attend under the grant.

John C. Bigelow Scholarship

Sponsor: The Seattle Foundation
Web Site: http://www.collegeplan.org/cpnow/pnwguide/onlineaps/jbigonap.htm
Amount of Scholarship: $1,500
Number of Awards: 1
Deadline: April 15
Education Level: high school seniors
Eligibility: Applicant must attend a Seattle School District public high school, have a minimum 3.0 GPA, enroll as a full-time student at a public two-year or four-year college, and demonstrate financial need.

At the top of this Web page you'll find a list of eligibility requirements for the scholarship. Beneath that are instructions for submitting the application package and a list of materials that you'll need to include in the package. Scroll to the bottom of the page to find an application form that you can fill out within your Web browser window and then print for mailing.

Philip B. Swain Scholarship

Sponsor: Alliance for Education
Web Site: http://www.collegeplan.org/cpnow/pnwguide/onlineaps/pbsonap.htm
Amount of Scholarship: $1,000 (renewable for four years)
Number of Awards: 1
Deadline: June 14
Education Level: high school seniors
Eligibility: Applicant must graduate from a public high school in Seattle and enroll as a full-time student at a two-year or four-year college.

Read about the purpose of this scholarship, the eligibility requirements, the selection criteria, and the application procedures at the top of this Web page. Scroll to the bottom of the page to find an electronic application that you can submit online.

Robert C. Byrd Scholarship

Sponsor: Office of the Superintendent of Public Instruction
Web Site: http://www.hecb.wa.gov/paying/aidprograms.html
Amount of Scholarship: not given
Number of Awards: not given
Deadline: not given
Education Level: high school seniors
Eligibility: Applicant must be a Washington resident.

To learn more about this scholarship, scroll down the Web page until you see the name of the award. You cannot apply directly for this scholarship. Instead, you will be invited to apply based on your test scores, GPA, and academic core subjects. The Web page tells you how to contact the scholarship sponsor directly if you need more information.

State Need Grant

Sponsor: Washington Higher Education Coordinating Board
Web Site: http://www.hecb.wa.gov/paying/aidprograms.html
Amount of Scholarship: not given
Number of Awards: not given
Deadline: not given
Education Level: high school seniors and college undergraduates
Eligibility: Applicant must be a Washington resident, enroll at a two-year or four-year col-

lege in Washington, and demonstrate financial need.

You will find a description of this educational grant program at the top of the Web page. The short paragraph lists the eligibility requirements and tells you how to apply. You will automatically be considered for the grant when you file the FAFSA.

Walter H. Meyer-Garry L. White Memorial Scholarship

Sponsor: College Planning Network and Walter H. Meyer-Garry L. White Memorial Educational Fund
Web Site: http://www.collegeplan.org/cpnow/pnwguide/onlineaps/mwonap.htm
Amount of Scholarship: $2,000
Number of Awards: not given
Deadline: February 15
Education Level: high school seniors, college undergraduates, and graduate students
Eligibility: Applicant must be a Washington resident; enroll at a two-year college, four-year college, or graduate school in the U.S., Canada, or Europe; and demonstrate financial need.

At the top of this Web page you'll find a list of eligibility requirements and a list of documents that you must submit to apply for the scholarship. Scroll to the bottom of the page to find an electronic application that you can submit online.

Washington Promise Scholarship

Sponsor: Washington Higher Education Coordinating Board
Web Site: http://www.hecb.wa.gov/paying/Promise/pm2000.html
Amount of Scholarship: $1,641 (renewable for one year)

Number of Awards: not given
Deadline: May 1
Education Level: high school seniors
Eligibility: Applicant must attend high school in Washington, rank in the top 15 percent of the high school class, enroll at an accredited two-year or four-year college in Washington, not pursue a degree in theology, and demonstrate financial need.

This Web page goes over the eligibility requirements for Washington's scholarship for low- and middle-income students, including the financial need income cutoffs your family must meet in order for you to qualify. Click the Application and Fact Sheet link to open a PDF copy of the application form that you can print out.

Washington Scholars

Sponsor: Washington Higher Education Coordinating Board
Web Site: http://www.hecb.wa.gov/paying/aidprograms.html
Amount of Scholarship: up to full tuition
Number of Awards: not given
Deadline: not given
Education Level: high school seniors
Eligibility: Applicant must be a Washington resident, rank in the top 1 percent of the high school class, and enroll at a college in Washington.

Three high school seniors from each legislative district in the state receive scholarships under this program. To learn more about it, scroll down the Web page until you see the name of the scholarship. The short paragraph following describes the purpose of the scholarship, the nomination process, and the scholarship amount. Your high school principal must nominate you for this scholarship, so contact your principal or guidance counselor to find out how to apply.

Windermere Foundation Scholarship

Sponsor: Windermere Foundation and College Planning Network
Web Site: http://www.collegeplan.org/cpnow/pnwguide/onlineaps/wfonap.htm
Amount of Scholarship: $1,000
Number of Awards: 7
Deadline: March 31
Education Level: high school seniors
Eligibility: Applicant must graduate from an eligible public high school in Seattle and enroll as a full-time student at a two-year or four-year college.

Read about the purpose of this scholarship, the eligibility requirements, the selection criteria, and the application procedures at the top of this Web page. A list of eligible high schools is given at the very top of the page. Scroll to the bottom of the page to find an application form that you can fill out inside your Web browser and then print with your answers intact.

Yes You Can (Y.Y.C.) Scholarship

Sponsor: The Seattle Foundation
Web Site: http://www.collegeplan.org/cpnow/pnwguide/onlineaps/yyconap.htm
Amount of Scholarship: $2,000
Number of Awards: not given
Deadline: February 15
Education Level: high school seniors and college undergraduates
Eligibility: Applicant must live in King or Snohomish County; be African-American; major in business, communications, computer science, or education; demonstrate financial need; and have a minimum 2.5 GPA.

Be sure to read through all the eligibility requirements and conditions of this scholarship.

They are very restrictive, and you must meet all of them to qualify. If you do qualify, you can submit an electronic application online. You will also have to mail in several additional documents, listed at bottom of the Web page, to complete your application package. To be safe, you should also print out a copy of the electronic application with your responses to the application questions typed in and include it with your application package; note that some parts of the application form must be completed by hand.

ZymoGenetics Scholarship for the Advancement of Science

Sponsor: ZymoGenetics
Web Site: http://www.collegeplan.org/cpnow/pnwguide/onlineaps/zgonap.htm
Amount of Scholarship: $1,000
Number of Awards: 5
Deadline: March 31
Education Level: high school seniors
Eligibility: Applicant must attend a public high school in Seattle; major in biology, biotechnology, or chemistry; have completed at least 25 hours of community service; and have a minimum 3.3 GPA.

Read the applicant criteria listed at the top of this Web page to be sure that you meet all of the conditions for this scholarship. Note that priority is given to minority applicants. Beneath the application criteria is a list of supporting documents that you must send in, in addition to your application. Scroll to the bottom of the page to find an electronic application form that you can either submit online or print out and mail in.

Also see the following scholarships:

• Audra M. Edwards Scholarship: Chapter 9, "Gay and Lesbian" section

- Bank of America ADA Abilities Scholarship: Chapter 10, "Any Disability" section
- Burlington Northern Santa Fe Foundation Scholarship: Chapter 9, "Native American" section
- Careers in Agriculture Scholarship: Chapter 6, "Agriculture" section
- GSBA, Pride, and INBA Scholarships: Chapter 9, "Gay and Lesbian" section
- HSF High School Scholarship: Chapter 9, "Hispanic" section
- Northshore Youth Soccer Association Scholarship: Chapter 8, "Athletics" section
- Oregon Nurserymen's Foundation Scholarships: Chapter 6, "Horticulture" section
- Regional EAGLE Scholarship: Chapter 9, "Gay and Lesbian" section
- State Funeral Director Associations Scholarships: Chapter 6, "Funeral Service and Mortuary Science" section

West Virginia

Robert C. Byrd Honors Scholarship

Sponsor: West Virginia State College and University Systems and West Virginia Department of Education
Web Site: http://www.scusco.wvnet.edu/www/stserv/FCTSTBYR.HTM
Amount of Scholarship: $1,500 (renewable for four years)
Number of Awards: 39
Deadline: March 15
Education Level: high school seniors
Eligibility: Applicant must be a West Virginia resident, enroll at an accredited postsecondary institution, meet minimum academic standards, and be a U.S. citizen or permanent resident.

This Web page provides a complete description of the scholarship program, including the average academic qualifications of scholarship recipients, which will help you decide if you would make a good candidate. You must apply through your high school guidance counselor. Contact information for the scholarship sponsor is provided on the Web page if you have further questions, though.

West Virginia Higher Education Grant

Sponsor: West Virginia State College and University Systems
Web Site: http://www.scusco.wvnet.edu/www/stserv/GRANT.HTM
Amount of Scholarship: $350 to $2,446 (renewable for four years)
Number of Awards: 39
Deadline: March 1
Education Level: high school seniors and college undergraduates
Eligibility: Applicant must be a West Virginia resident, enroll as a full-time student at an approved college in West Virginia or Pennsylvania, demonstrate financial need, and be a U.S. citizen.

On this Web page you will find all the facts about West Virginia's educational grant program for needy students, including eligibility requirements and selection criteria. To apply, you must submit the FAFSA and the Supplemental Grant Report Form, which is linked to the page.

Also see the following scholarships:

- David J. Clark Memorial Scholarship Grant: Chapter 6, "Film and Television" section
- Sidney B. Meadows Scholarship: Chapter 6, "Horticulture" section
- State Funeral Director Associations Scholarships: Chapter 6, "Funeral Service and Mortuary Science" section

- Underwood-Smith Teacher Scholarship: Chapter 6, "Education" section

Wisconsin

Academic Excellence Scholarship

Sponsor: State of Wisconsin Higher Educational Aids Board
Web Site: http://heab.state.wi.us/programs.html
Amount of Scholarship: $2,250
Number of Awards: not given
Deadline: February 15
Education Level: high school seniors
Eligibility: Applicant must attend high school in Wisconsin, have a GPA among the highest in the state, and enroll as a full-time student at a participating college in Wisconsin.

Scroll down the page until you see the scholarship description. There you will find the basic facts about the scholarship program and a link to a Frequently Asked Questions page. You don't apply directly for this scholarship. Instead, your high school must nominate you for the award, based on your outstanding grades.

Talent Incentive Program Grant

Sponsor: State of Wisconsin Higher Educational Aids Board
Web Site: http://heab.state.wi.us/programs.html
Amount of Scholarship: $250 to $1,800 (renewable for five years)
Number of Awards: not given
Deadline: not given
Education Level: high school seniors and college undergraduates
Eligibility: Applicant must be a Wisconsin resident, enroll at a college in Wisconsin, and demonstrate financial need.

Scroll down the page until you see the grant description. There you will find the basic facts about the grant program and contact information if you have further questions. Contact the financial aid officer at your college if you would like to apply for this grant.

Wisconsin Higher Education Grant

Sponsor: State of Wisconsin Higher Educational Aids Board
Web Site: http://heab.state.wi.us/programs.html
Amount of Scholarship: $250 to $1,800 (renewable for five years)
Number of Awards: not given
Deadline: not given
Education Level: high school seniors and college undergraduates
Eligibility: Applicant must be a Wisconsin resident, enroll at a public college or technical college in Wisconsin, and demonstrate financial need.

Scroll down the page until you see the grant description. There you will find the basic facts about the grant program and contact information if you have further questions. You will automatically be considered for this grant when you file the FAFSA.

Wisconsin Tuition Grant

Sponsor: State of Wisconsin Higher Educational Aids Board
Web Site: http://heab.state.wi.us/programs.html
Amount of Scholarship: $250 to $2,300 (renewable for five years)

Number of Awards: not given
Deadline: not given
Education Level: high school seniors and college undergraduates
Eligibility: Applicant must be a Wisconsin resident, enroll at a private college in Wisconsin, and demonstrate financial need.

Scroll down the page until you see the grant description. There you will find the basic facts about the grant program and contact information if you have further questions. You will automatically be considered for this grant when you file the FAFSA.

Also see the following scholarships:

- Careers in Agriculture Scholarship: Chapter 6, "Agriculture" section
- Catholic Aid Association College Tuition Scholarship: Chapter 11, "Catholic" section
- Hearing and Visually Handicapped Student Grant: Chapter 10, "Hearing Impaired" section

- Indian Student Assistance Grant: Chapter 9, "Native American" section
- Madison Jazz Society Scholarship: Chapter 8, "Performing Arts" section
- Minority Undergraduate Retention Grant: Chapter 9, "All Minorities" section
- State Funeral Director Associations Scholarships: Chapter 6, "Funeral Service and Mortuary Science" section

Wyoming

See the following scholarships:

- Careers in Agriculture Scholarship: Chapter 6, "Agriculture" section
- Regional EAGLE Scholarship: Chapter 9, "Gay and Lesbian" section
- State Funeral Director Associations Scholarships: Chapter 6, "Funeral Service and Mortuary Science" section

COLLEGE-SPECIFIC SCHOLARSHIPS

This chapter lists the Web addresses for the sites of accredited four-year colleges and universities in the United States that publish detailed scholarship information online. The colleges' scholarship sites are organized by state for easy reference. The best of these Web sites list all scholarships offered by the school to incoming freshmen, continuing students, transfer students, and graduate students. You can search for athletic and artistic scholarships, scholarships awarded by academic departments, scholarships for female and minority students, alumni scholarships, and general academic scholarships. At many of these sites you can even apply for scholarships online by submitting an electronic form, or you can download an application in PDF format. At the very least, you should find contact information, so you can get in touch with someone who can tell you how to apply.

Whether you are already enrolled in college or you are just starting a college search, you should take advantage of these online resources to help you find money to pay for your education. Keep in mind that many colleges don't publish scholarship information on the Web, so you should directly contact the financial aid offices of colleges not listed here to learn about scholarship opportunities. Even if your school doesn't publish extensive scholarship information online, you are bound to find some financial aid information on the school's Web site—definitely check it out.

A list of cross references to other scholarships listed in this book that you can use at each school follows each college's scholarship site, where applicable. This will help you track down even more scholarship money to help pay your tuition bills.

College and University Scholarship Web Sites

Alabama

Alabama A&M University

Web Site: http://www.aamu.edu/ Financial_Aid/Scholarships/scholarships.html

Also see the following scholarships:

- Army ROTC Scholarship for Historically Black Colleges and Universities: Chapter 13, "Army and Army ROTC" section
- Competitive Edge Scholarship: Chapter 6, "Engineering" section
- IFT Scholarships: Chapter 6, "Food Science and Nutrition" section
- NPSC Graduate Fellowships in the Physical Sciences: Chapter 7, "Sciences" section
- U.S. Department of Agriculture/Woodrow Wilson Fellowship: Chapter 6, "Agriculture" section

Auburn University

Web Site: http://www.auburn.edu/ student_info/student_affairs/scholarship/ index.html

Also see the following scholarships:

- Competitive Edge Scholarship: Chapter 6, "Engineering" section
- GEM Fellowships: Chapter 9, "All Minorities" section
- IFT Scholarships: Chapter 6, "Food Science and Nutrition" section
- International Study Programs Scholarship: Chapter 6, "Study Abroad" section

- NBAA Aviation Scholarship: Chapter 6, "Aviation" section
- NPSC Graduate Fellowships in the Physical Sciences: Chapter 7, "Sciences" section
- Search for Excellence National Scholarship: Chapter 5, "Academic Scholarships" section
- Thread Committee Excellence in Manufacturing Scholarship: Chapter 6, "Textile Science and Fiber Arts" section

Birmingham Southern College

Web Site: http://www.bsc.edu/fa/

Also see the following scholarship:

- International Study Programs Scholarship: Chapter 6, "Study Abroad" section

Jacksonville State University

Web Site: http://www.jsu.edu/depart/finaid/finaid.html

Oakwood College

Web Site: http://www.oakwood.edu/finaid/scholarships.html

Also see the following scholarships:

- COHEAO Scholarship: Chapter 5, "Academic Scholarships" section
- McDonald's UNCF Tri-State Scholarship: Chapter 9, "African-American" section
- UNCF Scholarships: Chapter 9, "African-American" section

Southeastern Bible College

Web Site: http://www.sebc.edu/finaid/sebc.htm

Troy State University Montgomery

Web Site: http://www.tsum.edu/scholar

Tuskegee University

Web Site: http://www.tusk.edu/finaid/scholarships.htm

Also see the following scholarships:

- Arkansas Health Education Grant: Chapter 15, "Arkansas" section
- Army ROTC Nurse Scholarships: Chapter 13, "Army and Army ROTC" section
- Army ROTC Scholarship for Historically Black Colleges and Universities: Chapter 13, "Army and Army ROTC" section
- Development Fund for Black Students in Science and Technology Scholarship: Chapter 12, "African-American" section
- GEM Fellowships: Chapter 9, "All Minorities" section
- McDonald's UNCF Tri-State Scholarship: Chapter 9, "African-American" section
- UNCF Scholarships: Chapter 9, "African-American" section
- U.S. Department of Agriculture/Woodrow Wilson Fellowship: Chapter 6, "Agriculture" section

University of Alabama

Web Site: http://www.ua.edu/academic/financial/skolar.html

Also see the following scholarships:

- Competitive Edge Scholarship: Chapter 6, "Engineering" section
- FEF Scholarships: Chapter 6, "Materials Science and Metallurgy" section
- GEM Fellowships: Chapter 9, "All Minorities" section
- International Study Programs Scholarship: Chapter 6, "Study Abroad" section
- NEHA/AAS Scholarship: Chapter 6, "Health Care" section

- NPSC Graduate Fellowships in the Physical Sciences: Chapter 7, "Sciences" section
- Search for Excellence National Scholarship: Chapter 5, "Academic Scholarships" section

University of Alabama at Birmingham

Web Site: http://main.uab.edu/ show.asp?durki=4213

Also see the following scholarship:

- COHEAO Scholarship: Chapter 5, "Academic Scholarships" section

University of Alabama in Huntsville

Web Site: http://www.uah.edu/HTML/ Admissions/AdmisInfo/scholarship.html

University of Montevallo

Web Site: http://www.montevallo.edu/finaid/ scolarship.htm

University of West Alabama

Web Site: http://www.uwa.edu/transfer/ scholarships/scholarships.html

Alaska

University of Alaska Anchorage

Web Site: http://www.uaa.alaska.edu/finaid/ uaascholarship.htm

Also see the following scholarships:

- Competitive Edge Scholarship: Chapter 6, "Engineering" section
- NPSC Graduate Fellowships in the Physical Sciences: Chapter 7, "Sciences" section
- University of Alaska Scholars Award: Chapter 15, "Alaska" section

Arizona

Arizona State University

Web Site: http://www.asu.edu/fa/ scholarships/0001/index.htm

Also see the following scholarships:

- Competitive Edge Scholarship: Chapter 6, "Engineering" section
- GEM Fellowships: Chapter 9, "All Minorities" section
- Key Club International Scholarships: Chapter 8, "Clubs" section
- NBAA Aviation Scholarship: Chapter 6, "Aviation" section
- NPSC Graduate Fellowships in the Physical Sciences: Chapter 7, "Sciences" section
- Search for Excellence National Scholarship: Chapter 5, "Academic Scholarships" section
- SRC Master's Scholarship: Chapter 7, "Electronics" section

Northern Arizona University

Web Site: http://www.nau.edu/finaid/ Scholarship/index.html

Also see the following scholarships:

- COHEAO Scholarship: Chapter 5, "Academic Scholarships" section
- NPSC Graduate Fellowships in the Physical Sciences: Chapter 7, "Sciences" section

University of Arizona

Web Site: http://w3.arizona.edu/~scholar/ scholars.htm

Also see the following scholarships:

- Competitive Edge Scholarship: Chapter 6, "Engineering" section

- GEM Fellowships: Chapter 9, "All Minorities" section
- International Study Programs Scholarship: Chapter 6, "Study Abroad" section
- Luce Scholars: Chapter 7, "Study Abroad" section
- NPSC Graduate Fellowships in the Physical Sciences: Chapter 7, "Sciences" section
- SRC Master's Scholarship: Chapter 7, "Electronics" section
- Winston Churchill Foundation Scholarship: Chapter 7, "Study Abroad" section

Arkansas

Arkansas State University

Web Site: http://www.astate.edu/docs/admin/FinAid/scholarships.html

Also see the following scholarships:

- Army ROTC Nurse Scholarships: Chapter 13, "Army and Army ROTC" section
- Competitive Edge Scholarship: Chapter 6, "Engineering" section

Hendrix College

Web Site: http://www.hendrix.edu/FinancialAid/Scholarships.htm

John Brown University

Web Site: http://www.jbu.edu/finaid/scholarships/index.html

University of Arkansas

Web Site: http://www.uark.edu/admin/regrinfo/admiss/index.html

Also see the following scholarships:

- Competitive Edge Scholarship: Chapter 6, "Engineering" section

- IFT Scholarships: Chapter 6, "Food Science and Nutrition" section
- NPSC Graduate Fellowships in the Physical Sciences: Chapter 7, "Sciences" section
- Search for Excellence National Scholarship: Chapter 5, "Academic Scholarships" section

University of Arkansas at Little Rock

Web Site: http://www.ualr.edu/~adminfo/aid-2.htm

University of Arkansas at Pine Bluff

Web Site: http://www.uapb.edu/page30.html

Also see the following scholarships:

- Army ROTC Scholarship for Historically Black Colleges and Universities: Chapter 13, "Army and Army ROTC" section
- U.S. Department of Agriculture/Woodrow Wilson Fellowship: Chapter 6, "Agriculture" section

University of the Ozarks

Web Site: http://www.ozarks.edu/admissions/scholarships.html

Williams Baptist College

Web Site: http://wbc2.wbcoll.edu/admfa.htm

California

Azusa Pacific University

Web Site: http://www.apu.edu/services/sfs/institutionalAid.shtml

California Lutheran University

Web Site: http://www.clunet.edu/Admission/Undergraduate/FinancialAid/scholarships.htm

Also see the following scholarships:

- AAL Lutheran Campus Scholarship: Chapter 11, "Lutheran" section
- COHEAO Scholarship: Chapter 5, "Academic Scholarships" section
- Lutheran College Scholarships: Chapter 11, "Lutheran" section

California State University, Bakersfield

Web Site: http://www.csubak.edu/FinAid/aid/scholar.html

Also see the following scholarship:

- International Study Programs Scholarship: Chapter 6, "Study Abroad" section

California State University, Chico

Web Site: http://www.csuchico.edu/fa/home/types/schol.html

Also see the following scholarships:

- FEF Scholarships: Chapter 6, "Materials Science and Metallurgy" section
- International Study Programs Scholarship: Chapter 6, "Study Abroad" section

California State University, Dominguez Hills

Web Site: http://www.csudh.edu/fin_aid/scholarships.htm

Also see the following scholarship:

- International Study Programs Scholarship: Chapter 6, "Study Abroad" section

California State University, Fresno

Web Site: http://studentaffairs.csufresno.edu/financial_aid/99.20/schol/sch_enter.htm

Also see the following scholarships:

- International Study Programs Scholarship: Chapter 6, "Study Abroad" section
- NEHA/AAS Scholarship: Chapter 6, "Health Care" section

California State University, Fullerton

Web Site: http://sa.fullerton.edu/financialaid/scholar/

Also see the following scholarships:

- COHEAO Scholarship: Chapter 5, "Academic Scholarships" section
- Hispanic Education Endowment Fund General Scholarships: Chapter 15, "California" section
- International Study Programs Scholarship: Chapter 6, "Study Abroad" section

California State University, Long Beach

Web Site: http://www.csulb.edu/enrollment/html/scholarships.html

Also see the following scholarship:

- International Study Programs Scholarship: Chapter 6, "Study Abroad" section

California State University, Los Angeles

Web Site: http://www.calstatela.edu/univ/finaid/scholar.htm

Also see the following scholarship:

- International Study Programs Scholarship: Chapter 6, "Study Abroad" section

California State University, Northridge

Web Site: http://www.csun.edu/finaid/scholarships.html

Also see the following scholarships:

- GEM Fellowships: Chapter 9, "All Minorities" section
- International Study Programs Scholarship: Chapter 6, "Study Abroad" section
- NEHA/AAS Scholarship: Chapter 6, "Health Care" section

California State University, Sacramento

Web Site: http://www.csus.edu/faid/finschlr.html

Also see the following scholarships:

- International Study Programs Scholarship: Chapter 6, "Study Abroad" section
- SRC Master's Scholarship: Chapter 7, "Electronics" section

California State University, San Bernardino

Web Site: http://finaid.csusb.edu/scholars.htm

Also see the following scholarship:

- International Study Programs Scholarship: Chapter 6, "Study Abroad" section

California State University, San Marcos

Web Site: http://ww2.csusm.edu/financial_aid/scholarship/cscholarship.html

Also see the following scholarship:

- International Study Programs Scholarship: Chapter 6, "Study Abroad" section

California State University, Stanislaus

Web Site: http://www.csustan.edu/FinAid/dept/scholar.html

Also see the following scholarship:

- International Study Programs Scholarship: Chapter 6, "Study Abroad" section

Mount St. Mary's College

Web Site: http://www.msmc.la.edu/Admissions/Financing/grants_%20and_%20scholarships.htm

Also see the following scholarships:

- International Study Programs Scholarship: Chapter 6, "Study Abroad" section
- Search for Excellence National Scholarship: Chapter 5, "Academic Scholarships" section

San Francisco State University

Web Site: http://www.sfsu.edu/finaid/scholarships/main.htm

Also see the following scholarship:

- Markowski-Leach Scholarship: Chapter 9, "Gay and Lesbian" section

Sonoma State University

Web Site: http://www.sonoma.edu/Scholarship

University of California, Berkeley

Web Site: http://uga.berkeley.edu/fao/scholarships.html

Also see the following scholarships:

- Civilian Radioactive Waste Management Fellowship: Chapter 7, "Waste Management" section
- COHEAO Scholarship: Chapter 5, "Academic Scholarships" section
- Competitive Edge Scholarship: Chapter 6, "Engineering" section

- Consortium for Graduate Study in Management Fellowship: Chapter 7, "Business" section
- Donald A. Strauss Scholarship: Chapter 6, "Government and Public Service" section
- GEM Fellowships: Chapter 9, "All Minorities" section
- Hertz Foundation Fellowship: Chapter 7, "Sciences" section
- International Predissertation Fellowships: Chapter 7, "Social Sciences" section
- International Study Programs Scholarship: Chapter 6, "Study Abroad" section
- Luce Scholars: Chapter 7, "Study Abroad" section
- Markowski-Leach Scholarship: Chapter 9, "Gay and Lesbian" section
- NPSC Graduate Fellowships in the Physical Sciences: Chapter 7, "Sciences" section
- Search for Excellence National Scholarship: Chapter 5, "Academic Scholarships" section
- SRC Master's Scholarship: Chapter 7, "Electronics" section

University of California, Davis

Web Site: http://faoman.ucdavis.edu/schol.htm

Also see the following scholarships:

- Donald A. Strauss Scholarship: Chapter 6, "Government and Public Service" section
- GEM Fellowships: Chapter 9, "All Minorities" section
- Hertz Foundation Fellowship: Chapter 7, "Sciences" section
- IFT Scholarships: Chapter 6, "Food Science and Nutrition" section
- International Study Programs Scholarship: Chapter 6, "Study Abroad" section
- NPSC Graduate Fellowships in the Physical Sciences: Chapter 7, "Sciences" section
- Search for Excellence National Scholarship: Chapter 5, "Academic Scholarships" section

University of California, Irvine

Web Site: http://www.fao.uci.edu

Also see the following scholarships:

- COHEAO Scholarship: Chapter 5, "Academic Scholarships" section
- Donald A. Strauss Scholarship: Chapter 6, "Government and Public Service" section
- GEM Fellowships: Chapter 9, "All Minorities" section
- Hertz Foundation Fellowship: Chapter 7, "Sciences" section
- International Study Programs Scholarship: Chapter 6, "Study Abroad" section
- NPSC Graduate Fellowships in the Physical Sciences: Chapter 7, "Sciences" section

University of California, Los Angeles

Web Site: http://www.saonet.ucla.edu/fa/scholar/index.htm

Also see the following scholarships:

- COHEAO Scholarship: Chapter 5, "Academic Scholarships" section
- Competitive Edge Scholarship: Chapter 6, "Engineering" section
- Donald A. Strauss Scholarship: Chapter 6, "Government and Public Service" section
- D.W. Simpson & Company Actuarial Science Scholarships: Chapter 6, "Actuarial Science" section
- GEM Fellowships: Chapter 9, "All Minorities" section
- Hertz Foundation Fellowship: Chapter 7, "Sciences" section
- International Predissertation Fellowships: Chapter 7, "Social Sciences" section
- International Study Programs Scholarship: Chapter 6, "Study Abroad" section
- Luce Scholars: Chapter 7, "Study Abroad" section

- NHFA Entertainment Industry Scholarship: Chapter 9, "Hispanic" section
- NPSC Graduate Fellowships in the Physical Sciences: Chapter 7, "Sciences" section
- SRC Master's Scholarship: Chapter 7, "Electronics" section
- Winston Churchill Foundation Scholarship: Chapter 7, "Study Abroad" section

University of California, Riverside

Web Site: http://www.finaid.ucr.edu/scholarships.html

Also see the following scholarships:

- COHEAO Scholarship: Chapter 5, "Academic Scholarships" section
- Donald A. Strauss Scholarship: Chapter 6, "Government and Public Service" section
- Hertz Foundation Fellowship: Chapter 7, "Sciences" section
- International Study Programs Scholarship: Chapter 6, "Study Abroad" section
- NPSC Graduate Fellowships in the Physical Sciences: Chapter 7, "Sciences" section
- SRC Master's Scholarship: Chapter 7, "Electronics" section

University of California, San Diego

Web Site: http://orpheus-1.ucsd.edu/finaid/Scholarships/SCHToc00.htm

Also see the following scholarships:

- COHEAO Scholarship: Chapter 5, "Academic Scholarships" section
- Donald A. Strauss Scholarship: Chapter 6, "Government and Public Service" section
- GEM Fellowships: Chapter 9, "All Minorities" section
- Hertz Foundation Fellowship: Chapter 7, "Sciences" section

- International Predissertation Fellowships: Chapter 7, "Social Sciences" section
- International Study Programs Scholarship: Chapter 6, "Study Abroad" section
- NPSC Graduate Fellowships in the Physical Sciences: Chapter 7, "Sciences" section
- SRC Master's Scholarship: Chapter 7, "Electronics" section

University of California, Santa Barbara

Web Site: http://www.finaid.ucsb.edu/scholarships.htm

Also see the following scholarships:

- COHEAO Scholarship: Chapter 5, "Academic Scholarships" section
- Donald A. Strauss Scholarship: Chapter 6, "Government and Public Service" section
- GEM Fellowships: Chapter 9, "All Minorities" section
- Hertz Foundation Fellowship: Chapter 7, "Sciences" section
- International Study Programs Scholarship: Chapter 6, "Study Abroad" section
- NPSC Graduate Fellowships in the Physical Sciences: Chapter 7, "Sciences" section
- SRC Master's Scholarship: Chapter 7, "Electronics" section

University of California, Santa Cruz

Web Site: http://www2.ucsc.edu/fin-aid/typesd.html

Also see the following scholarships:

- COHEAO Scholarship: Chapter 5, "Academic Scholarships" section
- Donald A. Strauss Scholarship: Chapter 6, "Government and Public Service" section

- Hertz Foundation Fellowship: Chapter 7, "Sciences" section
- International Study Programs Scholarship: Chapter 6, "Study Abroad" section
- NPSC Graduate Fellowships in the Physical Sciences: Chapter 7, "Sciences" section
- SRC Master's Scholarship: Chapter 7, "Electronics" section

University of Southern California

Web Site: http://www.usc.edu/dept/fao/scholar.html

Also see the following scholarships:

- Army ROTC Nurse Scholarships: Chapter 13, "Army and Army ROTC" section
- COHEAO Scholarship: Chapter 5, "Academic Scholarships" section
- Consortium for Graduate Study in Management Fellowship: Chapter 7, "Business" section
- GEM Fellowships: Chapter 9, "All Minorities" section
- International Study Programs Scholarship: Chapter 6, "Study Abroad" section
- Luce Scholars: Chapter 7, "Study Abroad" section
- NHFA Entertainment Industry Scholarship: Chapter 9, "Hispanic" section
- NPSC Graduate Fellowships in the Physical Sciences: Chapter 7, "Sciences" section
- SRC Master's Scholarship: Chapter 7, "Electronics" section

Colorado

Colorado Christian University

Web Site: http://www.ccu.edu/tuition/institutional.htm

Colorado School of Mines

Web Site: http://www.mines.edu/Admin/fin_aid/aid_available_frameset.html

Colorado State University

Web Site: http://www.colostate.edu/Depts/SFServices/index11.htm

Also see the following scholarships:

- COHEAO Scholarship: Chapter 5, "Academic Scholarships" section
- Competitive Edge Scholarship: Chapter 6, "Engineering" section
- IFT Scholarships: Chapter 6, "Food Science and Nutrition" section
- International Study Programs Scholarship: Chapter 6, "Study Abroad" section
- NEHA/AAS Scholarship: Chapter 6, "Health Care" section
- NPSC Graduate Fellowships in the Physical Sciences: Chapter 7, "Sciences" section

Fort Lewis College

Web Site: http://www.fortlewis.edu/stu-aff/finaid/index.html

Mesa State College

Web Site: http://www2.mesastate.edu/enrollmentmanagement/scholarships.htm

University of Colorado

Web Site: http://www.colorado.edu/finaid

Also see the following scholarships:

- Astronaut Scholarship: Chapter 6, "Sciences" section
- COHEAO Scholarship: Chapter 5, "Academic Scholarships" section

- Competitive Edge Scholarship: Chapter 6, "Engineering" section
- Eisenhower-Evans Scholarship: Chapter 8, "Work" section
- GEM Fellowships: Chapter 9, "All Minorities" section
- International Study Programs Scholarship: Chapter 6, "Study Abroad" section
- NPSC Graduate Fellowships in the Physical Sciences: Chapter 7, "Sciences" section
- Search for Excellence National Scholarship: Chapter 5, "Academic Scholarships" section
- SRC Master's Scholarship: Chapter 7, "Electronics" section

University of Colorado, Colorado Springs

Web Site: http://www.uccs.edu/~finaidse/scholarship/index.html

Also see the following scholarship:

- Competitive Edge Scholarship: Chapter 6, "Engineering" section

University of Colorado, Denver

Web Site: http://finaid.cudenver.edu/public/scholarships/scholarships.htm

Also see the following scholarships:

- ACMPE Scholarships: Chapter 6, "Health Care" section
- COHEAO Scholarship: Chapter 5, "Academic Scholarships" section
- Competitive Edge Scholarship: Chapter 6, "Engineering" section

University of Northern Colorado

Web Site: http://www.unco.edu/sfr/scholarships/scholarships.html

Also see the following scholarship:

- COHEAO Scholarship: Chapter 5, "Academic Scholarships" section

Western State College of Colorado

Web Site: http://www.western.edu/finaid/fainfo/scholarship.htm

Delaware

Goldey-Beacom College

Web Site: http://goldey.gbc.edu/advisement/scholarships.html

University of Delaware

Web Site: http://www.udel.edu/admissions/viewbook/finance/

Also see the following scholarships:

- B. Bradford Barnes Memorial Scholarship: Chapter 15, "Delaware" section
- Competitive Edge Scholarship: Chapter 6, "Engineering" section
- GEM Fellowships: Chapter 9, "All Minorities" section
- IFT Scholarships: Chapter 6, "Food Science and Nutrition" section
- NPSC Graduate Fellowships in the Physical Sciences: Chapter 7, "Sciences" section
- Search for Excellence National Scholarship: Chapter 5, "Academic Scholarships" section
- SRC Master's Scholarship: Chapter 7, "Electronics" section

District of Columbia

Georgetown University

Web Site: http://www.georgetown.edu/students/student-aid/schships.htm

Also see the following scholarships:

- COHEAO Scholarship: Chapter 5, "Academic Scholarships" section
- Economics Doctoral Research Fellowship: Chapter 7, "Economics and Finance" section
- International Study Programs Scholarship: Chapter 6, "Study Abroad" section
- Luce Scholars: Chapter 7, "Study Abroad" section
- Search for Excellence National Scholarship: Chapter 5, "Academic Scholarships" section

Florida

Florida A&M University

Web Site: http://www.famu.edu/students/ scholarship/index.htm

Also see the following scholarships:

- Army ROTC Nurse Scholarships: Chapter 13, "Army and Army ROTC" section
- Army ROTC Scholarship for Historically Black Colleges and Universities: Chapter 13, "Army and Army ROTC" section
- Competitive Edge Scholarship: Chapter 6, "Engineering" section
- Development Fund for Black Students in Science and Technology Scholarship: Chapter 12, "African-American" section
- Florida Engineering Society Scholarships: Chapter 6, "Engineering" section
- GEM Fellowships: Chapter 9, "All Minorities" section
- McKnight Doctoral Fellowship: Chapter 9, "African-American" section
- Southern Scholarship: Chapter 15, "Florida" section
- U.S. Department of Agriculture/Woodrow Wilson Fellowship: Chapter 6, "Agriculture" section

Florida Gulf Coast University

Web Site: http://condor.fgcu.edu/ES/FASO/ lg_faschol.htm

Florida International University

Web Site: http://www.fiu.edu/orgs/admiss/ scholarships.html

Also see the following scholarships:

- AHF Scholarships: Chapter 6, "Hotel and Restaurant Management" section
- International Study Programs Scholarship: Chapter 6, "Study Abroad" section
- McKnight Doctoral Fellowship: Chapter 9, "African-American" section
- Search for Excellence National Scholarship: Chapter 5, "Academic Scholarships" section

Florida State University

Web Site: http://admissions.fsu.edu/ fin-004.html

Also see the following scholarships:

- Army ROTC Nurse Scholarships: Chapter 13, "Army and Army ROTC" section
- COHEAO Scholarship: Chapter 5, "Academic Scholarships" section
- Competitive Edge Scholarship: Chapter 6, "Engineering" section
- Florida Engineering Society Scholarships: Chapter 6, "Engineering" section
- GEM Fellowships: Chapter 9, "All Minorities" section
- Lucent Florida Universities Fellowship: Chapter 15, "Florida" section
- McKnight Doctoral Fellowship: Chapter 9, "African-American" section
- NPSC Graduate Fellowships in the Physical Sciences: Chapter 7, "Sciences" section
- Search for Excellence National Scholarship: Chapter 5, "Academic Scholarships" section
- Southern Scholarship: Chapter 15, "Florida" section

University of Central Florida

Web Site: http://pegasus.cc.ucf.edu/~finaid/ mainpage.htm

Also see the following scholarships:

- AHF Scholarships: Chapter 6, "Hotel and Restaurant Management" section
- Astronaut Scholarship: Chapter 6, "Sciences" section
- GEM Fellowships: Chapter 9, "All Minorities" section
- Lucent Florida Universities Fellowship: Chapter 15, "Florida" section
- McKnight Doctoral Fellowship: Chapter 9, "African-American" section
- Search for Excellence National Scholarship: Chapter 5, "Academic Scholarships" section
- SRC Master's Scholarship: Chapter 7, "Electronics" section

University of Florida

Web Site: http://www.ufsa.ufl.edu/SFA/programs

Also see the following scholarships:

- Civilian Radioactive Waste Management Fellowship: Chapter 7, "Waste Management" section
- COHEAO Scholarship: Chapter 5, "Academic Scholarships" section
- Competitive Edge Scholarship: Chapter 6, "Engineering" section
- Florida Engineering Society Scholarships: Chapter 6, "Engineering" section
- GEM Fellowships: Chapter 9, "All Minorities" section
- IFT Scholarships: Chapter 6, "Food Science and Nutrition" section
- International Study Programs Scholarship: Chapter 6, "Study Abroad" section
- Lucent Florida Universities Fellowship: Chapter 15, "Florida" section
- McKnight Doctoral Fellowship: Chapter 9, "African-American" section

- NPSC Graduate Fellowships in the Physical Sciences: Chapter 7, "Sciences" section
- Southern Scholarship: Chapter 15, "Florida" section
- SRC Master's Scholarship: Chapter 7, "Electronics" section
- Winston Churchill Foundation Scholarship: Chapter 7, "Study Abroad" section

University of Miami

Web Site: http://www.miami.edu/financial-assistance/Scholarship/SchoCmbo.html

Also see the following scholarships:

- COHEAO Scholarship: Chapter 5, "Academic Scholarships" section
- Florida Engineering Society Scholarships: Chapter 6, "Engineering" section
- McKnight Doctoral Fellowship: Chapter 9, "African-American" section

University of North Florida

Web Site: http://www.unf.edu/finaid/2000-2001/scholarship.html

University of South Florida

Web Site: http://usfweb.usf.edu/finaid/Scholarship%20Information%20Page.html

Also see the following scholarships:

- Florida Engineering Society Scholarships: Chapter 6, "Engineering" section
- Lucent Florida Universities Fellowship: Chapter 15, "Florida" section
- McKnight Doctoral Fellowship: Chapter 9, "African-American" section
- NPSC Graduate Fellowships in the Physical Sciences: Chapter 7, "Sciences" section

University of West Florida

Web Site: http://www.uwf.edu/finaid/
uwfschprg.html

Also see the following scholarship:

• Florida Engineering Society Scholarships:
Chapter 6, "Engineering" section

Georgia

Clayton College and State University

Web Site: http://adminservices.clayton.edu/
financialaid/frames/scholar_frame.htm

Also see the following scholarships:

• AIFS International Scholarships: Chapter 6,
"Study Abroad" section
• PROMISE Teacher Scholarship: Chapter 6,
"Education" section

Columbus State University

Web Site: http://enroll.colstate.edu/finaid/
scholarship.htm

Also see the following scholarships:

• AIFS International Scholarships: Chapter 6,
"Study Abroad" section
• Competitive Edge Scholarship: Chapter 6,
"Engineering" section
• HOPE Teacher Scholarship: Chapter 7, "Ed-
ucation" section
• PROMISE Teacher Scholarship: Chapter 6,
"Education" section

Georgia College and State University

Web Site: http://www.gcsu.edu/acad_affairs/
enrl_srvcs/fin_aid

Also see the following scholarships:

• AIFS International Scholarships: Chapter 6,
"Study Abroad" section
• HOPE Teacher Scholarship: Chapter 7, "Ed-
ucation" section
• PROMISE Teacher Scholarship: Chapter 6,
"Education" section

Georgia Southern University

Web Site: http://www2.gasou.edu/sta/finaid/
schapps.htm

Also see the following scholarships:

• Army ROTC Nurse Scholarships: Chapter 13,
"Army and Army ROTC" section
• COHEAO Scholarship: Chapter 5, "Academic
Scholarships" section
• HOPE Teacher Scholarship: Chapter 7, "Ed-
ucation" section
• PROMISE Teacher Scholarship: Chapter 6,
"Education" section

Kennesaw State University

Web Site: http://www.Kennesaw.EDU/
scholarships

Also see the following scholarships:

• AIFS International Scholarships: Chapter 6,
"Study Abroad" section
• HOPE Teacher Scholarship: Chapter 7, "Ed-
ucation" section
• PROMISE Teacher Scholarship: Chapter 6,
"Education" section

Life University

Web Site: http://www.life.edu/newlife/
FinancialAid/scholarships.html

Also see the following scholarship:

COLLEGE AND UNIVERSITY SCHOLARSHIP WEB SITES

- Arkansas Health Education Grant: Chapter 15, "Arkansas" section

Savannah College of Art and Design

Web Site: http://www.scad.edu/lowFILES/main.htm

University of Georgia

Web Site: http://www.uga.edu/fas

Also see the following scholarships:

- AIFS International Scholarships: Chapter 6, "Study Abroad" section
- HOPE Teacher Scholarship: Chapter 7, "Education" section
- IFT Scholarships: Chapter 6, "Food Science and Nutrition" section
- International Study Programs Scholarship: Chapter 6, "Study Abroad" section
- NEHA/AAS Scholarship: Chapter 6, "Health Care" section
- NPSC Graduate Fellowships in the Physical Sciences: Chapter 7, "Sciences" section
- PROMISE Teacher Scholarship: Chapter 6, "Education" section
- Search for Excellence National Scholarship: Chapter 5, "Academic Scholarships" section

Valdosta State University

Web Site: http://www.valdosta.peachnet.edu/finaid/framedhome.html

Also see the following scholarships:

- AIFS International Scholarships: Chapter 6, "Study Abroad" section
- HOPE Teacher Scholarship: Chapter 7, "Education" section
- PROMISE Teacher Scholarship: Chapter 6, "Education" section
- Search for Excellence National Scholarship: Chapter 5, "Academic Scholarships" section

Hawaii

Brigham Young University—Hawaii

Web Site: http://www.byuh.edu/studentlife/scholarship

Hawaii Pacific University

Web Site: http://www.hpu.edu/index.cfm?section=financialaid

Idaho

Albertson College of Idaho

Web Site: http://www.acofi.edu/admissions/finaid.htm

Also see the following scholarship:

- ISGC Scholarships and Fellowships: Chapter 6, "Space Sciences" section

Boise State University

Web Site: http://stuaff.boisestate.edu/financialaid/Scholarship.htm

Also see the following scholarships:

- COHEAO Scholarship: Chapter 5, "Academic Scholarships" section
- Competitive Edge Scholarship: Chapter 6, "Engineering" section
- ISGC Scholarships and Fellowships: Chapter 6, "Space Sciences" section
- Luce Scholars: Chapter 7, "Study Abroad" section
- NEHA/AAS Scholarship: Chapter 6, "Health Care" section

Idaho State University

Web Site: http://www.isu.edu/departments/scholar/index.html

Also see the following scholarships:

- Competitive Edge Scholarship: Chapter 6, "Engineering" section
- ISGC Scholarships and Fellowships: Chapter 6, "Space Sciences" section
- International Study Programs Scholarship: Chapter 6, "Study Abroad" section
- Search for Excellence National Scholarship: Chapter 5, "Academic Scholarships" section

Lewis-Clark State College

Web Site: http://www.lcsc.edu/financialaid/aidschol.html

Also see the following scholarships:

- ISGC Scholarships and Fellowships: Chapter 6, "Space Sciences" section
- Search for Excellence National Scholarship: Chapter 5, "Academic Scholarships" section

Northwest Nazarene College

Web Site: http://web.nnc.edu/admissions/begin/fascholarships.htm

Also see the following scholarship:

- ISGC Scholarships and Fellowships: Chapter 6, "Space Sciences" section

University of Idaho

Web Site: http://www.uidaho.edu/sfas/scholar.htm

Also see the following scholarships:

- ACMPE Scholarships: Chapter 6, "Health Care" section
- Competitive Edge Scholarship: Chapter 6, "Engineering" section
- ISGC Scholarships and Fellowships: Chapter 6, "Space Sciences" section

- IFT Scholarships: Chapter 6, "Food Science and Nutrition" section
- International Study Programs Scholarship: Chapter 6, "Study Abroad" section
- NPSC Graduate Fellowships in the Physical Sciences: Chapter 7, "Sciences" section
- Search for Excellence National Scholarship: Chapter 5, "Academic Scholarships" section

Illinois

Benedictine University

Web Site: http://www.ben.edu/Pages/Prospective/A1c.html

Bradley University

Web Site: http://www.bradley.edu/admissions/student/scholarships.html

Also see the following scholarships:

- FEF Scholarships: Chapter 6, "Metallurgy and Materials Science" section
- International Study Programs Scholarship: Chapter 6, "Study Abroad" section

DePaul University

Web Site: http://www.depaul.edu/admission/admfin/financial/freshman/scholar.htm

Also see the following scholarships:

- COHEAO Scholarship: Chapter 5, "Academic Scholarships" section
- Search for Excellence National Scholarship: Chapter 5, "Academic Scholarships" section

Eastern Illinois University

Web Site: http://www.eiu.edu/~finaid/psa1.htm

Also see the following scholarship:

- COHEAO Scholarship: Chapter 5, "Academic Scholarships" section

Elmhurst College

Web Site: http://www.elmhurst.edu/finaid/ Scholarships.htm

Illinois Institute of Technology

Web Site: http://216.47.147.209/frontend/ merit.asp

Also see the following scholarships:

- COHEAO Scholarship: Chapter 5, "Academic Scholarships" section
- GEM Fellowships: Chapter 9, "All Minorities" section

Illinois State University

Web Site: http://www.ts.ilstu.edu/ finschla.htm

Also see the following scholarships:

- COHEAO Scholarship: Chapter 5, "Academic Scholarships" section
- International Study Programs Scholarship: Chapter 6, "Study Abroad" section
- NEHA/AAS Scholarship: Chapter 6, "Health Care" section

Knox College

Web Site: http://www.knox.edu/knoxweb/ admission/scholarships.html

Also see the following scholarship:

- Search for Excellence National Scholarship: Chapter 5, "Academic Scholarships" section

MacMurray College

Web Site: http://www.mac.edu/financial/ sch_info.html

Also see the following scholarship:

- COHEAO Scholarship: Chapter 5, "Academic Scholarships" section

Northern Illinois University

Web Site: http://www.niu.edu/scholarships

Also see the following scholarships:

- COHEAO Scholarship: Chapter 5, "Academic Scholarships" section
- International Study Programs Scholarship: Chapter 6, "Study Abroad" section

Southern Illinois University Edwardsville

Web Site: http://www.finaid.siue.edu/ finaprog/schlships.html-ssi

Also see the following scholarship:

- NBAA Aviation Scholarship: Chapter 6, "Aviation" section

University of Illinois at Springfield

Web Site: http://www.uis.edu/~enroll/ scholarship.html

Also see the following scholarships:

- COHEAO Scholarship: Chapter 5, "Academic Scholarships" section
- D.W. Simpson & Company Actuarial Science Scholarship: Chapter 6, "Actuarial Science" section
- GEM Fellowships: Chapter 9, "All Minorities" section

- IFT Scholarships: Chapter 6, "Food Science and Nutrition" section
- NBAA Aviation Scholarship: Chapter 6, "Aviation" section

University of Illinois at Urbana-Champaign

Web Site: http://www.osfa.uiuc.edu/Scholarships/scholar.htm

Also see the following scholarships:

- COHEAO Scholarship: Chapter 5, "Academic Scholarships" section
- Competitive Edge Scholarship: Chapter 6, "Engineering" section
- Hertz Foundation Fellowship: Chapter 7, "Sciences" section
- International Predissertation Fellowships: Chapter 7, "Social Sciences" section
- International Study Programs Scholarship: Chapter 6, "Study Abroad" section
- Luce Scholars: Chapter 7, "Study Abroad" section
- NPSC Graduate Fellowships in the Physical Sciences: Chapter 7, "Sciences" section
- SRC Master's Scholarship: Chapter 7, "Electronics" section
- Winston Churchill Foundation Scholarship: Chapter 7, "Study Abroad" section

Western Illinois University

Web Site: http://www.student.services.wiu.edu/mifina/broch/aidpack/scholar.asp

Indiana

Ball State University

Web Site: http://www.bsu.edu/finaid/scholars/dircover.html

Also see the following scholarships:

- COHEAO Scholarship: Chapter 5, "Academic Scholarships" section
- D.W. Simpson & Company Actuarial Science Scholarship: Chapter 6, "Actuarial Science" section
- Project Excellence Scholarships: Chapter 9, "African-American" section

DePauw University

Web Site: http://www.depauw.edu/admin/financial/paying/index.asp

Also see the following scholarships:

- Bonner Scholars: Chapter 8, "Community Service" section
- COHEAO Scholarship: Chapter 5, "Academic Scholarships" section
- International Study Programs Scholarship: Chapter 6, "Study Abroad" section
- Key Club International Scholarships: Chapter 8, "Clubs" section
- Project Excellence Scholarships: Chapter 9, "African-American" section

Indiana State University

Web Site: http://web.indstate.edu/top/schol-aid

Also see the following scholarships:

- COHEAO Scholarship: Chapter 5, "Academic Scholarships" section
- NEHA/AAS Scholarship: Chapter 6, "Health Care" section

Indiana University Bloomington

Web Site: http://www.indiana.edu/~sfa/types_aid/index.html

Also see the following scholarships:

- COHEAO Scholarship: Chapter 5, "Academic Scholarships" section
- Competitive Edge Scholarship: Chapter 6, "Engineering" section
- Consortium for Graduate Study in Management Fellowship: Chapter 7, "Business" section
- International Predissertation Fellowships: Chapter 7, "Social Sciences" section
- International Study Programs Scholarship: Chapter 6, "Study Abroad" section
- NPSC Graduate Fellowships in the Physical Sciences: Chapter 7, "Sciences" section
- Search for Excellence National Scholarship: Chapter 5, "Academic Scholarships" section
- Winston Churchill Foundation Scholarship: Chapter 7, "Study Abroad" section

Indiana University-Purdue University Fort Wayne

Web Site: http://www.ipfw.edu/finaid/scholarships/Freshman.html

Indiana University-Purdue University Indianapolis

Web Site: http://www.iupui.edu/~scentral

Indiana University South Bend

Web Site: http://www.iusb.edu/~admissio/scholars.html

Indiana University Southeast

Web Site: http://www.ius.indiana.edu/UD/scholarships.htm

Purdue University

Web Site: http://www.adpc.purdue.edu/Admissions/Expenses/

merit_based_scholarships/merit_based_scholarships.html

Also see the following scholarships:

- Army ROTC Nurse Scholarships: Chapter 13, "Army and Army ROTC" section
- ASHRAE Scholarships: Chapter 6, "Heating, Refrigeration, and Air Conditioning" section
- Civilian Radioactive Waste Management Fellowship: Chapter 7, "Waste Management" section
- COHEAO Scholarship: Chapter 5, "Academic Scholarships" section
- Competitive Edge Scholarship: Chapter 6, "Engineering" section
- FEF Scholarships: Chapter 6, "Materials Science and Metallurgy" section
- GEM Fellowships: Chapter 9, "All Minorities" section
- Hertz Foundation Fellowship: Chapter 7, "Sciences" section
- IFT Scholarships: Chapter 6, "Food Science and Nutrition" section
- International Study Programs Scholarship: Chapter 6, "Study Abroad" section
- NBAA Aviation Scholarship: Chapter 6, "Aviation" section
- NPSC Graduate Fellowships in the Physical Sciences: Chapter 7, "Sciences" section
- SRC Master's Scholarship: Chapter 7, "Electronics" section
- USAIG PDP Scholarship: Chapter 6, "Aviation" section
- Winston Churchill Foundation Scholarship: Chapter 7, "Study Abroad" section

Purdue University Calumet

Web Site: http://esc.calumet.purdue.edu/finaid/scholarships

Wabash College

Web Site: http://www.wabash.edu/admin/financial/Merit.htm

Also see the following scholarship:

- Key Club International Scholarships: Chapter 8, "Clubs" section

Iowa

Clarke College

Web Site: http://www.clarke.edu/financialaid/excellence.htm

Also see the following scholarship:

- Carver Scholars: Chapter 15, "Iowa" section

Coe College

Web Site: http://www.coe.edu/Admission/Scholarships.html

Also see the following scholarships:

- Carver Scholars: Chapter 15, "Iowa" section
- COHEAO Scholarship: Chapter 5, "Academic Scholarships" section

Drake University

Web Site: http://www.drake.edu/finaid/types.html

Also see the following scholarships:

- Carver Scholars: Chapter 15, "Iowa" section
- COHEAO Scholarship: Chapter 5, "Academic Scholarships" section
- D.W. Simpson & Company Actuarial Science Scholarship: Chapter 6, "Actuarial Science" section
- International Study Programs Scholarship: Chapter 6, "Study Abroad" section

Iowa State University

Web Site: http://www.iastate.edu/~fin_aid_info

Also see the following scholarships:

- Carver Scholars: Chapter 15, "Iowa" section
- COHEAO Scholarship: Chapter 5, "Academic Scholarships" section
- Competitive Edge Scholarship: Chapter 6, "Engineering" section
- GEM Fellowships: Chapter 9, "All Minorities" section
- IFT Scholarships: Chapter 6, "Food Science and Nutrition" section
- NPSC Graduate Fellowships in the Physical Sciences: Chapter 7, "Sciences" section
- Project Excellence Scholarships: Chapter 9, "African-American" section

University of Iowa

Web Site: http://www.uiowa.edu/finaid/scholframes.htm

Also see the following scholarships:

- Carver Scholars: Chapter 15, "Iowa" section
- COHEAO Scholarship: Chapter 5, "Academic Scholarships" section
- Competitive Edge Scholarship: Chapter 6, "Engineering" section
- International Study Programs Scholarship: Chapter 6, "Study Abroad" section
- Luce Scholars: Chapter 7, "Study Abroad" section
- NPSC Graduate Fellowships in the Physical Sciences: Chapter 7, "Sciences" section
- SRC Master's Scholarship: Chapter 7, "Electronics" section
- Winston Churchill Foundation Scholarship: Chapter 7, "Study Abroad" section

University of Northern Iowa

Web Site: http://www.uni.edu/finaid/scholarship.html

Also see the following scholarships:

- Carver Scholars: Chapter 15, "Iowa" section

- FEF Scholarships: Chapter 6, "Materials Science and Metallurgy" section
- Search for Excellence National Scholarship: Chapter 5, "Academic Scholarships" section

Kansas

Fort Hays State University

Web Site: http://www.fhsu.edu/finaid/scholarships.html

Also see the following scholarships:

- COHEAO Scholarship: Chapter 5, "Academic Scholarships" section
- Hays Medical Center Scholarships: Chapter 6, "Health Care" section

Kansas State University

Web Site: http://www.ksu.edu/sfa/q7.html

Also see the following scholarships:

- Competitive Edge Scholarship: Chapter 6, "Engineering" section
- GEM Fellowships: Chapter 9, "All Minorities" section
- IFT Scholarships: Chapter 6, "Food Science and Nutrition" section
- NPSC Graduate Fellowships in the Physical Sciences: Chapter 7, "Sciences" section
- Search for Excellence National Scholarship: Chapter 5, "Academic Scholarships" section

Pittsburg State University

Web Site: http://www.pittstate.edu/finaid/pssf.html

Also see the following scholarship:

- FEF Scholarships: Chapter 6, "Materials Science and Metallurgy" section

University of Kansas

Web Site: http://www.admissions.ku.edu

Also see the following scholarships:

- Competitive Edge Scholarship: Chapter 6, "Engineering" section
- GEM Fellowships: Chapter 9, "All Minorities" section
- International Study Programs Scholarship: Chapter 6, "Study Abroad" section
- NPSC Graduate Fellowships in the Physical Sciences: Chapter 7, "Sciences" section
- Winston Churchill Foundation Scholarship: Chapter 7, "Study Abroad" section

Washburn University

Web Site: http://www.washburn.edu/financial-aid

Also see the following scholarship:

- Army ROTC Nurse Scholarships: Chapter 13, "Army and Army ROTC" section

Kentucky

Kentucky State University

Web Site: http://www.kysu.edu/Admission/finaid.htm

Also see the following scholarships:

- COHEAO Scholarship: Chapter 5, "Academic Scholarships" section
- U.S. Department of Agriculture/Woodrow Wilson Fellowship: Chapter 6, "Agriculture" section

Morehead State University

Web Site: http://www.morehead-st.edu/units/finaid/scholar.html

Also see the following scholarships:

- Competitive Edge Scholarship: Chapter 6, "Engineering" section

Murray State University

Web Site: http://www.murraystate.edu/scholarships

Northern Kentucky University

Web Site: http://www.nku.edu/~ofa

University of Kentucky

Web Site: http://www.uky.edu/Admissions/merit_scholarship.html

Also see the following scholarships:

- Astronaut Scholarship: Chapter 6, "Sciences" section
- COHEAO Scholarship: Chapter 5, "Academic Scholarships" section
- Competitive Edge Scholarship: Chapter 6, "Engineering" section
- IFT Scholarships: Chapter 6, "Food Science and Nutrition" section
- International Study Programs Scholarship: Chapter 6, "Study Abroad" section
- SRC Master's Scholarship: Chapter 7, "Electronics" section

Louisiana

Louisiana College

Web Site: http://www.lacollege.edu/admissions/scholarships.html

Louisiana State University and A&M College

Web Site: http://www.sao.lsu.edu

Also see the following scholarships:

- Arkansas Health Education Grant: Chapter 15, "Arkansas" section
- Civilian Radioactive Waste Management Fellowship: Chapter 7, "Waste Management" section
- Competitive Edge Scholarship: Chapter 6, "Engineering" section
- GEM Fellowships: Chapter 9, "All Minorities" section
- IFT Scholarships: Chapter 6, "Food Science and Nutrition" section
- LaSPACE Fellowship: Chapter 7, "Aerospace Sciences and Engineering"
- LaSPACE Undergraduate Student Scholarship: Chapter 6, "Aerospace Sciences and Engineering" section
- NPSC Graduate Fellowships in the Physical Sciences: Chapter 7, "Sciences" section

Northeast Louisiana University

Web Site: http://www.nlu.edu/enrollment/scholarships.html

Also see the following scholarship:

- LaSPACE Undergraduate Student Scholarship: Chapter 6, "Aerospace Sciences and Engineering" section

Southeastern Louisiana University

Web Site: http://www.selu.edu/enroll/faid/s_ship.htm

Also see the following scholarships:

- LaSPACE Fellowship: Chapter 7, "Aerospace Sciences and Engineering"
- LaSPACE Undergraduate Student Scholarship: Chapter 6, "Aerospace Sciences and Engineering" section

Tulane University

Web Site: http://www.tulane.edu/~finaid/table.html

Also see the following scholarships:

- International Study Programs Scholarship: Chapter 6, "Study Abroad" section
- LaSPACE Fellowship: Chapter 7, "Aerospace Sciences and Engineering"
- LaSPACE Undergraduate Student Scholarship: Chapter 6, "Aerospace Sciences and Engineering" section
- Luce Scholars: Chapter 7, "Study Abroad" section
- NPSC Graduate Fellowships in the Physical Sciences: Chapter 7, "Sciences" section
- Winston Churchill Foundation Scholarship: Chapter 7, "Study Abroad" section

University of Louisiana Lafayette

Web Site: http://www.louisiana.edu/ Admissions/Scholarships

Also see the following scholarships:

- Competitive Edge Scholarship: Chapter 6, "Engineering" section
- LaSPACE Fellowship: Chapter 7, "Aerospace Sciences and Engineering"
- LaSPACE Undergraduate Student Scholarship: Chapter 6, "Aerospace Sciences and Engineering" section
- NPSC Graduate Fellowships in the Physical Sciences: Chapter 7, "Sciences" section

Maine

University of Maine

Web Site: http://www.ume.maine.edu/ ~stuaid/restrict.html

Also see the following scholarships:

- Army ROTC Nurse Scholarships: Chapter 13, "Army and Army ROTC" section
- Competitive Edge Scholarship: Chapter 6, "Engineering" section

- IFT Scholarships: Chapter 6, "Food Science and Nutrition" section
- International Study Programs Scholarship: Chapter 6, "Study Abroad" section

University of Maine at Farmington

Web Site: http://gladiola.umfacad.maine.edu/ ~finaid/ grant_and_scholarship_informatio.htm

University of Maine at Machias

Web Site: http://www.umm.maine.edu/ finaid.html

University of Southern Maine

Web Site: http://www.usm.maine.edu/fin/ schint00.htm

Also see the following scholarships:

- Competitive Edge Scholarship: Chapter 6, "Engineering" section
- Search for Excellence National Scholarship: Chapter 5, "Academic Scholarships" section

Maryland

Frostburg State University

Web Site: http://www.fsu.umd.edu/ungrad/ scholar/scholar.htm

Goucher College

Web Site: http://www.goucher.edu/programs/ programs_scholarship.cfm

Also see the following scholarship:

- Search for Excellence National Scholarship: Chapter 5, "Academic Scholarships" section

Johns Hopkins University

Web Site: http://www.jhu.edu/~finaid/scholarship

Also see the following scholarships:

- Competitive Edge Scholarship: Chapter 6, "Engineering" section
- GEM Fellowships: Chapter 9, "All Minorities" section
- Hertz Foundation Fellowship: Chapter 7, "Sciences" section
- International Study Programs Scholarship: Chapter 6, "Study Abroad" section
- Luce Scholars: Chapter 7, "Study Abroad" section
- NPSC Graduate Fellowships in the Physical Sciences: Chapter 7, "Sciences" section
- SRC Master's Scholarship: Chapter 7, "Electronics" section
- Winston Churchill Foundation Scholarship: Chapter 7, "Study Abroad" section

Towson University

Web Site: http://onestop.towson.edu/finaid

Also see the following scholarship:

- International Study Programs Scholarship: Chapter 6, "Study Abroad" section

University of Maryland

Web Site: http://www.inform.umd.edu/CampusInfo/Departments/FIN/OSFA/UGST/index.html

Also see the following scholarships:

- ADHA Institute for Oral Health Scholarships: Chapter 6, "Dentistry and Dental Hygiene" section
- Competitive Edge Scholarship: Chapter 6, "Engineering" section
- Economics Doctoral Research Fellowship: Chapter 7, "Economics and Finance" section

- GEM Fellowships: Chapter 9, "All Minorities" section
- IFT Scholarships: Chapter 6, "Food Science and Nutrition" section
- International Study Programs Scholarship: Chapter 6, "Study Abroad" section
- NPSC Graduate Fellowships in the Physical Sciences: Chapter 7, "Sciences" section
- Search for Excellence National Scholarship: Chapter 5, "Academic Scholarships" section
- SRC Master's Scholarship: Chapter 7, "Electronics" section

University of Maryland, Baltimore County

Web Site: http://www.umbc.edu//undergrad/index.html?I1=financialaid&

Also see the following scholarships:

- COHEAO Scholarship: Chapter 5, "Academic Scholarships" section
- NPSC Graduate Fellowships in the Physical Sciences: Chapter 7, "Sciences" section

Villa Julie College

Web Site: http://www.vjc.edu/admissions/scholarships/index_scholarships.htm

Massachusetts

Anna Maria College

Web Site: http://www.anna-maria.edu/amcpage/finaid/scholar.htm

Boston University

Web Site: http://www.bu.edu/finaid/merit_fr.html

Also see the following scholarships:

- GEM Fellowships: Chapter 9, "All Minorities" section

- Massachusetts Space Grant Consortium Graduate Fellowship: Chapter 7, "Space Sciences" section
- Search for Excellence National Scholarship: Chapter 5, "Academic Scholarships" section

Bridgewater State College

Web Site: http://www.bridgew.edu/depts/finaid/scholbroc.htm

Also see the following scholarship:

- COHEAO Scholarship: Chapter 5, "Academic Scholarships" section

Clark University

Web Site: http://www2.clarku.edu/offices/admissions/scholarships_dom.html

Also see the following scholarship:

- International Study Programs Scholarship: Chapter 6, "Study Abroad" section

Stonehill College

Web Site: http://academics.stonehill.edu/studentaid/Restricted-Endowed%20Scholarship%20Search.htm

University of Massachusetts Amherst

Web Site: http://www.umass.edu/umfa/pages/scholarships.html

Also see the following scholarships:

- COHEAO Scholarship: Chapter 5, "Academic Scholarships" section
- Competitive Edge Scholarship: Chapter 6, "Engineering" section
- IFT Scholarships: Chapter 6, "Food Science and Nutrition" section

- International Study Programs Scholarship: Chapter 6, "Study Abroad" section
- Massachusetts Space Grant Consortium Graduate Fellowship: Chapter 7, "Space Sciences" section
- NPSC Graduate Fellowships in the Physical Sciences: Chapter 7, "Sciences" section
- NSF/STEMTEC Teaching Scholars: Chapter 6, "Education" section

University of Massachusetts Dartmouth

Web Site: http://www.umassd.edu/FinancialAid/Scholarships/welcome.html

Also see the following scholarship:

- Thread Committee Excellence in Manufacturing Scholarship: Chapter 6, "Textile Science and Fiber Arts" section

Michigan

Baker College

Web Site: http://www.baker.edu/departments/finaid/schship.html

Calvin College

Web Site: http://www.calvin.edu/admin/finaid/merit.htm

Eastern Michigan University

Web Site: http://www.emich.edu/public/fin_aid/scholar/ugscholar.html

Also see the following scholarships:

- NBAA Aviation Scholarship: Chapter 6, "Aviation" section

- USAIG PDP Scholarship: Chapter 6, "Aviation" section

Ferris State University

Web Site: http://www.ferris.edu/htmls/admision/financialaid

Also see the following scholarship:

- NEHA/AAS Scholarship: Chapter 6, "Health Care" section

Hope College

Web Site: http://www.hope.edu/admissions/scholarship

Also see the following scholarship:

- International Study Programs Scholarship: Chapter 6, "Study Abroad" section

Kettering University

Web Site: http://www.kettering.edu/FinAid/schols.htm

Also see the following scholarship:

- FEF Scholarships: Chapter 6, "Materials Science and Metallurgy" section

Lake Superior State University

Web Site: http://www.lssu.edu/finaid/scholarships.html

Northwood University

Web Site: http://www.northwood.edu/admissions/pds/index.html

University of Michigan—Ann Arbor

Web Site: http://www.finaid.umich.edu/scholar.htm

Also see the following scholarships:

- ADHA Institute for Oral Health Scholarships: Chapter 6, "Dentistry and Dental Hygiene" section
- Army ROTC Nurse Scholarships: Chapter 13, "Army and Army ROTC" section
- Civilian Radioactive Waste Management Fellowship: Chapter 7, "Waste Management" section
- COHEAO Scholarship: Chapter 5, "Academic Scholarships" section
- Competitive Edge Scholarship: Chapter 6, "Engineering" section
- Consortium for Graduate Study in Management Fellowship: Chapter 7, "Business" section
- FEF Scholarships: Chapter 6, "Materials Science and Metallurgy" section
- GEM Fellowships: Chapter 9, "All Minorities" section
- Hertz Foundation Fellowship: Chapter 7, "Sciences" section
- International Predissertation Fellowships: Chapter 7, "Social Sciences" section
- International Study Programs Scholarship: Chapter 6, "Study Abroad" section
- NEHA/AAS Scholarship: Chapter 6, "Health Care" section
- NPSC Graduate Fellowships in the Physical Sciences: Chapter 7, "Sciences" section
- Search for Excellence National Scholarship: Chapter 5, "Academic Scholarships" section
- SRC Master's Scholarship: Chapter 7, "Electronics" section
- Winston Churchill Foundation Scholarship: Chapter 7, "Study Abroad" section

University of Michigan—Flint

Web Site: http://www.flint.umich.edu/Departments/FINAID

Wayne State University

Web Site: http://www.financialaid.wayne.edu

Also see the following scholarships:

- Competitive Edge Scholarship: Chapter 6, "Engineering" section
- NPSC Graduate Fellowships in the Physical Sciences: Chapter 7, "Sciences" section
- SRC Master's Scholarship: Chapter 7, "Electronics" section

Western Michigan University

Web Site: http://www.wmich.edu/finaid/ Scholarships/wmu_scholarships.html

Also see the following scholarships:

- Competitive Edge Scholarship: Chapter 6, "Engineering" section
- FEF Scholarships: Chapter 6, "Materials Science and Metallurgy" section
- International Study Programs Scholarship: Chapter 6, "Study Abroad" section
- NBAA Aviation Scholarship: Chapter 6, "Aviation" section

Minnesota

Bemidji State University

Web Site: http://info.bemidji.msus.edu/ Admissions/financialaid/scholarships/ index.html

College of Saint Benedict and Saint John's University

Web Site: http://www.csbsju.edu/prospective/ finaid/default.htm

Also see the following scholarships:

- Army ROTC Nurse Scholarships: Chapter 13, "Army and Army ROTC" section

- COHEAO Scholarship: Chapter 5, "Academic Scholarships" section
- International Study Programs Scholarship: Chapter 6, "Study Abroad" section

Gustavus Adolphus College

Web Site: http://www.gustavus.edu/ prospective/9899/fin/schgr/index.html

Also see the following scholarships:

- AAL Lutheran Campus Scholarship: Chapter 11, "Lutheran" section
- International Study Programs Scholarship: Chapter 6, "Study Abroad" section
- Lutheran College Scholarships: Chapter 11, "Lutheran" section

Minnesota Bible College

Web Site: http://www.mnbc.edu/ Financial_Aid/Scholarships/ scholarships.htm

Moorhead State University

Web Site: http://www.moorhead.msus.edu/ finaid/funds.htm

Also see the following scholarship:

- Competitive Edge Scholarship: Chapter 6, "Engineering" section

St. Olaf College

Web Site: http://www.stolaf.edu/services/ financial_aid/mbfa.html

Also see the following scholarships:

- AAL Lutheran Campus Scholarship: Chapter 11, "Lutheran" section
- International Study Programs Scholarship: Chapter 6, "Study Abroad" section
- Lutheran College Scholarships: Chapter 11, "Lutheran" section

- Search for Excellence National Scholarship: Chapter 5, "Academic Scholarships" section

University of Minnesota

Web Site: http://admissions.tc.umn.edu/Costs/scholarships/index.html

Also see the following scholarships:

- Astronaut Scholarship: Chapter 6, "Sciences" section
- COHEAO Scholarship: Chapter 5, "Academic Scholarships" section
- Competitive Edge Scholarship: Chapter 6, "Engineering" section
- GEM Fellowships: Chapter 9, "All Minorities" section
- Hertz Foundation Fellowship: Chapter 7, "Sciences" section
- International Predissertation Fellowships: Chapter 7, "Social Sciences" section
- International Study Programs Scholarship: Chapter 6, "Study Abroad" section
- Luce Scholars: Chapter 7, "Study Abroad" section
- NPSC Graduate Fellowships in the Physical Sciences: Chapter 7, "Sciences" section
- SRC Master's Scholarship: Chapter 7, "Electronics" section
- Winston Churchill Foundation Scholarship: Chapter 7, "Study Abroad" section

Mississippi

Mississippi State University

Web Site: http://www.msstate.edu/dept/sfa/howto.htm

Also see the following scholarships:

- Arkansas Health Education Grant: Chapter 15, "Arkansas" section
- Competitive Edge Scholarship: Chapter 6, "Engineering" section

- GEM Fellowships: Chapter 9, "All Minorities" section
- IFT Scholarships: Chapter 6, "Food Science and Nutrition" section

University of Mississippi

Web Site: http://www.olemiss.edu/depts/financial_aid/scholarships

Also see the following scholarships:

- Competitive Edge Scholarship: Chapter 6, "Engineering" section
- GEM Fellowships: Chapter 9, "All Minorities" section
- International Study Programs Scholarship: Chapter 6, "Study Abroad" section
- NPSC Graduate Fellowships in the Physical Sciences: Chapter 7, "Sciences" section
- Search for Excellence National Scholarship: Chapter 5, "Academic Scholarships" section

Missouri

Central Missouri State University

Web Site: http://web0.cmsu.edu/admit/scholarship

Also see the following scholarships:

- NBAA Aviation Scholarship: Chapter 6, "Aviation" section
- USAIG PDP Scholarship: Chapter 6, "Aviation" section

Missouri Western State College

Web Site: http://www.mwsc.edu/~finaid/scholar.html

Northwest Missouri State University

Web Site: http://www.nwmissouri.edu/financialaid/SCHOLARSHIPS.HTML

Ozark Christian College

Web Site: http://www.occ.edu/admissions/scholarships.htm

Saint Louis University

Web Site: http://www.slu.edu/services/fin_aid/programs.htm

Also see the following scholarship:

- Army ROTC Nurse Scholarships: Chapter 13, "Army and Army ROTC" section

Southeast Missouri State University

Web Site: http://www2.semo.edu/finaid/scholars

Also see the following scholarships:

- COHEAO Scholarship: Chapter 5, "Academic Scholarships" section
- Competitive Edge Scholarship: Chapter 6, "Engineering" section
- Missouri Department of Agriculture Scholarship: Chapter 15, "Missouri" section

Southwest Missouri State University

Web Site: http://www.smsu.edu/FinAid/finaid.html

Also see the following scholarships:

- Competitive Edge Scholarship: Chapter 6, "Engineering" section
- Missouri Department of Agriculture Scholarship: Chapter 15, "Missouri" section
- Search for Excellence National Scholarship: Chapter 5, "Academic Scholarships" section

University of Missouri—Columbia

Web Site: https://sfa.missouri.edu/scholar.html

Also see the following scholarships:

- Arkansas Health Education Grant: Chapter 15, "Arkansas" section
- Civilian Radioactive Waste Management Fellowship: Chapter 7, "Waste Management" section
- GEM Fellowships: Chapter 9, "All Minorities" section
- IFT Scholarships: Chapter 6, "Food Science and Nutrition" section
- Missouri Department of Agriculture Scholarship: Chapter 15, "Missouri" section
- NPSC Graduate Fellowships in the Physical Sciences: Chapter 7, "Sciences" section
- Project Excellence Scholarships: Chapter 9, "African-American" section

University of Missouri—Kansas City

Web Site: http://www.sfa.umkc.edu/UMKCAidPrograms/aidprograms.cfm

Also see the following scholarships:

- ADHA Institute for Oral Health Scholarships: Chapter 6, "Dentistry and Dental Hygiene" section
- Arkansas Health Education Grant: Chapter 15, "Arkansas" section

University of Missouri—Rolla

Web Site: http://www.umr.edu/admissions/afford.html

Also see the following scholarships:

- Competitive Edge Scholarship: Chapter 6, "Engineering" section
- FEF Scholarships: Chapter 6, "Materials Science and Metallurgy" section
- GEM Fellowships: Chapter 9, "All Minorities" section

- NPSC Graduate Fellowships in the Physical Sciences: Chapter 7, "Sciences" section

University of Missouri—St. Louis

Web Site: http://www.umsl.edu/services/finaid/scholarships/fd.htm

Also see the following scholarship:

- Arkansas Health Education Grant: Chapter 15, "Arkansas" section

Washington University in St. Louis

Web Site: http://www.wustl.edu/prospective/default.htm

Also see the following scholarships:

- Astronaut Scholarship: Chapter 6, "Sciences" section
- Consortium for Graduate Study in Management Fellowship: Chapter 7, "Business" section
- GEM Fellowships: Chapter 9, "All Minorities" section
- NPSC Graduate Fellowships in the Physical Sciences: Chapter 7, "Sciences" section
- SRC Master's Scholarship: Chapter 7, "Electronics" section
- Winston Churchill Foundation Scholarship: Chapter 7, "Study Abroad" section

Webster University

Web Site: http://www.websteruniv.edu/finaid/scholarships/html/scholshp.html

Montana

Montana State University—Billings

Web Site: http://www.msubillings.edu/finaid/Scholarships.htm

Also see the following scholarships:

- Baker Grant: Chapter 15, "Montana" section
- Montana Space Grant Consortium Scholarships and Fellowships: Chapter 6, "Aerospace Sciences and Engineering" section

Montana State University—Bozeman

Web Site: http://www.montana.edu/wwwfa/fa_schol.html

Also see the following scholarships:

- Army ROTC Nurse Scholarships: Chapter 13, "Army and Army ROTC" section
- Baker Grant: Chapter 15, "Montana" section
- Competitive Edge Scholarship: Chapter 6, "Engineering" section
- Montana Space Grant Consortium Scholarships and Fellowships: Chapter 6, "Aerospace Sciences and Engineering" section
- NPSC Graduate Fellowships in the Physical Sciences: Chapter 7, "Sciences" section

Montana Tech

Web Site: http://www.mtech.edu/admission_test/scholarship_form.htm

Also see the following scholarships:

- Baker Grant: Chapter 15, "Montana" section
- Montana Space Grant Consortium Scholarships and Fellowships: Chapter 6, "Aerospace Sciences and Engineering" section

University of Montana—Missoula

Web Site: http://www.umt.edu/finaid/scholar.htm

Also see the following scholarships:

- Baker Grant: Chapter 15, "Montana" section

- Montana Space Grant Consortium Scholarships and Fellowships: Chapter 6, "Aerospace Sciences and Engineering" section
- Search for Excellence National Scholarship: Chapter 5, "Academic Scholarships" section

Nebraska

Chadron State College

Web Site: http://admissions.csc.edu/scholarships.html

Also see the following scholarship:

- NASA Nebraska Space Grant and EPSCoR Programs Scholarships and Fellowships: Chapter 6, "Aerospace Sciences and Engineering" section

University of Nebraska—Lincoln

Web Site: http://www.unl.edu/nuhusker/tsfa/scholar.html

Also see the following scholarships:

- Competitive Edge Scholarship: Chapter 6, "Engineering" section
- D.W. Simpson & Company Actuarial Science Scholarship: Chapter 6, "Actuarial Science" section
- GEM Fellowships: Chapter 9, "All Minorities" section
- IFT Scholarships: Chapter 6, "Food Science and Nutrition" section
- International Study Programs Scholarship: Chapter 6, "Study Abroad" section
- NASA Nebraska Space Grant and EPSCoR Programs Scholarships and Fellowships: Chapter 6, "Aerospace Sciences and Engineering" section
- NPSC Graduate Fellowships in the Physical Sciences: Chapter 7, "Sciences" section
- Project Excellence Scholarships: Chapter 9, "African-American" section

- Search for Excellence National Scholarship: Chapter 5, "Academic Scholarships" section
- Winston Churchill Foundation Scholarship: Chapter 7, "Study Abroad" section

New Hampshire

Daniel Webster College

Web Site: http://www.dwc.edu/content/academics/scholarship

Also see the following scholarship:

- NBAA Aviation Scholarship: Chapter 6, "Aviation" section

New Jersey

Drew University

Web Site: http://www.drew.edu/finan/programs.html

Also see the following scholarship:

- COHEAO Scholarship: Chapter 5, "Academic Scholarships" section

Rutgers The State University of New Jersey

Web Site: http://studentaid.rutgers.edu/aid/sch.htm

Also see the following scholarships:

- C. Clyde Ferguson Law Scholarship: Chapter 7, "Law" section
- COHEAO Scholarship: Chapter 5, "Academic Scholarships" section
- Competitive Edge Scholarship: Chapter 6, "Engineering" section
- IFT Scholarships: Chapter 6, "Food Science and Nutrition" section
- International Study Programs Scholarship: Chapter 6, "Study Abroad" section

- NPSC Graduate Fellowships in the Physical Sciences: Chapter 7, "Sciences" section
- Project Excellence Scholarships: Chapter 9, "African-American" section
- Search for Excellence National Scholarship: Chapter 5, "Academic Scholarships" section
- SRC Master's Scholarship: Chapter 7, "Electronics" section

Seton Hall University

Web Site: http://www.shu.edu/admit/scholarship

Also see the following scholarships:

- Army ROTC Nurse Scholarships: Chapter 13, "Army and Army ROTC" section
- C. Clyde Ferguson Law Scholarship: Chapter 7, "Law" section

William Patterson University

Web Site: http://ww2.wpunj.edu/admissn/schol.cfm

Also see the following scholarship:

- Search for Excellence National Scholarship: Chapter 5, "Academic Scholarships" section

New Mexico

New Mexico State University

Web Site: http://www.nmsu.edu/~finaid/scholarships/index.html

Also see the following scholarships:

- Competitive Edge Scholarship: Chapter 6, "Engineering" section
- GEM Fellowships: Chapter 9, "All Minorities" section
- NPSC Graduate Fellowships in the Physical Sciences: Chapter 7, "Sciences" section

New Mexico Tech

Web Site: http://www.nmt.edu/mainpage/finaid

University of New Mexico

Web Site: http://www.unm.edu/~schol/schol.html

Also see the following scholarships:

- Competitive Edge Scholarship: Chapter 6, "Engineering" section
- GEM Fellowships: Chapter 9, "All Minorities" section
- International Study Programs Scholarship: Chapter 6, "Study Abroad" section
- NPSC Graduate Fellowships in the Physical Sciences: Chapter 7, "Sciences" section
- Search for Excellence National Scholarship: Chapter 5, "Academic Scholarships" section

New York

Adelphi University

Web Site: http://www.adelphi.edu/prepare/finaid/au_scholarships_grants.shtml

Also see the following scholarships:

- COHEAO Scholarship: Chapter 5, "Academic Scholarships" section
- International Study Programs Scholarship: Chapter 6, "Study Abroad" section

Alfred University

Web Site: http://www.alfred.edu/admissions/html/scholarships.html

Binghamton University

Web Site: http://bingfa.binghamton.edu

Also see the following scholarships:

- Search for Excellence National Scholarship: Chapter 5, "Academic Scholarships" section
- Winston Churchill Foundation Scholarship: Chapter 7, "Study Abroad" section

Hofstra University

Web Site: http://www.hofstra.edu/College/FA/scholarships.html

State University of New York—Empire State College

Web Site: http://www.esc.edu/ESConline/Across_ESC/Finaid.nsf/frameset1?openform&ESC+Funds+Search

University at Stony Brook

Web Site: http://naples.cc.sunysb.edu/Prov/scholarships.nsf

Also see the following scholarships:

- NPSC Graduate Fellowships in the Physical Sciences: Chapter 7, "Sciences" section
- SRC Master's Scholarship: Chapter 7, "Electronics" section
- Winston Churchill Foundation Scholarship: Chapter 7, "Study Abroad" section

University of Rochester

Web Site: http://www.rochester.edu/admissions/RC/aid/merit.html

Also see the following scholarships:

- Consortium for Graduate Study in Management Fellowship: Chapter 7, "Business" section
- Hertz Foundation Fellowship: Chapter 7, "Sciences" section
- International Study Programs Scholarship: Chapter 6, "Study Abroad" section
- NPSC Graduate Fellowships in the Physical Sciences: Chapter 7, "Sciences" section

- Project Excellence Scholarships: Chapter 9, "African-American" section
- SRC Master's Scholarship: Chapter 7, "Electronics" section
- Winston Churchill Foundation Scholarship: Chapter 7, "Study Abroad" section

North Carolina

Appalachian State University

Web Site: http://www.appstate.edu/www_docs/admissions/scholarship.html

Also see the following scholarships:

- ACMPE Scholarships: Chapter 6, "Health Care" section
- North Carolina Teaching Fellows: Chapter 6, "Education" section
- Search for Excellence National Scholarship: Chapter 5, "Academic Scholarships" section

East Carolina University

Web Site: http://www.ecu.edu/financial/homschol.htm

Also see the following scholarships:

- NEHA/AAS Scholarship: Chapter 6, "Health Care" section
- North Carolina Nurse Scholars Program Master's Scholarship: Chapter 7, "Nursing" section
- North Carolina Teaching Fellows: Chapter 6, "Education" section
- University of North Carolina Board of Governors Medical School Scholarship: Chapter 7, "Medicine" section

North Carolina A&T University

Web Site: http://www.ncat.edu/finaid/Scholarships.html

Also see the following scholarships:

- Army ROTC Nurse Scholarships: Chapter 13, "Army and Army ROTC" section
- Army ROTC Scholarship for Historically Black Colleges and Universities: Chapter 13, "Army and Army ROTC" section
- Astronaut Scholarship: Chapter 6, "Sciences" section
- Competitive Edge Scholarship: Chapter 6, "Engineering" section
- Development Fund for Black Students in Science and Technology Scholarship: Chapter 12, "African-American" section
- GEM Fellowships: Chapter 9, "All Minorities" section
- North Carolina Teaching Fellows: Chapter 6, "Education" section
- U.S. Department of Agriculture/Woodrow Wilson Fellowship: Chapter 6, "Agriculture" section

North Carolina State University

Web Site: http://www2.ncsu.edu/ncsu/ stud_affairs/merit_awards/index.html

Also see the following scholarships:

- Astronaut Scholarship: Chapter 6, "Sciences" section
- Aubrey Lee Brooks Scholarship: Chapter 15, "North Carolina" section
- Civilian Radioactive Waste Management Fellowship: Chapter 7, "Waste Management" section
- Dr. Wade H. Atkinson Scholarship: Chapter 15, "North Carolina" section
- GEM Fellowships: Chapter 9, "All Minorities" section
- IFT Scholarships: Chapter 6, "Food Science and Nutrition" section
- International Study Programs Scholarship: Chapter 6, "Study Abroad" section
- North Carolina Teaching Fellows: Chapter 6, "Education" section

- NPSC Graduate Fellowships in the Physical Sciences: Chapter 7, "Sciences" section
- SRC Master's Scholarship: Chapter 7, "Electronics" section
- Thread Committee Excellence in Manufacturing Scholarship: Chapter 6, "Textile Science and Fiber Arts" section
- Turrentine Scholarship: Chapter 15, "North Carolina" section

University of North Carolina Charlotte

Web Site: http://www.uncc.edu/admissions/ Freshman/schlbrochure.htm

Also see the following scholarships:

- Competitive Edge Scholarship: Chapter 6, "Engineering" section
- International Study Programs Scholarship: Chapter 6, "Study Abroad" section
- North Carolina Nurse Scholars Program Master's Scholarship: Chapter 7, "Nursing" section
- North Carolina Teaching Fellows: Chapter 6, "Education" section

University of North Carolina Greensboro

Web Site: http://www.uncg.edu/fia/merit

Also see the following scholarships:

- Aubrey Lee Brooks Scholarship: Chapter 15, "North Carolina" section
- Dr. Wade H. Atkinson Scholarship: Chapter 15, "North Carolina" section
- North Carolina Nurse Scholars Program Master's Scholarship: Chapter 7, "Nursing" section
- North Carolina Teaching Fellows: Chapter 6, "Education" section
- Turrentine Scholarship: Chapter 15, "North Carolina" section

Wake Forest University

Web Site: http://www.wfu.edu/admissions/finaid/merit-based-aid.html

Also see the following scholarships:

• Luce Scholars: Chapter 7, "Study Abroad" section
• University of North Carolina Board of Governors Medical School Scholarship: Chapter 7, "Medicine" section

North Dakota

Mayville State University

Web Site: http://www.masu.nodak.edu/main.cfm?page=admissions scholarships

Minot State University

Web Site: http://warp6.cs.misu.nodak.edu/finaid/html/scholarships.html

Also see the following scholarship:

• COHEAO Scholarship: Chapter 5, "Academic Scholarships" section

North Dakota State University

Web Site: http://www.ndsu.nodak.edu/finaid/scholarship/scholarship.html

Also see the following scholarships:

• Astronaut Scholarship: Chapter 6, "Sciences" section
• COHEAO Scholarship: Chapter 5, "Academic Scholarships" section
• Competitive Edge Scholarship: Chapter 6, "Engineering" section
• IFT Scholarships: Chapter 6, "Food Science and Nutrition" section

University of North Dakota

Web Site: http://www.und.edu/dept/finaid

Also see the following scholarships:

• Competitive Edge Scholarship: Chapter 6, "Engineering" section
• NBAA Aviation Scholarship: Chapter 6, "Aviation" section
• NPSC Graduate Fellowships in the Physical Sciences: Chapter 7, "Sciences" section
• Search for Excellence National Scholarship: Chapter 5, "Academic Scholarships" section
• USAIG PDP Scholarship: Chapter 6, "Aviation" section

Valley City State University

Web Site: http://www.vcsu.nodak.edu/offices/finaid

Ohio

Capital University

Web Site: http://www.capital.edu/admissio/admmerit.htm

Also see the following scholarships:

• AAL Lutheran Campus Scholarship: Chapter 11, "Lutheran" section
• Army ROTC Nurse Scholarships: Chapter 13, "Army and Army ROTC" section
• Lutheran College Scholarships: Chapter 11, "Lutheran" section

Case Western Reserve University

Web Site: http://finaid.cwru.edu/types.asp#scholars

Also see the following scholarships:

- FEF Scholarships: Chapter 6, "Materials Science and Metallurgy" section
- GEM Fellowships: Chapter 9, "All Minorities" section
- OSGC Graduate Fellowship: Chapter 7, "Aerospace Sciences and Engineering" section
- OSGC Scholarships: Chapter 6, "Aerospace Sciences and Engineering" section
- Winston Churchill Foundation Scholarship: Chapter 7, "Study Abroad" section

College of Mount St. Joseph

Web Site: http://www.msj.edu/admissions/sfs/scholarship.htm

Also see the following scholarship:

- COHEAO Scholarship: Chapter 5, "Academic Scholarships" section

Franklin University

Web Site: http://www.franklin.edu/paying/scholarships.html

Ohio State University

Web Site: http://www.ohio-state.edu/prospective/costs.html

Also see the following scholarships:

- Civilian Radioactive Waste Management Fellowship: Chapter 7, "Waste Management" section
- COHEAO Scholarship: Chapter 5, "Academic Scholarships" section
- Competitive Edge Scholarship: Chapter 6, "Engineering" section
- FEF Scholarships: Chapter 6, "Materials Science and Metallurgy" section
- GEM Fellowships: Chapter 9, "All Minorities" section

- IFT Scholarships: Chapter 6, "Food Science and Nutrition" section
- International Study Programs Scholarship: Chapter 6, "Study Abroad" section
- NBAA Aviation Scholarship: Chapter 6, "Aviation" section
- NPSC Graduate Fellowships in the Physical Sciences: Chapter 7, "Sciences" section
- OSGC Graduate Fellowship: Chapter 7, "Aerospace Sciences and Engineering" section
- OSGC Scholarships: Chapter 6, "Aerospace Sciences and Engineering" section
- Project Excellence Scholarships: Chapter 9, "African-American" section
- Winston Churchill Foundation Scholarship: Chapter 7, "Study Abroad" section

Ohio University

Web Site: http://www-sfa.chubb.ohiou.edu/scholar/scholar_about.html

Also see the following scholarships:

- International Study Programs Scholarship: Chapter 6, "Study Abroad" section
- NEHA/AAS Scholarship: Chapter 6, "Health Care" section
- OSGC Graduate Fellowship: Chapter 7, "Aerospace Sciences and Engineering" section
- OSGC Scholarships: Chapter 6, "Aerospace Sciences and Engineering" section

Otterbein College

Web Site: http://www.otterbein.edu/admission/finaid.htm

University of Akron

Web Site: http://www.uakron.edu/finaid/link2.html

Also see the following scholarships:

- Army ROTC Nurse Scholarships: Chapter 13, "Army and Army ROTC" section
- OSGC Graduate Fellowship: Chapter 7, "Aerospace Sciences and Engineering" section
- OSGC Scholarships: Chapter 6, "Aerospace Sciences and Engineering" section

University of Dayton

Web Site: http://admission.udayton.edu/finscholarship.asp

Also see the following scholarships:

- COHEAO Scholarship: Chapter 5, "Academic Scholarships" section
- OSGC Graduate Fellowship: Chapter 7, "Aerospace Sciences and Engineering" section
- OSGC Scholarships: Chapter 6, "Aerospace Sciences and Engineering" section
- Search for Excellence National Scholarship: Chapter 5, "Academic Scholarships" section

University of Toledo

Web Site: http://www.financialaid.utoledo.edu/scholarshipcontents.html

Also see the following scholarships:

- International Study Programs Scholarship: Chapter 6, "Study Abroad" section
- OSGC Graduate Fellowship: Chapter 7, "Aerospace Sciences and Engineering" section
- OSGC Scholarships: Chapter 6, "Aerospace Sciences and Engineering" section

Wilberforce University

Web Site: http://www.wilberforce.edu/services/fa/scholarships.htm

Also see the following scholarships:

- McDonald's UNCF Tri-State Scholarship: Chapter 9, "African-American" section
- OSGC Graduate Fellowship: Chapter 7, "Aerospace Sciences and Engineering" section
- OSGC Scholarships: Chapter 6, "Aerospace Sciences and Engineering" section
- UNCF Scholarships: Chapter 9, "African-American" section

Oklahoma

Oklahoma Panhandle State University

Web Site: http://www.opsu.edu/scholar.htm

Southeastern Oklahoma State University

Web Site: http://www.sosu.edu/enroll/scholar/frameIndex.html

Also see the following scholarship:

- NBAA Aviation Scholarship: Chapter 6, "Aviation" section

Southern Nazarene University

Web Site: http://www.snu.edu/scholars/index.htm

University of Oklahoma

Web Site: http://www.scholarships.ou.edu/form.taf

Also see the following scholarships:

- Arkansas Health Education Grant: Chapter 15, "Arkansas" section
- COHEAO Scholarship: Chapter 5, "Academic Scholarships" section
- Competitive Edge Scholarship: Chapter 6, "Engineering" section

- GEM Fellowships: Chapter 9, "All Minorities" section
- International Study Programs Scholarship: Chapter 6, "Study Abroad" section
- Search for Excellence National Scholarship: Chapter 5, "Academic Scholarships" section
- USAIG PDP Scholarship: Chapter 6, "Aviation" section

Oregon

Eastern Oregon University

Web Site: http://www.eou.edu/fao/schol.htm

Also see the following scholarship:

- OCECS Scholarship: Chapter 15, "Oregon" section

Marylhurst University

Web Site: http://www.marylhurst.edu/student/scholarships.html

Oregon State University

Web Site: http://osu.orst.edu/dept/foundation/scholarships/endowed/index.html

Also see the following scholarships:

- Competitive Edge Scholarship: Chapter 6, "Engineering" section
- IFT Scholarships: Chapter 6, "Food Science and Nutrition" section
- NEHA/AAS Scholarship: Chapter 6, "Health Care" section
- NPSC Graduate Fellowships in the Physical Sciences: Chapter 7, "Sciences" section
- OCECS Scholarship: Chapter 15, "Oregon" section
- Search for Excellence National Scholarship: Chapter 5, "Academic Scholarships" section

- SRC Master's Scholarship: Chapter 7, "Electronics" section

Portland State University

Web Site: http://www.oaa.pdx.edu/oaadoc/SCHOLARSHIPS/scholarshiphandbook.html

Also see the following scholarships:

- Competitive Edge Scholarship: Chapter 6, "Engineering" section
- International Study Programs Scholarship: Chapter 6, "Study Abroad" section
- OCECS Scholarship: Chapter 15, "Oregon" section
- Search for Excellence National Scholarship: Chapter 5, "Academic Scholarships" section

Southern Oregon University

Web Site: http://www.sou.edu/finaid

Also see the following scholarships:

- COHEAO Scholarship: Chapter 5, "Academic Scholarships" section
- OCECS Scholarship: Chapter 15, "Oregon" section

University of Oregon

Web Site: http://financialaid.uoregon.edu/SC-guide.htm

Also see the following scholarships:

- International Study Programs Scholarship: Chapter 6, "Study Abroad" section
- NPSC Graduate Fellowships in the Physical Sciences: Chapter 7, "Sciences" section
- OCECS Scholarship: Chapter 15, "Oregon" section
- Winston Churchill Foundation Scholarship: Chapter 7, "Study Abroad" section

Pennsylvania

Carnegie Mellon University

Web Site: http://www.cmu.edu/enrollment/admission/know/scholar.html

Also see the following scholarships:

- AISE Steel Foundation Scholarships: Chapter 14, "Unions and Professional Associations" section
- GEM Fellowships: Chapter 9, "All Minorities" section
- Hertz Foundation Fellowship: Chapter 7, "Sciences" section
- Luce Scholars: Chapter 7, "Study Abroad" section
- NPSC Graduate Fellowships in the Physical Sciences: Chapter 7, "Sciences" section
- Search for Excellence National Scholarship: Chapter 5, "Academic Scholarships" section
- SRC Master's Scholarship: Chapter 7, "Electronics" section
- Winston Churchill Foundation Scholarship: Chapter 7, "Study Abroad" section

Clarion University of Pennsylvania

Web Site: http://www.clarion.edu/admiss/scholar.htm

Also see the following scholarship:

- Pennsylvania's Outstanding Young Woman Scholarships: Chapter 12, "Female" section

East Stroudsburg University of Pennsylvania

Web Site: http://www.esu.edu/finaid/index.html

Lock Haven University of Pennsylvania

Web Site: http://www.lhup.edu/foundation/index.htm

Pennsylvania State University

Web Site: http://www.psu.edu/studentaid/html/schmain.html

Also see the following scholarships:

- Astronaut Scholarship: Chapter 6, "Sciences" section
- COHEAO Scholarship: Chapter 5, "Academic Scholarships" section
- Competitive Edge Scholarship: Chapter 6, "Engineering" section
- FEF Scholarships: Chapter 6, "Materials Science and Metallurgy" section
- GEM Fellowships: Chapter 9, "All Minorities" section
- IFT Scholarships: Chapter 6, "Food Science and Nutrition" section
- International Study Programs Scholarship: Chapter 6, "Study Abroad" section
- NPSC Graduate Fellowships in the Physical Sciences: Chapter 7, "Sciences" section
- Search for Excellence National Scholarship: Chapter 5, "Academic Scholarships" section
- SRC Master's Scholarship: Chapter 7, "Electronics" section

Slippery Rock University of Pennsylvania

Web Site: http://www.sru.edu/depts/fin_aid/schol/index.htm

Also see the following scholarships:

- COHEAO Scholarship: Chapter 5, "Academic Scholarships" section
- Search for Excellence National Scholarship: Chapter 5, "Academic Scholarships" section

Temple University

Web Site: http://sfsworld.temple.edu/temple_scholarships

Also see the following scholarships:

- COHEAO Scholarship: Chapter 5, "Academic Scholarships" section
- International Study Programs Scholarship: Chapter 6, "Study Abroad" section
- NPSC Graduate Fellowships in the Physical Sciences: Chapter 7, "Sciences" section

University of Pittsburgh

Web Site: http://www.pitt.edu/~oafa/schlrs.html

Also see the following scholarships:

- Army ROTC Nurse Scholarships: Chapter 13, "Army and Army ROTC" section
- COHEAO Scholarship: Chapter 5, "Academic Scholarships" section
- International Study Programs Scholarship: Chapter 6, "Study Abroad" section
- NPSC Graduate Fellowships in the Physical Sciences: Chapter 7, "Sciences" section

South Carolina

Clemson University

Web Site: http://www.clemson.edu/scholarships/index.htm

Also see the following scholarships:

- Army ROTC Nurse Scholarships: Chapter 13, "Army and Army ROTC" section
- Civilian Radioactive Waste Management Fellowship: Chapter 7, "Waste Management" section
- Competitive Edge Scholarship: Chapter 6, "Engineering" section
- GEM Fellowships: Chapter 9, "All Minorities" section
- IFT Scholarships: Chapter 6, "Food Science and Nutrition" section
- NPSC Graduate Fellowships in the Physical Sciences: Chapter 7, "Sciences" section

- Search for Excellence National Scholarship: Chapter 5, "Academic Scholarships" section
- Thread Committee Excellence in Manufacturing Scholarship: Chapter 6, "Textile Science and Fiber Arts" section

Furman University

Web Site: http://www.furman.edu/plan/design4/admissions/finaid.htm

Also see the following scholarships:

- Luce Scholars: Chapter 7, "Study Abroad" section
- Search for Excellence National Scholarship: Chapter 5, "Academic Scholarships" section

South Dakota

Black Hills State University

Web Site: http://www.bhsu.edu/studentlife/enrollment/financialaid/index.html

Dakota State University

Web Site: http://www.departments.dsu.edu/foundation/Scholarships/scholars.htm

University of South Dakota

Web Site: http://www.usd.edu/finaid

Also see the following scholarships:

- Competitive Edge Scholarship: Chapter 6, "Engineering" section
- Search for Excellence National Scholarship: Chapter 5, "Academic Scholarships" section

Tennessee

Middle Tennessee State University

Web Site: http://www.mtsu.edu/~admissn/scholar.html

Also see the following scholarship:

- NBAA Aviation Scholarship: Chapter 6, "Aviation" section

Tennessee Technological University

Web Site: http://www2.tntech.edu/scholarships

Also see the following scholarship:

- FEF Scholarships: Chapter 6, "Materials Science and Metallurgy" section

University of Tennessee, Knoxville

Web Site: http://web.utk.edu/~finaid/scholar2.html

Also see the following scholarships:

- Civilian Radioactive Waste Management Fellowship: Chapter 7, "Waste Management" section
- Competitive Edge Scholarship: Chapter 6, "Engineering" section
- GEM Fellowships: Chapter 9, "All Minorities" section
- IFT Scholarships: Chapter 6, "Food Science and Nutrition" section
- Search for Excellence National Scholarship: Chapter 5, "Academic Scholarships" section
- SRC Master's Scholarship: Chapter 7, "Electronics" section

Vanderbilt University

Web Site: http://www.vanderbilt.edu/FinancialAid/awdschlp.htm

Also see the following scholarships:

- COHEAO Scholarship: Chapter 5, "Academic Scholarships" section
- GEM Fellowships: Chapter 9, "All Minorities" section

- Hertz Foundation Fellowship: Chapter 7, "Sciences" section
- Homeland Ministries Scholarships: Chapter 11, "Christian Church (Disciples of Christ)" section
- International Study Programs Scholarship: Chapter 6, "Study Abroad" section
- Luce Scholars: Chapter 7, "Study Abroad" section
- NPSC Graduate Fellowships in the Physical Sciences: Chapter 7, "Sciences" section
- Project Excellence Scholarships: Chapter 9, "African-American" section
- SRC Master's Scholarship: Chapter 7, "Electronics" section
- Winston Churchill Foundation Scholarship: Chapter 7, "Study Abroad" section

Texas

Angelo State University

Web Site: http://www.angelo.edu/services/financial_aid/scholarships.htm

Also see the following scholarship:

- Teach for Texas Conditional Grant: Chapter 6, "Education" section

Sam Houston State University

Web Site: http://www.shsu.edu/~sfa_www/scholarships.html

Also see the following scholarship:

- Teach for Texas Conditional Grant: Chapter 6, "Education" section

Southern Methodist University

Web Site: http://www.smu.edu/~ofa/scholar.html

Also see the following scholarships:

- International Study Programs Scholarship: Chapter 6, "Study Abroad" section
- NASA/TSGC Graduate Fellowship: Chapter 7, "Space Sciences" section
- NASA/TSGC Space Grant Consortium Undergraduate Scholarship: Chapter 6, "Space Sciences" section
- NPSC Graduate Fellowships in the Physical Sciences: Chapter 7, "Sciences" section
- SRC Master's Scholarship: Chapter 7, "Electronics" section
- Teach for Texas Conditional Grant: Chapter 6, "Education" section

Southwest Texas State University

Web Site: http://www.swt.edu/financialaid/html/scholarships.html

Also see the following scholarships:

- FEF Scholarships: Chapter 6, "Materials Science and Metallurgy" section
- Search for Excellence National Scholarship: Chapter 5, "Academic Scholarships" section
- Teach for Texas Conditional Grant: Chapter 6, "Education" section

Stephen F. Austin State University

Web Site: http://www.sfasu.edu/faid/fa_scholarships/index.stm

Also see the following scholarship:

- Teach for Texas Conditional Grant: Chapter 6, "Education" section

Tarleton State University

Web Site: http://www.tarleton.edu/~scholars/index.html

Also see the following scholarship:

- Teach for Texas Conditional Grant: Chapter 6, "Education" section

Texas A&M University

Web Site: http://faid.tamu.edu

Also see the following scholarships:

- Astronaut Scholarship: Chapter 6, "Sciences" section
- Civilian Radioactive Waste Management Fellowship: Chapter 7, "Waste Management" section
- Competitive Edge Scholarship: Chapter 6, "Engineering" section
- GEM Fellowships: Chapter 9, "All Minorities" section
- Hertz Foundation Fellowship: Chapter 7, "Sciences" section
- IFT Scholarships: Chapter 6, "Food Science and Nutrition" section
- International Study Programs Scholarship: Chapter 6, "Study Abroad" section
- NASA/TSGC Graduate Fellowship: Chapter 7, "Space Sciences" section
- NASA/TSGC Space Grant Consortium Undergraduate Scholarship: Chapter 6, "Space Sciences" section
- NPSC Graduate Fellowships in the Physical Sciences: Chapter 7, "Sciences" section
- Teach for Texas Conditional Grant: Chapter 6, "Education" section

Texas Christian University

Web Site: http://www.fam.tcu.edu/fam

Also see the following scholarships:

- Army ROTC Nurse Scholarships: Chapter 13, "Army and Army ROTC" section
- International Study Programs Scholarship: Chapter 6, "Study Abroad" section
- NASA/TSGC Graduate Fellowship: Chapter 7, "Space Sciences" section
- NASA/TSGC Space Grant Consortium Undergraduate Scholarship: Chapter 6, "Space Sciences" section

- Teach for Texas Conditional Grant: Chapter 6, "Education" section

University of Houston

Web Site: http://www.uh.edu/enroll/sfa/ #schol

Also see the following scholarships:

- AHF Scholarships: Chapter 6, "Hotel and Restaurant Management" section
- GEM Fellowships: Chapter 9, "All Minorities" section
- NASA/TSGC Graduate Fellowship: Chapter 7, "Space Sciences" section
- NASA/TSGC Space Grant Consortium Undergraduate Scholarship: Chapter 6, "Space Sciences" section
- Teach for Texas Conditional Grant: Chapter 6, "Education" section

University of North Texas

Web Site: http://essc.unt.edu/finaid/ index.htm

Also see the following scholarships:

- Competitive Edge Scholarship: Chapter 6, "Engineering" section
- SRC Master's Scholarship: Chapter 7, "Electronics" section
- Teach for Texas Conditional Grant: Chapter 6, "Education" section

University of Texas at Arlington

Web Site: http://www2.uta.edu/fao/ Scholarships

Also see the following scholarships:

- NASA/TSGC Graduate Fellowship: Chapter 7, "Space Sciences" section
- NASA/TSGC Space Grant Consortium Undergraduate Scholarship: Chapter 6, "Space Sciences" section

- Teach for Texas Conditional Grant: Chapter 6, "Education" section

University of Texas at Austin

Web Site: http://www.utexas.edu/student/ finaid/info/assist2.html#non3

Also see the following scholarships:

- Civilian Radioactive Waste Management Fellowship: Chapter 7, "Waste Management" section
- Consortium for Graduate Study in Management Fellowship: Chapter 7, "Business" section
- D.W. Simpson & Company Actuarial Science Scholarship: Chapter 6, "Actuarial Science" section
- GEM Fellowships: Chapter 9, "All Minorities" section
- Hertz Foundation Fellowship: Chapter 7, "Sciences" section
- International Predissertation Fellowships: Chapter 7, "Social Sciences" section
- International Study Programs Scholarship: Chapter 6, "Study Abroad" section
- Luce Scholars: Chapter 7, "Study Abroad" section
- NASA/TSGC Graduate Fellowship: Chapter 7, "Space Sciences" section
- NASA/TSGC Space Grant Consortium Undergraduate Scholarship: Chapter 6, "Space Sciences" section
- NPSC Graduate Fellowships in the Physical Sciences: Chapter 7, "Sciences" section
- RTNDF Scholarships: Chapter 6, "Journalism" section
- Scott & White Nursing Scholarships: Chapter 6, "Nursing" section
- SRC Master's Scholarship: Chapter 7, "Electronics" section
- Teach for Texas Conditional Grant: Chapter 6, "Education" section

- Winston Churchill Foundation Scholarship: Chapter 7, "Study Abroad" section

University of Texas at Dallas

Web Site: http://financial-aid.utdallas.edu/AES/toppage1.htm

Also see the following scholarships:

- NASA/TSGC Graduate Fellowship: Chapter 7, "Space Sciences" section
- NASA/TSGC Space Grant Consortium Undergraduate Scholarship: Chapter 6, "Space Sciences" section
- SRC Master's Scholarship: Chapter 7, "Electronics" section
- Teach for Texas Conditional Grant: Chapter 6, "Education" section

University of Texas at El Paso

Web Site: http://www.utep.edu/schp

Also see the following scholarships:

- Army ROTC Nurse Scholarships: Chapter 13, "Army and Army ROTC" section
- Competitive Edge Scholarship: Chapter 6, "Engineering" section
- GEM Fellowships: Chapter 9, "All Minorities" section
- NASA/TSGC Graduate Fellowship: Chapter 7, "Space Sciences" section
- NASA/TSGC Space Grant Consortium Undergraduate Scholarship: Chapter 6, "Space Sciences" section
- NPSC Graduate Fellowships in the Physical Sciences: Chapter 7, "Sciences" section
- Teach for Texas Conditional Grant: Chapter 6, "Education" section

University of Texas at San Antonio

Web Site: http://www.utsa.edu/students/finance/sc01.htm

Also see the following scholarships:

- International Study Programs Scholarship: Chapter 6, "Study Abroad" section
- NASA/TSGC Graduate Fellowship: Chapter 7, "Space Sciences" section
- NASA/TSGC Space Grant Consortium Undergraduate Scholarship: Chapter 6, "Space Sciences" section
- Teach for Texas Conditional Grant: Chapter 6, "Education" section

West Texas A&M University

Web Site: http://www.wtamu.edu/administrative/vpa/em/scholidx.htm

Also see the following scholarships:

- NASA/TSGC Graduate Fellowship: Chapter 7, "Space Sciences" section
- NASA/TSGC Space Grant Consortium Undergraduate Scholarship: Chapter 6, "Space Sciences" section
- Teach for Texas Conditional Grant: Chapter 6, "Education" section

Utah

Brigham Young University

Web Site: http://ar.byu.edu/dept_scholarships/catalog.html

Also see the following scholarships:

- IFT Scholarships: Chapter 6, "Food Science and Nutrition" section
- Rocky Mountain NASA Space Grant Consortium Scholarships and Fellowships: Chapter 6, "Space Sciences" section

Southern Utah University

Web Site: http://www.suu.edu/ss/admissions/scholars.html

Also see the following scholarship:

- Rocky Mountain NASA Space Grant Consortium Scholarships and Fellowships: Chapter 6, "Space Sciences" section

University of Utah

Web Site: http://www.saff.utah.edu/finance/scholarships/index.htm

Also see the following scholarships:

- COHEAO Scholarship: Chapter 5, "Academic Scholarships" section
- Competitive Edge Scholarship: Chapter 6, "Engineering" section
- International Study Programs Scholarship: Chapter 6, "Study Abroad" section
- NPSC Graduate Fellowships in the Physical Sciences: Chapter 7, "Sciences" section
- Rocky Mountain NASA Space Grant Consortium Scholarships and Fellowships: Chapter 6, "Space Sciences" section
- Search for Excellence National Scholarship: Chapter 5, "Academic Scholarships" section
- SRC Master's Scholarship: Chapter 7, "Electronics" section

Utah State University

Web Site: http://www.usu.edu/%7Efinaid/scholarship.html

Also see the following scholarships:

- Competitive Edge Scholarship: Chapter 6, "Engineering" section
- IFT Scholarships: Chapter 6, "Food Science and Nutrition" section
- International Study Programs Scholarship: Chapter 6, "Study Abroad" section
- Rocky Mountain NASA Space Grant Consortium Scholarships and Fellowships: Chapter 6, "Space Sciences" section

Weber State University

Web Site: http://www.weber.edu/scholarships

Also see the following scholarship:

- Rocky Mountain NASA Space Grant Consortium Scholarships and Fellowships: Chapter 6, "Space Sciences" section

Virginia

James Madison University

Web Site: http://www.jmu.edu/finaid/schol.htm

Also see the following scholarships:

- International Study Programs Scholarship: Chapter 6, "Study Abroad" section
- Search for Excellence National Scholarship: Chapter 5, "Academic Scholarships" section

Old Dominion University

Web Site: http://web.odu.edu/af/finaid/finaid.htm

Also see the following scholarships:

- ADHA Institute for Oral Health Scholarships: Chapter 6, "Dentistry and Dental Hygiene" section
- Competitive Edge Scholarship: Chapter 6, "Engineering" section
- International Study Programs Scholarship: Chapter 6, "Study Abroad" section
- NEHA/AAS Scholarship: Chapter 6, "Health Care" section
- NPSC Graduate Fellowships in the Physical Sciences: Chapter 7, "Sciences" section
- VSGC Scholarships and Fellowships: Chapter 6, "Aerospace Sciences and Engineering" section

Virginia Tech

Web Site: http://wwwfinaid.es.vt.edu/scholarships.html

Also see the following scholarships:

- AHF Scholarships: Chapter 6, "Hotel and Restaurant Management" section
- Competitive Edge Scholarship: Chapter 6, "Engineering" section
- FEF Scholarships: Chapter 6, "Materials Science and Metallurgy" section
- GEM Fellowships: Chapter 9, "All Minorities" section
- IFT Scholarships: Chapter 6, "Food Science and Nutrition" section
- NPSC Graduate Fellowships in the Physical Sciences: Chapter 7, "Sciences" section
- VSGC Scholarships and Fellowships: Chapter 6, "Aerospace Sciences and Engineering" section

Washington and Lee University

Web Site: http://admissions.wlu.edu/frm_finance.htm

Also see the following scholarships:

- Luce Scholars: Chapter 7, "Study Abroad" section
- Project Excellence Scholarships: Chapter 9, "African-American" section
- United Daughters of the Confederacy Scholarships: Chapter 13, "Military Personnel and Veterans" section
- Virginia Division Scholarships: Chapter 13, "Military Personnel and Veterans" section

Washington

Central Washington University

Web Site: http://www.cwu.edu/~scholar

Also see the following scholarships:

- Competitive Edge Scholarship: Chapter 6, "Engineering" section
- FEF Scholarships: Chapter 6, "Materials Science and Metallurgy" section

Evergreen State College

Web Site: http://www.evergreen.edu/user/faid/scholars.htm

Seattle University

Web Site: http://www.seattleu.edu/admissions/finaid

Also see the following scholarships:

- Army ROTC Nurse Scholarships: Chapter 13, "Army and Army ROTC" section
- COHEAO Scholarship: Chapter 5, "Academic Scholarships" section
- International Study Programs Scholarship: Chapter 6, "Study Abroad" section
- Search for Excellence National Scholarship: Chapter 5, "Academic Scholarships" section

University of Washington

Web Site: http://www.washington.edu/students/ugrad/scholar

Also see the following scholarships:

- Astronaut Scholarship: Chapter 6, "Sciences" section
- COHEAO Scholarship: Chapter 5, "Academic Scholarships" section
- Competitive Edge Scholarship: Chapter 6, "Engineering" section
- GEM Fellowships: Chapter 9, "All Minorities" section
- Hertz Foundation Fellowship: Chapter 7, "Sciences" section
- International Predissertation Fellowships: Chapter 7, "Social Sciences" section

- International Study Programs Scholarship: Chapter 6, "Study Abroad" section
- NEHA/AAS Scholarship: Chapter 6, "Health Care" section
- NPSC Graduate Fellowships in the Physical Sciences: Chapter 7, "Sciences" section
- Search for Excellence National Scholarship: Chapter 5, "Academic Scholarships" section
- SRC Master's Scholarship: Chapter 7, "Electronics" section
- Winston Churchill Foundation Scholarship: Chapter 7, "Study Abroad" section

Washington State University

Web Site: http://faoservr.finaid.wsu.edu/finscol.htm

Also see the following scholarships:

- Civilian Radioactive Waste Management Fellowship: Chapter 7, "Waste Management" section
- Competitive Edge Scholarship: Chapter 6, "Engineering" section
- IFT Scholarships: Chapter 6, "Food Science and Nutrition" section
- International Study Programs Scholarship: Chapter 6, "Study Abroad" section
- NPSC Graduate Fellowships in the Physical Sciences: Chapter 7, "Sciences" section

Western Washington University

Web Site: http://www.ac.wwu.edu/~scholar

Also see the following scholarship:

- International Study Programs Scholarship: Chapter 6, "Study Abroad" section

West Virginia

West Virginia University

Web Site: http://www.wvu.edu/~finaid/scholar.htm

Also see the following scholarships:

- ADHA Institute for Oral Health Scholarships: Chapter 6, "Dentistry and Dental Hygiene" section
- Competitive Edge Scholarship: Chapter 6, "Engineering" section

Wisconsin

University of Wisconsin—Eau Claire

Web Site: http://www.uwec.edu/Admin/FinAid/schlrshp/maintoc.htm

University of Wisconsin—Green Bay

Web Site: http://www.uwgb.edu/FinancialAid/scholar2.htm

Also see the following scholarships:

- Competitive Edge Scholarship: Chapter 6, "Engineering" section
- International Study Programs Scholarship: Chapter 6, "Study Abroad" section

University of Wisconsin—Madison

Web Site: http://financial-aid.acadsvcs.wisc.edu/finaid

Also see the following scholarships:

- Civilian Radioactive Waste Management Fellowship: Chapter 7, "Waste Management" section
- COHEAO Scholarship: Chapter 5, "Academic Scholarships" section
- Competitive Edge Scholarship: Chapter 6, "Engineering" section
- Consortium for Graduate Study in Management Fellowship: Chapter 7, "Business" section
- FEF Scholarships: Chapter 6, "Materials Science and Metallurgy" section

- GEM Fellowships: Chapter 9, "All Minorities" section
- Hertz Foundation Fellowship: Chapter 7, "Sciences" section
- IFT Scholarships: Chapter 6, "Food Science and Nutrition" section
- International Predissertation Fellowships: Chapter 7, "Social Sciences" section
- International Study Programs Scholarship: Chapter 6, "Study Abroad" section
- Luce Scholars: Chapter 7, "Study Abroad" section
- NEHA/AAS Scholarship: Chapter 6, "Health Care" section
- NPSC Graduate Fellowships in the Physical Sciences: Chapter 7, "Sciences" section
- Search for Excellence National Scholarship: Chapter 5, "Academic Scholarships" section
- SRC Master's Scholarship: Chapter 7, "Electronics" section
- Winston Churchill Foundation Scholarship: Chapter 7, "Study Abroad" section

University of Wisconsin—Platteville

Web Site: http://vms.www.uwplatt.edu/~finaid

Also see the following scholarship:

- FEF Scholarships: Chapter 6, "Materials Science and Metallurgy" section

University of Wisconsin—River Falls

Web Site: http://www.uwrf.edu/financial-assistance

University of Wisconsin—Stevens Point

Web Site: http://www.uwsp.edu/admit/frshlist2.htm

Wyoming

University of Wyoming

Web Site: http://siswww.uwyo.edu/sfa/schlbook/schlbook.htm

Also see the following scholarships:

- COHEAO Scholarship: Chapter 5, "Academic Scholarships" section
- Competitive Edge Scholarship: Chapter 6, "Engineering" section
- International Study Programs Scholarship: Chapter 6, "Study Abroad" section
- Search for Excellence National Scholarship: Chapter 5, "Academic Scholarships" section

GLOSSARY

academic year Period of study usually consisting of two semesters or three trimesters, which determines a student's classification as freshman, sophomore, junior, or senior. Scholarships are usually awarded for one academic year.

accreditation Seal of approval by a regional accrediting agency or an academic-area accrediting agency, indicating that an institution of higher learning or an academic department has been recognized as providing an adequate education.

admissions officer Member of a college's admissions staff who recruits potential students, reads applications, and helps decide which applicants are admitted.

award letter The official document issued by the financial aid office that lists all of the financial aid that has been awarded to a student. The letter breaks down the aid package by the amount, source, and type of aid, includes the terms and conditions of granting the aid, and notes the total COA.

award year The academic year for which financial aid is requested.

campus-based program Federal Supplemental Educational Opportunity Grants, Federal Work-Study, and Federal Perkins Loan programs. These programs are called "campus-based" because the financial aid office at the school administers them from a fixed pool of federal funds.

class rank A student's standing in his or her high school graduating class relative to his or her peers. Class rank may be expressed as a raw number or as a rough percentile.

COA (cost of attendance) The total amount it costs a student to go to college, usually expressed as a yearly figure and including tuition and required fees, on-campus room and board, and allowances for books, supplies, transportation, loan fees, costs related to a disability, and miscellaneous expenses.

credit hour How a college course is measured. To earn one credit hour, a student must attend class for one classroom hour (usually 50 minutes) per week. College courses are offered in one- to five-credit-hour increments. Some scholarships are only awarded to students who have already earned a specified number of credit hours.

CSS/Financial Aid PROFILE Centralized financial aid application service operated by the College Scholarship Service (CSS) of the College Board, a nonprofit organization of universities, colleges, and other educational institutions. This financial aid form is required by many private colleges and universities to help determine financial aid awards.

EFC (expected family contribution) Figure that indicates how much of the family's financial resources should be used to help pay for a student's education. This number is subtracted from the COA to determine financial need and eligibility for campus-based programs.

endowment Funds owned by a college or university and invested to produce income. Many institutions devote a portion of this income to scholarships and other financial aid monies.

entitlement program Financial aid program in which every applicant who qualifies receives an award. The federal Pell Grant program is an example of an entitlement program.

extracurricular Any activity, such as clubs, work, sports, or volunteer service, that is performed outside of class.

FAFSA (Free Application for Federal Student Aid) Form used to apply for Pell Grants and other federal need-based financial aid programs. Most colleges require students to file the FAFSA to apply for college- and state-sponsored financial aid programs, as well.

Federal Perkins Loan Campus-based program that provides subsidized student loans to students with exceptional financial need. Perkins Loans have the lowest interest rate of any student loan.

Federal Supplemental Educational Opportunity Grant (FSEOG) Campus-based program that distributes grants to students with exceptional financial need. To qualify, the student must also be the recipient of a Pell Grant.

Federal Work-Study (FWS) Campus-based program that provides needy students with part-time employment to help pay school costs.

fellowship A stipend based on merit that is typically awarded to graduate students.

financial aid The money provided to a higher education student to help him or her pay the costs of higher education. Major forms of financial aid include loans, grants, scholarships, and work-study. Financial aid comes from many sources, including federal and state governments, colleges, and private organizations like companies, nonprofit organizations, and charitable foundations.

financial aid officer Person at a college who administers financial aid packages and determines how much aid to award to each student.

financial aid package The total amount of financial aid that a student receives, including federal, state, college, and private aid.

financial need The difference between the COA of a particular college and a student's EFC. Financial aid awards are based on this amount.

grade point average (GPA) System of scoring student achievement. A student's GPA is computed by multiplying the numerical grade received in each course by the number of credits offered for the course, and then dividing by the total number of credit hours studied. Many scholarship programs require applicants to have earned a minimum grade point average.

grant Type of need-based financial aid that the recipient does not have to repay. Grant awards are typically based on financial need and come from public sources, such as federal and state governments.

Historically Black Colleges and Universities (HBCUs) Schools that were founded when African-Americans were denied access to most other colleges and universities and that continue to serve predominantly African-American students today. Some scholarships are only awarded to students attending an HBCU.

honors program Advanced program of study offered by some colleges and universities to students with high academic qualifications. Many colleges give special scholarships to students who are admitted to their honors programs.

in-state student Student who meets the residency requirements to qualify for decreased tuition at a public college or university.

legacy A college or university applicant whose relative—typically a parent—is an alumnus or alumna of the school. Some schools offer special scholarships to legacy students.

major Academic area in which a student chooses to concentrate study when earning a bachelor's degree. Some scholarships are restricted to students who have declared a major in a specific subject.

merit-based aid Financial aid—typically a scholarship—awarded based on academic, artistic, or athletic merit, rather than on financial need.

National Merit Scholarship National scholarship program awarded based on PSAT/NMSQT scores. National Merit finalists can receive scholarships from the National Merit Scholarship Corporation, which sponsors the program, or from a participating college or corporate sponsor.

NCAA (National Collegiate Athletic Association) Organization that regulates athletic programs at the majority of colleges and universities. The NCAA establishes rules on academic eligibility, recruiting, and athletic scholarships.

need-based aid Financial aid based primarily on a student's financial need. All federal aid and most state aid is need-based.

non-need-based aid Broad category of financial aid that encompasses all aid based on criteria other than financial need, including merit-based aid and aid based on a student's ethnicity, gender, religion, or affiliation with a group.

outside scholarship A scholarship not awarded by the college that the student who receives the award is attending.

Pell Grant Federal financial aid program that awards grants to students with exceptional financial need.

PLUS (Parent Loans for Undergraduate Students) Federal education loans that are available to the parents of dependent students and may be used to pay the EFC. Qualification for a PLUS loan is not based on financial need.

private aid Financial aid that originates from private sources, such as private colleges and universities, foundations, nonprofit organizations, corporations, professional associations, and civic organizations.

private loan Student loan provided by a private lender, rather than by the federal or state government. Private loans are typically given to parents and are based on creditworthiness rather than financial need.

PSAT/NMSQT (Preliminary Scholastic Assessment Test/National Merit Scholarship Qualifying Test National standardized test, typically taken during the junior year of high school, that prepares students for taking the SAT. The score on this test determines a student's eligibility for a National Merit Scholarship.

public aid Financial aid that originates from publicly funded sources, such as federal, state, and local governments.

public school College or university that was founded by the state and is funded partly or fully by tax money. Public schools often offer reduced tuition to in-state students.

ROTC (Reserve Officers' Training Corps) On-campus extracurricular program that trains students for service as officers in a branch of the Armed Forces. Participants earn a small stipend as upperclassmen, and they often receive full-tuition scholarships; in return, students are expected to fulfill a service commitment in the Armed Forces after college.

SAR (Student Aid Report) The report that is returned after a student files the FAFSA, indicating the student's Pell Grant eligibility and EFC. The student must provide a copy of this report to the financial aid officer so that the college can put together a financial aid package.

SAT I National standardized college admissions test, widely given in the eastern and southern United States. Some scholarship programs require applicants to submit SAT I scores.

satisfactory academic progress A college's or university's standard of academic achievement that a student must maintain to remain eligible to receive federal financial aid or to retain a scholarship.

scholarship Form of financial aid that does not have to be repaid and is typically awarded based on merit or some other qualification rather than financial need.

Stafford Loan Federal education loan program that provides low-interest loans to students and parents.

student loan Form of financial aid that must be repaid with interest.

study abroad Program in which a student spends a semester or a year at a college in a foreign country. Some scholarships are awarded to help students pay for study abroad programs.

subsidized loan A federally guaranteed loan that is awarded based on financial need. The federal government pays the interest charges that accrue while the student who receives the loan is in school and for six months after graduation.

transcript The official record of a student's academic work. Many scholarship programs require applicants to submit transcripts with their applications.

transfer student A student who has completed one or more years of college-level education and who has transferred his or her enrollment and the college credits he or she has earned to a new school. Some colleges provide scholarships specifically for transfer students.

tuition The cost of a college education and required institutional fees for services provided by the college.

unmet need Any demonstrated financial need that is not met by a college's financial aid package.

unsubsidized loan A Stafford Loan that is not awarded based on financial need and thus may be used to help pay the EFC. The student must pay all of the interest charges that accrue on the loan.

work-study Type of financial aid that gives the student a part-time job, usually on campus. The student's paycheck is used to help pay college costs.

INDEX

Mercedes-Benz United States International, 104

Mercer County Bar Association, 189

Merck Company Foundation, 212

Mervyn's California, 226

MES Foundation, 373

Michigan Farm Bureau, 313

Microsoft, 82, 83

Millennium Society, 148

Milliman & Robertson, Inc., 315

The Minerals, Metals, & Materials Society (TMS), 129

Ministry of the United Methodist Church, 285

Minnesota Gay/Lesbian/Bisexual/Transgender Educational Fund, 262

Minnesota Higher Education Services Office, 330, 382, 383

Minnesota Masonic Foundation, Inc., 382

Miss America Organization, 290

Missouri Department of Agriculture, 385

Missouri Department of Higher Education, 324, 329

Missouri Department of Higher Education Student Assistance Division, 384, 385

Montana Bandmasters Association, 130

Montana Guaranteed Student Loan Program, 386

Montana Space Grant Consortium, 68

Morris K. Udall Foundation, 109, 177

The Morris Scholarship Fund, Inc., 253

Mousa Ler Association of California, 260

Moving Picture Technicians, Artists, 337

NACME, Inc., 104

NASA Nebraska Space Grant and EPSCoR Programs, 68

NASA/Texas Space Grant Consortium (TSGC), 144, 215

National Ad 2, 66

National Aeronautics and Space Administration (NASA), 157

National Association of Home Workshop Writers (NAHWW), 126

National Association of School Psychologists (NASP), 206

National Association of Secondary School Principals, 234, 239

National Association of the Deaf, 277

National Association of Water Companies (NAWC), 223

National Association of Women in Construction (NAWIC), 85

National Association for the Self-Employed (NASE), 336

National Bairy Promotion and Research Board (NDPRB), 71

National Beta Club, 231

National Black Law Students Association (NBLSA), 189

National Board for Respiratory Care (NBRC), 141

National Business Aviation Association (NBAA), 74, 76

National Council of State Garden Clubs, 121

National Collegiate Athletic Association (NCAA), 226

National Consortium for Graduate Degrees for Minorities in Engineering and Science, Inc. (GEM), 251

National Environmental Health Association (NEHA), 117

National Federation of Republican Women (NFRW), 288, 291

National Federation of the Blind, 279

National Foundation for Jewish Culture, 187

National Funeral Directors Association (NFDA), 113

National Gay and Lesbian Task Force (NGLTF), 125

National Gymnastics Foundation, 225

National Health Service Corps, 197

National Hispanic Foundation for the Arts (NHFA), 267

National Honor Society, 239

National Inventors Hall of Fame, 56

National Jewish Committee on Scouting, Boy Scouts of America, 281

Third Wave Foundation, 292
Time Magazine, 247
The Toro Company, 221
Toshiba Corporation, Toshiba, 57
Triangle Fraternity Education Foundation, Inc., 236
TROA Scholarship Fund, 323
Trust to Reach Education Excellence, 244
An Uncommon Legacy Foundation, Inc., 262
United Daughters of the Confederacy, 324
United Methodist Communications, 81, 187
United Nations Association of the United States of America (UNA-USA), 54
United Nations Development Programme, 54
United Negro College Fund (UNCF), 77, 118, 124, 211, 250, 256, 259
United States Achievement Academy (USAA), 47
United States Army Cadet Command Headquarters, 298, 300
United States Army, Navy, and Air Force, 210
United States Information Agency, 218
United Teachers of Dade (UTD), 173, 337
Universities Space Research Association (USRA), 145
University Aviation Association (UAA), 74
University Film and Video Foundation, 111
University of Alaska Statewide System, 340
University of North Carolina Board of Governors, 198
University Systems of West Virginia, 100
USA Gymnastics Junior Olympic Program Committee, 225
U.S. Aircraft Insurance Group (USAIG), 75
US Bank, 408
U.S. Department of Agriculture, 71
U.S. Department of Commerce, 124
U.S. Department of Education, 185
U.S. Department of Energy, 105
U.S. Department of Energy Office of Fusion Energy, 174

U.S. Department of Energy Office of Civilian Radioactive Waste Management, 222
U.S. Department of Energy (DOE) Office of Science and Office of Defense Programs, 209
U.S. Department of Health and Human Services, 118, 197
U.S. Department of State, 124, 186
U.S. Departments of Army, Navy, and Air Force, 58
U.S. Environmental Protection Agency (EPA), 108
U.S. State Department Bureau of Educational and Cultural Affairs, 218
Utah Highway Patrol Association, 330
Vaughan and Bushnell Manufacturing, 126
Vermont Student Assistance Corporation (VSAC), 417
Veterans Foundation for Monterey County, 346
Veterans of Foreign Wars of the United States, 55
Virginia Business and Professional Women (BPW) Foundation, 418
Virginia Smith Scholarship Trust, 347
Virginia Society for Clinical Laboratory Sciences (VSCLS), 80
Virginia Space Grant Consortium (VSGC), 69
Wachovia Bank, 412
Wal-Mart Foundation, 50, 103
Wal-Mart Stores, Inc., 246, 315
Walter H. Meyer-Garry L. White Memorial Educational Fund, 422
Walter Reed Army Medical Center, Psychology Department, 300
Warner-Lambert Company, 167
Washington Association of Wine Grape Growers, 72
Washington Crossing Foundation, 116
Washington Higher Education Coordinating Board, 420–422

ABOUT THE AUTHOR

Shannon R. Turlington is the author of 11 books about the Internet, college admissions, and college financing. Her first book was *Walking the World Wide Web,* a guide to the best of the Web (Ventana Press, 1995). Her more recent publications include *Field Guide to Colleges* (Arco, 1999), *The Unofficial Guide to Financing a College Education* (Arco, 1999), and *The Unofficial Guide to College Admissions* (Arco, 2000). Shannon is a proud graduate of the University of North Carolina at Chapel Hill, which she attended with the help of several scholarships. She currently lives and writes in Carrboro, North Carolina.